Communications
in Computer and Information Science 1577

More information about this series at https://link.springer.com/bookseries/7899

Juan Antonio Lossio-Ventura ·
Jorge Valverde-Rebaza · Eduardo Díaz ·
Denisse Muñante · Carlos Gavidia-Calderon ·
Alan Demétrius Baria Valejo ·
Hugo Alatrista-Salas (Eds.)

Information Management and Big Data

8th Annual International Conference, SIMBig 2021
Virtual Event, December 1–3, 2021
Proceedings

 Springer

Editors
Juan Antonio Lossio-Ventura ⓘ
National Institutes of Health
Bethesda, MD, USA

Jorge Valverde-Rebaza ⓘ
Visibilia
São Paulo, Brazil

Eduardo Díaz ⓘ
Universidad Peruana de Ciencias Aplicadas
Lima, Peru

Denisse Muñante ⓘ
ENSIIE and SAMOVAR
Evry, France

Carlos Gavidia-Calderon ⓘ
The Open University
Milton Keynes, UK

Alan Demétrius Baria Valejo ⓘ
Federal University of São Carlos
São Carlos, Brazil

Hugo Alatrista-Salas ⓘ
University of Engineering and Technology
UTEC
Lima, Peru

ISSN 1865-0929   ISSN 1865-0937 (electronic)
Communications in Computer and Information Science
ISBN 978-3-031-04446-5   ISBN 978-3-031-04447-2 (eBook)
https://doi.org/10.1007/978-3-031-04447-2

This Springer imprint is published by the registered company Springer Nature Switzerland AG
The registered company address is: Gewerbestrasse 11, 6330 Cham, Switzerland

Preface

SIMBig 2021[1], the 8th edition of the International Conference on Information Management and Big Data, presented novel methods for the analysis and management of large volumes of data, covering fields such as Artificial Intelligence (AI), Data Science, Machine Learning, Natural Language Processing, Semantic Web, Data-driven Software Engineering, Health Informatics, among others. The SIMBig conference series goal is to promote cooperation between national and international researchers to improve data-driven decision making by using new technologies dedicated to analyzing data.

SIMBig 2021 also encouraged proposals on the COVID-19 pandemic, with the goal of informing Latin American policy makers (specially in South America). SIMBig is a convivial place where participants present their scientific contributions in the form of full and short papers. This book contains the entire proceedings of the 8th edition of SIMBig, a full-virtual conference held between December 1 and December 3, 2021. For this edition, 23 long papers and four short papers were selected for publication, giving an acceptance rate of 40.3%.

Keynote Speakers' Resumes

SIMBig 2021 featured eight keynote speakers. Dr. Marinka Zitnik, from Harvard University, USA, presented her research group's work for infusing structure and knowledge into biomedical AI. Grand challenges in biology and medicine often lack annotated examples and require generalization to entirely new scenarios not seen during training. However, standard supervised learning is incredibly limited in scenarios such as designing novel medicines, modeling emerging pathogens, and treating rare diseases. In this talk, Dr. Zitnik presented their efforts to overcome these obstacles by infusing structure and knowledge into learning algorithms. First, Dr. Zitnik presented general-purpose and scalable algorithms for few-shot learning on graphs. At the core is the notion of local subgraphs that transfer knowledge from one task to another, even when only a handful of labeled examples are available. This principle is theoretically justified as the evidence for predictions can be found in subgraphs surrounding the targets. Dr. Zitnik concluded with applications in drug development and precision medicine where the algorithmic predictions were validated in human cells and led to the discovery of a new class of drugs.

Dr. Natasha Noy, from Google, USA, talked about the project Google Dataset Search that seeks to build an open ecosystem for dataset discovery. There are thousands of data repositories on the Web, providing access to millions of datasets. National and regional governments, scientific publishers and consortia, commercial data providers, and others publish data for fields ranging from social and life sciences through high-energy physics to climate science and more. Access to this data is critical to facilitating reproducibility of research results, enabling scientists to build on others' work, and providing data

---
[1] https://simbig.org/SIMBig2021/.

journalists easier access to information and its provenance. This talk gave an overview of Dataset Search by Google, which provides search capabilities over potentially all dataset repositories on the Web, and Dr. Noy discussed the open ecosystem for describing datasets that they hope to encourage.

Dr. Andrei Broder, from Google, USA, presented a point of view about the Web Advertising Ecosystem. The World Wide Web is arguably an engineering artifact and social environment that defines our era. A large part of it is made possible by money generated via advertising. The goal of Dr. Broder's talk was to give an introduction to the web advertising ecosystem and illuminate the complex relations between consumers, publishers, and advertisers.

Dr. Jiawei Han, from the University of Illinois Urbana-Champaign, USA, discussed their work to convert unstructured text data to structured knowledge. The real-world big data are largely dynamic, interconnected, and unstructured text. It is highly desirable to transform such massive unstructured data into structured knowledge. Many researchers rely on labor-intensive labeling and curation to extract knowledge from such data. Such approaches, however, are not scalable. We envision that massive text data itself may disclose a large body of hidden structures and knowledge. Equipped with pretrained language models and text embedding methods, it is promising to transform unstructured data into structured knowledge. In this talk, Dr. Han introduced a set of methods developed recently in his group for such an exploration, including joint spherical text embedding, discriminative topic mining, taxonomy construction, text classification, and taxonomy-guided text analysis. Dr. Han showed that a data-driven approach could be promising at transforming massive text data into structured knowledge.

Dr. Vipin Kumar, from the University of Minnesota, USA, focused on the opportunities and challenges for machine learning on topics related to big data in water. Water resources worldwide are coming under stress due to increasing demand from a growing population, increasing pollution, and depleting or uncertain supplies due to changing climate in which drought and floods have both become more frequent. As domains associated with water continue to experience tremendous data growth from models, sensors, and satellites, there is an unprecedented opportunity for machine learning to help address urgent water challenges facing humanity. Dr. Kumar's talk examined the role that big data and machine learning can play in advancing water science, challenges faced by traditional machine learning methods in addressing the domain of water, and some early successes.

Dr. Jian Pei, from Simon Fraser University, Canada, talked about relevant aspects such as interpretability, fairness, and marketplaces towards trustworthy data science. We believe data science and AI will change the world. No matter how smart and powerful an AI model we can build, the ultimate testimony of the success of data science and AI is users' trust. How can we build trustworthy data science? At the level of user-model interaction, how can we convince users that a data analytic result is trustworthy? At the level of group-wise collaboration for data science and AI, how can we ensure that the parties and their contributions are recognized fairly, and establish trust between the outcome (e.g., a model) of the group collaboration and the external users? At the level of data science participant eco-systems, how can we effectively and efficiently connect many participants of various roles and facilitate the connection between supplies and demands of data and models? Dr. Pei's talk brainstormed possible directions to the above questions in the context of an end-to-end data science pipeline. To strengthen trustworthy interactions between models and users, Dr. Pei advocated exact and consistent interpretation of machine learning models. His recent results showed that exact and consistent interpretations are not just theoretically feasible, but also practical even for API-based AI services. To build trust in collaboration among multiple participants in coalition, Dr. Pei reviewed some progress in ensuring fairness in federated learning, including fair assessment of contributions and fairness enforcement in collaboration outcomes. Last, to address the need of trustworthy data science eco-systems, Dr. Pei reviewed some latest efforts in building data and model marketplaces and preserving fairness and privacy. Through reflection Dr. Pei discussed some challenges and opportunities in building trustworthy data science for possible future work.

Dr. Francisco Pereira, from the National Institutes of Health (NIH), USA, presented his research aiming at revealing interpretable object representations from human behavior. Objects can be characterized according to a vast number of possible criteria (e.g. animacy, shape, color, function), but some dimensions are more useful than others for making sense of the objects around us. Dr. Pereira described an ongoing effort by his collaborators to collect a behavioral dataset of millions of odd-one-out similarity judgements on thousands of objects, and a new approach to identify the "core dimensions" of object representations used in those judgements. His approach models each object as a sparse, non-negative embedding, and judgements as a function of the similarity of those embeddings. The resulting model predicts subject behaviour on test data, as well as the fine-grained structure of object similarity. The dimensions of the embedding space are coherently interpretable by test subjects, and reflect degrees of taxonomic membership, functionality, and perceptual or structural attributes, among other characteristics. Further, naive subjects can accurately rate objects along these dimension, without training. Collectively, these results demonstrate that human similarity judgments can be captured by a fairly low-dimensional, interpretable embedding that generalizes to external behavior.

Dr. Jean Vanderdonckt, from the Université catholique de Louvain, Belgium, provided an overview of dimension reduction by model-based approaches and its application to gesture recognition. Machine learning algorithms used for 2D/3D gesture recognition typically require a large training set of templates having many dimensions, depending on the sensor used. Instead of applying classical methods for reducing the dimensionality of these templates, Dr. Vanderdonckt proposed relying on a model-based approach where the problem is first mathematically described and then submitted to machine learning algorithms.

Juan Antonio Lossio-Ventura
Jorge Valverde-Rebaza
Jorge Díaz
Denisse Muñante
Carlos Gavidia-Calderon
Alan Demétrius Baria Valejo
Hugo Alatrista-Salas

Organization

Organizing Committee

General Chairs

Juan Antonio Lossio-Ventura   National Institutes of Health (NIH), USA
Hugo Alatrista-Salas   Universidad de Ingeniería y Tecnología (UTEC),
                              Peru

SNMAM Track Organizers

Jorge Valverde-Rebaza   Visibilia, Brazil
Alan Demétrius Baria Valejo   Federal University of São Carlos, Brazil
Thiago de Paulo Faleiros   University of Brasília, Brazil

DISE Track Organizers

Denisse Muñante   ENSIIE and SAMOVAR, France
Carlos Gavidia-Calderon   The Open University, UK
Jorge Díaz   Universidad Peruana de Ciencias Aplicadas, Peru

BIOMEDS Track Organizers

Pablo Fonseca   Universidad Peruana Cayetano Heredia, Peru
José Ferrer   Universidad Peruana Cayetano Heredia, Peru
Mabel K. Raza   Universidad Peruana Cayetano Heredia, Peru
Joseph Pinto   Auna, Peru

Local Organizers

Jesús Bellido-Angulo   Universidad de Ingeniería y Tecnología, Peru
Yamilet Serrano-Llerena   Universidad de Ingeniería y Tecnología, Peru
Cristhian Ganvini Valcarcel   Universidad Andina del Cusco, Peru
Armando Fermín Pérez   Universidad Nacional Mayor de San Marcos, Peru
José A. Herrera-Quispe   Universidad Nacional Mayor de San Marcos, Peru

Program Committee

SIMBig Program Committee

Asma Ben Abacha   National Institutes of Health, USA
Nathalie Abadie   COGIT, IGN, France
Amine Abdaoui   Huawei Research, France

Pedro Marco Achanccaray Diaz	Pontifical Catholic University of Rio de Janeiro, Brazil
Hugo Alatrista-Salas	Universidad de Ingeniería y Tecnología, Peru
Marco Alvarez	University of Rhode Island, USA
Yuan An	Drexel University, USA
Sophia Ananiadou	University of Manchester, UK
Erick Antezana	Norwegian University of Science and Technology, Norway
Ghislain Atemezing	Mondeca, France
John Atkinson	Universidad Adolfo Ibañez, Chile
Jérôme Azé	University of Montpellier, France
Imon Banerjee	Mayo Clinic, USA
Patrice Bellot	Aix-Marseille Université, France
Cesar Beltrán	Pontificia Universidad Católica del Perú, Peru
Farah Benamara	Université Paul Sabatier, France
Elena Beretta	Vrije Universiteit Amsterdam, The Netherlands
Giacomo Bergami	Newcastle University, UK
Jose David Bermudez Castro	Pontifical Catholic University of Rio de Janeiro, Brazil
Jiang Bian	University of Florida, USA
Selen Bozkurt	Flatiron Health, USA
Carmen Brando	École des hautes études en sciences sociales, France
Sandra Bringay	Paul Valéry University, France
Andrei Broder	Google, USA
Jean-Paul Calbimonte Pérez	University of Applied Sciences and Arts Western Switzerland, Switzerland
Hugo David Calderon Vilca	Universidad Nacional Mayor de San Marcos, Peru
Guillermo Calderón-Ruiz	Universidad Católica de Santa María, Peru
Mete Celik	Erciyes Üniversitesi, Turkey
Qingyu Chen	National Institutes of Health, USA
Davide Chicco	Peter Munk Cardiac Centre, Canada
Diego Collarana Vargas	Fraunhofer IAIS, Germany
Nelly Condori-Fernandez	Universidade da Coruña, Spain
Adrien Coulet	Inria, Paris, France
Bruno Cremilleux	Université de Caen Normandie, France
Fabio Crestani	University of Lugano, Switzerland
Gabriela Csurka	NAVER LABS Europe, France
Nuno Datia	ISEL, Portugal
Jessica de Faria Dafflon	National Institutes of Health, USA
Jos De Roo	Ghent University, Belgium
Dina Demner-Fushman	National Institutes of Health, USA

Bart Desmet	National Institutes of Health, USA
Damiano Distante	University of Rome Unitelma Sapienza, Italy
Marcos Aurélio Domingues	State University of Maringá, Brazil
Catherine Dominguès	IGN, France
Martín Ariel Domínguez	Universidad Nacional de Córdoba, Argentina
Alexandre Donizeti	UFABC, Brazil
Dejing Dou	University of Oregon, USA
Brett Drury	Liverpool Hope University, UK
Jocelyn Dunstan	University of Chile, Chile
Tome Eftimov	Jožef Stefan Institute, Slovenia
Okyaz Eminaga	Stanford University, USA
Almudena Espin Perez	Stanford Universiry, USA
Jacinto Estima	INESC-ID and Universidade Europeia, Portugal
Paula Estrella	Universidad Nacional de Córdoba, Argentina
Karina Figueroa Mora	Universidad Michoacana de San Nicolás de Hidalgo, Mexico
Frédéric Flouvat	University of New Caledonia, New Caledonia
Cidália Fonte	University of Coimbra and INESC Coimbra, Portugal
Markus Forsberg	University of Gothenburg, Sweden
Carlos Gavidia	Pontifica Universidad Católica del Perú, Peru
Andrew Gentles	Stanford University, USA
Olivier Gevaert	Stanford University, USA
Ayush Goyal	Texas A&M University-Kingsville, USA
Natalia Grabar	University of Lille, France
Irlán Grangel-González	Robert Bosch GmbH, Germany
Juan Gutierrez Alva	Universidad de Ingeniería y Tecnología, Peru
Adrien Guille	Université Lumière Lyon 2, France
Yi Guo	University of Florida, USA
Thomas Guyet	Agrocampus Ouest and IRISA, France
Zhe He	Florida State University, USA
Diana Inkpen	University of Ottawa, Canada
Clement Jonquet	University of Montpellier, France
Jennifer Joseph	Abbott, USA
Frank Dennis Julca-Aguilar	Algolux, Canada
Maulik Kamdar	Elsevier Inc., USA
Maria Keet	University of Cape Town, South Africa
Ravi Kumar	Google, USA
Ka Chun Lam	National Institutes of Health, USA
Juan Lazo Lazo	Universidad del Pacífico, Peru
Florence Le Ber	Université de Strasbourg and ENGEES, France
Cédric López	Emvista, France

Maysa Macedo	IBM Research, Brazil
Sanjay Kumar Madria	Missouri University of Science and Technology, USA
Sabrine Mallek	ICN Business School, France
Ricardo Marcacini	University of São Paulo, Brazil
Marcos Martínez-Romero	Stanford University, USA
Bruno Martins	INESC-ID, Portugal
Florent Masseglia	Inria, France
Patrick McClure	National Institutes of Health, USA
Rosario Medina Rodriguez	Pontificia Universidad Católica del Perú, Peru
Guillaume Metzler	Université Lumière Lyon 2, France
Claudio Miceli	Federal University of Rio de Janeiro, Brazil
Nandana Mihindukulasooriya	IBM Research, USA
Adam Miner	Stanford University, USA
André Miralles	Irstea, France
Antonio Miranda	Barcelona Supercomputing Center, Spain
Avdesh Mishra	Texas A&M University-Kingsville, USA
Pritam Mukherjee	Stanford University, USA
Denisse Muñante	ENSIIE and SAMOVAR, France
Mark Musen	Stanford University, USA
Behzad Naderalvojoud	Stanford University, USA
Nhung Nguyen	University of Manchester, UK
Mais Nijim	Texas A&M University-Kingsville, USA
Jordi Nin	Universitat Ramon Llull and ESADE, Spain
Miguel Nuñez-del-Prado-Cortéz	Universidad del Pacífico, Peru
José Eduardo Ochoa Luna	Universidad Católica San Pablo, Peru
Maciej Ogrodniczuk	Institute of Computer Science of the Polish Academy of Sciences, Poland
Matilde Pato	ISEL, Portugal
Jessica Pinaire	Kalya, France
Jorge Poco	Universidad Católica San Pablo, Peru
Pascal Poncelet	University of Montpellier, France
Mattia Prosperi	University of Florida, USA
Marcos Quiles	Federal University of São Paulo, Brazil
Julien Rabatel	Catholic University of Leuven, Belgium
Mabel Raza	Universidad Peruana Cayetano Heredia, Peru
José Fabián Reyes Román	Universitat Politècnica de València, Spain
Justine Reynaud	University of Normandie, France
Edgar Rios	Genentech, USA
Mathieu Roche	CIRAD, France
Nancy Rodriguez	University of Montpellier, France
Alejandro Rodríguez-Gonzales	Universidad Politécnica de Madrid, Spain

Edelweis Rohrer	Universidad de la República, Uruguay
Rafael Rossi	University of São Paulo, Brazil
Silvia Rueda Pascual	University of Valencia, Spain
Jose M. Saavedra	Orand, Chile
Arnaud Sallaberry	Paul Valéry University, France
Christian Sallaberry	UPPA, France
Shengtian Sang	Stanford University, USA
Rafael Santos	Instituto Nacional de Pesquisas Espaciais, Brazil
Edgar Sarmiento-Calisaya	Universidad Nacional de San Agustín, Peru
Lucile Sautot	AgroParisTech, France
José Segovia-Juárez	INIA, Peru
Nazha Selmaoui-Folcher	University of New Caledonia, New Caledonia
Matthew Shardlow	University of Manchester, UK
Pedro Nelson Shiguihara Juárez	Universidad San Ignacio de Loyola, Peru
Diego Silva	Universidade Federal de São Carlos, Brazil
João Simões	Cron.Studio, Portugal
Wenyu Song	Harvard University, USA
Aurea Rossy Soriano Vargas	University of Campinas, Brazil
Victor Stroele	Universidade Federal de Juiz de Fora, Brazil
Madhumita Sushil	University of California, San Francisco, USA
Silvia Lizeth Tapia Tarifa	University of Oslo, Norway
Maguelonne Teisseire	INRAE, France
Paul Thompson	University of Manchester, UK
Camilo Thorne	Elsevier, Germany
Sanju Tiwari	Universidad Autonoma de Tamaulipas, Mexico
Turki Turki	King Abdulaziz University, Saudi Arabia
Willy Ugarte	Universidad Peruana de Ciencias Aplicadas, Peru
Carlos Vázquez	École de Technologie Supérieure, Canada
Antonio Vetro	Politecnico di Torino, Italy
Maria-Esther Vidal	Universidad Simón Bolívar, Venezuela
Edwin Rafael Villanueva Talavera	Pontificia Universidad Católica del Perú, Peru
Boris Villazon-Terrazas	Fujitsu Laboratories of Europe, Spain
Sebastian Walter	Semalytix GmbH, Germany
Florence Wang	Telstra, Australia
Lana Yeganova	National Institutes of Health, USA
Sarah Zenasni	ICube and Strasbourg University, France
Chryssa Zerva	Instituto de Telecomunicações, Portugal
Yuan Zhao	National Institutes of Health, USA
Charles Zheng	National Institutes of Health, USA
Lu Zhou	Kansas State University, USA
Pierre Zweigenbaum	Université Paris-Saclay, CNRS, and LISN, France
Ivan Dimitry Zyrianoff	University of Bologna, Italy

SNMAM Program Committee

Alexandre Donizeti	Federal University of ABC, Brazil
Alexandre Luis Magalhães Levada	Federal University of São Carlos, Brazil
Ankur Singh Bist	Signy Advanced Technology, India
Aurea Soriano Vargas	University of Campinas, Brazil
Brett Drury	INESC TEC, Portugal
Celia Ghedini Ralha	University of Brasília, Brazil
Cesar Henrique Comin	Federal University of São Carlos, Brazil
Daniela Godoy	UNICEN, Argentina
Dibio Leandro Borges	University of Brasília, Brazil
Diego Furtado Silva	Federal University of São Carlos, Brazil
Geraldo Pereira Rocha Filho	University of Brasília, Brazil
Guilherme Novaes Ramos	University of Brasília, Brazil
Heloísa de Arruda Camargo	Federal University of São Carlos, Brazil
José Reinaldo da Cunha Santos Aroso Vieira da Silva Neto	University of Brasília, Brazil
Jorge Poco	Fundação Getulio Vargas, Brazil
Luca Rossi	Queen Mary University of London, UK
Maria Da Conceição Rocha	INESC TEC, Portugal
Mathieu Roche	Cirad-TETIS, France
Newton Spolaôr	State University of Western Paraná, Brazil
Pascal Poncelet	University of Montpellier, France
Paulo Eduardo Althoff	University of Brasília, Brazil
Pedro Nelson Shiguihara Juárez	Universidad San Ignacio de Loyola, Peru
Rafael Delalibera Rodrigues	University of São Paulo, Brazil
Rafael Giusti	Federal University of Amazonas, Brazil
Rafael Santos	National Institute for Space Research, Brazil
Ronaldo Prati	Federal University of ABC, Brazil
Tiago Colliri	University of São Paulo, Brazil
Victor Stroele	Federal University of Juiz de Fora, Brazil
Vinicius Ruela Pereira Borges	University of Brasília, Brazil
Willy Ugarte	Peruvian University of Applied Sciences, Peru

DISE Program Committee

José Ignacio Panach Navarrete	Universitat de València, Spain
José Fabián Reyes Román	Universitat Politécnica de València, Spain
Carlos Efraín Iñiguez Jarrín	Escuela Politécnica Nacional, Ecuador
Silvia Rueda Pascual	Universitat de València, Spain
Damiano Distante	University of Rome Unitelma Sapienza, Italy
Otto Parra	Universidad de Cuenca, Ecuador
Vincent Lalanne	Université de Pau et des Pays de l'Adour, France
Aurea Rossy Soriano Vargas	University of Campinas, Brazil

Lenis Wong	Universidad Peruana de Ciencias Aplicadas, Peru
Glen Rodriguez	Universidad Nacional de Ingeniería, Peru
Jose Antonio Pow-Sang	Pontificia Universidad Catolica del Perú, Peru
Yudith Cardinale	Universidad Simón Bolívar, Peru
Manuel Munier	Université de Pau et Pays de l'Adour, France
Roxana Lisette Quintanilla Portugal	PUC-Rio, Brazil

Organizing Institutions and Sponsors

Organizing Institutions

Universidad de Ingeniería y Tecnología UTEC, Peru[2].
National Institutes of Health, USA[3].

Collaborating Institutions

Universidad Andina del Cusco, Peru[4].
Universidad Nacional Mayor de San Marcos, Peru[5].
Université de Montpellier, France[6].
Visibilia, Brazil[7].

---

[2] https://www.utec.edu.pe/en.
[3] https://www.nih.gov/.
[4] http://www.uandina.edu.pe/.
[5] http://www.unmsm.edu.pe/.
[6] https://www.umontpellier.fr/.
[7] http://visibilia.net.br.

Contents

Data Mining and Applications

Automatic Data Imputation in Time Series Processing Using Neural Networks for Industry and Medical Datasets

Juan Ignacio Porta[1,2]($\boxtimes$), Martín Ariel Domínguez[1,3]($\boxtimes$), and Francisco Tamarit[1,2]($\boxtimes$)

[1] FaMAF, Universidad Nacional de Córdoba, Córdoba, Argentina
juan.porta@mi.unc.edu.ar, {martin.dominguez,francisco.tamarit}@unc.edu.ar
[2] Instituto de Física Enrique Gaviola, IFEG (UNC-CONICET), Córdoba, Argentina
[3] Sección de Ciencias de la Computación, Córdoba, Argentina

Abstract. Time series classification and regression techniques help solve problems in many knowledge areas, including medicine, electronics, industry, and even music. When we apply them to real-life issues, a common obstacle is the lack of data in intervals within a time series. Usually, to solve it, the missing data is populated with information highly dependent on available datasets, which requires prior analysis. This paper addresses the problem in a novel way, automatically filling the missing data using a mixture of techniques and letting the prediction model decide which filling is better. We tested our approach for classification in industrial and medical datasets and for regression, we used a dataset containing COVID-19 information.

Our results are very competitive, and our approach improves the state-of-the-art models. We obtain better performance in all the experiments for the selected quality measures. Most importantly, the improvement is more statistically significant when the amount of missing data is higher.

Keywords: Time series classification · Regression · Deep learning · Convolutional networks · Long short-term memory

1 Introduction

Classifying a time series into specific categories predefined by experts has been a task of great interest in different areas of knowledge, such as medicine, music, and electronics, among others, [23,28,36]. This type of technique is highly versatile and applicable to endless tasks that range from abnormalities detection in electrocardiograms [28] to detecting failures in electronic components during production [23]. There are different approaches to time series classification, which vary from classical statistical methods to rule-based systems. This research line experienced a re-growth with the increase of computing capability and the creation of specific hardware that enabled significant improvement in the training

J. A. Lossio-Ventura et al. (Eds.): SIMBig 2021, CCIS 1577, pp. 3–16, 2022.
https://doi.org/10.1007/978-3-031-04447-2_1

of deep learning models. In particular, models based on recurrent Long Short-Term Memory (LSTM)-type networks [16], and Convolutional Neural Networks (CNN) [8] have shown the highest performances for this task. In 2016, Cui, Chen, and Chen [8] addressed this problem with a novel method that incorporates a peculiar feature engineering. They used CNN architectures and fed it simultaneously with different preprocessed versions of a given time series.

In this work, we tackle a common obstacle that time-series datasets usually present in natural environments: time intervals with missing data. This problem is particularly relevant when dealing with sensor measurements, which can fail for various reasons, including the lack of power, signal, and memory, among others. In addition, it is common for missing data to appear in the health area, as in the case of discontinued records of data on patients, either due to irregularities in their measurements or absences. Many classical statistical methods overcome this problem, such as interpolation or forward filling, but these approaches strongly depend on the specific dataset analyzed.

Inspired by the work of Cui, Chen, and Chen [8], we present two models that take time series as input: one for classification and one for regression. The models presented can develop the tasks based on an input with missing data, generate different filling treatments in parallel, and take advantage of the information from each of these inputs to maximize performance in the specific task.

For the classification task, we test our model using two industrial datasets (Wafer and Ford). We also include a medical dataset, Mimic-III, which, unlike the previous ones, incorporates multivariable time series. Both methods use deep learning to choose and extract relevant information. Starting with a complete-time series, we emulate data loss by randomly sampling time intervals and removing them from the time series in different sizes. Our model outperforms other methods, and the performance is even more expressive as the number of missing data increases.

Additionally, we address the data imputation problem for regression. A common task in time series is regression; that is, given a series, one must try to predict a value in a region of $\mathbb{R}^n$. Regression is a widespread task in areas such as public health, econometrics, and meteorology. The best tools to learn regression models for time series are recurrent neural networks, such as LSTM [11] or GRU [7]. To address the lack of data intervals in regression time series, we develop a regression model based on an LSTM, similar to the one we use for the classification task. To test our approach, we use a dataset of COVID-19 cases in Argentina. We took the ideas from [1] where the authors use forecasting methods and interpolation to predict the total number of people infected and the number of active cases for COVID-19 propagation in a global dataset. We construct an iterative method based on cubic spline interpolation and Euler's method, which is an improvement over the two latter methods. Our model outperforms state-of-the-art methods, although the task is more complex than in classification, and therefore, the model is more sensitive to missing data.

This paper is structured as follows. The next section analyzes the related work for time series classification and data imputation. In Sect. 3, we describe the datasets used for both classification and regression. In Sect. 4, we address the problem of TSC with missing data and the problem of TSR with missing data. In particular, we define a baseline model adapted from [8] and a new Automatic Data imputation model, and we analyze the experimental setup of our models and the baseline models. In Sect. 5, we describe the experimental results and compare the performance of both models. Finally, in 6, we present our conclusion and possible extensions of this work.

2   Related Work

In this Section we describe the most relevant previous work related to our models.

Formally, a time series is a set of real numbers measured in chronological order. We denote a time series as $T = \{V_{t_1}, ..., V_{t_n}\}$, where $V_i = (v_1, \ldots, v_k)$ is a vector of dimension k of v_i values at time t_i with data recorded at n different times for each series.

A labeled time series dataset is denoted as $D = \{(T_j, y_j)\}_{j=1}^{N}$, which contains N time series with their corresponding tags. In this paper, we consider classification and regression tasks, then, for classification, y_i is a categorical value at $C = \{1, ..., c\}$ where $c \in \mathbb{Z}^+$ is the number of different labels or categories. In contrast, for regression task, y_i is a number belonging to an interval of $\mathbb{R}$.

As Cui, Chen, and Chen mentioned, many specific difficulties arise when dealing with time series that make it very difficult for machine learning models to deal with the classification tasks. Among the most relevant ones, we can mention, for instance, the need for features at different time scales, strongly depending on the dataset used and the handling of random noise.

2.1   Cui Chen and Chen MCNN

To address these issues, the authors introduced a Multi-scale Convolutional Neural Network (MCNN). They have addressed the TSC problem using CNN and obtained excellent results compared with previous ones. They compared their results with Dynamic Time Warping (DTW) with a warping window constraint set through cross-validation(DTW CV) [25], Fast Shapelet (FS) [26], Symbolic Aggregate approXimation (SAX) with Vector Space (SV) model [34], Bag-of-SFA-Symbols (BOSS) [32], Shotgun Classifier (SC) [31], Time Series based on a Bag-of-Features (TSBF) [5], Proportional Elastic Ensemble (PROP) [3], 1-NNBag-Of-SFA-Symbols in Vector Space (BOSSVS) [33], Learn Shapelets Model (LTS) [10] and the Shapelet Ensemble (SE) model [4]. The proposed model by Cui, Chen, and Chen, proved to be very powerful for carrying out this difficult task. The architecture proposed can be divided into three different stages:

1. *Transformation Stage*: from the input time series, they build three different transformations, namely, (a) a time compression, (b) spectral transformations in frequency and, (c) a direct mapping, and these three series feed the local stage. Each one of these transformations is called *a branch*.

2. *Local convolution stage*: for each of the three branches, we apply sequentially several convolutional layers to implement a feature extraction. At this stage, the convolutions are independent of each branch.
3. *Global convolution stage*: finally, they concatenate the output of the convolutional layers into a single layer, on which new convolutional nuclei are applied, ending in a completely connected architecture with two linear output neurons with softmax activation functions, which is a function that normalizes the outputs of the linear layer.

It is worth mentioning that the results obtained in [8] outperform all previous models at that time.

2.2   State-of-the-Art for Data Filling

The problem of filling data in a time series has been widely studied in the literature, the most relevant ones are: soft impute [22] xgboost-based model [39] ST-MVL [37], adversarial training [19]. Next, we describe more in the deep Soft Impute and Xgboost-based Model used in our approach. .

- **Soft Impute** [22]: In this work, the authors replace the missing elements with those obtained from a soft threshold Singular Value Decomposition (SVD). With the help of warm starts, they efficiently calculate a complete solution regularization path on a grid of regularization parameter values. This model shows great performance as a filling data technique, showing better performance than Hard-impute [22], SVT [6] and OptSpace [17], and a similar performance to MMMF [35].
- **Xgboost-based Model** [39]: this approach combines an unsupervised pre-filling strategy with a supervised machine learning approach, using extreme gradient boosting (XGBoost). This combination leverage both types of context for imputation purposes: Contextual information in individuals and laboratory test variables. The resulting model outperforms 3D-MICE [21], and even a combination of local mean and soft impute in most datasets presented.

3   Dataset

This section describes the datasets used in this work. The first dataset we use is the Wafer dataset generated by R. Olszewski. This time series dataset consists of measurements obtained during the semiconductor circuit production process and binary classification of it: normal or abnormal. The dataset essentially consists of 152 temporary features. This corpus is split in two with distribution not suitable to test the models; consequently, we generate a new distribution. We join the previous sets and create a new partition of 80% of the data for training (5731 entries), and the resulting 20% is assigned as the test set (1433). The dataset is highly unbalanced, with 10.7% of the training set and 12.1% of the test set belonging to the abnormal class.

The following explored dataset is the **FordA** and **FordB** dataset, which is a dataset initially used in a competition at the IEEE World Congress on Computational Intelligence, 2008. Its objective is to classify the existence or absence of a particular symptom in an. Each time series consists of a record of engine noise and a binary objective of 1 or -1.

The last classification dataset to use is the Medical Information Mart for Intensive Care III database version 1.4 (MIMIC III v1.4) which includes information on 46,520 patients who were admitted to various ICUs of BIDMC in Boston, Massachusetts from 2001 to 2012 [9,15,24]. Adult patients who were diagnosed with sepsis-3 were included in the study. The criterion used was the same as in Hou, Nianzong, et al. (2020) [12]. Patients were divided into two groups based on whether they were dead or alive within 30 days, and a binary variable was generated based on this. A total of 4559 sepsis-3 patients are included in our study, in which 889 patients died and 3670 survived after 30 days.

Finally, to test our approach for regressor models, we use a COVID-19 dataset from Argentina [2]. These time series include the number of new daily cases and the average age of people infected. The time frame considered was between March 1, 2020, and August 1, 2021. Taking this freely available data, we generate 400 series of 30 days in length. We split it into two subsets for training a test dataset with 80 and 20%, respectively. The target is to predict the number of cases 15 days in the future.

4   Experimental Setup

This section describes the pipeline, and the network architecture that we propose to address the imputation of missing data in time series processing. We also clarify the differences in our approach with that introduced in [8], which inspired our work.

Based on the first two datasets previously described, each series randomly removes missing data taking into account different percentages. Let $D = \{(V_{t_1}, y_{t_1}), \ldots, (V_{t_N}, y_{t_N})\}$ be a labeled time series. We build different datasets, with different percentages of missing data from the original dataset D. We call D_{-f} the dataset resulting from deleting a percentage f. We construct D_{-f} by generating sets of disjoint time intervals $I_f = [t_{i_1}^l, t_{i_1}^r] \ldots [t_{i_k}^l, t_{i_k}^r]$ where $t_i < t_{i_1}^l < ti_1^{\ r} < \ldots < ti_k^{\ l} < ti_k^{\ r} < t_N$ and the resulting series D_{-f} has an f percentage of less vectors than D. This deletion is carried out by replicating real-life sensor time series: it has one or more missing subsets of data that are continuous over time, and it has an average controlled amount of fewer data.

For Wafer and Ford datasets, we tested our model for D_{-f} with percentage $f \in \{10, 30, 50, 60, 70, 80, 90\}$. The percentage f of data deletion is randomly selected, then, to validate the statistical significance of our results, for each percentage f, we build 10 random deleted datasets. Because of how data erasure is designed, the type of missing data that our models address is missing at random (MAR) because the data deletion is random, but missing data cannot appear in the first or last values of the series [27].

The MIMIC dataset is more complex than previous datasets, and it has real missing data; then, the data deletion was carried out only until having 30% of missing data. Although in the case of medical datasets, it makes more sense to find missing data in all variables simultaneously, as in certain variables, we also trained on the mimic-III dataset with independent deletion per column. This idea tries to test the model on a dataset multivariable that may present this characteristic more frequently in sensor systems. To do so, we apply the deletion of the univariable datasets to each column of the mimic-III dataset.

In the COVID-19 dataset, the data deletion was carried out only until having 30% of missing data.

4.1   MCNN Baseline Model

Before we introduce our model, let us briefly describe the modification implemented on the model presented in [8], which we will call our baseline model. This modification seeks to handle smaller datasets and thus avoid overfitting. First, we eliminate the convolutional layers in the global stage, leaving only a single one, a fully connected global layer. The base model is structured as follows:

– **Coord Conv Channel**: A general problem that convolutional networks present when analyzing time series, compared to recurrent networks (RNN), is that the former lacks a structure that allows full exploitation of the time relationship between the values of the time series. A suitable property of the convolutional network is that it uses the "closeness" in time of two values when they are at a distance less than the size of the convolutional nucleus. However, when this does not happen, the layers have no information on where in the series it is located. For regular series, this can be of great importance. Therefore, we propose to use a variant of the idea stated in [20]. In this work, the authors added a channel to the network's entrance, which provides spatial information in convolutional neural networks of images, while our proposal provides temporal information and allows the model to locate itself in time. We call this the time *CoordConv* channel.
– **Transformation stage**: In the transformation stage, downsampling is performed every five temporary events to generate a temporarily compressed version of the original series. We also perform a moving average with a window of 5 consecutive events to generate a smoothing transformation in frequency.
– **Local convolution stage**: each branch of Local convolution stage in Fig. 1 consists of 3 convolutional layers in parallel of 32 kernels, with a kernel height of 1, 3, and 5 respectively, each with batch normalization [14] and followed by a linear layer of 10 neurons each with a dropout of 0.3 (Fig. 2). The number of branches is 12, 4 for each of the transformed series because the baseline model has the same number of parameters as the one that we will present later.
– **Global stage**: We concatenate the outputs by using a linear layer of 2 neurons, followed by a softmax.

Unlike the original Cui *et al.* model, the applied model works on the complete time series.

4.2 LSTM Baseline Model

The model used as a baseline for regression-based in LSTM follows the same ideas of the CNN classification model. It is set up in the following way:

- **Coord Conv Channel**: As in the MCNN model, we add a Time *CoordConv* channel, which allows the model to locate itself in time.
- **Transformation stage**: In the transformation stage, downsampling is performed every five temporary events to generate a temporarily compressed version of the original series. We also perform a moving average with a window of 5 consecutive events to generate a smoothing transformation in frequency.
- **local LSTM stage**: each branch of local recurrent stage in Fig. 1 consists of 1 LSTM layer, with 100 hidden states, followed by a linear layer of 10 neurons each with a dropout of 0.3 (Fig. 3). The number of branches is 12, 4 for each of the transformed series because the baseline model has the same number of parameters as the one that we will present later.
- **global stage**: we concatenate the outputs by using a linear layer of 1 neuron.

Keep in mind that both baselines are state of the art in data filling.

4.3 Our Approach for Automatic Imputation Model

In this subsection, we describe our model, which, as we will see in short, improves results obtained with the baseline model. As we mentioned previously, our work is based on Cui Chen and Chen's idea; we added new branches, which use different methods of data imputation. We combine the standard techniques of imputation in statistical analysis for time series, such as linear interpolation and forward filling, with the state-of-the-art techniques, such as soft impute, which repeatedly fills in missing values with the current prediction, and then solves an optimization problem on the complete matrix using a soft-thresholded SVD [22], and an xgboost-based model [39]. We combine each of these methods with frequency and time scale transformations. The idea is that the model can combine the robustness provided by multi-scale and multi-frequency to extract information from different methods of data imputation.

In the rest of this section, we describe our extension for CNN and LSTM models for automatic data imputation.

CNN Imputation Data Classification Model

In Fig. 1, we schematize our model architecture. Next, we enumerate how we extend the Cui *et al.* model [8]:

- The repeated branches in the baseline model are replaced with the chosen mechanisms for data imputation previously described.
- We add a temporary feature channel. The temporal information added in the new channel is only a list of index $1, 2, ..., n - 1, n$, which corresponds with a column of the temporal series, and n is the number of its elements.

- As in the Baseline model, each branch of Local convolution stage in Fig. 1 consists of 3 convolutional layers in parallel of 32 kernels, with a kernel height of 1, 3, and 5 respectively, each with batch normalization [14] and followed by

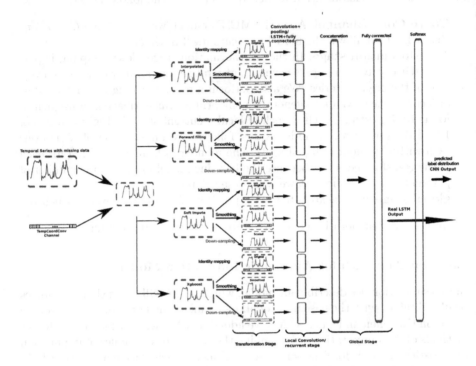

Fig. 1. MCNN/LSTM architecture scheme with data imputation.

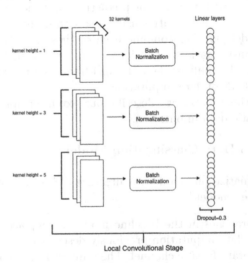

Fig. 2. Scheme of one branch in local convolution stage.

a linear layer of 10 neurons each with a dropout of 0.3 (Fig. 2). The number of branches is 12, 4 data filling techniques, and 3 transformations for each of the techniques 2.

LSTM Imputation Data Regression Model

In Fig. 1, we schematize our model architecture. The differences between the baseline model 4.2 and our model are as follows:

- The repeated branches in the baseline model are replaced with the same mechanisms for data imputation that were applied in the CNN model (forward filling, linear regression, soft impute, and Xgboost).
- We add a temporary feature channel, same as the CNN model.
- As in the baseline model, each branch of local recurrent stage in Fig. 1 consists of 1 LSTM layer, with 100 hidden states, followed by a linear layer of 10 neurons each with a dropout of 0.3 (Fig. 3). The number of branches is 12,4 data filling techniques, and 3 transformations for each of the techniques 3.

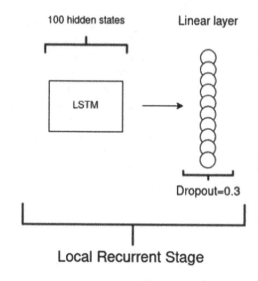

Fig. 3. Scheme of one branch in local recurrent stage.

5 Results

In this section, we present the evaluation of models proposed in the previous one.

5.1 Classification

We perform experiments for classification using "Wafer" and "Ford" datasets, with percentages 10, 30, 50, 60, 70, 80 and 90 of missing data in each time series as we described in Sect. 3. For mimic we use 10, 20 and 30. It is important to remark that for each percentage of missing data, we generate ten different datasets. In Tables 1, 2, 3 and 4 we compare the results of our data imputation with the baseline model described in the previous section. We report the performance for each percentage f of deleted data by using the standard quality measure. The selected measures were the average of $ROC - AUC$ measure $(\overline{AUC})$, and the standard deviation of $ROC - AUC$ (σ_{AUC}). The results show that our model exceeds the baseline even more while increasing the percentage of deleted data. It is important to note that the baseline model has a higher standard deviation in the results when the loss of data increases. The pertinent t-tests were carried out for these datasets, and it was found that, for the wafer and ford datasets, the models evaluated with data erasure between 50% and 90% are statistically different in 95% of the cases. In the Mimic-III dataset, it is found that they are different when the models are evaluated with data erasure above 10%.

It is remarkable how for classification models, our approach consistently outperforms the baseline. In simpler datasets, such as wafer or ford, it is found that when we evaluate the models by deleting time intervals up to 70%, the model continues to perform well and is consistently better than the baseline. For higher percentages, the performance decreases, which is to be expected.

For more complex datasets, such as mimic-III, it is observed that when 20% of data is deleted, the performance drops considerably, however our model is still consistently better.

The behavior of the models for those datasets without data deletion is the same, which is to be expected since by not having data deleted, both models are essentially the same.

In the case of the mimic-III dataset with global deletion, it is observed that the behavior of the model is worse than in the single variable datasets. It must be considered that we perform the data deletion, erasing all variables at the same time. This means that we delete patients and this makes the prediction more difficult. Additionally, the target variable is more complex than in previous datasets. In order to simulate a more realistic experiment in which only some features of patients are missing, we create a new datasets with deletion of data by column. Better results are observed since the model can use information from one variable to estimate the behavior at the time when another variable is absent.

Table 1. Performance of our model against the Baseline in Wafer Dataset.

%f of Del.	Our model		Baseline	
	$\overline{AUC}$	σ_{AUC}	$\overline{AUC}$	σ_{AUC}
0	99.2%	1.0%	99.2%	1.0%
10	99.1%	1.1%	99.1%	1.0%
30	98.3%	2.3%	98.1%	1.2%
50	95.3%	2.3%	92.8%	3.7%
60	94.8%	1.5%	90.5%	5.3%
70	94.1%	2.2%	87.1%	3.1%
80	76.1%	5.1%	70.5%	5.7%
90	56.7%	8.4%	53.0%	9.6%

Table 2. Performance of our model against the Baseline in Ford Dataset.

%f of Del.	Our model		Baseline	
	$\overline{AUC}$	σ_{AUC}	$\overline{AUC}$	σ_{AUC}
0	97.9%	1.3%	97.9%	1.3%
10	95.2%	2.2%	95.1%	1.7%
30	93.4%	3.1%	93.1%	3.3%
50	91.9%	2.7%	88.3%	3.2%
60	91.3%	2.5%	85.5%	3.3%
70	88.7%	2.7%	84.2%	2.1%
80	69.3%	6.2%	65.1%	7.4%
90	54.1%	7.7%	54.7%	9.4%

Table 3. Performance of our model against the Baseline in MIMIC-III Dataset.

%f of Del.	Our model		Baseline	
	$\overline{AUC}$	σ_{AUC}	$\overline{AUC}$	σ_{AUC}
0	91.2%	1.2%	91.2%	1.2%
10	89.4%	1.1%	87.5%	1.0%
15	71.7%	3.4%	66.8%	4.2%
20	64.3%	4.3%	60.1%	5.0%
25	59.7%	5.0%	57.3%	6.6%
30	56.4%	7.3%	55.5%	8.3%

Table 4. Performance of our model against the Baseline in MIMIC-III Dataset, with independent deletion per column.

%f of Del.	Our model		Baseline	
	$\overline{AUC}$	σ_{AUC}	$\overline{AUC}$	σ_{AUC}
0	91.2%	1.2%	91.2%	1.2%
10	90.2%	1.1%	89.2%	1.2%
15	75.3%	2.4%	72.9%	2.6%
20	68.9%	2.9%	64.4%	3.7%
25	60.2%	4.4%	59.2%	4.8%
30	56.6%	7.3%	55.8%	7.5%

5.2 Regression

We perform experiments for regression using the COVID-19 dataset, with percentages 10, 20, and 30 of missing data. It is important to remark that for each percentage of missing data, we generate ten different datasets. We report the performance for each percentage f of deleted data by using the standard quality measure. The selected measures were the average of the Percentage Prediction Error measure $(\overline{PPE})$ [1], and the standard deviation of PPE (σ_{PPE}).

The results in Table 5 show that our model exceeds the baseline consistently while increasing the percentage of deleted data. However, the problem seems to be more sensitive to data loss; for values over 30%, the PPE is too big. To validate our results, we perform t-tests, obtaining that the results of the regression models are statistically different in 95% of the cases in the regression for a value above 10% of the data deletion. In addition, with no data erasure (0%), both the proposed model and the baseline converge to the same model, as we expected.

Table 5. Performance of our LSTM model against the Baseline in COVID-19 dataset.

$\%f$ of Del.	Our model		Baseline	
	$\overline{PPE}$	σ_{PPE}	$\overline{PPE}$	σ_{PPE}
0	26.4%	14.7%	26.4%	14.7%
10	31.3%	23.4%	39.7%	26.3%
15	38.1%	27.2%	47.1%	31.2%
20	53.9%	39.3%	60.5%	35.1%
25	64.5%	41.1%	70.1%	35.6%
30	80.5%	42.4%	86.9%	46.5%

6   Conclusions and Future Work

As a general conclusion, we find that our model is a suitable method for the automatic imputation of missing data in temporal series classification and regression. The results obtained show that our approach outperforms a very competitive method combined with a standard interpolation. Another remarkable property is that our model's imputation is automatic, while this task is usually dependent on the dataset statistical analysis. For the classification task, our results show that our models outperform the state-of-the-art baseline in the three considered dataset, obtaining better $(\overline{AUC})$ and minor variance when the drop of data is higher. We obtain a similar result in the regression task, but the improvement in the quality measure $(\overline{MPE})$ is even more significant.

This research opens many doors to evolve the model. Next, we describe the most relevant ones. First, we can include any new data filling techniques in our model. Another line of investigation, especially with multi-class classification, involves using Generative Adversarial Network (GAN) [38] for generating the missing time series data. Finally, we can extend the model to apply it not only as a classifier and regressor of time series, but also as a forecast. In this sense, we could include state of the art models of forecasting and let the learning models choose the best option. Some of the possible combinations to use are: DeepAR [30], which is based on LSTM or GRU neurons; combined models of RNN as in [29], LSTNet [18], which is a mixture of CNN and RNN; or finally, augmented LSTM [13], which combines LSTM with autoencoders. In addition, we can make the approach more complex by exploring mixed problems of regression and forecasting.

References

1. Comparison of some forecasting methods for COVID-19. Alexandria Eng. J. **60**(1), 1565–1589 (2021)
2. Covid-19. casos registrados en la república argentina. http://datos.salud.gob.ar/dataset/covid-19-casos-registrados-en-la-republica-argentina
3. Bagnall, A.: Time series classification with ensembles of elastic distance measures. Data Min. Knowl. Disc. **29**(3), 565–592 (2014). https://doi.org/10.1007/s10618-014-0361-2
4. Bagnall, A., Lines, J., Hills, J., Bostrom, A.: Time-series classification with cote: the collective of transformation-based ensembles. IEEE Trans. Knowl. Data Eng. **27**, 2522–2535 (2015)
5. Baydogan, M., Runger, G., Tuv, E.: A bag-of-features framework to classify time series. IEEE Trans. Patt. Anal. Mach. Intell. **35**, 2796–2802 (2013)
6. Cai, J.F., Candès, E.J., Shen, Z.: A singular value thresholding algorithm for matrix completion. SIAM J. Optim. **20**(4), 1956–1982 (2010)
7. Cho, K., et al.: Learning phrase representations using RNN encoder-decoder for statistical machine translation. arXiv preprint arXiv:1406.1078 (2014)
8. Cui, Z., Chen, W., Chen, Y.: Multi-scale convolutional neural networks for time series classification. ArXiv (2016)
9. Goldberger, A.L., et al.: Physiobank, physiotoolkit, and physionet: components of a new research resource for complex physiologic signals. Circulation **101**(23), e215–e220 (2000)
10. Grabocka, J., Schilling, N., Wistuba, M., Schmidt-Thieme, L.: Learning time-series shapelets. In: Proceedings of the 20th ACM SIGKDD International Conference on Knowledge Discovery and Data Mining, pp. 392–401 (2014)
11. Hochreiter, S., Schmidhuber, J.: Long short-term memory. Neural Comput. **9**, 1735–80 (1997)
12. Hou, N., et al.: Predicting 30-days mortality for MIMIC-III patients with sepsis-3: a machine learning approach using XGboost. J. Transl. Med. **18**(1), 1–14 (2020)
13. Hsu, D.: Time series forecasting based on augmented long short-term memory. arXiv preprint arXiv:1707.00666 (2017)
14. Ioffe, S., Szegedy, C.: Batch normalization: accelerating deep network training by reducing internal covariate shift (2015)
15. Johnson, A.E., et al.: MIMIC-III, a freely accessible critical care database. Sci. Data **3**(1), 1–9 (2016)
16. Karim, F., Majumdar, S., Darabi, H., Harford, S.: Multivariate LSTM-FCNs for time series classification. Neural Netw. **116**, 237–245 (2019)
17. Keshavan, R.H., Montanari, A., Oh, S.: Matrix completion from a few entries. IEEE Trans. Inf. Theory **56**(6), 2980–2998 (2010)
18. Lai, G., Chang, W.C., Yang, Y., Liu, H.: Modeling long-and short-term temporal patterns with deep neural networks. In: The 41st International ACM SIGIR Conference on Research & Development in Information Retrieval, pp. 95–104 (2018)
19. Lin, S., Wu, X., Martinez, G., Chawla, N.V.: Filling missing values on wearable-sensory time series data. In: Proceedings of the 2020 SIAM International Conference on Data Mining, pp. 46–54. SIAM (2020)
20. Liu, R., et al.: An intriguing failing of convolutional neural networks and the Coord-Conv solution. In: Advances in Neural Information Processing Systems, vol. 31, pp. 9605–9616. Curran Associates, Inc. (2018)

21. Luo, Y., Szolovits, P., Dighe, A.S., Baron, J.M.: 3D-MICE: integration of cross-sectional and longitudinal imputation for multi-analyte longitudinal clinical data. J. Am. Med. Inform. Assoc. **25**(6), 645–653 (2018)
22. Mazumder, R., Hastie, T., Tibshirani, R.: Spectral regularization algorithms for learning large incomplete matrices. J. Mach. Learn. Res. **11**, 2287–2322 (2010)
23. Mohammed, B., Awan, I., Ugail, H., Younas, M.: Failure prediction using machine learning in a virtualised HPC system and application. Cluster Comput. **22**(2), 471–485 (2019). https://doi.org/10.1007/s10586-019-02917-1
24. Oweira, H., et al.: Comparison of three prognostic models for predicting cancer-specific survival among patients with gastrointestinal stromal tumors. Future Oncol. **14**(4), 379–389 (2018)
25. Rakthanmanon, T., et al.: Searching and mining trillions of time series subsequences under dynamic time warping, vol. 2012, August 2012
26. Rakthanmanon, T., Keogh, E.: Fast Shapelets: A Scalable Algorithm for Discovering Time Series Shapelets, pp. 668–676, May 2013
27. Rubin, D.B.: Inference and missing data. Biometrika **63**(3), 581–592 (1976)
28. Salem, A.M., Revett, K., El-Dahshan, E.A.: Machine learning in electrocardiogram diagnosis. In: 2009 International Multiconference on Computer Science and Information Technology (2009)
29. Salinas, D., Bohlke-Schneider, M., Callot, L., Medico, R., Gasthaus, J.: High-dimensional multivariate forecasting with low-rank gaussian copula processes. arXiv preprint arXiv:1910.03002 (2019)
30. Salinas, D., Flunkert, V., Gasthaus, J., Januschowski, T.: DeepAR: probabilistic forecasting with autoregressive recurrent networks. Int. J. Forecast. **36**(3), 1181–1191 (2020)
31. Schäfer, P.: Towards time series classification without human preprocessing, pp. 228–242, January 2014
32. Schäfer, P.: The BOSS is concerned with time series classification in the presence of noise. Data Min. Knowl. Disc. **29**(6), 1505–1530 (2014). https://doi.org/10.1007/s10618-014-0377-7
33. Schäfer, P.: Scalable time series classification. Data Min. Knowl. Disc. **30**(5), 1273–1298 (2015). https://doi.org/10.1007/s10618-015-0441-y
34. Senin, P., Malinchik, S.: SAX-VSM: interpretable time series classification using SAX and vector space model (2013)
35. Srebro, N., Rennie, J.D., Jaakkola, T.S.: Maximum-margin matrix factorization. In: NIPS, vol. 17, pp. 1329–1336. Citeseer (2004)
36. Wyse, L.L.: Audio spectrogram representations for processing with convolutional neural networks. ArXiv (2017)
37. Yi, X., Zheng, Y., Zhang, J., Li, T.: ST-MVL: filling missing values in geo-sensory time series data (2016)
38. Yoon, J., Jarrett, D., van der Schaar, M.: Time-series generative adversarial networks. In: Advances in Neural Information Processing Systems 32. Curran Associates, Inc. (2019)
39. Zhang, X., Yan, C., Gao, C., Malin, B.A., Chen, Y.: Predicting missing values in medical data Via XGBoost regression. J. Healthc. Inform. Res. **4**(4), 383–394 (2020). https://doi.org/10.1007/s41666-020-00077-1

Calibration of Traffic Simulations Using Simulated Annealing and GPS Navigation Records

Carlos Gamboa-Venegas[1,2]([✉]) [ID], Steffan Gómez-Campos[3] [ID], and Esteban Meneses[1,2] [ID]

[1] School of Computing, Costa Rica Institute of Technology, Cartago, Costa Rica
{cgamboa,emeneses}@cenat.ac.cr
[2] Advanced Computing Laboratory, Costa Rica National High Technology Center, San José, Costa Rica
[3] State of the Nation Program/CONARE, San José, Costa Rica
sgomez@estadonacion.or.cr

Abstract. A traffic simulation tool provides a virtual environment to efficiently analyze current traffic conditions and quickly measure the impact of changes to either transport infrastructure or driving rules. Realizing the full potential of traffic simulations depends on correct parameter setting. In this work, we propose a method to calibrate traffic simulations using available transportation data from Costa Rica. The data comes from Global Position System (GPS) navigation records that only show the traffic speed in different sectors. The calibration algorithm aims to solve the inverse problem of finding the actual traffic flows in all routes to accurately reproduce real traffic conditions. We managed to calibrate the simulations for four case studies and leveraged our program to design solutions that ease traffic conditions in those scenarios. The impact and applications of this work are plenty. First, additional calibration techniques can be explored. Second, available data for more general settings can be exploited. Third, our tool can be integrated as a useful resource for analysis and decision making in urban mobility studies.

Keywords: Simulation optimization · Simulated annealing · Traffic simulation

1 Introduction

The *Gran Area Metropolitana (GAM)* of Costa Rica, the principal urban and industrial region in the country, has severe traffic congestion and public and private transportation problems [9]. The reasons for that situation include a significant lag in traffic infrastructure development and an extremely large amount of vehicles concentrated in a small region. This behaviour worsens during rush hours and affects much of the population. Traffic congestion leads to several problems affecting the environment and quality of life of the population [19].

J. A. Lossio-Ventura et al. (Eds.): SIMBig 2021, CCIS 1577, pp. 17–33, 2022.
https://doi.org/10.1007/978-3-031-04447-2_2

These problems include air and sound pollution, increment in fuel consumption, delays in commute time and emergencies, traffic accidents, and more.

An Intelligent Transportation System (ITS) [22] is traditionally used to help in solving pressing traffic problems. An ITS is a tool that gathers several types of traffic and social data from different sources. Such as traffic sensors, GPS, video detectors, autonomous and connected vehicles. For analysis and decision making on temporal or permanent solutions. Transportation authorities in Costa Rica have not implemented an ITS yet. Therefore, we must resort to computer traffic simulations to understand traffic patterns and propose alternatives that alleviate critical problems. A traffic simulation tool builds a virtual environment with the goal of performing analysis about the current traffic conditions and exploring potential changes to transport infrastructure or driving rules. Although promising, traffic simulations require a substantial calibration effort of all system parameters. Otherwise, it may not be possible to obtain an accurate and adequate simulation. Parameter adjustment is achieved with methods to optimize simulations, mostly calibration, validation and verification [6,15].

In this paper, we present a method to calibrate traffic simulations using Global Position System (GPS) navigation records, collected from Waze, a commercial mobile application widely popular among Costa Rican drivers. Data was obtained from previous studies performed by State of Nation Program (PEN) [5,7,19]. These navigation records only report traffic speed in road segments. Therefore, our proposed method must solve an inverse problem. Traffic flows in all possible routes in a sector have to be calibrated to reproduce the same traffic speed. The whole calibration process requires selecting locations for study, preprocessing the GPS navigation data, processing and adjusting the network files of the virtual roads for the simulation, executing the calibration method as a software tool to perform experiments, evaluating results, and proposing solutions for each location.

2   Background

2.1   SUMO and Traffic Simulations

Computer simulations help emulate real traffic situations, show weak points in the road network and predict traffic conditions. Simulations are useful when there is no available real traffic flow information and traffic behavior is complex. The ultimate aim of traffic simulation is to create a virtual environment to understand traffic patterns difficult to capture and analyze from real scenarios. Modern data analysis and hardware advanced technologies have intensified the use of traffic applications to increase drivers safety, energy efficiency, user navigation system experience, and road infrastructure planning. Many of these problems are complex and can scale significantly. Therefore, we should rely on traffic simulation models that can be more accurate and dynamic than traditional analytical methods to suggest solutions for the aforementioned problems [6].

SUMO (Simulation of Urban MObility) [13] is a traffic simulation software created to simulate traffic conditions in a city. Specifically, its goal is to unveil the underlying model that produces traffic patterns, comparing features like speed simulation or the capacity to represent reality from other models. Created in the Centre for Applied Informatics at Cologne, Germany, it has been a popular tool to simulate and study traffic flow models, with additional tools to simplify processes like converting to different formats and creating routes to describe city transportation environments.

Past developments and SUMO applications are presented in a study [11]. SUMO simulates vehicular communication to: *i*) study the effect of vehicle-to-vehicle and vehicle-to-infrastructure communication where a combined simulation of traffic and communication is necessary; *ii*) optimize traffic light algorithms to make traffic lights capable of adapting to current traffic situations; *iii*) evaluate traffic surveillance systems to develop surveillance technology, and *iv*) use image processing of simulated areas to predict weather that could trigger critical traffic situations. A very interesting work is the calibration of the car-model in real sectors of American roads. In that research, they calibrated travel times compared with data from simulated traffic detectors. They managed to reduce the simulation error from 40% to a 15% [12].

Taking advantage of that SUMO simulates route choice and dynamic navigation. The work of the authors in [21] concentrates on traffic flow generation using an origin-destination (O-D) matrix with data from induction loop measurements available from traffic authorities, and then it uses DFROUTER (a SUMO tool to reroute vehicles), along with a heuristic, to generate an O-D matrix for traffic that resembles the real traffic distribution. Simulation results are validated against real data.

Similar work was done by Celick and Karadeniz [3], using SUMO simulator as we did in this paper. They aimed at optimizing the traffic flow, depending on the traffic density. Their approach takes an intersection and examines all the lanes on each side and processes traffic based on the lane where the longest tail is located. Then, it develops a real-time traffic light optimization system to set new light configuration, creating a smart intersection system. The most important conclusion is that for traffic light optimization the real-time analysis and change method gives better results than a fixed time and green wave method. The latter method is based on the principle that most cars which pass on green light encounter green light again at the traffic lights on the next intersection.

Flow [10] is another work where researches used reinforcement learning with SUMO to analyze traffic dynamics and perform optimization. Flow provides users with the ability to easily implement, through TraCI's Python API, hand-designed controllers for any components of the traffic environment such as calibrated models of human dynamics or smart traffic light controllers. Together with the dynamics built into SUMO, Flow allows users to design rich environments with complex dynamics. A central focus in the design of Flow is the ease of modifying road networks, vehicle characteristics, and infrastructure within an experiment, along with an emphasis on enabling reinforcement learning control over not just vehicles, but traffic infrastructure as well.

Additional to the studies using SUMO, other authors have summarized several consideration while performing traffic simulations. Li *et al.* [14] describe the process of traffic optimization and organization, both processes were implemented using the combination of static channelized of road junction and signal optimization. For signal optimization, they used a model called simultaneous perturbation stochastic approximation, an approach that approximates the gradient of the objective function through finite differences. This method achieves an important reduction in computational cost compared to traditional stochastic approximation methods. The article presents a case study where they analyze one sector of 1.68 km with 7 signal intersections, during morning rush hours where the average speed of vehicles was around 10 and 15 km/h. They used data from a historical database of the traffic flow in the road. The final results show that the signal optimization method for the simulation model and the implementation were effective and feasible, increasing the average car speed after the optimization.

And finally, works like Paternina *et al.* 1 [17] proposed the use of artificial intelligence-based techniques, such as reinforcement learning and artificial neural networks, to design a global optimization approach that is coupled with discrete-event computer simulation models to efficiently resolve practical problems.

2.2   Simulation Optimization Techniques

A simulation model is based on a mathematical model which is used to implement a computer program. By running the simulation model with specific values for the input variables, we can examine the behavior of a system. We can define a simulation experiment as one or several tests in which meaningful changes are made to the input variables of a simulation model to observe and identify the reasons for changes in the output. We selected *random (heuristic) search methods* for our calibration process. These methods are part of direct search methods, and they are used to find a way to organize the search process and avoid searching over all possible solutions. Instead, these methods turn into a low-cost search that is likely to discover a good, or near-optimal solution. Providing an efficient global search strategy, because they balance exploration with exploitation [1]. The heuristic as a rule-of-thumb may not guarantee convergence and optimality, making heuristic methods vulnerable to falling into local optima.

Simulated annealing (SA) is a stochastic search method commonly used to solve deterministic optimization problems and combinatorial problems in traffic assignment [16]. The concept of annealing comes from thermodynamics, which emulates how a fluid slowly cools down into a solid to produce a stronger, more stable product. Simulated annealing as an optimization tool has been used in different fields for several decades now. The method is a variation of conventional iterative improvement methods that begin with an initial feasible solution, repeatedly generate and consider changes in the current configuration, and accept only those that improve the objective function. This improvement mechanism has a probabilistic factor, in which non-improving moves are occasionally made, and it therefore offers a way to avoid getting stuck in local optima, while keeping track of the best overall solution, expecting to arrive to a global optimum [20]. To avoid the undesired convergence to a local optimum that characterizes deterministic local heuristic methods, simulated annealing methods probabilistically accept configurations that temporarily deteriorate the quality of the system being optimized. An acceptance probability is computed, based on the change in the objective function and a temperature parameter. As the temperature is appropriately reduced (this is called an annealing schedule or a cooling schedule), fewer non-improving moves are accepted. Thus, a coarse global search evolves into a fine local search for optimality, and the probabilistic jumps provide avenues to avoid sinking into non-global optima [2]. Implementation of simulated annealing requires choosing parameters of the initial and final temperatures, the cooling schedule, and a number of function evaluations at each temperature.

3 Solution Overview

The principal goal of this work is to create a tool to calibrate a traffic simulation in SUMO, being able to represent the real-world traffic situation on specific road sectors in a determined period. This calibration is done with GPS records from the Waze application. The data is used to compare the reported speed with results from simulation. Using an optimization algorithm we adjust traffic flow in all routes to represent real traffic conditions as close as possible.

3.1 Scenario Selection

Rush hour in Costa Rica is problematic. Several locations of the GAM show heavy traffic and congestion affecting a substantial amount of people daily. Selecting a road sector to analyze their traffic flow is not an easy task. The government is already working in some sections of the road network, for example *Circunvalación*, the principal bypass in the capital city of San José. Currently, this ring is being completed with a brand new north segment, and some secondary roads are suffering changes to create more lanes and new signaling. Considering that, we focus on sectors that represent a problematic case and, at the moment, may not be receiving total attention from the corresponding authorities.

We then chose four road sectors from different areas, considering the importance of the location, the impact of current traffic congestion, and the feasibility to create new infrastructure. From the study called *Congestion of Vehicular Flow of GAM* by CFIA [4], we considered the reasons for traffic congestion together with some ways to address the road congestion to select the scenarios. Including on these reasons are the traffic demand in rush hours, the limited road spaces, the elevated cost of road infrastructure, the negative impact of heavy congested junctions, the traffic light coordination timing and the priority to public transportation. We describe the four chosen sectors next.

(a) Sector 1: Plaza Mayor, Rohrmoser (original map and segment overlay)

(b) Sector 2: Taras three-way junction (original map and segment overlay)

(c) Sector 3: Sabanilla road east: (original map and segment overlay)

(d) Sector 4: Road Heredia to Barva (original map and segment overlay)

Fig. 1. Maps of sectors in the study along with their corresponding segment overlay (Color figure online)

Figure 1 shows the map of segments (in purple) per sector. Each segment is 100 m long or less, depending the split of each road length. In red numbers are annotated the main segments we chose to evaluate the traffic flow. These segments are the more relevant according with the observed traffic congestion, and the vehicle flow moving to the focal point in the sector.

Sector 1 is a main junction in Plaza Mayor, Rohrmoser, visible in Fig. 1(a). It presents traffic congestion in all directions, specially in the direction north to south. The north road comes from an uphill road and a bridge and stops at a traffic light, which aggravates the jam on the north side of the intersection. The traffic light is necessary because it is a junction with 5 routes and 8 turns. In this sector, we are looking into reducing that north-south jam, showing the impact of some simple changes. The districts at this location are Uruca and Pavas. This information is important because it is part of the filtering process to extract the involved road segments. Sector 2 (see Fig. 1(b)) presents a three-way junction without traffic lights, which is overly problematic. Sector 3 (see Fig. 1(c)) and Sector 4 (see Fig. 1(d)) are similar. Their location represents a main road that has heavy traffic flow mainly in one direction and has several secondary ways that introduce more complexity and vehicles to the actual traffic congestion.

3.2   Data Preparation from Waze

The data used to calibrate the simulation are GPS navigation records from the commercial mobile application Waze. A collaboration among State of the Nation Program (PEN), Ministry of Public Transportation of Costa Rica (MOPT) and Waze allows us to use data coming from jams and incidents reported since 2018. Even though the raw data is not available for this study. We used different data layers provided by a previous team of researchers that worked on the processing of this raw data [5, 7, 9]. They worked on cleaning and organizing the records in data frames of R programming language, and saving them on an RDS file. Using this data, we performed our filters to select the GPS records from the time frame and the appropriate location. The new data contains records with the following variables: *city, length, speed, anno, hour, delay, line, startNode, month, day-Week, endNode, roadType, street, day*. We only need *speed* and *line* information for each record, but the filters are executed considering other variables.

For this work, we have data from the whole 2018 and part of 2019. The first filter selects records from the weekdays and the evenings rush hours. After that, it selects two variables: *line* and *speed*. The first one contains the geometric information required to intersect with spatial information from SUMO and other sources. The second one is the average reported speed of the jams in that moment. Then, we took only one-hour records during the rush hour in the work days, specifically 17th h (5 p.m.). We focused the study on that specific hour to try to avoid errors caused by the unstable conditions of the beginning and the ending of the rush hour. We assume this is the steady-state of the system.

The next step converts those records into spatial data. The spatial data structure includes points, lines, polygons and grids; each of them with or without attribute data [18]. Then, using the dataset *RedVial*, a dataset prepared from the previous studies of Gómez-Campos and Cubero [5, 9], the algorithm takes the district IDs to extract the 100-m road segments for each district. Finally, it intersects the GPS records with the road segments to once again reduce the amount of data and canalize only the required information.

At this stage, the workflow aggregates the data and gets the statistics of speed for each segment, resulting in a new data frame with the segments of road organized by id and their respective average speed reported for one hour, specifically at hour 17 (5 p.m.). This information is saved as a csv (comma-separated values) file that is used during the calibration process to compare with the speeds resulting from the simulation.

3.3   Calibration Algorithm Implementation

We developed the solution in Python and R languages. Python was chosen to facilitate the programming and take advantage that SUMO is written in Python. R was chosen to reuse the existing code elaborated by Cubero *et al.* [5] as a base for the spatial data processing, and specifically the parallel code execution to intersect road networks.

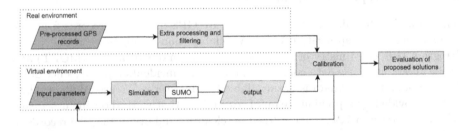

Fig. 2. General workflow of the solution

Figure 2 shows an overview diagram of our simulation optimization solution. The virtual environment component starts with preparing the input parameters that include the time period for vehicle insertion in specific routes of the sector. SUMO runs the simulation and generates an output that is the aggregated data of the road segment by a time interval. This output is used in combination with the GPS records to compare them and calculate the measure of performance (MoP) of the data, starting the calibration algorithm to find new parameters to simulate again. Each iteration the algorithm will perform the same procedure, generating new parameters, executing the simulation and calculating the MoP to verify and validate the alternative solution. The process stops when the indicated iterations are performed. The final step is the statistical test to validate the best found solution, to decide if it is truly useful.

3.4   Calibration Algorithm

The input parameters of the traffic simulation are the vehicles flows created manually in a *routes* file. Each flow (or route) contains an initial node (*from*) and final node (*end*). Those nodes are manually set according to the study and visualization of real conditions of the sector where more traffic flow is created.

Attributes like *departLane, departPos, departSpeed* are set to random values to include variability. The most important attribute is **period**, this parameter is the spawning time in seconds between vehicles in the respective route. If those values are tiny, the simulation generates a high traffic flow, but it may cause deadlocks on the roads.

The chosen algorithm used as a base for the design of the solution was Simulated Annealing (SA). This algorithm takes an initial set of parameters to run a simulation once to create the *initial solution*. This initial parameters are the spawning periods for the initial set of routes indicated in the *routes* file. The first solution is set as the *best solution* that will work as a comparison start point. Then, the algorithm chooses a combination of parameters based on the initial input to generate an alternative solution (also called neighbor), either worse or better. Being this new solution stored in a *routes* file. The value of this new solution will be compared with the previous best solution, and the best of both will be set as the new best solution. On each iteration, the algorithm attempts to generate and select a better solution.

In our traffic simulations, the solution is a set of values describing the average speed by segment. We represent two sets of values (from GPS records and from simulation) as two vectors (V_{waze} and V_{sim} respectively), on which we compute a distance function. That is why we need close enough vectors to affirm that the simulation is representing a real situation of traffic congestion in the studied sector. To compare those two sets of values and obtain a measure of the solution, first we calculate the MoP using the mean relative error (MRE) using the formula $MRE = (\sum (|V_{sim} - V_{waze}|/V_{waze}))/size(V_{waze})$, which gives us a value of the distance of the vectors. With this result, we have an idea of how close those vectors are and we can put a single number on each solution. The final aim of the calibration method is to minimize that distance, trying to get the most similar values as possible and the lowest MRE. At the end of the process, the statistical test Paired Sample T-Test is calculated to determine if the best solution we found is statistically relevant, and thus we verify whether the calibration algorithm succeeded.

Algorithm 1 shows the core steps. In summary, the first part calculates the solution of the initial parameter configuration. Those parameters are given by a random value in a specific range to generate some traffic flow. This initial calculation involves processing the simulation output, intersecting the resulting road sectors with the Waze data to calculate the MoP, and setting the value as the first point of comparison. After that, the iterative algorithm starts. Based on the last solution parameters, SA will choose several neighbors indicated as a parameter. For each neighbor, the program will run a simulation, intersect the results with the GPS records and get an MRE value. Each time, the new solution will be compared with the last best solution found and changing it if a better solution is found. Neighbors are chosen using the property of temperature of the SA. The nature of the algorithm is that a temperature variable resembles the temperature in the original process in metallurgy. This variable starts at a high value and it is reduced at each iteration, similar to the cooling process. So,

---

Algorithm 1: Simulated Annealing for parameter calibration

Result: Best parameter combination

`Calculate initial solution with default parameters`

runSUMOSimulation(*routes file*)

processSimulationResults()

intersectGPSRecords()   `// implemented in R`

actualSolution = calculateMRE() ;

// $MRE = (\sum (|V_{sim} - V_{waze}|/V_{waze}))/size(V_{waze})$

for *temp in temperatures* **do**

    bestSolution = actualSolution()

    allNeighbors = calculateNeighbors()

    for *neighbor in allNeighbors* **do**

        runSUMOSimulation(neighbor/*new routes file*))

        processSimulationResults()

        intersectGPSRecords()   `// implemented in R`

        actualSolution = calculateMRE()

        if *newSolution < bestSolution* **then**

         | bestSolution = newSolution

        end

        change = actualSolution - bestSolution

        if *change > 0* **then**

         | actualSolution = bestSolution

        else

            if *probBest (change, currentTemp)* **then**

             | actualSolution = bestSolution

            end

        end

    end

end

---

the higher the temperature, the more the input parameters will change in the simulation. That is, the period of the flows in the routes. On each iteration we expect we get closer to the best solution, selecting every time the lowest MRE. The cooling factor reduces each time the change of temperature in the neighbors, meaning the change in the input parameters is less vigorous every time. Also, cooler temperatures reduce the chances of getting many different neighbors and trying to converge to an optimal global solution. The cooling factors can be set manually in the configuration file before starting the program.

In the calibration process we calculated the initial MRE for each sector with the default parameter configuration, the algorithm searched for a better MRE to optimize on each iteration and found the possible solution. We aimed to optimize each sector using a significance level of 0.5, given the statistical test is proving that the final speed vector should be the same or at least show statistical evidence that they are the same. In the results we present a deeper description for each sector that helps to understand and explain the experimental setup and the obtained results.

4   Results and Analysis

4.1   Calibration Results

Sector 1 (see Fig. 1(a)) has 15 routes which create heavy traffic in the main junction and in the north-south road. Those 15 parameters are the focus of our calibration. In the process, every iteration the algorithm calculates 50 neighbors from each solution changing three values at a time and iterating over five temperature levels.

The initial value of the period of the input parameters is a random number from 20 to 30 s, with which we obtained an initial MRE of 4.842. Once the calibration algorithm ends, we obtained the final MRE of 0.478. That final value is significantly smaller than the initial 4.842. The final two-sample paired T-test gives us a p-value of 0.717, with α equals to 0.5 to that the H_0 can not be rejected. On the contrary, we accept H_0 having statistical evidence that indicates the two speed vectors are similar enough, supporting and validating the calibration algorithm results.

Table 1 summarizes the simulation results of the initial MRE, the final MRE once the calibration is run and the final p-value of the statistical test.

Table 1. Measure of Performance and p-value calculation of the studied sectors

Sector	Initial MRE	Final MRE	p-value	n-size
1	4.842	0.478	0.717	14
2	2.297	0.265	0.583	8
3	1.360	0.286	0.500	15
4	1.066	0.176	0.396	15

Sector 2 (see Fig. 1(b)) only has 8 routes: three routes coming from the north side of the highway, one route going south in the same road, one going east to segment 15 and the third going southeast to segment 4. One route in the highway going from south to north that increases traffic in the junction in segments 7 and 6 (not in image). Two more routes from segment 15 to north and south, and the last two routes going from south (segment 4) to east and north.

The algorithm runs with 5 levels of temperature, selecting 40 neighbors for each solution found and changing 3 values of those 8 parameters at the time to choose a new combination of parameters. The initial value of the MRE with periods from 15 to 30 s is 2.297. The calibration algorithm ran until we obtained a final MRE of 0.265, a huge difference compared with the initial value. To validate results the p-value of the T-test is 0.583. Again, we accept H_0 with α equals to 0.5 indicating both resulted vectors are statistically similar.

For the last studied sectors, we present two important cases of heavy traffic in the most complex conditions. A main road moves a heavy traffic flow to a specific direction while other routes fight each other for right of way, hindering the constant flow and reducing the speed in the majority of the segments. In addition, it generates a chain of situations that impact negatively the general traffic conditions. Sector 3 (see Fig. 1(c)) is a clear example of that. In rush hour at 5pm the main traffic flow moves from west to east. This sector has 3 traffic lights that complicate matters even more. We created 15 routes that generate the most of the traffic flow. In summary, there are three routes coming from the west, four coming from the east to different directions, three routes from the north, two coming from point 13 and two more from point 12. Details can be found in the configuration file. We focus on the amount of routes that create heavy traffic, even so, initial results show that we need to calibrate those spawning times. With periods from 15 to 25 s, we obtained an initial MRE of 1.360. The simulation runs with five levels of temperature, selecting for each solution 60 neighbors and changing 3 values at the time. The final MRE was 0.286, an adequate result. The statistical p-value gives us 0.5, enough to accept H_0 to indicate both result vectors are similar. With these results the calibration process on these complex scenarios is satisfactory.

Lastly, in sector 4 buses have the most negative impact on traffic conditions. There are 16 routes created manually using observations of the common paths used by vehicles. Bus routes, however, have only one direction and there are several bus destinations that need to share the main route (route 126 in the map). East and west are the origin of two spawn points each one, having a total of four spawning points. This sector clearly illustrates the worst traffic conditions during rush hour in the country. An initial MRE of 1.066 was obtained with initial periods from 20 to 25 s. Simulation ran with 5 levels of temperature and selecting 50 neighbor per solution, changing 3 values each time. With that, the calibration algorithm results in a final MRE of 0.176, with a p-value of 0.396 rejecting H_0 with α of 0.5. This case requires more study because several runs did not calibrate the sector with the expected precision.

4.2   Evaluation of Proposed Traffic Solutions

To evaluate the proposed traffic solutions and test if they produce a positive impact on traffic conditions, we ran a new simulation using the initial parameters of the optimized simulation and the changes applied in the network road and/or traffic rules. It is important to clarify that solution were proposed by expert opinion related with the main cause of the traffic congestion on each sector. We took the resulting speeds for each involved road segment and we compared them with the result of the optimized simulation. Showing the differences for each speed per segment and calculating the speed increment rate to quantify the impact of the proposals. Figure 3 illustrates the proposed solutions.

Beginning with Sector 1, we focused on the 11 segments marked on Fig. 1(a), chosen strategically to test specific traffic conditions and have better control of the situation. The traffic flow in segments 5, 6, 7 and 8 going to south warning about a necessity of a possible solution. Because of this, we created a new lane for turning right in the way to the west trying to reduce the amount of vehicles going to south and east. Figure 4(a) shows the values of speed in the selected

(a) Sector 1: extra lane coming down from the north to the junction in the south

(b) Sector 2: traffic light in junction allowing right turns in red

(c) Sector 3: adjusted timing in 3 traffic lights

(d) Sector 4: creation of off-line bus stop

Fig. 3. SUMO visualization of proposed solutions for each sector. Black lines represents roads. Red sections are junctions, inside them are different colors lines representing the direction of turning. In sector 3 a small icons indicates the traffic light in the junction. In Sector 4 the wide blue line represents a off-line bus stop. (Color figure online)

segments for the optimized simulation and the proposed solution. For Segment 5 the difference is not substantial because it is the closest segment to the junctions where cars need to stop on the traffic light. However, the other three segments show a difference of more than 14 m/s (50 km/h) in average. This means that cars coming from north have good speed and cars that need to turn right have complete free right-of-way to do it. The speedups in segments 5, 6, 7, and 8 are 1.78, 13.98, 12.07 and 9.04, respectively.

Sector 2 shows an increase of speed in 8 of the 15 segments, and a small slowdown in 4 segments. Segments 2, 3, 4 and 5 present a slowdown because we are allowing more traffic to cross from north to east. In that route, segments 7, 8, 9, 12, 13, 14 and particularly 15 show a significant acceleration.

Sector 3 is more complicated (see Fig. 1(c)). It has a lot of routes and several limitations about the structural road changes that we can propose. The simplest solution is to adjust the timing of the existing traffic lights at the east of the map (traffic lights shown in Fig. 1(c)). That solution involves setting a higher duration for routes in the main road, meaning the way from west to east will have more time to go through. The secondary turn time is reduced or adjusted according to the real time at the moment. In chart 3(c) we see the values of segments 1 and 2 that are the road segment closest to the traffic lights, here the average speed almost does not change. However, this effect can be caused by the natural stopping of vehicles approaching the junctions. After that, in the other segments the speed increases, exhibiting the most important differences from

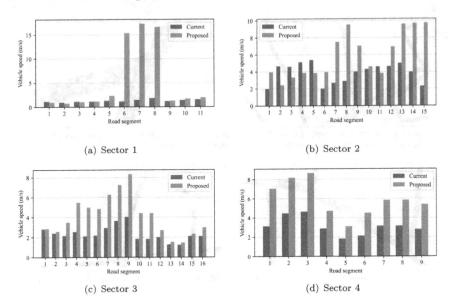

(a) Sector 1

(b) Sector 2

(c) Sector 3

(d) Sector 4

Fig. 4. Comparison of original speed for all sectors in the study against speed obtained after apply the alternatives proposed. Each bar shows the average speed in m/s for vehicles in the respective road segment.

segment 4 to 11. The majority of segments show an increase of approximately the double of speed. This behavior is clear evidence that simulation shows a benefit in the speed of vehicles in the segments approaching the traffic lights, implying an improvement of the traffic jam.

Finally, in Sector 4 (Fig. 4(d)) all 9 segments showed a speed increment, being the most successful solution to the traffic congestion. The acceleration on every segment was close to 2x. The proposed solution included adding a bus bay for the bus stop along the main road. Currently, buses stop on the road and create a delay for the entire traffic at every stop.

4.3 Sensitivity Analysis

The objective of sensitivity analysis is to detect routes that are more sensitive to segment speed variations and change the best MRE that results in an optimal configuration of the spawning periods. We present results with route ids and the numbers of seconds added to the optimal value that changes the new MRE in more than 1, making the final solution not optimal. We verify this by running the same two-paired T-test we used in the calibration process to evaluate the statistical relevance of the solution.

Starting with Sector 1, the minimum change is 1 s, where two routes going from west to north and east respectively, affect the solution when their period changes −1 s, and a route south-to-east affects the solution when 1 s is added. That means those routes are extremely sensitive and with minimum changes the traffic flow in the sector is affected and the simulation can not represent the scenario observed on the GPS records. That implies that those three routes can be the main cause of traffic congestion in the sector. It is important that route coming from the south highway, entering the main road and going north, starts changing the solution when we add 3 s and more. That delay in spawning time is causing a low traffic flow reflecting in the average speed in the roads segments and again, not representing the real traffic conditions.

The same happens in Sector 2 results. It shows the north-east to north route is the most sensitive when we subtract -4, -3, and -2 s from the spawning time. Then, north-east to south-east route is sensitive when we start adding seconds, indicating that those two routes are crucial for the traffic congestion.

Sector 3 is peculiar, with only route going from west to north that affects the optimal solution after adding more than 6 s. That means this route is the one that has a real impact in the traffic flow, generating the largest number of vehicles going from the west to the east. And showing what happens in real life during rush hours, because it is one the principal roads to leave that sector. A future approach to calibrate and propose a solution for the real traffic problems around that place must focus on this specific road.

Finally, Sector 4 is chaotic, almost every route is susceptible to changes. Even the minimum change of 1 s alters the final solution and 10 routes reflect this behavior. Thus, we could instead search for the route that is least affected. But, in the shorter range from -2 to 2 s there is no clear route that is less involved. This could be a reason why the calibration algorithm was more complicated to set up for this sector.

5 Conclusions and Future Work

We successfully created a pipeline of computational tools to implement a method to calibrate traffic simulations for all studied sectors. The pipeline is adaptable for other locations and it can also scale in size to model bigger sectors. We can ensure the results from simulations and GPS records are statistically similar, supporting the successful calibration of the simulation. With this calibrated simulations we were able to analyze the impact of proposed solutions to traffic problems. We created new simulations to measure the speed in the involved road segments, and we observed improvements in multiple segments at each sector.

For data processing we recommend exploring and using a faster and more reliable file format for GPS records. If a not-optimized data file format is used in R, then it can affect the processing time of data. Using a more optimized format such as Parquet [8], we can reduce data wrangling time and improve testing and implementation of experiments.

Future work should focus on simulation of public transportation and changes in traffic rules and their acceptance by the drivers. This can be a crucial aspect of designing new rules for buses, the most important public transport in Costa Rica. Giving new guides to create bus-bays, rules to follow their right-of-way and measure the efficiency of those solutions.

Acknowledgements. This research was partially supported by a machine allocation on Kabré supercomputer at the Costa Rica National High Technology Center.

References

1. Carson, Y., Maria, A.: Simulation optimization: methods and applications. In: Winter Simulation Conference Proceedings, pp. 118–126 (1997)
2. Carter, M.W., Price, C.C., Rabadi, G.: Operations Research. A Practical Introduction, 2nd edn. CRC Press, Boca Raton (2019)
3. Celik, Y., Karadeniz, A.T.: Urban traffic optimization with real time intelligence intersection traffic light system. Int. J. Intell. Syst. Appl. Eng. **3**(6), 214–219 (2018)
4. Colegio Federado de Ingenieros y Arquitectos de Costa Rica, CFIA: Congestionamiento del flujo vehicular en la gran Área metropolitana de san josÉ: recopilación, análisis y posicionamiento (2005)
5. Cubero-Corella, M., Durán-Monge, E., Díaz, W., Meneses, E., Gómez-Campos, S.: Modelling road saturation dynamics on a complex transportation network based on GPS navigation software data. In: Crespo-Mariño, J.L., Meneses-Rojas, E. (eds.) CARLA 2019. CCIS, vol. 1087, pp. 136–149. Springer, Cham (2020). https://doi.org/10.1007/978-3-030-41005-6_10
6. Daamen, W., Buisson, C., Hoogendoorn, S.P.: Traffic Simulation and Data: Validation Methods and Applications. CRC Press, Boca Raton (2014)
7. de la Nación, P.E., Gómez Campos, S., Cubero, M.: Capítulo 7 : Patrones de la movilidad en tiempos de pandemia: una aproximación con técnicas del "big data" [Informe Estado de la Nación 2020], pp. 231–254 (2020)
8. Foundation., A.S.: Apache parquet. https://parquet.apache.org/documentation/latest/. Accessed 30 Apr 2021
9. Gómez Campos, S., Cubero, M.: Congestión vial en los cantones de Costa Rica (2019)
10. Kheterpal, N., Parvate, K., Wu, C., Kreidieh, A., Vinitsky, E., Bayen, A.: Flow: deep reinforcement learning for control in SUMO. In: SUMO 2018- Simulating Autonomous and Intermodal Transport Systems, vol. 2, pp. 134–115 (2018)
11. Krajzewicz, D., Erdmann, J., Behrisch, M., Bieker, L.: Recent development and applications of SUMO - Simulation of Urban MObility. Int. J. Adv. Syst. Meas. **5**(3), 128–138 (2012)
12. Krajzewicz, D., Hertkorn, G., Wagner, P., Rössel, C.: An example of microscopic car models validation using the open source traffic simulation SUMO. In: Proceedings of Simulation in Industry 14th European Simulation Symposium, pp. 318–322 (2002)
13. Krajzewicz, D., Hertkorn, G., Wagner, P., Rössel, C.: SUMO (Simulation of Urban MObility) an open-source traffic simulation. In: Symposium on Simulation, pp. 63–68 (2002)
14. Li, S.B., Wang, G.M., Wang, T., Ren, H.L.: Research on the method of traffic organization and optimization based on dynamic traffic flow model. Discrete Dyn. Nat. Soc. **2017** (2017)
15. Ozbay, K., Mudigonda, S., Morgul, E., Yang, H.: Big data and the calibration and validation of traffic simulation models. Transp. Res. Board **2015** (2015)
16. Pardalos, P.M., Du, D.Z., Graham, R.L.: Handbook of Combinatorial Optimization, vol. 1–5 (2013)

17. Paternina Arboleda, C.D., Montoya Torres, J.R., Fábregas Ariza, A.: Simulation-optimization using a reinforcement learning approach. In: Proceedings - Winter Simulation Conference, pp. 1376–1383 (2008)
18. Pebesma, E., Bivand, R.S.: Classes and Methods for Spatial Data: the sp Package (2015)
19. Programa Estado de la Nación: Informe 2018, Estado de la Nación en desarrollo humano sostenible, chap. 6. Transporte y movilidad: retos en favor del desarrollo urbano. Estado de la Nación (2018)
20. Wang, L.F., Shi, L.Y.: Simulation optimization: a review on theory and applications. Zidonghua Xuebao/Acta Automatica Sinica **39**(11), 1957–1968 (2013)
21. Zambrano, J.L., Calafate, C.T., Soler, D., Cano, J.C., Manzoni, P.: Using real traffic data for ITS simulation: procedure and validation. In: 2016 International IEEE Conferences on Ubiquitous Intelligence & Computing, Advanced and Trusted Computing, Scalable Computing and Communications, Cloud and Big Data Computing, Internet of People, and Smart World Congress, pp. 161–170 (2016)
22. Zhang, J., Wang, F.Y., Wang, K., Lin, W.H., Xu, X., Chen, C.: Data-driven intelligent transportation systems: a survey. IEEE Trans. Intell. Transp. Syst. **12**(4), 1624–1639 (2011)

Predicting Daily Trends in the Lima Stock Exchange General Index Using Economic Indicators and Financial News Sentiments

Adrian Ulloa, Soledad Espezua, Julio Villavicencio, Oscar Miranda, and Edwin Villanueva$^{(\boxtimes)}$

Pontifical Catholic University of Peru, Lima, Peru
ervillanueva@pucp.edu.pe

Abstract. Predicting the future trend of the Lima Stock Exchange market is challenging because of its high volatility, transaction costs, and illiquidity. In this work, we investigate machine learning models able to use technical indicators, economic variables, and financial news sentiments to forecast the daily return trend of the S&P/BVL Peru General Index.

To the best of our knowledge, no other published S&P/BVL predicting tool considered these joint sources of information as relevant input features.

To do so, fifteen economic indicators relevant to the local market and sentiment-tagged financial news headlines were used as extra input features for multiple machine learning classification models and feature selection methods. In addition, the performance of the static learning approach (the only one used for this particular problem so far) was compared against an online learning approach, which could dynamically better adapt to such a volatile, emergent market.

The results showed an increase in performance when using the economic variables and news sentiment in comparison to existing predicting tools of the local market. When comparing both learning approaches, online learning yielded better predictive accuracy than its static counterpart.

To the best of our knowledge, this is the first effort to include all these novel features for predicting trends in the Lima Stock Exchange.

Keywords: Stock market trend prediction · News sentiment analysis · S&P/BVL · Machine learning

1 Introduction

Predicting future trends in stock indices remains a challenging problem. A reliable trend-predicting tool has the potential to provide investors with information

Supported by Pontifical Catholic University of Peru.

on the expectations of the behavior and movement of the economy, as well as the performance obtained by a specific investment portfolio. It can also represent a form of early warning for investors, especially for short-term investors, against sudden falls in the market.

Initial research on the prediction of trends in stock markets resulted in the efficient market hypothesis and the random walk hypothesis [23,24,48]. These early models suggested that security prices always fully reflect all available information (e.g. news, or blog posts), rather than current and/or past prices. In practice, however, the efficient market hypothesis is not verified [2,36,37,43]. This is because markets are imperfect and the economic agents that operate in them have non-uniform information about prices or present some bias when making decisions [53,54]. Moreover, the degree of market efficiency is linked to factors such as: the number of competitors in the market, the magnitude of profit opportunities available, and the adaptability of the market participants [35].

Although the vast majority of stock market prediction models uses technical analysis of stock indices, different ways of supplementing this information have been proposed in the literature: by artificially constructing stock indices by grouping stock prices of shares with the same economic segments [29,33,42], statements of public sentiment extracted from social networks [9,12,28], opinions and criticisms of the products of the companies to be evaluated and financial news from verifiable sources [27,30,57], among others.

We can cluster the different variables proposed for stock market prediction into the following groups: technical variables, economic and financial variables, and investor sentiment variables. Technical variables are the historical prices of a security. The economic indicators are important as they determine the environment that will influence the firm's performance. Examples of economic indicators are the exchange rates, the expected inflation, and the expected growth rate, among others. The financial variables, like the world stock indices, constitutes the systematic risk factor that will affects the evolution of individual stock prices. Investor sentiment variables assess the investor optimism or pessimism about the future stock price ([7]).

Behavioral economics tells us that investor sentiments are of high importance because they can profoundly affect individual behavior and decision-making, influencing their trading activities and, as a consequence, the stock market in general [10,16,34]. Financial news are useful indicators of economic and political conditions and can reflect or influence investor sentiments. Financial news are especially valuable in countries with fewer real time data sources [8]. Moreover, the empirical results of [20] show that sentiment is not an individual investor phenomenon that affects only small capitalization stocks, but a systematic risk.

Even though there is a growing financial literature that indicate that investor sentiment information could be a useful predictor of future stock market returns ([5,6,14]), the complexity of the relation between the sentiment variables and the stock market trends produced studies that dispute those results [13,18,51]. Others found that this dispute arrives when the market scenario is not classified according to investor's sentiment, suggesting a no linear relation [50].

On the other hand, stock markets rarely remain stable: approaches that are highly predictive at one point may become less so as more traders spot the patterns employed and adjust their trading techniques. This then causes the tools developed with a static analysis to become ineffective for investors when the market changes to different dynamics from those that were present in the data used for its implementation.

The Lima Stock Exchange is a small stock market that has been little studied. Few prediction tools have been proposed for predicting its future trends [17]. High transaction costs and illiquidity issues make its prediction more challenging. In this paper we address the daily prediction of the Lima Stock Exchange, represented by the S&P/BVL Peru General Index. We hypothesize that we can obtain better results if we adjust models able to consume the three mentioned data sources: technical variables, economic and financial variables, and sentiments from financial news. It is expected that the news information may have more impact in the stock returns predictions than in emerging markets because its high costs of trade, its high volatility, and because of the fact that is not possible to short assets [49]. We also propose to address the dynamism of the market by using a online learning approach.

Previous efforts in predicting the S&P/BVL index posed static approaches and/or did not consider the sentiment information contained in the local news [15,17,19,32,38,44,45,52]. Our paper adds two important contributions to the literature: First of all, it provides further support to the hypothesis that news from local financial media contribute to predict stock returns if there is a complex relation (which could be dynamically modeled), even in a non-liquid emerging market like the Lima Stock Exchange. This paper also contributes, as far as we know, to provide the first study that incorporates investor sentiment information embedded in local news, to predict the S&P/BVL index behavior. This latest contribution is particularly important because there is few evidence of this kind of analysis in illiquid markets, like the Peruvian stock market, since there is a generalized assumption than only international or foreign financial news matter to predict stock returns in these small markets.

The paper is structured as follows. Section 2 describes the materials and methods proposed and gives details of the data used. Section 3 present the experiments and results achieved: compares the learning approaches and assess the impact of the technical, economic and sentiment indicators on the forecasting accuracy. Section 4 concludes and discusses further research.

2   Materials and Methods

The S& P/BVL Peru General (Peru) Index. The Lima Stock Exchange General Index (S&P/BVL) is the most representative stock index of the Peruvian stock market. It comprises 34 national company shares, mainly from the financial, mining, and energy sectors.

We defined the target feature to predict as the upward or downward trend of the daily closing price of the S&P/BVL Peru General (Peru) Index. To do so, we collected the historical opening, closing, daily high and daily low prices as technical indicators in the last 15 years (as of the start of the project, from March 31st 2006 to March 31st 2021) as available data.

Fig. 1. Daily values of the General Index of the Lima Stock Exchange, 2006–2021.

The logarithmic daily returns for each of the last business 5 days of the 4 indicators were calculated and the connection was made to the Yahoo Finance interface to extract the information in real time. In other words, for all the conducted experimentation, we consider only the 5 past continuous logarithmic returns of the available time series as input features, and the discrete closing trend of the day under consideration as the target output (with a value of 1 if the closing price of the day is higher than the previous closing price and 0 if the price is lower or equal).

We also considered variables derived from the properties and relationships between the 5-day window of each of the 4 time series, generated using the TFresh tool and filtered by their relevance in a classification problem. Among the acquired variables we have, for each window: the mean, median, minimum, number of positive returns and the sum of returns, among others.

Economic Indicators. To obtain the necessary indices and find the historical daily values of economic indicators, we used the Central Reserve Bank of Peru API Tool for Developers (*BCRPData API*), which provides us with historical data that is updated daily. As a representative part of the economic indicators, the daily price and logarithmic return at the closing price of copper, silver, gold, oil, wheat, corn and soybean oil were considered, since these commodities have the most impact on the macroeconomics of Peru: they determine changes in the terms of trade, which has been historically related to an increase in investment, productivity and growth [25,39].

In addition, the closing sale price of the interbank exchange rate from dollars to soles (local currency) was considered as a relevant economic indicator in our emerging market economy. This is because a significant portion of the debt held by firms is denominated in US dollars [1, 26, 46]. This is visualized in Fig. 2.

Fig. 2. Normalized daily values of financial indicators, 2006–2021.

To finish, the international equity risk premium of investing in the international stock market was also considered. This premium was estimated using the daily returns of the S&P500 (the high-risk investment) and the daily yield of the 3-month US bond (the risk-free investment). Both indices were fetched from Yahoo Finance.

Financial News. Before all else, the appropriate sources of the most relevant news for the national stock market were identified. After a conversation with finance experts, it was concluded that the best financial, local news sources are the newspaper *Gestion*, edited by *Grupo El Comercio*; and the magazine *Semana Economica* (SE), edited by *Perú Economico S.A.*

Since a publicly available corpus of news published in either source was not found, we had to create one. To do this, we first fetched the headlines and news publication dates from both sources, and then tagged the polarity of each headline with an appropriate text classification model for this problem. That is, classified whether the news was "positive", "neutral" or "negative" in terms of the impact it would have on the Lima Stock Exchange.

For the construction of the corpus, a web scraper was developed, which recovered 13,547 financial news headlines published across the total archives of *Gestion* and *SE* (spanning 8 years, from 2014 to 2021), by extracting them through the static files available on their HTML web pages.

Once the headlines and dates were fetched, several text classification models were considered, from simple models like bag-of-words, to more complex language models based on neural networks, such as BERT (Bidirectional Encoder Representations from Transformers) [21]. After a thorough comparison between all the available models, we decided to use a pre-trained language model, based on the BERT base architecture, fitted with 1.8 million financial news published by Reuters and specifically adapted for the sentiment analysis of financial texts [4]. This model is publicly available for use through the Hugging Face platform with v4.7.0 Transformers [56]. However, this model is capable of processing financial news in English. To solve this problem, the free web service Google Translation API was used to translate the Spanish headlines into English.

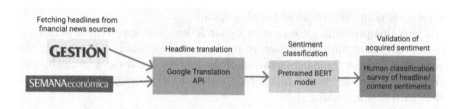

Fig. 3. Illustrative diagram of the process of obtaining the financial news headlines corpus and the sentiment polarity labels.

To sum up, a corpus with 13,547 rows and 5 features is obtained: the text of the headline, in Spanish and English, the date of publication, the source and the polarity of the news ('positive', 'neutral', or 'negative'). In addition, this corpus is condensed into a daily summary with the amount of positive, neutral and negative news published in both sources, for the last 8 years, together with a polarity indicator, obtained by averaging the published news in each day and considering a score of 1 for positive news, 0.5 for neutral and 0 for negative.

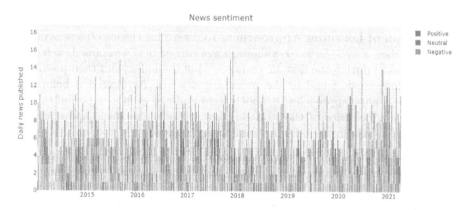

Fig. 4. Daily financial news concerning the Lima Stock Exchange, by polarity.

Learning Approaches. There are two common learning approaches for prediction models: traditional learning (static approach over time) and incremental or online learning (dynamic approach). In the static approach, the tool is trained with historical data from the series to predict future information. This approach is appropriate when the behavior of the target variable is usually relatively constant over time.

However, in the case of volatile variables such as those of the stock market, the performance of tools with this approach tends to decrease with respect to what was observed in the training stage as time goes by, since they do not consider this volatility and market change in their predictions and assume it remains as it is in the historical training data.

To face this problem, an online or dynamic learning approach is performed in the development and production of modern models, which continuously and incrementally adjust the representation of the market behavior, adding the data points of each new day to the historical corpus and re-training the classification models with this new data.

Classification Models. In reviewing the state of the art, we found that the majority of published stock market trend prediction tools employ the following machine learning classification models: Random Forests [22,31,40], Support Vector Machines [9,55], and Neural Networks (both traditional Multi-layer Perceptron [28,41,47], and recurrent architecture networks, such as LSTM [11,27]). Therefore, these four classification models were considered in the experimentation for both learning approaches.

To evaluate the performance of each experiment, the balanced accuracy metric was chosen: it consists of the mean average of the sensitivity and specificity of the models; that is, how much the model correctly detects the ups and downs of the index, based on its predictions.

3   Experiments and Results

Comparison of Learning Approaches. To determine the effectiveness of the two approaches, a walk-forward evaluation was carried out: we trained each classification model during the first 12 years (80%) of the index, and then predicted its up or downwards trend in the remaining 3 years. As discussed before, in the dynamic/online approach the models were updated each new period to represent the new behavior of the stock market; while in the static approach the representation built in the original training is preserved.

Classification Models Experimentation. For Random Forest Classifiers (RFCs), the very structure of the model makes incremental learning impossible, so its online updating was simulated by training the model with data of size N of the 4 most recent time series in each iteration, where N is the original training size before the walk-forward evaluation. As hyper-parameters to fit in the random forests, the number of estimators in the forest was varied from 100 to 500, and the maximum depth from 3 to 5 separations.

For the case of Support Vector Machines (SVM), we experimented with two kernel functions: linear and radial basis functions (RBF), with a regularization parameter C varying geometrically from 1 to 1000 and a kernel coefficient from 0.0001 to 1. However, the dynamic approach in this model type is only possible if the kernel function of the machine is linear, in which the model then can be reduced to a linear classifier with stochastic gradient descent with standard L2 regularizer and hinge loss function.

For the experiments with Multi-Layer Perceptron neural networks (MLP), the evaluations were carried out considering a single hidden layer of perceptrons in the network, the Adam optimization algorithm and varying the L2 regularization parameter from 0.00001 to 0.01 and the size of the hidden layer in between 5 to 15 units.

Finally, for the experiments for recurrent neural networks with LSTM architecture, a single layer of the LSTM type was used for prediction, varying the size of the output units from 1 to 5. Furthermore, different sizes of input time windows were experimented, from 3 to 21 data points prior to the target day.

In addition, through a grid or iterative search for each model, the best hyperparameters that define the structure of the models and that maximize the evaluation metric were chosen for both approaches and both datasets. The 16 searches were carried out 5 times and the best result was chosen from them. As a summary, the entire machine learning classification model experimentation strategy for each approach is visualized in Fig. 5.

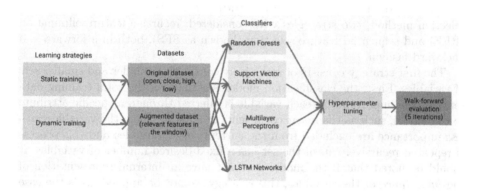

Fig. 5. Illustrative diagram of the machine learning experimentation pipeline used to evaluate each of the approaches.

To contrast the results by learning approach, the best balanced accuracy value was collected from across all scenarios. Then, the best metrics for each model used in experimentation. These can be seen in Fig. 6. Observing these, and as a summary across all results, it can be said that the dynamic approach performs better than its counterpart. In other words, there is evidence of a trend that favors the dynamic approach, having a higher balanced accuracy in 3 of the 4 models (with the exception of the LSTM network), with the MLP showing a greater improvement than change approaches. To sum up, a dynamic or online approach generally provides better results in predicting trends in the Lima Stock Exchange.

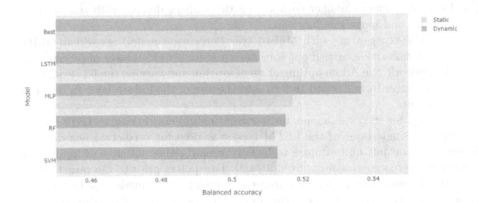

Fig. 6. Balanced accuracy for static (light green) and dynamic approaches (green) and the different classification models trained with the technical data. The *Best* bar indicates the best result of the total experimentation (MLP). (Colors figure online)

Feature Importance of Economic Indicators. When choosing a variable selection method, two strategies were considered: recursive feature elimination (RFE) and sequential feature selection (known as SFS), both in a forward and backward fashion.

The first strategy consists of recursively considering smaller and smaller sets of variables. First, the classification model is trained on the total training data set, and the importance of each variable is inferred through a specific attribute to the model, such as the linear coefficients of a SVM. Then, the variables with less importance are excluded from the current set of variables and this process is repeated recursively, until the set has a fixed desired number of variables. It should be noted that if the model does not have an internal representation of the *importance* of the variables, this strategy cannot be applied, as is the case with multi-layer neural networks. Therefore, experiments with this strategy were performed only on SVMs.

This recursive elimination strategy was applied to the complete dataset, considering the minimum number of variables to be considered as 1, since the objective is to extract the order of importance of all variables, that is, which ones were eliminated first and which ones are the model considers the most, equally important in the dataset (of order 1). The cross-evaluation metric obtained (balanced accuracy), based on the number of variables selected in each stage of the elimination, is shown in Fig. 7. Here, we observed that the balanced accuracy of the model tends to improve as more variables are used, reaching its peak in between 35 to 45 features selected.

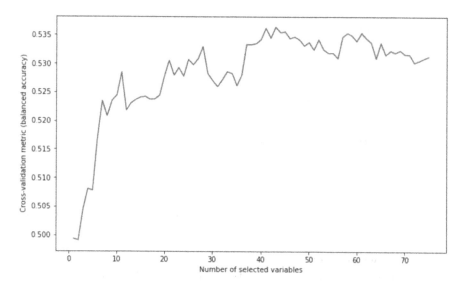

Fig. 7. Number of variables selected by RFE vs validation metric - balanced accuracy.

The second strategy, sequential feature selection (SFS), consists of adding (forward selection) or removing (backward selection) the input variables to form subsets of the data body in a manner similar to a greedy algorithm. That is, in each iteration of the strategy, the best variable to add or remove is chosen based on the best cross-validation metric obtained from all possible subset variables.

As this strategy does not depend on internal parameters of the models, it can be applied to all estimators under consideration. To do this, the complete training data set is used and the best 40 variables are searched (to provide a better comparison with RFE-chosen features) by selecting sequentially both forward and backward. Finally, for all input variables, their inclusion in all sets of selected variables was counted, and the 40 most frequent variables throughout the sets were taken as the most important in the prediction problem.

When grouping the variables selected through all the methods in their original time series (Fig. 8), it is observed that the most frequent (and therefore, most relevant to the problem) are the close price return of the index (as expected, since its the quantified target output for the days before) and the closing copper (most exported commodity) and oil (most imported commodity) return, followed by various returns of key export commodities in the national market. At the bottom, we have the international series: the return on the USD
PEN exchange rate, and the closing return of the S & P500 index, which represents the stock market situation in the United States.

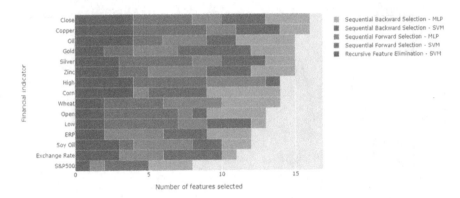

Fig. 8. Most relevant financial indicators, for each feature selection strategy and model.

Financial News Impact

As a first step, we continued to use the 5-day window like previous results to transform the daily news dataset in an equivalent way. However, adding these variables to the current data set is not as simple as adding an additional column, since there is historical data for the time series worked on for the last 15 years (2006–2021), while the news corpus only comprises the last 8 years (2014–2021).

In order to not lose valuable training data by truncating the first set by half, we employ a combiner machine learning model, which consists of designing and training two intermediate models, and then combining them to arrive at a final prediction.

The first intermediate model considers only as input features the 11 time series with a 5-day window and a historical range of 15 years (12 years of training and 3 years of testing), with the 40 variables of greatest importance; and the output variable would be the probability of the upward and downward trend in the closing price the following business day.

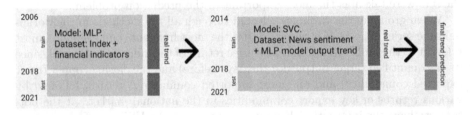

Fig. 9. Combiner model diagram, for the MLP x SVC combination. Here, the SVC model takes as an input variable the prediction probability of the MLP model to make the final prediction.

Then, the second intermediate model takes as the input variable, together with the news sentiment features, the output feature of the first intermediate model in the last 8 years (5 years of training and 3 last of tests). Figure 9 graphically presents the structure of the chosen combiner model.

For both the first and second intermediate models, we experimented with support vector machines and multi-layer neural networks, adjusting the hyperparameters of both by grid search and optimizing for a better balanced accuracy.

The final performance increase of utilizing the financial news sentiment is presented in Fig. 10, based on the balanced accuracy metric. There, we see that for all combinations of estimators in the combiner model, the addition of news sentiments in the trend prediction increased the overall performance. In other words, for all experimentation iterations, a slight improvement of 4 points in balanced accuracy was observed when incorporating the polarity of financial news as a feature. This result is aligned with was found in the literature [16,34] and could be generalized to other emergent stock markets that present similarly reliable, local news sources.

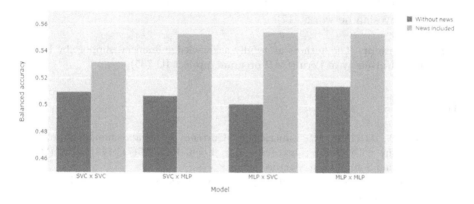

Fig. 10. Balanced accuracy of models with and without news sentiment information, for each type of combiner model considered (MLP and SVM).

4   Conclusion

A comparative analysis of the static and dynamic approach prediction tools was carried out. During the analysis, the dynamic approach was found to perform better in predicting the S&P/BVL Peru General Index. This result could be generalized to related problems, such as trend prediction in other representative indices of stock markets with similar characteristics.

Using both technical and economic indicators results in better forecasting performance, when compared to using only technical features. Furthermore, using an optimal subset of features was found to be preferable to using all available. It is important to note that the best variables chosen by the selection strategies are consistent with what is established in the national economic literature [25,39].

When comparing the performance of the prediction models that use financial news sentiment information in contrast to the models that do not, for all the experiments carried out, the balanced accuracy improved significantly. As far as we know, this work is the first to employ news sentiment data to improve trend prediction in the S&P/BVL Peru General Index.

For **future work**, we propose to construct a personalized, polarity model fine-tuned to the local national reality. In order to do so, key concepts specific to the Lima Stock Exchange that usually appear in financial news and their either positive or negative impact on it must be identified and quantified.

Also, it would be of interest to consider other relevant features with non-daily periods, such as the annual inflationary expectation, the monthly variation of the foreign trade terms of trade, or the GDP and domestic demand annualized variations[3].

Finally, the dynamic ability to adapt the prediction model to continuously use the best features as the market changes and evolves is an interesting future work that would require different tools and machine learning models, such as the use of Bayesian networks [17].

Acknowledgment. The authors gratefully acknowledge financial support by Pontifical Catholic University of Peru (CAP program, project ID 735).

References

1. Aghion, P., Bacchetta, P., Banerjee, A.: Currency crises and monetary policy in an economy with credit constraints. Eur. Econ. Rev. **45**(7), 1121–1150 (2001). international Seminar On Macroeconomics
2. Alexander, S.: Price movement in speculative markets: Trend or random walks. Industrial Management Review (1964)
3. Aycaya, J.L.A.: Factores económicos que afectan el rendimiento del Índice selectivo de la bolsa de valores de lima - isbvl, periodo 2015–2018 (2018). https://repositorio. upt.edu.pe/handle/20.500.12969/755
4. Araci, D.: FINBERT: Financial sentiment analysis with pre-trained language models. CoRR abs/1908.10063 (2019)
5. Baker, M., Stein, J.C.: Market liquidity as a sentiment indicator. J. Finan. Mark. **7**(3), 271–299 (2004)
6. Baker, M., Wurgler, J., Yuan, Y.: Global, local, and contagious investor sentiment. J. Finan. Econom. **104**(2), 272–287 (2012)
7. Baker, M., Wurgler, J.: Investor sentiment and the cross-section of stock returns. J. Finan. **61**(4), 1645–1680 (2006)
8. Baker, S.R., Bloom, N., Davis, S.J.: Measuring economic policy uncertainty. Q. J. Econom. **131**(4), 1593–1613 (2016)
9. Batra, R., Daudpota, S.M.: Integrating stocktwits with sentiment analysis for better prediction of stock price movement. In: 2018 International Conference on Computing, Mathematics and Engineering Technologies (iCoMET), pp. 1–5. IEEE (2018)
10. Bollen, J., Mao, H., Zeng, X.: Twitter mood predicts the stock market. J. Computat. Sci. **2**(1), 1–8 (2011)

11. Botunac, I., Panjkota, A., Matetic, M.: The importance of time series data filtering for predicting the direction of stock market movement using neural networks. In: Proceedings of the 30th DAAAM International Symposium (2019)
12. Bouktif, S., Awad, M.A.: Predicting stock market movement: an evolutionary approach. In: 2015 7th International Joint Conference on Knowledge Discovery, Knowledge Engineering and Knowledge Management (IC3K), vol. 1, pp. 159–167. IEEE (2015)
13. Brown, G.W., Cliff, M.T.: Investor sentiment and the near-term stock market. J. Empirical Finan. **11**(1), 1–27 (2004)
14. Brown, G.W., Cliff, M.T.: Investor sentiment and asset valuation. J. Bus. **78**(2), 405–440 (2005)
15. Gamarra, J.E.C.: Modelación de la volatilidad del índice general de la bolsa de valores de lima, periodo 2009–2011 (2014). http://repositorio.lamolina.edu.pe/handle/UNALM/2276
16. Chan, W.S.: Stock price reaction to news and no-news: Drift and reversal after headlines. S&P Global Market Intelligence Research Paper Series (2001)
17. Chapi, D., Espezua, S., Villavicencio, J., Miranda, O., Villanueva, E.: Modeling and predicting the lima stock exchange general index with Bayesian networks and information from foreign markets. In: Information Management and Big Data, pp. 154–168. Springer International Publishing (2021)
18. Clarke, R.G., Statman, M.: Bullish or bearish? Finan. Anal. J. **54**(3), 63–72 (1998)
19. Cunya, J.A.O., Rodríguez, G.: An application of a random level shifts model to the volatility of Peruvian stock and exchange rate returns. Macroecon. Finan. Emerg. Mark. Econ. **9**(1), 34–55 (2016)
20. De Long, J.B., Shleifer, A., Summers, L.H., Waldmann, R.J.: Noise trader risk in financial markets. J. Polit. Econ. **98**(4), 703–738 (1990)
21. Devlin, J., Chang, M.W., Lee, K., Toutanova, K.: BERT: pre-training of deep bidirectional transformers for language understanding. In: Proceedings of the 2019 Conference of the North American Chapter of the Association for Computational Linguistics: Human Language Technologies, vol. 1 (Long and Short Papers), pp. 4171–4186, June 2019
22. Elagamy, M.N., Stanier, C., Sharp, B.: Text mining approach to analyse stock market movement. In: The International Conference on Advanced Machine Learning Technologies and Applications (AMLTA2018), pp. 661–670. Springer International Publishing (2018)
23. Fama, E.F.: The behavior of stock-market prices. J. Bus. **38**(1), 34–105 (1965)
24. Fama, E.F.: Efficient capital markets a review of theory and empirical work. In: The Fama Portfolio: Selected Papers of Eugene F. Fama, pp. 76–121. University of Chicago Press (2021)
25. Florián, D., Aguilar, J., Toma, H., Velásquez, C.: Impacto de los cambios anticipados de los términos de intercambio en la economía. Revista Moneda **174**, 21–25 (2018)
26. Gondo, R., Orrego, F.: Dedollarization and financial robustness. Working Papers 2011–022, Banco Central de Reserva del Perú, December 2011
27. Jiawei, X., Murata, T.: Stock market trend prediction with sentiment analysis based on LSTM neural network. In: International Multiconference of Engineers and Computer Scientists, pp. 475–9 (2019)
28. Khan, W., Malik, U., Ghazanfar, M.A., Azam, M.A., Alyoubi, K.H., Alfakeeh, A.S.: Predicting stock market trends using machine learning algorithms via public sentiment and political situation analysis. Soft Comput. **24**(15), 11019–11043 (2019). https://doi.org/10.1007/s00500-019-04347-y

29. Kia, A.N., Haratizadeh, S., Shouraki, S.B.: A hybrid supervised semi-supervised graph-based model to predict one-day ahead movement of global stock markets and commodity prices. Expert Syst. Appl. **105**, 159–173 (2018)
30. Krysovatyy, A., Vasylchyshyn, O., Desyatnyuk, O., Galeshchuk, S.: News feed for stock movement prediction. In: ICTERI (2019)
31. Labiad, B., Berrado, A., Benabbou, L.: Machine learning techniques for short term stock movements classification for Moroccan stock exchange. In: 2016 11th International Conference on Intelligent Systems: Theories and Applications (SITA), pp. 1–6 (2016)
32. Lecca, E.R., Guevara, L.R., Atúncar, C.Q.: Aplicación de la metodología garch al precio de cierre en la bolsa de valores de lima. Ind. data **15**(2), 96–105 (2012)
33. Li, C., Song, D., Tao, D.: Multi-task recurrent neural networks and higher-order Markov random fields for stock price movement prediction: Multi-task RNN and higer-order MRFs for stock price classification. In: Proceedings of the 25th ACM SIGKDD International Conference on Knowledge Discovery and Data Mining, pp. 1141–1151 (2019)
34. Li, Q., Wang, T., Li, P., Liu, L., Gong, Q., Chen, Y.: The effect of news and public mood on stock movements. Inf. Sci. **278**, 826–840 (2014)
35. Lo, A.W.: Reconciling efficient markets with behavioral finance: the adaptive markets hypothesis. J. Investment Consult. **7**, 21–44 (2005)
36. Lo, A.W., MacKinlay, A.C.: Stock market prices do not follow random walks: evidence from a simple specification test. Rev. Finan. Stud. **1**(1), 41–66 (1988)
37. Lo, A.W., MacKinlay, A.C.: A Non-random Walk Down Wall Street. Princeton University Press, Princeton (1999)
38. Ruíz, B.L.M.: Modelación del índice general de la bolsa de valores de lima con series de tiempo (2017). https://dspace.unitru.edu.pe/handle/UNITRU/7979
39. Mendoza, E.G.: The terms of trade, the real exchange rate, and economic fluctuations. Int. Econ. Rev. 101–137 (1995)
40. Misra, P., Chaurasia, S.: Forecasting direction of stock index using two stage hybridization of machine learning models. In: 2018 7th International Conference on Reliability, Infocom Technologies and Optimization (Trends and Future Directions) (ICRITO), pp. 533–537, August 2018
41. Moews, B., Herrmann, J.M., Ibikunle, G.: Lagged correlation-based deep learning for directional trend change prediction in financial time series. Expert Syst. Appl. **120**, 197–206 (2019)
42. Nelson, D.M., Pereira, A.C., de Oliveira, R.A.: Stock market's price movement prediction with LSTM neural networks. In: 2017 International Joint Conference on Neural Networks (IJCNN), pp. 1419–1426. IEEE (2017)
43. Niederhoffer, V., Osborne, M.F.M.: Market making and reversal on the stock exchange. J. Am. Stat. Assoc. **61**(316), 897–916 (1966)
44. Gavilán, J.C.O.: Uso de los modelos heterocedásticos con bootstrap en el análisis del índice general de la bolsa de valores de lima (2019)
45. Cornejo, B.P.: Comparación de modelos de cálculo estocástico y su aplicación en el modelamiento del índice general de la bolsa de valores de lima y la tasa de rendimiento del bono del gobierno peruano (2019)
46. Ramírez-Rondán, N.R.: Balance sheet and currency mismatch: evidence for Peruvian firms. Emp. Econ. **57**(2), 449–473 (2019)
47. Ratto, A.P., Merello, S., Ma, Y., Oneto, L., Cambria, E.: Technical analysis and sentiment embeddings for market trend prediction. Expert Syst. Appl. **135**, 60–70 (2019)

48. Samuelson, P.A.: Proof that properly anticipated prices fluctuate randomly. Manage. Rev. **6**(2) (1965)
49. Segura, A., Villavicencio, J.: Análisis de los posibles impactos de una reclasificación de msci perú de mercado emergente a frontera y propuestas para reducir la probabilidad que suceda. Bolsa de Valores de Lima (2019)
50. Sheu, H.J., Lu, Y.C., Wei, Y.C.: Causalities between sentiment indicators and stock market returns under different market scenarios. Int. J. Bus. Finan. Res. **4**(1), 159–171 (2010)
51. Solt, M.E., Statman, M.: How useful is the sentiment index? Finan. Anal. J. **44**(5), 45–55 (1988)
52. Tirado, N.A.S.: Análisis técnico como herramienta para optimizar la evaluación de alternativas de inversión en la bolsa de valores de lima-2014 (2014)
53. Tversky, A., Kahneman, D.: Judgment under uncertainty: heuristics and biases. Science **185**(4157), 1124–1131 (1974)
54. Tversky, A., Kahneman, D.: The framing of decisions and the psychology of choice. In: Behavioral Decision Making, pp. 25–41. Springer (1985). https://doi.org/10.1007/978-1-4613-2391-4_2
55. Upadhyay, V.P., Panwar, S., Merugu, R., Panchariya, R.: Forecasting stock market movements using various kernel functions in support vector machine. In: Proceedings of the International Conference on Advances in Information Communication Technology and Computing. AICTC 2016. Association for Computing Machinery, New York, NY, USA (2016)
56. Wolf, T., et al.: Transformers: state-of-the-art natural language processing. In: Proceedings of the 2020 Conference on Empirical Methods in Natural Language Processing: System Demonstrations, pp. 38–45. Association for Computational Linguistics, Online, October 2020
57. Xu, B., Zhang, D., Zhang, S., Li, H., Lin, H.: Stock market trend prediction using recurrent convolutional neural networks. In: Natural Language Processing and Chinese Computing, pp. 166–177. Springer International Publishing, Cham (2018)

Government Public Services Presence Index Based on Open Data

Miguel Nunez-del-Prado[1,2](✉)[iD] and Leibnitz Rojas-Bustamante[3][iD]

[1] Instituto de Investigación de la Universidad Andina del Cusco, Cusco, Peru
[2] Peru Research, Developmente, and Innovation Institute, Lima, Peru
miguel.nunez@peruidi.com
[3] Pontificia Universidad Catolica del Perú, Lima, Peru
leibnitz.rojas@pucp.edu.pe

Abstract. Public services are essential to satisfy the needs of health-care, education, justice, *etc.* in citizens' daily life. Thus, individuals need these services in a certain proximity to their homes. Nonetheless, in big cities, some public services are not close enough. To tackle this problem, we propose a methodology to compute a *Government Public Services Presence Index* for measuring how well different zones are in a city are served. We apply our methodology to the city of Lima, showing the utility of the index while being simple to understand. We profile fifty different districts in four groups, allowing policymakers and urban planners to observe the lack of public services.

Keywords: Public service · Index computation · Data mining

1 Introduction

Public service is defined as the assistance to the inhabitant provided by the government, on aspects such as health, education, or justice, among others. These services are essential to citizens' daily life through hospitals, schools, police stations, etc. Thus, individuals need these services in a certain proximity to their homes. Nevertheless, in big cities, some public services are not close enough, generating food deserts [11], and segregation [18]. Hence, metrics to measure the absence of the State are necessary to help policymakers. Therefore, different efforts have been done to propose different vulnerability indices in health [6,17], hazard [3,5], energy [8], food [16], jobs [2,14], and public services [7,19,20]. The main limitation in previous works is the isolated analysis of the indices in different sectors. Hence, we propose a novel methodology to build an index to quantify the proximity or absence of various public services in urban areas in the current effort. Our methodology has five steps: street network construction, administrative boundary partition, distance to public service measure, index computation, and unsupervised learning profiling. The idea behind this index is to profile urban areas to understand the presence or absence of certain public services to

Table 1. Summary of different methods to create index in different context.

Authors	Index	Domain	Technique
Daras *et al.* [6]	Vulnerability index for Covid-19	Health	Multivariable Poisson regression
Moore *et al.* [17]	Health vulnerability index	Health	Qualitative weighting
Aksha *et al.* [3]	Social vulnerability index	Hazard	Principal component analysis
Cutter *et al.* [5]	Social vulnerability to environmental hazards	Hazard	Principal component analysis
Gatto and Busato [8]	Global energy vulnerability index	Energy	Principal component analysis
Meenar [16]	Place-Based Food index	Food	Adding the values of the different layers
Barboza *et al.* [2]	Accessibility measure index	Job	Balancing Time
Kelobonye *et al.* [14]	Job accessibility index	Job	Cumulative opportunities model
Neutens *et al.* [20]	Space-time accessibility measures	Public service	Open time tables analysis
Delafontaine and Neutens [7]	Accessibility to libraries	Public service	Utilitarian and egalitarian models
Neutens *et al.* [19]	Spatiotemporal gaps in public service delivery	Public service	Accessibility and demand using origin-destination matrices

help policymakers and urban planners to approach public services infrastructure and services to citizens.

The present document is organized as follows. Section 2 describes the related work in the literature about indexes in different sectors. Then, Sect. 3 presents our methodology to build the *Government Public Services Presence Index*, while Sect. 4 depicts the results of our experiments applied to Lima city. Finally, Sect. 5 concludes our work and presents new research avenues.

2 Related Work

Citizens demand different kinds of services from governments, ranging from health, to education, justice, and food access. Therefore, in the present section, we describe work in the literature measuring accessibility and vulnerability to health, energy, food, jobs, and public services. Table 1 summarizes different techniques to build indices in the aforementioned sectors.

Concerning health vulnerability, Daras *et al.* [6] proposed a vulnerability index for Covid-19 based on age, ethnicity, poverty, the prevalence of long-term health conditions, living in care homes, and living in overcrowded housing in England. They relied on multivariable Poisson regression models to estimate the index. The authors found the geographic communities with higher risk to a pandemic second wave. Another example of infectious disease vulnerability index is the proposal of Moore *et al.* [17]. They proposed an index based on demographic, health care, public health, disease dynamics, political-domestic, political-international, and economical. The tool allows marking the risk in each indicator as low, medium, and high risk to generate a risk map for policymakers.

Regarding social and energy vulnerability, Aksha *et al.* [3] proposed a *social vulnerability index* (SoVI) using 39 variables reduced to only seven factors explaining 63.02% of variance in the data through the principal component analysis. The analyzed factors were age, built environment, education, ethnicity, family structure, gender, employment, medical services, migration, occupation, population change, renters, socioeconomic level, special needs population, and urban, rural densities. Thus, the SoVI scores were computed by summing all seven principal components based on their cardinality, mean and standard deviations. Cutter *et al.* [5] proposed an index of social vulnerability to environmental hazards. The authors used 42 variables reduced to eleven factors to implement this index using a factor analytic approach. The factors explaining 72% of the variance are personal wealth, age, the density of the built environment, single-sector economic dependence, housing stock and tenancy, race-African American, ethnicity-Hispanic, ethnicity-Native American, race-Asian, occupation, and infrastructure dependence. Authors applied the State of Chicago index finding spatial patterns with the most vulnerable counties clustered in metropolitan counties in the east, south Texas, and the Mississippi Delta region.

With reference to energy, Gatto and Busato [8] suggested a global energy vulnerability index considering the electricity access, energy intensity, energy import, renewable energy consumption, greater energy consumption, fuel export, and renewable energy output variables. The authors applied a principal component analysis as a multivariate analysis method to calculate the final index. This index allows one to measure and rank worldwide energy vulnerability, addressing the increasing need to understand global vulnerability and resilience and energy policy scopes.

With respect to food vulnerability, Meenar [16] developed a Place-Based Food Insecurity and Vulnerability Index (PFIVI), which takes into account six indicators and 30 variables applied to the context of Philadelphia. The basic idea is to show how environmental factors influence food security and vulnerability. Thus, to implement this idea, the author conducted several interviews to understand the importance of hunger and food hardship; lower access to healthy food; poor food habits; poor public health condition; lower community engagement; and at-risk population and places indicators. Once the relevance of the indicators was clear, the author used ESRI ModelBuilder to build the indicators layers. Hence, the vulnerability index was obtained by adding the values of the different layers over a given area. With regard to job accessibility, Barboza *et al.* [2] provided a new accessibility measure that considers the competition effects, which is practical, intuitive, and transferable. The Balancing Time proposed indicator assesses job accessibility inequality for 160 neighborhoods in Rio de Janeiro. The researchers aim to compare this metric to the cumulative opportunities measure. The results show that Balancing Time overcomes some limitations of the cumulative opportunities metric. In addition, the Balancing Time is a helpful tool for city planners in cities with job opportunities focused on central regions. Besides, this metric works in contexts where data is limited and personal have low-skilled technical staff. Finally, Kelobonye *et al.* [14] studied the accessibility for different urban services like jobs, primary/secondary education, and shopping. The authors added a competition component to the cumulative opportunities model for highlighting the impact of addressing competition for different services. The results showed that when taking competition into account, the service equity and accessibility spatial patterns change. Besides, this study reveals demand-supply imbalances and determines accessibility inequalities. The authors also found that the three services had different levels and spatial accessibility patterns. Therefore, relying on a single service to assess spatial accessibility could be misleading.

With reference to public service, Neutens *et al.* [20] studied the accessibility to public services in terms of space and time in Ghent, Belgium using space-time accessibility measures (STAM). Their analysis showed that the changes influence the space-time accessibility average level in the temporal opening of public services. Finally, the authors showed that accessibility varies day-to-day and hour-to-hour. In the same spirit, Delafontaine and Neutens [7] study the accessibility to libraries in Ghent city. The authors modeled the citizens' activities as a set of sequential triplets containing a given activity in a certain location in a given period. Based on these representations, the authors use the utilitarian and egalitarian models to measure accessibility from randomly selected households using bicycles and vehicles as transportation modes for accessibility. They conclude that opening hours play an important role as well as spatial accessibility. Besides, Neutens *et al.* [19] studied the spatiotemporal gaps in public service delivery. They modeled the spatiotemporal accessibility of services, the demand for services, and the difference between accessibility and demand using origin-destination matrices. They used as a study case the government office service in Genth. The authors found spatial deprivation patterns using two different time intervals. Their methodological approach may help to improve or complement the static indicators for public services.

As mentioned in [14], the accessibility metric should not take into account a single service. Therefore, we propose a vector accessibility metric that considers access distance to justice, health, primary/secondary education, superior education (university), and food. In addition, our methodology does not depend on local-specific datasets. On the contrary, it uses open data from OpenStreetMap.

3   Methodology

In the present section, we introduce our methodology to compute a *Government Public Services Presence Index* for measuring the presence of the government to fulfill basic service for citizens. Figure 1 depicts the five steps to produce the *Government Public Services Presence Index* beginning with the graph construction, administrative level or area partition, distance measuring, index calculation, and profiling area. In the following paragraphs, we detail each step of our proposal.

Street
network
construction

Fig. 1. Government public services presence index methodology.

Street Network Construction generates a graph $G(V, R, E)$, where V are the nodes representing entities like street intersections and public service amenities. R is the relation between entities that captures the connection between adjacent street intersections or from one street intersection to a public service amenity. Finally, E connects the nodes in the graph. Since the challenges to calculate an index are the absence of information, gathering relevant information through interviews, and collecting different datasets to put them together, we simplified this process by using open data available for different cities. In our case, we relied on the OSMnx Python [4] library, which allows one to gather data from *OpenStreetMap* [10].

Administrative Boundary Partition allows one to segment geographic areas using different administrative levels[1] or a custom form. To section the geographic areas, we relied either on OSMnx Python [4] or the Geopandas [13] library to work with shape files[2].

Distance to Public Service Measure quantifies the minimal distance in the graph G to reach a given public service from all nodes in the graph representing an administrative level or custom area. In our methodology, the minimal distance is computed using the Dijkstra algorithm[3] implemented in NetworkX [9] weighted by the street distance.

Index Computation needs as input a set of amenities, namely hospitals, schools, universities, marketplaces, among overs. Therefore these amenities represent public services like health, education, financial services, food, *etc.*. Without loss of generality, one can add other amenities to enrich the index. Hence, the distance represented as a vector $v \in \mathbb{R}^n$ of average distances from all nodes in street network to a set of amenities in a given administrative area, where n is the number of evaluated public services presence. Finally, to have a single comprehensible metric, the average of the distance in the vector v was computed. Hence, the metric is simple to understand, not only for policymakers but for citizens. The idea behind this metric is to quantify the public services presence

---

[1] Administration Level Definitions: https://sedac.ciesin.columbia.edu/povmap/ds_defs_admin.jsp.

[2] ESRI shape file: https://www.esri.com/content/dam/esrisites/sitecore-archive/Files/Pdfs/library/whitepapers/pdfs/shapefile.pdf.

[3] Python recipe: https://code.activestate.com/recipes/119466/.

in terms of distance as proposed in [2]. Thus, distance is easy to understand, simplifying more abstract models such as principal component analysis.

Unsupervised Learning Profiling allows us to group administrative areas sharing a similar index value (*i.e.*, profile). The *Government Public Services Presence Index* allows having a single metric to rank different administrative areas based on their level. Therefore, to cluster the different regions, we relied on the k-Means clustering algorithm [15] using the Euclidean distance function. The clustering algorithm take as input the distance vectors v to output groups of areas with the same characteristics.

4 Experiments and Results

In the present section, we present the results of the experiments performed in *Lima* the capital city of Peru and *Callao*, which is a seaside city and part of the region on the Lima metropolitan area. Thus, we built the street networks of the 43 districts in Lima and seven districts in Callao representing $147\,km^2$ with 10.7 millions of inhabitants. To achieve this, we used *OSMnx*, a Python library that implements several methods to gather data from OpenStreetMap. This data is generally taken as a graph where nodes are street intersections and edges represent streets. For instance, Fig. 2A depicts the nodes and edges for Lince district. In the same spirit, amenities such as bank, courthouse, hospital, marketplace, police, school, and university in Lima and Callao were gathered with the same library. In this case, each amenity was represented by a geographical point on a map as shown in Fig. 2B.

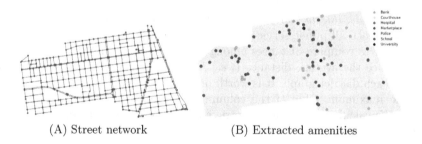

(A) Street network   (B) Extracted amenities

Fig. 2. Example of graph and amenities for Lince district.

To asses the distance to the amenities representing the public service in the fifty graphs corresponding to all districts of Lima and Callao, we measured the shortest path distance to reach each amenity from all the nodes V in a given graph representing a district. Basically, for each district we built an origin-destination matrix M_{OD} as follow:

$$M_{OD} = \begin{array}{c} \\ node_1 \\ node_2 \\ \\ node_n \end{array} \begin{pmatrix} p & h & b & c & s & u & m \\ 2.4 & 1.3 & 0.7 & 1.2 & 3.7 & 4 & 0.8 \\ 1.4 & 2.3 & 1.7 & 0.2 & 2.7 & 2 & 1.8 \\ \multicolumn{7}{c}{\ldots} \\ 2.1 & 0.3 & 4.3 & 2.3 & 1.3 & 1.2 & 2.2 \end{pmatrix}$$

Where in the columns we have the shortest distance to police (p), hospital (h), bank (b), courthouse (c), school (s), university (u), and marketplace (m) amenities from $node_n$. To achieve this results, we used GostNets[4] and NetworkX libraries, which implement Dijkstra's algorithm weighted by the street distance to consider spatial distance instead of number of hops.

Once the distance matrix for each district was built, we can understand the density distribution of served nodes depending on the distance. Therefore, Figure 3 shows the percent of nodes reaching a given amenity, representing public services, within a certain distance. Thus, depending on the districts, there are different situations. The first case is the absence of public services. For instance, *Santa Rosa*, *Pucusana* or *Mi Peru* do not have all the amenities. Besides, we noted district having all amenities. Nonetheless, some of them are far away compared to the average distance of the other districts. For example, in *Lurigancho* district, to reach a hospital, 60% of inhabitants must travel more than 20 km. In *Ancon* district to attain a police station, 90% of nodes need to travel 22 km. In *Villa Maria del Triunfo* district for all nodes getting to a university, it is necessary a 20 km. trip. In *Ate* district to arrive to a bank, 80% of the nodes need to travel 15 km. In *Pachacamac* individuals need to travel 15, 18, and 20 km. to reach a hospital, a bank, and a university, respectively. Then, districts such as *Ventanilla*, *Villa el salvador*, *Santiago de Surco*, *Los Olivos*, *La Molina*, *Lurin*, *Comas*, and *Cieneguilla* satisfy the public service demand in less than 10 km. Finally, in districts like *Miraflores*, *San Borja*, *Magdalena*, *Lince*, *Surquillo*, *San Isidro*, *San Luis*, *Pueblo Libre*, *Barranco La Perla*, *La Victoria*, and *Jesus Maria*, nodes can reach all public service in less than 5 km.

In order to compare distances among all districts, we built Table 2 in which we introduce the average distance (*i.e.*, *Index*) to reach all amenities from all nodes of each district graph. It is worth noting that missing values are replaced with the maximum value of the column to penalize the absence of a public service. We calculated the *Index* metric considering the average distances of all amenities per district as follow in Eq. 1:

$$index_j = \frac{\sum d_i}{n} \tag{1}$$

where i corresponds to each amenity $amenity = \{p, h, b, c, s, u, m\}$ and j represents each district from Lima and Callao. Furthermore, if d_i is unavailable, we take the maximum distance on the amenity over all districts. We obtained how far or how close public services are located in each district of Lima and Callao with this measure. Finally, the higher the index is the less presence of

---

[4] GostNets: https://github.com/worldbank/GOSTnets.

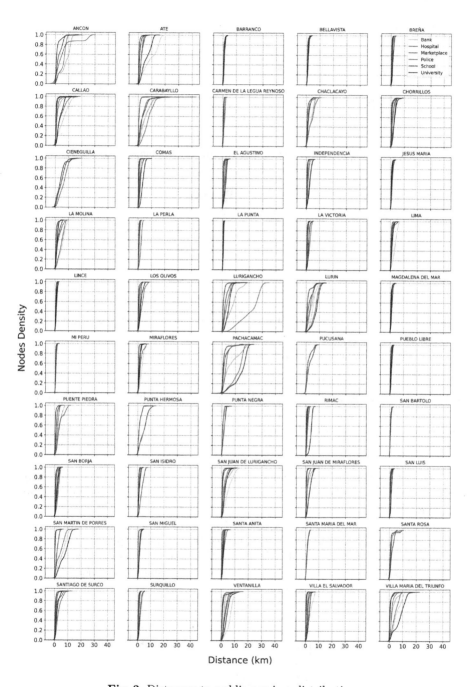

Fig. 3. Distances to public services distribution.

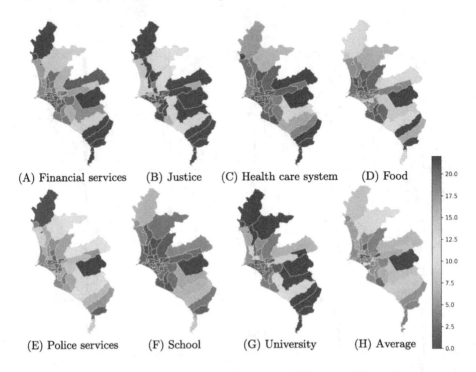

(A) Financial services   (B) Justice   (C) Health care system   (D) Food

(E) Police services   (F) School   (G) University   (H) Average

Fig. 4. Heatmap of the average distance to different public services.

government public services we have. Figure 4 shows the heatmap of the average distances to all the amenities considered for this study as well as the Public Service Presence Index previously calculated. The heatmap reveals that districts in the periphery are the ones that have less presence of the Government of Public Services.

The last part of our methodology was about clustering districts into groups with similar characteristics in terms of distances to public services. For this aim, we used k-means algorithm [12,21] and the elbow to find the optimal number of clusters k. As illustrated in Fig. 5A, the distortion score and the fit time intersects at $k = 4$ for 0.1 and 0.018, respectively. The output of the k-means algorithm is depicted in Fig. 5B. To obtain this result, the clustering algorithm takes as input the average distances vectors for all districts, as follows :

$$
\begin{array}{c}
\begin{array}{ccccccc}
p & h & b & c & s & u & m
\end{array} \\
\begin{array}{c}
district_1 \\
district_2 \\
\\
district_n
\end{array}
\left(
\begin{array}{ccccccc}
4.4 & 3.1 & 5.7 & 8.2 & 13.7 & 11 & 9.8 \\
11.4 & 7.3 & 8.7 & 7.2 & 8.7 & 9 & 7.8 \\
\multicolumn{7}{c}{\ldots} \\
12.1 & 15.3 & 14.3 & 2.3 & 6.3 & 8.2 & 5.2
\end{array}
\right)
\end{array}
$$

To describe the profile of each cluster, we utilize a radial graph for district profiling visualisation as depicted in Fig. 6.

Table 2. District distance to different public services in Lima city.

District	Bank	Courthouse	Hospital	Marketplace	Police	School	University	Index	Cluster
Ancon	7.70	–	5.70	2.78	6.07	1.34	–	6.61	0
Ate	2.27	9.00	2.41	1.17	2.28	0.55	6.03	3.39	1
Barranco	0.74	–	–	1.03	0.98	0.49	1.03	4.9	3
Bellavista	1.20	–	0.89	0.76	0.90	0.60	1.17	2.08	1
Breña	0.73	–	1.48	0.57	0.90	0.31	1.43	2.06	1
Callao	1.71	5.94	4.04	0.88	1.42	0.56	3.51	2.58	1
Carabayllo	5.09	5.30	7.45	3.45	3.44	0.71	–	5.59	0
Carmen de la Legua Reynoso	1.05	1.05	1.21	0.43	0.64	0.35	–	2.63	0
Chaclacayo	3.17	3.35	3.68	1.28	1.66	0.65	–	3.93	0
Chorrillos	1.55	–	2.33	0.80	1.49	0.44	2.70	2.62	1
Cieneguilla	–	–	–	4.56	6.23	3.80	–	9.43	2
Comas	1.24	–	1.94	0.69	1.64	0.31	3.57	2.63	1
El Agustino	1.65	–	1.49	0.82	0.75	0.30	2.18	2.31	1
Independencia	1.29	2.30	2.32	0.59	1.11	0.33	2.48	1.49	1
Jesus Maria	0.59	–	0.86	1.07	1.32	0.48	0.67	2.0	1
La Molina	1.18	5.08	4.38	2.07	2.48	0.67	1.39	2.46	1
La Perla	0.77	1.36	2.22	0.88	0.85	0.46	–	2.89	0
La Punta	0.47	–	–	0.47	0.44	0.30	0.77	4.64	3
La Victoria	0.52	–	2.38	0.81	0.88	0.40	1.71	2.24	1
Lima	1.00	3.35	1.52	0.88	0.93	0.43	1.32	1.35	1
Lince	0.46	1.22	1.17	0.70	1.29	0.45	0.99	0.9	1
Los Olivos	1.08	–	3.18	0.85	1.66	0.36	2.34	2.64	1
Lurigancho	7.32	–	21.05	2.38	3.40	0.95	4.79	6.98	3
Lurin	3.68	5.10	6.74	2.52	3.13	1.37	7.53	4.29	0
Magdalena del Mar	0.61	–	1.05	1.36	0.86	0.48	0.83	2.03	1
Mi Peru	–	–	–	0.71	0.92	0.47	–	7.65	2
Miraflores	0.49	3.06	1.40	1.30	2.24	0.47	1.23	1.45	1
Pachacamac	6.47	–	11.45	2.07	3.07	1.25	13.70	6.72	0
Pucusana	–	–	–	2.62	2.57	1.54	–	8.31	2
Pueblo Libre	0.71	–	1.29	0.83	1.23	0.39	0.88	2.05	1
Puente Piedra	3.26	–	3.96	1.27	2.04	0.48	–	4.82	0
Punta Hermosa	–	–	4.68	–	4.64	1.44	–	6.53	0
Punta Negra	–	–	–	1.68	1.66	0.75	–	7.93	2
Rimac	1.36	–	1.19	0.55	0.82	0.30	3.84	2.44	1
San Bartolo	–	–	–	–	0.74	0.50	–	8.18	2
San Borja	0.81	–	2.66	2.06	1.05	0.57	1.69	2.55	1
San Isidro	0.59	–	–	3.15	1.09	0.55	1.32	5.25	3
San Juan de Lurigancho	2.68	5.13	2.76	0.81	1.87	0.47	2.76	2.36	1
San Juan de Miraflores	1.67	–	3.03	0.51	1.26	0.33	3.00	2.69	1
San Luis	0.91	–	–	0.72	0.54	0.36	1.42	4.86	3
San Martin de Porres	1.92	5.72	4.28	0.52	2.02	0.32	7.38	3.17	0
San Miguel	1.01	–	1.42	1.39	1.43	0.34	1.48	2.3	1
Santa Anita	1.11	1.16	1.27	0.76	1.80	0.28	1.44	1.12	1
Santa Maria del Mar	–	–	–	–	1.03	1.17	–	8.32	2
Santa Rosa	–	–	–	2.00	1.38	0.98	–	7.97	2
Santiago de Surco	0.95	–	3.24	1.14	1.90	0.61	2.07	2.7	1
Surquillo	0.92	2.42	1.13	0.62	0.69	0.46	1.98	1.17	1
Ventanilla	2.14	6.35	3.30	1.31	2.82	0.89	4.36	3.02	1
Villa El Salvador	1.45	3.53	1.27	0.56	1.79	0.32	2.59	1.64	1
Villa Maria del Triunfo	2.62	5.48	4.29	0.84	1.96	0.69	7.82	3.39	1

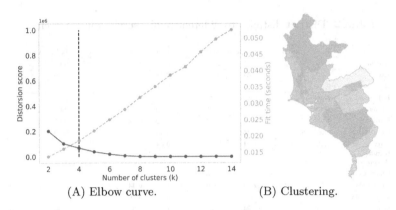

(A) Elbow curve.   (B) Clustering.

Fig. 5. District clustering.

It is essential to remind that k-means algorithm clusters data by separating samples in k groups of equal variance, minimizing a criterion known as inertia [1,21]. Please note that other kinds of clustering algorithms can be used without loss of generality. Finally, we can also observe the group number, ranging from 1 to 4, of each district in the *cluster* column in Table 2. Each radial graph contains seven axes representing the amenities' distance. Where each amenity provides a public service to the given district. Then, inner circles symbolize the distance in Km. Hence, we observe, in each radial graph, different profiles belonging to grouped districts. For example, *Cluster 0* shows a lack of services in terms of higher education, security, and justice, where the districts belonging to this cluster are *Ancon, Carabayllo, Carmen de la Legua Reynoso, Chaclacayo, La Perla, Lurin, Pachacamac, Puente Piedra, Punta Hermosa, San Martin de Porres*, and *Villa Maria del Triunfo*. Regarding *Cluster 1*, the present cluster evinces a lack of justice service represented by courthouses. This cluster is composed of *Ate, Bellavista, Callao, Chorrillos, Comas, Independencia, Jesus Maria, La Molina, La victoria, Lima, Lince, Los Olivos, Magdalena, Miraflores, Pueblo Libre, Rimac, San Juan de Lurigancho, San Juan de Miraflores, San Miguel, Santa Anita, Santiago de Surco, Surquillo, Ventanilla*, and *Villa el Salvador* districts. Concerning *Cluster 2*, we note the absence of health and higher education services. Besides, some of the districts like *Cieneguilla, Pucusana, San Bartolo, Santa Maria del Mar*, and *Santa Rosa* are seasonal living districts. Finally, *Cluster 3* groups *Barranco, La Punta, Lurigancho, San Isidro*, and *San Luis* districts, which do not possess a public hospital infrastructure.

Consequently, the Government Public Services Presence Index profiling allows one to communicate what districts lack public service easily. Hence, the index is a tool for policymakers, urban planners, and citizens to understand and quantify in terms of access based on the distance the presence of the State.

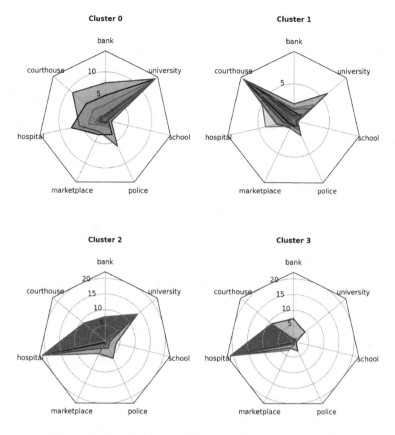

Fig. 6. Radial district profiling based on distance in Km.

5   Conclusion

In the current effort, we described the new methodology to build the *Government Public Services Presence Index*. This index overcomes the problem of gathering too specific data, sometimes missing, especially in developing countries, of cities using open data from the OpenStreetMap platform. Besides, the (public) services to quantify are configurable depending on the study. In this particular case, we used as a study case Lima city to apply our methodology. We considered public health, justice, security, education, and financial services. Thus, we have extracted all amenities from OpenStreetMap, representing the before-mention services. The results show different districts' profiles based on access, in terms of distance, to public services. Table 2 and Fig. 6 show how intuitive and interpretable the index is. In the future, we would like to test different clustering algorithms based on density and hierarchy. In addition, we would like to measure accessibility in terms of time and monetary units based on public service transport.

References

1. Clustering - scikit-learn 0.24.2 documentation. https://scikit-learn.org/stable/modules/clustering.html#k-means
2. Barboza, M.H., Carneiro, M.S., Falavigna, C., Luz, G., Orrico, R.: Balancing time: using a new accessibility measure in Rio de Janeiro. J. Transp. Geogr. **90**, 102924 (2021)
3. Berrouet, L., Villegas-Palacio, C., Botero, V.: A social vulnerability index to changes in ecosystem services provision at local scale: a methodological approach. Environ. Sci. Policy **93**, 158–171, 102924 (2019)
4. Boeing, G.: OSMnx: a Python package to work with graph-theoretic openstreetmap street networks. J. Open Source Softw. **2**(12) (2017)
5. Cutter, S.L., Boruff, B.J., Shirley, W.L.: Social vulnerability to environmental hazards. Soc. Sci. Q. **84**(2), 242–261 (2003)
6. Daras, K., Alexiou, A., Rose, T.C., Buchan, I., Taylor-Robinson, D., Barr, B.: How does vulnerability to COVID-19 vary between communities in England? Developing a small area vulnerability index (SAVI). J. Epidemiol. Community Health **75**, 729–734 (2021)
7. Delafontaine, M., Neutens, T.: Accessibility and the temporal organisation of public service facilities. In: 37th Colloquium Vervoersplanologisch Speurwerk (CVS-2010). Dipas Druk & Print (2010)
8. Gatto, A., Busato, F.: Energy vulnerability around the world: the global energy vulnerability index (GEVI). J. Clean. Prod. **253**, 118691 (2020)
9. Hagberg, A., Conway, D.: NetworkX: Network analysis with Python
10. Haklay, M., Weber, P.: OpenStreetMap: user-generated street maps. IEEE Pervasive Comput. **7**(4), 12–18 (2008)
11. Hillier, A., Cannuscio, C.C., Karpyn, A., McLaughlin, J., Chilton, M., Glanz, K.: How far do low-income parents travel to shop for food? Empirical evidence from two urban neighborhoods. Urban Geogr. **32**(5), 712–729 (2011)
12. Jin, X., Han, J.: K-means clustering. In: Sammut, C., Webb, G.I. (eds.) Encyclopedia of Machine Learning, pp. 563–564. Springer, Boston (2010). https://doi.org/10.1007/978-0-387-30164-8_425
13. Jordahl, K.: GeoPandas: Python tools for geographic data (2014). https://github.com/geopandas/geopandas
14. Kelobonye, K., Zhou, H., McCarney, G., Xia, J.C.: Measuring the accessibility and spatial equity of urban services under competition using the cumulative opportunities measure. J. Transp. Geogr. **85**, 102706 (2020)
15. Likas, A., Vlassis, N., Verbeek, J.J.: The global k-means clustering algorithm. Pattern Recogn. **36**(2), 451–461 (2003)
16. Meenar, M.R.: Using participatory and mixed-methods approaches in GIS to develop a place-based food insecurity and vulnerability index. Environ. Plan A **49**(5), 1181–1205 (2017)
17. Moore, M., Gelfeld, B., Adeyemi Okunogbe, C.P.: Identifying future disease hot spots: infectious disease vulnerability index. Rand Health Q. **6**(3) (2017)
18. Moro, E., Calacci, D., Dong, X., Pentland, A.: Mobility patterns are associated with experienced income segregation in large us cities. Nat. Commun. **12**(1), 1–10 (2021)
19. Neutens, T., Delafontaine, M., Scott, D.M., De Maeyer, P.: A GIS-based method to identify spatiotemporal gaps in public service delivery. Appl. Geogr. **32**(2), 253–264 (2012)

20. Neutens, T., Schwanen, T., Witlox, F., De Maeyer, P.: Evaluating the temporal organization of public service provision using space-time accessibility analysis. Urban Geogr. **31**(8), 1039–1064 (2010)
21. Yeturu, K.: Machine learning algorithms, applications, and practices in data science. In: Handbook of Statistics, vol. 43, pp. 81–206 (2020)

Clustering Analysis for Traffic Jam Detection for Intelligent Transportation System

Edwin Alvarez-Mamani[1(✉)], Harley Vera-Olivera[1,2],
and José L. Soncco-Álvarez[1]

[1] Department of Informatics, Universidad Nacional de San Antonio Abad del Cusco,
Cusco, Peru
{edwin.alvarez,jose.soncco}@unsaac.edu.pe
[2] Department of Computer Science, Universidade de Brasília, Brasília, D.F., Brazil

Abstract. The growth of cities and the mobility of their inhabitants often generate traffic jams. In order to diminish this problem, cities began to implement Intelligent Transportation Systems (ITS), such as real-time control and monitoring of public transportation buses, smart traffic lights, mobile applications to inform passengers. ITS are a reliable source of data collection for further analysis. This research aims to perform a clustering analysis to detect traffic jams, for which the Parallel Social Spider Optimization (P-SSO) algorithm was used. The choice of the P-SSO algorithm was made based on the previous results where the P-SSO algorithm was compared with the K-means and Social Spider Optimization (SSO) algorithms to solve clustering problems. On the first stage of this research, the P-SSO algorithm was used to define traffic jam states. In the second stage, the P-SSO algorithm was used to detect traffic jam areas based on the geospatial data generated by public transport buses in Cusco-Perú. This clustering analysis was performed on the main streets of the city between June and August 2019. Further, an application was developed that allows to check graphically the clusters obtained.

Keywords: Clustering · Traffic jam detection · Intelligent transportation systems · Parallel social spider optimization

1 Introduction

Traffic jam is a permanent problem faced by city dwellers. According to a study carried out by IBM [1], between 2000 and 2050, the most used means of transport will be the bus from public transport. In the process of becoming a Smart City, Cusco started to implement Intelligent Transportation Systems (ITS), such as charge tickets using RFID technology that give information to passengers through mobile applications, real-time monitoring of public transport fleets, intelligent traffic lights, to name a few examples. Each of these examples is a reliable source of data collection.

J. A. Lossio-Ventura et al. (Eds.): SIMBig 2021, CCIS 1577, pp. 64–75, 2022.
https://doi.org/10.1007/978-3-031-04447-2_5

The motivation to carry out this work arose from seeing all the opportunities mentioned in [2] for transport planning using GPS data to analyze urban mobility. For detecting traffic jams, are used algorithms such as K-means, K-metoids, and DBSCAN. However, new algorithms with better accuracy were proposed, such as the sequential Social Spider Optimization (SSO) bio-inspired algorithm for clustering [3]. The SSO algorithm consists of simulating the behavior and interaction of male and female spiders based on the biological laws of a spider colony. In [3] it was reported that the SSO algorithm has better accuracy than the K-means algorithm and the experiments were performed over five datasets taken from the UCI Machine Learning Repository. Later, we implemented the parallel version of the SSO algorithm, called Parallel Social Spider Optimization (P-SSO) [4]. P-SSO produced similar results as the SSO algorithm. Regarding execution time, P -SSO is 28 times faster than the SSO algorithm. For this reason, in this research work, the geospatial data generated by public transport buses in Cusco-Perú was analyzed, using the P-SSO algorithm for clustering and the OSMnx module for detecting traffic jams in a study area.

The graph obtained shows the streets with a traffic jam on OpenStreetMap (OSM), based on five states of traffic jams found in this analysis. Therefore, these results will help improve the management of transport and traffic in cities to become Smart Cities.

The present work is organized as follows; in Sect. 2, we present the literature review. In Sect. 3, the methodology is presented for the clustering analysis. A case study and the results are presented in Sect. 4. Finally, in Sect. 5, the discussions and conclusions are presented.

2 Related Works

The authors conducted a literature review, considering the following question: What clustering algorithms are applied to detect traffic jams? The following summarizes those research papers that used a given clustering algorithm to detect traffic jams.

Zhou, Q. [5] studied the traffic jam at intersections in Zhenjiang to alleviate bottlenecks, adopted the hierarchical clustering method and the K-means algorithm. The congestion flow is divided according to the value that k takes (number of centers). The results of the comparative analysis show that the hierarchical clustering method is better than the K-means algorithm.

Pholsena, K., and Pan, L. [6] evaluated the state of vehicular congestion applying a new congestion assessment model based on possibilistic fuzzy c-means (PFCM). Four states of congestion were considered: traffic jam, congested flow, steady flow, and free flow. For the experiments, it was used the dataset of the Caltrans performance measurement system (PeMS) and compared the PFCM and fuzzy c-means (FCM) algorithms, where the proposed model evaluated the state of congestion more efficiently.

Mondal, M. A., and Rehena, Z. [7] analyzed the problem of traffic jams in different career segments. The analysis is carried out on the density of the congestion and the average speed of the vehicles, with data captured by stationary sensors. The K-means algorithm was applied to classify congested road segments. Four clusters were found: high density-low speed (cluster 1), medium density-low speed (cluster 2), medium density-moderate speed (cluster 3), and low density-high speed (cluster 4).

Wang, H., and Si, Y. [8] proposed a method to detect traffic jams anomalies based on clustering of GPS data from taxis in Beijing. They apply the Non-Negative Matrix Factorization (NMF) method to extract congestion patterns and the K-means algorithm to detect neighboring roads. They also define a function to determine the probability that a specific route is abnormal. The results mention that this method is entirely accurate, as it provides detection through horizontal and vertical comparisons.

Huertas, J. A. et al. [9] studied the level of Traffic Jams Stress (LTS) of cyclists in Bogotá (Colombia) and considered four categories of LTS: low, medium, high, and extremely high. In the cluster analysis, they used the K-medoids algorithm on government data. Comparing the results with city reports, it was found that the number of fatal and non-fatal cyclist collisions per kilometer is positively correlated.

Toshniwal, D. et al. [10] applied the clustering algorithms Partitioning Around Medoids (PAM), Agglomerative Nesting (AGNES), and DBSCAN for the analysis of clustering on Spatio-temporal data of the urban congestion of Aarhus, the second-largest city in Denmark. Finally, they analyzed the results to determine the various factors that affect congestion flow patterns in a metropolitan area.

Hasan, MM, and Oh, JS [11] developed a GIS-based Multivariate Spatial Clustering (SMVC) approach to recognize state-level congestion patterns based on temporal and spatial variables of the departments of transportation (DOT) in the city of Michigan. The proposed clustering approach was compared and validated based on machine learning classifiers. Results showed that it outperforms Michigan DOT's traditional pooling approach.

3 Methodology

The following aspects are considered for this research: data pre-processing using ETL techniques, OSMnx module application, clustering analysis and graphic visualization of the results (See Fig. 1).

3.1 Data Preprocessing

The geospatial data was generated by the ITS to control and monitor urban transport in Cusco city [12]. Because of the enormous amount of data generated by the GPS devices in the public transport units, for this study, the data generated between June and August of the year 2019 was considered. Each public transport unit generates data every 30 s on average, this data is stored in a PostgreSQL database with a frequency of approximately five records per second.

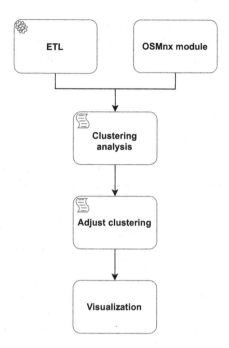

Fig. 1. Workflow for clustering analysis of the geospatial data by the ITS

The data has the following attributes *ID, date, time, latitude, longitude, speed, bearing, lap,* and *vehicle_id.*
Extract: At this stage, the data generated by the ITS system was restored to a PostgreSQL database and then exported to a *.csv* file for subsequent transformation.
Transform: After doing data extraction, the data was filtered by taking into consideration only the following attributes: *date, time, latitude, longitude, speed,* and *bearing.* Where, *latitude* and *longitude* were put together in a single attribute called *lat_lon,* with the data type POINT.
Load: Finally, the transformed data were stored in the PostGIS database for further analysis using a Python script.

3.2   Module OSMnx

For the data analysis, it is necessary to consider a region or area of study enclosed by a polygon. OSMnx [13] is a python package that allows downloading geospatial data from OpenStreetMap and modeling street networks; it also has modules and functions for geospatial geometry that enable interacting with this data. This work uses OSMnx to obtain the nodes and edges representing the selected area's street networks. These data will be necessary to perform the clustering analysis described in Sect. 3.1. In the same way, the "osmnx.distance.nearest_nodes" method was used to find the closest node to a point and the "osmnx.stats.intersection_count" method to determine the number of intersections in a network of streets, this last data will serve as a parameter of algorithms for clustering analysis. The module OSMnx are available at https://osmnx.readthedocs.io/en/stable/.

3.3 Clustering Analysis

This research aims to find the areas of traffic jams within an area of study, for which the analysis of geospatial data is carried out. In related works (Sect. 2) was found that the K-means, K-metoids, and DBSCAN algorithms are applied to detect traffic jams. According to [3], the sequential SSO algorithm for clustering has better precision (sum of Euclidean distances) than the K-means algorithm. Likewise, the parallel version of the SSO algorithm, called P-SSO [4], has similar results as the SSO algorithm, but it is 28 times faster than the SSO algorithm.

For this analysis, it is proposed to use the bio-inspired P-SSO algorithm. The purpose of the P-SSO algorithm is to solve clustering problems using all computational resources of a computer. The pseudocode for P-SSO is shown in Algorithm 1. P-SSO receives as parameter the geospatial data, the number of iterations (generations), the number of clusters K. This value is obtained from the number of intersections that exist in the area of study. Additionally, the P-SSO algorithm receives migration parameters that take the following values: number of islands: 24, migration topology: network B, type of migrant individual: better, type of immigrant individual: random, emigration policy: clone, political immigration: replace, number of emigrants/immigrants: 3 and migration interval: 1.

The clustering analysis was carried out in two stages. In the first stage, the time and speed attributes of the geospatial data were used, and the clusters representing the states of traffic jam were obtained as a function of speed. For the second stage, the latitude and longitude attributes were used. As is well known, the result of the clustering algorithms returns the centroids and the labels that verify the association of each geospatial data to the clusters. But the centroids that are obtained do not necessarily coincide with an intersection of the streets. For this reason, each centroid is approximated to the closer intersection (node), for which the methods implemented in OSMnx were used. This procedure was called clustering adjustment.

3.4 Visualization

The information resulting from applying the P-SSO algorithm for stages 1 and 2, explained in Sect. 3.3, is used to show (graphically) the state of traffic jam on the OSM, where the streets (nodes) belong to the area of study. To color the streets, a scale that represents the state of the traffic is considered. This value can be defined based on the density (No. of vehicles/t), where t represents a unit of time and the speed of the vehicles (Km/hr) [6,7,14–17]. For example, in [6] is considered 4 states (free flow, steady flow, congested flow, traffic jam), in [7] is considered 4 states(high density-low speed, medium density-low speed,

---

Algorithm 1: Parallel SSO (P-SSO) [4]

Input: A dataset N-dimensional points, $D = \{d_1, d_2, \ldots, d_m\}$; number of
clusters, $k > 0$; *numberGenerations*; *parameters* of migration
Output: *Centroids* of the clusters found and *Labels*

1 MPI_Init;
2 MPI_Comm_rank get process id ($rank$);
3 MPI_Comm_size get the number of processes ($size$);
4 Read dataset D;
5 Read initial population P;
6 Calculate fitness of population P;
7 Calculate weight of population P;
8 **for** $i \leftarrow 2$ **to** *numberGenerations* **do**
9 | Cooperative operator for female spiders;
10 | Cooperative operator for male spiders;
11 | Mating operator;
12 | Replacement of spider in P;
13 | Calculate fitness of population P;
14 | Calculate weight of population P;
15 | MPI_Barrier;
16 | Run migration according to *parameters*;
17 **if** $rank == 0$ **then**
18 | **for** $i \leftarrow 1$ **to** $size - 1$ **do**
19 | | MPI_Recv the metric $\mathcal{M}$ from process i and keep the best one;
20 **else**
21 | MPI_Send the best metric $\mathcal{M}$ to process 0;
22 MPI_Finalize;
23 **return** *Centroids and Labels*

---

medium density-moderate speed, low density-high speed), in [14] is considered
4 states, in [15] is considered 3 states($0 \leq v \leq 42$ km/h for wide moving jam,
43 km/h $\leq v \leq 74$ km/h for the synchronized phase and 74 km/h $\leq v \leq 120$ km/h
for the free flow), in [16] is considered 5 states(free flow, steady flow, unstable
flow, limited flow, forced limit), and in [17] is considered 5 states (speed level 1:
> 45 km/h, level 2: 35 km/h $< v \leq 45$ km/h, level 3: 25 km/h $< v \leq 35$ km/h,
level 4: 15 km/h $< v \leq 25$ km/h, level 5: ≤ 15 km/h).

In this work, the traffic states were determined based on the time, speed
(Km/hr), and five traffic states.

4   Case Study and Results

4.1   Case Study

The methodology proposed in Sect. 3 is applied to find traffic jam in the city
of Cusco. As indicated in Sect. 3.1, the source of the data used in this study is
generated by urban transport buses. This data is analyzed applying clustering
algorithms, and finally, the results are shown using OSM.

● date	● time	▣ lat_lon	123 speed	123 bearing
1	2019-06-03	07:00:00	POINT (-13.5466 -71.8884)	7	6
2	2019-06-03	07:00:00	POINT (-13.5208 -71.9489)	9	2
3	2019-06-03	07:00:00	POINT (-13.5365 -71.9545)	26	6
4	2019-06-03	07:00:00	POINT (-13.5205 -71.9687)	34	2
5	2019-06-03	07:00:00	POINT (-13.5229 -71.9968)	30	1
6	2019-06-03	07:00:00	POINT (-13.5451 -71.8994)	29	2
7	2019-06-03	07:00:01	POINT (-13.5443 -71.9868)	7	1
8	2019-06-03	07:00:01	POINT (-13.5357 -71.9566)	23	2
9	2019-06-03	07:00:01	POINT (-13.522 -71.9762)	16	6
10	2019-06-03	07:00:01	POINT (-13.5499 -71.891)	35	2
11	2019-06-03	07:00:01	POINT (-13.5193 -71.9748)	8	7
12	2019-06-03	07:00:01	POINT (-13.5392 -71.9423)	20	6
13	2019-06-03	07:00:01	POINT (-13.5405 -71.927)	12	6
14	2019-06-03	07:00:01	POINT (-13.5352 -71.9613)	11	1
15	2019-06-03	07:00:02	POINT (-13.5226 -71.9696)	13	7
16	2019-06-03	07:00:02	POINT (-13.5466 -71.8884)	10	6
17	2019-06-03	07:00:02	POINT (-13.5266 -71.9387)	10	6

Fig. 2. Geospatial data

The geospatial data selected for this case study is from June 03 to August 03 in 2019 between 05 h and 22 h and has a total of 4 051 667 records. The format of these data is displayed in Fig. 2. The selected area, enclosed by a polygon (Fig. 3(a)), represents the area of study of the city of Cusco. The vertices of the polygon (Fig. 3(b)) are the latitudes and longitudes, with an area of 11.1213 km^2. For better visualization, an example of a smaller selected area is shown in Fig. 4(a) and its respective polygon in Fig. 4(b). Our interface allows analysis of any area of the city in a specific date and time range.

4.2   Experiments and Results

The clustering analysis was run on a computer with two Intel Xeon Gold 6134 s processors, each processor having 8 cores with hyper-threading, a maximum speed clock of 3.7 GHz, and 128 GB of RAM memory. The Python programming language and the Django Rest backend framework were used to perform the operations and calculations. The VueJS frontend framework was used together with NuxtJS to select a study area, a range of dates, a range of hours for the query, and to show the results more interactively. Finally, PostgreSQL was used as a database manager with the PostGIS extension. A web application was built to analyze vehicular traffic more interactively using these technologies.

The experiments were executed in two stages. In the first stage, the P-SSO algorithm was conducted to obtain the traffic jams states clusters. For the second stage, the P-SSO algorithm was executed to obtain the clusters representing the intersections of streets with an accumulation of geospatial points.

The following parameters were considered for the first stage, $K = 5$ (number of clusters), 100 iterations (generations), a population of 120 individuals. Finally, time and speed columns from the database, divided into two ranges of hours from 05:00 h to 12:59 h and 13:00 h to 22:00 h. The results are shown in Table 1 and Fig. 5. The execution of this first experiment resulted in five states

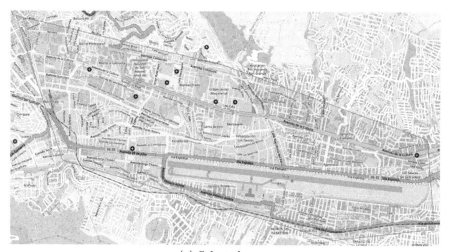

(a) Selected area

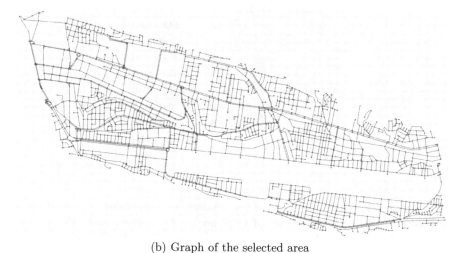

(b) Graph of the selected area

Fig. 3. Study area

(clusters) for each range of hours. The average of each minimum value of the states was calculated similarly for each maximum value to determine the final states. Finally, the following traffic jams states were obtained based on time and speed: State 1, from 1 to 12 km/h; State 2, from 13 to 21 km/h; State 3, from 22 to 31 km/h; State 4, from 32 to 44 km/h; and State 5, from 45 to 99 km/h.

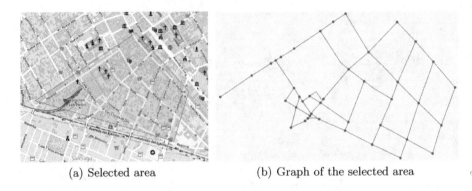

(a) Selected area   (b) Graph of the selected area

Fig. 4. Study area, city center

Table 1. Clustering analysis for traffic jams states based on speed

Interval	No. records	States	Min	Max
05 h–12:59 h	1 955 100	1	1.0	13.0
		2	14.0	22.0
		3	23.0	31.0
		4	32.0	44.0
		5	45.0	99.0
13 h–22 h	2 096 567	1	1.0	12.0
		2	13.0	21.0
		3	22.0	31.0
		4	32.0	44.0
		5	45.0	99.0

For the second stage, the graph of the selected area was taken into considera-tion (See Fig. 3(b)), which consists of 1 827 nodes, 2 686 edges, and 425 intersec-tions formed at least by the intersection of 4 streets. Then the P-SSO algorithm was executed with the following parameters, $K = 425$ (number of intersections),

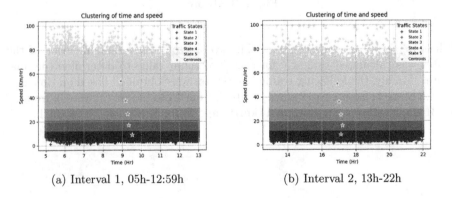

(a) Interval 1, 05h-12:59h   (b) Interval 2, 13h-22h

Fig. 5. Clustering analysis for traffic jams states

100 iterations (generations), a population of 120 individuals, and latitude, longitude columns from the database (1 732 825 records). The P-SSO algorithm returns the labels and the corresponding centroids after performing the clustering analysis. But the location of the centroids does not always coincide with a real intersection of the streets. For this reason, it is necessary to move each centroid to the closest intersection, as seen in Fig. 6, where the red point is the original centroid, and the green point is the new centroid.

Fig. 6. Clustering centroid fixing

Finally, this approach will help to color the streets according to the 5 traffic states found in the first stage of the experiments. Nodes, graph vertices, and the average of the speeds of each node (centroid) are used to paint the streets. The final result can be seen in Fig. 7 and 8, where the color scale represents the level of traffic jams on the streets. The redder the street, the greater the traffic jams.

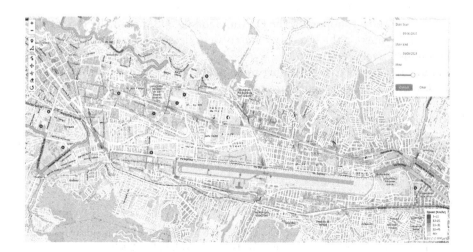

Fig. 7. Detection of traffic jam in the selected area of the city according to the 5 states

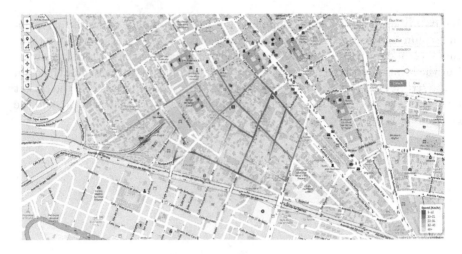

Fig. 8. An analysis of traffic jams in a more specific area.

5 Discussion and Conclusions

The detection of traffic jams using the P-SSO algorithm shows encouraging results, according to the five traffic jams states found in this research, the streets with the highest traffic jams in a selected area can be seen on the OSM map. In the literature review, the K-means, K-medoids, and DBSCAN algorithms are used. In this research, the P-SSO algorithm is used because of the faster times regarding the sequential SSO, which has better results than the K-means algorithm. Another essential aspect found in this research is the state of traffic jams for the case study; five states are considered based on the time and speed of the geospatial data. The speed intervals for each jam state found in this research differ from those found in other research works. This difference is due to the nature of the geospatial data and the case study context.

Finally, with the support of the OSMnx module, OSM, and the P-SSO algorithm, traffic jams in the streets of Cusco were detected, showing encouraging results interactively.

As future work, we are planning to compare the P-SSO algorithm with the K-means and DBSCAN algorithms for detecting the traffic jams.

Acknowledgment. The authors thank Dr. Germain Garcia Zanabria for guiding us in using the OSM and OSMnx modules, the Algorithms and Data Analysis Laboratory (LAAD) of the UNSAAC for providing us with their equipment and facilities. Finally, the company TRYS (http://www.gpstrys.com/) for providing us with the data for the study.

References

1. Houghton, J., Reiners, J., Lim, C.: Transporte inteligente cómo mejorar la movilidad en las ciudades. IBM Institute for Business Value, 20 (2009)

2. Puebla, J.G., et al.: Cómo aplicar big data en la planificación del transporte: El uso de datos de gps en el análisis de la movilidad urbana (2020)
3. Vera-Olivera, H., Soncco-Álvarez, J.L., Enciso-Rodas, L.: Social spider algorithm approach for clustering. In: Proceedings of the 3rd Annual International Symposium on Information Management and Big Data (SIMBig), pp. 114–121 (2016). CEUR Workshop Proceedings 1743
4. Alvarez-Mamani, E., Enciso-Rodas, L., Ayala-Rincón, M., Soncco-Álvarez, J.L.: Parallel social spider optimization algorithms with island model for the clustering problem. In: Lossio-Ventura, J.A., Valverde-Rebaza, J.C., Díaz, E., Alatrista-Salas, H. (eds.) SIMBig 2020. CCIS, vol. 1410, pp. 122–138. Springer, Cham (2021). https://doi.org/10.1007/978-3-030-76228-5_9
5. Zhou, Q.: Traffic flow data analysis and mining method based on clustering recognition algorithm. Adv. Transp. Stud. **3** (2018)
6. Pholsena, K., Pan, L.: Traffic status evaluation based on possibilistic fuzzy c-means clustering algorithm. In: 2018 IEEE Third International Conference on Data Science in Cyberspace (DSC), pp. 175–180. IEEE (2018)
7. Mondal, M.A., Rehena, Z.: Identifying traffic congestion pattern using k-means clustering technique. In: 2019 4th International Conference on Internet of Things: Smart Innovation and Usages (IoT-SIU), pp. 1–5. IEEE (2019)
8. Wang, H., Si, Y.: Detection of traffic abnormity based on clustering analysis of taxi GPS data. In: Proceedings of the 2019 2nd International Conference on Data Science and Information Technology, pp. 219–224 (2019)
9. Huertas, J.A., et al.: Level of traffic stress-based classification: a clustering approach for Bogotá, Colombia. Transp. Res. Part D Transp. Environ. **85**, 102420 (2020)
10. Toshniwal, D., Chaturvedi, N., Parida, M., Garg, A., Choudhary, C., Choudhary, Y.: Application of clustering algorithms for spatio-temporal analysis of urban traffic data. Transp. Res. Procedia **48**, 1046–1059 (2020)
11. Hasan, M.M., Oh, J.-S.: GIS-based multivariate spatial clustering for traffic pattern recognition using continuous counting data. Transp. Res. Rec. **2674**(10), 583–598 (2020)
12. Mamani, E.A.: Sistema de transporte inteligente (sti), para el control y monitoreo del servicio urbano en la ciudad del cusco. Universidad Nacional de San Antonio Abad del Cusco (2018)
13. Boeing, G.: OSMnx: new methods for acquiring, constructing, analyzing, and visualizing complex street networks. Comput. Environ. Urban Syst. **65**, 126–139 (2017)
14. Zhao, L., Li, Y.: Study on urban road network traffic district division based on clustering analysis. In: 2018 Chinese Automation Congress (CAC), pp. 3556–3560. IEEE (2018)
15. Esfahani, R.K., Shahbazi, F., Akbarzadeh, M.: Three-phase classification of an uninterrupted traffic flow: a k-means clustering study. Transportmetrica B Transp. Dyn. (2018)
16. Dai, Y., Lu, W., Huang, H., Liu, L.: Threshold division of urban road network traffic state based on macroscopic fundamental diagram and k-means clustering. In: ICTE 2019, pp. 31–39. American Society of Civil Engineers Reston, VA (2020)
17. Wang, W.-X., Guo, R.-J., Yu, J.: Research on road traffic congestion index based on comprehensive parameters: taking Dalian city as an example. Adv. Mech. Eng. **10**(6), 1687814018781482 (2018)

Deep Learning and Applications

A Study of Dynamic Convolutional Neural Network Technique for SCOTUS Legal Opinions Data Classification

Eya Hammami[1(✉)], Rim Faiz[2], and Sami Ben Slama[3]

[1] LARODEC Laboratory, ISG, University of Tunis, Tunis, Tunisia
hammami.eya@isg.u-tunis.tn
[2] LARODEC Laboratory, IHEC, University of Carthage, Tunis, Tunisia
rim.faiz@ihec.ucar.tn
[3] King Abdul Aziz University, Jeddah, Saudi Arabia

Abstract. The quantity of legal information that is being produced on a daily basis in courts is growing enormously. The processing of such data has been gaining considerable attention thanks to their availability in an electronic form and the advancement made in Artificial Intelligence applications. Indeed, deep learning has offered promising results when used in the field of natural language processing (NLP). Neural Networks such as recurrent neural network and convolutional neural networks have been used for different NLP tasks like information retrieval, document classification and sentiment analysis. In this paper, we present a Neural Network based model with a dynamic input length for classifying legal opinions from cases seen by the Supreme Court of the United States (SCOTUS) (https://www.kaggle.com/gqfiddler/scotus-opinions). The proposed model, tested over a real-world legal opinions dataset, by the way, proved better performance than the other baseline methods.

Keywords: Text classification · Natural language processing · Legal text · Artificial intelligence · Deep learning · Neural networks

1 Introduction

The continued application of computational intelligence in legal domain has shown a lot of attention in the last recent years. With the expanded accessibility of legal text in digital form a vast variety of applications, including translation, summarization [1], classification [2], reasoning, text analytics, and others have been focused on within the legal field. In this work we principally take on the text classification task. Indeed, there are a lot of applications that demand the subdividing of natural language data into groups, e.g. filtering spam emails or classifying opinions retrieved from social media sites, etc.

In this paper, we attest that law experts would appreciably gain advantages

SIMbig 2021.

from the potential outfitted by machine learning. This is specifically the case for legal experts who have to take hard decisions concerning varied sides of a given case. Given machine learning techniques and data availability, it is conceivable to train text classification systems to predict some of these decisions. Such systems can rendering as a decision support system for legal experts. Several methods have been proposed for this task of classification to mention, Support Vector Machine, Logistic Regression, Naive Bayes classifier, and most lately deep learning models [3,4], like Convolutional Neural Network [5,6], Recurrent Neural Network and Long Short Term Memory [7]. Most of these models are not principally addressed for the legal domain, which make them not appropriate to be used for Legal texts. Indeed, this kind of text has a specific vocabulary, that demands more pre-processing to achieve good accuracy results and capture the hidden characteristics and hidden semantics.

In this work, we propose Neural Network based model with dynamic input length layer to deal with SCOTUS legal opinions data. We also show a comparative study between our proposal and certain baseline approaches. This paper is organized as follows: we present in Sect. 2 a state of the art that examines the different approaches for text classification. In Sect. 3, we present the architecture of our proposal in detail. Finally, the experimental results of our proposed model compared to the different methods used in the literature are presented in Sect. 4.

2   Related Work

This section presents a brief discussion on the text classification task and on the application of deep learning to legal domain which includes various models developed for retrieving and classifying relevant legal text. Text classification is a necessary task in Natural Language Processing. Linear classifiers were frequently used for text classification [9,10]. According to [11] these linear models could scale up to a very huge dataset rapidly with a proper rank constraint and a fast loss approximation. Deep learning methods, such as recurrent neural networks (RNN) and Long Short Term Memory (LSTM) have been widely used in language modeling. Those methods are adapted to natural language processing because of their ability to extract features from sequential data, to mention the Convolutional Neural Network (CNN) which is usually used for computer vision tasks like in [12–14]. This model has been adopted in NLP for the first time in [15]. In this work the authors presented a new global max-pooling operation, which was revealed to be efficient for text, as an alternative to the conventional local max-pooling of the original LeNet architecture [16]. Furthermore, they suggested to transfer task-specific information by co-training different deep models on many tasks.

Inspired by the original work of [12,15] introduced a simpler architecture with modifications consisting of fixed pre-training word2vec embeddings. They proceed that both multitask learning and semi-supervised learning enhance the generalization of the shared tasks, resulting in state-of the-art-performance. Moreover, in [17], the authors demonstrated that this model can actually achieve state-of-the-art performances on many small datasets. Dynamic Convolutional Neural Network (DCNN) is a type of CNN which is introduced by [18]. Their approach outperforms other methods on sentiment classification. They use a new pooling layer called a dynamic K-max pooling. This dynamic k-max pooling is a generalization of the max pooling operator, which computes a new adapted K value for each iteration. Thus, their network can read any length of an input. Character-level Convolutional Neural Network (Char-CNN) which is introduced by [13] also yields better results than other methods on sentiment analysis and text classification. In the same context, [19] shows that a character-based embedding in CNN is an effective and efficient technique for sentiment analysis that uses less learnable parameters in feature representation. Their proposed method performs sentiment normalization and classification for unstructured sentences. A new Char-CNN model proposed by [20] and inspired from the work presented in [13], allows any length of input by employing k-max pooling before a fully connected layer to categorize Thai news from a newspaper. Furthermore, the work in [21] presented a character aware neural language model by combining a CNN on character embeddings with a Highway-LSTM on subsequent layers. Their results suggest that on many languages, character inputs are relevant for language modeling. In addition, [22] analyzed a multiplicative LSTM (mLSTM) on character embeddings and found out that a basic logistic regression learned on this representation can reach state-of-the art results on the Sentiment TreeBank dataset [23] with a few hundred labeled examples.

We have noticed a rather small body of previous works about automatic text classification for legal documents. For example, support vector machines (SVMs) have been used to classify legal documents like legal docket entries in [24]. The authors developed simple heuristics to address the conjunctive and disjunctive errors of classifiers and improve the performance of the SVMs. Based on the prescience gained from their experiments, they also developed a simple propositional logic based classifier using hand labeled features, that addresses both types of errors simultaneously. They proved that this simple approach outperforms all existing state-of the-art ML models, with statistically significant gains. A mean probability ensemble system combining the output of multiple SVM classifiers to classify legal texts, was also developed by [25]. They reported accuracy scores of 98% for predicting a case ruling, 96% for predicting the law area of a case and 87.07% on estimating the date of a ruling. A preliminary study addressing deep learning for text classification in legal documents was proposed in [26]. They compared deep learning results with results obtained using SVM algorithm on four datasets of real legal documents. They demonstrated that CNN present better accuracy score with a training dataset of larger size and can be improved for text classification in the legal domain. Neural Networks such as CNN, LSTM and RNN have also been used for classifying English legal court opinions of Washington University School of Law Supreme Court Database (SCDB) in [27]. The authors compared the machine learning algorithms with several Neural Networks systems and they found out that CNN combined with Word2vec performed better compared to the other approaches and gave an accuracy around 72.7%. Based on the Brazilian Court System representing the biggest judiciary system in the world, and receiving an extremely high number of lawsuits every day, the work in [28] presented a CNN based approach that helps analyse and classify these cases, in order to be associated to relevant tags and allocated to the right team. The obtained results are very promising.

However, most of the mentioned approaches are generally based on the CNN model and usually use a static input length. Therefore, we propose a Neural Network model with a dynamic input length to classify SCOTUS legal Opinions data. Experiments on real dataset highlight the relevance of our approach and open up many perspectives.

3   Proposed Model

The architecture of our proposed approach, drawn in Fig. 1, is based on the Convolutional Neural Network technique [27], represented by a max pooling layer, which is a method for down sampling data by employing a gliding window on a row of data and choosing a cell which contains a maximum value to be utilized in the next layer. It conducts out an operation on 1D CNN and it is calculated by the following formula (1) which is suggested in [20]:

$$P_{r,c} = max_{j=1}^{s} M_{r,s(c-1)+j} \tag{1}$$

where:

- M is an input matrix with a dimension of $n \times l$
- s is a pooling size
- P is an output matrix with a dimension of $n \times \frac{l}{s}$
- c is a column cell of matrix P
- r is a row cell of matrix P

In this work we try to experiment a new pooling layer, therefore we use the k-max pooling layer instead than the max-pooling layer. Indeed the k-max pooling operation enables to pool the k maximum active features in P, also, it conserves the order of the features, but it is unresponsive to their accurate positions. It can then catch more finely the number of times where the feature is activated in P. The k-max pooling operator is applied in the network after the highest convolutional layer. This grants the input to the fully connected layers to detach from the length of the input sentence. Furthermore, in the middle of the convolutional layers, the pooling parameter k is not fixed, but is chosen in a dynamic way to permit a sleek extraction of a longer-range and higher order features [18]. This dynamic pooling layer is calculated by the following formula (2) which is defined by Koomsubha and Vateekul [20]:

$$P_{r,*} = kmax_{j=1}^{l} M_{r,j} \tag{2}$$

where:

- M is an input matrix with a dimension of $n \times l$
- K is an integer value
- P is an output matrix with a dimension of $n \times k$
- $*$ shows that all columns in a row are calculated together
- r is a row cell of matrix P

The major difference between these two kinds of pooling layer depends in the use of a gliding window. Max pooling is a method for down sampling data by employing a gliding window on a row of data and selecting a cell which consists of a maximum value to be moved to the next layer [20]. Nonetheless, k-max pooling doesn't have a window, but it has a choosing operation which takes out all data in a row. Then, top k cells which have maximum value are picked to be employed in the up-coming layer [20]. By adopting K-max pooling in a convolutional neural network, as we propose, we can certainly have a matrix which is ready to fit into a fully connected layer regardless of the length of an input. Figure 1 clarify in details our proposed approach.

On the convolutional and pooling layers, the length of data belongs to the input. Although, after the k-max pooling layer, the length of data in each document is coequal. Therefore, our neural network classification model is a little bit similar to the one defined by [12], but we changed the layers, by adding other layers and adjusted some of the original hyperparameters in order to achieve a better-performed text categorization model. Our model first composed of an embedding layer using word2vec as a pre-trained word embedding, and next builds a matrix of documents represented by 300-dimensional word embedding. As we all know when applying machine learning approaches in NLP, most of the studies use 200 or 300 dimensional vectors, but 300-dimensional embedding save more information, therefore, is considered to produce better performance outcomes. Then, we integrate the following sets of parameters: A dropout of 0.5, because it helps to change the concept of learning all the weights together, to learn a fraction of the weights in the network in each training iteration; a convolution layer of 128 filters with a filter size of 3, according to the literature, we set the k value to 5. We also add a dense layer composed of 128 units between two dropouts of 0.5 to avoid overfitting. Finally, the last layer (output layer) is a dense layer with a size of 3 equal to the number of labels in our dataset.

4 Experiments and Results

We show in this part the experimental results of our proposal compared to the different approaches presented in the literature. In order to evaluate the performance of our proposed model and the baseline methods, we adopt the accuracy and the F_1 scores as measures to evaluate these models.

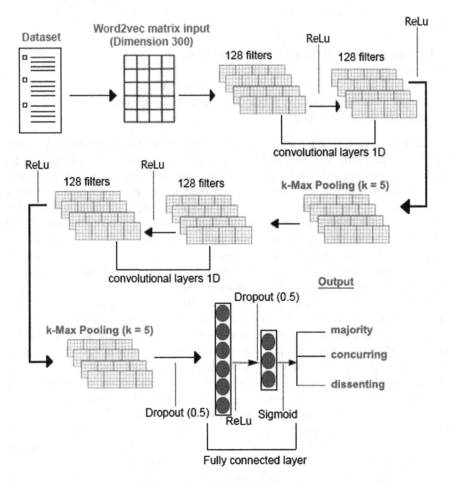

Fig. 1. Proposed architecture.

4.1   Dataset

We tested the performance of our proposed model using a real-world dataset of SCOTUS legal Opinions which is collected from Courtlistener.com[1]. It is a free legal research website that holds millions of legal opinions from state courts and federal. The dataset includes 36,000 opinions from 1970 through 2020, organized into 4 categories (see Table 1). After the pre-processing, we randomly divide it into train and test sets, with 80% and 20% split. To have a clear idea about the SCOTUS legal Opinions we present the number of opinions written by each recent justice, by category in the Fig. 2.

---

[1] https://www.courtlistener.com/.

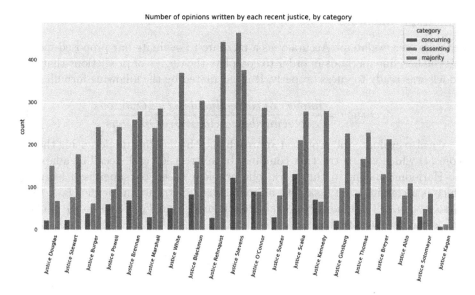

Fig. 2. Number of opinions written by each recent justice, by category.

4.2 Pre-processing

Our model first gets rid of special characters like stopwords, punctuation, whitespaces, and numbers. The elimination of these special characters will permit us to have classes that are illustrative of the words, which are recurring in our legal texts. Second, we continue with lemmatization by utilizing the TreetaggerWrapper module and taking off the named entities after recognizing them with Spacy and NLTK modules to authorize a more careful interpretation of the data. We chose to proceed with lemmatization otherwise stemming because lemmatization takes into account the context and switches the word to its significant base form, while stemming just removes the last few characters, overwhelmingly conduct to incorrect meanings. Finally, each word in the texts is mapped to a word2vec vector before being fed into the CNN for the classification.

Table 1. Number of opinions for each category.

Opinions	Categories
24840	Majority
5040	Dissenting
5760	Concurring
360	Other

4.3 Experiments

In this paper, we adapt Accuracy as a measure to evaluate our proposed model and the baseline methods in order to complete the degree of predictions that the models was ready to guess properly. It is calculated by the following formula (3):

$$Accuracy = \frac{number\ of\ correctly\ classified\ Opinions}{total\ number\ of\ classified\ Opinions} \tag{3}$$

We also evaluate the proposed approach and the baseline models using the F_1 score (4) which is a metric that combines both Precision and Recall by adapting the Harmonic mean. In this work, our problem based on supervised learning which is a classification task with an imbalanced distribution for the class, thus F_1 score is a suitable metric to evaluate our model on. $F_{1,i}$ refers to F_1 of class i, C is the number of labels:

$$F_1 = \frac{\sum_{i=1}^{C} F_{1,i}}{|C|} \tag{4}$$

where:

$$F_{1,i} = 2 \cdot \frac{precision_i \cdot recall_i}{precision_i + recall_i} \tag{5}$$

Besides, we experimented two other CNN based approaches which are CNN with a simple max-pooling layer and CNN with the global max-pooling layer. In the CNN with a simple max pooling, we use the same hyperparameters as the CNN with the global max pooling, but we switch the pooling size to 3. Accordingly, the implementation of these three architectures is executed using Keras which permit users to select whether the models they construct are running on Theano or TensorFlow. In our situation the models run on TensorFlow.

Regularization of Hyperparameters: In our experiments, we tested our model with several various hyperparameters. But we discovered that the model performed best when adapting 128 filters for each of the convolutional layers. Furthermore, each of the models is regulated with a dropout [30], which works by dropping out a proportion p of hidden units during training. We uncovered that a dropout of 0.5 with a batch size of 256 performs better for our CNNs models, by applying the Adam optimizer [29].

Results of Our First Experiment When the K Value Set to 5: As displayed in Table 2, CNN by using max pooling layer achieves better results. It can attain an accuracy of 82,60 %, which outperforms the CNN with dynamic k-max pooling layer (our proposed model) and CNN with the global max pooling layer. We think that this could be due to the restricted length of texts in the SCOTUS opinions dataset.

Table 2. Results of first experiments when the k value was fixed to 5.

Method	Accuracy (%)	F1 (%)
CNN-kmax pooling	79.93	78.80
CNN-max pooling	82,60	82.61
CNN-global max pooling	81,84	82.30

Results of Our Second Experiment When the K Value Set to 3: In this second experiment, we reduce the k parameter to 4 then to 3. The target of this experiment was trying if we could get better accuracy when altering K parameter with the proposed K-max pooling model. As displayed in Table 3, our model outperforms the other models with 85.01% accuracy when K is fixed to 3.

Table 3. Results of second experiments when k value was fixed to 3.

Method	Accuracy (%)	F1 (%)
CNN-kmax pooling (K = 3)	**85.01**	**84.50**
CNN-kmax pooling (K = 4)	83,05	83.70
CNN-max pooling	82,60	82.61
CNN-global max pooling	81,84	82.30

As follows we demonstrate two plots of Cross Entropy and Accuracy for the second experiment: Fig. 3 present the regression of the Cross Entropy and the progression of the accuracy for CNN using k-max pooling (k = 3) layer approach correspondent to the number of epochs for both training and test sets. The red curve belongs to the validation and the blue curve belongs to the training. In this two graphics we observed that the line plot is fully converged for the two curves and gives no sign of under or over fitting.

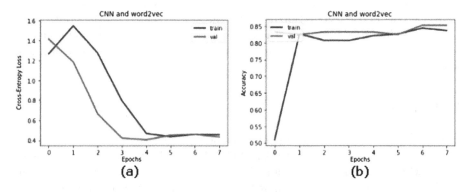

Fig. 3. Line plot of cross entropy loss over training epochs.

Comparison with Baseline Methods: We proceed also with the comparison of the CNN based methods to three traditional approaches: Naive Bayes Classifier using TF-IDF [31] to represent the SCOTUS opinions texts, Logistic Regression [32] with Word2vec embedding and SVM [24]. The results are drawn in Table 4 as we can note that the CNN with k-max pooling model outperforms also the non NN based models.

Table 4. Comparison with baseline methods.

Method	Accuracy (%)	F1 (%)
CNN-kmax pooling	**85.01**	**84.50**
CNN-max pooling	82,60	82.61
CNN-global max pooling	81,84	82.30
Naive Bayes classifier	50,91	48,15
Word2vec and Logistic Regression	75,78	76,12
SVM	77,89	78,67

5   Discussion

Dynamic max pooling [20], ordinarily demonstrated to perform much better compared to simple max pooling and other baseline models. But according to our first experiment, the simple max pooling outperforms all other approaches by achieving an accuracy of 82.60%. Next in our second experiment, we tried to adjust the value of the parameter K of the Dynamic max pooling to 3, as a consequence the Dynamic max pooling attain accuracy result of 85.01%. Besides, it outperforms all other approaches. In this work we take into account that with dynamic k-max pooling layer, the value of the parameter k rely on the input shape. The concept is that longer sentences can take higher k values. But in our situation, the sentence's length that we have, are not sufficient to set higher K value. We take into consideration also that the words included in the pre-trained word embedding may not detect the particularity of languages in legal domain. Hence, we think maybe for these reasons our results may not be very optimal exceptionally for our first experiment.

6   Conclusion

In this work, we focused on the use of dynamic input length in the Convolutional Neural Network algorithm to classify SCOTUS legal opinions. Our proposed model, which can take into account longer input length, perform better than the original model with a fixed input length according to the accuracy measure. Besides, a variety of attractive future work has to be mentioned:

Firstly, we plan to re-adjust the approach architecture by using some newer word embedding models like ELMO, Fast Text, and especially using the transformers, to better capture the characteristics of SCOTUS legal opinions.

Secondly, we should train our proposed method on new datasets to validate its performance.

Finally, we can extend our reflections to the classifications of handwritten documents and not be limited to electronic versions.

Acknowledgments. This work is supported by LARODEC laboratory of the Higher Institute Management, University of Tunis.

References

1. Doan, T.M., Jacquenet, F., Largeron, C., Bernard, M.: A study of text summarization techniques for generating meeting minutes. In: Proceedings of the 14th International Conference on Research Challenges in Information Science, RCIS, pp. 522–528 (2020)
2. Stead, C., Smith, S., Busch, P., Vatanasakdakul, S.: Towards an academic abstract sentence classification system. In: Proceedings of the 14th International Conference on Research Challenges in Information Science, RCIS, pp. 562–568 (2020)
3. Bochie, K., Gilbert, M.S., Gantert, L., Barbosa, M.S.M., Medeiros, D.S.V., Campista, M.E.M.: A survey on deep learning for challenged networks: applications and trends. J. Netw. Comput. Appl. **194**, 103213 (2021)
4. Chakma, K., Das, A., Debbarma, S.: Summarization of Twitter events with deep neural network pre-trained models. In: Lossio-Ventura, J.A., Valverde-Rebaza, J.C., Díaz, E., Alatrista-Salas, H. (eds.) SIMBig 2020. CCIS, vol. 1410, pp. 45–62. Springer, Cham (2021). https://doi.org/10.1007/978-3-030-76228-5_4
5. Li, Y.D., Hao, Z.B., Hang, L.: Survey of convolutional neural network. J. Comput. Appl. **36**, 2508–2515 (2016)
6. Saad, A., Abed, M.T., Saad, A.-Z.: Understanding of a convolutional neural network. In: International Conference on Engineering and Technology, ICET, pp. 1–6 (2017)
7. Hochreiter, S., Schmidhuber, J.: Long short-term memory. Neural Comput. **9**, 1735–1780 (1997)
8. Litvak, M.: Deep dive into authorship verification of email messages with convolutional neural network. In: Lossio-Ventura, J.A., Muñante, D., Alatrista-Salas, H. (eds.) SIMBig 2018. CCIS, vol. 898, pp. 129–136. Springer, Cham (2019). https://doi.org/10.1007/978-3-030-11680-4_14
9. Joachims, T.: Text categorization with support vector machines: learning with many relevant features. In: Nédellec, C., Rouveirol, C. (eds.) ECML 1998. LNCS, vol. 1398, pp. 137–142. Springer, Heidelberg (1998). https://doi.org/10.1007/BFb0026683
10. Andrew, M., Kamale, N.: A comparison of event models for Naive Bayes text classification. In: AAAI 1998 Workshop on Learning for Text Categorization, pp. 41–48 (1998)
11. Joulin, A., Grave, E., Bojanowski, P., Mikolov, T.: Bag of tricks for efficient text classification. In: Proceedings of the 15th Conference of the European Chapter of the Association for Computational Linguistics, pp. 427–431 (2017)

12. Kim, Y.: Convolutional neural networks for sentence classification. In: Proceedings of the 2014 Conference on Empirical Methods in Natural Language Processing (EMNLP), pp. 1746–1751 (2014)
13. Zhang, X., Zhao, J., Lecun, Y.: Character-level convolutional networks for text classification. In: Proceedings of the 29th Conference on Neural Information Processing Systems, NIPS 2015, Advances in Neural Information Processing Systems, pp. 649–657 (2015)
14. Conneau, A., Schwenk, H., Barrault, L., Lecun, Y.: Very deep convolutional networks for text classification. In: Proceedings of the 15th Conference of the European Chapter of the Association for Computational Linguistics, pp. 1107–1116 (2017)
15. Ronan, C., Jason, W.: A unified architecture for natural language processing: deep neural networks with multitask learning. In: Proceedings of the 25th International Conference on Machine Learning, ICML, pp. 160–167 (2008)
16. LeCun, Y., Bottou, L., Bengio, Y., Haffner, P.: Gradient-based learning applied to document recognition. Proc. IEEE **86**, 2278–2324 (1998)
17. Mikolov, T., Chen, K., Corrado, G.S., Dean, J.: Efficient estimation of word representations in vector space. In: International Conference on Learning Representations (2013)
18. Kalchbrenner, N., Grefenstette, E., Blunsom, P.: A convolutional neural network for modelling sentences. In: Proceedings of the 52nd Annual Meeting of the Association for Computational Linguistics, pp. 655–665 (2014)
19. Arora, M., Kansal, V.: Character level embedding with deep convolutional neural network for text normalization of unstructured data for Twitter sentiment analysis. Soc. Netw. Anal. Min. **9**(1), 1–14 (2019). https://doi.org/10.1007/s13278-019-0557-y
20. Thanabhat, K., Peerapon, V.: A character-level convolutional neural network with dynamic input length for Thai text categorization. In: Proceedings of the 9th International Conference on Knowledge and Smart Technology, KST, pp. 101–105 (2017)
21. Kim, Y., Jernite, Y., Sontag, D., Rush, A.M.: Character-aware neural language models. In: Proceedings of the Thirtieth AAAI Conference on Artificial Intelligence (2016)
22. Radford, A., Jozefowicz, R., Sutskever, I.: Learning to generate reviews and discovering sentiment. In: International Conference on Learning Representations, ICLR (2018)
23. Socher, R., et al.: Recursive deep models for semantic compositionality over a sentiment treebank. In: Proceedings of Conference on Empirical Methods in Natural Language Processing, pp. 1631–1642 (2013)
24. Nallapati, R., Manning, C.D.: Legal docket classification: where machine learning stumbles. In: Proceedings of the 2008 Conference on Empirical Methods in Natural Language Processing, pp. 438–446 (2008)
25. Sulea, O.-M., Zampieri, M., Malmasi, S., Vela, M., Dinu, L.P., van Genabith, J.: Exploring the use of text classification in the legal domain. In: Proceedings of 2nd Workshop on Automated Semantic Analysis of Information in Legal Texts, ASAIL (2017)
26. Wei, F., Qin, H., Ye, S., Zhao, H.: Empirical study of deep learning for text classification in legal document review. In: International Conference on Big Data, pp. 3317–3320 (2018)
27. Undavia, S., Meyers, A., Ortega, J.E.: A comparative study of classifying legal documents with neural networks. In: Federated Conference on Computer Science and Information Systems, FedCSIS, pp. 515–522 (2018)

28. Da Silva, N.C., et al.: Document type classification for Brazil's supreme court using a convolutional neural network. In: Proceedings of the Tenth International Conference on Forensic Computer Science and Cyber Law-ICoFCS, pp. 7–11 (2018)
29. Kingma, D.P., Ba, J.: Adam: a method for stochastic optimization. In: International Conference on Learning Representations (2015)
30. Srivastava, D., Hinton, G., Krizhevsky, A., Sutskever, I., Salakhutdinov, R.: Dropout: a simple way to prevent neural networks from over fitting. J. Mach. Learn. Res. 15, 1929–1958 (2014)
31. Yoo, J.-Y., Yang, D.: Classification scheme of unstructured text document using TF-IDF and Naive Bayes classifier. J. Mach. Learn. Res. 111, 263–266 (2015). Proceedings of 3rd International Conference on Computer and Computing Science, COMCOMS
32. Pranckevičius, T., Marcinkevičius, V.: Comparison of Naive Bayes, random forest, decision tree, support vector machines, and logistic regression classifiers for text reviews classification. Baltic J. Mod. Comput. 5, 221 (2017). University of Latvia

Hydra: Funding State Prediction for Kickstarter Technology Projects Using a Multimodal Deep Learning

Alonso Puente$^{(\boxtimes)}$ and Marks Calderón

ESAN University, Alonso de Molina No. 1652, Lima, Peru
15101383@ue.edu.pe,mcalderon@esan.edu.pe
https://www.ue.edu.pe

Abstract. Since crowdfunding started, thousands of entrepreneurs have presented their projects to the public to fund them. During the 2009–2019 period, 37% of all Kickstarter projects, one of the most popular crowdfunding platforms, were successfully funded. Different Machine Learning algorithms have been used, considering all the categories in this platform to develop predictive models. However, their research works only reached 20% for the Technology category. The main aim of this study is to develop a Multimodal Deep Learning model with three layers: a Multilayer Perceptron for metadata, a Convolutional Neural Network for project descriptions, and a Bidirectional LSTM model for backers comments. This proposal can predict funding state of Technology projects on Kickstarter. In order to train the model, we created a dataset with 27K Technology projects on Kickstarter between 2009 and 2019. The performance of this proposal reached an AUC value of 93%. Thus, the problem was solved with a different approach that combinates different types of networks to improve results.

Keywords: Crowdfunding · Project · Multimodal Deep Learning · Funding · Convolutional Neural Network · Recurrent Neural Network

1 Introduction

Currently, many entrepreneurs present their projects on the Internet to attract investors. For this reason, a few web platforms have been created to accelerate the interaction between projects published for at least one month and the community that wishes to collaborate with an amount of money. Website of crowdfunding show projects and campaign promotions. The project goal would be funded until a deadline, and so it becomes a reality. This activity is known as crowdfunding [25], which reached more than 6 million worldwide campaigns in 2019 [23].

Since Kickstarter, one of the most popular crowdfunding websites and Indiegogo, was launched in 2009, 6.3 billion dollars has been pledged, more than 212 thousand projects have been successfully funded, and 16 million contributors were registered. Kickstarter is a platform for creative projects, including movies, games, music, art, design, and technology. The platform uses a funding model called "All-or-nothing," which means a project only will carry on pledged money if it reaches at least its funding goal during the campaign [12]. While backers support these projects for many reasons without getting ownership or income from projects they funded, but rather creators keep all of their work [11].

Until 2019, the technology category had the lowest success rate on the Kickstarter site, reaching only 20%. The average ratio of all categories between 2009 and 2019 was 37%. The main reason for the low success ratio is high goal values, 23 thousand dollars on average, and only 32% of successful Technology projects raise at least this amount [24]. It denotes a great challenge for project creators to reach the goal during the campaign, especially in this category.

Our proposal will support entrepreneurs to predict (as many times as they require) whether their campaign will or will not be funded once it is launched, reducing the risk of uncertainty about the campaign's performance to make better decisions before the deadline. Therefore, we developed a Multimodal Deep Learning model using quantitative variables (metadata) and textual content (project description written by creators and backer's comments) provided from Technology projects between 2009 and 2019. Additionally, we analyzed the state of art techniques on Machine and Deep Learning in this field.

In Sect. 2, we described works related to successful crowdfunding prediction; in Sect. 3, we presented the methodology of this work; Sect. 4 shows the results, and finally, in Sect. 5, we discuss the main conclusions of the investigation.

2 Related Works

In this section, we presented related works predicting crowdfunding projects' funding state that apply classical Machine Learning and Deep Learning models in order to predict the campaign and how they were trained with metadata information about projects, such as pledged amounts, the number of backers, and other variables; textual, visual, and multimodal data.

Classical Machine Learning models can predict with 90% accuracy in average using metadata to feed the model. For instance: [4] used an SVM model with features from the project campaign such as number of pledged projects by its creator, number of projects created by its creator, whether or not it has a video and project goal. They got 90% accuracy for real-time projects that they could analyze through an Android mobile app and a Google Chrome extension. Another author [21] also developed an SVM model that trained metadata using Part-of-speech (POS) Tagging as a feature selection method. Thus, they got success with 92% accuracy. [14] formulated a survival analysis problem to predict with 74% AUC the success of a project, applying the Censored Regression approach, implementing a Logistic Regression model and a log-logistic regression model using a more than 2 K projects dataset. In addition, the distribution of the project's time of success was studied. Next, [9] implemented a system with Machine Learning techniques (Decision Tree, Random Forest, Artificial Neural Network, KNN algorithm, and Naive Bayes) and then trained with main project section features (metadata) to predict with 94% accuracy the project funding state. This research cited [4] and [15] in their state-of-the-art.

On the other hand, other works applied on Deep Learning models such as [26] that developed a Multilayer Perceptron, which trained with campaign metadata of 378K crowdfunding projects between May 2009 and March 2018, and this work got 93.23% AUC funding success of a crowdfunding project prediction, which was contrasted with Machine Learning models from the literature to determine if it performed better than them. [8] developed a Seq2seq model with SMP architecture to predict with 96% Decoder accuracy the distribution of promises and the correct duration of the campaign to achieve funding success using metadata and feedback from 14 K Indiegogo projects.

Now, we are going to present works based on textual analytics. Phrases that propel the funding success of a crowdfunding project from the textual content extracted from its description and reward information were determined by [15]. This proposal got 2.4% cross-validation error and was trained with more than 45 K Kickstarter projects with a penalized logistic regression model to protect against collinearity. [27] implemented a framework established on a hybrid of DC-LDA to determine topical features that transform input data for a Random Forest model, to predict with 91% F1-Score the collection of crowdfunding projects using textual data from 2 Chinese websites. Later, [13] designed a Deep Neural Network to predict with 80% accuracy the funding state of Technology projects using only textual content (campaign description, updates, comments, and words obtained from the main video) from 23 K Kickstarter Technology projects between April 2009 and August 2017. Next, [5] studied the impact of textual content in a Kickstarter project from analyzing its keywords to determine the funding success ratio, used to create two SVM-RFE models with different tools each. The best result was 78.90% accuracy. On the other hand, [3] developed an algorithm to extract product keywords in textual information (title, summary, and description) from 246 Kickstarter projects to determine its effect on advertising crowdfunding campaigns.

Finally, for Multimodal data, we reviewed previous works which used two different modals. [6] studied the influence of sophisticated interactions between textual, visual, and metadata modals on the prediction of project success, building advanced Neural Networks schemes to predict with 83.26% accuracy the project funding state using only pre-posting information. The author [22] developed an integrated system for recommending crowdfunding projects with LSTM- LDA architecture from textual analysis of 504 K comments in 600 projects and used it to identify potential fraudulent projects when analyzing discussion trends. The best result was 96% accuracy using an RNN-LDA model with 300 epochs. Moreover, [7] made clusters using the K-means algorithm to identify the creator of the potential group and define strategies to lead a project to success, identifying attributes of the successfully funded project and defined behavioral stereotypes associated with new projects.

3 Methodology

CRISP-DM methodology deploys six stages for this proposal, as Fig. 1 presents. [7] used this approach in their work. Some previous works [6,8,22] applied methodologies with stages on CRISP-DM. Therefore, this technique can be an excellent alternative to develop this research work. Finally, the following subsections describe each stage for CRISP-DM in this study.

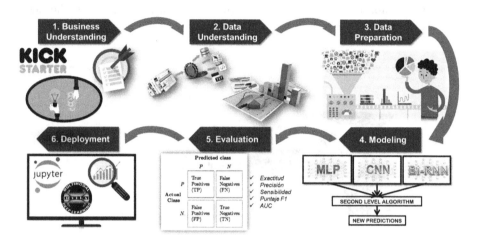

Fig. 1. Implementation of CRISP-DM methodology.

3.1 Business Understanding

In this stage, we defined the problems and objectives of this work, the methodology built on crowdfunding, similar predecessors on solving problems of funding classification in crowdfunding campaigns, and technical bases on Artificial Intelligence, Deep Learning, and Natural Language Processing.

3.2 Data Understanding

In this step, we collected data for each modal. This process builds data sets with three different sources. Finally, we carried out an exploratory analysis of each variable for the data.

We started with the metadata dataset building process, downloading monthly data scraped between 2015 and 2019 by the website Web Robots. Each file had at least 27 variables that were completed to reach 37, the maximum number of variables over all datasets. After downloading and unzipping those files, they were merged into one using Alteryx Designer software. Then, we discarded variables unconsidered in state-of-the-art (*converted_pledged_amount*, *creator*, *currency_symbol*, *currency_trailing_code*, *current_currency*, *disable_communication*, *friends, fx_rate, is_backing, is_starrable, is_starred, location, name, permissions, photo, profile, slug, source_url, spotlight, staff_pick, state_changed_at, static_usd_rate, usd_type).* Next, we dropped rows of projects whose financing status differed from "Successful" or "Failed" and removed duplicate records, keeping only ones corresponding to the Technology category.

Then, we designed a web scraping algorithm to search descriptions using metadata's *urls* variable to redirect itself to the project page. Metadata and description were scraped from the main section (as shown in Fig. 2), while comments were made from its section (as shown in Fig. 3), keeping only the ones from the backers.

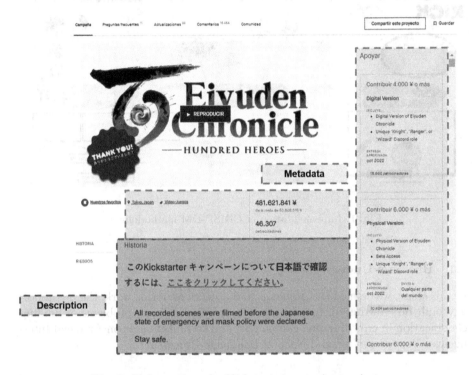

Fig. 2. Main section of a Kickstarter campaign project.

We realized an exploratory analysis of the three modals' variables upon data collection. We observed that the ratio of successful and unsuccessful projects in the observed periods is 28% and 72%, respectively, as shown in Fig. 4. This pie chart shows the distribution of the qualitative variables and box-and-whisker plots for quantitative ones Fig. 5.

Fig. 3. The comments section of a Kickstarter campaign project.

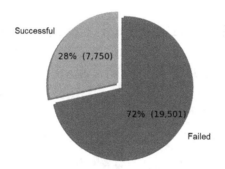

Fig. 4. Distribution of technological projects according to their funding state.

Almost all projects had descriptions (98%). However, less than a third had comments (29%). We created word clouds to know which words they frequent the most on campaigns, such as those received in the social interaction.

3.3 Data Preparation

This stage carried out the pre-processing of each kind of data. For the Metadata submodel, the financial characteristics of the campaign added seven quantitative variables founded on creating a correlation matrix to evaluate variables (Fig. 6). Therefore, eight combinations of variables that have a correlation value less or equal to 0.30 [16], to which they were normalized using Min-Max Scaler.

For textual content (Description and Comments models), three processes find to clean and reduce dimensions; these are text cleaning (Fig. 7) and word vectorization and creation of word embeddings matrix (Fig. 8). Text cleaning consisted of reducing each word to its minimal expression. For this, text words

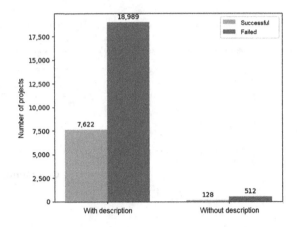

Fig. 5. Projects distribution grouped by presence of description and funding state.

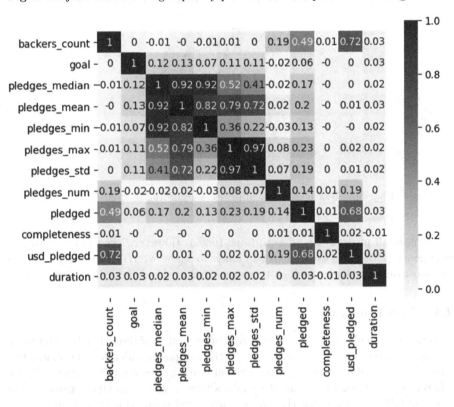

Fig. 6. Quantitative variables correlation matrix.

were tokenized to delete special characters and stop words, and finally to lemmatize them. After processing, textual variables (Description and Comments) were split the dataset into 80% and 20% to create training and test subsets, respectively.

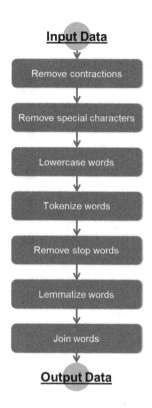

Fig. 7. Text cleaning pipeline.

According to Fig. 8a, for the process of representing words as numerical vectors. In order to train models, we created a tokenizer that used a training subset, which will detect each unique input word and assign a code to it. The value $<OOV>$ will be assigned if the term is undetected. This action was applied to two subsets mentioned above. In addition to the encoding, the function creates a vector whose size is the maximum length of the rows, 3,671 words for the Description dataset and 30,072 for the Comments dataset. In the last case, to avoid the high computational cost required by that size, the maximum length was limited to 5,000. Those vectors of coded words, whose records are shorter than those established, were filled on the right with 0.

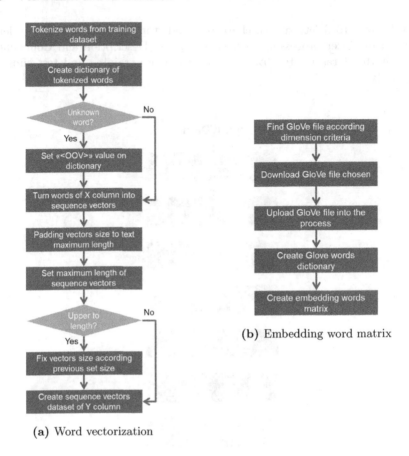

(a) Word vectorization

(b) Embedding word matrix

Fig. 8. Word vectorization process and embedding word matrix creation.

In Fig. 8b, the embedding matrix of each textual modal was elaborated to use in the embedding layer of their respective models. For this, we implemented the 100-dimensional GloVe algorithm [17]. The reason for using this tool was to create a dictionary with trained word representations from a considerably large corpus, related by their meaning in a vector space of words. Finally, *vocabulary size x maximum word length* defines the matrix dimension.

3.4 Modeling

We built our Multimodal model based on a stacked model in this stage. It resulted from merging other submodels, as [6] presented in their work, with better results than independent models. The dataset split 80% for training and 20% testing, respectively, according to [5, 15, 21, 26, 27]. Before building the three submodels architectures in Table 1, following steps by [26] and Rules of Thumb by [20], we made other models for Metadata and Description. For the first case, we built an MLP and an SVM model [1, 4, 21], while two SVM models for the second one, with the TF-IDF and BoW algorithms [5, 21], using the same database to compare later with them as baseline [18]. Our initial hypothesis was that the Multimodal model would have a better performance against both the three submodels built and the baseline. For this reason, we made neural networks to join them later from their last layers like [2, 6].

The first submodel built was a Multilayer Perceptron (MLP) for metadata, as applied in [6, 9, 26]. This architecture was built of one input layer, two dense layers, two deactivation layers, and one output layer.

The second submodel built was a Convolutional Neural Network (CNN) for description, as applied in [6] but focused on texts. This architecture consisted of one input layer, one Embedding layer, one Conv1D layer, one GlobalMaxPooling1D layer, one dense layer, and one output layer.

The third submodel built was a Recurrent Neural Network (RNN) for comments, as applied in [8, 22]. This architecture consisted of one input layer, one Embedding layer, one Dropout layer, one Bidirectional LSTM layer, and one output layer.

Table 1. The structure of each submodel

Model	Layer type		Output shape	Parameter
MLP	Input layer	Input	(None, 6)	0
	Dense 1	Dense	(None, 32)	224
		ReLU	(None, 32)	0
		Dropout	(None, 32)	0
	Dense 2	Dense	(None, 16)	528
		Tanh	(None, 16)	0
		Dropout	(None, 16)	0
	Classification layer	Dense	(None, 1)	17
		Sigmoid	(None, 1)	0
CNN	Input layer	Input	(None, 3,671)	0
	Embedding layer	Embedding	(None, 3,671, 100)	14,827,000
	Convolutional layer	Conv1D	(None, 3,667, 128)	64,128
		ReLU	(None, 3,667, 128)	0
		GlobalMaxPooling1D	(None, 128)	0
	Dense 1	Flatten	(None, 128)	0
		Dense	(None, 64)	8,256
		Tanh	(None, 64)	0
	Classification layer	Dense	(None, 1)	65
		Sigmoid	(None, 1)	0
RNN	Input layer	Input	(None, 5,000)	0
	Embedding layer	Embedding	(None, 5,000, 100)	7,409,600
		Dropout	(None, 5,000, 100)	0
	Bidirectional layer	Bidirectional (LSTM)	(None, 256)	234,496
	Classification layer	Dense	(None, 1)	257
		Sigmoid	(None, 1)	0

Final variables used both in the submodels and in the stacked model are presented in Table 2.

Table 2. Data dictionary of the final trained dataset

Variable	Detail
Independent variables	
goal	Project funding money goal
completeness	Percentage of funding
duration	Campaign duration (in days)
pledges_num	Number of pledges available
pledged	Pledged money in the campaign
pledges_median	Average of pledges available
description	Project description
comments	Backers comments about the project
Dependent variable	
state	Funding state of the project campaign

Once the models for each modal were built, our Multimodal model is presented in Fig. 9.

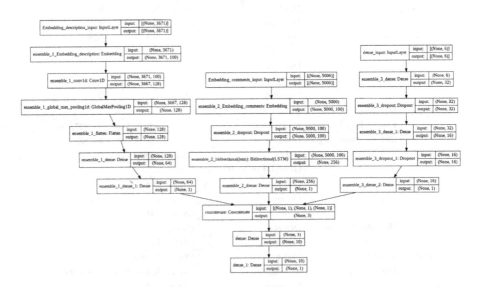

Fig. 9. Final stacked model architecture.

The architecture consisted of loading previous trained submodels, assigning their layers as *trainable = False* to avoid that their weights will not be updated during the training phase of the proposed model and only occur for the weights of the new hidden layer and the output. After the concatenated layer, a dense layer was added to deepen the created network further and achieve better model performance. Finally, the output layer conducts the classification.

We proposed to build a Multimodal Deep Learning model as in [6] founded on choosing the three best modals of a Kickstarter project campaign. From previously works cited on the state-of-art, there was listed five kind of modals on a campaign: metadata [1,4,6–10,14,15,21,26,27], project description [3,5, 6,8,9,13,15,21,27], backers comments [8,13,14,22], updates/rewards [13], and multimedia content [6].

We realized that campaign updates were not relevant to models because they were not present and did not mention much information about the project. Rewards only explained more detail about shipping and obtaining way, as additional information to pledges. Furthermore, the leading video/image of a Technology Kickstarter project was also discarded due to the infeasibility of finding patterns among their multimedia content features when testing CNN models.

Finally, we added dynamic data as backers comments to our Multimodal model static data (metadata and project descriptions) to analyze the impact during the campaign time. It helped us determine the favorable or unfavorable conditions of using a variable that did not directly depend on the characteristics of the project assigned by the creator.

3.5   Evaluation

For evaluation of the trained models, we have been used the following metrics: accuracy (Eq. 1), precision (Eq. 2), recall (Eq. 3), F1-Score (Eq. 4), AUC (area under the curve) (Eq. 5), and confusion matrix. Those were chosen according to [1,27] (except for AUC), [6,10], and [5] (except for recall and AUC).

$$Accuracy = \frac{TP + TN}{TP + TN + FP + FN} \tag{1}$$

$$Precision = \frac{TP}{TP + FP} \tag{2}$$

$$Recall = \frac{TP}{TP + FN} \tag{3}$$

$$F1 - Score = \frac{2 * precision * recall}{precision + recall} \tag{4}$$

$$AUC = \int TPRd(FPR) \tag{5}$$

3.6 Deployment

In the last stage of our methodology, we built the system prototype for project creators from the Technology category that includes data collection for different modals from the web address of a project consulted as the input value.

This software consisted of a web platform to demonstrate the proposed classification model in real-time, as shown in Fig. 10.

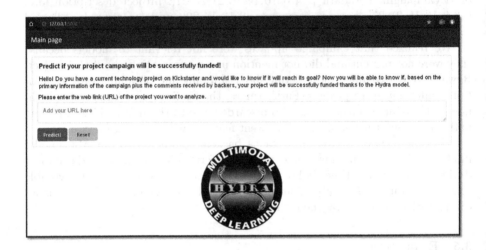

Fig. 10. Web interface demo.

After extracting and pre-processing the project information, the loaded model *Hydra* receives this data as input to concatenate it internally and follow the process of predicting the funding state. If the probability threshold is at least 0.50, the result will be **SUCCESSFUL**. Otherwise, it will be **FAILED**. In both cases, the probability is displayed below the result.

4 Results

Table 3 summarizes results after experiments with classical Machine Learning models and our proposal. The baseline used a Support Vector Machine (SVM) for metadata and an SVM trained with TF-IDF algorithm for description.

We used the same databases (Kickstarter Technology projects completed between 2009 and 2019 that can be downloaded from [19]) for both modals to compare our developed models with the baseline and the same metrics to evaluate each model. Training time from the antecedent mentioned above was longer (approximately 16 s for metadata and 4 h for the description), in contrast to our current work (approximately 38 s for the metadata and two and a half hours for the description).

Table 3. Comparison of proposed models results with baseline

Models		Accuracy	Precision	Recall	F1-Score	AUC
Classical machine learning [18]	Metadata	0.89	0.86	0.72	0.75	0.84
	Description	0.75	0.59	0.53	0.35	0.68
Proposal	Metadata	0.93	0.91	0.92	0.92	0.92
	Description	0.77	0.72	0.75	0.73	0.75
	Comments	0.85	0.87	0.75	0.79	0.75
	Hydra	**0.93**	**0.91**	**0.93**	**0.92**	**0.93**

From Table 3, we concluded that the Multimodal Deep Learning model was affected by elements considered in its development, since it presented better performance both against its submodels and against Classical Machine Learning models evaluated by the five chosen metrics, being 0.01 the difference against the second-best model under the AUC value and 0.57 against the worst model under F1-Score. However, the disadvantage of the research proposal is that the absence or negligible presence of data in any of the text-based modals decreases the predicted success rate for a project. Due to this, it is prone to failure, which was observed when testing the prototype with Technology projects with such characteristics as concise descriptions or few comments received by backers.

5 Conclusions

This work contributes to predicting the funding state of technology projects that implement a Multimodal Deep Learning model called *Hydra*. The main aim of this proposal is to join features that are used independently by other authors. This work joined textual content and metadata models to find a better performance. Although Description and Comments models presented overfitting after 20 epochs, the Multimodal model maintained even levels of accuracy and loss (using validation data set) during its training. We achieved thanks to the balanced weights of classes and the assignment of an early stopper in the model from the detection of overfitting during five consecutive epochs. On the other hand, the Metadata submodel was essential in the final architecture due to boost results above 90% of other modals such as textual because of the inability to reach the root of some words for description and comments dictionaries. The absence of at least one backer comment at more than 70% of the sample represented a big challenge. We fill null values with a random value out of topic for those projects without comments. Grammatical errors generated by the lemmatizing algorithm probably limited the implementation of textual models. Hydra accomplishes better results because the current model merges the best characteristics of each independent model to balance the performance; we can see this if we compare it with other models that used independent features without joining models. Furthermore, Hydra could be integrated into a website app to predict real-time projects. Finally, we suggest that researchers continue developing these tools to support crowdfunding sites' funding projects.

References

1. Beckwith, J.: Predicting Success in Equity Crowdfunding. Degree thesis, University of Pennsylvania (2016). http://repository.upenn.edu/joseph_wharton_scholars/25
2. Brownlee, J.: Stacking ensemble for deep learning neural networks in python (2018). https://machinelearningmastery.com/stacking-ensemble-for-deep-learning-neural-networks/
3. Chaichi, N., Anderson, T.: Deploying natural language processing to extract key product features of crowdfunding campaigns: the case of 3d printing technologies on Kickstarter. In: 2019 Portland International Conference on Management of Engineering and Technology (PICMET), pp. 1–9. PICMET 2019. IEEE (2019). https://doi.org/10.23919/PICMET.2019.8893839
4. Chen, K., Jones, B., Kim, I., Schlamp, B.: Kickpredict: Predicting Kickstarter success. Technical report, California Institute of Technology (2013). http://courses.cms.caltech.edu/cs145/2013/blue.pdf
5. Chen, L.S., Shen, E.L.: Finding the keywords affecting the success of crowdfunding projects. In: 2019 IEEE 6th International Conference on Industrial Engineering and Applications (ICIEA). ICIEA 2019, pp. 567–571. IEEE (2019). https://doi.org/10.1109/IEA.2019.8714815
6. Cheng, C., Tan, F., Hou, X., Wei, Z.: Success prediction on crowdfunding with multimodal deep learning. In: Twenty-Eighth International Joint Conference on Artificial Intelligence. IJCAI 2019, pp. 2158–2164 (2019). https://doi.org/10.24963/ijcai.2019/299
7. Fernández-Blanco, A., Villanueva-Balsera, J., Rodríguez-Montequin, V., Morán-Palacios, H.: Key factors for project crowdfunding success: an empirical study. Sustainability 12(2), 599 (2020). https://doi.org/10.3390/su12020599
8. Jin, B., Zhao, H., Chen, E., Liu, Q., Ge, Y.: Estimating the days to success of campaigns in crowdfunding: a deep survival perspective. In: 33rd AAAI Conference on Artificial Intelligence (AAAI 2019), AAAI 2019, vol. 33, pp. 4023–4030. Association for the Advancement of Artificial (2019). https://doi.org/10.1609/aaai.v33i01.33014023
9. Kamath, R.S., Kamat, R.K.: Supervised learning model for Kickstarter campaigns with r mining. Int. J. Inf. Technol. Model. Comput. (IJITMC) 4(1) (2018). https://doi.org/10.5281/zenodo.1228716
10. Kaur, H., Gera, J.: Effect of social media connectivity on success of crowdfunding campaigns. Procedia Comput. Sci. 122, 767–774 (2017). https://doi.org/10.1016/j.procs.2017.11.435
11. Kickstarter: About: Kickstarter. https://www.kickstarter.com/about
12. Kickstarter: Why is funding all-or-nothing? https://help.kickstarter.com/hc/en-us/articles/115005047893-Why-is-funding-all-or-nothing-
13. Lee, S., Lee, K., Kim, H.C.: Content-based success prediction of crowdfunding campaigns: a deep learning approach. In: 2018 ACM Conference on Computer Supported Cooperative Work and Social Computing. CSCW 2018, Association for Computing Machinery (ACM), Nueva York, United States of America, pp. 193–196 (2018). https://doi.org/10.1145/3272973.3274053
14. Li, Y., Rakesh, V., Reddy, C.K.: Project success prediction in crowdfunding environments. In: Ninth ACM International Conference on Web Search and Data Mining, WSDM 2016, pp. 247–256. Association for Computing Machinery (ACM) (2016). https://doi.org/10.1145/2835776.2835791

15. Mitra, T., Gilbert, E.: The language that gets people to give: phrases that predict success on Kickstarter. In: 17th ACM conference on Computer supported cooperative work & social computing. CSCW 2014, pp. 49–61. Association for Computing Machinery (ACM) (2014). https://doi.org/10.1145/2531602.2531656
16. Mukaka, M.M.: Statistics corner: a guide to appropriate use of correlation coefficient in medical research. Malawi Med. J. **24**(3), 69–71 (2012). https://www.researchgate.net/publication/236604665_Statistics_Corner_A_guide_to_appropriate_use_of_Correlation_coefficient_in_medical_research
17. Pennington, J., Socher, R., Manning, C.D.: Glove: global vectors for word representation. Technical report, Stanford University (2014). https://nlp.stanford.edu/pubs/glove.pdf
18. Puente, A.: Bachelor thesis - full material, December 2019. https://github.com/AlonsoPuente/BachelorThesis_Codes
19. Puente, A.: Degree thesis - full material, September 2020. https://github.com/AlonsoPuente/DegreeThesis_Codes
20. Ranjan, C.: Rules-of-thumb for building a neural network, July 2019. https://towardsdatascience.com/17-rules-of-thumb-for-building-a-neural-network-93356f9930af
21. Sawhney, K., Tran, C., Tuason, R.: Using language to predict Kickstarter success. Reporte técnico, Stanford University (2016). https://stanford.edu/~kartiks2/kickstarter.pdf
22. Shafqat, W., Byun, Y.C.: Topic predictions and optimized recommendation mechanism based on integrated topic modeling and deep neural networks in crowdfunding platforms. Appl. Sci. **9**(24), 5496 (2019). https://doi.org/10.3390/app9245496
23. Shepherd, M.: Crowdfunding statistics (2021): Market size and growth, February 2020. https://www.fundera.com/resources/crowdfunding-statistics
24. The Hustle: What are your chances of successfully raising money on kickstarter? February 2019. https://thehustle.co/crowdfunding-success-rate
25. Universo Crowdfunding: ¿qué es el crowdfunding? https://www.universocrowdfunding.com/que-es-el-crowdfunding/
26. Yu, P.F., Huang, F.M., Yang, C., Liu, Y.H., Li, Z.Y., Tsai, C.H.: Prediction of crowdfunding project success with deep learning. In: 2018 IEEE 15th International Conference on e-Business Engineering (ICEBE). ICEBE 2018, pp. 1–8. IEEE (2018). https://doi.org/10.1109/ICEBE.2018.00012
27. Yuan, H., Lau, R.Y., Xu, W.: The determinants of crowdfunding success: a semantic text analytics approach. Dec. Supp. Syst. **91**, 67–76 (2016). https://doi.org/10.1016/j.dss.2016.08.001

Composite Recommendations with Heterogeneous Graphs

Naomi Rohrbaugh[1] and Edgar Ceh-Varela[2(✉)]

[1] University of Pittsburgh, Pittsburgh, PA, USA
ncr19@pitt.edu
[2] Eastern New Mexico University, Portales, NM, USA
eduardo.ceh@enmu.edu

Abstract. Recommender systems (RS) help users to deal with the problem of information overload. These systems suggest items to users based on their preferences. Traditionally, RS recommend a single item to the user, such as a movie, a song, or a place to eat. In some real-life situations, the user's preference for a particular item could be influenced by the entity (e.g., a brewery, a restaurant) that sells or produces the item (e.g., a beer, a hamburger). For example, when suggesting a hamburger, the recommendation might be enhanced by considering the user's liking for the restaurant that serves it. Therefore, the user's preference for the entity's characteristics must also be considered when recommending an item. This paper presents a recommender system model for composite recommendations. We define a *composite recommendation* as the recommendation of items with a "Has-a" relationship. For example, a restaurant "has-a" hamburger or a brewery "has-a" beer. Therefore, our model can recommend a tuple ⟨*entity, item*⟩ instead of a single item as traditional RS. As a basis, we use *metapath2vec* to obtain node embeddings from a heterogeneous graph. We formed the heterogeneous graph using features and user-entity, user-item, and entity-item interactions. The node embeddings for entities with a composite relationship are aggregated during recommendation to account for the user's preference for these entities. Our proposed model was tested with a real-life dataset composed of users, breweries, and beers. The results show that our proposed approach obtains better results than a baseline model, which does not consider the composite relationship.

Keywords: Recommender system · Graph neural network · Composite recommendation

1 Introduction

Recommender systems (RS) are valuable tools that use information related to a user, such as behavior, demographics, and social information, to predict a user's preferences for items [3]. Businesses with online platforms and social media websites often use RS to increase profitability by inferring users' preferences from

J. A. Lossio-Ventura et al. (Eds.): SIMBig 2021, CCIS 1577, pp. 108–121, 2022.
https://doi.org/10.1007/978-3-031-04447-2_8

past interactions [25]. Traditional RS present to customers a list of suggestions. Each suggestion consists of a single type of item, such as a book or a movie. These RS use the user-item interactions to make recommendations [16]. Other types of RS are used to a provide personalized recommendation of a point of interest (POI) [8]. These POIs can be anything, including restaurants, hotels, parks, or museums. In this type of RS, the recommendation is made by analyzing the user's interactions with different POIs.

There has been a recent increase in the use of graph neural networks (GNN) as part of RS to make accurate predictions of a user's preferences [25]. GNN do this prediction using the observed user-item interactions from the graph. Heterogeneous graphs could be formed by multi-typed nodes and edges [26]. In these types of graphs, representation learning is used to obtain a lower-dimensional vector representation (i.e., embeddings) for each node while preserving the graph structure. A well-known method to get node embeddings in heterogeneous graphs is *metapath2vec* [6]. *Metapath2vec* uses random walks through the nodes and edges of a graph to learn vector representations of each node. The algorithm uses metapaths [6,22] to capture the node relations. As similar node representations are placed close together in the latent space, the proximity of nodes can be used in different applications such as node classification, link prediction, and recommender systems.

In this paper, we address a new type of recommendation called composite recommendations. We use composite items to refer to items with a "Has-a" relationship (e.g., restaurant-hamburger, brewery-beer). For example, when recommending a hamburger, the recommendation could be improved by accounting for user preference of the restaurant that sells the food (i.e., the restaurant "Has-a" hamburger). On the one hand, a hamburger could be perfectly suited to a user's preferences but is sold at a restaurant with poor service or unhygienic practices, where the user does not want to eat. On the other hand, a restaurant might have the perfect vibe for a user but does not sell a hamburger that the user would enjoy. To remedy this predicament, the recommendation must consider the user's preferences for both restaurant and hamburger. Thus, composite recommendations that account for users' preferences for items in a "Has-a" relationship are needed.

We use the *metapath2vec* algorithm to obtain the node representations of a heterogeneous graph containing users, vendors, and items to produce composite recommendations. Then, our model performs a feature aggregation step to incorporate the user's representation and preferences for the venues that have a "Has-a" relationship with the items. The resulting user representation is then used to find a list with top-n items to be recommended.

The remainder of this paper is organized as follows: Sect. 2 presents the related literature. The problem is defined in Sect. 3. Section 4 details the proposed method. Section 5 outlines the experimental settings used to test our proposed model. The results showing the validity of our proposed method and its effectiveness are in Sect. 6. Finally, our conclusions are in Sect. 7.

2   Related Work

Recommender systems (RS) suggest new items or places to users based on past item interactions or using the interactions of similar users [4]. [1] proposes a meal recommendation system that the food chain sector may use to continuously update the options from their menu, based on customer likes, interests, and order history. In [5], user ratings and user reviews from an online beer community are used to recommend a beer to a user. Similarly, [11] presents a beer recommender system for Android mobile devices. This system uses fuzzy ontologies to represent pieces of information and semantic reasoners to infer implicit knowledge. In [12], a system to recommend POIs is presented. This system uses the relationship of textual information to model underlying patterns for POI recommendations. Similarly in [2], a POI recommender system is created by modeling users and POIs using the aspects posted on user reviews as a bipartite graph. In [7], a restaurant recommender system is proposed using user-based collaborative filtering. This system uses ratings given by users attending and restaurant location data. Likewise, in [10], an intelligent decision support model was created to recommend restaurants for individuals or groups. It uses features such as customer interest, price/budget, distance, and taste rating.

Recommendations can be generated using a bipartite graph where nodes are the users and items, and a link between these nodes represents an interaction between a user and an item. GNN has recently been used to learn user and item representations (i.e., embeddings) based on their features and interaction [25].

Representation learning assigns nodes in a graph to a lower-dimensional space while preserving the structure of the graph. Several methods have been used to obtain node representations. *Node2vec* [9], based on *DeepWalk* [18], defines a node's graph neighborhood and uses a biased random walk procedure to explore neighborhoods. This procedure allows the mapping of nodes to a low-dimensional space of features that maximizes the likelihood of preserving graph neighborhoods of nodes. Another approach based on *DeepWalk* is *"LINE"* [24]. This model learns the embedding of a graph while preserving the node's first- and second-order proximities (i.e., local and global graph structures).

However, there could be multiple types of nodes with different features and structural positions in a graph. The complication of making a GNN with heterogeneous nodes has inspired past researchers to develop graph embedding frameworks to preserve semantic relationships between different types of nodes [6].

A *heterogeneous graph* is defined in [6] as the graph $G = (V, E, T)$, where each node v has a mapping function $\phi(v) : V \to T_V$, and each edge e has a mapping function $\varphi(e) : E \to T_E$. The sets of objects and relation types are denoted as T_V and T_E, respectively, where $|T_V| + |T_E| > 2$.

Applying homogeneous graph methods for node representations on heterogeneous graph produce sub-optimal representations [25]. The *metapath2vec* [6] algorithm is a state-of-the-art method for representation learning of heterogeneous nodes. Metapath2vec uses latent space representations to place similar nodes close together without directly connecting them. This representation is accomplished by specifying *metapaths* used on the random walks through the graph.

Some works have used the node representations obtained by metapath2vec to make recommendations. In [22], a recommender system is presented to recommend authors to any author in DBLP for citation purposes. The system creates a Heterogeneous User-Item (HUI) graph, and it is traversed using metapath2vec to capture the structural and semantic relationships between nodes. Similarly, [21] uses the node embeddings obtained from metapath2vec to recommend items and friends. The model uses cosine similarity between the node embeddings to generate a recommendation list.

The works presented in this section only recommend a single item (i.e., food, beer) and a single POI (i.e., restaurant). They do not consider how the user preference for the venue influences the user preference for a particular item being sold or produced in that place.

3   Problem Statement

We call composite items i and j to those items having a "Has-a" relationship.

$$i \xrightarrow{\text{"Has-a"}} j$$

For example, a brewery i *produces/sells* ("Has-a") a beer j. Moreover, i might have more than one item. In this case, we have $i \xrightarrow{\text{"Has-a"}} J_i$ (e.g., a restaurant sells burgers, burritos, and ice-creams). In a composite relationship, selecting an item j implicitly contains the item i that produces or contains j. Therefore, a tuple $\langle i, j \rangle$ can be generated containing the related items.

For example, when recommending a beer, the recommendation would be improved by accounting for the user preference of the brewery that produces that type of beer (i.e., the brewery "Has-a" beer). On the one hand, a beer could be perfectly suited to a user's preferences but is sold/produced at a venue with poor service or lousy ambiance, aspects that are not to the user's liking. On the other hand, a brewery might have the perfect vibe for a user, but the kinds of beers produced in that venue do not meet user requirements. Therefore, the recommendation of a beer must consider the user's preferences for both breweries and beers.

Thus, having a set of users U, a set of items I, and a set of items J, where items from I have a composite relationship with items from J, the problem is to recommend an item j (e.g., beer) considering the characteristics of item i (e.g., brewery).

4   Proposed Approach

4.1   Generating a Heterogeneous Graph

Let us have the set of users U who have interacted with a set of items I (i.e., restaurants). Items I have a composite relationship (i.e., "Has-A") with the set of items J_i (i.e., item i has items J).

The elements of these sets and their relationship can be represented as nodes and edges in a heterogeneous graph $G = (V, E, T)$ (see Fig. 1 in Sect. 5.2). Each user node u_m and item node i_n are connected by an edge if user u_m has reviewed item i_n. Similarly, there is an edge between nodes u_m and j_l if there is a review from u_m to item j_l. Finally, an edge can be created between nodes i_n and j_l if i_n has an item j_l.

4.2   Obtaining the Node Embeddings

We are interested in the node embeddings for the elements in U, I, and J_i. To preserve the context of the nodes in an heterogeneous graph we employ a metapath strategy with unbiased random walks. With this strategy, we can incorporate semantic relationships between the different types of nodes.

The metapath2vec algorithm allows the construction of node representations as a vector considering the context of nodes conditioned on their types in a heterogeneous context.

A metapath is defined in a heterogeneous graph $G = (V, E, T)$ as [6, 22]

$$P : V_1 \xrightarrow{R_1} V_2 \xrightarrow{R_2} \cdots V_t \xrightarrow{R_t} V_{t+1} \cdots \xrightarrow{R_{l-1}} V_l \tag{1}$$

where $R = R_1 \circ R2 \circ \cdots \circ R_{l-1}$ defines the relationship between node types V_1 and V_l.

Moreover, the transition probability for each step i is calculated as follows

$$p(v^{i+1}|v_t^i, P) = \begin{cases} \frac{1}{|N_{t+1}(v_t^i)|} & (v^{i+1}, v_t^i) \in E, \phi(v^{i+1}) = t+1 \\ 0 & (v^{i+1}, v_t^i) \in E, \phi(v^{i+1}) \neq t+1 \\ 0 & (v^{i+1}, v_t^i) \notin E \end{cases}$$

where $v_t^i \in V_t$ and $N_{t+1}(v_t^i)$ denotes the V_{t+1} type of node neighborhood of v_t^i. This indicates that the walker's direction is determined by the metapath defined in Eq. 1. As metapaths are usually symmetrical [22, 23], the transition probability can be simplified using recursion as

$$p(v^{i+1}|v_t^i) = p(v^{i+1}|v_1^i), if t = 1$$

4.3   Feature Aggregation

For clarity, we use bold lowercases for vectors and bold uppercases for matrices. For each user u_m who has not reviewed an item i_n, we compute a score based on cosine similarity (CS) and select the top-k items with the highest score. CS is suitable for metric learning given that the resulting similarity measure is always within the range of -1 and $+1$ [17]. A value close to -1 indicates low similarity, while a value close to $+1$ shows high similarity. Therefore, our score is defined as

$$score = CS(\mathbf{u_m}, \mathbf{i_n}) = \frac{\mathbf{u_m} \cdot \mathbf{i_n}}{||\mathbf{u_m}|| \cdot ||\mathbf{i_n}||} \tag{2}$$

where $\mathbf{u_m}$ and $\mathbf{i_n}$ are the user and item embedding vectors, respectively. After this step, we obtain a set $I_{u_m}^k$ with the k items (e.g., breweries) having the highest scores for user u_m.

To incorporate the features of the set of items $I_{u_m}^k$ having the set of items J_i (e.g., set of items J being sold by the business i) into a user's representation, we use the following:

$$\mathbf{u}'_{\mathbf{m}} = \frac{1}{|I_{u_m}^k| + 1} \cdot \left(\mathbf{u_m} + \sum_{I_{u_m}^k} \mathbf{i_k} \right) \tag{3}$$

where $\mathbf{u}'_{\mathbf{m}}$ is the new user representation (i.e., embedding) having the embeddings of the most preferred items i incorporated. $I_{u_m}^k$ is the set of the k most similar items i to u_m, $|\cdot|$ is the cardinality of the set, $\mathbf{u_m}$ is the user's embedding, and $\mathbf{i_k} \in \mathbf{I_{u_m}^k}$ the item's embedding.

4.4   Composite Recommendations

Traditionally, a dot product has been used to combine embeddings and calculate similarity [19]. To capture the interest of a user u_m for an item j_l, we use a generalization of matrix factorization, which uses the dot product [14] for recommendations.

$$\mathbf{r_{u_m}} = \mathbf{u}'^{\top}_{\mathbf{m}} \bullet \mathbf{J_{I_{u_m}^k}} \tag{4}$$

where $\mathbf{r_{u_m}}$ is a vector of scores for the items J_i not already rated by the user u_m, $\mathbf{J_{I_u^k}}$ is a matrix having the embeddings for each item j belonging to the set $I_{u_m}^k$, $\mathbf{u}'_{\mathbf{m}}$ comes from Eq. 3, and $\bullet$ is the dot product.

Finally, $\mathbf{r_{u_m}}$ is sorted and the top-n items j are used in a tuple with their corresponding item i (i.e., $\langle i, j \rangle$), in a recommendation list.

5   Experimental Settings

5.1   Dataset

To evaluate our proposed model, we generated a dataset with real-world data collected for two weeks in June 2021 from *BeerAdvocate.com*. The dataset contains information of users, breweries, and beers. For the study, we selected breweries from the state of California, USA. Moreover, the dataset includes user-beer and user-brewery interactions (i.e., reviews and ratings). Given that a brewery has beers, we can use this relationship for our composite recommendation.

Our dataset consists of 23,324 users, 959 breweries, and 39,349 beers. In total, we collected 273,831 records for user-beer interactions and 5,359 records for user-brewery interactions. On average, each brewery has 54.62 beers, each user has reviewed 12.07 beers and 2.73 breweries, and each beer has 17.20 user reviews. We split the dataset into 70% for training and 30% for testing.

5.2 Graph Creation

We represent the dataset as a heterogeneous graph. We use the user IDs, beer IDs, and brewery IDs as node labels. Moreover, three different types of edges are created to represent the interaction between the different nodes (i.e., *User-Brewery, User-Beer, Beer-Brewery*). Table 1 shows the different features for the node types and for two of the edges (i.e., *user-brewery* and *user-beer*). The *beer-brewery* edge does not have additional features.

Table 1. Node and edge features

B(rewery)	b(eer)	U(ser)	U-B	U-b
Name	Name	Username	Username	Username
Beer Rating	Style	Location	Location	Location
# Beers Sold	ABV		Rating	Rating
Rating	Score		Vibe	Taste
Location	Location		Quality	Smell
	Availability		Service	Feel
	Rating		Selection	Look
			Food	Overall

Figure 1 shows a representation of the heterogeneous graph. In total, the graph has 318,539 edges.

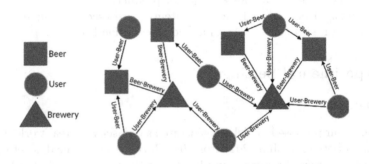

Fig. 1. Heterogeneous graph

5.3 Node Representations

To get each node representation (i.e., embeddings), we use the metapath2vec algorithm with symmetrical metapaths (i.e., same first and last node type). We use an embedding dimension of 64, a window's size of 5, 100 random walks per node, and each random walk with a length of 1. These values were selected after testing different ranges. A set of random walks through the metapaths can train the GNN in a way that preserves structural correlations between nodes [6].

The following metapaths were considered (see Sect. 6.6): *Beer-Brewery-Beer*, *Beer-User-Beer*, *User-Brewery-User*, *User-Beer-User*, and *User-Beer-Brewery-Beer-User*.

Figure 2 shows in a 2D space the embeddings for users (in green), breweries (in purple), and beers (in yellow). From this figure, we can observe clusters of the different nodes. These clusters indicate the similarity existing among nodes. For example, users with similar preferences given the beers and breweries rated will be placed in the same cluster of nodes.

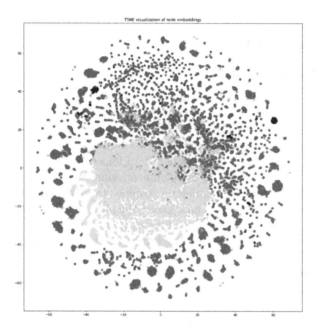

Fig. 2. Node embeddings visualization. Users in green, breweries in purple, and beers in yellow. (The figure is best understood in color.) (Color figure online)

5.4   Evaluation Metrics

We use *Hit Ratio* (*HR@n*) [13] to evaluate the performance of the composite recommendations. In this metric, n represents the length of the recommendation list. *HR@n* is computed by determining whether a hit exists within the top-n items in the list. The hit ratio is defined as [15]

$$HR@n = \frac{1}{U_T} \sum_{u=1}^{U_T} 1_{R_u \leq n} \tag{5}$$

where U_T is the set of test users, R_u indicates the relative rank of the item in the recommendation list, and 1_X indicates the event X ($1_X = 1$ iff X is a hit and 0 otherwise.)

Having an *HR@n* of 1 indicates that the recommender system can always recommend the items from the test set. On the other hand, a value of 0 indicates that the system is not able to find any of the test items [20].

5.5 Baseline

To compare our model, we use the model proposed in [21] as the baseline. This model also uses the metapath2vec algorithm to get the node embeddings. Then, using the user's embeddings, it recommends the top-n most similar items using cosine similarity.

6   Experimental Results

6.1   Model's Performance

We tested the composite and baseline recommender systems with the test set. For our tests, we varied the size of the recommendation list (i.e., top-n) from 1 to 20 items. In our recommendation process, we use a value of $k = 7$ for Eq. 3. Similarly, we ran the tests five times for each model, and the average is presented. Table 2 displays the average HR@n for our composite model and the baseline model when used for beer recommendations

Compared to the baseline model, our composite model consistently had significantly higher performance, regardless of the size of the recommendation list (i.e., top-n). These results indicate that integrating the information for the breweries that are more likely to be liked by the user to the user profile improves the recommendation for the beers that the user will like. The results align with our initial hypothesis that the user preference for a particular item could be influenced by the venue's characteristics and user preference for those characteristics.

Table 2. HR@n Performance comparison for beer recommendations varying the size of the recommendation list

	Baseline	Composite (ours)
n = 1	0.0045	**0.0376**
n = 3	0.0195	**0.1030**
n = 5	0.0304	**0.1537**
n = 7	0.0405	**0.1802**
n = 10	0.0511	**0.1983**
n = 15	0.0656	**0.2221**
n = 20	0.0768	**0.2328**

6.2 Effect of the Number of Similar Items (k)

We vary the value of k to determine how this value affects the model's performance. The value of k determines how many item i representations (e.g., breweries) are aggregated with the user representation.

Figure 3 shows the results of HR@n when varying the value k for beer recommendations while fixing the size list to $n = 10$. We can see that the best result are obtained when k is between $k = 5$ to $k = 7$. Low values of k seem not to completely capture the characteristics of the most likely breweries, and higher values of k start introducing confusion to the model.

6.3 Effect of the Embedding Dimension

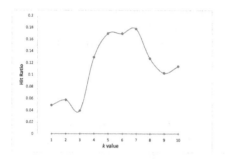

Fig. 3. Effect of the value k **Fig. 4.** Effect of embedding dimension

Figure 4 shows the model's performance when varying the dimension for the embeddings.

The results show that the model performs better with an embedding dimension of 64. These results indicate that embeddings of lower dimensions cannot capture the full extent of the graph with latent space representations. Moreover, it also shows that a higher embedding dimension is likely to introduce noise to the node representations.

6.4 Effect of the Random Walk Length

Figure 5 shows the model performance when varying the length of the random walk for the metapath2vec algorithm. The results show that with random walk lengths of 100, the model performs the best. From the results, we also can see that the performance is reduced as the length of the walk grows. This reduction in performance could result from uncertainty introduced to the model because of the use of information of less similar nodes.

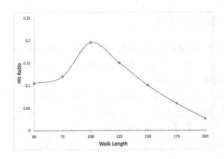
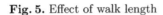
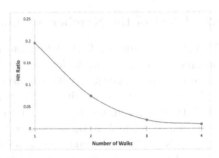

Fig. 5. Effect of walk length   **Fig. 6.** Effect of number of walks

6.5   Effect of the Number of Random Walks

Figure 6 shows the model's performance when varying the number of random walks for the metapath2vec algorithm. From the results, we can see that only one walk is enough. More walks per node could have introduced too much inconsistency to the system, causing decreased performance.

6.6   Effect of the Metapaths

We wanted to test if the selection of metapaths influences the model's performance. We initially defined the following set of metapaths: *Beer-Brewery-Beer, Brewery-User-Brewery, Beer-User-Beer, User-Brewery-User, User-Beer-User, User-Beer-Brewery-Beer-User,* and *User-Beer-Brewery-User.* To choose the best subset of metapaths from the set initially defined, we excluded one metapath at a time and tested the model's performance using the remaining metapaths. The resulting HR@n was compared to the average HR@n for all metapaths to determine whether excluding the metapath had improved the performance.

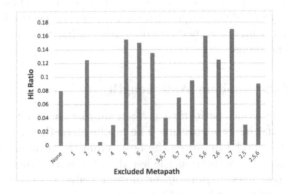

Fig. 7. Effect of metapaths

Figure 7 shows the model's performance when excluding metapaths from the initial set. The results show that the model's performance increases when removing the individual metapaths 2, 5, 6, and 7.

We further test if excluding combinations of these metapaths affected the model's performance. The results from these tests show that excluding the combination of metapaths 2 and 7 yielded the best results. As a result, the following metapaths were used: *Beer-Brewery-Beer, Beer-User-Beer, User-Brewery-User, User-Beer-User, User-Beer-Brewery-Beer-User.*

Using a set of diverse metapaths seemed to maximize results. This result was made clear when removing similar metapaths caused an increase in performance.

Surprisingly, not using metapaths with breweries as endpoints improves the performance of the recommendations. This outcome could happen because the brewery's representation is implicitly obtained by the preferences of the users who attend and the characteristics of the beers sold, mainly because each beer belongs only to one brewery.

7   Conclusions

This work proposes a composite recommender system model that accounts for user preferences of items in a "Has-a" relationship (e.g., brewery has a beer). Therefore, our model can recommend a tuple $\langle entity, item \rangle$ instead of a single item as traditional RS.

The proposed system uses metapaths based on random walks to improve the Graph Neural Network's ability to model the dataset. The recommender system model accurately captures user preferences by embedding a heterogeneous graph with nodes for users, vendors, and items. The use of feature aggregation to account for a user's vendor preferences in selecting an item improves the recommendation by considering all aspects of the recommended set. The composite recommender system significantly outperformed the baseline model.

Acknowledgment. This work is partially supported by the NSF grant #1950121.

References

1. Ahuja, K., Goel, M., Sikka, S., Makkar, P.: What-to-taste: a food recommendation system (2020)
2. Baral, R., Zhu, X., Iyengar, S., Li, T.: Reel: review aware explanation of location recommendation. In: Proceedings of the 26th Conference on User Modeling, Adaptation and Personalization, pp. 23–32 (2018)
3. Bobadilla, J., Ortega, F., Hernando, A., Gutiérrez, A.: Recommender systems survey. Knowledge-Based Syst. **46**, 109–132 (2013)
4. Ceh-Varela, E., Cao, H.: Recommending packages of multi-criteria items to groups. In: 2019 IEEE International Conference on Web Services (ICWS), pp. 273–282. IEEE (2019)

5. Chinchanachokchai, S., Thontirawong, P., Chinchanachokchai, P.: A tale of two recommender systems: the moderating role of consumer expertise on artificial intelligence based product recommendations. J. Retail. Consum. Serv. **61**, 102528 (2021)
6. Dong, Y., Chawla, N.V., Swami, A.: metapath2vec: scalable representation learning for heterogeneous networks. In: Proceedings of the 23rd ACM SIGKDD International Conference on Knowledge Discovery and Data Mining, pp. 135–144 (2017)
7. Fakhri, A.A., Baizal, Z., Setiawan, E.B.: Restaurant recommender system using user-based collaborative filtering approach: a case study at Bandung Raya region. J. Phys. Conf. Ser. **1192**, 012023 (2019). IOP Publishing
8. Gottapu, R.D., Monangi, L.V.S.: Point-of-interest recommender system for social groups. Procedia Comput. Sci. **114**, 159–164 (2017)
9. Grover, A., Leskovec, J.: node2vec: scalable feature learning for networks. In: Proceedings of the 22nd ACM SIGKDD International Conference on Knowledge Discovery and Data Mining, pp. 855–864 (2016)
10. Hartanto, M., Utama, D.N.: Intelligent decision support model for recommending restaurant. Cogent Eng. **7**(1), 1763888 (2020)
11. Huitzil, I., Alegre, F., Bobillo, F.: Gimmehop: a recommender system for mobile devices using ontology reasoners and fuzzy logic. Fuzzy Sets Syst. **401**, 55–77 (2020)
12. Khanthaapha, P., Pipanmaekaporn, L., Kamonsantiroj, S.: Topic-based user profile model for poi recommendations. In: Proceedings of the 2nd International Conference on Intelligent Systems, Metaheuristics & Swarm Intelligence, pp. 143–147 (2018)
13. Koren, Y.: Factorization meets the neighborhood: a multifaceted collaborative filtering model. In: Proceedings of the 14th ACM SIGKDD International Conference on Knowledge Discovery and Data Mining, pp. 426–434 (2008)
14. Koren, Y., Bell, R., Volinsky, C.: Matrix factorization techniques for recommender systems. Computer **42**(8), 30–37 (2009)
15. Li, D., Jin, R., Gao, J., Liu, Z.: On sampling top-k recommendation evaluation. In: Proceedings of the 26th ACM SIGKDD International Conference on Knowledge Discovery & Data Mining, pp. 2114–2124 (2020)
16. Mu, R.: A survey of recommender systems based on deep learning. IEEE Access **6**, 69009–69022 (2018)
17. Nguyen, H.V., Bai, L.: Cosine similarity metric learning for face verification. In: Kimmel, R., Klette, R., Sugimoto, A. (eds.) ACCV 2010. LNCS, vol. 6493, pp. 709–720. Springer, Heidelberg (2011). https://doi.org/10.1007/978-3-642-19309-5_55
18. Perozzi, B., Al-Rfou, R., Skiena, S.: Deepwalk: online learning of social representations. In: Proceedings of the 20th ACM SIGKDD International Conference on Knowledge Discovery and Data Mining, pp. 701–710 (2014)
19. Rendle, S., Krichene, W., Zhang, L., Anderson, J.: Neural collaborative filtering vs. matrix factorization revisited. In: Fourteenth ACM Conference on Recommender Systems, pp. 240–248 (2020)
20. Sieg, A., Mobasher, B., Burke, R.: Improving the effectiveness of collaborative recommendation with ontology-based user profiles. In: proceedings of the 1st International Workshop on Information Heterogeneity and Fusion in Recommender Systems, pp. 39–46 (2010)
21. Sowmya, A., Shebin, K.M., Mohan, A., et al.: Social recommendation system using network embedding and temporal information. In: 2020 5th International Conference on Computing, Communication and Security (ICCCS), pp. 1–7. IEEE (2020)

22. Sun, Y., Han, J.: Mining heterogeneous information networks: principles and methodologies. Synthesis Lect. Data Min. Knowl. Disc. **3**(2), 1–159 (2012)
23. Sun, Y., Han, J., Yan, X., Yu, P.S., Wu, T.: Pathsim: meta path-based top-k similarity search in heterogeneous information networks. Proc. VLDB Endowment **4**(11), 992–1003 (2011)
24. Tang, J., Qu, M., Wang, M., Zhang, M., Yan, J., Mei, Q.: Line: large-scale information network embedding. In: Proceedings of the 24th International Conference on World Wide Web, pp. 1067–1077 (2015)
25. Wu, S., Sun, F., Zhang, W., Cui, B.: Graph neural networks in recommender systems: a survey. arXiv preprint arXiv:2011.02260 (2020)
26. Zhang, C., Song, D., Huang, C., Swami, A., Chawla, N.V.: Heterogeneous graph neural network. In: Proceedings of the 25th ACM SIGKDD International Conference on Knowledge Discovery & Data Mining, pp. 793–803 (2019)

Energy Efficiency Using IOTA Tangle
for Greenhouse Agriculture

Arturo Flores[1] , Alessandro Morales[2] , Gianfranco Campos[3]([✉]) ,
and Jorge Gelso[4]

[1] Robotics Engineer of IRIS, Lima, Peru
[2] Zignar Technologies, Lima, Peru
[3] Zignar Technologies, Alberta, Canada
go@zignar.tech
[4] Zignar Technologies, Kuala Lumpur, Malaysia

Abstract. Greenhouse farmers around the world face multiple challenges imposed by manual tasks and must deal with complex relationships among growth environment variables. Usually, tasks are accomplished with low efficiency and high uncertainty, which becomes evident
when evaluating the impact introduced by adjustments to these variables.
These challenges have led to the appearance of the precision agriculture industry, as farmers attempt to automate the agricultural and com-
mercialization processes using solutions based on the Internet of Things
(IoT), Artificial Intelligence (AI) and Cloud Computing. Although these
novel technological solutions seem to tackle some of the challenges, several concerns about centralization and data silos throughout the supply
chain have arisen. Thus, we propose the Interplanetary Precision Agriculture (IPA) project as an alternative to an increasing demand for better
technological solutions in the sustainable food supply, required by the
long-term presence of humans in any given environment. The current
project aims to improve the cultivation process on and off Earth, by
implementing solutions based on the IoT, AI, and Distributed Ledger
Technologies (DLT). Hence, a "system of systems" is laid out. First,
Magrito, a holonomic autonomous rover, is introduced to capture crop
performance parameters (output variables). Second, Precision Habitat
PRO, the environment controlling device, is deployed to capture growing parameters (input variables). Third, a commercial Bluetooth scale is
added. Last, a Farm Management System is utilized to correlate the data
captured by IoT devices with business logic. The resulting information is
sent to the IOTA Tangle network to render it immutable and interoperable, at zero network processing fees with minimal energy consumption.

Keywords: Agriculture · Internet of Things · Artificial Intelligence ·
Distributed ledger technologies

1 Introduction

Greenhouse farmers around the world deal with challenges imposed by multiple
manual tasks related to agricultural processes, when trying to maximize yield

J. A. Lossio-Ventura et al. (Eds.): SIMBig 2021, CCIS 1577, pp. 122–138, 2022.
https://doi.org/10.1007/978-3-031-04447-2_9

in their crops. Moreover, farmers must manage dozens of environment variables that are interrelated in a complex manner. These repetitive tasks are normally performed with very low efficiency, and the impact on the yield caused by adjustments of crop growing conditions is usually not measured. These challenges have been extensively documented in various studies emphasizing the need for sustainable agricultural systems [1–3].

The need for better agricultural practices has led to the development of platforms based on exponential technologies such as the Internet of Things (IoT), Artificial Intelligence (AI), and Cloud Computing or On-Prem Installations [4] that take upon the task of automating, monitoring, and commercializing the agricultural production process. However, the use of centralized architectures, cloud or on-premise, come at a cost that is not evident at first glance. Although centralization facilitates data handling and storage, it introduces a single point of failure and undermines autonomy [5]. Another nondesirable characteristic of centralization is the proliferation of data silos that limit the visibility of information through the supply chain, which in turn leads to additional management procedures that restrict value and decision-making constraints derived from different stakeholders, based on the status of this supply chain [6].

The Distributed Ledger Technology (DLT) industry, through Blockchain, has proposed an alternative to centralized platforms. However, energy consumption, scalability limitations and networks fees have become an impediment for a tangible adoption of this technology by agro-industry. Also, greenhouse farming on-earth has suggested an alternative for traditional farming, but the high energy consumption along with high initial investment is slowing down adoption. These two technologies have an impending requirement: efficient use of energy needs to be considered.

Furthermore, the current space exploration efforts are paving the way to the establishment of human settlements in near-earth celestial bodies. Therefore, farming will eventually play a crucial role in providing food for crew living in microgravity aboard spacecraft, or in planetary bases [7]. For instance, greenhouses in planetary bases are envisioned to be composed of large modules with conventional vertical growing areas that will sustain a controlled environment for farming staple crops (e.g., wheat, soybean, potato, and rice). Hence, monitoring and harvesting these crops will represent a challenging human activity for settlers, if not automated. The overarching goal is the expansion of several greenhouses within basecamps and other settlements, that will welcome a source of valuable, rich data for our very first space farmers.

In this context, we propose the Interplanetary Precision Agriculture (IPA) project, based on exponential technologies such IoT, AI, and DLT, and seeking to introduce game-changing aspects to the lives of farmers on and off Earth. IPA utilizes the IOTA DLT Framework applied to the agriculture industry, which has an impact in the following three key areas: IoT communication security, Machine-to-Machine (M2M) payments at zero network fees [8], and energy efficiency.

IPA's proof of concept was conducted during a five-day experiment in a greenhouse located in the base camp of Mars-Moon Astronautics Academy & Research

Science institute (MMAARS) in the Mojave Desert, United States. The objective was to monitor and collect data related to the cultivation of grapes and tomatoes using protocols that analog astronauts can complete in Isolated Confined Environments (ICE). Analog missions are field tests carried out in locations that attempt to reproduce physical characteristics like extreme space environments. There, scientists collaborate by gathering requirements and testing technologies in harsh environments before they are used in space [9]. In this regard, we were motivated to test our IoT devices - rover, environment controller, and scale - in the extreme conditions of the Mojave Desert with temperatures of up to 45 °C, high-speed winds, and dust abundance.

The performance of the hardware tested during the analog mission was sufficient to conduct all the experiments successfully, despite the extreme conditions. The results showed the strengths and weaknesses of the system as a whole and set the targets for improvement in upcoming versions of IPA. The specific contribution of this study is to show that the combination of IoT, AI and DLT is technically feasible, economically viable, and energy efficient, even in energy restrictive conditions.

Following this introduction, Sect. 2 presents a general overview of the main components of the proposed solution. Section 3 describes the materials and methods implemented in the project. Section 4, provides a summary of the theoretical concepts and calculations used thorough this work. Section 5 introduces IPA proof of concept evaluated during the Astronaut Analog Mission. Finally, Sects. 6, and 7 present the results of the project and further elaborate on the next steps for the development of IPA.

2   Interplanetary Precision Agriculture Components

IPA is an integral, end-to-end solution which general architecture is depicted as a system of systems (see Fig. 1). First, Magrito v1.0, a holonomic autonomous rover, is introduced to capture crop performance parameters (system output variables). Second, the environment controllers Precision Habitat PRO and Precision Water PRO are tested and deployed to capture the growing parameters (system input variables). However, for the final experiment only Precision Habitat PRO is used. Third, a commercial Bluetooth scale is integrated. Fourth, the Farm Management System (FMS) correlates the data captured by all the devices to provide context and interpretation capabilities (business logic). All the data is forwarded to a private instance of IOTA Tangle. Further development of the system considers Machine Learning (ML) models to be trained on past data to understand crops' behavior under various conditions. This knowledge will allow to determine the optimal growing conditions for future growing seasons.

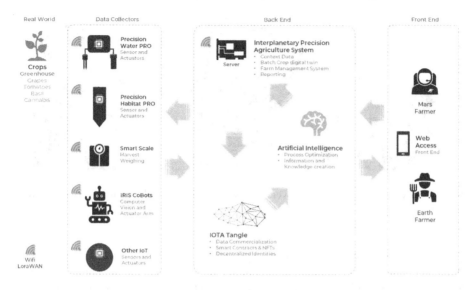

Fig. 1. IPA conceptual diagram

3   Material and Methods

Three IoT devices, plus a FMS, and a DLT, were implemented.

3.1   Holonomic Autonomous Rover: Magrito

A holonomic omnidirectional mobile robot is an IoT device with three degrees
of freedom in a plane. This type of robot can move in any direction with, or
without changing their orientation on the plane, giving the rover the ability to
avoid obstacles without changing its orientation, moving in constrained spaces,
and tracking a target [10].

Magrito Rover dynamics have the capability to assist with greenhouse-related
tasks because its mobility is based on two independent driven wheels placed on
both sides of the robot body and an additional castor wheel.

Magrito's mechanical structure allows the incorporation of additional hardware that can further enhance its performance. For instance, the rover has an
extra mast that can be utilized to attach an additional navigation camera placed
behind the Intel Real Sense Depth Camera. There is also enough internal free
space to add a GPS module to geo-tag video readings and on the upper surface
to fix a LIDAR sensor.

In addition, the rover's frame protective cover and wheels can be developed
with different material technologies to adapt to a particular environment. Comparing Magrito (Fig. 2) to four-wheel rovers, we find that the solution is more
versatile, which remains a key factor when selecting this type of robot for this
specific experiment.

Fig. 2. Rover 3D design (left), Rover Prototype (center), and Precision Habitat PRO (right)

Hereby we present a general overview of all the Rover's technical specifications (see Table 1). Thanks to its modularity, the end user can tailor Magrito's feature set to comply with any specific requirements. For example, if the production application requires the recognition of apples or oranges, a Mask R - Convolutional Neural Network (CNN) [11] model can be trained for that specific purpose and the software on the main board can be updated accordingly.

Table 1. Summary of main specifications and technologies of Magrito

Feature	Description
Dimensions	45.3 cm (W) × 41.8 cm (L) × 41.8 cm (H)
Weight	7 kg
Maximum Speed	0.2 m/s
Camera	Real Sense D435i
Software packages	Ubuntu 18.04, ROS, Melodic, Gazebo
DL algorithm architecture	Mask R-CNN
Battery System	Talent Cell Battery 12 VDC 3000 mAh
Packaging material	White PLA - Thickness 3 mm

3.2 Precision Habitat PRO

This IoT device was used to capture data related to the environment. Designed with ESP32 microcontrollers [12] and Wi-Fi connectivity at 2.4 GHz, the average range for this device is 30 m to an available access point which adequate for greenhouses.

On the other hand, if longer distances are required, the devices are also built to support LoRaWAN connectivity. This type of connectivity allows for longer ranges (>1 km) and a higher quantity of devices (or nodes) per gateway (≈1,000).

The static device works as a weather station and integrates five different sensors with two actuators (relays). All the sensors are connected to the ESP32 microcontroller. Since its location is fixed, it does not require a GPS; however, each sensor reading (see Fig. 3) is associated to specific plots or sections within the farm from the FMS (see Sect. 3.3). The technical specifications of the device can be found in the product datasheet [13].

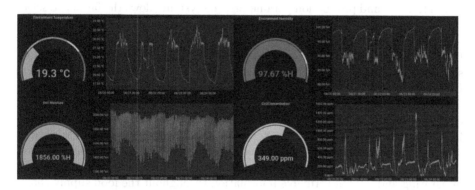

Fig. 3. Grafana dashboard showing temperature, humidity, soil moisture, and CO_2

3.3 Farm Management System

The purpose the FMS is to allow farmers to add and correlate business logic to the data collected by IoT and Deep Learning (DL) and generate information with ML models. In particular, the main use cases deployed in this research project were focused on seed management, plot or section management, and crop planning (see Fig. 4).

Fig. 4. Crop Planning use case to manage plots/sections and crop stages

The collection of data allows to have a clear understanding of what resources have been used to produce a given crop batch. All the details can be stored locally, in the cloud, or made immutable using IOTA Tangle (see Sects. 3.5, 4.1, 4.2).

For example, the farmer can record descriptive attributes of the seeds used in a specific crop, its batch number, supplier, and available supply, among other characteristics, and trigger rules based on specific criteria. Having specified the characteristics and production parameters, the system allows the farmer to select specific plots or sections of the greenhouse where a batch of seeds was planted, and automatically correlate sensor data to the crop. As crops evolve in time, the farmer can update this transition from one stage to the next one (i.e., from sowing to harvesting, etc.). During harvesting, a commercial scale connected via Bluetooth or Wi-Fi allows to record the partial weights of a given batch. In upcoming developments, the weight data will be used as a reference variable to estimate the performance of the whole farm. In addition, calculations derived from the DL components will be included, thereby detecting growth variations and aggregating existing data. This set of mechanisms, and further digital twin tracking, will allow the farmer to certify the quality of the final product, by integrating and adding verifiable information throughout the food supply chain.

Moreover, the Magrito Rover currently allows the automation of the physical task of surveying. With a robotic arm, other tasks such as cleaning, sampling and harvesting will be possible. The task automation feature is a proposition aligned with the Machine-to-Machine (M2M) economy where machines become autonomous economic agents.

Tasks Automation and Rover Integration. In the current version the rover can be manually paid for specific tasks using IOTA tokens [14] with M2M transactions (see Sect. 4.3). In future versions of the platform, the system will include an option to pre-program tasks requests automatically, depending on specific needs of the farm's production environment.

The regulated use of energy is a vital responsibility within the crew (see Sect. 1). For instance, during the analog mission, a clear priority was established among all the crew activities - daily chores, projects, charging devices, and so forth. Moreover, current literature in energy-consumption of CNN deployed in real devices states that the processing consumes high energy because of its computational complexity [15], which signaled us to carefully consider the design of the solution to comply with the available power resources. An online implementation of the Mask R-CNN model is possible, but the energy consumption of the rover would increase.

In this context, the rover was configured to process offline crop recognition, and CNN was trained with a collection of photos of vineyard grapes and cherry tomatoes, which can be requested to any of the authors of this manuscript. Four agents are required for this: the rover, the storage platform (Amazon S3), a droplet (Digital Ocean) containing an API, the Mask R-CNN model for crop recognition, and the IPA's FMS. This solution was done in five steps:

- The Rover sends the unprocessed video captured by the depth camera to the storage platform using a Python executable and the unprocessed video is stored.
- Then, an API developed in python requests this video from the storage platform.
- Later, the feeding and processing with the deep learning algorithm begins.
- Then, the processed video is uploaded to the storage platform.
- Finally, the API requests the processed video from storage and broadcasts the result via the MQTT protocol [16] to the FMS.

3.4 IOTA Private Tangle

Another objective is to provide secure communication and data storage using a DLT with energy efficiency. To implement this, a Raspberry Pi 4 was used to run a private version of IOTA Tangle detached from the public IOTA Network. The messages coming from the IoT devices (see Sect. 3) are immutably anchored in the private tangle while using the IOTA Streams Framework and Channels Protocol (see Sect. 4.2).

Due to the lightweight nature of the IOTA protocol, a Coordinator and three Hornet nodes can operate in a low power device such as the Raspberry Pi 4, allowing full support for transactions and data streams; the spamming was set up to run at 6 Messages Per Second (MPS). The three hornet nodes were only propagating messages, and the coordinator was running all the Proof of Work (see Sect. 4.1), this scenario is also known as Easy PoW [17].

3.5 Proposed Data Flow Towards IOTA Tangle

For data messages from IoT devices, AI, or the FMS the following steps were laid out:

- First, the sensor measures in the IoT device a specific environmental condition and sends an electrical signal to the ESP32 microprocessor of the IoT Devices described in Sect. 3.
- Second, the ESP32 processes the signal and creates a message in JSON format that is sent to a topic in the MQTT Broker. A variation of this is the AI or the FMS sending a JSON message to an MQTT topic.
- Third, Node-RED [18], a web browser-based visual programming tool that allows a user to add, eliminate and connect nodes, is listening to the MQTT topics, thereby receiving the message with data.
- Fourth, the IOTA Streams API encrypts and routes the data to any of the three load-balanced hornet nodes running in the Raspberry Pi 4 where the private tangle is implemented by using the IOTA Streams Framework and implementing the IOTA Channels Protocol. It primarily has three functions: CreateAuthor, SendOne, and FetchAll that have been developed following the IOTA Streams Specification for "Single Branching" (see Sect. 4.2). Each function operates as follows:

- CreateAuthor: Creates the author, defines the branch type as single branch and announces the Channel.
- SendOne: Imports the author to send a message to the tangle with the Keyload and starts the sequence counting.
- FetchAll: Creates a subscriber, receives the channel address to listen and returns the messages sent by the author.

For value transactions, the user enters data such as the amount, an additional transaction message and the receiving address. Then the front-end generates a JSON message that is sent to a custom API that supports the IOTA wallet (IOTA Wallet API was developed by Zignar Technologies). The wallet API organizes the data, prepares it, and sends the transaction to the tangle. Once the transaction has been approved, the API obtains a transaction identifier from the tangle and forwards it to the frontend to be shown to the user. Finally, the user can view the details of the completed transaction, with the option of verifying the transaction in the IOTA explorer.

Therefore, for data messages and value transactions, end-to-end communication is technically viable when utilizing IoT, AI, and DLT.

4   Theory and Calculation

In this section, the core technologies and concepts that allow interoperability between machines for the purpose of IPA are summarized and explained.

4.1   Distributed Ledger Technologies

It is important to differentiate Blockchain from DLT as separate concepts [19]. Blockchain is a data structure that was first proposed in 1982 [20], and Bitcoin is the most popular implementation of this data structure, especially because of the secure techniques applied when transmitting messages from one node to another [21].

The IoT and AI industries require a secure communication layer that can be used when transmitting data, or messages generated by IoT-enabled smart meters or small sensors. This platform should be capable of meeting three basic requirements: accepting data, transmitting data, and fetching data, with the additional need of being energy efficient and frictionless [22].

Nevertheless, all Blockchains rely on miners and fees to secure the network. This fact has two main implications; first, energy required by miners to process transactions; second, the fees required to process transactions that create friction because each message comes at an additional cost. Also, Proof of Work (PoW) is one of the methods used by blockchains to secure the network and consists in finding a correct combination expressed by a hashing function such that the output begins with a certain number of zeros in its binary representation [23]. PoW is expensive in terms of calculation and energy consumption, when utilized in the specific manner that blockchain requires (i.e., miners competing for fees).

An alternative data structure that promises to solve and improve on the limitations inherent to a blockchain is the Directed Acyclic Graph (DAG). DAGs are by design more expressive than a sequential model. Also, when implemented properly, their data structure is nimbler and more lightweight. Therefore, this approach can be utilized to solve diverse problems.

One of the first DLT projects that proposed the use of a DAG as data structure was IOTA [24]. In the paper of IOTA-Next Generation Blockchain [25], the authors mentioned that "The Tangle is a new data structure based on a Directed Acyclic Graph. As such it has no Blocks, no Chain, and no Miners".

The IOTA token has been designed for IoT optimizing micropayments (value) and messaging (data) within the same protocol [26]. The Tangle as a data structure eliminates the need for specialized hardware and excessive energy consumption required by blockchain to secure the network. Due to all these characteristics, IOTA is an energy efficient choice when it comes to designing applications for distributed communication of IoT devices. Therefore, adopting the Tangle as the supporting DLT is naturally a much better option for this research project, as opposed to Blockchain technology.

4.2   IOTA Streams and IOTA Channels

IOTA Streams is a framework that structures and navigates secured data through the Tangle. It organizes data by ordering it in an interoperable structure. It has been created by the IOTA Foundation to allow the development of cryptographic protocols on top of The Tangle.

IOTA Streams provides a toolset for structuring and transforming data for application-specific purposes, to be communicated over any transportation layer. IOTA Channels is a Streams protocol implementation that uses the IOTA network as a transportation layer. [27]. Its core functionality is achieved through the following features:

- Maintains Streams state through an internal link store mechanism.
- Numerous predefined message types (Announce, Signed Packets, Keyloads, tagged packets, Subscribe, Unsubscribe, and Sequence).
- Decentralized transportation and storage through the usage of the Tangle.
- Message types for managing cryptographic access control to data branches.
- Uses a pub/sub model with key sharing for access management.

IOTA Channel supports two configurations: "Single Branching" and "Multi Branching". These refer to the delineation for participant management within a channel and the sequencing model that all participants in the channel will be configured with.

Finality refers to the time when it becomes impossible to remove a message or transaction from the ledger [28], and in the case of IOTA it represents the probability that the message becomes final, guaranteeing that the message is deep in the tangle and will not be orphaned [30]. The finality time directly impacts the user experience and the overall perception of the DLT, our assumption is that anything beyond 10 s of finality is not practical for mainstream adoption, and the ideal should be under 5 s. Message finality directly impacts the user experience and the overall perception of the DLT. Is our rational assumption that a message finality above 10 s is not practical for mainstream adoption, and a message finality under 5 s is convenient for human-to-human interaction.

In the experiment, response rate, when sending and fetching messages with a payload of up to 32 Kb [27] using the private tangle, the finality averaged at 50 ms for 4320 messages. Conversely, when using the public IOTA Mainnet network, the finality averaged at 4 s; showing that the message finality is at desirable levels, and validating the technical feasibility of combining IoT, AI, and DLT. These findings are aligned with message finality theoretical values that are being developed and yet to be benchmarked in the production version of the IOTA Network [29].

4.3   Machine-to-Machine Economy

The M2M Economy implies machines becoming independent economic entities that make decisions on their own and react to the world around them without waiting for specific instructions. For example, a parked autonomous vehicle contracting a micro insurance with provider A and switching to insurance provider B when driving on the highway, all of this without asking to the owner, but taking the best decision based on predefined owner's interests [30,31]. This concept can be extended to space settlements where machines will be providing or buying services at different levels to other machines and humans.

4.4   Energy Consumption with IOTA Streams

Firstly, the energy consumption of a greenhouse farm is a sensitive matter, especially for operations that apply artificial lighting to speed up the growth process of crops. This consumption increases proportionally according to the location's latitude to keep the environment temperature at acceptable levels for the crops.

Secondly, the availability of energy for space settlements is very limited. For instance, the International Space Station produces on average 84 to 120 kWh of electricity with eight solar arrays [32].

For the experiment, two EF ECOFLOW Portable Power Stations (3300 W) were used to store all the energy collected by solar panels. The ECOFLOW power stations were powering one Precision Habitat PRO, and two Raspberry Pi 4 Single Board Computers; the first Raspberry Pi 4 was running the full IPA FMS application, including backend and frontend, with a friendly Avahi Protocol [33] address defined as agri-mars.local. The second Raspberry Pi 4 was hosting the private tangle at friendly address defined as tangle-mars.local.

According to calculated benchmarks, the energy requirement to write the IoT data to a private tangle under Easy PoW (see Sect. 3.4) is 1.18 MJ at 100 MPS and 1.21 MJ at 50 MPS [17]. These referential values are used to calculate the linear regression function (see Eq. 1) to estimate the energy cost per transaction at 6 MPS, where x is the MPS, and y is the energy in millijoules.

Then, at 6 MPS the estimated energy per message/transaction is 1.23 MJ or 3.41×10^{-10} kWh.

$$y = -0.0006x + 1.24 \tag{1}$$

The set frequency for our IoT controllers was one JSON message every minute.

$$Messages = days \cdot hours \cdot minutes \tag{2}$$

The mission run the equipment for three days, giving us a total of 4320 messages (see Eq. 2).

$$Energy = messages \cdot energy/message \tag{3}$$

The estimated total energy spent to process the 4320 messages was 5.313 J (see Eq. 3) or 1.47×10^{-6} kWh.

As part of the experiment, value transactions were also performed between the platform and the rover to pay for surveying the farm. These transactions were confirmed in the private tangle showing that the technology can also be used as a payment layer for machines, at a very low energy cost.

Using IOTA Tangle, the energy cost required to issue one value transaction is equivalent as the one required for one data message. As previously calculated in our experiment, it equals 1.23 MJ. This amount of energy is trivial when compared to the energy requirements of centralized payment networks such Visa, where a single transaction within the network consumes around 10,566 J or 2.935×10^{-3} kWh [34,35]. Furthermore, the energy required by PoW of a single Bitcoin transaction is calculated to be 1827.75 kWh, as of September 2021 [36,37], and a single Hedera Hashgraph transaction consumes 39.70×10^{-6} kWh [35]. In perspective an average north American household consumes about 877 kWh/month [38].

Thus, since energy is a very limited resource for on-earth and off-earth farming, it makes sense to implement a comprehensive solution that uses this resource most efficiently. The IOTA network amply meets the criteria.

5   Case Study: Astronaut Analog Mission

The case study was conducted on an MMAARS' greenhouse (referred to as "GreenHab") located in Mojave Desert, California, USA, during a five-day analog mission (see Fig. 2). The GreenHab was used for research of different types of vegetables. It also intends to closely reproduce Martian environmental conditions.

The objective of this case study was to monitor and collect data derived from the cultivation of grapes and tomatoes in the GreenHab through analogous protocols, routines, and methodologies that astronauts could perform and reproduce in Isolated Confined Environments (ICE), considering constraints on internet connection, Wi-Fi signal, energy supply, coupled with extreme temperatures of up to 43 °C (113 °F). Moreover, the dust lifted by the strong winds of the Mojave Desert seeped into the hardware and caused some glitches. Therefore, we defined the following objectives for the experiment to validate the success of the proof of concept of IPA:

- Magrito's Recognition Algorithm shall accurately recognize and count most of the grape and tomato fruits that are in the GreenHab.
- Habitat Precision PRO shall gather environment data such temperature, humidity, soil moisture, and CO_2.
- IOTA Private Tangle shall secure the data and value with greatly reduced energy consumption.

Throughout the five-day Analog Mission conducted by the MMAARS institute, IPA was implemented on the first days of the mission. The experiment was performed in the afternoons of August 22nd, 23rd, 24th to harness colder temperatures. The referential location of the Habitat (basecamp) was seven miles northeast of the Best Western Hotel, California City.

5.1   Space Analog Mission Protocols

As part of the simulation, some tomatoes and grapes were planted on the first tier of the GreenHab racks to be detected by Magrito's camera. Also, the Precision Habitat PRO was installed next to the crops with its sensors. During the analog mission, A. M. Flores, the crew member responsible of IPA, conducted a two-hour protocol to run the experiments. First, the Precision Habitat PRO module was plugged into the power supply; then, the local Wi-Fi Network was initiated along with the IPA server and then private tangle was started. Later, the system started to collect data. Finally, Magrito's work plan in the GreenHab followed a route that covered all the crops in the GreenHab.

6   Results

The standard security protocols to grant access to third parties to the data require the setup of private and centralized TCP/IP networks (VPNs) or Web APIs. The proof of concept showed that multiple types of data sources (IoT, FMS, AI) can write data messages through the IOTA Channels Protocol, allowing data to be fetched from third parties using the same protocol without centralized VPNs or Web APIs.

For the agriculture industry, this enables traceability and interoperability since the digital twins of crop batches can be accessed by third parties to audit the production data, information, or knowledge related to the end products.

Furthermore, the calculations introduced in Sect. 4.4, estimate 1.23 MJ per message. The set up included one IoT Device (see Sect. 3) sending data every minute, the IPA system, and the private tangle. Two EF ECOFLOW Portable Power Stations (3300 W) were used to support these systems demonstrating that the energy required to write/read data on IOTA network is very low. Even when processing value transactions the energy consumption is trivial compared to networks like VISA. During the experiment message spammers were set to a required minimum of 6 MPS to keep the network running. In a real scenario, spammers can be deployed on other nodes communicating through IOTA network and reaching higher numbers of MPS.

On the other hand, we can appreciate that the Mask R-CNN is framing the recognized grapes and tomatoes (See Fig. 5), respectively; in the lower right corner of the image, the algorithm is counting the number of recognized fruits.

Fig. 5. Deep Learning algorithms identifying tomatoes (N = 167) and grapes (N = 8)

Finally, the DL model is accurately framing the fruits but is failing to count the exact number. This can be improved by tuning hyper-parameters in the layers of the Mask R-CNN and testing the model's performance by comparison in each tuning [39]. Nonetheless, the first implementation in extreme conditions of this algorithm demonstrates good potential for future improvements and capabilities to add more data collectors.

7   Discussion and Conclusion

The specific contribution of this study during the Analog Astronaut Mission is to show that the combination of IoT, AI and DLT is technically feasible, economically viable, and energy efficient. The feeless DLT enables M2M communication and monetary transactions without friction, as shown in Sects. 4.4 and 3.3. Its implementation in a hostile environment was motivated due to the possible identification of strengths and weaknesses in the current IPA's systems version. Despite the extreme environmental conditions, and energy constraints, the performance of data collectors selected was not affected. In fact, valuable crop data and observations were collected during the analog mission that will serve to the betterment of the general concept of IPA.

These exponential technologies can be developed and integrated with the goal of increasing yield by extending the automation in a greenhouse on-earth. As result, the cost of the crop production decreases significantly [40,41]. In addition, the low energy consumption and the portability of the systems allow replicability required for off-planet missions. As on-earth greenhouse adoption increases, along with its automation [42], the performance and capabilities of the proposed systems may improve. These more advanced versions would increase its usefulness for future off-earth greenhouses.

Future improvements will entail an increase in the deep learning model's precision used for identifying and counting the fruits, the addition of a robotic arm for automatic harvesting purposes, the re-engineering of Precision Habitat PRO (see Sect. 3.2 to have modularized boards that can be used in other applications, the development of new features for the FMS (see Sect. 3.3), the improvement of IOTA Streams API to support multibranching (see Sect. 4.2), the addition of IOTA Smart Contracts for Tasks Automation (see Sect. 3.3), and the use of ML to evaluate the impact of growing condition adjustments in the cultivation process. The collected data will be used to train regression models that would predict the resulting yield for each type of crop. Thus, our explanation variables consist of time series for each measured variable while the response variable corresponds to the resulting yield. The structure of the given problem is suitable for the use of sequential models such as long-short term memory modules (LSTMs).

Moreover, in the next iteration, IOTA 2.0, the Tangle is evolving into a new solution that incorporates Sharding and Multiverse [43–45]; in an off-planet situation, considering communication constraints imposed by planet distance, both Sharding and Multiverse would be characteristics desirable for any DLT.

Acknowledgements. We thank all the collaborators from IRIS Corporation and Zignar Technologies for their effort in developing the software and hardware of all the systems presented in this article, and for the showcasing of the solution at the AGS-mart Expo 2021, AB, Canada [46] and the analog mission of MMAARS 2021 [47]. Likewise, we thank the MMAARS institute for providing all the resources to adapt the crops in the greenhouse for the space analog mission. Finally, we thank Giorgio Morales, Lead Data Scientist at Zignar Technologies and PhD Student in Computer Science at Montana State University; Pablo Bellido, IoT Engineer at Zignar Technologies and Bachelor of Electronic Engineering from the National University San Luis Gonzaga; and Oliver Stehr, Software Engineer at Zignar Technologies and Computer Science student at Universidad Adolfo Ibáñez, for assisting with technical writing in the elaboration of this document.

References

1. Buttel, H.: The US Farm Crisis and the Restructuring of American Agriculture: Domestic and International Dimensions, pp. 46–83. Palgrave Macmillan UK (1989)
2. Butterfield, K.L.: The social problems of American farmers. Am. J. Sociol. **10**(5), 606–622 (1905)
3. Hanson, J., et al.: Challenges for maintaining sustainable agricultural systems in the United States. Renew. Agric. Food Syst. **23**, 325–334 (2008)
4. Zhang, Y.: Design of the node system of wireless sensor network and its application in digital agriculture. In: 2011 International Conference on Computer Distributed Control and Intelligent Environmental Monitoring, pp. 29–35 (2011)
5. Enrique, J.E.: Data centralisation, the challenge it poses and its benefits - Emiral, April 2020. https://tinyurl.com/76DatCen. Accessed 13 Oct 2021
6. Patel, J.: Overcoming data silos through big data integration. Int. J. Educ. (IJE) **3**(01), 1–6 (2019)

7. Monje, O., et al.: Farming in space: environmental and biophysical concerns. Adv. Space Res. **31**(1), 151–167 (2003)
8. Popov, S.: IOTA: Feeless and Free. IEEE Blockchain Technical Briefs (2019)
9. National Aeronautics and Space Administration (NASA): About Analog Missions. https://tinyurl.com/76AnalogMission. Accessed 13 Oct 2021
10. de Silva, R., et al.: Development of a holonomic mobile robot for field applications. In: International Conference on Industrial and Information Systems, p. 500 (2009)
11. He, K., Gkioxari, G., Dollár, P., Girshick, R.: Mask R-CNN. In: 2017 IEEE International Conference on Computer Vision (ICCV), pp. 2980–2988 (2017)
12. Espressif Systems: ESP32 Wi-Fi & Bluetooth MCU I Espressif Systems (2021). https://tinyurl.com/76ESP32. Accessed 13 Oct 2021
13. Zignar Technologies: Precision Habitat Pro datasheet (2021). https://bit.ly/habitatpro. Accessed 13 Oct 2021
14. Interplanetary Precision Agriculture: Zignar Technologies Message ID: 02c8e5a881fd76bec19e564f4dd0b4394220287cbebfc818a94f3feec68d38c9, IOTA Explorer. https://tinyurl.com/M4GR1T0. Accessed 13 Oct 2021
15. Yang, T.J., Chen, Y.H., Sze, V.: Designing energy-efficient convolutional neural networks using energy-aware pruning. In: 2017 IEEE Conference on Computer Vision and Pattern Recognition (CVPR), pp. 6071–6079 (2017)
16. International Business Machines Corporation (IBM) and Eurotech: MQTT V3.1 Protocol Specification. https://tinyurl.com/76MQTT. Accessed 13 Oct 2021
17. Ramachandran, N.: Energy Benchmarks for the IOTA Network (Chrysalis Edition), May 2021. https://tinyurl.com/IOTA-EB. Accessed 13 Oct 2021
18. Lee, C.: Security and Trust in IoT Data Streams using Tangle Distributed Ledger and Node-Red Technology, School of Electronic Engineering and Computer Science, Queen Mary University of London (2021). https://tinyurl.com/76SecurityWithTangle. Accessed 13 Oct 2021
19. Ganne, E.: Can Blockchain revolutionize international trade? https://tinyurl.com/76Blockchain. Accessed 13 Oct 2021
20. Sherman, A., et al.: On the origins and variations of blockchain technologies. IEEE Secur. Priv. **17**(1), 72–77 (2019)
21. Rahouti, M., Xiong, K., Ghani, N.: Bitcoin concepts, threats, and machine-learning security solutions. IEEE Access **6**, 67189–67205 (2018)
22. Anadiotis, G.: A better blockchain: Bitcoin for nothing and transactions for free? — ZDNet (2017). https://tinyurl.com/76FreeTran. Accessed 13 10 2021
23. Attias, V., et al.: Implementation Study of Two Verifiable Delay Functions — IOTA Foundation (2020). https://tinyurl.com/76Delay. Accessed 13 Oct 2021
24. Ivancheglo, S.: IOTA — Bitcointalk (2015). https://bitcointalk.org/index.php?topic=1216479.0. Accessed 13 Oct 2021
25. Divya, M., et al.: IOTA-next generation block chain. Int. J. Eng. Comput. Sci. **7**(04), 23823–23826 (2018)
26. Popov, S.: The Tangle, Version 1.4.3 (2018). https://tinyurl.com/76TheTangle143. Accessed 13 Oct 2021
27. Chapman, D.: Streams Specification Rev:1.0 A, IOTA Foundation, Initial Release (2020). https://tinyurl.com/76IotaStreamsSpecs. Accessed 13 Oct 2021
28. Anceaume, E., et al.: On Finality in Blockchains (2020). https://tinyurl.com/76FinalityBitcoins. Accessed 13 Oct 2021
29. IOTA Foundation: Fully decentralized IOTA 2.0 explained in under 3 minutes. https://tinyurl.com/76IotaDescentralised (2020). Accessed 23 Oct 2021

30. Banerjee, A., et al.: Efficient, Adaptive and Scalable Device Activation for M2M Communications, School of Computing (2015). http://www.cs.umd.edu/~slee/pubs/m2m-secon15.pdf. Accessed 13 Oct 2021

31. Rajasingham, D.: Commonwealth Bank of Australia, Welcome to the machine-to-machine economy (2017). https://tinyurl.com/76MTM. Accessed 13 Oct 2021

32. Garcia, M.: About the Space Station Solar Arrays, NASA (2017). https://tinyurl.com/76NASASolarArrays. Accessed 13 Oct 2021

33. Avahi 0.8 (2020). https://www.avahi.org/. Accessed 13 Oct 2021

34. VISA: Environmental, Social & Governance Report (2020). https://tinyurl.com/76VISAReport. Accessed 13 Oct 2021

35. EU Blockchain Observatory and Forum: Energy Efficiency of Blockchain Technologies (2021). https://tinyurl.com/76EnergEffic. Accessed 13 Oct 2021

36. de Vries, A., Stoll, C.: Bitcoin's growing e-waste problem. Resour. Conserv. Recycl. **175**, 105901 (2021)

37. Digiconomist: Bitcoin Energy Consumption Index, Single Bitcoin Transaction Footprint (2021). https://tinyurl.com/76EnergTran. Accessed 13 Oct 2021

38. U.S. Energy Information Administration: Frequently Asked Questions, How much electricity does an American home use? (2020). https://tinyurl.com/76USEnergy. Accessed 13 Oct 2021

39. Chon, S.: Hyper-parameter Optimization of a Convolutional Neural Network (2019). https://scholar.afit.edu/etd/2297. Accessed 13 Oct 2021

40. Padmanabhan, P., et al.: Solanaceous fruits including tomato, eggplant, and peppers. In: Encyclopedia of Food and Health, pp. 24–32. Academic Press (2016)

41. Kozai, T., et al.: Plant Factory: An Indoor Vertical Farming System for Efficient Quality Food Production. Academic Press (2019)

42. Lowenberg-DeBoer, J., et al.: Economics of robots and automation in field crop production. Precision Agric. **21**(2), 278–299 (2020)

43. Moog, H.: Scaling IOTA Part 1 - A Primer on Sharding (2020). https://tinyurl.com/76IOTAShardingMultiverse. Accessed 13 Oct 2021

44. Moog, H.: Scaling IOTA Part 2 - Untangling the Tangle (2019). https://tinyurl.com/76UntanglingIOTA. Accessed 13 Oct 2021

45. Moog, H.: A New, "Consensus": The Tangle Multiverse [Part 1] (2019). https://tinyurl.com/76IOTAMultiverse1. Accessed 13 Oct 2021

46. Campos, G., et al.: Interplanetary Precision Agriculture, Zignar Technologies (2021). https://tinyurl.com/76DemoZignar. Accessed 13 Oct 2021

47. Cerron, B., et al.: Interplanetary Precision Agriculture - Demo: Analog Mission, MMAARS (2021). https://tinyurl.com/DemoIr. Accessed 13 Oct 2021

Data-Driven Software Engineering

Multiphase Model Based on K-means and Ant Colony Optimization to Solve the Capacitated Vehicle Routing Problem with Time Windows

Airton Huamán[ID], Marco Huancahuari[ID], and Lenis Wong[(✉)][ID]

Universidad Peruana de Ciencias Aplicadas, Lima 15023, Peru
lwongpuni@gmail.com

Abstract. The delivery of products on time while reducing transportation costs has become an issue for retail companies in Latin America due to the rise of the e-commerce market in recent years. The Vehicle Routing Problem (VRP) is one of the most studied topics in operations research. This work addresses the Capacitated Vehicle Routing Problem with Time Windows (CVRPTW). The problem focuses on finding optimal routes for each vehicle to serve customers on time and minimal transportation costs under capacity and time constraints. Previous research has addressed the issue by proposing non-exact and exact techniques. This paper aims to select a proper approach and algorithms to present a model to solve the CVRPTW in real-world scenarios by incorporating a Google distance matrix, the empirical knowledge of delivery zones, and a solution relatively easy to deploy in a cloud environment. The proposed model consists of four phases: order scheduling, client clustering, delivery route generation, and operator assignment. We use the *K-means* algorithm to cluster customers and assign them to vehicles and the Ant Colony Optimization (ACO) algorithm to generate optimal routes. The proposed model was validated through a case study for a retail company in Lima, Perú. The results show that the proposed model reduces the route generation execution time by 95% of the average time. It also cuts travel distance and time by around 182 km and 532 min in 5-day periods.

Keywords: Vehicle routing problem · Capacitated vehicle routing problem with time windows · K-means · Ant colony optimization · Vehicle scheduling problem

1 Introduction

Transportation accounts for one-third of logistic costs having a significant impact on supply chain performance [1]. Therefore, solving the Vehicle Routing Problem (VRP) significantly impacts cost reduction, timely delivery, and increased customer satisfaction. The *VRP* is one of the most studied optimization problems in operations research [2]. It was proposed by [3], and its variants continue to grow as real-world scenarios appear. Taxonomic studies such as [4] and [5] confirm its validity in scientific research.

The Capacitated Vehicle Routing Problem with Time Windows (CVRPTW) is the topic of this work. Among the papers reviewed, [1] presents a modular algorithm based

J. A. Lossio-Ventura et al. (Eds.): SIMBig 2021, CCIS 1577, pp. 141–157, 2022.
https://doi.org/10.1007/978-3-031-04447-2_10

on historical data to solve any variant of the *VRP*. [2] proposes a five-phase approach based on the Savings Matrix and 2-OPT algorithms. [6] presents an improved Ant Colony Optimization (ACO) algorithm that optimizes the routes with the local search algorithm. However, many medium/small size companies from the retail industry don't have enough historical data to use a data-driven approach, the computational infrastructure needed, or qualified personnel to select and implement complex optimization algorithms. Also, the reviewed works don't consider the empirical knowledge from drivers, essential in Latin American cities. This paper aims to choose a proper technique and algorithms to present a model to solve the *CVRPTW* in real-world scenarios by incorporating a Google distance matrix, the empirical knowledge of delivery zones, and that is relatively easy to deploy in a cloud environment.

The proposal consists of a multiphase model to solve the *CVRPTW*. It has four phases: order scheduling, client clustering, delivery route generation, and operators assignment. It is achieved by applying a modified *K-means* algorithm for client clustering and a modified *ACO* algorithm for route generation.

This work is organized as follows: In Sect. 2, the literature review is carried out. Section 3 presents the proposed model. The validation of the study is carried out in Sect. 4. The results and discussion are shown in Sect. 5. Finally, in Sect. 6, the conclusions and future work are presented.

2 Related Work

This section presents a systematic review of the literature on the *VRP* and its variants. It comprises three phases: planning, development, and findings.

In the planning phase, we executed the following steps: *(i)* formulation of research questions, *(ii)* scientific databases, *(iii)* keywords selection, and *(iv)* definition of inclusion and exclusion criteria. The research questions defined were Q1: What techniques do the researchers currently use to address the *VRP* problem? Q2: What phases do the proposed techniques have? Q3: What algorithms do the found approaches employ to build a VRP solution? Q4: How to determine the quality of a VRP solution?

The following keywords were defined: "vehicle routing problem"; "vehicle scheduling problem"; "CVRPTW"; "Capacitated vehicle routing problem"; "route optimization"; "K-means"; and "Ant colony optimization". The multidisciplinary databases selected were Scopus and Web of Science. The research articles considered were from scientific journals published after 2017, and answer one or more research questions.

We followed the flow chart elaborated based on the search protocols defined in the previous development phase. Finally, 21 studies were selected and analyzed through a proposed taxonomy related to the research questions posed (see Table 1).

Table 1. Classification of studies.

Category	References	Quantity
Techniques (Q1)	[1, 2, 7–15]	11
Phases (Q2)	[1, 2, 13, 14, 16]	5
Algorithms (Q3)	[4, 6, 10, 16–23]	11
Quality (Q4)	[1, 6, 10, 13, 18, 19]	6

The "Techniques" identified are exact and non-exact. In [7], the authors propose *K-means* to assign groups of customers to each vehicle and a genetic algorithm to generate optimal routes. In [2], a five-phase solution is presented. The phases are initialization, distance calculation, grouping, route prioritization, and final optimization based on the Savings Matrix and 2-OPT algorithms. The authors of [11] present a comparison of the Exact and Metaheuristic techniques, concluding that the latter is more dynamic and has better processing times.

Three typical "phases" were identified in *VRP* solutions: *(i)* scheduling phase; it determines the delivery date and the priority; *(ii)* clustering phase, it assigns customer groups to delivery operators and *(iii)* routing phase, which sorts the delivery points for each vehicle [14]. On the other hand, only two phases were defined in [20], clustering and routing, and the scheduling phase is part of the routing phase.

To create solutions for the *CVRPTW*, a wide range of "algorithms" are used. According to the review, non-exact techniques are the most used, and *ACO* is the most successfully employed algorithm in non-exact methods. It is important to highlight that techniques are procedures that tell how to solve the *CVRPTW* using many algorithms.

The quality metrics identified for the "Quality" category were processing time, distance traveled, number of vehicles, capacity compliance, and efficiency in route execution by operators. Solomon benchmark datasets are used in five research articles, and [18] proposes new validation datasets. [20] and [14] use numerous Solomon benchmarks during its validation processes. On the other hand, five studies employ historical data from the case study. We can point to the paper [1], which builds its approach on historical data analysis and validates it with Solomon benchmark datasets. It isn't possible to use public datasets to validate the proposed model because our approach employs a distance matrix of Lima. The validation will be done using historical data from the case study.

Our findings conclude that the best approach to solving the *CVRPTW* is the non-exact techniques consisting of various phases. Non-exact methods use less computational resources than the exact methods and provide good enough results for the real-world scenarios where the solution is applied. In addition, having many stages allows us to split the problem into small ones making it easier to solve.

The *K-means* algorithm was chosen for the clustering phase based on the results from [19]. The authors conclude that *K-means* performs better than the other clustering algorithms testest. The metrics used were traveled distance, waiting time, vehicle number, and computational time. Finally, the route generation phase will employ the *ACO* algorithm. In [14], authors use *ACO* successfully, reducing the routing distance and improving the completed shipments from 80% to 93% per day. The implementation of *ACO* in [8] allows the authors to optimize resources in terms of traveled km, load factor, and the number of vehicles. In [18] and [15], authors go one step further optimizing *ACO*. However, the standard ACO algorithm performs well in most of the datasets used in their comparisons. In addition, [15] confirms that *ACO* was used successfully with actual distance instead of spatial distance.

3   Proposed Model

Figure 1 depicts the multiphase model proposed to solve the *CVRPTW*. The model is fed relevant information on orders, customers, vehicles, and applicable business rules for prioritization and dispatch as inputs. The model's first phase is called "order scheduling." During this phase, orders are prioritized based on the purchase date applying the first-in, first-out rule, the sales value of the products, and the available capacity. The second phase is called "client clustering", and it consists of creating clusters of customers based on available vehicles. The optimal delivery sequence is assigned using the *ACO* algorithm during the "delivery routes generation" phase. Finally, the "operator assignment" phase sets the appropriate driver based on geofences of delivery area knowledge.

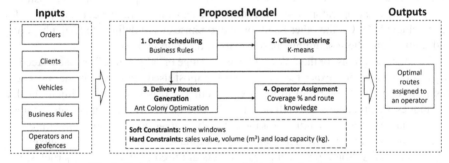

Fig. 1. Proposed multiphase model to solve the *CVRPTW*.

3.1   Phases of the Proposed Model

Phase 1: Order scheduling. This phase's goal is to prioritize and schedule the attention of pending deliveries. The inputs are the pending orders, available vehicles, and the dates to schedule. The model performs the following steps: *(i)* Get the available vehicles and their capacity. *(ii)* The total capacity is calculated per day by adding the individual capacities of each vehicle in terms of load (kg), volume (m^3), and sales value (PEN). *(iii)* All pending orders are sorted by purchase date and sales value descendingly, then a priority is assigned based on the position. Higher positions have preference over lower positions. *(iv)* Finally, this phase assigns a delivery date to each prioritized order until the scheduled orders reach the maximum normalized capacity possible per day. This step normalizes the demand of each order in terms of load (kg), volume (m^3), and sales value (PEN) by representing them as percentage values of the total capacity calculated previously. Then, it selects the maximum percentage value as the normalized demand.

Pending orders that couldn't be scheduled due to capacity constraints or incompleted ones from previous days will be prioritized for the following scheduling process due to having older purchase dates.

As output, this phase provides orders with an assigned service date. Figure 2 shows the steps during Phase 1. The variables used in this diagram are as follows: available vehicles (*v*), total capacity (*tc*), range of scheduling days (*sDays*), current day (*sDay*), pending orders (*o*), normalized demand of the pending orders (*o.nDemand*), scheduled day for delivery (*o.ScheduledDay*), and accumulated demand (*aDemand*).

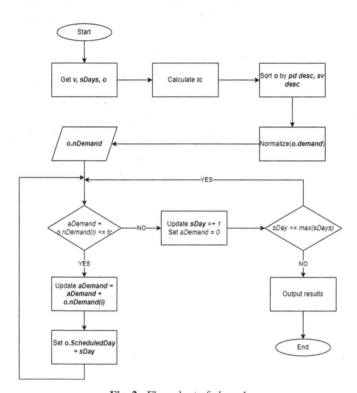

Fig. 2. Flow chart of phase 1.

Phase 2: Client Clustering. This stage takes the previous phase's results, available vehicles, and capacities. There are two business rules: *(a)* a customer cluster cannot exceed the capacity restrictions, and *(b)* the total sales value of orders assigned to a vehicle cannot exceed 25,000.00 PEN. This phase uses a modified *K-means* algorithm to generate customer clusters based on their location using a Google distance matrix, where *k* represents the number of vehicles employed to satisfy the demand. According to [7], *K-means* outperforms other clustering algorithms for *VRPTW* problems.

The steps of this phase are: *(i)* Get the available vehicles, scheduled orders, and the range of planned dates. *(ii)* Calculate the total capacity per day in terms of load (kg), volume (m³), and sales value (PEN). *(iii)* Normalize the demand of the scheduled orders. The demand normalization consists of converting the demand of kg, m³, sales value to its percentage value and selecting the maximum value as the normalized demand (nDemand). *(iv)* The numbers of clusters are calculated using the function *CalculateK( )* that receives the scheduled orders as parameters. This function uses the elbow method and the normalized demand to calculate k. The elbow method determines k based on the dispersion of the data points in the map, and the normalized demand calculates k based on the number of vehicles needed to satisfy the demand from the scheduled orders. Then returns the highest value between them to set k. *(v)* In this step, we use the algorithm *K-means++* to choose the initial values or seeds for the centroids in *K-means* clustering. The algorithm receives as parameters the localization points of the customers and the normalized demand. It boosts the performance by avoiding poor initial centroids, a common problem of the standard *K-means* algorithm. *(vi)* Finally, we validate that a cluster k does not exceed a vehicle's available capacity using the normalized demand in every clustering iteration.

All steps must be repeated per each scheduled day. Figure 3 shows the basic idea of the modified *K-means* algorithm in a flowchart. The variables used in this diagram are as follows: Scheduled orders (*so*), the demand of a scheduled order (*so.demand*), accumulated demand of a cluster (*k.aDemand*), and the total capacity of a cluster (*k.tc*).

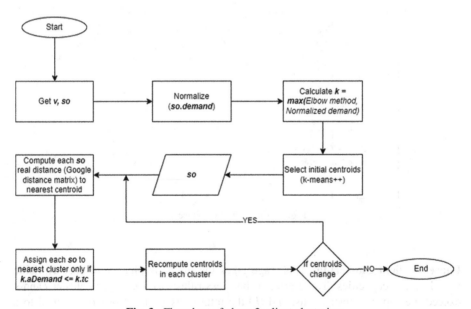

Fig. 3. Flowchart of phase 2: client clustering.

Table 2 shows the pseudocode of the modified *K-means* implemented in the proposed model.

Table 2. Modified *K-means algorithm.*

Algorithm 1. K-means
1: Get available vehicles (*v*), scheduled orders (*so*).
2: Normalize the demand of the scheduled orders.
3: Calculate ke with the ElbowMethod(o.latitud, o.longitud).
4: Calculate kd = RoundUp(total demand / total capacity per vehicle).
5: Set k = max(ke,kd); k <= v.count().
6: Initialize k centroids using the k-means++ (k, so) algorithm.
7: **repeat**
8:    expectation: Assign each customer to its closest centroids based on the Google distance matrix
9:    without exceeding the total cluster capacity (ktc)
10:   maximization: Compute the new centroids of each cluster.
11: **until** The centroid positions do not change.
12: **output**: A set of k clusters.

Phase 3: Delivery Routes Generation. This phase creates optimal delivery routes that each operator must complete. Its inputs are the location of the depot, generated clusters, time windows of each clustered order, and the available vehicles.

The *ACO* algorithm has been used successfully in [6, 8, 18], and [22]. Table 3 shows the pseudocode for the *ACO* algorithm that was implemented. It performs the following steps: *(i)* Define the optimization variant Near-to-Far of *ACO*. *(ii)* Execute *ACO* to generate delivery routes based on time windows and the distance matrix. The algorithm receives three types of time windows: default (all day), morning (from 8 a.m. to 1 p.m.), and afternoon (from 2 p.m. to 6 p.m.). When the *ACO* algorithm constructs

Table 3. Modified *ACO* algorithm.

Algorithm 2. ACO
1: Get *k* clusters
2: Set ACO optimization variant to Near-to-Far.
3: Load the distance matrix from Google: *getDistanceMatrix()*
4: **For** all clusters
5:   Initialize standard ACO parameters (AntK=100, iteration=2000, evaporation rate=0.95)
6:   **repeat**
7:   **do** for all ants *Antk = 1, ..., Antk$_{max}$*
8:   **set** *ant path*
9:   **do** for all decision points
10:   Select next point based on the desired time window and distance from Google dm
11:   Update the *ant path* with the point
12:   **end do**
13:   **end do**
14:   **do** for all ants
15:   Evaluate paths and select the best route
16:   **end do**
17:   Update pheromones on the best route
19:   iteration = iteration + 1, nSolutions = nSolutions + 1
20:   **until** *iteration > I$_{max}$ and nSolutions > maxNSolutions*
21: **end for**

the routes, it validates the time window selected for each decision point. If two or more decision points have the same time window, it measures the distance (using Google distance matrix) from the current point to the decision points. If *ACO* can't meet a time window, it assigns a new one to the order since the model considers time windows as soft constraints. The output is a set of optimal routes for each vehicle.

In addition, Fig. 4 shows the steps followed by the modified *ACO* algorithm.

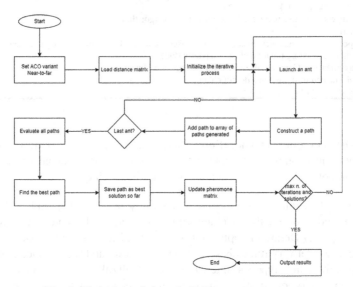

Fig. 4. Flow chart of phase 3: Delivery routes generation

Phase 4: Operators Assignment. This phase aims to assign an operator as the route's responsible. We first interviewed the drivers to obtain information about the delivery zones they know well, then transformed them into geographical coordinates on the map, forming a geofence. The inputs of this phase are the operators available, their geofences, and the set of routes generated in phase 3. The steps are as follows: *(i)* Get the list of the operators and the coordinates of their geofences. *(ii)* This step evaluates each route and then assigns the operator if the geofence covers the maximum number of customer locations. The output result is a set of optimal routes assigned to the most suitable operator.

4   Validation

The validation of the model was through a case study for a retail company in Lima, Perú. The current solution that the company uses is partially manual. The person in charge of the route generation process starts by downloading an excel report of prioritized pending orders from the Sales system. Then, based on his experience, assign the orders to vehicles available, and generate the routes.

We implemented the proposed model in a scheduling and route generation system. The physical architecture uses the serverless model on Microsoft Azure. Figure 5 depicts the system's physical architecture, where the web system, the Android application, REST API services, and the scheduling and routing engine are the four main modules. The web system was developed with the qualities of the software requirements in mind [24].

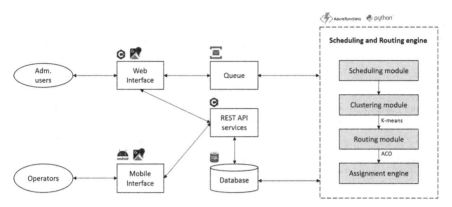

Fig. 5. Proposed System Architecture.

The primary customers in this case study are final buyers. Under the parameters defined in Table 4, the problem has been formulated as the *CVRPTW*.

Table 4. General configuration parameters.

Parameters	Values
Number of warehouses	1
Vehicle fleet	20
Uniform fleet	Yes
Vehicle load capacity (kg)	1,800 kg
Vehicle volume capacity (m^3)	9
Maximum sale value limit (vv)	25,000.00 PEN
Service hours per vehicle	8 h
N.° of routes assigned to a vehicle per day	1
Time Windows	Yes

Table 5 shows the input parameters and metrics that were used to validate each phase with the proposed system modules.

Table 5. Input parameters and metrics.

#	Module	Parameters	Metrics
1	Order scheduling	• Number of days to be scheduled • Number of clients • Available capacity • Capacity demanded	• Number of scheduled clients per day
2	Clustering client	• Number of clients • Number of vehicles • Capacity s.v • Capacity kg • Capacity m^3	• Number of clusters • Compliance with capacity restrictions • % of capacity utilized (kg, m^3, sv)
3	Route generation	• Number of clusters • Number of vehicles	• Number of routes that need manual intervention • Compliance with time constraints
4	Assignment	• Knowledge geofences • Available operators • Optimized routes	• Adequate operator assignment

5 Results and Discussion

The retail company provided information from 19,407 deliveries from 2019 to test the efficiency of the proposed model. This section shows the execution results for 1,469 deliveries completed in 5 days.

5.1 Phase 1: Order Scheduling

The deliveries were planned using the scheduling module over five business days, and the number of scheduled deliveries per day was the metric under consideration. The results are shown in Table 6.

Table 6. Results of order scheduling in phase 1.

Day	Scheduled orders (propose model)	Scheduled orders (current solution)
1	300	289
2	300	305
3	300	299
4	300	310
5	269	266

Orders for the proposed model are scheduled to adhere to the maximum capacity of 300 deliveries per day for 20 vehicles. Nonetheless, the current solution exceeds capacity on days 2 and 4, and it does not use the capacity to its full potential on the remaining days.

Figure 6 depicts the distribution of delivery points scheduled by the proposed model on a map of Lima, Peru.

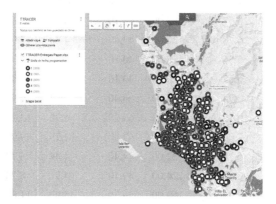

Fig. 6. Distribution of delivery points in the city of Lima, Peru.

In phase 2, we use the *K-means* algorithm to form clusters of customers and assign them to a vehicle. The calculation is made using the distances provided by a Google distance matrix of Lima. Table 7 compares the clustering performed by the proposed model and the current solution.

Table 7. Comparative results of the proposed model and the current one.

Día	Proposed model			Current solution		
	Num. of clients	Vehicles	k clusters	Num. of clients	Vehícles	k clusters
1	300	20	20	289	20	20
2	300	20	20	305	20	22
3	300	20	20	299	20	20
4	300	20	20	310	20	24
5	269	20	18	266	20	19
Total	**1469**	**20**	**98**	**1469**	**20**	**105**

After several simulations, the model generates an average of 7 to 10 fewer clusters every five days. It means an 8% improvement in fleet utilization efficiency, a reduction in route execution time of 10%, and, consequently, it impacts the reduction of delivery times. Table 8 shows the execution results for day 4.

Table 8. Results of the client clustering phase for 20 operators on day 4.

Vehicle	Clients	Demand (kg)		Demand (m^3)		Demand (s.v.)	
k		% utilised	Qty	% utilised	Qty	% utilised	Qty
A2I997	16	7.39	133.00	48.40	4.84	9.60	2400.00
A2K667	20	10.67	192.00	64.10	6.41	12.84	3210.00
A3U889	15	6.78	122.00	43.40	4.34	7.94	1985.00
A5U779	12	6.56	118.00	40.10	4.01	6.94	1735.00
A8N702	12	6.67	120.00	40.10	4.01	6.90	1725.00
A9L179	2	0.94	17.00	6.40	0.64	0.92	230.00
A9M088	22	10.22	184.00	69.20	6.92	13.46	3365.00
A9U334	17	7.06	127.00	47.90	4.79	9.98	2495.00
AT3776	14	6.78	122.00	44.40	4.44	8.74	2185.00
AUB922	16	6.89	124.00	49.10	4.91	8.24	2060.00
B3U830	19	9.39	169.00	59.70	5.97	11.88	2970.00
C1O888	22	9.22	166.00	62.90	6.29	12.32	3080.00
C1O890	16	7.94	143.00	50.90	5.09	8.88	2220.00
C9P856	4	1.78	32.00	13.00	1.30	3.14	785.00
D1P877	20	8.11	146.00	58.60	5.86	11.18	2795.00
F3V720	22	10.78	194.00	70.20	7.02	14.22	3555.00
H6K088	1	0.44	8.00	3.20	0.32	0.90	225.00
H7B345	15	7.33	132.00	49.40	4.94	7.72	1930.00
P1L864	15	7.56	136.00	50.40	5.04	10.38	2595.00
PIK891	20	11.17	201.00	67.60	6.76	13.40	3350.00

The capacity constraints were satisfied. Due to a small number of assigned orders, anomalies were discovered for the vehicles A9L179, H6K088, and C9P856. Following the analysis, it was found that the delivery areas are remote, requiring the attention of a vehicle, and unable to be included in other customer clusters.

Figures 7(a) and 7(b) depicts the distribution of scheduled and clustered deliveries on the map for days 1 and 4 respectively, and we can see that the clusters are correctly defined based on the distance matrix used.

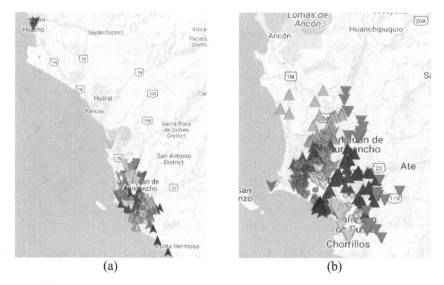

(a)   (b)

Fig. 7. Distribution of clients clusters generated on day 1 (a) and day 4 (b).

5.2 Phase 3: Delivery Routes Generation

We use the standard ACO algorithm to generate optimal routes for each cluster generated in the previous phase. Table 9 summarizes the results of phase 3, where k is the number of clusters.

Table 9. Results of the "Delivery routes generation" phase using the ACO algorithm.

Day	Proposed Model				Current Model			
	Clients	k	Distance (km)	Time (min)	Clients	k	Distance (km)	Time (min)
1	300	20	706.98	2068	289	20	739	2160
2	300	20	558.19	1736	305	22	603	1863
3	300	20	648	1962	299	20	685	2051
4	300	20	667	1988	310	24	701	2091
5	269	18	663	1865	266	19	698	1973

Compared to the current case study model, using the ACO algorithm reduces the distance traveled to complete the routes by 182 km. On the other hand, there is a 532-min reduction in travel time.

The visit sequence generated for vehicle H7B345 is depicted in Fig. 8(a). Figure 8(b) shows that operator 6's knowledge geofence covers 91.67% of the delivery points on the route for which it was chosen, whereas operator "1" only covers 26.67%.

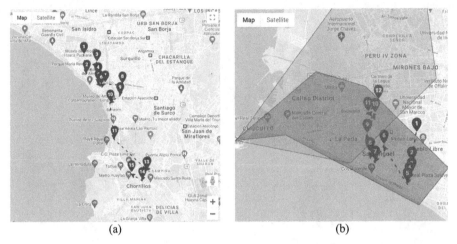

(a)   (b)

Fig. 8. Route of vehicle A3U889 (a). A graphic example of the evaluation of knowledge geofence (b).

5.3   Phase 4: Operator Assignment

This section uses a custom procedure to evaluate the routes generated in the previous phase based on each operator's geofence of knowledge and availability. Table 10 shows the results obtained.

Table 10. Results of the "Operator assignment" phase.

Vehicle (k)	Clients	Districts	Assigned operator	Coverage
C1O890	16	San Martin de Porres, Callao, Carmen de la Legua	1	81.18%
C9P856	4	Huacho, Hualmay	2	90.50%
F3V720	22	San Isidro, Jesus Maria, Lince	3	75.89%
A9L179	2	San Antonio	4	70.30%
A2K667	20	Rímac, San juan de Lurigancho, El Agustino	5	90.00%
A8N702	12	San Miguel, Bellavista	6	91.67%
H7B345	15	San Miguel, Bellavista, Callao	7	86.70%
A9U334	17	Magdalena del Mar, Pueblo Libre	8	82.65%
A5U779	12	San Juan de Lurigancho, Carabayllo	9	91.66%
B3U830	19	Comas, Los Olivos, San Martin de Porres	10	94.74%

(*continued*)

Table 10. (*continued*)

Vehicle (k)	Clients	Districts	Assigned operator	Coverage
C1O888	22	Santiago de Surco, San Borja, San Isidro	11	81.83%
PIK891	20	San Martin de Porres, Independencia, Los Olivos	12	75.00%
D1P877	20	Los Olivos, Comas, San Martin de Porres	13	85.00%
AUB922	16	San Juan de Miraflores, La Molina, Villa María del Triunfo	14	93.75%
A2I997	16	Carabayllo, Puente Piedra, Ventanilla	15	87.50%
H6K088	1	Lurigancho	16	100.00%
P1L864	15	Cercado de Lima, San Martin de Porres	17	93.33%
AT3776	14	Los Olivos, Callao	18	85.71%
A3U889	15	Miraflores, Chorrillos, Barranco	19	86.67%
A9M088	22	San Juan de Lurigancho, Santa Anita, Santiago de Surco	20	96.36%

In all cases, the assigned operators' percentage of coverage exceeds 70%, confirming that the assignment is correct. The algorithm chose the operator with the highest range for the evaluated route.

We evaluate the proposed model's performance in terms of execution time after validating each phase. Table 11 displays the execution times for each day of the sample.

Table 11. Execution times of the proposed model.

Proposed model				Current solution		
Days	Clients	Execution times (mn:ss)		Days	Clients	Execution times (mn:ss)
1	300	02:20		1	289	45:00
2	300	02:21		2	305	46:00
3	300	02:48		3	299	45:00
4	300	02:49		4	310	47:00
5	269	02:47		5	266	42:00

The model's average execution time is 02:37 (mm: ss), representing a 95% reduction compared to the case study's current solution, which runs at an average time of 45 min according to the owner of the process.

6   Conclusions and Future Work

A multiphase model based on the *K-means* and *ACO* algorithms was proposed in this paper to solve the *CVRPTW* in capillary logistics. The main contributions were: a model applicable to other case studies, the selection of algorithms that provide optimal performance in *CVRPTW*, the improvement of *K-means* by initializing it with the elbow method and *K-means++*, the use of the distance matrix in clustering and route generation, and the use of empirical knowledge of the operators.

The results demonstrated that using the proposed model reduces the execution time for route generation by 95% on average. Furthermore, it shortened the distance and time of travel by 182 km and 532 min, respectively. The model complied with the capacity and time constraints. The operators assigned to each route covered more than 70% of the delivery points.

Future research should apply the proposed model to other *VRP* variants in real-world scenarios. An improvement could be, the parameters: number of warehouses, the inclusion of a diverse fleet of vehicles, and partial deliveries should be configurable. Another significant improvement is implementing a learning module that dynamically manages the business rules, analyzes route execution data, and provides input that optimizes the results generated by the proposed model. Finally, implement new instances that support load balancing to test the model's scalability.

References

1. Žunić, E., Đonko, D., Buza, E.: An adaptive data-driven approach to solve real-world vehicle routing problems in logistics. Complexity (2020)
2. Cassettari, L., Demartini, M., Mosca, R., Revetria, R., Tonelli, F.: A Multi-Stage Algorithm for a Capacitated Vehicle Routing Problem with Time Constraints. Multidisciplinary Digital Publishing Institute (2018)
3. Dantzig, G., Ramser, J.: The truck dispatching problem. Manage. Sci. 6, 80–91 (1959)
4. Braekers, K., Ramaekers, K., Van, I.: The vehicle routing problem: State of the art classification and review. Comput. Ind. Eng. 99, 300–313 (2016)
5. Eksioglu, B., Vural, A., Reisman, R.: The vehicle routing problem: a taxonomic review. Comput. Ind. Eng. 57, 1472–1483 (2009)
6. Mutar, M., Burhanuddin, M., Hameed, A., Yusof, N., Mutashar, H.: An efficient improvement of ant colony system algorithm for handling capacity vehicle routing problem. Int. J. Ind. Eng. Comput. 11, 549–564 (2020)
7. Alfiyatin, N., Mahmudy, W., Anggodo, Y.: K-means clustering and genetic algorithm to solve vehicle routing problem with time windows problem. Indonesian J. Elect. Eng. Comput. Sci. 11, 462–468 (2018)
8. Calabrò, G., Torrisi, V., Inturri, G., Ignaccolo, M.: Improving inbound logistic planning for large-scale real-world routing problems: a novel ant-colony simulation-based optimization. Eur. Transp. Res. Rev. 12, 1–11 (2020). https://doi.org/10.1186/s12544-020-00409-7

9. Nicola, D., Vetschera, R., Dragomir, A.: Total distance approximations for routing solutions. Comput. Oper. Res. **102**, 67–74 (2018)
10. Florian, A., Michel, G., Kenneth, S.: Efficiently solving very large-scale routing problems. Comput. Oper. Res. **107**, 32–42 (2019)
11. Nuha, H., Wati, P., Widiasih, W.: A comparison of exact method - metaheuristic method in determination for vehicle routing problem. In: MATEC Web of Conferences, (2018)
12. Lukmandono, Basuki, M., Hidayat, M., Aji, F.: Application of saving matrix methods and cross entropy for capacitated vehicle routing problem (CVRP) resolving. In: IOP Conference Series: Materials Science and Engineering (2018)
13. Oudouar, F., El Fallahi, A., Zaoui, E.: An improved heuristic based on clustering and genetic algorithm for solving the multi-depot vehicle routing problem. J. Recent Technol. Eng. **8**, 6535–6540 (2019)
14. López, E., Rodriguez-Vásquez, W., Méndez, G.: A hybrid expert system, clustering and ant colony optimization approach for scheduling and routing problem in courier services. J. Ind. Eng. Comput. **9**, 369–396 (2018)
15. Muniz de Miranda, S., Maghrebi, M.: A more realistic approach towards concrete delivery dispatching problem: using real distance instead spatial distance. Aust. J. Civ. Eng. **16**, 1–11 (2018)
16. Wicaksono, P., Puspitasari, D., Ariyandanu, S., Hidayanti, R.: Comparison of simulated annealing, nearest neighbour, and tabu search methods to solve vehicle routing problems. In: IOP Conference Series: Earth and Environmental Science (2020)
17. Granada-Echeverri, M., Toro, E., Santa, J.: A mixed integer linear programming formulation for the vehicle routing problem with backhauls. J. Ind. Eng. Comput. **10**, 295–308 (2019)
18. Haitao, X., Pan, P., Feng, D.: Dynamic vehicle routing problems with enhanced ant colony optimization. discrete dynamics in nature and society (2018)
19. Gocken, T., Yaktubay, M.: Comparison of different clustering algorithms via genetic algorithm for VRPTW. Int. J. Simul. Model. **8**, 574–585 (2019)
20. Pérez, M., Loaiza, R., Flores, P., Ponce, P., Peralta, C.: A heuristic algorithm for the routing and scheduling problem with time windows: a case study of the automotive industry in Mexico. Algorithms (2019)
21. Cui, H., Ruan, G., Xue, J., Xie, R., Wang, L., Feng, X.: A collaborative divide-and-conquer K-means clustering algorithm for processing large data. In: Proceedings of the 11th ACM Conference on Computing Frontiers, New York (2014)
22. Malik, H., Amir, M., Mazhar, B., Ali, S., Jalil, R., Khalid, J.: A hybrid expert system, clustering and ant colony optimization approach for scheduling and routing problem in courier services. Int. J. Adv. Comput. Sci. Appl. **9**, 384–390 (2018)
23. Wang, L., Cai, J., Li, M., Liu, Z.: Flexible job shop scheduling problem using an improved ant colony optimization. Sci. Program. (2017)
24. Wong, L., Mauricio, D.S.: Qualities that the activities of the elicitation process must meet to obtain a good requirement. J. Eng. Sci. Technol. (JESTEC) **14**(5), 2883–2912 (2019)
25. The dataset used to support this paper is deposited in the following repository: https://git hub.com/MarcoHuancahuari/ttracerproject/blob/d77b555fb391d8bfd972b5232d6d4480b fc812c4/Sample%20Dataset%20TTRACER.xlsx

Enterprise Architecture Based on TOGAF for the Adaptation of Educational Institutions to e-Learning Using the DLPCA Methodology and Google Classroom

Geraldine Puntillo⬤, Alonso Salazar⬤, and Lenis Wong⁽⊠⁾⬤

Universidad Peruana de Ciencias Aplicadas, Lima 15023, Perú
lwongpuni@gmail.com

Abstract. Given the current situation of online classes, it is necessary to implement a Business Architecture model in order to facilitate the adaptation of virtual teaching, since 97.4% of teachers give up the use of information systems for learning. In addition, up to 80% of students experience stress with this new modality of learning. Based on this context, we can identify the gap in the adaptation to the virtual class process as a latent problem. Therefore, a model composed of 3 stages (Analysis, design, and validation) is proposed. Stage 1 includes the analysis of components on which the model will be developed. Stage 2 describes the Open Group Architecture Framework (TOGAF) on which the model will be developed, and the Discover, Learn, Practice, Collaborate, and Assignment (DLPCA) e-learning Methodology as the basis of the business process to be proposed. Finally, in stage 3, the model was validated in a private school in Lima with 70 students, 2 teachers, and 1 director, where it was shown that our proposal increased user satisfaction by 18.97%, positively increased adaptation to virtual classes by 28.50%, and also obtained a 75.34% acceptance of our proposal by the subjects of study, which shows the effectiveness of our solution to the problem.

Keywords: E-learning · Google classroom · TOGAF · Enterprise architecture · Educational institution

1 Introduction

For years there have been alarming data among private schools in Lima, for example is worrying that only 62% of these have access to Technology of the information and communication (ICTs) [1], 97.4% of teachers prefer physical materials due to their lack of knowledge about e-learning platforms [2], and 43.3% of teachers do not have a good management of their time as well as 51.2% of students [3]. Having access to this information, little has been done to combat this data until the emergence of the COVID19 pandemic, when the education sector decided to take action against this situation as it has been one of the most affected by this new normality [4].

Unfortunately, due to inadequate integration between their processes, current technology, and the people who manage them in schools, 90% of the student delayed the

J. A. Lossio-Ventura et al. (Eds.): SIMBig 2021, CCIS 1577, pp. 158–173, 2022.
https://doi.org/10.1007/978-3-031-04447-2_11

start of their classes following the onset of pandemic [5]. This is alarming because one year after this crossroads began, the great gap in the adaptation to the process of virtual teaching classes has not been able to be diminished. For example, in a study at National Autonomous University of Mexico (UNAM) it was detected that 5 platforms are used as communication resources, 8 platforms as academic work resources, 4 platforms as storage resources, and 7 platforms as synchronous work resources, all in a single educational institution causing an excess of excessive use of technologies and that increased stress in students by up to 80% [3]. A study was also carried out in all the national universities of Peru where it was found that 5 virtual education platforms, 4 instant messaging platforms, and 4 email platforms are used [6]. Therefore, it is relevant to undo or reduce this gap between the academic environment and the management of information technology.

As a result of this, proposals have emerged to reduce the problem, explaining the implementation of an enterprise architecture focused on business processes such as student enrolment and staff recruitment in order to automate their activities.

This shows that the problem exists and needs to be reduced, since by not decreasing the detected gap there is the threat of opening schools in a face-to-face way in the middle of the conjuncture as it is in countries of Chile, Uruguay, and Argentina despite the fact that the risk of infection has not decreased, this justifying itself in the elevation of academic dropout, the lack of access, and adaptation to ICTs [7].

It is worth mentioning that, the aforementioned proposals would not directly attack the detected problem instead our proposal will present an Enterprise Architecture aligned to the TOGAF framework [8] to follow the correct guidelines for its development, it will focus on the business process of delivering virtual classes based on the DLPCA e-learning Methodology [9] for the standardization of teaching and will be incorporated into the Google Classroom e-learning Platform [10] to meet the necessary criteria for student and teacher satisfaction.

The paper is organized in this way. Section 2 presents related works. The details of the stages of the proposed model (Stage 1, Stage 2, and Stage 3) are presented in Sect. 3. Section 4 presents the results of the project validation. Finally, the conclusions and future work are presented in Sect. 5.

2 Related Works

For the analysis of related work, a systematic review of the literature was conducted [11]. Starting with 4 questions related to e-learning methodologies, e-learning platforms, enterprise architectures, and factors that have affected distance learning: What e-learning methodologies and under what criteria have been applied in virtual classes? (Q1), What e-learning platforms and under what criteria have they been applied in virtual classes? (Q2), Which enterprise architecture models and under what criteria have they been applied in virtual classrooms? (Q3), and What factors affect learning in virtual classrooms? (Q4).

After that, the articles were searched in information sources such as: Scopus, ScienceDirect, and IEEE Xplorer; for which keywords such as: "e-learning", "satisfaction", "e-learning platforms", "e-learning methodologies", "EA frameworks", "Enterprise Architecture", "TOGAF", "Zachman", and "FEAF - Federal enterprise architecture " were used. The choice of the article depended on it being no more than 3 years old, belonging to Quartile 1 or Quartile 2 according to Scimago, and being a scientific article or book chapter.

It is also worth mentioning that, for the analysis of the articles, a taxonomy related to each of the questions initially posed was applied (see Table 1).

Table 1. Articles according to the proposed taxonomy.

Taxonomy	Source
Methodologies (Q1)	[9, 12–19]
Platforms (Q2)	[10, 14, 20–29]
Architectures (Q3)	[8, 30–32]
Factors (Q4)	[10, 12, 24, 26, 33–37]

Regarding the "methodologies" found, five were obtained, which are: DLPCA [9], the Collaborative [13], DynaMap Remediation Approach (DMRA) [14], the Integrative Methodology [12] and CUSIT [15]. The most relevant are DLPCA, Collaborative and DMRA; as they obtained a successful result in their case study. Therefore, these articles will serve as a reference when choosing the appropriate e-learning methodology, this choice will be based on the evaluation criteria that allow choosing a favorable e-learning methodology for those involved, [16–19].

On the other hand, with respect to the "platforms" found, five were obtained which are: Google Classroom [10, 20–22], Zoom [10, 23], Moodle [14, 24, 25], D2L Brightspace [21], and Google Meet [26]. The most relevant are Google Classroom and Moodle because they have a great potential to be applied in virtual classrooms, so these platforms will be analyzed for one of them to be used in the project based on the evaluation criteria that allow choosing the platform e-learning adaptable to our objective of the process of teaching virtual classes [27–29].

Likewise, with respect to the "architectures" found, the one based on TOGAF covers more processes and components relevant to our investigation [8]; while the other architecture based on Zachman is only referred to administrative management [30]. Because of this, we conclude that TOGAF would be the best option to implement the enterprise architecture of our project due to its holistic approach that has been evaluated under the necessary criteria [31, 32].

Finally, within the articles found, the most outstanding "factors" were: poor access to ICTs and low socio-economic status [33–38].

3 Proposed Model

This article proposes an enterprise architecture based on TOGAF that seeks to align the defined strategies to the process of teaching virtual classes using the DLPCA e-learning methodology. In addition, this process will be integrated to the e-learning platform Google Classroom and other platforms belonging to the Google G-suite to streamline and facilitate the management of distance learning.

For the development of the proposed enterprise architecture, 3 stages have been defined: Stage 1, Stage 2, and Stage 3 (see Fig. 1). In Stage 1 the analysis of the components is carried out, this will help to design the final artefact by accessing information about frameworks, e-learning methodologies, and e-learning platforms. In Stage 2, the design of the proposal is carried out, where the phases of the TOGAF framework will be developed. Finally, in Stage 3, the implementation of the proposed enterprise architecture will be defined and planned based on instruments such as Google Forms surveys.

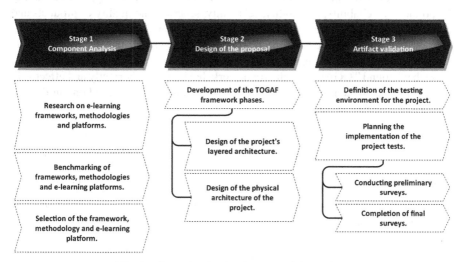

Fig. 1. Phases for the development of the project.

3.1 Stage 1: Component Analysis

Research on Frameworks, Methodologies, and e-Learning Platforms. For this first activity, four questions were formulated: What business architecture models and under what criteria have they been evaluated and applied in virtual classrooms? (Q1) What frameworks are used for learning in virtual classrooms? (Q2) What e-learning methodologies and under what criteria have they been evaluated and applied in virtual classes? (Q3), and What e-learning platforms and under what criteria have they been evaluated and applied in virtual classes? (Q4), obtaining a total of 22 articles.

For Q1, studies have been found that have used e-learning platforms for the management of academic progress but not as a tool for delivering the virtual classes themselves. In addition, they have focused on automating enrollment, attendance and assessment processes, but not the actual delivery of classes. Therefore, our differentiator from these proposals is the focus on the process of delivering virtual classes, the use of a learning methodology designed for e-learning and the incorporation of e-learning platforms that meet the necessary criteria of satisfaction.

That is why, in order to design our proposal it is pertinent to perform 3 benchmarking related to questions Q2, Q3, and Q4, where we analyze and select the best component that aligns to the desired proposal. It is worth mentioning that the 3 benchmarking will be based on the numerical Likert scale that allows the components to be evaluated within a range of values and not have as an option only the extremes (for example: yes or no) [39].

Benchmarking of Frameworks, Methodologies, and e-Learning Platforms. For question Q2, we performed a benchmarking on Table 2 of architecture frameworks where we evaluated 7 main quality attributes: alignment and integrity, maintainability and portability, reliability, reusability, scalability, security, and quality of products and services [31]. It has been evaluated from 0–5 on a Likert scale where 0 means does not comply, 5 if it complies and the intermediate numbers are the scale between the extremes. In addition, we compared the Zachman, TOGAF, and FEAF [31] frameworks, of which we found TOGAF to be the framework that integrates correctly and effectively with this project, since it is the framework with the highest score based on our defined comparison criteria (see Table 2).

Table 2. Benchmarking of architecture frameworks.

Criteria/framework	Zachman	TOGAF	FEAF
Alignment and integrity	5	5	5
Maintenance and portability	3	4	3
Reliability	5	5	5
Reuse	0	5	4
Scalability	5	5	3
Security	5	5	5
Quality of products and services	4	5	3
Total	27	34	28

For question Q3, we benchmark e-learning methodologies on Table 3 where we will evaluate 9 criteria, which are: general quality (QGEN), which encompasses quality of service (QSERV), system (QSIST), information (QINF), service compatibility (COMP), user satisfaction (SA), in actual use (USE), technology fit (TTF), and performance effect (PE) [16]. It has been evaluated from 0–5 on a Likert scale where 0 means does not comply, 5 if it complies and the intermediate numbers are the scale between the extremes. These criteria have been analyzed for DLPCA, Collaborative, and DMRA methodologies that were found in the previous analysis. After the necessary comparative, DLPCA was found as the e-learning methodology that integrates with this project in a better way (see Table 3), because, of the two methodologies with the highest score, in the case of DMRA we would need access to the prototype application with which its operation is supplied. Whereas, in the case of DLPCA it uses easily accessible platforms and also generates a positive impact on student learning.

Table 3. Benchmarking of e-learning methodologies.

Criteria/Methodology	DLPCA Methodology	Collaborative methodology	DMRA Methodology
System quality (QSIST)	5	3	5
Quality of information (QINF)	5	5	5
Quality of service (QSERV)	4	5	5
General quality (QGEN)	4	4	5
Compatibility (COMP)	5	5	4
Actual use (USE)	5	3	5
User satisfaction (SA)	5	2	5
Task technology framework (TTF)	5	4	4
Performance effect (PI)	5	5	5
Total	43	36	43

Finally, for Q4, a benchmarking of e-learning platforms on Table 4 was conducted where the learning approach, communication, and productivity were evaluated [27]. It has been evaluated from 0–1 on the Likert scale where 0 means does not comply and 5 if it complies. This was analysed for the e-learning platforms Moodle, Google Classroom, and SAKAI which are in the top 10 best e-learning platforms for virtual classes [27]. At the end of the comparison we have found Google Classroom as the e-learning platform that integrates with this project in a correct and effective way, since it is the e-learning platform with the highest score based on our selected comparison criteria (see Table 4).

Selection of the Framework, Methodology, and e-Learning Platform. The comparisons made in the respective benchmarking have given us the basis for the beginning of the design of our proposal, which is why in Stage 2 we will develop the TOGAF framework in integration with the selected DLPCA methodology and the Google Classroom platform.

3.2 Stage 2: Design of the Proposal

Development of the TOGAF Framework Phases. The first framework phase analysis activity consists of identifying the 9 phases of the TOGAF Architecture Development Method (ADM), from the Preliminary Phase to the Change Management Phase.

Preliminary Phase. For this first phase, the context analysis was carried out and the business requirements on which the business architecture will be designed were set out:

Table 4. Benchmarking of e-learning platforms.

Criteria/Platform	Subcriteria	Moodle	Google Classroom	Sakai
Learning	Enable Conferencing	1	1	1
	Allow examples and tasks, such as documents	1	1	1
	Allow assignments and exercises as quizzes	1	1	1
	Enable gamification	0	1	0
	Allows students to be assessed	1	1	1
Communication	Allow chat	1	1	1
	Allow Forums	1	1	1
	Allow sending e-mail messages	1	1	1
Productivity	Allows you to upload or download various types of documents	1	1	1
	Allows you to add, edit or delete data for students	1	1	1
	Allows analysis of student outcomes	1	1	1
	Features cross-platform support	1	1	1
	Features security and protection of user data	1	1	1
	Presents the creation of a backup copy of the data	1	1	1
	Allow a system administrator to manage all user roles on the platform	1	1	1
	Features web-based software development technology	1	1	1
	Allows you to use the online platform (installation required)	0	1	1
	Self Registration	1	1	1
Total		16	18	17

it is necessary to train teachers on the new information systems, reduce the excessive use of technologies, and standardize the use of e-learning platforms with similar interfaces to reduce the stress of adaptation of students and teachers. Then we will define the principles that would affect the development of the architecture: the same e-learning methodology should be maintained in all sections and the applications to be used should be unique for the same purpose.

Likewise, as one of the main activities of this stage we have the design of the architecture in layers, which will cover from the Architecture Vision to the Technological Architecture.

Phase A: Architecture Vision. In this phase the motivational layer of the layered architecture is defined. In Fig. 2, it will be observed how students, teachers, principals, and parents of private schools in Lima have been identified as Stakeholders, the 3 strategies (teacher training, group work, and implementation of asynchronous learning) that will support the achievement of specific objectives and the identification of access to ICT as the main constraint.

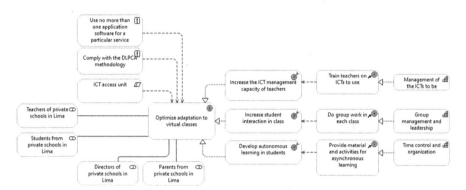

Fig. 2. Motivation layer.

Phase B: Business Architecture. For this phase the business layer is defined (see Fig. 3), where the business process "Process of teaching virtual classes" is proposed, which is directly related to the DLPCA e-learning methodology. This methodology has 5 sections (Discover, Learn, Practice, Collaborate, and Evaluate) and two more sections will be added: Training and Classroom creation, the Training section will help in solving the cause of the problem that describes how some teachers prefer the use of physical teaching materials because they do not have the proper training on the information systems and finally the class creation section will be necessary to interact with the selected e-learning platform (Google Classroom) and start teaching classes.

Phase C: Information Systems Architecture. Based on the design of the process described in the previous phase, it is necessary to connect with application components that provide the service of: Virtual Learning Space, Class Dictation, Communication Media, and Work Repository (see Fig. 4 and Fig. 5).

Phase D: Technological Architecture. For the technological layer, the four respective platforms were defined for each application service (Google Classroom, Google Meet, Gmail, and Google Drive) that can be accessed through a computer or mobile devices that must be updated periodically to access the necessary functionalities of the platforms (see Fig. 6).

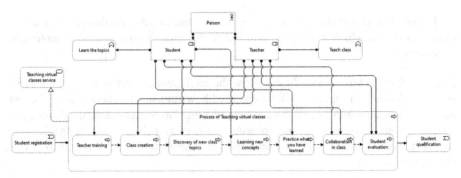

Fig. 3. Business layer.

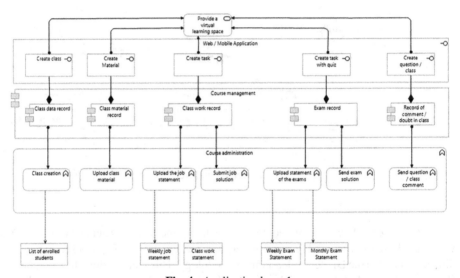

Fig. 4. Application layer 1.

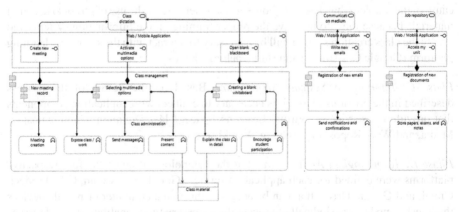

Fig. 5. Application layer 2.

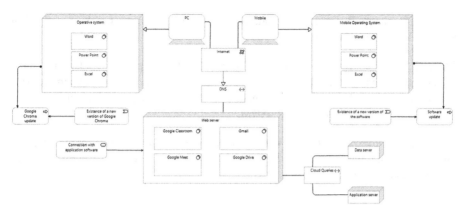

Fig. 6. Technology layer.

Also, within this phase D we have another key activity which is the design of the physical architecture that will be developed to support the technological layer (see Fig. 7) and demonstrate the access of e-learning platforms to their data in the cloud and the need to access the system software such as Word, Power Point, and Excel to properly develop virtual classes.

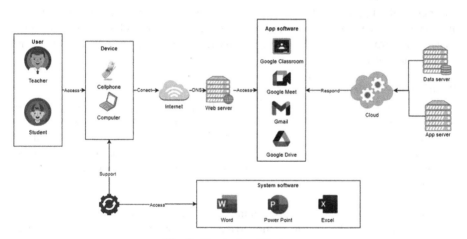

Fig. 7. Physical architecture.

Phase E: Opportunities and Solutions. For this phase we identified that all the proposed software is free and reusable for activities other than the process on which this enterprise architecture is focused, mostly for office, and administrative activities such as staff coordination meetings or meetings between students through Google Meet.

Phase F: Migration Planning. For this phase, due to the naturalness of the project, we will not make a migration plan but we will detail the implementation of the design proposed in phases B, C, and D. In addition, this implementation will be described in Stage 3: Validation of the artifact.

Phase G: Implementation Governance. This phase within our project is detailed in Stage 3: Validation of the artifact. for there is monitoring and supervision over the implementation and will ensure that the implementation is aligned to the proposed architecture as defined in this phase of the TOGAF ADM.

Phase H: Architecture Change Management. In this last phase, continuous post-implementation monitoring of the architecture is requested in order to be aware of and anticipate changes over time.

3.3   Stage 3: Artifact Validation

Definition of the Testing Environment for the Project. To start with the validation of the project it is important to define that the study will have as population the private schools of Lima, having as sample the private school of Lima "Miguel de Cervantes - Don Quijote" of the district of Puente Piedra, of which the subjects of study will be a director, two teachers of different courses and 4 sections of students of the same grade, all belonging to the same private school of Lima. Also, it is important to mention that before the implementation of the project, this school did not have any business architecture framework, it had a 4-step e-learning methodology (class creation, identify, analyze, and evaluate) that did not consider asynchronous sessions and used Edusys and Zoom as an e-learning platform.

Planning the Implementation of the Project Tests. To start with the implementation of the project, a meeting was scheduled with the principal, teachers, and students of the private school of Lima "Miguel de Cervantes - Don Quijote", during which an explanation of the structure designed for the proposed enterprise architecture was given. Once the principal accepted the implementation of the project in his school, the respective preliminary surveys were sent (see Table 5) to obtain the necessary data before the implementation of the project.

Likewise, it is worth mentioning that the proposed process in the business layer will be implemented from the training section to the collaboration section due to the time that the tests will take. Once the implementation and testing of this process was completed, all test participants were sent their final surveys (see Table 6).

4   Results and Discussion

The implementation of the project was carried out with a total of 70 students during 2 weeks of classes, with which 3 indicators were measured: %SAT (Satisfaction percentage), %ADP (Adaptation percentage) and %ACP (Adaptation percentage) where we obtained favorable results since it was demonstrated that our proposal increased by 18.97% the user satisfaction increased positively by 28.50% the adaptation to virtual

Table 5. Preliminary survey questions.

Question
Are you satisfied with the current process of teaching virtual classes?
Are you satisfied with the policies and mechanisms in place to encourage student participation?
Do you consider that the platforms contribute to the teacher's explanation?
Do you think that students' performance has decreased after the implementation of virtual classes?
From which device did you connect to the virtual classroom?
Was it easy for you to adapt to virtual classes?
What difficulties did you encounter when teaching your virtual classes?
Have you actively participated in the courses during your virtual classes?
If yes, how much have you participated in the courses?
Do you understand the topics of the subjects when you are in virtual classes with the current methodology?
Would you recommend using the same methodology to all teachers?
How did you feel when you started your virtual classes? (You can check more than one option)

Table 6. Final survey questions.

Question
Do you think that Enterprise Architecture has improved the adaptation to virtual classrooms?
Are you satisfied with the policies and mechanisms in place to encourage student participation?
Do you feel that the platforms have been underst, able, and appropriate?
Do you think that with the implementation of our process of teaching virtual classes the performance of the students could be equivalent to when the classes were face-to-face?
In terms of how virtual classes were given before, did you find it easy to adapt to this new methodology?
What difficulty did you encounter in the test class?
Have you actively participated during the trial period of the course?
Do you underst the topics of the subjects when you are in virtual classes with the methodology in test?
How did you feel during the trial period of the course? (You can check more than one option)
Do you think that all teachers using the same methodology would facilitate their learning?

classes, and an acceptance of 75.34% of our proposal was also obtained by the subjects of study (see Table 7).

For the %SAT indicator, 3 measurement factors (participation, understanding, and use of platforms) were considered, in which an increase in satisfaction was obtained of

Table 7. Validation results.

Process: Delivering Virtual Classes	
INDICATORS	RESULTS
%SAT: Increase in the % of user satisfaction	18.97%
%SAPA (Satisfaction percentage based on participation): Increase in % of user satisfaction based on participation	25.50%
%SAEN (Satisfaction percentage based on understanding): Increase in the % of student satisfaction based on understanding	27.10%
%SAPL (Satisfaction percentage based on platforms): Increase in % of student satisfaction based on platforms	4.30%
%ADP: Increase of the % of user adaptation	28.50%
Process: Project Implementation	
INDICATORS	RESULTS
%ACP: % of majority acceptance of the submitted proposal	75.34%

25.50%, 27.10%, and 4.30% respectively. This allowed the %SAT to increase by 18.97% with the implementation of the Project.

Regarding the %ADP indicator, we obtained an increase of 28.50% of adaptation to virtual classes with our proposal, which directly reduces the gap detected in the analysis of the problem of the project.

And on the %ACP indicator, a total of 75.34% of acceptance and conformity to our proposal was obtained, so that it can be implemented with the support of stakeholders.

It should also be noted that before implementation, the existence of the exposed problem could be validated since it was obtained that 68.6% of the students had difficulties adapting to virtual classes, 63% experienced stress and fatigue and both teachers surveyed agreed that they did not there is sufficient training on the information systems they use.

5 Conclusions and Future Work

For the present project an analysis was carried out based on four key questions that define the main components to be used and integrated within the proposed Enterprise Architecture. After choosing the TOGAF framework, the DLPCA e-learning Methodology, and the Google Classroom e-learning Platform, the design of the architecture in layers of the proposal is carried out, defining in the motivation layer the strategies, the restrictions, and the Stakeholders of the business, Then, in the business layer the process of teaching virtual classes integrated to the selected e-learning methodology is proposed, in the application layer the application services that will be integrated to the proposed business process will be defined and finally in the technology layer the e-learning platforms such as Google Classroom that will support the defined application services are defined. For the validation of this project, it was necessary to consider groups of students from different sections to have a better view of the results.

Also, as a conclusion of the tests carried out during the validation period, the main result obtained was an increase of 28.5% in the adaptation to the teaching of virtual classes involving user acceptance based on participation, understanding, and chosen platforms.

Finally, for future work it is recommended to analyze platforms that support the security of information exchange between teachers and students through e-learning platforms, as this aspect is also a fundamental part of the problem and should be studied in detail. It will also be important to carry out the validation with a sample of 89 private schools in Lima based on a population of 1200 schools, since in the present work the ideal sample was not achieved due to time factors.

References

1. Arias Gallegos, W.L.: Tecnologías de la información y la comunicación en colegios públicos y privados de Arequipa. Interacciones **1**, 11–28 (2015)
2. Tafur Puente, R., de la Vega Ramirez, A.: El acceso a los recursos educativos por los docentes de educación secundaria: un estudio exploratorio. Educación **XIX**(37), 29–46 (2018)
3. Sánchez Mendiola, M., et al.: Rendón Cazales, Retos educativos durante la pandemia de COVID-19: una encuesta a profesores de la UNAM, Mexico: Revista Digital Universitaria (2020)
4. Britez, M.: La educación ante el avance del COVID-19 en Paraguay, Paraguay: Scientific Electronic Library Online (2020)
5. UNESCO, Cómo estás aprendiendo durante la pandemia de COVID-19?, 07 07 2020. https://es.unesco.org/covid19/
6. Gómez Arteta, I., Escobar Mamani, F.: Educación virtual en tiempos de pandemia: incremento de la desigualdad social en el perú, Lima: SciELO Preprint (2021)
7. FRANCE24, "FRANCE 24," 04 03 2021. https://www.france24.com/es/am%C3%A9rica-latina/20210304-regreso-clases-presenciales-chile-uruguay-argentina
8. Moscoso-Zea, O., Castro, J., Paredes-Gualtor, J., Luján-Mora, S.: A hybrid infrastructure of enterprise architecture and business intelligence & analytics for knowledge management in education. IEEE Access, pp. 1–12 (2019)
9. Lapitan, L., Tiangco, C., Sumalinog, D., Sabarillo, N., Diaz, J.: An effective blended online teaching and learning strategy during the COVID-19 pandemic. Education for Chemical Engineers, pp. 116–131 (2021)
10. Asanov, I., Flores, F., McKenzie, D., Mensmann, M., Schulte, M.: Remote-learning, time-use and mental health of Ecuadorian high-school students during the COVID-19 quarantine. World Development, p. 1–9 (2021)
11. Wong, L., Mauricio, D., Rodriguez, G.: A systematic literature review about software requirements elicitation. J. Eng. Sci. Technol. **12**, 296–317 (2017)
12. Money, W.H., Dean, B.P.: Incorporating student population differences for effective online education: a content-based review and integrative model. Comput. Educ. **138**, 57–82 (2019)
13. Herrera-Pavo, M.Á.: Collaborative learning for virtual higher education. Learning, Culture, and Social Interaction, pp. 1–11 (2021)
14. Marzano, A., Miranda, S.: The DynaMap Remediation Approach (DMRA) in online learning environments. Comput. Educ. 162, 1–30 (2021)
15. Habib, M.N., Jamal, W., Khalil, U., Khan, Z.: Transforming universities in interactive digital platform: case of city university of science and information technology. Educ. Inf. Technol. **26**, 517–541 (2020)

16. Isaac, O., Aldholay, A., Abdullah, Z., Ramayahd, T.: Online learning usage within Yemeni higher education: the role of compatibility and task-technology fit as mediating variables in the IS success model. Comput. Educ. **136**, 113–129 (2019)
17. Rajhans, V., Memon, U., Patil, V., Goyal, A.: Impact of COVID-19 on academic activities and way forward in Indian Optometry. J. Optometry **13**, 216–226 (2020)
18. Vasconcelos, P., Sucupira, E., Plácido Pinheiro, F., Furtado, L.: Multidisciplinary criteria for the quality of e-learning services design. Computers in Human Behavior, pp. 1–12 (2020)
19. Peñarrubia-Lozano, C., Segura-Berges, M., Lizalde-Gil, M., Bustamante, J.C.: A qualitative analysis of implementing e-learning during the covid-19 lockdown. Sustainability (Switzerland), pp. 1–28 (2021)
20. Abdullah, M.H., Sulong, M.A., Rahim, M.A.: Development and validation of the music education teaching practice e-supervision system using the google classroom application. Int. J. Innov. Creativity Change **11**, 102–116 (2020)
21. Francom, G.M., Schwan, A., Nuatomue, J.N.: Comparing Google classroom and D2L brightspace using the technology acceptance model. TechTrends **65**, 111–119 (2020)
22. Kumar, J.A., Bervell, B.: Google Classroom for mobile learning in higher education: Modelling the initial perceptions of students. Education and Information Technologies, pp. 1–25 (2019)
23. Joia, L.A., Lorenzo, M.: Zoom In, Zoom Out: The Impact of the COVID-19 Pandemic in the Classroom. Sustainability, pp. 1–18 (2021)
24. Milićević, V., et al.: E-learning perspectives in higher education institutions. Technological Forecasting and Social Change, pp. 1–5 (2021)
25. Costa, A., Costa, A., Olsson, I.A.S.: Students' acceptance of e-learning approaches in Laboratory Animal Science Training. Laboratory Animals, pp. 487–497 (2020)
26. Qazi, A., et al.: Conventional to online education during COVID-19 pandemic: Do develop and underdeveloped nations cope alike. Children and Youth Services Review, pp. 1–22 (2020)
27. Kraleva, R., Sabani, M., Kralev, V.: An analysis of some learning management systems. Int. J. Adv. Sci. Eng. Inf. Technol. **9**, 1190–1198 (2019)
28. Jeong, J.S., González-Gómez, D.: Assessment of sustainability science education criteria in online-learning through fuzzy-operational, multi-decision analysis, and professional survey. Heliyon **6**, 1–11 (2020)
29. Al-Fraihat, D., Joy, M., Masa'deh, R., Sinclair, J.: Evaluating E-learning systems success: an empirical study. Comput. Hum. Behav. **102**, 67–86 (2020)
30. Setyawan, A.H., Atmaja, R.A., Wang, G., Legowo, N.: Designing effective E-learning system in Kanisius school with Zachman framework. Int. J. Adv. Trends Comput. Sci. Eng. **9**, 2619–2624 (2020)
31. Mirsalaria, S.R., Ranjbarfard, M.: A model for evaluation of enterprise architecture quality. Eval. Program Plann. **60**, 1–12 (2020)
32. Shanks, G., Gloet, M., Asadi Someh, I., Frampton, K., Tamm, T.: Achieving benefits with enterprise architecture. J. Strategic Inf. Syst. **27**, 139–156 (2018)
33. Catalano, A.J., Torff, B., Anderson, K.S.: Transitioning to online learning during the COVID-19 pandemic: differences in access and participation among students in disadvantaged school districts. Int. J. Inf. Learn. Technol., 258–270 (2021)
34. Anakwe, A., Majee, W., Noel-London, K., Zachary, I., Belue, R.: Sink or swim: Virtual life challenges among African American families during covid-19 lockdown. Int. J. Environ. Res. Public Health, 1–12 (2021)
35. Izzeddin, A., RN, Ph.D.: Nursing students' and faculty members' perspectives about online learning during COVID-19 pandemic: a qualitative study. Teaching and Learning in Nursing, pp. 12–17 (2021)
36. Yang-Feng, G., et al.: Physical activity, screen exposure, and sleep among students during the pandemic of COVID-19. Scientific Reports, pp. 1–12 (2021)

37. Soeren Torrau, J.: Exploring teaching and learning about the Corona crisis in social studies webinars. J. Soc. Sci. Educ., 15–29 (2020)
38. Almetwazi, M., Alzoman, N., Al-Massarani, S., Alshamsan, A.: COVID-19 impact on pharmacy education in Saudi Arabia: Challenges and opportunities Saudi Pharmaceutical J., 1431–1434 (2020)
39. Wu, H., Leung, S.-O.: Se pueden tratar las escalas Likert como escalas de intervalo?. J. Soc. Serv. Res. (2017)

Quality Model for Educational Mobile Apps Based on SQuaRE and AHP

Pablo Del Aguila(ID), Dante Roque(ID), and Lenis Wong$^{(\boxtimes)}$ (ID)

Universidad Peruana de Ciencias Aplicadas, Lima 15023, Perú
lwongpuni@gmail.com

Abstract. During the last decade, there has been an increase in the demand of mobile apps in different download platforms, like Google Play Store, Apple App Store and Amazon App Store. Because of this, different approaches related to mobile app quality have surged, which tend to focus on assessing the general quality of an app without focusing on a specific sector. Because of this reason, the motivation to develop a quality model for mobile apps for the educational sector arises, using the System and Software Quality Requirements and Evaluation (SQuaRE) guidelines and the Analytic Hierarchy Process (AHP) weighting technique; the latter was used to prioritize the quality attributes. A quality model has been obtained, which consists of 8 characteristics, 19 sub-characteristics and 30 metrics. In order to corroborate the proposed model, 4 research questions and 2 case studies related to 2 mobile apps have been established. The results proved that *Google Classroom* and *Moodle* have very similar scores in each assessed characteristic; in the case of *Usability*, there is a difference of 0.006 in favor of *Moodle*, for *Portability*, there is a difference of 0.150 in favor of *Google Classroom*, and for *Security*, regarding authentication rules and mechanisms, both apps obtained the same result.

Keywords: Mobile apps · Quality model · Education · SQuaRE · AHP

1 Introduction

During the last decade, the demand of mobile apps has increased, and app stores have turned into a channel that leads the spread of mobile app products [1]. In 2017, there were around 3.5 million mobile apps on Google Play, around 2.2 million on Apple App Store, and around 385 thousand mobile apps on Amazon App Store [1].

Due to this demand, it is important to meet new software requirements, adapt to the new technological platforms and correct mistakes or improve the software's design. However, if this is not accomplished in an efficient way, the costs of software development and maintenance could be higher than expected. Some studies show that costs associated with software maintenance and development vary between 50% and 90% of the total cost, while other studies show that these costs are higher than the cost of the software's first version [2].

In addition, according to a survey done by Perfecto Mobile, it was shown that 44% of mobile app quality assurance (QA) comes from users [3]. The study also shows the most

© The Author(s), under exclusive license to Springer Nature Switzerland AG 2022
J. A. Lossio-Ventura et al. (Eds.): SIMBig 2021, CCIS 1577, pp. 174–186, 2022.
https://doi.org/10.1007/978-3-031-04447-2_12

frequent types of issues that are identified at the time of assessing mobile apps from the user's perspective. Among these, we have: issues related to user interface, which represent 58% of the cases, performance issues represent 52%, and device compatibility issues represent 45% [3].

There exist many approaches related to these issues. Gezici [2] proposed exploring the existing relationships between the external and internal quality of mobile apps, which he determined through comprehension of the relationship between metrics and established quality characteristics. Another approach that stands out is Mutia's [4], which evaluates the results of the maintainability quality measurements of the Study Plan Forms module on the myITS mobile app.

However, despite the existence of multiple approaches that focus on solving the problem, most of them only focus on one specific quality characteristic, while others focus on assessing the general quality of an app without focusing on a specific sector. For this reason, we propose an optimized mobile app quality model based on the SQuaRE [5] guidelines and the AHP weighting technique [6], which will allow assessing the quality of a mobile app of a specific sector through the prioritization of the essential quality characteristics, sub-characteristics and metrics for that type of mobile app.

This study is structured as follows. Section 2 describes work related to the topic of research. Section 3 shows the development of the proposed quality model. Section 4 presents the validation and execution of the model. Section 5 shows the compilation of the results obtained after having carried out the validation of the model. And finally, Sect. 6 presents the conclusions and related future work.

2   Related Work

Several studies had used the ISO/IEC 25010 [2, 8] and ISO/IEC 9126 [8–10] models for the quality assurance of mobile apps. Gezici et al. [2] apply ISO/IEC 25010 for the assessment of internal and external quality of open-source mobile apps. Manglapuz and Lacatan [8] also use this model, but to measure the performance of an Android app focused on the analysis of academic performance. Temkar and Bhaskar [10] apply AHP and ISO/IEC 9126 for the quality assurance of IoT apps.

In addition, different quality attributes have been considered for the quality assurance of mobile apps, such as characteristics and sub-characteristics. The following characteristics were found: reliability [2, 8, 11], usability [4, 8, 9], performance efficiency [4, 8, 11], security [8, 9, 12], functional suitability [8, 11, 12], compatibility [2, 9, 11], portability [2, 4, 9], maintainability [4, 8, 12], accuracy [8, 9, 11], flexibility [8, 12, 13] and interoperability [4, 9, 13]. And the following sub-characteristics were found: Learnability [2, 11, 12], Operability [2, 4, 8], Adaptability [9, 12, 13], Time Behavior [2, 8, 9], Fault Tolerance [8, 11, 13], Resource Utilization [2, 8, 13], Functional Completeness [4, 9, 11], Maturity [8, 9, 13], Accessibility [2, 8, 9], and Coexistence [2, 9, 12]. Finally, it was evidenced that the metrics were different for each author. In one of the paper [8] attributes were used for the quality assurance of an educational app.

It is important to mention that none of these studies were focused on the quality assurance of mobile apps directed to the educational sector.

3   Proposed Quality Model

The proposed model will be based on the characteristics, sub-characteristics and metrics established on the ISO/IEC 25000 standards (SQuaRE) and the AHP technique will be used to determine the weight of each of these quality attribute on the quality of mobile apps directed to the educational sector. The technique will be applied through the tool Super Decisions [14] by the selected experts. To design the model, a process was designed with the following activities: (1) Compilation of mobile app quality models, (2) Unification of characteristics and sub-characteristics, (3) Selection of experts in mobile app development and/or QA, (4) Prioritization of characteristics, sub-characteristics, and metrics, and (5) Obtaining the definitive quality model.

3.1   Quality Model Compilation

This section shows the quality models that were found in the state of the art. A total of 2 mobile app quality models have been obtained: ISO/IEC 25010 [7], in which 8 characteristics were identified (Functional suitability, Performance efficiency, Compatibility, Usability, Reliability, Security, Maintainability, and Portability), and ISO/IEC 9126 [15], which contained 7 characteristics (Functional suitability, Performance efficiency, Usability, Reliability, Maintainability, Portability, and Accuracy).

3.2   Unification of Characteristics and Sub-characteristics

Considering the critical analysis from each author of the quality models that were mentioned in Table 2, similarities were found between the sub-characteristics of each selected quality model regarding mobile app quality. One example of this is the term "Attractiveness" being used instead of "User Interface Aesthetics" in one of the analyzed papers [13]. With the list completed, 47 sub-characteristics were mentioned, which were unified afterwards, bringing the number down to 33 sub-characteristics.

3.3   Selection of Experts in Mobile Apps

Through the non-probabilistic snowball technique, used when respondents are hard to find [16], experts in IT, QA and mobile app development were contacted. A questionnaire was designed with the following selection criteria: Expert area of specialty, Years of experience by specialty and Quality model (ISO/IEC 25010 and ISO/IEC 9126). Each expert signed a consent form [17]. Based on the selection criteria, 5 out of 7 experts were selected, since they are specialized in mobile app development and are specialists in ISO/IEC 25010.

3.4   Prioritizing Characteristics, Sub-characteristics and Metrics with AHP

This section addresses the approach to apply the multi-criteria decision in the weighting of mobile app quality characteristics, sub-characteristics and metrics. For this, a process from Saaty [6] was used, which consists of 3 steps: structuring the problem hierarchy, making value judgments and calculating weights.

Hierarchy for Prioritization. Figure 1 shows the decision hierarchical tree composed of 3 levels. Level 0 represents the quality model (objective). Level 2 represents the 8 characteristics (criteria). Level 2 represents the 31 sub-characteristics (sub-criteria). Level 3 represents the 86-quality metrics (alternatives).

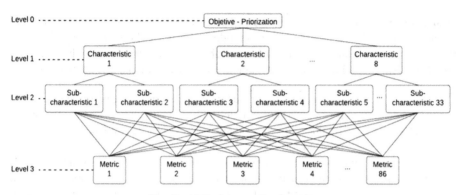

Fig. 1. AHP conceptualization [6].

Selecting a Tool. A comparison was carried out for 10 tools that focus on applying the AHP technique. For this, 2 criteria were considered: tool cost and whether it is a desktop or online application. The tool "SuperDecisions" was selected, due to it being free to use, being a desktop app and being constantly updated.

Figure 2 shows the hierarchy for the prioritization of characteristics, sub-characteristics and metrics with the *SuperDecisions* tool. For this, a cluster was made with the name "Objective: Prioritizing Characteristics, Sub-characteristics and Metrics",

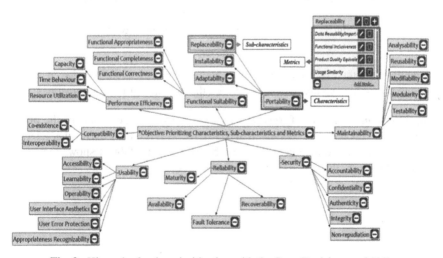

Fig. 2. Hierarchy for the prioritization with the SuperDecisions tool [14].

which is composed of a node named "Perceived Weight" (numeric value that the expert subjectively gives to each characteristic, sub-characteristic and metric). This node joins the "Objective" cluster with each of the 8 clusters that represent the SQuaRE quality characteristics; it also represents the weight of each one. In a similar manner, the rest of the clusters represent the quality sub-characteristics and metrics.

Prioritization by the Experts. Through a 1-h session, the experts were explained about the tool they would use and the type of mobile app they would focus on, by following these steps: (a) Introduction of a demo video about the tool, (b) Sending the AHP tool and its credentials and (c) Document that contains key definitions and Saaty scale.

After the training session, each expert subjectively registered the perceived weight of each characteristic, sub-characteristic and metric. Each expert was instructed to register their preferred numeric value, since the values for the prioritization would be extracted from these results. This lasted for 1 h.

Figure 3 shows the Judgement tab, in which the "Objective" cluster must be selected to carry out the assessment of quality characteristics with the "Direct" option, in which each characteristic was qualified in a 1 to 9 scale (higher number, more importance). Sub-characteristics and metrics were assessed in the same manner.

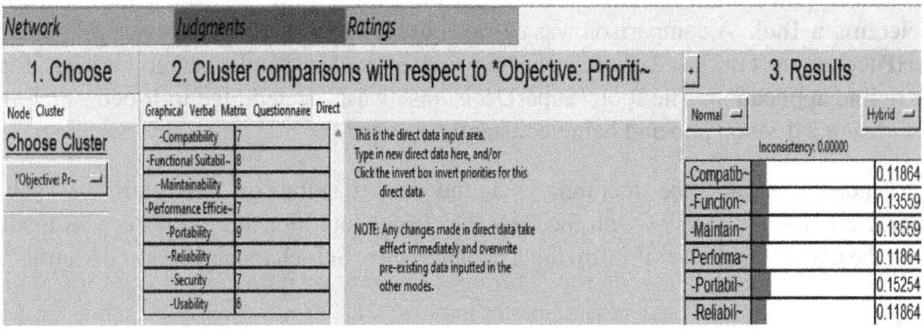

Fig. 3. Quality characteristic assessment interface [14].

Finally, once the experts were finished with the prioritization, they saved and sent the file to the authors so that they can compile the obtained prioritization values.

Compilation and Analysis of Results: This section shows the results of the prioritization process. Each expert was given an ID (E1, E2, E3, E4, E5). The characteristics were subjectively given a perceived weight by each expert. Table 1 shows the average result obtained from the experts for each characteristic (C).

Table 1. Prioritization of quality characteristics.

C	E1	E2	E3	E4	E5	Avg.
Usability (C1)	0.1400	0.1356	0.1200	0.1552	0.1111	0.1324
Portability (C2)	0.1800	0.1017	0.1200	0.1379	0.1111	0.1301
Security (C3)	0.1400	0.1186	0.1200	0.1207	0.1429	0.1284
Functional Suitability (C4)	0.1000	0.1186	0.1600	0.1207	0.1429	0.1284
Performance Efficiency (C5)	0.1400	0.1186	0.1000	0.1379	0.1111	0.1215
Compatibility (C6)	0.1400	0.1186	0.1000	0.1207	0.1270	0.1213
Reliability (C7)	0.1000	0.1525	0.1400	0.0862	0.1270	0.1211
Maintainability (C8)	0.0600	0.1356	0.1400	0.1207	0.1270	0.1167

Table 2 shows the 6 sub-characteristics (S) with the highest perceived weight out of a total of 33. In the same way, Table 3 shows the top 10 metrics (M) out of a total of 86.

Table 2. Prioritization of quality sub-characteristics.

C	S	E1	E2	E3	E4	E5	Avg.
C1	Learnability (S1)	0.0059	0.0039	0.0039	0.0078	0.0035	0.0050
C1	Operability (S2)	0.0056	0.0051	0.0043	0.0059	0.0037	0.0049
C1	Accessibility (S3)	0.0040	0.0062	0.0041	0.0064	0.0036	0.0048
C2	Adaptability (S4)	0.0058	0.0037	0.0043	0.0062	0.0040	0.0048
C1	User Error Protection (S5)	0.0048	0.0050	0.0044	0.0061	0.0037	0.0048
C3	Authenticity (S6)	0.0075	0.0032	0.0037	0.0055	0.0036	0.0047

Table 3. Prioritization of quality metrics.

C	S	M	E1	E2	E3	E4	E5	Avg.
C1	S1	User guidance completeness (M1)	0.0027	0.0033	0.0027	0.0035	0.0027	0.0030
C1	S1	Error messages understandability (M2)	0.0027	0.0023	0.0028	0.0040	0.0025	0.0028
C1	S2	Understandable categorization of information (M3)	0.0038	0.0030	0.0024	0.0029	0.0020	0.0028
C1	S2	Functional customizability (M4)	0.0012	0.0023	0.0017	0.0061	0.0017	0.0026

(*continued*)

Table 3. (*continued*)

C	S	M	E1	E2	E3	E4	E5	Avg.
C1	S3	Supported languages adequacy (M5)	0.0031	0.0026	0.0019	0.0031	0.0018	0.0025
C2	S4	Operational environment adaptability (M6)	0.0020	0.0025	0.0018	0.0034	0.0017	0.0023
C1	S5	User error recoverability (M7)	0.0016	0.0029	0.0021	0.0027	0.0017	0.0022
C2	S4	Hardware environmental adaptability (M8)	0.0028	0.0022	0.0021	0.0024	0.0015	0.0022
C3	S6	Authentication rules conformity (M9)	0.0023	0.0019	0.0018	0.0026	0.0022	0.0022
C3	S6	Authentication mechanism sufficiency (M10)	0.0022	0.0020	0.0022	0.0019	0.0023	0.0021

3.5   Obtaining the Quality Model

Table 4 shows the list of characteristics, sub-characteristics, and metrics with their respective average weight and ordered from highest to lowest. Only the top 30 metrics with the highest weights were selected. This was the case due to the limited time dedicated to this study, as well as following the time suggested by Humprey [18] for the testing of mobile apps. Therefore, the obtained mobile app quality model focused on the educational sector is composed of 8 characteristics (C1–C8), 19 sub-characteristics (S1–S19), and 30 metrics (M1–M30).

Table 4. Obtained final quality model.

C	S	M	Weight (Avg.)	Order	C	S	M	Weight (Avg.)	Order
C1	S1	M1	0.0030	1	C3	S10	M16	0.0018	16
C1	S1	M2	0.0028	2	C2	S9	M17	0.0018	17
C1	S2	M3	0.0028	3	C5	S10	M18	0.0018	18
C1	S2	M4	0.0026	4	C4	S11	M19	0.0018	19
C1	S3	M5	0.0025	5	C5	S12	M20	0.0017	20
C2	S4	M6	0.0023	6	C6	S13	M21	0.0017	21
C1	S5	M7	0.0022	7	C3	S14	M22	0.0017	22
C2	S4	M8	0.0022	8	C7	S15	M23	0.0016	23

(*continued*)

Table 4. (*continued*)

C	S	M	Weight (Avg.)	Order	C	S	M	Weight (Avg.)	Order
C3	S6	M9	0.0022	9	C1	S16	M24	0.0016	24
C3	S6	M10	0.0021	10	C7	S15	M25	0.0016	25
C4	S7	M11	0.0021	11	C7	S17	M26	0.0016	26
C5	S8	M12	0.0019	12	C8	S18	M27	0.0015	27
C5	S8	M13	0.0019	13	C8	S19	M28	0.0015	28
C2	S9	M14	0.0019	14	C8	S18	M29	0.0015	29
C5	S8	M15	0.0018	15	C8	S19	M30	0.0015	30

4 Experimentation

In this section, an experiment will be carried out to test the proposed mobile app quality model, only considering mobile apps for the educational sector. To accomplish this, 4 key activities will be applied, which will be explained bellow.

4.1 Selection of Cases of Study

Table 5 shows the most used mobile apps on the educational sector during the pandemic and the evolution of technologies, which were found in research articles and literature reviews. For this, a review of 8 articles was carried out, and for the selection of the mobile apps the following criteria was considered: (a) Article frequency, (b) Type of institution (c) App cost.

Table 5. Selection of mobile apps

Mobile app for education	Article frequency	Type of institution	App cost
Google Classroom	[19–25]	Educational	Free
Quizizz	[23]	Educational	30$/month – free
Edmodo	[22, 23]	Educational	Free
Moodle	[21–23, 25, 26]	Educational	Free
Google Meet	[20, 23, 24]	Business	6$/month – free
Zoom	[19–21, 23–25]	Business	15$/month – free
Blackboard	[21]	Educational	Free
Microsoft Team	[22]	Business	5$/month – free

From the comparison of the 10 mobile apps considered for the selection of cases of study, the "Google Classroom" and "Moodle" apps were selected, since their frequency in articles were of 7 and 5 respectively. Aside from this, their use is mostly centered in educational purposes and are completely free.

4.2 Experimental Definition and Planning

The objective of this experiment consisted of comparing the quality attributes of two education apps, which are "Google Classroom" and "Moodle". The experiment was carried out from the perspective of researchers and professionals that are testers interested in research on a mobile app quality model.

Selection of Quality Attributes. In this section, the quality characteristics, sub-characteristics and metrics will be selected based on the proposed mobile app quality model, since while obtaining said model prioritizations and analyses were carried out, from which the top 30 metrics were selected (see Table 6). The top 10 metrics will be used to validate the attributes of the model, since assessing 30 metrics would take too long for our approach and for experts.

Defining Research Questions. Next is the description of the research questions that were defined for this study, which were extracted from the selection of the quality attributes:

- Question 1: Is the usability of the "Google Classroom" mobile app similar to that of "Moodle"? Usability is measured by user guide completeness, error messages understandability, understandable categorization of information. *Hypothesis = The Google Classroom and Moodle mobile apps have similar usability.*
- Question 2: Is the portability of the "Google Classroom" mobile app similar to that of "Moodle"? Portability is measured by operational environment adaptability and hardware environmental adaptability. *Hypothesis = The Google Classroom and Moodle mobile apps have similar portability.*
- Question 3: Is the security of the "Google Classroom" mobile app similar to that of "Moodle"? Security is measured by authentication rules conformity and authentication mechanism sufficiency. *Hypothesis = The Google Classroom and Moodle mobile apps have similar security.*
- Question 4: Have the selected quality attributes been adequate for the assessment of mobile apps of the educational sector? *Hypothesis = The selected quality attributes are adequate for the assessment of mobile apps for the educational sector.*

Definition of Metrics. The 10 metrics that were previously mentioned have been defined based on the ISO/IEC 25023 standard [27] and their respective criteria: purpose, application method, formula, desired value, measure type and utilized resource.

4.3 Execution of the Mobile App Assessment

To execute the assessment, each characteristic, sub-characteristic, and metric would be evaluated according to the order of priority that resulted from obtaining the optimized quality model (see Table 6).

Assessment of Mobile Apps By the Experts. A procedure was defined for the experiment, which lasted for an hour and consisted of the following activities: introduction to the quality model, completion of a knowledge test, filling a demographic questionnaire, assessment of the mobile apps, filling an act with post-experiment observations.

4.4 Analysis of Results

This section shows the values obtained from each expert and how they were averaged at the level of metrics, sub-characteristics, and characteristics for the "Google Classroom" and "Moodle" mobile apps (see Table 6 and Table 7).

Table 6. Results for the Google Classroom app

Attributes			Testers			Attribute averages		
C	S	M	T1	T2	T3	M	S	C
C1	S1	M1	0.6667	1.0000	0.7105	0.7924	0.8052	0.8874
		M2	1.0000	0.8824	0.5714	0.8179		
	S2	M3	0.6000	1.0000	0.5385	0.7128	0.7444	
		M4	0.8000	0.9091	0.6190	0.7760		
	S3	M5	1.0000	1.0000	1.0000	1.0000	1.0000	
	S5	M7	1.0000	1.0000	1.0000	1.0000	1.0000	
C2	S4	M6	0.3333	1.0000	1.0000	0.7778	0.8056	0.8056
		M8	0.5000	1.0000	1.0000	0.8333		
C3	S6	M9	1.0000	1.0000	1.0000	1.0000	1.0000	1.0000
		M10	1.0000	1.0000	1.0000	1.0000		

Table 7. Results for the Moodle app

Attributes			Testers			Attribute averages		
C	S	M	T1	T2	T3	M	S	C
C1	S1	M1	0.6667	1.0000	0.9583	0.8750	0.8794	0.8932
		M2	1.0000	0.8333	0.8182	0.8838		
	S2	M3	0.7500	0.9091	0.6364	0.7652	0.8284	
		M4	0.8750	1.0000	0.8000	0.8917		
	S3	M5	0.5952	1.0000	1.0000	0.8651	0.8651	
	S5	M7	1.0000	1.0000	1.0000	1.0000	1.0000	
C2	S4	M6	0.3333	0.9130	0.8333	0.6932	0.6564	0.6564
		M8	0.3333	0.8333	0.6923	0.6197		
C3	S6	M9	1.0000	1.0000	1.0000	1.0000	1.0000	1.0000
		M10	1.0000	1.0000	1.0000	1.0000		

5 Discussion

This section contains the discussion of each defined research question.

- *Question 1:* The "usability" characteristic has values that are higher than the mean regarding its metrics, which demonstrates that the applied method to obtain the value of the variables were suitable. However, some metrics like M3 (Understandable categorization of information) were definitive to determine that Moodle has a light advantage over Google Classroom regarding the usability characteristic.
- *Question 2:* For "portability", the values are higher than the mean regarding its metrics, although in Google Classroom the experts assigned superior values to metrics M6 (Operational environment adaptability) and M8 (Hardware environmental adaptability) since they considered that the app can adapt to both operational and hardware environments. The opposite happened with Moodle, to which the experts assigned lightly inferior values to metrics M6 and M8, which caused a difference in favor of Google Classroom.
- *Question 3:* The "security" characteristic has the maximum values, since the experts, while assessing the "Google Classroom" and "Moodle" mobile apps, assigned the maximum values to metrics M9 (Authentication rules conformity) and M10 (Authentication mechanism sufficiency), considering that authentication in this apps is very important to validate the identity of a subject through its respective authentication rules.
- *Question 4:* The selected quality attributes had allowed the testers to assess the mobile apps with consistent results. The results for Google Classroom and Moodle on each assessed characteristic were very close; in the case of Usability, the scores had a difference of 0.006 in favor of Moodle, in Portability, the difference was of 0.150 in favor of Google Classroom, and in Security, both apps obtained the same result.

6 Conclusions and Future Work

In this study, a mobile app quality model was designed based on the ISO/IEC 25010 guidelines and the multi-criteria technique AHP, obtaining 8 characteristics, 19 sub-characteristics and 30 metrics. The model was obtained by carrying out the following activities: (1) compilation of quality models, (2) unification of characteristics and sub-characteristics, (3) selection of experts, (4) prioritization of quality attributes and (5) compilation and analysis of prioritization results.

To corroborate the validity of the proposed model, an experiment was carried out with two mobile apps related to the educational sector ("Google Classroom" and "Moodle") and 10 quality metrics to assess usability, portability, and security, which allowed measuring the quality of those apps. Additionally, 4 research questions were defined to validate the results.

The obtained results evidenced that the selected attributes to assess these mobile apps were adequate, since the obtained values for the usability, portability and security characteristics were similar between both apps.

As future work, research on mobile app quality models on other sectors is recommended. In addition, the design of a tool that supports the measurement of the quality model could be a good contribution. Finally, it is recommended to increase the number of apps and experts for the experiment to collect a larger variety of cases that are present during the execution of the activities.

References

1. Statista. Biggest app stores in the world 2020 (2020). https://www.statista.com/statistics/276 623/number-of-apps-available-in-leading-app-stores/. Accessed 09 Apr 2021
2. Gezici, B., Tarhan, A., Chouseinoglou, O.: Internal and external quality in the evolution of mobile software: an exploratory study in open-source market. Inf. Softw. Technol. **112**, 178–200 (2019). https://doi.org/10.1016/j.infsof.2019.04.002
3. Perfecto Mobile. WHY MOBILE APPS FAIL (2019). https://info.perfectomobile.com/rs/per fectomobile/images/why-mobile-apps-fail-report.pdf
4. Rahmi Dewi, M., Ngaliah, N.: Maintainability measurement and evaluation of myITS mobile application using ISO 25010 quality standard. In: Proceedings - 2020 International Seminar on Application for Technology of Information and Communication. IT Challenges Sustain. Scalability, Secur. Age Digit. Disruption, iSemantic 2020 (2020). https://doi.org/10.1109/iSe mantic50169.2020.9234283
5. ISO/IEC 25000. NORMAS ISO 25000 (2021). https://iso25000.com/index.php/normas-iso-25000?start=0. Accessed 30 Apr 2021
6. Saaty, R.W.: The analytic hierarchy process-what it is and how it is used. Math. Model. **9**(3–5), 161–176 (1987). https://doi.org/10.1016/0270-0255(87)90473-8
7. ISO/IEC 25000: La familia de normas ISO/IEC 25000 (2021). https://iso25000.com/index. php/normas-iso-25000/iso-25010. Accessed 30 Apr 2021
8. Manglapuz, S.J.R., Lacatan, L.L.: Academic management android application for student performance analytics: a comprehensive evaluation using ISO 25010:2011. Int. J. Innov. Technol. Explor. Eng. **8**(12), 5085–5089 (2019). https://doi.org/10.35940/ijitee.L2735.108 1219
9. Lechner, N.H., Strahonja, V.: Quality factors for mobile medical apps. Cent. Eur. Conf. Inf. Intell. Syst. **2014**, 229–236 (2017)
10. Temkar, R., Bhaskar, A.: Quality assurance of IoT based systems using analytic hierarchy process. Turkish J. Comput. Math. Educ. **12**(10), 6759–6767 (2021)
11. Falih, N., Firdaus, A.: Measuring performance, functionality and portability for mobile hybrid application. In: Proceedings - 1st International Conference on Informatics, Multimedia, Cyber and Information System, ICIMCIS 2019, pp. 195–200 (2019). https://doi.org/10.1109/ICI MCIS48181.2019.8985222
12. Santos, S.V., Ramos, F.R.S., Costa, R., da C. Batalha, L.M.: Assessment of the quality of a software application for the prevention of skin lesions in newborns. Rev. Lat. Am. Enfermagem **28**, 1–12 (2020). https://doi.org/10.1590/1518-8345.3711.3352
13. Idri, A., Sardi, L., Fernández-Alemán, J.L.: Quality evaluation of gamified blood donation apps using ISO/IEC 25010 standard. In: Health 2018 - 11th International Conference on Health Informatics, Proceedings; Part 11th International Joint Conference on Biomedical Engineering Systems and Technologies, BIOSTEC 2018, vol. 5, no. Biostec, pp. 607–614 (2018). https://doi.org/10.5220/0006724806070614
14. Super Decisions. Super Decisions (2021). http://www.superdecisions.com/. Accessed 28 June 2021
15. ISO. ISO 9126-1:2001 - Software engineering — Product quality — Part 1: Quality model (2018). https://www.iso.org/standard/22749.html. Accessed 07 Sep 2021

16. Baltar, F., Gorjup, M.T.: Online mixed sampling: an application in hidden populations. Intang. Cap. **8**(1) (2012). https://doi.org/10.3926/ic.294
17. Roque, D.: Selección de Expertos (2021). https://docs.google.com/forms/d/e/1FAIpQLSd 07GUtIhTjAmDhx4BY6kFhS_0iX3NxwnbGVn-GmBLXeJdqEw/viewform. Accessed 08 Sep 2021
18. Humphrey, J.: How Long Does It Take to Develop a Mobile App?. The Startup | Medium (2018). https://medium.com/swlh/how-long-does-it-take-to-develop-a-mobile-app-77574df9d18d. Accessed 21 June 2021
19. Demuyakor, J.: COVID-19 pandemic and higher education: leveraging on digital technologies and mobile applications for online learning in Ghana. Shanlax Int. J. Educ. **9**(3), 26–38 (2021). https://doi.org/10.34293/education.v9i3.3904
20. Mannong, A.B.M.: The students' eyesight: the effectiveness of learning-based applications on ELT in pandemic era. ETERNAL (English Teach. Learn. Res. J. **6**(2), 394 (2020). https://doi.org/10.24252/eternal.v62.2020.a14
21. Agormedah, E.K.: Online learning in higher education during COVID-19 pandemic: a case of Ghana. J. Educ. Technol. Online Learn. (2020). https://doi.org/10.31681/jetol.726441
22. Pramana, C.: Virtual learning during the Covid-19 pandemic, a disruptive technology in higher education in Indonesia. Int. J. Pharm. Res. **12**(2), 3209–3216 (2020). https://doi.org/10.31838/IJPR/2020.12.02.430
23. Natsir, I.: Implementation online lectures in Covid-19 pandemic: a student perception. ACM Int. Conf. Proc. Ser. (2020). https://doi.org/10.1145/3452144.3452203
24. Sofyan, H.: Online learning model in the pandemic time COVID 19 at SMK negeri 1 saptosari yogyakarta. J. Phys. Conf. Ser. **1700**(1) (2020). https://doi.org/10.1088/1742-6596/1700/1/012070
25. Hrydzhuk, O., Struhanets, L., Struhanets, Y.: Information technologies in language education during the COVID-19 pandemic. XLinguae **14**(1), 197–211 (2021). https://doi.org/10.18355/XL.2021.14.01.16
26. Subandowo, M.: Use of blended learning with Moodle: study effectiveness in elementary school teacher education students during the COVID-19 pandemic. Int. J. Adv. Sci. Technol. **29**(7), 3272–3277 (2020)
27. ISO/IEC 25023: Systems and software engineering — Systems and software Quality Requirements and Evaluation (SQuaRE) — Measurement of system and software product quality, vol. 1, p. 54 (2016)

Health, NLP, and Social Media

Automatic Detection of Levels of Intimate Partner Violence Against Women with Natural Language Processing Using Machine Learning and Deep Learning Techniques

Tereza Yallico Arias$^{(\boxtimes)}$ and Junior Fabian

ESAN University, Alonso de Molina No 1652, Lima, Peru
15101410@ue.edu.pe, jfabian@esan.edu.pe
https://www.ue.edu.pe/

Abstract. Violence against women continues to claim thousands of lives worldwide each year. The COVID-19 pandemic only aggravated the problem by confining many victims together with their aggressors. When a woman experiences this situation, she usually falls into denial, justifies the aggressive behavior of her partner, or even blames herself for provoking it. The sooner she realizes that she is experiencing intimate partner violence, she can act and prevent her advance in the violence cycle (from psychological violence to physical violence, which could lead to femicide). The work proposes a classifier artificial intelligence model to detect levels of psychological violence against women in written virtual expressions (messages 'from him to her' in a couple) to 'alert her' about the risk that she runs in that relationship. 5250 records in Spanish were extracted with 4 techniques from 6 different sources. Definition of 5 intimate partner psychological violence levels (0-Low Risk, 1-Emotional Blackmail, 2-Jealousy/Justification, 3-Insults/Humiliations, and 4-Threats/Possessiveness) and the data labeling were supervised by a psychologist expert on the problem. Techniques TF-IDF and Word2Vec were used to get the vectors and were tested five Machine Learning algorithms (SVM, MLP, Random Forest, Logistic Regression, and Naive Bayes) with various combinations of parameters. Too were tested pad sequences with LSTM and Bidirectional LSTM. The best result was 93.45% accuracy and 0.2476 categorical cross-entropy loss, obtained with extensive preprocessing, pad sequences, and LSTM.

Keywords: Violence against women · Detection of violence · Dating violence · Intimate partner violence · Domestic violence · Violence cycle · Natural Language Processing · Machine Learning · Deep Learning · Levels of psychological violence · Analysis in Spanish

© The Author(s), under exclusive license to Springer Nature Switzerland AG 2022
J. A. Lossio-Ventura et al. (Eds.): SIMBig 2021, CCIS 1577, pp. 189–205, 2022.
https://doi.org/10.1007/978-3-031-04447-2_13

1   Introduction

In Peru, between 6 and 7 women out of 10 have been victims of intimate partner violence at some point in their lives. Throughout 2020, 132 femicides and 204 attempts occurred, of which more than half occurred during the state of emergency [1]. The Ministry of Women and Vulnerable Populations of the Peruvian Government reported that only in the first three months of the COVID-19 pandemic 36 333 telephone calls were registered to Line 100 (an emergency line that receives reports of cases of violence against women and domestic violence) [2].

The quarantine as a measure to prevent the spread of the COVID-19 virus had as a collateral effect the confinement of victims with their aggressors, adding high levels of stress to the situation and reducing the possibility of moving away or requesting external help, made them even more vulnerable to experience violent episodes, especially Physical Violence (pushing, punching, kicking, hitting or others). This type of violence was the most attended in the first six months of the pandemic by the Peruvian Itinerant Team of Urgency in 2020 [3] being 46.19%, followed closely by Psychological Violence, with 37.64% (yelling, emotional abuse, humiliation, manipulation, threats, among other tactics).

Despite the efforts and campaigns to make the population aware of violence against women, it is still a deeply ingrained behavior in Peru, perpetuating this mindset by gender stereotypes, prejudices, and sexism that are very marked in the culture. The most dangerous aspect of this problem is its tendency to increase in the intensity of the violent episodes and the types of violence: psychological violence is usually only the beginning, the most 'silent' because there are no 'visible' or quickly evident marks, progressing slowly but steadily through the 'Cycle of Violence' [4] until breaks out in physical violence, economic violence, or in the most severe cases, sexual violence.

To explain why the victim does not leave the aggressor despite all the damage that he causes her, the psychologist Leonor Walker proposed a dynamic called 'Cycle of Violence' with three steps 1) Tension building phase with the couple (Disagreements, yelling, and later, insults), 2) The acute episode of Aggression (the aggressor loses control and lets out his anger in an outburst, the first times could be threats or blows to the wall or nearby objects, in the following iterations of the cycle could be slapping, hitting, there is physical or even sexual violence) and 3) Honeymoon Phase (the aggressor begs to be forgiven, fervently promises that it will never happen again, swears that he will change and that everything will be as at the beginning of the relationship if the victim gives him the opportunity). At some point, everything seems fine again, then the victim clings to the idea that her aggressor has changed, but tension returns to accumulate, and the cycle begins again. As a couple goes around this cycle, the episodes become more dangerous for the victim, and the 'peace period' becomes shorter than in the first turns. 'Cycle of Violence' just can be broken if the victim realizes her situation (by herself or by externals) and decides to take action (ask for help in their support network, withdraw from the aggressor, even file a restraining order or put a demand in severe cases) to avoid 'iterating in the circle' [5].

The factor that makes it more difficult for a woman to realize that she is experiencing intimate partner violence is that she usually normalizes these episodes excusing the aggressor, justifying him because "he has been stressed", "he is temperamental" or even blaming herself for 'having caused it', denying being in a dangerous situation despite having already experienced psychological, economic, physical or sexual violence. Many women in this situation avoid asking for help in their support network (family, friends, neighbors) to maintain the appearances of a loving and united couple or for fear of being judged as a victim, among other reasons [5]. As the Cycle of Violence progresses, the danger increases, but the sooner she realizes the risk they are running and takes action, the violence is prevented from advancing and may even end her life.

Our proposal is to develop a classifier model to detect intimate partner violence levels in the first type that is manifested, psychological (invisible in the victim's body but detectable in what the potential aggressor writes her virtually) using Natural Language Processing with techniques of Machine Learning or Deep Learning. It aims to alert the potential victim of the level of risk that she runs in that couple relationship, and she could act in time, avoiding the progress of the Cycle of Violence and helping her break it.

In order to train the mentioned model, first, we reviewed the state of art in Sect. 2. Then, we collected a dataset large enough to make the first approach to the exposed problem, in the social context of Latinoamerica, with this specific type of data (virtual messages from him to her) in Spanish. Dataset was labeled under the supervision of a specialist, to be later carefully preprocessed and used in training of the desired model, for which multiple experiments with distinct Machine Learning and Deep Learning techniques were performed. The entire process is exposed in detail in Sect. 3. The results of the multiple experiments are in Sect. 4. Finally, in Sect. 5, are exposed our conclusions and recommendations for future works.

2   Related Work

No antecedent has previously aborded the classification in intimate partner psychological violence levels in direct virtual communication specifically. However, there are studies related to violence against women and classifying aggression levels (in general, not necessarily in the couple dynamic).

In 2019, Subramani et al. [6] based on 1654 posts and comments drawn from the ten most active pages on Domestic Violence on Facebook, tried to classify them into five classes: Awareness, Empathy, Fundraising, General, and Experience. That is to speed up support group's responses by automatically locating possible reports of abuse or urgent requests for financial support, preventing these posts/messages from being lost among the rest of the content. The data labeling was supervised by an expert psychiatrist active in the field research of domestic violence. Classic Machine Learning algorithms were tested, such as Support Vector Machine, Logistic Regression, Naive Bayes, Decision Trees and Random Forests. The advanced Deep Learning techniques tested were Convolutional Neural Networks, Recurrent Neural Networks, Long Short-Term Memory networks, Gated Recurrent Units, and Bidirectional LSTMs. The vectorization techniques used were Bag of Words, Term Frequency Inverse Document Frequency, Word2Vec, and GloVe. The best result obtained was 91.78% from Accuracy through GRUs and GloVe.

In 2017, Escalante et al. [7] used three different data sources: a dataset called 'Detecting Insults in Social Commentary Daque' (3947 records) obtained from a Kaggle Challenge, provided by a company that had previously used it in research about aggressive text (Binary: Aggressive vs. Non-aggressive), a dataset of aggressive tweets (1570 records) from the UANL (Multiclass: Non-Aggressive, Aggressive, Extremely aggressive) that contains profanities widely used in the actual context of communication of that institution and, finally, a dataset called PAN-CLEF 12 (6588 records) that serves to identify sexual predators and includes a large number of virtual conversations (chats) with sexual predators. These authors sought to identify pedophile behavior and aggressive text early, through text analysis, not in forensic analysis, but in real-time conversation. They proposed an additive technique that for each word written generates a characteristic vector and after accumulated in a document that would represent the entire conversation through the Profile-Based Representation for early recognition and Suprofile. They used traditional techniques such as TF or TF-IDF to vectorize. The best result was 94.37% of Accuracy.

In 2018, Jimenez [10] manually consolidated 1,561 comments and publications from three social networks (Facebook, Twitter, and YouTube) to train a classifier of levels of aggressiveness (Multiclass: Very aggressive, aggressive, not very aggressive, or neutral). She applied extensive preprocessing because her dataset was in Spanish and presented much distortion for misspelling. It needs a good data cleaning before the vectorization to avoid train two words instead of one. Naive Bayes, Bayes Net, Decision Stump, IBK, K Start, and others were tested. The best result was 0.09 Mean Absolute Error with IBK.

3   Methodology

3.1   Database

- **Data Extraction:** No dataset made of virtual expressions 'from him towards her' denotes intimate partner psychological violence levels to train the desired model to alert directly to a victim. So had to be built a new dataset in Spanish able to train a functional model as part of our research based on different types of data (victim narratives, screenshots with evidence, key-phrases published by psychologists, video-dramatizations of prevention campaigns, analysis of warning signs, notes from emergency line operators, and comments in social networks) to which we could extract the needed expressions.

We obtained data from six different sources through four distinct techniques(manual copy, transcription from audio or video to text, scrapping, and a formal request to a State Organization). In Fig. 1 can be observed a diagram explaining the data collection process and the number of records extracted from each source, these are detailed following:

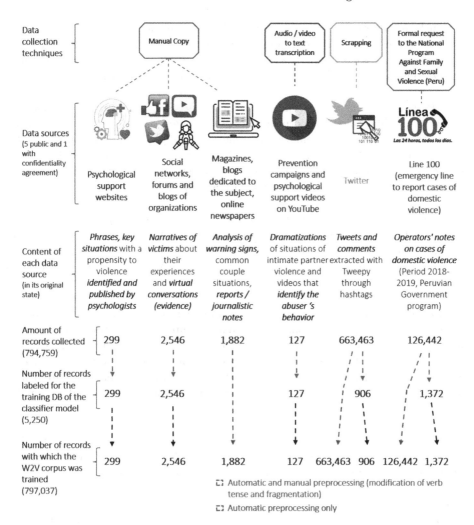

Fig. 1. Dataset collection process (both the labeled dataset to train the multiclass classifier model and the dataset to train the Word2Vec corpus)

SOURCE 1 - Psychological Support Websites: Many psychologists specialists in intimate partner violence have published on their support websites the keys to identifying the behavior of an abuser, sometimes even specific key phrases or common situations that put an aggressor in evidence. We manually searched and copied the relevant content from these web pages obtaining 299 records.

SOURCE 2 - Social Networks, Forums, Blogs of Organizations: Through various blogs (specialized in the fight against violence against women, forums, self-help web pages, and other virtual mass communication platforms), some victims or people who knew their stories shared these experiences of abuse (narrations), screenshots, and most significant phrases of the aggressor. Additionally, we manually extracted comments and posts on Facebook, Twitter, and Youtube as in our antecedents with topics of violence against women or abusive language in online context [6,8,14]. Consolidating, we obtained 2 546 records.

SOURCE 3 - Magazines, Blogs Dedicated to the Subject, Online Newspapers: Electronic publications have crucial because through journalistic notes, articles in magazines, and blogs, analyze the issues of a couple's relationship, too how to recognize a healthy relationship and difference to one with emotional dependence, sexism, reports of cases of violence, and the stage of recovery after having lived it, among other content. We copied manually 1 882 records.

SOURCE 4 - Prevention Campaigns and Psychological Support Videos on Youtube: Has been developed many video analyses of how to recognize a partner aggressor's behavior, characteristics, or explicit phrases. We obtained 127 records transcribing them from audio/video to text. Videos were mainly of two types:

Awareness Campaigns - Dramatizations: Many campaigns have been organized worldwide, including several short films that recreate situations that denote intimate partner violence (in adolescents, girlfriends/ boyfriends, and marriages) to show an example of the behavior of an aggressor in a concrete example, through a story where violent behavior occurs gradually (as in reality, dialogues are usually written with the guidance of an expert on the subject due to its educational purpose).

Emotional Education Videos - Psychological Support: These videos seek to teach how to recognize these behaviors even in their earliest state (expose situations of risk and specific phrases to be alert) and how to act accordingly.

SOURCE 5 - Twitter: This social network is frequently used to express thoughts, opinions, personal experiences, integrate support groups/collectives and propagate news, therefore many research of detection of aggressiveness or abusive language [8,14] have considered as a source. Through the Tweepy package, we scrapped 663 463 tweets and comments in several runs, of which 906 were processed and finally labeled for the classifier training dataset. The parameters were: Spanish language, date contained between 2015–2019, with the content of interest for the context of the phrases that denote intimate partner violence through hashtags like #NiunaMenos, #MeToo, #NovioCeloso, #NovioTóxico among others.

SOURCE 6 - Line 100: The Peruvian government's Program Against Family and Sexual Violence manages Line 100, providing 24/7 psychological and legal support to domestic or intimate partner violence victims. Victims can report their situation, request urgent help or orientation, and the operators take notes for the registered cases. Months later to have been presented the formal request and after the data had been anonymized for the Information Generation and Knowledge Management Unit team of the Ministry of Women and Vulnerable Populations of Peru, they sent it to us in an email. Obtained with a formal request and was received under a confidentiality agreement (Period 2018–2019). After inspection of the data, we maintained just the relevant content for this research keeping 126 442 operator's notes for cases registered, of which 1 372 were processed and finally labeled for the classifier training dataset.

Were extracted initially 794 759 records where each one contains an average of 92 characters (with a maximum of 288 and a minimum of 16), 18 words (with a maximum of 57 and a minimum of 3), and 2 sentences (with a maximum of 8 and a minimum of 1). Data in its 'original state' was used to train Word2Vec corpus (after 2 phases of automatic preprocessing). After, a part of it, 5250 registers, cross a manual phase of preprocessing to fragment each record and extract only the expression 'from him to her' and versioned it to the right verbal time (modifications will be explained after) to be finally labeled and used to train the multiclass classifier model. The versioned records were added to the Word2Vec corpus training dataset because they differed from their original version.

Definition of Levels and Labeling. This research aims to classify virtual expressions ('from him to her', in couple context) in five intimate partner psychological violence levels, these have been defined based on 'Violentometer' ('Violentómetro', in Spanish) [9] that is a tool currently used to measure intimate partner violence in cases in Mexico and was virtually published by the Mexican government (is relevant because social context is quite similar with Peru). As is detailed in Fig. 2, we considered only psychological violence manifestations of the tool and aggregated similar behaviors in only five levels. Then we validate if the levels were consistent with the context with the help of the psychologist expert in emotional containment of victims of family violence in a Women's Emergency Center in Lima, Peru. The final levels considered in multiclass classification were: 0-Low Risk, 1-Emotional Blackmail, 2-Jealousy/Justification, 3-Insults/Humiliations, and 4-Threats/Possessiveness.

There were established two criteria to label a record in one of the levels with the help and expert judgment of the mentioned specialist: 1) Topic of the content and 2) Inferable objective of the talker/writer. These are detailed as follows:

LEVEL 0 - 'Low Risk' - Example: "Good morning my love! it is everything okay?". The content of the record does not denote psychological violence; rather, it demonstrates a seemingly healthy couple relationship, can be observed mutual respect or interest in the welfare of the other.

LEVEL 1 - 'Emotional Blackmail' - Example: "If you leave me, I'll hurt myself, you can't do this to me! You never cared about me". The aggressor's goal will be to manipulate the victim through guilt, obligation, and fear of losing him/her fear of being alone to obtain attention, reassurance, and displays of affection. The potential aggressor will victimize himself, make the partner feel guilty for not making him feel 'loved enough', compare her to other women or threaten to harm himself if he does not get what he wants.

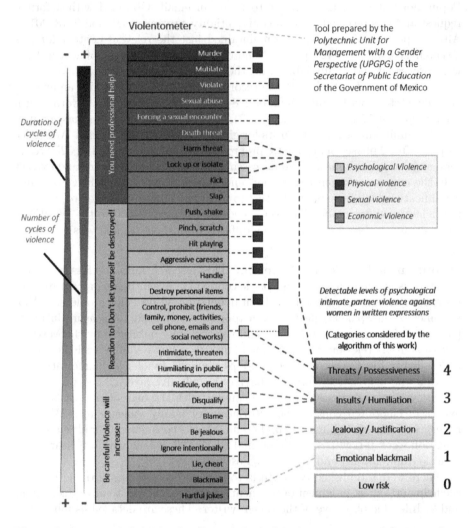

Fig. 2. Definition of the 5 levels of psychological intimate partner violence against women to be considered in the analysis obtained based on the Violentometer. Only psychological violence is considered as it is evident in virtual messages from a partner

LEVEL 2 - 'Jealousy/Justification' - Example: "Who are you talking to so much that you don't answer me? If you are online! I am your boyfriend! Are you cheating me?". The aggressor's objective is 'avoid losing his loved one' and 'prevent' infidelity, having her watched all the time closely and claiming her whenever he has a suspicion. Try always to know where and with whom his partner is, ask for evidence. In addition, he blames her for his behavior, arguing that 'she provokes it'.

LEVEL 3 - *'Insults/Humiliations'* - Example: "HOW DID I END UP WITH SUCH A STUPID WOMAN ?? GOOD FOR NOTHING!!!". Aggressor's objective will be to attack her, humiliate her, ridicule, belittle, decrease his self-esteem so that she does not defend herself. This messages content insults, offenses, devaluation of the person.

LEVEL 4 - *'Threats/Possessiveness'* - Example: "IF YOU LEAVE ME, I'LL NEVER LEAVE YOU ALONE !!! NOBODY LEAVES ME !!! IF YOU ARE NOT MINE YOU WILL BE NOBODY'S !!! I DON'T ALLOW YO !! ". The aggressor's objective is to force the victim to do what he demands by threatening to lose something valuable to her, to harm her or her loved ones (mostly her children). The messages contain threats to harm her physically or sexually. He also objectifies her, treating her as an object of his belonging that must always do what he wants. He shelters her from his friends and family and seeks to have her 'only for him'.

3.2   Preprocessing

With several data sources and quite heterogeneous data, the preprocessing had to be complex enough to eliminate everything in the records that were not useful for the analysis. The Fig. 3 illustrates the steps followed during the preprocessing in three stages, one manual and two automatic:

- First Automatic Phase: We applied this stage to 794 759 records (all data collected from six sources) to remove all that did not contribute to the analysis. Due to the typical format from records from social networks, we had to remove links (step a), replace emoticons (b) for tags that represent them (' :) ' for 'happy'), remove hashtags and mentions (c) of other users (mainly for Twitter's data). Then, we replace emojis (d) for tags because, like emoticons, contribute to understanding the emotions of the virtual writer (':poutingFace:', ':loudly-CryingFace:', ':faceBlowingAKiss:', among others), then we eliminate symbols, exclamation marks and numbers (e). To avoid duplicity of words trained in the corpus for a misspelling (a common situation in the Spanish language, especially in data from social networks), we removed accents and idiomatic characters (f) as accents, umlauts, diacritical marks, among others. In virtual context, the repetition of the last letter in a word is commonly used to express intensity or enthusiasm, too, to avoid a multiple training of the same word, we 'homologate' this reducing words wich their last letter was repeated ('nucaaaaaaaaa', 'nucaaaaa' and 'nucaa' are really the same word, we converted it to 'nunca', that means 'never') and finally we convert all text to lowercase (g).

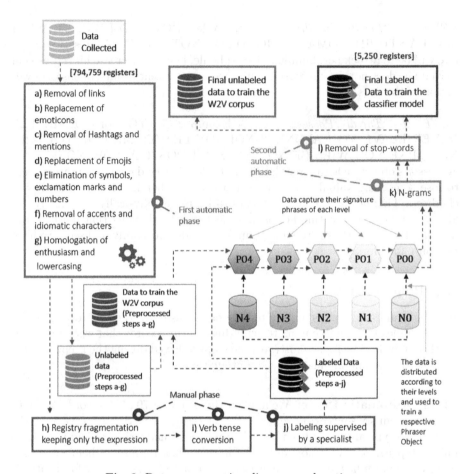

Fig. 3. Data preprocessing diagram explanation

- **Manual Phase:** Once the first automatic phase has preprocessed all collected data, a part of records was separated (only which clearly can be detected one of the intimate partner psychological violence defined levels). Only these records will pass through the manual phase. Considering that the input to be tested in the classifier model is directly the virtual messages from the potential aggressor to the potential victim, the records must have this form ('direct virtual message from him to her'). Because the data (coming from different sources and being so heterogeneous) does not come in the correct form, to train the classifier model, the records will be manually moved to the correct grammatical form, taking into account that it is the same form in that new records will be received to be tested.

To achieve this, first, in step h, considering that many records contain complete and explicit narratives by the victim (Translated input example: "Whenever we fought he would repeat the same thing to me, it sounded terrifying, he told me that I belonged to him and that I would never run away from him, that no matter how far I escaped, he would never allow me to be happy with another man. He said those exact words"), we fragmented these to eliminate narration of the episode or details and keep only the part of the record that includes the violent psychological expressions from the aggressor (Translated output example: "He told me that I belonged to him and that I would never run away from him, that no matter how far I escaped, he would never allow me to be happy with another man"). Second, in step i, we converted this fragment with a narrative form to a 'virtual written expression from him to her' form; verbal tense changed, but the record's content was preserved (Translated output example:"You are mine and you could never run away from me, no matter how far you escape I will never allow you to be happy with another man"). Then, in step j, under the strict supervision of the previously mentioned expert psychologist, 5 250 records were labeled (exactly 1050 records per level, to obtain a perfectly balanced dataset) to be later used to train the classifier model.

- **Automatic Second Phase:** The concept of phrases is very significant in one-to-one communication in the Spanish language, even more in a virtual couple's conversation. To capture the characteristic phrases of each violence level in the form of n-grams, we separate the data into five mini-datasets by their level and use each one to train a different Phraser Object (PO) with Gensim package, because if we use all data to train only one PO, the number of times a word was repeated caused too much distortion. Once the five POs were trained, the total labeled data (5 250 records) were exposed sequentially to each PO (initialing with PO trained with the data of Level-4 and finalizing with the PO trained with data of Level-0) to aggregate the words trained as phrases (step j), too we expose to POs the unlabeled data used to train the Word2Vec corpus. Then, in step k, we deleted stopwords (prepositions and articles needed to integrate phrases have already been captured in the last step).

3.3 Feature Extraction

For the extraction of characteristics, we tested two vectorization techniques (which model a sparsa-matrix, 'TF-IDF' and 'Word2Vec') for Machine Learning algorithms and one (in sequences, 'Pad Sequences') for Deep Learning models:

- **Term Frequency - Inverse Document Frequency (TF-IDF):** This technique were very recommended in related works to detection of violence [6,7]. In the experiments, we tuned the minDf parameter, which indicates the minimum number of times a word has to appear in the corpus to be considered in training of the vocabulary. Where obtained the feature vector sets TfIdf-FV1 (minDf = 3, 2821 trained words), TfIdf-FV2 (minDf = 6, 1684 trained words) and TfIdf-FV3 (minDf = 10 045 trained words)

- **Word2Vec:** We employed the Skip-gram scheme (based on one word predicts related words through back-propagation) because Mikolov and his collaborators recommend it to train with relatively short data [11]. This technique has been used in related research [6]. We trained the Word2Vec corpus with Gensim package and tuned the Size parameter, which refers to the dimension of the vectors of numbers that represent each trained word, values tested were 200, 300, and 350. obtaining the corpus W2V-C1 (size $= 200$, mincount $= 3, 60\,843$ trained words in 350 dimensions), W2V-C2 (size $= 300$, mincount $= 3, 46\,777$ trained words in 300 dimensions) and W2V-C3 (size $= 350$, mincount $= 3, 60\,843$ trained words in 200 dimensions).

- **Pad Sequences:** We used Keras package to convert text to pad sequences (vectors of numbers, where which one represent a word, padded with zeros) because was needed a compatible structure with LSTM, which, by definition, uses sequences to train. Were turned the parameter EmbeddingSize obtaining the feature vectors sets PadSeq-FV1 (tunned with value 128), PadSeq-FV2 (300), PadSeq-FV3 (400), PadSeq-FV4 (500) and PadSeq-FV5 (600). The corpus considered 6276 words, and the most extensive document includes 26 words.

3.4   Modeling

In Machine Learning experiments, we applied a perfectly balanced stratified sampling (labeled data contains 1 050 records of each of the five levels, having 5 250 records in total). 75% of the data were used for training and 25% for testing. We tested five Machine Learning algorithms due to the good performance in research with similar topics as hate classification, categorization of posts in pages of Domestic Violence, and toxicity detection, all in Online context [6,12,14]. These techniques were tested with the following parameters:

> - **Support Vector Machine (SVM):** C (values 50, 100, and 10000), gamma (scale, 0.001, 0.007, and 0.05), and kernel (RBF, Linear, and Poly).
> - **Logistic Regression (LR):** C (0.0004, 0.002, 0.05, 1, 10, and 100), solver (lbfgs and newton-cg), and multiClass (multinomial)
> - **Random Forest (RF):** nEstimators (100, 500, 1000, 1050, 2500, and 4000)
> - **Naive Bayes(NB):** alpha (0.001, 0.05, 1, 2, and 3)
> - **Multi-Layer Perceptron (MLP):** numInputNeurons (200, 300, 350, and 2821), numHiddenLayers (2, 4, and 5), activationFunctionHiddenLayer (tanh and sigmoid), numHiddenLayerNeurons (6, 8, 10, 12, and 20), activationFunctionOutputLayer (softmax), numOutputLayerNeurons (5), Dropout (0.2 and 0.5), and epochs (50, 100, 200 and 250).

About Deep Learning experiments, we tested two artificial recurrent neural network architectures which have good performance in detection of violence in virtual context [6] in combination with the following parameters:

- **Long Short Term Memory (LSTM):** activationFunction (relu), batchSize (64, 32, and 100), dropout (0.2 and 0.1), activationFinalLayer (softmax), this technique is too called Unidirectional LSTM.

- **Bidirectional LSTM:** activationFunction (relu), batchSize (64, 32, and 100), dropout (0.2 and 0.1), and activationFinalLayer (softmax).

The target variable (psychological violence level as a label) was converted into a dummy variable of length five to be predicted by the network.

3.5 Model Evaluation

The fact that the dataset is perfectly balanced (same number of records for each of the five levels) causes precision, recall, and F1-score to have similar results (which would not happen if there was an imbalance because it would be penalized) and makes proper to use Accuracy as a valid metric to compare the performance of the distinct models of Machine Learning. As loss in the experiments of Deep Learning, we used Categorical Cross-Entropy due to our related works that classify levels of aggression and recommended this metric [13]. Finally, we used the confusion matrix for the visualization of results.

4 Results

The comparison of results of the best combinations of parameters of the experiments with Machine Learning and Deep Learning techniques can be observed in Table 1.

Concerning Deep Learning techniques, the best result (93.45% Accuracy) was obtained with the combination of LSTM and Pad Sequences (specifically with the feature vector set PadSeq-FV2, with 300 of embedding size) due to the nature of the model, which uses the previous words to predict the next capturing the pattern of the content of each level. Deep Learning techniques usually present high levels of predictive power. Additionally, the metric of loss assigned in the model's training was Categorical Cross-Entropy loss, which is the most recommended loss metric by multiclass problems of classification, obtaining 0.2476 of loss. The confusion matrix of the best model of this research is displayed in Fig. 4.

About Machine Learning techniques, the best result was obtained with Naive Bayes (93.30% Accuracy), an algorithm with usually good performance in multiclass text classification [6], in combination with TF-IDF, specifically with the feature vector set TfIdf-FV1, that considers 2821 trained words, being the set which more words consider concerning others of this type (TfIdf-FV2, with 1684 words and TfIdf-FV3, with 1045 words). The second best combination for Machine learning was obtained combining SVM (92.38% Accuracy), too frequently recommended [6], and TfIdf-FV1.

Table 1. Comparison of the best results obtained, their type of vectorization, their algorithms, and their training parameters

Model	Accuracy (%)	Vectorization type	Parameters with best results
LSTM (DL)	93.45	PadSeq-FV2	activation = relu, batchSize = 64, dropout = 0.2, activationFinalLayer = softmax
NB (ML)	93.30	TfIdf-FV1	alpha = 1
SVM (ML)	92.38	TfIdf-FV1	C = 100, gamma = scale, kernel = RBF
LR (ML)	91.87	TfIdf-FV1	C = 10, solver = newton-cg, multiClass = multinomial
MLP (ML)	91.55	TfIdf-FV1	numInputNeurons= 2821; numHiddenLayers = 2; activationFunctionHiddenLayer = tanh; numHiddenLayerNeurons = 8; Dropout= 0.2; epochs= 50
Bidirectional LSTM (DL)	90.48	PadSeq-FV3	activation = relu, batchSize = 64, dropout = 0.2, activationFinalLayer = softmax
RF (ML)	89.69	TfIdf-FV1	nEstimators = 2500
SVM (ML)	86.21	W2V-C3	C = 100, gamma = scale, kernel = RBF
LR (ML)	84.68	W2V-C2	C = 0.05, solver = newton-cg, multiClass = multinomial
MLP (ML)	83.47	W2V-C2	numInputNeurons = 300; numHiddenLayer = 2; activationFunctionHiddenLayer = tanh; numHiddenLayerNeurons = 10; Dropout = 0.5; epochs = 50
RF (ML)	81.57	W2V-C2	nEstimators = 2500
NB (ML)	73.23	W2V-C3	alpha = 0.005

Fig. 4. Confusion matrix of the combination of techniques with the best performance: LSTM with Pad Sequences, with 93.45% of Accuracy

The fact that the extraction of characteristics with TF-IDF technique supers in performance to Word2Vec (which, with SVM, reaches 86.21% Accuracy, the eighth-best result of combinations) is due to the size of the training dataset. The labeled dataset has only 5250 records; it is very little data for a method based in neural networks (Word2Vec) to outperform a simple method as TF-IDF, above all because the mechanical to label a record of this technique is quite similar with the method of the expert psychologist to classify a message, based on 'key phrases' that reveals the objective of the potential aggressor.

Were used stratified sampling to obtain perfectly balanced data to train the classifier model. As a consequence, we obtained consistent results for Precision, Recall, and F1, which are exposed in Table 2.

Table 2. Comparison between metrics

Best model	Precision	Recall	F1	Accuracy
1 LSTM	93.47	93.45	93.45	93.45
2 NB	93.38	93.3	93.31	93.30
3 SVM	92.53	92.38	92.41	92.38

In Table 3 are detailed the comparative of Accuracy per level. As we can observe, the best-classified level is 'Low Risk' (Level 0) with 96.96% of Accuracy, and the worst is 'Emotional Blackmail' (Level 1). It occurs because there are many strategies to apply emotional blackmail (threats to withdraw attention or affection, compare the partner with other women to make them feel insecure, victimize to generate guilty, appeal to the fear of being left alone, among others) which makes the situations and, specifically, the words used in this records are not so repetitive, this content tend to be more diverse than at other levels.

Table 3. Comparison of Accuracy (%) by levels between the 3 best models

Best model	Low risk (L0)	Emotional blackmail (L1)	Jealousy/ Justification (L2)	Insults/ Humilia- tions (L3)	Threats/ Posses- siveness (L4)	Total
1 LSTM	96.96	91.22	94.3	92.75	92.02	93.45
2 NB	96.96	95.8	90.49	90.87	92.37	93.30
3 SVM	94.29	93.51	92.4	89.35	92.37	92.38

5   Conclusions and Recommendations

Was achieved the development of a model that automatically classifies with a 93.45% accuracy a written virtual expression ('from him to her', in a couple, in Spanish) in 5 intimate partner psychological violence levels. It aims alert her about the risk she runs in that relationship and she can take action to get out of the Cycle of Violence (the most challenging step to get out of it is to realize her violence8situation due to the usual denial or even justification), thus preventing her advance towards other more severe types of violence (physical, sexual, among others). There is no research with exactly the same objective, type of data and social context. However, considering the impact of this problem in society, the present work aims to contribute to research on technology to prevent intimate partner violence, demonstrating that it is possible to build tools with Artificial Intelligence techniques capable of facilitating detection and giving notice to possible victims in the most timely manner possible.

The good performance of the developed model was obtained despite all difficulties in obtaining data. We had to build an entirely new dataset and apply it in an extensive and intricate preprocessing to obtain records with the correct form for the objective in Spanish and from six different sources. With the legal and social movement against domestic violence and violence against women, we hope data related to the topic will becoming increasingly public. In the future, this could facilitate the extraction of more significant amounts of data (especially in Spanish, which is not a very analyzed language), in this case it would be helpful to include more psychologists experts in the labeling to give more reliability to the tool. More data too would permit make a more robust analysis and with more advanced Deep Learning techniques such as GRU or Transformers. Too can be proved other advanced tokenization techniques like Glove, Bert, and others.

The labeling step considered only records that manifested only one of the established levels. If they contained two levels in the same record, they were excluded. However, it could be contemplated to find two levels in the same record in future work, as it could occur in the actual violent couple context.

Too the model would be available in a web platform or an App directly for the population, to they can use it for themselves.

References

1. CIES (Consorcio de Investigación económica y social): INEI: La violencia contra las mujeres se ha convertido en 'la pandemia de la sombra' (2020). https://www.cies.org.pe/es/actividad/inei-la-violencia-contra-las-mujeres-se-ha-convertido-en-la-pandemia-de-la-sombra
2. CONVOCA: En cuarentena la línea 100 recibió más de 36333 llamadas sobre violencia familiar y contra la mujer (2020). https://convoca.pe/agenda-propia/en-cuarentena-la-linea-100-recibio-mas-de-36333-llamadas-sobre-violencia-familiar-y

3. MIMP (Ministerio de la Mujer y Poblaciones Vulnerables): Cartilla estadística 16 de marzo al 30 de setiembre 2020 - Estado de emergencia nacional - Cifras de Violencia (durante aislamiento social) (2020). https://portalestadistico.pe/wp-content/uploads/2020/10/Cartilla-Estadistica-AURORA-16-de-marzo-al-30-de-setiembre-2020.pdf
4. Walker, L.: The Battered Women. Harper & Row Publishers, New York (1979)
5. Pérez, M.M.C., Calvera, J.F.M.: Descripción y caracterización del Ciclo de Violencia que surge en la relación de pareja. Tesis Psicológica, vol. 8, no. 1, pp. 80–88. Fundación Universitaria Los Libertadores, Bogotá (2013)
6. Subramani, S., et al.: Deep learning for multi-class identification from domestic violence online posts. IEEE Access 7, 46210–46224 (2019). https://doi.org/10.1109/ACCESS.2019.2908827
7. Escalante, H.J., Villatoro-Tello, E., Garza, S.E., López-Monroy, A.P., Montes-y-Gómez, M., Villaseñor-Pineda, L.: Early detection of deception and aggressiveness using profile-based representations. Expert Syst. Appl. 89, 99–111 (2017). Elsevier. https://doi.org/10.1016/j.eswa.2017.07.040
8. Park, J.H., Fung, P.: One-step and two-step classification for abusive language detection on Twitter. In: ALW1: 1st Workshop on Abusive Language Online. Association for Computational Linguistics, Vancouver (2017). https://doi.org/10.18653/v1/W17-3006
9. Secretaría de Educación Pública del Gobierno de México: Violentómetro. https://www.ipn.mx/genero/materialesdeapoyo/violentometro.html. Accessed 1 Aug 2021
10. Jimenez, R.: Influencia del Aprendizaje Computacional Basado en Técnicas de Minería de Textos en la Clasificación de Comentarios de Textos Agresivos. UNAJMA (Universidad Nacional José María Arguedas), Apurímac, Perú (2018)
11. Mikolov, T., Sutskever, I., Chen, K., Corrado, G., Dean, J.: Distributed representations of words and phrases and their compositionality. In: Neural Information Processing Systems (NIPS) (2013). https://arxiv.org/pdf/1301.3781.pdf
12. Gunasekara, I., Nejadgholi, I.: A review of standard text classification practices for multi-label toxicity identification of online content. In: ALW2: Proceedings of the 2nd Workshop on Abusive Language Online. Association for Computational Linguistics, Brussels (2018). https://doi.org/10.18653/v1/W18-5103
13. Galery, T., Charitos, E., Tian, Y.: Aggression identification and multi lingual word embeddings. In: Proceedings of the First Workshop on Trolling, Aggression and Cyberbullying, Santa Fe, USA, pp. 74–79 (2018). https://aclanthology.org/W18-4409.pdf
14. Salminen, J., Hopf, M., Chowdhury, S.A., Jung, S., Almerekhi, H., Jansen, B.J.: Developing an online hate classifier for multiple social media platforms. HCIS 10(1), 1–34 (2020). https://doi.org/10.1186/s13673-019-0205-6

Deep Learning vs Compression-Based vs Traditional Machine Learning Classifiers to Detect Hadith Authenticity

Taghreed Tarmom$^{(\boxtimes)}$ [iD], Eric Atwell[iD], and Mohammad Alsalka[iD]

University of Leeds, Leeds LS2 9JT, UK
{sctat,E.S.Atwell,M.A.Alsalka}@leeds.ac.uk

Abstract. Due to the increasing numbers of Hadith forgeries, it has become necessary to use artificial intelligence to assist those looking for authentic Hadiths. This paper presents detailed research on ways to automatically detect Hadith authenticity in Arabic Hadith texts. It examines the utilization of deep learning-based and prediction by partial matching (PPM) compression-based classifiers, which have not been previously used in detecting Hadith authenticity. The proposed methods were compared with the most recent method used which is machine learning. In addition, there is a detailed description of the new Arabic Hadith corpus (non-authentic Hadith corpus) created for this study and the authors' experiments, which also used the Leeds University and King Saud University (LK) Hadith corpus. The experiments demonstrate that the authentication based on Isnad obtained accuracy ranging from 84% to 93%. The authentication based on Matan obtained an accuracy range of 55% to 93%, while the accuracy range for this experiment was from 55% to 85%, which means that Isnad is the most effective part of Hadith for automatically detecting authenticity. Moreover, the experiment proved that Matan can be used to judge Hadith authenticity with an accuracy of 85%. The study also showed that PPM and deep learning classifiers are effective means of automatically detecting authentic Hadith.

Keywords: Hadith authenticity · Hadith corpus · Deep learning · Arabic natural language processing

1 Introduction

Text classification is the process of classifying a set of written information into one of a number of predefined classes. Several methods can be used to accomplish this task, including prediction by partial matching (PPM) compression-based algorithms, machine learning (ML) algorithms and deep learning (DL) algorithms.

Most Arabic natural language processing (NLP) studies concentrate on Modern Standard Arabic (MSA), such as [1–3]. However, there is a paucity of research on the classification of Classical Arabic (CA) texts, such as Hadith.

J. A. Lossio-Ventura et al. (Eds.): SIMBig 2021, CCIS 1577, pp. 206–222, 2022.
https://doi.org/10.1007/978-3-031-04447-2_14

During prophet Muhammad's mission, which lasted 23 years, there was no official scribe recording his speeches, deeds, orders or his silent approvals. However, his companions (Arabic: Sahaba) memorized the prophet Muhammad's legacy and passed it on to others. From generation to generation, his legacy was transmitted in oral and/or written form [10], until Hadith scholars collected them in books.

Hadith-the second source of Islam-refers to any action, saying, order, silent approval or other aspect of the holy prophet Muhammad's life or legacy that was delivered through a chain of narrators. Each Hadith has an Isnad-the chain of narrators-and a Matan-the action of the prophet Muhammad. Figure 1 is an example of a Hadith written in CA, which is entirely different from MSA in both vocabulary and spelling.

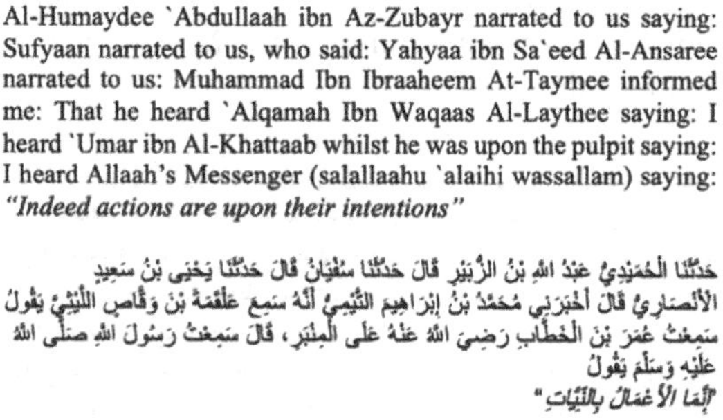

Al-Humaydee `Abdullaah ibn Az-Zubayr narrated to us saying: Sufyaan narrated to us, who said: Yahyaa ibn Sa`eed Al-Ansaree narrated to us: Muhammad Ibn Ibraaheem At-Taymee informed me: That he heard `Alqamah Ibn Waqaas Al-Laythee saying: I heard `Umar ibn Al-Khattaab whilst he was upon the pulpit saying: I heard Allaah's Messenger (salallaahu `alaihi wassallam) saying: *"Indeed actions are upon their intentions"*

حَدَّثَنَا الْحُمَيْدِيُّ عَبْدُ اللهِ بْنُ الزُّبَيْرِ قَالَ حَدَّثَنَا سُفْيَانُ قَالَ حَدَّثَنَا يَحْيَى بْنُ سَعِيدٍ الأَنْصَارِيُّ قَالَ أَخْبَرَنِي مُحَمَّدُ بْنُ إِبْرَاهِيمَ التَّيْمِيُّ أَنَّهُ سَمِعَ عَلْقَمَةَ بْنَ وَقَّاصٍ اللَّيْثِيَّ يَقُولُ سَمِعْتُ عُمَرَ بْنَ الْخَطَّابِ رَضِيَ اللهُ عَنْهُ عَلَى الْمِنْبَرِ، قَالَ سَمِعْتُ رَسُولَ اللهِ صَلَّى اللهُ عَلَيْهِ وَسَلَّمَ يَقُولُ
"إِنَّمَا الأَعْمَالُ بِالنِّيَّاتِ "

Fig. 1. An example of Hadith, Isnad in black and Matan in green. (Color figure online)

Hadith scholars are interested in studying the validity of Hadiths because they are important in every aspect of Muslim life. In contrast to the Quran, some Hadiths, which have been handed down over centuries, have been corrupted by incompetent narrators who incorrectly transferred them. Hadith scholars classify these texts as non-authentic Hadiths.

However, many forged Hadiths have also been circulated not only by incompetent Muslims but also by pious Muslims to encourage others to follow the religious and ethical advice contained in the Hadith. The Isnad exists to clarify the Hadith's reliability. Today, however, most Muslim scholars cite Hadiths without citing their Isnad, which is contrary to the early Islamic period, when Hadiths were not cited without mentioning their Isnad [10]. Today, increased access to the internet has expanded the threat by causing a steady climb in the numbers of forged Hadiths.

To determine the authenticity of a specific Hadith, Hadith scholars use both the Isnad and the Matan. In Isnad, the narrators must be connected, so scholars study the status of each narrator to ascertain whether they are reliably accurate and connected or not [4]. Figure 2 shows an example of a Hadith determined to be non-authentic due to weak and lying narrators (highlighted in yellow).

الحاكم) حدثنا القاسم بن غانم بن حمويه حدثنا محمد بن صالح بن هانئ حدثنا محمد بن إسحاق الهمداني حدثنا أبي حدثنا
محمد بن عمر القرشي عن نهشل بن سعيد عن أبي إسحاق الهمداني عن حبة العرني عن علي مرفوعاً من قرأ آية
الكرسي في دبر كل صلاة لم يمنعه من دخول الجنة إلا الموت ومن قرأها حين يأخذ مضجعه أمنه الله على داره ودار
جاره ودويرات حوله لا يصح حبة ضعيف ونهشل كذاب

Fig. 2. An example of a non-authentic Hadith due to weak and lying narrators. (Color figure online)

In Matan, Hadith scholars study whether it is in agreement with or contradictory to Arabic grammar, another authentic Hadith or what is mentioned in the Quran. Figure 3 illustrates a Hadith that was declared non-authentic for these reasons (highlighted in yellow). In other cases, the Matan contains unacceptable words or expressions that do not reflect the Prophet Muhammad's speech or Muslim beliefs. Figure 4 shows an example of a Matan that contains an unacceptable explanation of Allah.

العقيلي) حدثنا الفضل بن عبدالله العتكي حدثنا سهل المروزي حدثنا النضر بن محرز عن محمد بن المنكدر عن جابر
بن عبدالله عن النبي صلى الله عليه وسلم قال لأن يمتلئ جوف أحدكم قيحاً خير له من أن يمتلئ شعراً هجيت به،
موضوع: والنضر لا يتابع عليه ولا يجوز الاحتجاج به (قلت) عبارة العقيلي وإنما يعرف هذا الحديث بالكلبي عن أبي
صالح عن ابن عباس حدثنا محمد بن إسماعيل الصائغ حدثنا عثمان بن زفرة حدثنا محمد بن مروان السدي عن الكلبي
عن أبي صالح عن ابن عباس عن النبي صلى الله عليه وسلم بهذا وقد قال الحافظ ابن حجر في اللسان العقيلي يضعف
لمجرد المخالفة أو الإعراب والله أعلم.

Fig. 3. An example of a non-authentic Hadith because of the contradiction or the grammar. (Color figure online)

قال أبو الشيخ في العظمة حدثنا محمد بن العباس حدثنا الحسن بن الربيع حدثنا عبدالعزيز بن عبدالوارث حدثنا حرب بم
سريح حدثتنا زينب بنت يزيد العتكية قالت كنا عند عائشة رضي الله تعالى عنها فقالت سمعت رسول الله صلى الله عليه
وسلم يقول إن لله عز وجل ديكاً رجلاه تحت سبع أرضين ورأسه قد جاوز سبع سموات يسبح في أوقات الصلاة فلا يبقى
ديك من ديكة الأرض إلا أجابه

Fig. 4. An example of a Matan that contains an unacceptable explanation of Allah.

The process of distinguishing authentic Hadiths from non-authentic Hadiths is the task of Hadith judgement science. The researchers in [5] reported that Hadiths can be automatically judged using a computerized classifier, such as ML and DL classifiers, which can assist Hadith researchers in their task.

In this paper, we first aimed to produce a new free resource for Hadith research. This language resource is called the non-authentic Hadith corpus, and it contains text from lesser-known Hadith books. Our second aim was to identify which part of the Hadith (Isnad, Matan or both) is most effective for automatically detecting authenticity. Third, we aimed to examine the utilization of DL and PPM classifiers, which have not previously been used for detecting Hadith authenticity. The fourth aim was to compare the DL, ML and PPM classifiers to determine which is the most effective classifier when detecting the authenticity of a Hadith.

2 Related Work

Hadith authentication refers to the classification of Hadiths as authentic or non-authentic using artificial intelligence methods. Several types of NLP methods can be applied to solve the problem of Hadith authentication. However, very few studies have been published in this area. In this section, we present some of the prior studies that focused on determining Hadith authenticity.

Ghazizadeh et al. [6] pointed out that determining a Hadith's authenticity involves two parameters: (1) the reliability and honesty of the Hadith narrators and (2) whether the Hadith was continuous or discrete, as determined by the Isnad. They built a fuzzy rule-based system with these parameters and expert opinions that relied on two inference engines. In the first engine, each narrator was ranked according to reliability and honesty. The output from the first step was used as the input for the second engine. This second stage produces a Hadith validation rate. To test their system, they used the *Kafi* database, which is a reliable book of Hadiths, and achieved an accuracy rate of 94%.

Bilal and Mohsin [7] noted that classifying Hadiths is a sensitive and complex task that can only be accomplished by Hadith scholars with intimate knowledge of the large number of rules involved in the process. As a result, the *Muhadith* system was built to facilitate the Hadith classification process. The aims of the *Muhadith* are to automatically classify Hadiths by imitating Hadith scholars' ability to determine authenticity. It was designed by combining ideas from distributed computing systems, web technologies and Hadith scholars' knowledge. A user types a Hadith into a web-based interface, where the Hadith then passes to the web server, where the user's input is analysed and the required data extracted. This information is then sent to the fact extractor connected to the database, which returns the results and an explanation of the Hadith classification to the user.

In their research, Aldhaln et al. [8] used the decision tree (DT) algorithm to classify Hadiths according to degree (Sahih, Hasan, Daeef or Maudo). Their corpus consisted of 999 Hadiths from three different Hadith books: *Bukhari, Jami'u Al-Termithi* and *Silsilat Al-Ahadith Al-Dae'ifah w' Al-Mawdhu'ah*. In addition, it included both the Hadiths and their attributes, as included in the Hadith books, as a means of describing their individual degrees. However, some of the Hadiths did not clearly describe these attributes, which resulted in missing values. To solve this problem, the researchers used a missing data detector (MDD). The corpus was divided into two data sets, with 66.7% of the Hadiths comprising the training data set and 33.3% comprising the test data set. Their experiments showed that the MDD had a significant effect on the performance of the DT classifier, with accuracy rising from a rate of 50.1502% to 97.597%.

Najiyah et al. [9] asserted that non-authentic Hadiths can lead to misunder-standings of Islamic law, identifying a need to develop automatic classifications of authentic and non-authentic Hadiths. They classified Hadiths using expert systems and a DT classifier. First, they created an expert table of Hadiths by interviewing Hadith experts and confirming their findings using a variety of trusted Hadith books. They divided the Hadiths by degree into three groups: (1) Sahih, or authentic Hadiths with continuous, trustworthy Isnads and with Matan that did not contradict other authentic Hadiths; (2) Daeef, or Hadiths made weak by non-continuous Isnads, which they then divided into 17 sub-degrees; and (3) Maudo, or fabricated Hadiths created by inauthentic narrators. The degree of a Hadith can be determined by evaluating the Isnad and Matan, as authenticated by Hadith scholars. To evaluate their system, they built a training corpus containing 274 Hadiths and a test corpus containing 72 Hadiths. Their results showed that their classification model could be relied upon to classify Sahih Hadith with an error rate of only 0.00134%.

It is clear from this review of the existing research that, first, most Hadith authentication studies have focused on Isnad for automatically judging the authenticity of Hadiths, and a paper by Hakak et al. [4] indicated that authenti-cation based on Matan is one of the challenges facing the authenticating of digital Hadith. Second, none of the existing work examines the use of DL or PPM clas-sifiers to automatically detect a Hadith's authenticity. Thus, the present study aimed to fill these research gaps.

3   Proposed Data Sets

For this study, we selected two different Hadith corpora: a non-authentic Hadith (NAH) corpus [14] and the Leeds University and King Saud University (LK) Hadith corpus [15]. The main advantages of these corpora are that they are freely available to the Hadith research community and they have different Hadith structures.

3.1   Non-authentic Hadith (NAH) Corpus

Most NLP studies for Arabic Hadith research focus on the six canonical Hadith books, and there is a shortage of research into lesser-known Hadith books. There-fore, a corpus containing Arabic Hadith from lesser-known Hadith books, in particular, would provide a new resource for Hadith community research. Thus, the purpose of the NAH corpus was to build a corpus that contained text from lesser-known Hadith books. These books are considered challenging for many reasons, including being written in a very old style, lacking a clear structure and lacking any new revisions, restructuring or editing processes.

The NAH corpus is so named due to the large number of non-authentic Hadiths it contains, as compared to authentic Hadiths. The main features of this corpus are that it is freely available to the Hadith research community[1] and it contains 1,621,423 words from 15 non-famous Hadith books. Over 4,000 Hadiths were annotated manually according to the Hadith's *Isnad* and *Matan* in addition to *Authors comment, Hadith type, Hadith authenticity* and *Hadith topic*. These Hadiths were divided into over 7,000 Hadith records. Some of the Hadiths are classified as Hadith block, which refers to a complex kind of Hadith that contains several Isnads, Matans or author comments, and these were written sequentially. Figure 5 illustrates an example of a Hadith block. So, Hadith in Fig. 5 was divided into two records since it has two isnads and matans. Table 1 shows the corpus contents.

```
<Isnad1>حدثنا عمر له أن ابن موسى حدثنا موسى بن السندي حدثنا عثمان بن
عبدالرحمن الطرايفي حدثنا عمر بن موسى بن دحية عن القاسم عن أبي أمامة
أن لله إذا غضب أنزل الوحي بالعربية وإذا رضي أنزل <Matan1></Isnad1> مرفوعاً
قال ابن حبان هذا الحديث باطل لا<AuthorComment1></Matan1> الوحي بالفارسية
أخبرني عن محمد <Isnad2></AuthorComment1> أصل له عمر بن موسى بن دحية وضاع
بن الحسين بن فنجويه حدثنا أبي حدثنا محمد بن إبراهيم حدثنا محمد بن أحمد
التميمي حدثنا أبو عصمة عاصم بن عبيد الله البلخي حدثنا إسماعيل بن زياد عن
أبغض الكلام <Matan2></Isnad2> الغالب القطان عن المقبري عن أبي هريرة رفعه
إلى الله تعالى بالفارسية وكلام الشيطان الخوزية وكلام أهل النار البخارية وكلام
قال ابن حبان وضعه إسماعيل شيخ <AuthorComment2></Matan2> أهل الجنة العربية
دجال لا يحل ذكره في الكتب إلا على سبيل القدح فيه رواه عن عاصم بن عبيدالله
البلخي وهو موضوع لا أصل له من كلام رسول الله صلى الله عليه وسلم ولا حدث به أبو
</AuthorComment2> هريرة ولا المقبري ولا غالب
```

Fig. 5. An example of a Hadith block extracted from N3_1.

Table 1. The NAH corpus contents.

No.	Book Reference Name	Book's Title	Author	Book's Contents	Hadith's Type	No. of words	Annoted	verifed
1	N1	الأباطيل والمناكير والصحاح والمشاهير	أبو عبد الله الحمادي الجورقاني	Isnad/Matan/Comments	authentic and NAH	121,080	Yes	Yes
2	N2	مائة حديث ضعيف وموضوع منتشرة بين الخطباء والوعاظ	إحسان العتيبي	Matan/Comments	NAH	2,898	Yes	No
3	N3_1	اللآلئ المصنوعة في الأحاديث الموضوعة الجزء الأول ط. دار دار المعرفة	جلال الدين السيوطي	Isnad/Matan/Comments	authentic and NAH	15,421	Yes	Yes
4	N3_2	اللآلئ المصنوعة في الأحاديث الموضوعة الجزء الثاني ط. دار دار المعرفة	جلال الدين السيوطي	Isnad/Matan/Comments	authentic and NAH	151,382	Yes	Yes
5	N4	الأحاديث الضعيفة في كتاب رياض الصالحين	إحسان العتيبي	Isnad/Matan	NAH	5,675	Yes	No
6	N5	الجد الحثيث في بيان ما ليس بحديث ابو زيد دار الراية	أحمد بن عبد الكريم العامري	Matan/Comments	NAH	16,382	Yes	No
7	N6	القوائم المجموعة في الأحاديث الموضوعة ط. العلمية	الإمام محمد بن علي الشوكاني	Matan/Comments	NAH	139,786	Yes	Yes
8	N7	معرفة التذكرة في الأحاديث الموضوعة مؤسسة الكتب الثقافية	لابن ظاهر المقدسي	Matan/Comments	NAH	115,672	No	No
9	N8	جامع الأحاديث القدسية (الضعيفة) دار الريان للتراث	حسام الدين الصابني	Matan/Comments	NAH	246,141	No	No
10	N9	ضعيف سنن الترمذي	محمد ناصر الألباني	Isnad/Matan/Comments	NAH	663,783	No	No
11	N10	الموضوعات دار المأمون للتراث - دمشق	الحسن بن محمد الصغاني	Matan/Comments	NAH	13,508	No	No
12	N11	النخبة البهية في الأحاديث المكذوبة على خير البرية المكتب الإسلامي	محمد الأمير الكبير المالكي	Matan/Comments	NAH	13,508	No	No
13	N12	المصنوع في معرفة الحديث الموضوع	علي القاري الهروي المكي	Matan/Comments	NAH	33,037	No	No
14	N13	أحاديث الإحياء التي لا أصل لها	الإمام تاج الدين السبكي	Matan	NAH	55,917	No	No
15	N14	اللؤلؤ الموضوع فيما لا أصل له أو بأصله موضوع ط. دار البشائر + ط. قديمة	الشيخ أبي الحسن القاروني	Matan/Comments	NAH	27,233	No	No
Total	15					1,621,423		

Methodology. The Web as a corpus method [11], was used to collect Hadiths from the islamweb.net and almeshkat.net websites. Because the Web texts are

---

free and written by a wide variety of writers, there is a lack of interest in proof-reading [11]. We found numerous mistakes in our corpus, such as missing spaces عنمسروق رضياللهعنها, missing letters الل, and spelling errors مفوعاً, اتنهى, مرضوع. By comparing the *N3_1* Word file with the original book PDF file, we found some Hadiths missing from the Word file, and we left these errors as they were written in the source

الورد الأبيض خلق من عرقي ليلة المعراج والورد الأحمر خلق من عرق -78
جبريلوالورد الأصفر من عرق البراق وأورده ابن فارس عن عائشة

Fig. 6. An example of missing space in N5 (in bold).

Corpus Annotation. The NAH corpus contains two primary folders. The annotated folder contains seven comma-separated value (CSV) files encompassing the Hadith books that have been manually annotated for this study. The unannotated folder contains five CSV files that contain the Hadith books that have not been annotated (see Fig. 7). Every Hadith in the first folder has eight primary features or attributes. These are *No.*, *Full Hadith*, the *Isnad*, the *Matan*, the *Authors Comments*, the *Hadith Type*, *Authenticity* and *Topic*. The Authenticity feature is an important label in this study and the annotator copied the Hadith authenticity from Hadith book which was acknowledged by Hadith scholars. A description of the NAH corpus features is provided in Table 2.

Table 2. Features of the NAH corpus.

Features	Description
No.	The Hadith reference number
Full Hadith	The Hadith as it appears in the book without annotations
Isnad	The chain of narrators
Matan	The act of the Prophet Muhammad
Authors Comments	The author describes the authenticity of each Hadith
Hadith Type	The Hadith Type (Maqtu' مقطع, Mawquf موقف and Marfo (مرفوع) or Hadith degree (ضعيف, موضوع and so on)
Authenticity	Whether this Hadith is authentic or non-authentic
Topic	The chapter title

Corpus Evaluation. This section describes the various experimental analyses conducted to evaluate the corpus. First, cross-corpus evaluation was used to compare the classification results of the NAH corpus with other Hadith corpora using different DL classifiers. This assisted in verifying Hadith components (Isnad and Matan) by comparing them against existing Hadith corpora. Second, to verify the quality of the annotation, we applied an inter-annotator agreement (IAA) analysis.

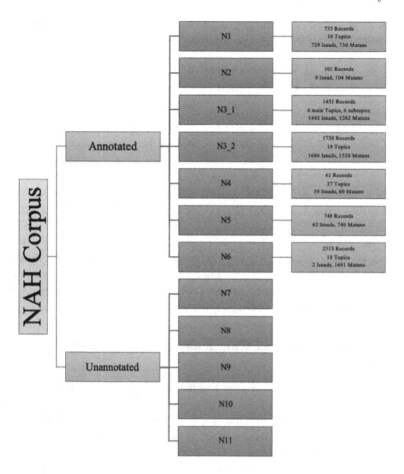

Fig. 7. The NAH corpus structure.

Cross-Corpus Evaluation. In order to evaluate the NAH corpus, we compared it with another existing corpus with similar features, the LK corpus [15]. In this experiment, we used one corpus as a training set and the other corpus as a testing set. The experiment used the convolutional neural network (CNN) and long short-term memory (LSTM) classifiers.

Table 3 shows that the NAH corpus identified 98% and 99% of the LK corpus using CNN and LSTM, respectively. The LK corpus identified 90% and 98% of the NAH corpus using CNN and LSTM, respectively. This demonstrates that even when using different classifiers, training models with the NAH corpus results in higher accuracy rates than training with the LK corpus.

Table 3. Cross-corpus evaluation using CNN and LSTM trained on the training datasets (rows) and tested on testing datasets (columns).

Classifier	Dataset	NAH	LK
CNN	NAH	-	98.39%
	LK	90.54%	-
LSTM	NAH	-	99.57%
	LK	98.06%	-

Inter-annotator Agreements. Annotation of the NAH corpus was carried out by two annotators with Arabic and Islamic backgrounds. To validate the quality of their annotation, the Kappa coefficient, K, [12] was chosen to calculate the IAA between the two annotators. This paid process is quite expensive, so we provided only three books to the annotators who took part in this research. These were *N3_1*, *N3_2* and *N6* from the NAH. Then the Kappa coefficient was calculated for the total of 4,338 Hadith records and obtained Kappa values between 0.9842 and 0.9983, which indicates perfect agreement, according to [13].

3.2 Leeds University and King Saud University (LK) Hadith Corpus

The LK corpus is a parallel corpus of English-Arabic Hadith built by [15], which containing 39,038 annotated Hadiths from the six canonical Hadith books. The main advantage of this corpus is that it is freely available[2] to the Hadith research community, while the main disadvantage is that the split into Isnad and Matan was automatically annotated and has only been manually verified for the *Bukhari* sub-corpus. This means that the other sub-corpora, such as Muslim, are noisy and need to be verified.

4 Deep Learning Classifiers

In this study, which used the CNN and LSTM basic models, we propose a hybrid model, the CNN-LSTM hybrid, that incorporates the advantages of each. The CNN captures the local features of the text, but with long sequences of words, it cannot preserve long-term dependencies. The LSTM overcomes the vanishing gradient problem by capturing any long-term dependencies in a lengthy sequence of words [16,17]. Zhang et al. [16] reported that this hybrid model enhanced the accuracy rate of text classification.

Word embeddings are standard representation of word meanings used in NLP [19]. Our DL models consist of an input embedding layer, a hidden layer and a dense output layer. The embedding layer is important for DL models because it

---

[2] https://github.com/ShathaTm/LK-Hadith-Corpus.

permits capturing relationships between words that are hard to capture otherwise. In this layer, each word in the input data is represented by a dense vector of fixed size. We used this layer to learn an embedding for all of the words in our training datasets.

The dense output layer takes the number of classes as its output dimension. Because this is a binary classification problem, the sigmoid function was used for activation.

The hierarchy of our DL models is as follows:

- CNN. The architecture of our CNN model consists of one CNN layer with 15 filters and a kernel size of 3, followed by global max-pooling with default values (see Fig. 8).
- LSTM. The architecture of our LSTM model consists of one LSTM layer with `hidden_nodes` = 15 and `return_sequences` = true. The `return_sequences` argument returns all the outputs of the hidden states of each time steps. The next layer is global max-pooling with default values (see Fig. 8).

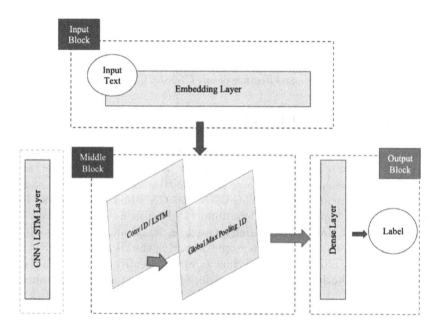

Fig. 8. The architecture of our CNN and LSTM models.

- CNN-LSTM. The architecture of this model consists of one CNN, one LSTM and global max-pooling with default values (see Fig. 9).

When fitting DL models, we used a `callbacks` function with the `early_stop` method to monitor our model's performance. This method halts the training process if accuracy stops improving. In addition, we added a `patience` argument with four epochs to delay this early stopping for a set number of unimproved epochs.

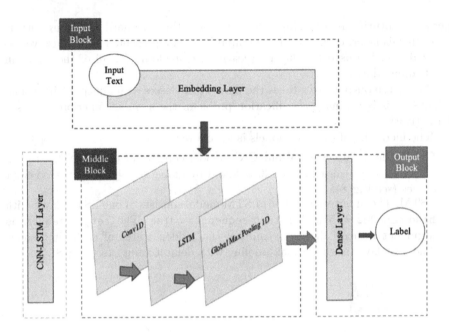

Fig. 9. The architecture of our CNN-LSTM model.

5   Experiments and Results

Three experiments were performed to evaluate the automatic detection of Hadith authenticity by the compression-based classifier [18]; ML classifiers, such as the support vector machine (SVM), naïve Bayes (NB) and DT classifiers; and DL classifiers, which includes the LSTM, CNN and CNN-LSTM classifiers. These experiments were conducted to determine (1) Hadith authenticity based on Hadith; (2) detect Hadith authenticity based on Isnad and (3) detect Hadith authenticity based on Matan. Aside from comparing the DL, ML and PPM classifiers, the primary aim of these experiments was to identify the part of a Hadith (Isnad, Matan or both) that is best used for effective automatic determination of authenticity.

These experiments used two data sets (*N3_1* and *N3_2*) from the NAH corpus and the *Bukhari* and *Muslim* data sets from the LK corpus, with the goal of determining authenticity. Each Hadith record was assigned to one of the following two classes:

- **Authentic** records that contained an authentic Hadith from the *Bukhari* or *Muslim* data sets.
- **Non-authentic** records that contained non-authentic Hadith from the *N3_1* or *N3_2* data sets.

To guarantee a balanced distribution in the classes, we limited the number of records per class, thereby ensuring that the training phases used an equal number of records per category. We used 1,264 Hadith records from *Bukhari* to train the authentic model, and we used 1,264 Hadith records from *N3_1* to train the non-authentic model. The testing file contained 2,996 Hadith records: 1,498 Hadith records from *N3_2* and 1,498 Hadith records from *Muslim*.

5.1   Authentication Based on Hadith

In this experiment, we extracted full Hadith records containing both Isnad and Matan from the *Bukhari* and *N3_1* data sets to train the authentic and non-authentic models, respectively. The PPM and CNN-LSTM classifiers achieved higher rates of accuracy than the other classifiers by reaching up to 93%. The LSTM classifier obtained 80% and the CNN 72%. The lowest accuracy reported was from the DT classifier, with 55%. Table 4 shows the results of this experiment.

Table 4. The results of the authentication in the Hadith-based experiment.

Classifier	Accuracy (%)	Recall	Precision	F-measure
PPM	**93**	**0.94**	**0.93**	**0.93**
SVM	61	0.61	0.78	0.54
NB	76	0.76	0.83	0.75
DT	55	0.55	0.76	0.44
LSTM	80	0.97	0.73	0.84
CNN	72	0.99	0.64	0.78
CNN-LSTM	**93**	**0.93**	**0.93**	**0.93**

Figure 10 illustrates some authentic Hadiths that were predicted to be non-authentic. This might be because the narrator أبو عقيل (highlighted in blue in Fig. 10) had been mentioned several times in *N3_1*, which was the non-authentic training set.

5.2   Authentication Based on Isnad

In this experiment, we extracted records that contained only Isnad from the *Bukhari* and *N3_1* data sets to train the authentic and non-authentic models, respectively. The CNN classifier achieved better accuracy than the other classifiers and reached up to 93%. This was followed by the PPM classifier, with 92%, and then the SVM classifier, with 91%. The lowest accuracy was reported for the CNN-LSTM classifier, with 84%. Table 5 presents the results of this experiment.

Table 5. The results of the authentication based on Isnad experiment.

Classifier	Accuracy (%)	Recall	Precision	F-measure
PPM	92	0.93	0.92	0.93
SVM	91	0.91	0.92	0.92
NB	89	0.89	0.90	0.89
DT	90	0.90	0.90	0.90
LSTM	90	0.95	0.87	0.90
CNN	**93**	**0.97**	**0.90**	**0.93**
CNN-LSTM	84	0.97	0.77	0.86

1.
<NonAuthentic>وحدثني أبو بكر بن النضر بن أبي
النضر قال حدثني أبو النضر هاشم بن القاسم
حدثنا أبو عقيل صاحب بهية قال كنت جالسا عند
القاسم بن عبيد الله ويحيى بن سعيد فقال يحيى
للقاسم يا أبا محمد إنه قبيح على مثلك عظيم أن
تسأل عن شيء من أمر هذا الدين فلا يوجد عندك
منه علم ولا فرج أو علم ولا مخرج فقال له القاسم
وعم ذاك قال لأنك ابن إمامي هدى ابن أبي بكر
وعمر قال يقول له القاسم أقبح من ذاك عند من
عقل عن الله أن أقول بغير علم أو آخذ عن غير ثقة
قال فسكت فما أجابه<\NonAuthentic>

2.
<NonAuthentic>وحدثني بشر بن الحكم العبدي قال
سمعت سفيان بن عيينة يقول أخبروني عن أبي
عقيل صاحب بهية أن أبناء لعبد الله بن عمر
سألوه عن شيء لم يكن عنده فيه علم فقال له
يحيى بن سعيد والله إني لأعظم أن يكون مثلك وأنت
ابن إمامي الهدى يعني عمر وابن عمر تسأل عن
أمر ليس عندك فيه علم فقال أعظم من ذلك والله عند
الله وعند من عقل عن الله أن أقول بغير علم أو أخبر
عن غير ثقة قال وشهدهما أبو عقيل يحيى بن
المتوكل حين قالا ذلك<\NonAuthentic>

Fig. 10. Sample of authentic Hadiths predicted to be non-authentic in the PPM output of the first experiment. (Color figure online)

Figure 11 illustrates an example of a non-authentic Isnad from *N3_2* that was predicted to be authentic. This is because the Isnad for this Hadith had a narrator, ابن عمر who is known to be a trustworthy narrator. It is possible that this Hadith was classified as authentic not because of any weakness in the Isnad but because of its Matan.

عن ابـن عمـر عن الـنبي صلى الله علـيـه<Authentic>
<Authentic\>   وسلم أن هقـال

Fig. 11. Example of a non-authentic Isnad from N3_2 predicted to be authentic in the PPM output of the second experiment.

5.3 Authentication Based on Matan

In this experiment, we extracted Matan records, which contained only Matan, from the *Bukhari* and *N3_1* data sets to train the authentic and the non-authentic models, respectively. The LSTM classifier achieved the highest rates of accuracy, reaching 85%, which is lower than the previous experiments. This was followed by the CNN and CNN-LSTM classifiers, with 84% and 82%, respectively. The PPM classifier obtained an accuracy of 79%. The lowest accuracy was reported by the SVM and DT classifiers, each with 55%. Table 6 provides the results of this experiment.

Table 6. The results of the authentication based on Matan experiment.

Classifier	Accuracy (%)	Recall	Precision	F-measure
PPM	79	0.79	0.79	0.79
SVM	55	0.56	0.75	0.45
NB	72	0.72	0.80	0.70
DT	55	0.56	0.75	0.45
LSTM	**85**	**0.80**	**0.90**	**0.85**
CNN	84	0.85	0.84	0.84
CNN-LSTM	82	0.87	0.79	0.83

Figure 12 illustrates an example of a non-authentic Matan from *N3_2* that was predicted to be authentic. This Matan was mentioned in the *Bukhari* data set several times. Furthermore, this Hadith might be narrated by different Isnad, and the Isnad mentioned in the *N3_2* data set constitutes a weakness.

بـين كـل أذ انـين صلاة<Authentic>   <Authentic\>

Fig. 12. Example of a non-authentic Matan from N3_2 predicted to be authentic in the PPM output of the third experiment.

The accuracy for the first experiment ranged from 55% to 93%. The accuracy for the second experiment was between 84% and 93%, while the accuracy for this third experiment ranged from 55% to 85%, which means that Isnad was the part of a Hadith that resulted in the most effective automatic determinations of authenticity. However, this experiment also proved that we could use the Matan to judge Hadiths with an accuracy rate of 85%. Figure 13 compares the performance of PPM classifier, three ML classifiers and three DL classifiers.

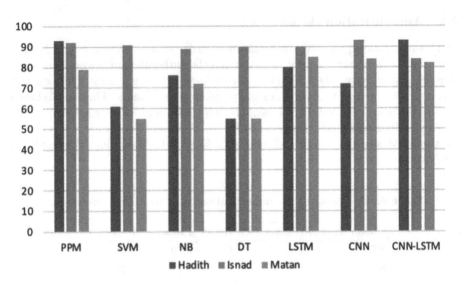

Fig. 13. A comparison of the accuracy rates using different parts of a Hadith.

6   Conclusion

This paper discussed our creation of a new Arabic corpus that uses the NAH containing samples of Arabic Hadith text from lesser-known Hadith books. Our experiments showed, first, that Isnad is the part of a Hadith that results in the most effective automatic determination of authenticity. Also proved was that Matan can be used to judge Hadiths with an accuracy rate of up to 85%. Finally, we also demonstrated that the PPM and DL classifiers were also helpful in obtaining an effective automatic determination of Hadith authenticity.

References

1. Khreisat, L.: A machine learning approach for Arabic text classification using N-gram frequency statistics. J. Informetr. **3**(1), 72–77 (2009). https://doi.org/10.1016/j.joi.2008.11.005

2. Duwairi, R., Al-Refai, M.N., Khasawneh, N.: Feature reduction techniques for Arabic text categorization. J. Am. Soc. Inf. Sci. Technol. **60**(11), 2347–2352 (2009). https://doi.org/10.1002/asi.21173

3. Alwedyan, J., Hadi, W.M., Salam, M., Mansour, H.Y.: Categorize Arabic data sets using multi-class classification based on association rule approach. In: Proceedings of the 2011 International Conference on Intelligent Semantic Web-Services and Applications, pp. 1–8. Association for Computing Machinery, New York (2011). https://doi.org/10.1145/1980822.1980840

4. Hakak, S., et al.: Digital Hadith authentication: recent advances, open challenges, and future directions. Trans. Emerg. Telecommun. Technol. (2020). https://doi.org/10.1002/ETT.3977

5. Najeeb, M.M.A.: Towards a deep learning-based approach for Hadith classification. Eur. J. Eng. Technol. Res. **6**(3), 9–15 (2021). https://doi.org/10.24018/ejeng.2021.6.3.2378

6. Ghazizadeh, M., Zahedi, M.H., Kahani, M., Bidgoli, B.M.: Fuzzy expert system in determining Hadith validity. In: Sobh, T. (ed.) Advances in Computer and Information Sciences and Engineering, pp. 354–359. Springer, Dordrecht (2008). https://doi.org/10.1007/978-1-4020-8741-7_64

7. Bilal, K., Mohsin, S.: Muhadith: A cloud based distributed expert system for classification of Ahadith. In 2012 10th International Conference on Frontiers of Information Technology, pp. 73–78, IEEE, New York (2012). https://doi.org/10.1109/FIT.2012.22

8. Aldhaln, K., Zeki, A., Zeki, A.: Knowledge extraction in Hadith using data mining technique. Int. J. Inf. Technol. Comput. Sci. **2**, 13–21 (2012)

9. Najiyah, I., Susanti, S., Riana, D., Wahyudi, M.: Hadith degree classification for Shahih Hadith identification web based. In: 2017 5th International Conference on Cyber and IT Service Management, pp. 1–6. IEEE, New York (2017). https://doi.org/10.1109/citsm.2017.8089304

10. Brown, J.A.C.: Hadith: Muhammad's Legacy in the Medieval and Modern World. One-world Publications, London (2017)

11. Kilgarriff, A., Grefenstette, G.: Introduction to the special issue on the web as corpus. Comput. Linguist. **29**(3), 333–347 (2003). https://doi.org/10.1162/089120103322711569

12. Cohen, J.: A coefficient of agreement for nominal scales. Educ. Psychol. Meas. **20**(1), 37–46 (1960). https://doi.org/10.1177/001316446002000104

13. Landis, J.R., Koch, G.G.: The measurement of observer agreement for categorical data. Biometrics **33**(1), 159–174 (1977). https://doi.org/10.2307/2529310

14. Tarmom, T., Atwell, E., Alsalka, M.: Non-authentic Hadith corpus: design and methodology. In: International Conference on Islamic Applications in Computer Science and Technologies (2019). http://www.sign-ific-ance.co.uk/index.php/IJASAT/article/view/2272

15. Altammami, S., Atwell, E., Alsalka M.A.: The Arabic-English parallel corpus of authentic Hadith. In: International Conference on Islamic Applications in Computer Science and Technologies (2019). http://www.sign-ific-ance.co.uk/index.php/IJASAT/article/view/2199

16. Zhang, J., Li, Y., Tian, J., Li, T.: LSTM-CNN hybrid model for text classification. In: 2018 IEEE 3rd Advanced Information Technology, Electronic and Automation Control Conference (IAEAC), pp. 1675–1680. IEEE, New York (2018). https://doi.org/10.1109/IAEAC.2018.8577620

17. Li, X., Ning, H.: Chinese text classification based on hybrid model of CNN and LSTM. In: Proceedings of the 3rd International Conference on Data Science and Information Technology, pp. 129–134. Association for Computing Machinery, New York (2020). https://doi.org/10.1145/3414274.3414493
18. Teahan, W.J.: A compression-based toolkit for modelling and processing natural language text. Information **9**(12), 294 (2018). https://doi.org/10.3390/info9120294
19. Daniel, J., Martin, J.H.: Speech and Languages Processing. Prentice-Hall, New Delhi (2000)

Classical Machine Learning vs Deep Learning for Detecting Cyber-Violence in Social Media

Randa Zarnoufi[1][(⊠)] and Mounia Abik[2]

[1] FSR, Mohammed V University in Rabat, Rabat, Morocco
randa_zarnoufi@um5.ac.ma
[2] ENSIAS, Mohammed V University in Rabat, Rabat, Morocco
mounia.abik@ensias.um5.ac.ma

Abstract. Cyber-violence is a largely addressed problem in e-health researches, its focus is the detection of harmful behavior from the online user-generated text in order to prevent and protect victims. In this work, we tackle the problem of Social Media (SM) text analysis to detect the harmful content that is the common characteristic of cyber-violence acts. For that, we use classical Machine Learning (ML) based on user psychological features that we compare with Deep Learning (DL) techniques in a small dataset setting. The results were in favor of classical ML. The findings highlight that psychological characteristics extracted from user-generated text are strong predictors of his harmful behavior.

Keywords: Social Media · Cyber-violence · Harmful behavior · Classical Machine Learning · Features engineering · Deep Learning

1 Introduction

Cyber-violence can be defined as: online abuse against an individual or group, often with disruptive effects on the victims. Cyber-violence has been widely discussed in the literature under different names such as cyberstalking, hate speech, and offensive, aggressive or toxic language. However, its interest remains the detection of violent contents to protect other users. Therefore, in the present study, we consider 'cyber-violence' as any act reflecting virtual violence.

For the techniques employed in the detection of cyber violence, and after a review of the literature, we have extracted the following conclusions:

- The most of related studies in the computational field have been mainly focused on supervised ML techniques based on features often of a technical nature (e.g., key-words, user and network information).
- The DL techniques, that have been used for performance improvement of existing systems without features engineering, require large amounts of annotated data.
- The previous studies have neglected important factors for detecting violent behavior, such as, personality and human behavioral characteristics [1].

J. A. Lossio-Ventura et al. (Eds.): SIMBig 2021, CCIS 1577, pp. 223–235, 2022.
https://doi.org/10.1007/978-3-031-04447-2_15

– Finally, psychological studies related to cyber-violence recommend studying the psychological characteristics of the perpetrators' personality [2, 3].

Following these recommendations, in this work, we study the impact of user' emotions and Big Five personality traits in detecting harmful content from its written text.

Our principal motivation behind extracting violent traits from individuals' writings comes from the strong relationship between language, personality and behavior. Indeed, a wide range of studies have been established on the correlation between language use and psychological traits. Some studies show that word use differs between individuals, but *correlates with their personalities and behaviors* [4–7]. Other studies confirm the *strong relationship between SM users' writing and personality traits* [8, 9].

Our approach has several advantages, first, the detection of the harmful behaviour is based on the language of emotions and personality traits that are present in almost all types of violence through the expressions written by cyber perpetrators. Second, the harmful behavior is considered to be the common characteristic of the most forms of cyber-violence. This means that our approach is generic and scalable to other forms of cyber violence. Finally, since it is based on classical ML it can work on small dataset for which DL cannot give good performance as we will prove in this paper.

The paper is organized as follows; we first present some related works to cyber-violence detection. Later we introduce our approach for harmful behavior detection based on psychological features with classical ML that we compare with DL architectures. Finally, we present and discuss the obtained results.

2   Related Works

Even if that cyber-violence includes several forms, the most covered one by the previous studies is cyber-bullying. Cyber-bullying is defined as an aggressive and repetitive act, however, by analyzing its related studies, we found that the majority of them were concerned about the harmful behavior of this act and ignored its repetitious nature [10]. It can, therefore be considered similar to other forms of violence (e.g. hate speech, offensive language...). Consequently, for the detection of the other forms of cyber-violence we can still use the same approaches as in these studies. In our case, this harmful content is considered as a sign of user behavior that will help in cyber-violence perpetrator detection.

In general, the detection task is carried out either through classical ML techniques or DL ones. ML techniques require the engineering of features and an algorithm that performs the detection. For DL, since the features are created in an autonomous way, the detection is only based on the used algorithm that requires large amounts of annotated data to ensure good performance. Here after, we present the previous works related to these techniques.

2.1 Classical ML

In classical ML, the detection process is based on two steps; the first is *features extraction* and the second is *learning* the ML model based on the extracted features.

Features Extraction
This step relies to human engineered features that aims to find the learning criterions, which here are the elements of a harmful content. According to the survey made by [10], four main categories are used; content (e.g. abusive/profane words), psychological characters (sentiments, emotions, personality traits), user (e.g. gender and age) and network (e.g. number of followers-following, the number of Likes) based features. For instance, in this work [11] the authors used Big Five and dark triad personality features in addition to network features. In our previous work [12] Big Five traits were employed effectively in harmful content detection. [13] used the emotional states of the victims after a cyber-violence episode. User's emotions were also used in our previous work [14]. In [15] they employed user, content, activity and network features to detect cyberbullying behavior. Also [16] extracted user, text, and network-based features.

ML Algorithms
Supervised learning is the most used technique for cyber-violence detection [10]. Among the used algorithms Support Vector Machine (SVM) classifier is the most used one, for instance, in [13, 17–19]. Whereas, other techniques are also used, in [11, 16] they used Random Forest classifier and they reached good performances in cyber-bullying detection. For the same purpose Al-garadi et al. [15] trained a Random Forest classifier in addition to LibSVM, the latter was the best performing model. Logistic regression was also used in many studies [20, 21] and it shows good performance.

2.2 DL Techniques

DL has been used significantly in recent years in cyber violence detection. In [22], they have addressed the problem of hate speech detection by applying different DL architectures, namely, CNN and LSTM that was the best performing one. Tommasel et al. [23] presented an approach for automatic aggression detection based on combining SVM and DL models. Their results show that aggression detection is a rather complex task, especially when it is expressed implicitly in the text (as in irony and sarcasm).

Transfer learning was also adopted in this task. Agrawal and Awekar [24] have tested transfer learning to investigate whether the knowledge gained from DL models (CNN, LSTM, BLSTM, and BLSTM with attention) on one dataset can be used to improve the performance of cyber-bullying detection on other datasets extracted from different SM platforms. In a similar study, Dadvar and Eckert [25] have replicated the same techniques by performing a transfer learning from Twitter to a YouTube dataset showing an increase in performance.

Recently, contextual embedding with BERT was used in a multilingual context to detect offensive language [26], misogyny and aggressiveness [27] while achieving very good performance.

In summary, supervised learning is the leading approach in cyber violence studies. DL techniques remain the most powerful, but require large annotated corpora. In a small dataset setting, we think that classical ML will be the right choice. However, these techniques need a careful features engineering. We have noticed that previous studies have focused on technical features and have not considered the users' psychological factors. Although, we believe that these factors can be very useful in the detection process.

Therefore, in this work, we will explore the relationship between the online user's emotions and Big Five personality traits and its harmful behavior to show their impact on cyber-violence detection. The details of our approach are given here after.

3   Approach and Method

In our approach, we assume that the harmful behaviour of the cyber-perpetrators can be identified from their emotions and personality traits.

To test this assumption, we have adopted the supervised learning approach with classical ML techniques that go through a feature extraction step followed by a learning step. First, we have extracted the features related to user' emotional states. On these features, we have trained Ensemble ML algorithms to predict the presence or absence of user's violent content. Second, we have applied the same process with the features based on the Big Five personality traits. After that, we have combined these two types of features. Finally, we have compared the performance of the generated models with those of DL based on CNN, RNN and transformer models architectures. The objective is to prove that classical ML are more convenient in small dataset setting than DL, which will allow us to save both time and computational efforts.

As use case, we have applied our approach on the detection of cyber-harassment, which is a common form of cyber violence.

We mention that, even if our approach deals with each tweet independently; however, if we can collect a set of tweets generated by the same user, we can get a clear overview of his online behaviour.

3.1   Features Extraction

In our approach, to extract linguistic features, we adopt the open vocabulary approach [9] and [20] rather than the use of special lexicon like Linguistic Inquiry and Word Count (LIWC) [28]. The main advantage of open vocabularies is that linguistic features are automatically identified and extracted from texts written by the users themselves. Special lexicons, on the other hand, are limited to predefined word lists, therefore they cannot largely cover the words used in different types of self-expressions.

For this purpose, we have used two types of features: based on emotions lexicon and based on Big Five personality traits. To extract these features from the dataset, in addition to lexical matching we use semantic similarity with word embedding to better contextualize the matching process between words from lexicons with posts' words from the dataset. For each post word, we calculate the cosine similarity between the word vectors of that word and each word from lexicon. the effectiveness of semantic similarity has been proven in our previous work [14].

Emotions. For features we have used EmoLex [29], a lexicon extracted from tweets containing words related to the eight basic emotions proposed by Plutchik [30]: anticipation, anger, fear, confidence, surprise, sadness, joy, and disgust.

Big Five Personality Traits. As features, we have chosen the Big Five personality facets (Agreeableness, Conscientiousness, Extraversion, Neuroticism and Openness. To enlarge the coverage of this lexicon we have applied a reinforcement technique based on semantic similarity using word embedding.

3.2 ML Algorithms

After features extraction, we have trained supervised learning models to predict the presence or not of harmful content. The prediction task is a binary classification.

Since the dataset used for our implementation is of a limited size, therefore, classical ML is the most convenient. Furthermore, the dataset suffers from imbalanced classes distribution with 86% for negative class and 14% for positive one. This imbalance will create a bias in the model's decision function in favor to the majority class during the learning step, and consequently it will induce errors during the prediction step. To solve this problem, we have chosen Ensemble classifiers based on decision trees which are well known for their ability to handle imbalanced data. The idea behind Ensemble ML is that by combining weak learning models, we can produce a strong prediction model and thus improve the overall result. Namely, we have used Random Forest, Gradient Boosting, XGBoost and Adaboost, their performance will be proved in the evaluation section.

4   Evaluation

The goal of the evaluation is validating the efficiency of emotion-based and Big Five-based features in comparison with DL techniques. Further details will be presented in this section, but first we will present the resources on which we have applied our classifiers.

4.1   Materials

The used materials in our experiments are Lexicons and Dataset. The used lexicons in features extraction step are of two types: the first is related to Plutchik eight emotions and the second is related to Big Five personality traits.

Emotion's Lexicons. We have compiled these features from EmoLex[1] or NRC Sentiment and Emotion Lexicons with size of 17k unigram weighted words (see example in Table 1). NRC tool contains nine lexicons types that represent the relationship between words/phrases and the eight emotions: anger, fear, anticipation, trust, surprise, sadness, joy, and disgust.

---

[1] https://www.saifmohammad.com/WebPages/NRC-Emotion-Lexicon.htm.

Table 1. Examples of emotions lexicon

Emotion	Word	Weight
Anticipation	#expecting	2.237478095
Anger	jerk	0.593667390
Fear	security	0.518031195
Trust	admitting	1.485154665
Surprise	tricks	0.936144418
Sadness	hibernate	1.067902590
Joy	yey	1.747070367
Disgust	#vomit	1.518608679

Table 2. Example of agreeableness lexicon

Word	Weight
Amazing	0.056682
A great	0.056981
Fuck	−0.120624
Fucking	−0.113133

Big Five Traits' Lexicons. The second features are based on Big Five personality traits (Agreeableness, Conscientiousness, Extraversion, Neuroticism and Openness). For that, we have used the lexicon (see Table 2 for an example of agreeableness lexicon) elaborated in the work of Schwartz[2] [9]. The original lexicon is composed of 200 entries for each Big Five trait. As we mentioned earlier this lexicon was reinforced to extend its coverage (from 1000 entries to 10000 entries in total) and hence improve the models performances as proved in our previous work [12].

Dataset. We have applied our solution on a cyber-violence dataset[3] dedicated to online harassment detection in twitter posts [31], it contains 25,000 annotated tweets labeled with "Harassing" or "Not harassing". This dataset captures five different types of harassment content: sexual, racial, appearance-related, intellectual, and political. We have decided to use the "racial" dataset, one of the most common forms of online violence, it is composed of 5000 tweets. Table 3 shows an example of two entries from this dataset.

Since this dataset is provided in raw form, we first performed a preprocessing to exclude non-meaningful elements such as URLs, stop words, @ mentions and digits.

---

[2] https://wwbp.org/data.html.
[3] https://github.com/Mrezvan94/Harassment-Corpus.

Table 3. Racial dataset examples

Decision	Tweet
Harassing	@asadowaisi his father forgot to board train to lahore in 1947 and left this paki pig in india
Not harassing	@brandonlee161 paki haha i'm joking how are you mate?

4.2 Experiments

Classical ML

The conducted experiments aim to explore the performance of the different ML techniques first with emotions lexicon and Big Five personality traits as features independently, and second with their combination.

After features extraction, we have run each of the four classifiers on the training dataset that we split into 80% for training and 20% for test.

We have conducted five experiments each with a ML algorithm: Random Forest, Gradient Boosting, XGBoost and AdaBoost. In addition to that, we have run Penalized SVM as baseline, this classifier is considered as a very good variant of SVM and can handle imbalanced data more accurately. Moreover, it is the most used algorithm in cyberbullying detection. These experiments are as follows:

1. Penalized SVM with class_weight = 'balanced'.
2. Random Forest classifier with 100 as the maximum number of estimators (the number of trees in the forest).
3. Gradient Boosting classifier with 100 estimators.
4. XGBoost with its basic parameters without any adjustment, except the number of estimators which we fixed at 200.
5. AdaBoost with Random Forest as the base estimator, and 100 as the maximum number of estimators.

We note that all our ML methods were implemented using Scikit-Learn[4] library.

DL Techniques

To further evaluate our models, we have conducted several experiments with the DL architectures: CNN [32], RNN-BLSTM [33] and fine-tuned transformer models like BERT [34]. Next, we will give the details of each of these experiments.

CNN. CNN network is used in many NLP tasks such as text classification while showing a good performance. In our case the built model contains:

– Input layer: a 300-dimensional embedding layer.

---

[4] Scikit-Learn is an open-source python machine learning library.

– Hidden layers: is a CNN (1D) with 128 convolution kernels, followed by a second Conv1D layer of 64 kernels, then a pooling layer, all separated by dropout rates of 0.3.
– Output layer: a dense layer composed of a single unit, it uses a 'sigmoid' activation function to provide probability values between 0 and 1. The closer these values are to 0, the more non-violent the content of the tweet is, and the closer these values are to 1, the more violent the content is.

RNN-BLSTM. BLSTM is a variant of LSTM working in two directions. Their advantage is that they can capture patterns, perhaps omitted by the unidirectional network, and thus build more meaningful text representations. Our BLSTM model is composed of:

– Input layer: a 300-dimensional embedding layer.
– Hidden layers: two BLSTM layers of 128 and 64 units respectively, separated by a dropout of 0.3.
– Output layer: a dense layer to recover the results with a single unit and a sigmoid activation function.

We have also tested a hybridization of CNN and BLSTM networks. We have connected a Conv1D layer of 128 units with a BLSTM type GRU layer of 64 units whose output is fed into a pooling layer.

Transformer Models. Are the latest language models that have surpassed all performance records in several NLP tasks. The most known one is BERT. Their success is primarily due to their bidirectional encoder that considers the context before and after the word. Secondly, their architecture allows parallel processing of input sequences, which results in a huge gain in computation time. These models have been used as a transfer learning in text classification with fine tuning for adaptation to specific tasks since they have been pre-trained on a general domain.

In this experiment we have used the BERT-base-uncased model (12 layers of encoders, 768-hidden, 12 attention heads, and 110M parameters), in addition to RoBERTa-base (12-layer, 768-hidden, 12-heads, 125M parameters) that is an optimized version of BERT and finally, Twitter RoBERTa fine-tuned for offensive language detection.

In our test, the models fine tuning is performed as following:

– First, the input text is pre-processed to generate the tokens and attention mask identifiers required by these models.
– Then, each model is combined with a classifier, in our case it is composed of a dropout followed by a dense layer.

All over these models, we have used the optimization function 'adam', and the loss function 'binary_crossentropy', since we target a binary classification. The network was trained on 10 epochs with a batch size equal to 100. The implementations were done using TensorFlow library, especially the Keras API. For transformer models we have used the *transformers* library developed by Hugging Face[5].We mention that we have split the racial dataset into 70% for training, 20% for validation and 10% for testing.

4.3 Results and Discussion

Evaluation Metrics. As we said before, our dataset is imbalanced (86% for negative class and 14% for positive one). Consequently, a classifier that does not take into consideration the imbalanced class issue will generate an overfitting by only predicting the majority class with a high accuracy. In such situation, Accuracy is no longer a suitable metric. This is why we have chosen the AUC (Area Under the Curve ROC) associated with the ROC (Receiver Operating Characteristic) curve as the main metric:

$$AUC = \frac{1 + TP_{Rate} - FP_{Rate}}{2} \tag{1}$$

AUC (formula 1) is widely used as an evaluation metric in case of imbalanced class distribution. The ROC curve plots the true positive rate (TP_{rate}) against the false positive rate (FP_{rate}), allowing the separation of signal (TP) from noise (FP). The AUC is the area under the ROC curve and is considered as a summary of the ROC curve. The AUC measures the ability of a model to differentiate between classes. The larger the AUC value, the better the model is at differentiating between positive and negative classes.

Results. The results obtained from the different experiments are illustrated in the tables below. We note that all metrics are given in macro-average.

Classical ML Results
a. *Emotions-based learning results*
   Table 4 illustrate the results given by the five classifiers, as it is shown, XGBoost has achieved the best results in terms of AUC 0.75. The second to best classifier was Gradient Boosting with an AUC score of 0.73, then Adaboost with 0.72. Among the five classifiers, the penalized SVM scored the lowest in all metrics.

Table 4. Classifiers' performance results with Emotions as features

Classifier	AUC	Precision	Recall	F1
Penalized SVM	0.53	0.42	0.50	0.45
Random forest	0.71	0.78	0.58	0.66
gradient boosting	0.73	0.73	0.54	0.62
XGBoost	0.75	0.74	0.55	0.63
AdaBoost	0.72	0.71	0.59	0.64

b. *Big Five-based learning results*
   Table 5 shows the results obtained from the experiments where we compare the performance of the five classifiers (with lexicon reinforcement).

---

[5] https://huggingface.co.

Table 5. Classifiers' performance results with Big Five as features

Classifier	AUC	Precision	Recall	F1
Penalized SVM	0.5	0.79	0.54	0.64
Random Forest	0.73	0.77	0.64	0.69
Gradient Boosting	0.71	0.75	0.52	0.61
XGBoost	0.72	0.65	0.65	0.65
AdaBoost	0.72	0.82	0.61	0.69

As shown in this Table 5, the best AUC score was achieved by Random Forest (0.73). AdaBoost achieved the best results in terms of precision and F1 (0.82, 0.63 respectively). XGBoost reached the highest recall among all other classifiers (0.65). Finally, among the five classifiers, penalized SVM performed the lowest in all metrics except precision (0.79) where SVM was ranked second.

c. *Emotions and Big Five traits Combination*

To evaluate the impact of emotions and Big Five features combination on this task, we have conducted this third experiment. The results are presented in Table 6 showing an increase in performance especially in AUC that has reached 0.80, which means that the combination of personality features was more efficient in this task.

Table 6. Results of emotions and Big Five features combination

Classifier	AUC	Precision	Recall	F1
Penalized SVM	0.38	0.13	0.50	0.20
Random Forest	0.73	0.70	0.54	0.60
Gradient Boosting	0.79	0.76	0.57	0.65
XGBoost	0.80	0.77	0.59	0.66
AdaBoost	0.74	0.79	0.56	0.65

Next, we give the results of harmful content detection with DL techniques.

DL Results

Table 7 presents the results given by the DL architectures CNN, BLSTM in addition to transformer models: BERT, RoBERTa and Twitter RoBERTa for offensive language detection. As observed, all DL models show poor performance over all metrics except for RoBERTa fine-tuned on offensive language which has achieved quite good results.

In summary, ensemble ML techniques have proved their performance for the case of small and imbalanced dataset. Although DL techniques are known for their high performance in many NLP tasks, however, they require large amounts of data to achieve such performance. This was confirmed by the low scores of different evaluation metrics.

Table 7. Performance of DL architectures CNN, BLSTM and transformer models

Classifier	AUC	Precision	Recall	F1
CNN	0.53	0.43	0.50	0.46
BLTSM	0.49	0.43	0.50	0.46
CNN + BLSTM (GRU)	0.42	0.43	0.50	0.46
BERT	0.57	0.58	0.62	0.59
RoBERTa	–	0.43	0.50	0.46
Twitter RoBERTa Offensive	0.67	0.67	0.77	0.71

In contrast to classical ML techniques which can achieve good results even with a small dataset. Regarding transformer models, as they were trained on a very large amount of general domain corpora, they need to be fine-tuned on specific domain to provide better results, which was proven by the good recall reached by RoBERTa for offensive language model. Finally, these findings show that user psychological characteristics extracted from its written text can be good indicators of its online harmful behavior.

5   Conclusion

To help in individuals' well-being, we are interested in this study in finding a mean to automatic detection of harmful behavior from the online users' generated text. Which can lead to the detection of cyber-perpetrators.

Psychologists state that cyber-violence act is related to the perpetrator's psychology. Along this study, we tried to demonstrate the validity of this assumption, where, we extracted features related to personality and we trained supervised models on racial harassment dataset. In particular, we used Ensemble Machine Learning that have shown good performance in dealing with imbalanced dataset.

We have also proved that classical ML can outperform DL techniques in a small dataset context while saving computational efforts. However, transfer learning with transformer models is still appealing in case of further fine-tuning with specific dataset.

The obtained results show that individual's psychological features are correlated with his/her harmful behavior. Furthermore, our solution can be generalized to be employed in detecting other type of cyber-violence where harmful behaviors are present as in hate speech for instance. Finally, these findings may be exploited in e-health interventions by the organizations interested to this phenomenon.

References

1. Sanchez, H., Kumar, S.: Twitter bullying detection. In: NSDI, pp. 15–22 (2011)
2. Kowalski, R.M., Giumetti, G.W., Schroeder, A.N., Lattanner, M.R.: Bullying in the digital age: a critical review and meta-analysis of cyberbullying research among youth. Psychol. Bull. © 2014 Am. Psychol. Assoc. **140**, 1073–1137 (2014)

3. Paul, S., Smith, P.K., Blumberg, H.H.: Investigating legal aspects of cyberbullying. Psicothema **24**, 640–645 (2012)
4. Davahli, M.R., et al.: Personality and text: quantitative psycholinguistic analysis of a stylistically differentiated Czech text. Psychol. Stud. (Mysore). **12**, 1–23 (2020)
5. Moreno, J.D., Martínez-Huertas, J., Olmos, R., Jorge-Botana, G., Botella, J.: Can personality traits be measured analyzing written language? A meta-analytic study on computational methods. Pers. Individ. Dif. **177** (2021)
6. Tausczik, Y.R., Pennebaker, J.W.: The psychological meaning of words: LIWC and computerized text analysis methods. J. Lang. Soc. Psychol. **29**, 24–54 (2010)
7. Yarkoni, T.: Personality in 100,000 words: a large-scale analysis of personality and word use among bloggers. J. Res. Pers. **44**, 363–373 (2010)
8. Azucar, D., Marengo, D., Settanni, M.: Predicting the big 5 personality traits from digital footprints on social media: a meta-analysis. Pers. Individ. Dif. **124**, 150–159 (2018)
9. Schwartz, H.A., et al.: Personality, gender, and age in the language of social media: the open-vocabulary approach. PLoS ONE **8**, e73791 (2013)
10. Salawu, S., He, Y., Lumsden, J.: Approaches to automated detection of cyberbullying: a survey. IEEE Trans. Affect. Comput. **3045**, 1–20 (2017)
11. Balakrishnan, V., Khan, S., Fernandez, T., Arabnia, H.R.: Cyberbullying detection on twitter using big five and dark triad features. Pers. Individ. Dif. **141**, 252–257 (2019)
12. Zarnoufi, R., Abik, M.: Big five personality traits and ensemble machine learning to detect cyber-violence in social media. In: Serrhini, M., Silva, C., Aljahdali, S. (eds.) EMENA-ISTL 2019. LAIS, vol. 7, pp. 194–202. Springer, Cham (2020). https://doi.org/10.1007/978-3-030-36778-7_21
13. Dadvar, M., Ordelman, R., de Jong, F., Trieschnigg, D.: Towards user modelling in the combat against cyberbullying. In: Bouma, G., Ittoo, A., Métais, E., Wortmann, H. (eds.) NLDB 2012. LNCS, vol. 7337, pp. 277–283. Springer, Heidelberg (2012). https://doi.org/10.1007/978-3-642-31178-9_34
14. Zarnoufi, R., Boutbi, M., Abik, M.: AI to prevent cyber-violence: harmful behaviour detection in social media. Int. J. High Perform. Syst. Arch. **9**, 182–191 (2020)
15. Algaradi, M.A., Varathan, K.D., Ravana, S.D.: Computers in human behavior cybercrime detection in online communications: the experimental case of cyberbullying detection in the Twitter network. Comput. Human Behav. **63**, 433–443 (2016)
16. Chatzakou, D., Kourtellis, N., Blackburn, J., De Cristofaro, E., Stringhini, G., Vakali, A.: Mean birds: detecting aggression and bullying on Twitter. In: Proceedings of the 2017 ACM on Web Science Conference, New York, USA, pp. 13–22 (2017)
17. Dadvar, M., de Jong, F., Ordelman, R., Trieschnigg, D.: Improved cyberbullying detection using gender information. In: 12th - Dutch-Belgian Information Retrieval Workshop. DIR'2012, pp. 22–25 (2012)
18. Hosseinmardi, H., Mattson, S.A., Rafiq, R.I., Han, R., Lv, Q., Mishra, S.: Detection of cyberbullying incidents on the Instagram social network. In: 13th Annual International Conference on Mobile Systems, Applications, and Services, Florence, 18–22 May 2015, p. 481. ACM (2015)
19. Robinson, D., Zhang, Z., Tepper, J.: Hate speech detection on Twitter: feature engineering v.s. feature selection. In: Gangemi, A., et al. (eds.) ESWC 2018. LNCS, vol. 11155, pp. 46–49. Springer, Cham (2018). https://doi.org/10.1007/978-3-319-98192-5_9
20. Stillwell, D., Matz, S.: Latent human traits in the language of social media: an open-vocabulary approach latent human traits in the language of social media. PLoS ONE **13**(11) (2018)
21. Waseem, Z., Hovy, D.: Hateful symbols or hateful people? Predictive features for hate speech detection on Twitter. In: Proceedings of NAACL-HLT, pp. 88–93 (2016)

22. Badjatiya, P., Gupta, S., Gupta, M., Varma, V.: Deep learning for hate speech detection in tweets. In: Proceedings of the 26th International Conference on World Wide Web Companion, pp. 759–760 (2017)
23. Tommasel, A., Rodriguez, J.M., Godoy, D.: Textual aggression detection through deep learning. In: Proceedings of the First Workshop on Trolling, Aggression and Cyberbullying, pp. 177–187 (2018)
24. Agrawal, S., Awekar, A.: Deep learning for detecting cyberbullying across multiple social media platforms. In: Pasi, G., Piwowarski, B., Azzopardi, L., Hanbury, A. (eds.) ECIR 2018. LNCS, vol. 10772, pp. 141–153. Springer, Cham (2018). https://doi.org/10.1007/978-3-319-76941-7_11
25. Dadvar, M., Eckert, K.: Cyberbullying detection in social networks using deep learning based models; a reproducibility study. In: DaWaK, pp. 1–13 (2018)
26. Ranasinghe, T., Zampieri, M., Hettiarachchi, H.: BRUMS at HASOC 2019: deep learning models for multilingual hate speech and offensive language identification. In: FIRE 2019 (2019)
27. Samghabadi, N.S., Patwa, P., Pykl, S., Mukherjee, P., Das, A., Solorio, T.: Aggression and misogyny detection using BERT: a multi-task approach. In: Proceedings of the Second Workshop on Trolling, Aggression and Cyberbullying LREC 2020, pp. 126–131 (2020)
28. Pennebaker, J.W., Boyd, R.L., Jordan, K., Blackburn, K.: The development and psychometric properties of LIWC2015 (2015)
29. Mohammad, S.M., Turney, P.D.: Crowdsourcing a word-emotion association lexicon. Comput. Intell. **29**, 436–465 (2013)
30. Plutchik, R.: Emotion: a psychoevolutionary synthesis (1980)
31. Rezvan, M., Shalin, V.L., Sheth, A.: A quality type-aware annotated corpus and lexicon for harassment research. In: WebSci 2018, Web Science. ACM (2018)
32. Lecun, Y., et al.: Handwritten digit recognition with a back-propagation network. In: NIPS, pp. 396–404 (1990)
33. Schuster, M., Paliwal, K.K.: Bidirectional recurrent neural networks. IEEE Trans. Sig. Process. **45**, 2673–2681 (1997)
34. Devlin, J., Chang, M., Lee, K., Toutanova, K.: BERT: pre-training of deep bidirectional transformers for language understanding. In: Proceedings of NAACL-HLT 2019, pp. 4171–4186 (2019)

Automatic Detection of Deaths
from Social Networking Sites

Nuhu Ibrahim$^{(\boxtimes)}$ ⓘ and Riza Batista-Navarro$^{(\boxtimes)}$ ⓘ

The University of Manchester, Oxford Road, Manchester M13 9PL, UK
nuhu.ibrahim@postgrad.manchester.ac.uk, riza.batista@manchester.ac.uk

Abstract. The automatic detection of deaths of users of social networking sites provides a step towards the creation and adoption of an international standard for transferring digital estates to the next-of-kin of Internet users who die a sudden death. In this work, we develop a natural language processing (NLP)-based method for detecting deaths from posts and comments of concerned followers associated with user profiles. We analysed the differences between linguistic characteristics and practices in pre- and post-mortem contents, and developed text classifiers that achieved satisfactory performance in detecting deaths from the online posts. A new corpus was developed by leveraging data from Wikidata and Twitter. Machine learning models, both traditional (RF, KNN, LR and SVM) and deep learning (BiLSTM, CNN and BERT) were trained on features extracted using a variety of techniques: TF-IDF and pre-trained embeddings (Glove, Word2Vec and Fasttext) to classify pre- and post-mortem contents. The results obtained showed that BERT model outperformed all other models. Analysing the linguistic characteristics and practices showed, not surprisingly, that feelings that suggest negativity are dominant in post-mortem tweets and feelings that suggest positivity are dominant in pre-mortem tweets. It was also found that the number of words, personal pronouns, verbs, and family, religious, death, and swear words are higher in post-mortem tweets, whereas, the number of impersonal pronouns and informal words are higher in pre-mortem tweets.

Keywords: Grief · Digital estates · Text classification

1 Introduction

Boyd and Ellison [1] defined social networking sites (*SNSs*) as online platforms that allow individuals to "construct a public or semi-public profile" and connect with others within a "bounded system". SNSs have continued to gain significant popularity from the late 20th through to the 21st century [18] and have grown to become an inextricable part of life as they keep people company between leaving their beds at dawn and returning to them at dusk.

Due to the increasing relevance of SNS-based interactions to many people's social life, significant events including but not limited to graduations, marriage

© The Author(s), under exclusive license to Springer Nature Switzerland AG 2022
J. A. Lossio-Ventura et al. (Eds.): SIMBig 2021, CCIS 1577, pp. 236–252, 2022.
https://doi.org/10.1007/978-3-031-04447-2_16

proposals, marriages, childbirths, etc., are now experienced in part through SNSs [2]. This remains true even after the death of these SNSs' users, as *concerned followers* often express their shock and grief on the deceased's profile page following their death. In this paper, we define "concerned followers" of a SNS user, U, as consisting of other users who have posted messages on the profile of U. Hence they might be family members/relatives, friends or concerned admirers of U.

Though the use of the Internet has been growing year on year since it became available to the public in the 1980s [7], the COVID-19 pandemic has caused a further conspicuous spike in the use of the Internet, and the data created, captured, copied, and consumed [13]. This data is continuously composing into larger series of digital assets for all Internet users [37]. Digital assets may include digital images or videos; subscribed financial, cryptocurrency or cloud services; electronic bank and investment account statements; e-mail records and associated passwords; and SNSs' accounts [33]. The combination of these digital assets forms a person's digital estate [19].

Sadly, despite this vast acceptance and use of the Internet, there is still no working standard for transferring digital estates to the next-of-kin of Internet users who die a sudden death. Currently, financial institutions, for instance, still depend on clients' relatives to manually report their deaths before their estates get appropriately passed on. Also, most SNSs rely on people to report the death of a user [22]. For example, Facebook supports its users to nominate another user who should be allowed access to change their profile after they die [28]. But this takes months or sometimes years, because some relatives are unaware of all the services that the deceased was subscribed to.

Meanwhile, some cloud platforms have also implemented measures to facilitate the transfer of data to others upon detection of the possibility of death. For example, Google implemented an Inactive Account Manager to help users to share parts of their account data or notify someone if they have been inactive for a certain period [17]. This method is flawed because it would take some user-specified amount of time to finally conclude that a client is dead, and even though inactivity provides a helpful signal to detect if someone is dead, it is not reliable as inactivity could be caused by many different reasons other than death.

The use of these Internet-based services has increased because of the vast "stay at home" COVID-19 national directives around the world. Regulators' failure to properly manage digital estates of the deceased has increased the risks of subscribers dying and leaving their digital estates that are presumably important to their relatives or friends in the coffers of online-service providers.

The growth in the use of SNSs encouraged a linguistic study of the wall posts of memorialised SNSs profiles where it was found that condolences wall posts show higher rates of negative emotion than their regular equivalents [3, 4, 16]. These studies further suggest that social network profiles can be carefully studied and analysed to find generalisable conditions that could be used to detect whether the SNSs profiles' owners are dead or still alive. These, hence, shine a ray of hope that there could be a solution to the lack of a mechanism for automatically detecting service subscribers' deaths to facilitate the transfer of their digital estates to their next-of-kin.

The aim of this work is to develop *natural language processing (NLP)*-based methods to analyse differences in the linguistic characteristics and practices in pre- and post-mortem contents and automatically detect deaths of SNSs users from the posts of concerned followers associated with their profiles.

2   Related Work

This section reviews studies on the use of SNSs as platforms for grieving and memorialising the dead. We also discuss previously proposed NLP methods for detecting deaths and how our work differs from them.

2.1   SNSs as Platforms for Grieving and Memorialising the Dead

Expressing grief and memorialising the dead has been done online since the early stages of the Internet [3]. Initially, individual websites were created and maintained for the dead, then numerous "virtual cemeteries" where visitors can leave messages about a deceased became widely used [34]. However, from the late 20th through to the 21st century, when SNSs gained significant popularity [18], users started expressing grief and memorialising the deceased on their SNSs profile pages [5] and creating groups on SNSs to memorialise the dead [11].

Moore et al. [29] conducted a comprehensive study investigating what motivates mourners to utilise SNSs during bereavements. They found several reasons: "(a) sharing information with family or friends and (sometimes) beginning a dialogue, (b) discussing the deceased's death with others, (c) discussing death with a broader mourning community, and (d) commemorating and continuing connection to the deceased." Gathman [15] also suggests that users may use SNSs for grieving or disclosing deaths to avoid the discomfort of having to tell the news over and over again. Dickinson [12] notes that allowing others to partake in grief, even if they are merely strangers, helps consoling those in grief. Besides, receiving consolations over SNSs also helps the bereaved feel that they are not alone [23].

Though people still go through the usual physical grieving process, i.e., sometimes wearing black or dark colours to rituals, Carroll and Laundry [6] noted that there had been a shift in the expression of grief. The bereaved are now discouraged from showing too many emotions and are instead motivated to limit their time in mourning. Only a little time is now used to grief, "which is perhaps part of the reason why the use of SNSs as forums of grief expression has become increasingly more popular" [18]. This is similar to an observation by Romanoff & Tenezio [35] that, on the one hand, traditional mourning rituals are, over time, getting replaced, decreased or eliminated; on the other hand, online mourning rituals are increasingly becoming more popular.

2.2 NLP Methods for Detection of Deaths

Large scale text mining and NLP approaches have been successfully used in many recent pieces of research to quantify and predict mental illness severity in online pro-eating disorder communities [8], identify emotional distress and depression [3,10,24], identify mothers at risk of postpartum depression [10], analyse the response of users of SNSs to terrorism [27] and classify post-mortem contents on SNSs [4,22,26].

These researches found that positive emotions provide a basis for detecting the expression of joy [3,30] and negative emotions provide a basis for detecting sadness [3,10,16]. Specifically, Getty et al. [16] and Jiang & Brubaker [4,22] found that post-mortem posts show higher rates of negative emotion and has higher number of word counts, first person pronoun, second person pronouns and past tense than pre-mortem equivalents. Overall, these studies show great successes and potentials in using computational linguistics to analyse differences in annotated texts and inspire this work.

To our knowledge, only a few works have attempted to classify online data based on their owners' living or death status. Ma et al. [26] differentiated relinquished sites from deceased sites on CaringBridge[1], an online platform similar to a blog that helps users support and follow patients' health journeys by using a combination of unigram features detected from Language Inquiry and Word Count (LIWC), e.g., "funeral", "died", "grief", etc., and n-gram features that were manually identified from the training dataset, e.g., "went to heaven", "with our Lord", "in lieu of flowers", etc., that are not included in LIWC death category. They calculated the term frequency of these death words and divided the number of occurrences of each unigram and n-gram by the total number of words in the three previous updates about the subject whose profile is to be checked. These features were then prepared and fed into traditional machine learning algorithms to train models that can predict whether the owner of the profile is deceased or not. However, this research was based on an online health community platform where the linguistic practices are different and not diverse as in real SNSs. Another limitation of Ma et al. [26] is that the results presented were derived from a limited dataset; only 388 and 202 profiles were used in training and testing, respectively.

Jian and Brubaker [21,22] also used computational linguistic analysis on a dataset collected from the profiles of MySpace users in April 2010 and developed classifiers to detect mortality from these profiles and comments. Similar to Ma et al. [26], they used features detected through LIWC but also used n-gram features (with n = 1, 2, or 3) detected from Term Frequency-Inverse Document Frequency (TF-IDF) weights and compared using features from either of these methods (i.e., TF-IDF or LIWC) and the combination of both. Features generated from these three feature engineering techniques were then prepared and fed into traditional machine learning algorithms to train models that can predict whether a piece of text is pre- or post-mortem. A limitation of this work

---

[1] https://www.caringbridge.org.

is the inefficient generalisability of the trained classifiers to other contexts, i.e., dataset from other SNSs and the changes in linguistic practices since the dataset was drawn from over eleven years ago. Though [21,22] tested their classifiers to see how they will generalise to data from other platforms and time frames and achieved promising results, the new test datasets were from Facebook memorial groups and newspapers obituaries. The Facebook memorial groups' dataset contained messages posted in groups created by friends and family to memorialise the deceased and the dataset collected from newspaper obituaries was not from social media and consisted more formal writing styles. Overall, similar to the dataset collected from MySpace, the limitation of these datasets is that they do not include pre-mortem contents posted by either the deceased or the survivors and only comprise contents in which friends or relatives are memorialising loved ones.

In addition, recent text mining and NLP advancements that have achieved outstanding performances, i.e., deep learning algorithms like Bidirectional Long Short-Term Memory (BiLSTM), Convolutional Neural Network (CNN) or Bidirectional Encoder Representations from Transformers (BERT), pre-trained word embeddings as features (e.g., Word2Vec, Glove or Fasttext), were not explored in Ma et al. [26] and Jian and Brubaker [21,22].

This work takes a different approach by using SPARQL over Wikidata to mine celebrities' data, i.e., status, whether deceased or alive; date of death if dead; and social media handles, which will be used to collect posts from their SNSs' profiles. The training of classifiers was done using posts collected from individual users' profiles containing both pre- and post-mortem contents that span through many years and contain recent content, rather than just post-mortem content from several years ago that may not generalise to recent linguistic practices. Additionally, more recently proposed NLP techniques that have achieved outstanding performance (as mentioned above) were explored and compared with traditional machine learning and feature engineering techniques.

3 Methodology

In this section, the methodology employed to achieve the objectives of this work is discussed. Figure 1 depicts the different steps involved in our methodology.

3.1 Data Collection and Annotation

Twitter was selected as the SNS where the data used in this experiment were mined; this choice was influenced by the free, open and easily accessible nature of Twitter's data. However, it is not possible to get post- and pre-mortem tweets about deceased celebrities from Twitter without their Twitter usernames. Therefore, SPARQL was used over Wikidata to mine 1,639 deceased celebrities usernames, that were then used to mine pre- and post-mortem tweets from Twitter. Altogether, a total number of 79,431 pre-mortem and 46,180 post-mortem tweets were extracted from Twitter. The pre-mortem tweets are tweets posted before

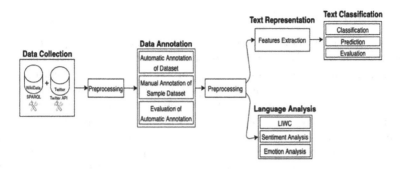

Fig. 1. Steps involved in our methodology

the day the celebrity died; whereas, post-mortem tweets are those posted after his or her death.

The unit of analysis in this work is a collection of tweets that are either pre- or post-mortem but containing the Twitter username of a subject celebrity between a selected time of analysis. In this experiment, the desired maximum size of a collection was 10, i.e., every unit of analysis consists at most 10 exclusive post or pre-mortem tweets about a celebrity.

Collecting and manually annotating corpora to develop gold standard datasets is laborious, time-consuming and expensive [14]. This has encouraged researchers to question whether these gold standard datasets can be satisfactorily replaced with automatically annotated data, i.e., silver standard datasets. In this research, hundreds of thousands of tweets were collected and later compacted into thousands of units of analysis; we argue that it is time-consuming and laborious for human annotators to manually read through the tweets in each unit, comprehend them and decide if they convincingly communicate whether or not the celebrity it was written about is deceased. Thus, this work adopts the approach of automatically annotating the units of analysis to develop a large silver standard dataset.

To achieve this, all the units obtained using tweets extracted from Twitter that were posted after the death of celebrities were assigned a label, "Deceased" to denote that they are post-mortem, and all the units obtained using tweets extracted from Twitter that were posted before the death of celebrities were assigned a label, "Alive" to denote that they are pre-mortem. This resulted in 8,494 and 5,178 units of analysis that are pre-mortem and post-mortem, respectively.

To ensure no information leaks to the machine learning algorithms during validation or testing, all pre- and post-mortem units about a particular celebrity can only appear in a single subset; training, validation or testing. Hence, the validation and testing subsets are totally unseen pre- and post-mortem units belonging to celebrities whose units were not involved in the training process. Division of the usernames was done in the following proportions: 68% training, 17% validation and 15% testing.

3.2   Pre-processing

Tweets are generally short, and this means it will usually be required for Twitter users to include abbreviations, phonetic substitutions, emoticons, emojis and ungrammatical structures that text-processing tools struggle with [36]. Pre-processing was done in two stages: first, to remove unnecessary information and make it conducive for human annotators to annotate a subset of the dataset for evaluation purposes (see Sect. 4.1); second, to bring the dataset to a normalised form for further text analysis: text classification, sentiment analysis and emotion analysis tasks. Figures 2 and 3 show the different stages of steps that were applied to remove unnecessary information from the dataset.

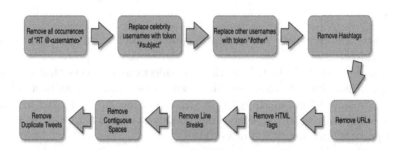

Fig. 2. Text pre-processing procedures applied to extracted tweets to remove unnecessary information before manual annotation

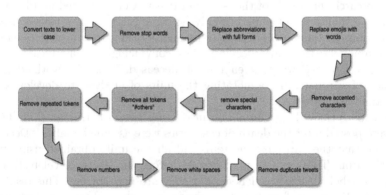

Fig. 3. Text pre-processing procedures applied to extracted tweets to normalise the dataset before text classification

3.3   Text Representation and Classification

We applied different techniques for text representation (TF-IDF, Word2Vec, Glove and Fasttext) on the dataset and trained a number of traditional machine learning algorithms: Random Forest (RF), K-Nearest Neighbours (KNN), Logistic Regression (LR), Support Vector Machine (SVM), and deep learning machine learning algorithms (BiLSTM and CNN). Additionally, we fine-tuned the state-of-the-art BERT embeddings, on the dataset using the pre-trained *bert-base-uncased* model made easily available by Huggingface[2]. Table 1 summarises the selected machine learning algorithms and feature extraction techniques applied to classify pre-mortem and post-mortem contents.

Table 1. Machine learning algorithms with feature engineering techniques

Concept	Model	Feature
Traditional	Baseline	
	NB	TF-IDF, Glove, Word2Vec and Fasttext.
	KNN	TF-IDF, Glove, Word2Vec and Fasttext.
	LR	TF-IDF, Glove, Word2Vec and Fasttext.
	SVM	TF-IDF, Glove, Word2Vec and Fasttext.
Deep Learning	CNN	Glove, Word2Vec and Fasttext
	BiLSTM	Glove, Word2Vec and Fasttext
	BERT	bert-base-uncased

3.4   Analysis of Linguistic Characteristics and Practices

The collected post-mortem and pre-mortem tweets were separately analysed using various techniques and tools to detect and discuss the embedded linguistic characteristics and practices. The sentiments (positive, negative or neutral), emotions (happy, sad, angry, surprise or fear) and linguistic practices expressed in the collected pre-mortem and post-mortem tweets were separately estimated using Valence Aware Dictionary and Sentiment Reasoner (VADER) [20], Text2emotion[3], and LIWC [32], respectively.

4   Evaluation

This section presents and discusses the results obtained in the experiments conducted in this work.

4.1   Inter-annotator Agreement

A great concern when using a silver standard dataset is the correctness and accuracy of the annotations. Therefore, a sample of about 10% of the silver standard was randomly selected equally from both the pre-mortem and post-mortem units

---

[2] https://huggingface.co.
[3] https://pypi.org/project/text2emotion/.

to be manually annotated by humans. Following the annotation of the selected sample by two human annotators, Cohen's Kappa [9] was then used to estimate the agreement between these two annotators and between the two annotators and the silver standard dataset. Table 2 shows the kappa scores and agreements for each comparison combination, i.e., between Annotator 1 and Annotator 2, Annotator 1 and silver standard, and Annotator 2 and silver standard. In all of the comparisons conducted, kappa scores (k) between 0.63 and 0.68 that can be interpreted as "substantial agreement" [25], were obtained. These scores altogether indicate strong agreement between the human annotators and between the human annotators and the automatic annotation; thus, instills confidence in the automatic annotation procedure.

Table 2. Agreements between two human annotators and automatic annotation

Annotators	Kappa score (k)	Agreement
Annotator 1 & Annotator 2	0.68	Substantial Agreement
Annotator 1 & Automatic Annotation	0.65	Substantial Agreement
Annotator 2 & Automatic Annotation	0.63	Substantial Agreement

4.2   Classification of Pre- and Post-mortem Contents

Classification Results Table 3 shows the performance of each machine learning model with the different feature engineering techniques. It was observed that the baseline classifier that applied the most frequent selection strategy did not perform well; it achieved precision, recall, accuracy, F1-score and AUC of 24.95%, 50.00%, 49.90%, 33.29% and 50.00%, respectively. It was also interesting that all the trained models in this experiment significantly outperformed the baseline model. The best model, BERT, achieved an outstanding accuracy of 91.60%, recall of 91.59%, F1-score of 91.59% and AUC score of 92.00%.

The results of the experiment show that for all the models trained using the traditional machine learning algorithms (RF, KNN, LR and SVM), RF has the best recall, accuracy, F1-score and AUC, i.e., 91.20%, 91.21%, 91.20%, and 91.00%, respectively and SVM has the best precision, i.e., 91.81%; also, all traditional machine learning models trained on features extracted using TF-IDF consistently outperformed others trained on features extracted using Glove, Word2Vec and Fastest.

Furthermore, for the models trained using deep learning algorithms (BiL-STM and CNN), BiLSTM has the best precision, recall, accuracy, F1-score and AUC, i.e., 91.09%, 91.08%, 91.08%, 91.08%, and 91.00%, respectively; also, all deep learning models trained on features extracted using Word2Vec consistently outperformed others trained on features extracted using Glove and Fasttext.

Generally, it was observed that the deep learning algorithms (BiLSTM and CNN) outperformed the traditional machine learning algorithms (RF, KNN, LR and SVM) when they are all applied on pre-trained embeddings (Glove,

Word2Vec and Fasttext). Although the BERT model that is a deep learning concept outperformed all other models trained in this experiment, the precision, recall and F1-score obtained in LR and SVM trained using TF-IDF as features outperformed BiLSTM and CNN trained on pre-trained word embeddings (Glove, Word2Vec and Fastext); though it was only with metrics less than 0.5% in most cases when compared to the performance obtained by the BiLSTM model trained on Word2Vec features.

Table 3. Performance metrics of the trained machine learning models. **Note:** Model with the best in every metric is shown in **bold** and all metrics are in **percentages**.

Concept	Classifier	Feature	Precision	Recall	Accuracy	F1	AUC
Traditional	Baseline		24.95	50.00	49.90	33.29	50.00
	RF	TF-IDF	91.33	91.20	91.21	91.20	91.00
		Glove	82.11	81.89	81.90	81.87	82.00
		Word2Vec	86.22	85.70	85.71	85.66	86.00
		Fasttext	84.48	84.22	84.23	84.20	84.00
	KNN	TF-IDF	74.55	73.52	73.50	73.22	74.00
		Glove	76.80	74.82	74.79	74.32	75.00
		Word2Vec	78.14	75.66	75.63	75.09	76.00
		Fasttext	75.77	73.40	73.37	72.75	73.00
	LR	TF-IDF	91.76	91.07	91.08	91.04	91.00
		Glove	83.58	83.58	83.58	83.58	84.00
		Word2Vec	88.64	88.42	88.43	88.41	88.00
		Fasttext	86.74	86.61	86.62	86.61	87.00
	SVM	TF-IDF	**91.81**	91.20	91.21	91.18	91.00
		Glove	84.50	84.48	84.49	84.48	84.00
		Word2Vec	90.20	89.78	89.79	89.76	90.00
		Fasttext	88.55	88.42	88.42	88.42	88.00
Deep Learning	BiLSTM	Glove	90.33	90.23	90.24	90.23	90.00
		Word2Vec	91.09	91.08	91.08	91.08	91.00
		Fasttext	90.26	90.24	90.24	90.24	90.00
	CNN	Glove	87.19	87.13	87.14	87.13	87.00
		Word2Vec	90.29	90.17	90.17	90.18	90.00
		Fasttext	89.01	88.88	88.87	88.88	89.00
	BERT	bert-base-uncased	91.66	**91.59**	**91.60**	**91.59**	**92.00**

Classification Error Analysis. The misclassified test samples for each model were obtained and closely observed; the observations are described below. Importantly, it was ensured that only tweets or a collection of tweets that cannot be easily traced back through web or Twitter search to the Twitter usernames they originated from are presented. Also, the names, usernames or hashtags in the presented tweets have been omitted according to ethical requirements.

We observed that most of the misclassified pre-mortem samples actually resemble post-mortem messages because they use words that indicate death, and most of the misclassified post-mortem samples are either very short or use words that do not clearly show that the subject is being grieved or memorialised. For instance, the test sample *"i love you mum. i will spend the rest of my life trying to be as amazing as u. RIP. _*_ Happy Birthday booboo I love you, I hope it's one for the books. Hopefully I'll see you soon _*_ this will make your whoooole daaaay. BRO."* was misclassified as post-mortem. The reason for the misclassification may be because it contains the word "RIP" that strongly suggests that the subject the texts were written about is deceased. However, this is particularly a scenario in which the author of this tweet is the subject celebrity and they are memorialising their mum.

Furthermore, the misclassified examples in high performing models, i.e., RF trained using TF-IDF as features, BiLSTM trained on Word2Vec features and BERT were investigated. It was observed that out of the around 140 test samples misclassified by these best three models, slightly over 60% were similarly misclassified by all the models. This indicates that although these models were trained using different algorithms and feature extraction techniques, they misclassified similar testing samples. This shows that most misclassifications are not a result of poor algorithm architecture, hyperparameter tuning or feature engineering technique but likely from text inconsistencies in social media data due to its unregulated and noisy nature [38].

4.3   Analysis of Linguistic Characteristics and Practices

Figures 4a and 4b show the results of using VADER to estimate the sentiments expressed in the pre- and post-mortem tweets. It was found that the post-mortem tweets have a significantly higher proportion of negative sentiments, i.e., 24.04%, than the pre-mortem counterparts, i.e., 13.61%. Additionally, although the difference between the proportion of positive sentiments expressed in the pre-mortem tweets and that expressed in the post-mortem tweets is just slightly over 1%, the difference between the proportion of neutral sentiments expressed in both categories is quite significant, with the pre-mortem and post-mortem tweets expressing neutral sentiments of 38.07% and 26.36%, respectively. This shows that although pre-mortem and post-mortem tweets express almost the same extent of positive sentiments, post-mortem tweets more strongly express negative sentiments while the pre-mortem tweets tend to express neutral sentiments.

Beyond estimating the sentiments in the collected tweets, Text2emotion was used to separately extract five different feelings, i.e., *happy, sad, angry, surprise* and *fear*, from the tweets. Figures 5a and 5b show the results of using Text2emotion to estimate the emotions expressed in pre-mortem and post-mortem tweets. It was found that the proportion of *sad, angry, surprise* and *fear* feelings expressed in the post-mortem tweets, i.e., 16.57%, 4.99%, 18.73%, and 16.44%, respectively, are higher than those expressed in the pre-mortem tweets, i.e., 11.48%, 3.45%, 17.67%, and 15.75%, respectively. Among all the five feelings

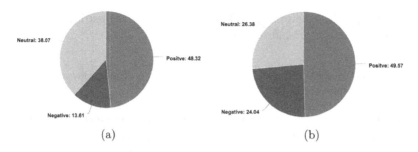

Fig. 4. (a) Proportion of sentiments expressed in pre-mortem tweets. (b) Proportion of sentiments expressed in post-mortem tweets.

that were estimated, only the proportion of *happy* feelings expressed in the pre-mortem tweets, i.e., 51.65%, is higher than that expressed in the post-mortem tweets, i.e., 43.28%. Thus, this shows that feelings that suggest negativity, i.e., *sad, angry, surprise,* and *fear,* are dominant in post-mortem tweets than in pre-mortem tweets and the feeling that suggests positivity, i.e., *happy,* is dominant in pre-mortem tweets than in post-mortem tweets.

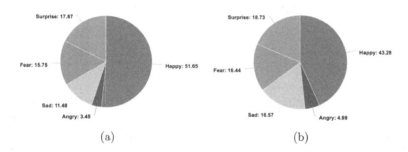

Fig. 5. (a) Proportion of the five feelings, *happy, sad, angry, surprise* and *fear,* expressed in pre-mortem tweets. (b) Proportion of the five feelings, *happy, sad, angry, surprise* and *fear,* expressed in post-mortem tweets.

Lastly, LIWC was used to separately analyse the pre-mortem and post-mortem tweets. The mean of every LIWC metric for all the tweets in every category (pre-mortem and post-mortem) was estimated, and only the metrics that are related to the conducted experiment in this work and that shows a significant difference between linguistic characteristics in pre-mortem and post-mortem tweets were selected. Table 4 juxtaposes the results obtained for both pre-mortem and post-mortem tweets in the selected LIWC metrics. It was found that the number of words, personal pronouns, verbs, family words, religious words, death words, and swear words in post-mortem tweets are higher than those in pre-mortem tweets; whereas, the number of impersonal pronouns and informal words in pre-mortem tweets are higher than those in post-mortem tweets. Additionally, analytical thinking [31] is more expressed in post-mortem conversations than in pre-mortem conversations.

Table 4. LIWC analysis of pre- and post-mortem tweets. Categories with the higher LIWC metric is shown in **bold**.

LIWC metric	Pre-mortem tweets (Mean)	Post-mortem tweets (Mean)
Word count	13.22	**16.41**
Analytical thinking	55.27	**58.12**
Personal pronouns	5.65	**7.07**
Impersonal pronouns	**15.54**	12.19
Verb	9.98	**11.32**
Family words	0.32	**0.55**
Friend words	0.39	**0.59**
Religious words	0.478	**0.65**
Death words	0.19	**1.01**
Informal	**2.99**	2.05
Swear words	0.27	**0.31**
Exclamations	**5.57**	2.5

5 Conclusion

To avoid similar limitations as in Ma et al. [26] and Jian & Brubakar [21,22], where the datasets used for training classifiers are not as diverse as in real SNSs, are drawn from so many years ago and may not capture the recent linguistic practices used on SNSs or do not include pre-mortem contents, this work developed a new dataset from open-source platforms by using SPARQL over Wikidata and the Twitter academic research API. Because of the excessive labour, cost and time required to develop gold standard datasets through manual annotation, automatic annotation approaches were adopted to develop a silver standard dataset. Two human annotators were then recruited to annotate a sample of this developed silver standard dataset to establish confidence in the automatic annotation procedure. There is substantial agreement between the human annotators, and between the human annotators and the automatic annotation.

It was found that all the traditional machine learning models (RF, KNN, LR and SVM) trained on features extracted using TF-IDF consistently outperformed those trained on features extracted using pre-trained word-embeddings, i.e., Glove, Word2Vec and Fastext. Also, it was observed that BiLSTM and CNN outperformed the traditional machine learning algorithms when applied on pre-trained embeddings. However, the precision, recall and F1-score obtained in LR and SVM trained using TF-IDF as features outperformed BiLSTM and CNN trained on pre-trained word embeddings, although it was only with a margin less than 0.5% in most cases when compared to the performance obtained by the BiLSTM trained on Word2Vec features. These results show that TF-IDF is still highly relevant for consideration in text classification problems. Finally, the BERT model outperformed all other models in this task, which is not usually the case when the texts are long. But in this case, the units are a maximum of 10 tweets, likely short enough for BERT to do well.

The extent of sentiments (i.e., positive, negative or neutral), feelings (i.e., *happy, sad, angry, surprise* or *fear*), and other linguistic characteristics expressed in the collected pre- and post-mortem tweets were separately estimated using VADER, Text2Emotion and LIWC, respectively; this is to enable a comprehensive comparison between the similarities and differences in post-mortem and pre-mortem linguistic practices. Similar to the results obtained by Getty et al. [16] and Jiang & Brubaker [4,22], it was found that post-mortem tweets more strongly express negative sentiments while pre-mortem tweets express more neutral sentiments. Similarly, feelings that suggest negativity are more dominant in post-mortem tweets than in pre-mortem tweets and the feeling that suggests positivity is more dominant in pre-mortem tweets than in post-mortem tweets. Additionally, the number of words, personal pronouns, verbs, family words, religious words, death words and swear words in post-mortem tweets are higher than those in pre-mortem tweets; whereas, the number of impersonal pronouns and informal words in pre-mortem tweets are higher than those in post-mortem tweets. Also, analytical thinking is more expressed in post-mortem conversations than in pre-mortem conversations.

This work's significant contribution is the successful development of a machine learning approach for the distinction between pre- and post-mortem posts of concerned followers associated with SNSs profiles to automatically detect deaths. This technique is a potential solution that can be used as part of the tools required for the creation and adoption of an international standard for transferring digital estates to the next-of-kin of Internet users who die a sudden death. This has the potential to reduce the risk of subscribers dying and leaving their digital estates that are presumably important to their relatives or friends in the coffers of online-service providers.

6   Future Work

Although this work succeeded in training high performing models to classify pre- and post-mortem contents, there are still existing limitations in the methods adopted in the experiments. Based on these limitations, we propose the following future work.

1. **Training classifiers on tweets in all languages.** The text classifiers trained in this experiment can only classify pre- and post-mortem contents if they are written in English. Thus, there is still a need to train text classifiers that would be able to generalise well on texts that span many different languages.

2. **Training machine learning classifiers to contextually detect post-mortem languages.** There is a need to train the machine learning classifiers to detect post-mortem language contextually, so that death is not reported only because of the presence of post-mortem words but because of how those post-mortem words have been used. For example, the best model trained in this experiment would classify the text sample "[subject]'s performance in his most recent series 'RIP to him' is phenomenal. I love how he acted at the funeral of his child, and I will miss the series so much now that it has come to an end" as post-mortem because of the presence of the post-mortem words "RIP", "funeral", and "miss"; however, a human would be able to detect that the text is only describing a scenario in which the "[subject]" acted in a series and not expressing the death of the "[subject]".

3. **Test classifiers with posts and comments of concerned followers associated with celebrities' profiles collected from other SNSs.** There is a need to evaluate the performance of trained classifiers on text data collected from other social networking platforms like Facebook, Instagram, etc. This is to assess whether the trained machine learning classifiers would generalise well and remain accurate when evaluated on testing subset collected from a different platform from where the training and validation subsets were collected.

References

1. Boyd, D.M., Ellison, N.B.: Social network sites: definition, history, and scholarship. J. Comput.-Mediat. Commun. **13**(1), 210–230 (2007)
2. Brubaker, J., Swaine, F., Taber, L., Hayes, G.: The language of bereavement and distress in social media. In: AAAI (2011)
3. Brubaker, J., Kivran-Swaine, F., Taber, L., Hayes, G.: Grief-stricken in a crowd: the language of bereavement and distress in social media. In: Proceedings of the International AAAI Conference on Web and Social Media, vol. 6 (2012)
4. Brubaker, J.R., et al.: Describing and classifying post-mortem content on social media. In: Twelfth International AAAI Conference on Web and Social Media (2018)
5. Brubaker, J., Hayes, G., Dourish, P.: Beyond the grave: Interpretation and participation in peri-mortem behavior on facebook. Inf. Soc. Int. J. **3**, 152–163 (2012)
6. Carroll, B., Landry, K.: Logging on and letting out: Using online social networks to grieve and to mourn. Bull. Sci. Technol. Soc. **30**(5), 341–349 (2010)
7. Cerf, V., Aboba, B.: How the Internet Came To Be. The On-line User's Encyclopedia: Bulletin Boards and Beyond. Addison-Wesley, Reading (1993)
8. Chancellor, S., Lin, Z., Goodman, E.L., Zerwas, S., De Choudhury, M.: Quantifying and predicting mental illness severity in online pro-eating disorder communities. In: Proceedings of the 19th ACM Conference on Computer-Supported Cooperative Work & Social Computing, pp. 1171–1184 (2016)
9. Cohen, J.: A coefficient of agreement for nominal scales. Educ. Psychol. Measur. **20**(1), 37–46 (1960)
10. De Choudhury, M., Gamon, M., Counts, S., Horvitz, E.: Predicting depression via social media. In: Seventh International AAAI Conference on Weblogs and Social Media (2013)

11. DeGroot, J.M.: Facebook memorial walls and CMC's effect on the grieving process. In: Annual Meeting of the National Communication Association, San Diego, CA (2008)
12. Dickinson, G.: Shared grief is good grief. In: Phi Kappa Phi Forum, vol. 91, pp. 10–12. Honor Society of Phi Kappa Phi (2011)
13. Feldmann, A., et al.: The lockdown effect: Implications of the COVID-19 pandemic on internet traffic. In: Proceedings of the ACM Internet Measurement Conference, pp. 1–18 (2020)
14. Filannino, M., Di Bari, M.: Gold standard vs. silver standard: the case of dependency parsing for italian. CLiC it, p. 141 (2015)
15. Gathman, E.C.H.: "Where everybody knows your name... and can call bullshit": collaborative self-presentation and information disclosure on Facebook. The University of Wisconsin-Madison (2014)
16. Getty, E., Cobb, J., Gabeler, M., Nelson, C., Weng, E., Hancock, J.: I said your name in an empty room: Grieving and continuing bonds on facebook. In: Proceedings of the SIGCHI Conference on Human Factors in Computing Systems, pp. 997–1000 (2011)
17. Google: About inactive account manager (2021). https://support.google.com/accounts/answer/3036546
18. Hillis, J.: Digitalizing Death: A Study of the Influence of Social Media on the Grieving Process. Ph.D. thesis, Boston College. College of Arts and Sciences (2018)
19. Hopkins, J.P.: Afterlife in the cloud: managing a digital estate. Hastings Sci. Tech. LJ **5**, 209 (2013)
20. Hutto, C., Gilbert, E.: Vader: A parsimonious rule-based model for sentiment analysis of social media text. In: Proceedings of the International AAAI Conference on Web and Social Media, vol. 8 (2014)
21. Jiang, J., Brubaker, J.: Describing and classifying post-mortem content on social media. In: Proceedings of the International AAAI Conference on Web and Social Media, vol. 12 (2018)
22. Jiang, J.A., Brubaker, J.R.: Tending unmarked graves: Classification of post-mortem content on social media. In: Proceedings of the ACM on Human-Computer Interaction 2(CSCW), pp. 1–19 (2018)
23. Katims, L.: Grieving on facebook: How the site helps people. Time/CNN (2010)
24. Kotikalapudi, R., Chellappan, S., Montgomery, F., Wunsch, D., Lutzen, K.: Associating depressive symptoms in college students with internet usage using real internet data. IEEE Technol. Soc. Mag. **31**(4), 73–80 (2012)
25. Landis, J.R., Koch, G.G.: The measurement of observer agreement for categorical data. Biometrics **33**, 159–174 (1977)
26. Ma, H., et al.: Write for life: Persisting in online health communities through expressive writing and social support. In: Proceedings of the ACM on Human-Computer Interaction 1(CSCW), pp. 1–24 (2017)
27. Mansour, S.: Social media analysis of user's responses to terrorism using sentiment analysis and text mining. Procedia Comput. Sci. **140**, 95–103 (2018)
28. McCallig, D.: Facebook after death: an evolving policy in a social network. Int. J. Law Inf. Technol. **22**(2), 107–140 (2014)
29. Moore, J., Magee, S., Gamreklidze, E., Kowalewski, J.: Social media mourning: Using grounded theory to explore how people grieve on social networking sites. OMEGA-J. Death Dying **79**(3), 231–259 (2019)
30. Pang, B., Lee, L., Vaithyanathan, S.: Thumbs up? sentiment classification using machine learning techniques. arXiv preprint cs/0205070 (2002)

31. Pennebaker, J.W., Chung, C.K., Frazee, J., Lavergne, G.M., Beaver, D.I.: When small words foretell academic success: The case of college admissions essays. PLoS ONE **9**(12), e115844 (2014)
32. Pennebaker, J.W., Francis, M.E., Booth, R.J.: Linguistic inquiry and word count: Liwc 2001. Mahway: Lawrence Erlbaum Associates **71**(2001), 2001 (2001)
33. Perrone, M.: What happens when we die: estate planning of digital assets. Comm-Law Conspectus **21**, 185 (2012)
34. Roberts, P., Vidal, L.A.: Perpetual care in cyberspace: a portrait of memorials on the web. OMEGA-J. Death Dying **40**(4), 521–545 (2000)
35. Romanoff, B.D.: Rituals and the grieving process. Death Stud. **22**(8), 697–711 (1998)
36. Sproat, R., Black, A.W., Chen, S., Kumar, S., Ostendorf, M., Richards, C.: Normalization of non-standard words. Comput. Speech Lang. **15**(3), 287–333 (2001)
37. Walker, R.: Cyberspace when you're dead. New York Times 5 (2011)
38. Zhang, D.: Inconsistencies in big data. In: 2013 IEEE 12th International Conference on Cognitive Informatics and Cognitive Computing, pp. 61–67. IEEE (2013)

Model Comparison for the Classification of Comments Containing Suicidal Traits from Reddit via NLP and Supervised Learning

Camila Mantilla-Saavedra and Juan Gutiérrez-Cárdenas[✉][iD]

Universidad de Lima, Lima, Peru
20172324@aloe.ulima.edu.pe, jmgutier@ulima.edu.pe

Abstract. In recent years, suicide has become one of the most critical issues regarding public health between teenagers and adults. On the other hand, the growth and wide-spread of social networks and mobile devices have allowed us to compile relevant information that helps us understand the thoughts, feelings, and emotions extracted from these platforms. The detection of suicidal traits on social media has be-come one relevant research topic. It has permitted the identification of probable suicide traits among media users by examining their posts on known social net-works such as Reddit. For that reason, the purpose of the present research is to compare different supervised classification models such as Logistic Regression, Support Vector Machines, Random Forest, AdaBoost, Gradient Boosting, and XGBoost; together with feature extraction techniques such as TF-IDF and Glove. The results from our experiments show that the best model is SVM with TF-IDF obtaining metrics of 91.50% in Accuracy, 92.40% in Precision, 90.30% in Re-call, and 91.50% regarding the F1-score. This study also shows that TF-IDF for feature extraction outperforms Glove when applied to the different models tested.

1 Introduction

Suicide is a global situation that has markedly increased over the years. The WHO [1] points out that each year, approximately 800 000 people die because of committing suicide and define this as an issue of public health, which is preventable to a large extent (pp. 02–03). Samah J. Fodeh et al. [2] mention that suicide is, actually, the tenth principal cause of deaths in the United States, with an approximate cost of 51 thousand million dollars per year; because of that, it is not only a concern of public health but also an issue of economic magnitude (p. 941).

J. A. Lossio-Ventura et al. (Eds.): SIMBig 2021, CCIS 1577, pp. 253–263, 2022.
https://doi.org/10.1007/978-3-031-04447-2_17

In this context, estimating the risk of committing a suicide act is not an easy task. Coppersmith Glen et al. [3] mentioned two factors that do not directly relate to understanding each patient's personal history. The first one is the short time between the beginning of a suicide attempt and a suicide action. The second factor is that the most successful methods to detect a suicide risk demand that the patient reveal their desire to inflict self-harm to a health professional. Additionally, the authors point out that social networks could offer a new type of data that could aid in understanding the behavior of persons with suicide traits. McHugh et al. [4] mention that the suicide risk cannot be predicted efficiently by using traditional clinical practices, i.e., asking patients about their suicidal thoughts.

The authors found that approximately 80% of the patients studied were not under psychiatric treatment, and those who died when alive neglected any suicidal thoughts when a general practitioner asked them. Similarly, and after reviewing approximately 365 studies, Franklin et al. [5] conclude that the capacity to predict suicidal thoughts suicidal behavior (STB) has not improved through 50 years of different studies. Nock et al. [6] reinforce this idea stating that there is a lack of an adequate understanding of the fundamental properties on which STB are based.

Some studies suggested using mobile apps, mobility detection systems, application of algorithms or models to perform behavior analysis for gathering the thoughts or ideas of probable patients. For example, behavior showed in their homes and the communication they establish with people surrounding them. All these methods have the goal to obtain data that could identify when somebody is a potential risk to commit a suicidal act and, in great measure, try to prevent it [7–9].

Additionally, further studies [10–13] show that it is possible to identify people with suicidal traits from their language in their publications on social networks. This identification occurs because those sites promote or encourage users to show or expose their suicidal thoughts outside a traditional clinical environment [3]. It is important to emphasize that an early detection on these social sites could help a potential suicidal to seek help before his situation evolves to a tragic outcome. Coppersmith et al. [3] used NLP techniques and Deep Learning to propose a model capable of analyzing and estimating the suicidal risk by analyzing their Twitter posts. Similarly, Roy et al. [14] used a set of neural networks that received as input psychological constructs to predict the state of suicidal risk from a user.

The present study aims to test different machine learning classification models: Logistic Regression, Support Vector Machines, Random Forest, AdaBoost, Gradient Boost, and XGBoost to detect probable suicidal trends by using the information from the SuicideWatch from Reddit. Additionally, we decide to test if these ML models have results comparable to those found in the literature and if the application of an embedding model such as Glove performs better or worse than a classical TF-IDF-based model.

2   State of the Art

Diverse authors such as Sawhney, R et al. [15] and Tadesse, M et al. [13] have employed social networks because they contain information posted by users about mental health issues. Therefore, the analysis of the information that entails this published online data has found an interesting niche in the field of Machine and Deep Learning. For example, Sawhney et al. used TF-IDF and word embedding to transform the original data to serve as input to different neural network models such as RNN, Logistic Regression (LR), SVM, LSCM, and C-LTSM. Tadesse et al. used n-grams combined with TF-IDF and word embedding with models such as Random Forest (RF), SVM, Naive Bayes, and XGBoost. Both authors concluded that the model with the best performance was the one that combined the CNN and LSTM models. Sawhney et al. [15] obtained metrics closed to 81% in Accuracy, 78% in Precision, 87% in Recall, and an 83% in F1-Score. Tadesse [13] managed to acquire an accuracy of 81%, Precision of 78%, Recall of 87%, and an F1 score of 83%. In other studies, we can mention the one of Coppersmith et al. [3]. They employed Glove as a word embedding technique joined with a bidirectional LSTM and applied a SoftMax layer for the posterior classification. Even though these authors recognized those persons at risk of committing suicide, they suggest that their practical utility should only be used in the early phases of these disorders and for making direct interventions.

In relationship with techniques based on automatic learning, we could mention the work of Birjali, M. et al. [10], who built a vocabulary related to suicidal terms. These compiled data were pre-processed by finding the relevant and most frequent words, n-grams, and categorizing the information using grammatical rules. The models used for classifying their results were SVM, Maximum Entropy, and Naive Bayes. In the end, the authors concluded that the SVM model with a Sequential Minimum Optima (SMO) was the best model related to the metrics of Precision with 89.5%, Recall 89.11%, and F1-score with 89.3%. Huang, X. et al. [16] used different classification models with a cross-validation technique of 10 folds to evaluate their results. The models used were Naive Bayes, Logistic Regression, J48, Random Forest, SMO, and SVM. They concluded that the best model was the SVM with an Accuracy of 94%, Recall of 60.3%, Precision of 78.9%, and F-measure of 68.3%.

We can also mention the study of Ji, S et al. [11], who compiled information previously labeled from Reddit and Twitter; pre-processed and cleaned it using segmenta-tion and tokenization techniques. Afterward, they applied TF-IDF, and word embedding joined with Latent Dirichlet Allocation for extracting the topics related to each publication. In the end, the authors used an LSTM in an attempt to capture the dependencies between posts. The classification models employed were SVM, Random Forest, Gradient Boost, XGBoost, and a Multiple Layer Feed Forward Neural Net-work using cross-validation of 10 folds to validate each model. They concluded that the model that obtained the best performance was Random Forest with an Accuracy and Precision of 96.4%, Recall of 99.1%, F1-score of 96.5%, and an AUC of 98.6%. Vioules, M. et al. [17] proposed using models such as SMO, Naive Bayes, J48, 1B1, and Random Forest with the techniques of Pointwise Mutual Information, n-grams, and Unified Strangeness Measure. After comparing the results from their different models, they concluded that the best model was Random Forest with a Precision of 57.1%, Recall of 55.9%, and an F-measure of 51.8%.

Similarly, Mbarek, A. et al. [12] and Rajesh Kumar et al. [18] concluded that the Random Forest model was the one that gave the best results compared with models such as Naive Bayes Logistic Regression, Random Forest, and XGBoost. The techniques used by the authors were similar to others exposed in this section, with the use of tokenization, bag-of-words, frequency of words, and word embedding. The n-grams technique was used to perform a phrase search, and the tool named Vader for sentiment analysis was also relevant. The authors obtained an Accuracy of 99.6%

Finally, the authors Chiong, R. et al. [19] used two public datasets from Twitter [20,21] to train the models. The pre-processing techniques were spelling error correction, elongation word correction, negative word correction, and POS tagging with lemmatization. The models employed were Logistic Regression, SVM, MLP, Decision Trees, Random Forest, Adaptive Boosting, Bagging Predictors, and Gradient Boosting. The datasets used for testing were different from the ones employed in the training phase utilizing the Koda dataset [22–24]. The authors concluded that the best model was Logistic Regression with an Accuracy of 90.40%.

3 Background

3.1 SuicideWatch

Reddit is a popular online discussion forum with a posting boards form. This site has more than one million communities called "Subreddits" where a different topic is covered in each of them. Suicide Watch[1] is a subreddit that is a "Peer support for anyone struggling with suicidal thoughts." In this subreddit, users could post personal stories related to suicide feelings to obtain support and advice from other members and moderators. The persons in charge are constantly monitoring the posts to guarantee the users' protection and security with rules for posting and answering. It is essential to mention that, even though the data in Reddit is publicly available and that the users can post anonymously, all the discussions on this site contain sensitive information. They, therefore, should be treated with an adequate level of ethics when using it [25].

3.2 TF-IDF

TF-IDF is a technique that allows determining the relative frequency of words in a document compared with the inverse proportion of the same word in all the document corpus [26]. Therefore, instead of just counting the frequency of words in each document like Bag-of-Words, it computes the normalized count of words

---

[1] https://www.reddit.com/r/SuicideWatch/.

divided by the number of documents in which that particular word appears. It is essential to mention that when a queried word appears on a scarce number of documents, it has an important meaning for those documents and obtains a higher score because of its high IDF.

3.3 Glove

Global Vectors or Glove is an unsupervised machine learning model that obtains the vector representation of the words. The training of this model is made on non-zero entries of a global array of co-occurrences word-word, which tabulates the coexistence between words given a particular corpus [27]. In other words, this model adopts an array that represents the frequency of the words in a given text and calculates a scoring of the generated vectors by considering the co-occurrences of the words in a specific context [28].

4 Methodology

In Fig. 1, we can observe the methodology followed, which has as an initial part the gathering of data extracted from the Suicide Watch forum in Reddit; this dataset comprises approximately 232074 posts in English previously labeled[2]. The data is distributed in two columns, one concerning the posted publications and related to two labels: "suicidal" or "non-suicidal." We worked only with 20000 samples distributed evenly considering each label; the decision was due to limited computational resources for testing the complete dataset. After loading the data, we cleaned it using segmentation and tokenization techniques. We applied regular expressions to remove hashtags or other non-relevant terms, stopwords elimination, and lemmatization by using the NLTK toolkit. Afterward, we made a feature extraction using TF-IDF and Glove to obtain vector representations of each post which would serve as an input to a set of classification models. Finally, we applied ten-fold cross-validation in the validation step to obtain the relevant metrics and compare the selected models.

5 Experimentation

5.1 Compiling, Loading and Data Cleaning

As we mentioned before, we worked with a dataset obtained from the subreddit known as Suicide Watch, which contains 232074 posts in English with their respective labeling. As a first step, we loaded the data on a Data frame considering two columns: text and class. After this step, we segment the sentences into words and clean the data by using regular expressions. We removed the whitespaces and special characters such as "#" and "@" punctuation symbols, emoticons, digits, web tags, and web links; we also eliminated those words with

---

[2] https://www.kaggle.com/nikhileswarkomati/suicide-watch.

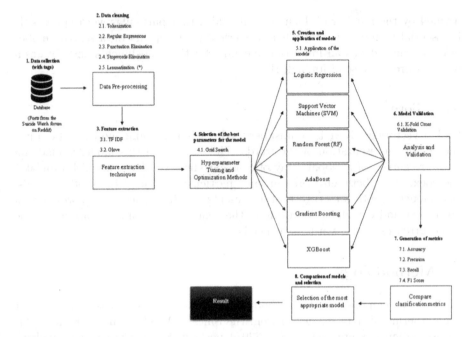

Fig. 1. Methodology followed. (*) The lemmatization process will only be used with the TF-IDF technique.

less than three characters. When the data was clean, we performed a lemmatization of the words, which allowed us to obtain the root of each term. For this operation, we used the WordNetLemmatizer from the corpus WordNet. It is important to mention that this lemmatization process was only performed when we used the TF-IDF technique.

5.2   Feature Extraction

This step aimed to convert the text into a numerical representation to serve as an input for the different classification models. It is valuable to mention that for the TF-IDF technique, we will be using bi-grams. Additionally, for the application of the Glove technique, we have used the library named Zeugma[3], which contains a set of packages for using a set of pre-trained embedded words that used the Glove model.

5.3   Classification Models

We implemented six classification models to test which one would better classify the posts into a probable suicidal or non-suicidal trait. The models we used were: Logistic Regression, SVM, Random Forest, Ada Boost, Gradient Boosting, and

---

[3] https://pypi.org/project/zeugma/.

XGBoost. We tuned the hyperparameters from each model using the Grid Search technique with cross-validation of ten folds; these are depicted in Table 1. The models were implemented by using de scikit-learn package.

Table 1. Best hyperparameters found for each model.

Logistic Regression	TF-IDF	Glove	SVM	TF-IDF	Glove	Random Forest	TF-IDF	Glove
Penalty	l2	l1	Kernel	linear	poly	Max depth	300	50
C	1	10	C	1	10	Number of estimators	500	500
Solver	sag	liblinear	Degree	-	5	Max features	sqrt	log2
			Gamma	-	-			

AdaBoost	TF-IDF	Glove	Gradient Boosting	TF-IDF	Glove	XGBoost	TF-IDF	Glove
Number of estimators	300	500	Number of estimators	500	50	Booster	gbtree	gbtree
Base estimators	-	-	Learning rate	0.3	0.3	Subsample	0.3	0.7
Learning rate	1	0.6	Max depth	7	15	Eta	0.01	0.1
						Gamma	5	5
						Max depth	15	30
						Min child weight	15	30
						Colsample bytree	0.3	0.3

After identifying the best hyperparameters, we implemented the different classification models and validated our results using ten-fold cross-validation. The metrics obtained for comparing our different models were Accuracy, Precision, Recall, and F1-score.

6 Results

The different metrics from the implemented models can be observed in Table 2:

Table 2. Metrics of evaluation.

Model		Accuracy	Precision	Recall	F1-Score
Logistic regression	TF-IDF	91.3% ± 0.9%	**92.5% ± 0.9%**	89.9% ± 1%	91.2% ± 0.9
	Glove	83.1% ± 0.6%	80.6% ± 0.9%	87.4% ± 0.7%	83.1% ± 0.7%
SVM	TF-IDF	**91.5% ± 0.7%**	92.4% ± 0.7%	**90.3% ± 0.8%**	**91.5% ± 0.6%**
	Glove	86.9% ± 0.6%	85.9% ± 0.9%	88.3% ± 1.0%	86.9% ± 0.6%
Random forest	TF-IDF	89.2% ± 0.8%	89.7% ± 0.9%	88.5% ± 1.2%	89.2% ± 1.0%
	Glove	86.3% ± 0.6%	87.6% ± 1.1%	84.5% ± 0.8%	86.3% ± 0.6%
AdaBoost	TF-IDF	89.7% ± 0.7%	91% ± 0.7%	88% ± 1.0%	89.7% ± 0.7%
	Glove	85.2% ± 0.8%	83.8% ± 1.3%	87.3% ± 0.8%	85.2% ± 0.8%
Gradient boosting	TF-IDF	89.6% ± 0.8%	91% ± 0.7%	88% ± 1.4%	89.6% ± 0.8%
	Glove	86.2% ± 0.7%	85.6% ± 1.1%	87% ± 1.0%	86.1% ± 0.8%
XGBoost	TF-IDF	88.5% ± 1.0%	90.5% ± 1.1%	86% ± 1.3%	88.5% ± 1.0%
	Glove	86.1% ± 0.7%	86% ± 1.1%	86.2% ± 0.9%	86.1% ± 0.7%

In Table 2, we can see the results from the different models considering their average and standard deviation, which were computed after applying cross-validation with ten folds. As we can observe, the Logistic Regression model was the one that obtained the best Precision score; however, the SVM with a linear kernel managed to get better results considering the different metrics evaluated.

7   Discussion

Considering the results shown in 2, we can observe that the model with the best performance was SVM with TF-IDF. This model obtained 91.50% in Accuracy, 92.40% in Precision, 90.30% in Recall, and 91.50% in F1-score. Another model that showed interesting results was Logistic Regression, TF-IDF, with 91.30% in Accuracy, 92.50% in Precision, 89.90% in Recall, and 91.20% in Precision F1-score.

We can see that the models with the best scores used the TF-IDF for feature extraction, which is a very classical model used in NLP before other methods, such as Word Embeddings, appeared. The reason that the former, on some occasions, perform better than the latter could be the specific characteristics that have the text to be evaluated [28]. Dessi et al. [28] stated that the TF-IDF-based models performed better when the data was strongly biased than using other more advanced techniques. Also, the study of Piskorski, J. et al. [29], in which they compared TF-IDF over word embeddings by using an SVM model, showed the combination of n-grams TF-IDF work better than embedded methods such as Glove, Bert, and FastText. However, considering the general data, this could only work when the training data is not below 3%.

It is important to mention that other authors such as Wang, Y. et al. [30] also observed a high performance in SVM models by also using TF-IDF. These authors compared different classification models such as Naive Bayes, Decision Tree, KNN, Logistic Regression, and SVM with feature extraction techniques such as Word2Vec, Doc2Vec, and TF-IDF. Also, they mentioned that the Logistic regression model showed high precision values, with 84.22% being better than the SVM model. Additionally, studies like the one from Birjali, M. et al. [10] concluded that the SVM model, while compared with other models such as Maximum Entropy and Naive Bayes, obtained satisfactory results with an accuracy of 94%, Recall of 60.3%, Precision of 78.9% and F-measure of 68.3%.

On the other hand, researchers such as Aladağ, A. et al. [31] also used information extracted from Reddit with matrix extraction techniques such as LIWC, Sentiment Matrix, and Document Term Matrix. The classification models the authors applied were Logistic Regression, SVM, ZeroR, and Random Forest; the authors concluded that the best models were Logistic Regression and SVM, both with 92% approximately in the different metrics evaluated.

Regarding the dataset employed in the present research [23], we found that the authors Chiong, R. et al. [19] also used it. However, it was only used to test the performance of different classification models such as Logistic Regression, LSVM, MLP Classifier, Decision Tree, AdaBoost, BPClassifier, Gradient Boosting, and Random Forest. These authors used two public datasets for training their models and obtained from Twitter [20,21]. The evaluation of the models mentioned above showed that the Logistic Regression model is the one that performed better compared to the other models with an accuracy of 90.40%, being the second-best model LSVM with 85.92%; results are closely related to the ones obtained in the present research.

References

1. World Health Organization Prevención del suicidio: un imperativo global. http://apps.who.int/iris/bitstream/10665/136083/1/9789275318508_spa.pdf. Accessed 1 Oct 2020
2. Fodeh, S., et al.: Using machine learning algorithms to detect suicide risk factors on Twitter. In: 2019 International Conference on Data Mining Workshops (ICDMW), pp. 941–948. IEEE, Beijing (2019). https://doi.org/10.1109/ICDMW.2019.00137
3. Coppersmith, G., Leary, R., Crutchley, P., Fine, A.: Natural language processing of social media as screening for suicide risk. Biomed Inform Insights. **10**, 117822261879286 (2018). https://doi.org/10.1177/1178222618792860
4. McHugh, C.M., Corderoy, A., Ryan, C.J., Hickie, I.B., Large, M.M.: Association between suicidal ideation and suicide: meta-analyses of odds ratios, sensitivity, specificity and positive predictive value. BJPsych open. **5**, e18 (2019). https://doi.org/10.1192/bjo.2018.88
5. Franklin, J.C., et al.: Risk factors for suicidal thoughts and behaviors: a meta-analysis of 50 years of research. Psychol. Bull. **143**, 187–232 (2017). https://doi.org/10.1037/bul0000084
6. Nock, M.K., Ramirez, F., Rankin, O.: Advancing our understanding of the who, when, and why of suicide risk. JAMA Psychiat. **76**, 11 (2019). https://doi.org/10.1001/jamapsychiatry.2018.3164
7. Nobles, A.L., Glenn, J.J., Kowsari, K., Teachman, B.A., Barnes, L.E.: Identification of imminent suicide risk among young adults using text messages. In: Proceedings of the 2018 CHI Conference on Human Factors in Computing Systems, pp. 1–11. ACM, Montreal (2018). https://doi.org/10.1145/3173574.3173987
8. Canzian, L., Musolesi, M.: Trajectories of depression: unobtrusive monitoring of depressive states by means of smartphone mobility traces analysis. In: Proceedings of the 2015 ACM International Joint Conference on Pervasive and Ubiquitous Computing - UbiComp 2015, pp. 1293–1304. ACM Press, Osaka (2015). https://doi.org/10.1145/2750858.2805845
9. Sinha, P.P., Mishra, R., Sawhney, R., Mahata, D., Shah, R.R., Liu, H.: #suicidal - a multipronged approach to identify and explore suicidal ideation in Twitter. In: Proceedings of the 28th ACM International Conference on Information and Knowledge Management, pp. 941–950. ACM, Beijing (2019). https://doi.org/10.1145/3357384.3358060
10. Birjali, M., Beni-Hssane, A., Erritali, M.: Machine learning and semantic sentiment analysis based algorithms for suicide sentiment prediction in social networks. Procedia Comput. Sci. **113**, 65–72 (2017). https://doi.org/10.1016/j.procs.2017.08.290
11. Ji, S., Yu, C.P., Fung, S., Pan, S., Long, G.: Supervised learning for suicidal ideation detection in online user content. Complexity **2018**, 1–10 (2018). https://doi.org/10.1155/2018/6157249
12. Mbarek, A., Jamoussi, S., Charfi, A., Ben Hamadou, A.: Suicidal profiles detection in Twitter. In: Proceedings of the 15th International Conference on Web Information Systems and Technologies, pp. 289–296. SCITEPRESS - Science and Technology Publications, Vienna, Austria (2019). https://doi.org/10.5220/0008167602890296

13. Tadesse, M.M., Lin, H., Xu, B., Yang, L.: Detection of suicide ideation in social media fo-rums using deep learning. Algorithms **13**, 7 (2019). https://doi.org/10. 3390/a13010007
14. Roy, A., Nikolitch, K., McGinn, R., Jinah, S., Klement, W., Kaminsky, Z.A.: A machine learning approach predicts future risk to suicidal ideation from social media data. npj Digit. Med. **3**, 78 (2020). https://doi.org/10.1038/s41746-020-0287-6
15. Sawhney, R., Manchanda, P., Mathur, P., Shah, R., Singh, R.: Exploring and learning sui-cidal ideation connotations on social media with deep learning. In: Proceedings of the 9th Workshop on Computational Approaches to Subjectivity, Sentiment and Social Media Analysis, pp. 167–175. Association for Computational Linguistics, Brussels (2018). https://doi.org/10.18653/v1/W18-6223
16. Huang, X., Zhang, L., Chiu, D., Liu, T., Li, X., Zhu, T.: Detecting Suicidal Ideation in Chinese Microblogs with Psychological Lexicons. In: 2014 IEEE 11th Intl Conf on Ubiquitous Intelligence and Computing and 2014 IEEE 11th Intl Conf on Autonomic and Trusted Computing and 2014 IEEE 14th Intl Conf on Scalable Computing and Communications and Its Associated Workshops. pp. 844–849. IEEE, Bali (2014). https://doi.org/10.1109/UIC-ATC-ScalCom.2014.48
17. Vioules, M.J., Moulahi, B., Aze, J., Bringay, S.: Detection of suicide-related posts in Twitter data streams. IBM J. Res. Dev. **62**, 7:1–7:12 (2018). https://doi.org/10.1147/JRD.2017.2768678
18. Rajesh Kumar, E., Rama Rao, K.V.S.N., Nayak, S.R., Chandra, R.: Suicidal ideation prediction in twitter data using machine learning techniques. J. Interdisciplinary Math. **23**, 117–125 (2020). https://doi.org/10.1080/09720502.2020.1721674
19. Chiong, R., Budhi, G.S., Dhakal, S., Chiong, F.: A textual-based featuring approach for de-pression detection using machine learning classifiers and social media texts. Comput. Biol. Med. **135**, 104499 (2021). https://doi.org/10.1016/j.compbiomed.2021.104499
20. Eye, B.B.: Depression Analysis. 1 edn., Kaggle (2020)
21. Shen, G., Jia, J., Nie, L., Feng, F., Zhang, C., Hu, T., Chua, T.-S., Zhu, W.: Depression detection via harvesting social media: a multimodal dictionary learning solution. In: Proceedings of the Twenty-Sixth International Joint Conference on Artificial Intelligence, pp. 3838–3844. International Joint Conferences on Artificial Intelligence Organization, Melbourne, Australia (2017). https://doi.org/10.24963/ijcai.2017/536
22. Tanwar, R.: Victoria Suicide Data. Kaggle (2020)
23. Komati, N.: r/SuicideWatch and r/depression posts from Reddit. Kaggle (2020)
24. Virahonda, S.: Depression and anxiety comments. 1 edn. Kaggle (2020)
25. Benton, A., Coppersmith, G., Dredze, M.: Ethical research protocols for social media health research. In: Proceedings of the First ACL Workshop on Ethics in Natural Language Processing, pp. 94–102. Association for Computational Linguistics, Valencia (2017). https://doi.org/10.18653/v1/W17-1612
26. Ramos, J.: Using TF-IDF to determine word relevance in document queries. In: Proceedings of the First Instructional Conference on Machine Learning, vol. 4, pp. 94–102 (2003)
27. Pennington, J., Socher, R., Manning, C.: Glove: global vectors for word representation. In: Proceedings of the 2014 Conference on Empirical Methods in Natural Language Processing (EMNLP), pp. 1532–1543. Association for Computational Linguistics, Doha (2014). https://doi.org/10.3115/v1/D14-1162

28. Dessi, D., Helaoui, R., Recupero, D.R., Riboni, D.: TF-IDF vs Word Embeddings for Morbidity Identification in Clinical Notes: An Initial Study. arXiv preprint (2021). 2105.09632
29. Piskorski, J., Jacquet, G.: TF-IDF Character N-grams versus word embedding-based models for fine-grained event classification: a preliminary study. In: Proceedings of the Workshop on Automated Extraction of Socio-political Events from News 2020(9), pp. 26–34 (2020)
30. Wang, Y., Zhou, Z., Jin, S., Liu, D., Lu, M.: Comparisons and selections of features and classifiers for short text classification. IOP Conf. Ser.: Mater. Sci. Eng. **261**, 012018 (2017). https://doi.org/10.1088/1757-899X/261/1/012018
31. Aladağ, A.E., Muderrisoglu, S., Akbas, N.B., Zahmacioglu, O., Bingol, H.O.: Detecting suicidal ideation on forums: proof-of-concept study. J. Med. Internet Res. **20**(6), e9840 (2018)

A Data-Driven Score Model to Assess Online News Articles in Event-Based Surveillance System

Syed Mehtab Alam[1,4]([✉]), Elena Arsevska[2,5], Mathieu Roche[1,4], and Maguelonne Teisseire[3,4]

[1] CIRAD, UMR TETIS, 34398 Montpellier, France
{mehtab-alam.syed,mathieu.roche}@cirad.fr
[2] CIRAD, UMR ASTRE, 34398 Montpellier, France
elena.arsevska@cirad.fr
[3] INRAE, UMR TETIS, 34398 Montpellier, France
maguelonne.teisseire@inrae.fr
[4] TETIS, Univ Montpellier, AgroParisTech,
CIRAD, CNRS, INRAE, Montpellier, France
[5] ASTRE, Univ Montpellier, CIRAD, INRAE, Montpellier, France

Abstract. Online news sources are popular resources for learning about current health situations and developing event-based surveillance (EBS) systems. However, having access to diverse information originating from multiple sources can misinform stakeholders, eventually leading to false health risks. The existing literature contains several techniques for performing data quality evaluation to minimize the effects of misleading information. However, these methods only rely on the extraction of spatiotemporal information for representing health events. To address this research gap, a score-based technique is proposed to quantify the data quality of online news articles through three assessment measures: 1) news article metadata, 2) content analysis, and 3) epidemiological entity extraction with NLP to weight the contextual information. The results are calculated using classification metrics with two evaluation approaches: 1) a strict approach and 2) a flexible approach. The obtained results show significant enhancement in the data quality by filtering irrelevant news, which can potentially reduce false alert generation in EBS systems.

Keywords: Text mining · Natural language processing · Data quality

1 Introduction

Outbreaks of infectious diseases pose serious threats to public health and safety [21]. Infectious disease outbreaks affect not only public health but also the national and international economy and global awareness [31]. It is important to implement public health surveillance methods to recognize potential infectious

© The Author(s), under exclusive license to Springer Nature Switzerland AG 2022
J. A. Lossio-Ventura et al. (Eds.): SIMBig 2021, CCIS 1577, pp. 264–280, 2022.
https://doi.org/10.1007/978-3-031-04447-2_18

disease outbreaks and to minimize their associated devastating effects on society. In the existing literature [28,31], there are two main types of public health surveillance strategies: 1) event-based surveillance (EBS) and 2) indicator-based surveillance (IBS). Both of these surveillance strategies complement one another in terms of benefits due to their unique data collection, monitoring, assessment, and data interpretation processes [28] and are treated as fundamental in constructing a comprehensive surveillance system [5]. This research focuses on EBS, whereas IBS is outside the scope of this article.

EBS is the organized process of detecting and reporting information (i.e., represented as events) to healthcare authorities by rapidly capturing information from different unstructured data sources [5]. It enables concerned authorities to be better prepared for endemic and pandemic disease outbreaks by functioning as a key component of an effective early warning system [5,28]. For information acquisition, online information sources (e.g., news articles, blogs, rumors, social media (such as Twitter, etc.), and other ad hoc reports, etc.) have gained great attention in implementing "web-based" or "internet-based" EBS systems [34] compared to traditional data collection methods, which are labor intensive [10] and restricted by interobserver variability [24]. The working efficiency of web-based EBS systems in terms of detecting true outbreaks to protect public health against the spread of infectious diseases depends on the quality of the information collected from online news sources [34]. As online news information is diverse and collected from heterogeneous online data sources, it is crucial to verify this unstructured information to avoid misinformation (i.e., a piece of information that is false or having no scientific evidence) [40] and disinformation (i.e., intentionally generated false information) [6] that can pose serious threats to public health.

Unstructured news information sources are in a common textual format [9,34]. Large amounts of textual information from diverse information sources can overwhelm web-based EBS systems. Existing EBS-based methods exploiting different text mining techniques transform online textual data into a computer-readable format to enable the extraction of relevant news information from existing textual sources per human needs [2,34]. However, this method not only relies on the extraction of spatiotemporal information (i.e., when-where questions) for representing health events but also does not adequately evaluate the accuracy of these executed mapping processes for extracting the correct information for generating true health alerts [17].

The work presented in this paper aims to address these research gaps by 1) including data quality attributes based on metadata and news content through the extraction of epidemiological information (in addition to the extraction of spatiotemporal data) to identify relevant information. This epidemiological information is extracted using a pattern-based text mining approach. This concerns the epidemiological concepts and terms related to infectious diseases and particularly avian influenza. 2) Then, news sources are labeled into two different groups of news articles, relevant (outbreak-related) and irrelevant, based on the data quality scores. Consequently, the proposed method prioritizes outbreak-related news by discarding irrelevant news in real time to minimize false health alerts in EBS systems.

The paper is structured as follows: Sect. 2 describes the state-of-the-art literature related to quality attributes and the evaluation of online news sources. Section 3 presents the proposed methodology. Section 4 presents the results of experiments, and Sect. 5 discusses the proposed work. Finally, Sect. 6 presents the conclusion and outlines future work.

2   State of the Art

Research on data quality, which is crucial for evaluating online news sources and constructing EBS systems, began in the 1990s. Wang and Strong [37] defined data quality as "the information which is fit for use". The dimensions for assessing data quality are a set of attributes representing single or multiple aspects of data, including the currency, accuracy, relevance, authority, and purpose of information [7]. In the existing literature, there is a degree of overlap identified among the data quality dimensions and their assessment methods. For instance, Mandalios and Jane [26] used the following assessment criteria to evaluate online sources: purpose, authority and credibility, accuracy and reliability, currency and timeliness and objectivity. In addition, Zhu and Gauch [41] proposed six quality metrics, including currency, availability, information-to-noise ratio, authority, popularity and cohesiveness, for investigating the assessment of online sources. Additionally, Nozato and Yoshiko [27] stated that the timeliness, depth, reputation, and accuracy of online sources are the most important data quality dimensions. Another study [4] used the quality attributes of the respondents and general perception of the news sources for news classification. Moreover, another study [8] investigated news credibility assessments by comparing crowds and expert opinions to understand the differentiation in the rating of the source.

In addition to the data quality dimensions and their assessment methods as described above, there exist different studies that employ various state-of-the-art techniques [10] based on information retrieval, machine learning, deep learning and knowledge representation graphs for assessing the relevance of news sources. For example, Essam and Elsayed [16] defined a specialized information retrieval technique by assessing the topics and subtopics of the news to identify highly relevant background articles. Elhadad et al. [15] adopted a machine learning technique for extracting features from the news content and prepared a complex set of metadata for identifying the credibility of the news sources. Another study [19] proposed a method based on deep learning techniques to find patterns in news sources to avoid false information, rumors, spam, fake news, and disinformation. Moreover, Hu et al. [18] analyzed the visual layout information of news homepages to utilize the mutual relationship that exists between news articles and news sources using a semi-supervised learning algorithm. However, this approach is not only based on a computationally expensive learning model to establish a relationship between new articles and sources but also limited to small news corpora. To address this limitation, a system named MediaRank was designed [39] to incorporate large datasets for measuring the quality of news sources by a mix of computational signals reflecting peer reputation, reporting bias, bottom-line pressure, and popularity. A study employing the application of knowledge graphs by Rudnik et al. [33] implemented a method using a Wikidata knowledge base for generating the semantic annotation of news articles to filter relevant news articles.

As stated above, substantial efforts have been made in news article classification using different data quality dimensions and methods. However, these studies have been centered on generalized news article classification problems. For designing a web-based EBS system, a domain-oriented news article classification approach is needed to filter relevant news articles. In the literature, there exist numerous EBS systems that not only perform manual curation of spatiotemporal entities but also map them with domain-specific (thematic) entities [2]. Therefore, the accuracy of these event-related extracted information from the processed mapping process is inappropriate for generating true alerts [17]. For instance, the existing HealthMap system provides the latitude and longitude coordinates linked to each event. However, the accuracy of the extracted geographical features has never been evaluated. Moreover, various other state-of-the-art systems, including HealthMap [17,34], use the news publication date to determine the occurrence date of the event. However, the extraction of temporal information directly from news articles has not yet been sufficiently explored and validated. To fill this research gap, a study proposed by Alomar et al. [1] that is based on a domain-oriented news article classification problem, is taken as fundamental to this research and used to develop the proposed approach. Alomar et al. [1] discussed a direct method (i.e., identification, review and evaluation of known sources to find relevant information sources) and an indirect method that assesses quality attributes of news content and metadata. Using the identified attributes by Alomar et al. [1], this work presents its extension by presenting the implementation and automatic extraction of attributes required for news article classification problems. To extend the baseline approach identified by Alomar et al. [1] for extracting relevant news articles, this work reports a 3-step process of information extraction that uses state-of-the-art text mining techniques. The 1st step involves the automatic extraction of the metadata information (i.e., publisher, subject, description, type, source, language, rights, and date) of the news article. This information is used to determine the trustworthiness of the article. The 2nd step consists of evaluating the news article's content in terms of accessibility, relevance, accuracy, clarity, timeliness, and reputation parameters. Last, the 3rd step, which is the main contribution of this work, introduces an epidemiological entity extraction approach (E3A) to weight the epidemiological context.

3 Proposed Work

Online information sources are the major information providers for event-based surveillance (EBS) systems. Therefore, the verification of these heterogeneous data sources is the primary concern of event-based systems. Thus, it is important to rate the data quality of online news sources by data quality scores before considering this news source information as part of an EBS system. In the proposed work, the data quality of online news sources is computed from three principal components: 1) metadata, 2) news content and 3) an epidemiological entity extraction approach (E3A). The main contribution of the E3A approach is introduced to improve the results by filtering out relevant news articles. The process workflow with all components is shown in Fig. 1.

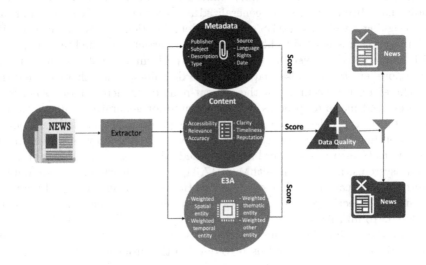

Fig. 1. Process workflow

3.1   Data Quality Measures (DQM)

Data quality measures (DQMs) are metrics used for ranking high-quality and low-quality elements to filter reliable news sources from the perspective of relevance, accuracy and reputation [36]. There are many criteria used to compute the data quality of online news sources, i.e., metadata attributes and content analysis by attributes [1]. The proposed approach allows us to measure the metadata score (MS) from metadata components, the content score (CS) by the content component and the epidemiological entity extraction score (E3S) calculated with weighted named entities (i.e., spatiotemporal entities with epidemiological entities). The E3S is computed from weighted named entities using the E3A. These components are discussed in the subsequent sections.

3.1.1   Metadata
Metadata are the core components of data used to establish quick information [11]. Therefore, metadata are defined and used to find relevant results quickly in search engines from millions of online sources [11]. There are some tags defined

by each reliable online source that are analyzed and fetched by search engines to provide ranked results.

There are different metadata attributes that are considered in the assessment of metadata from news sources [1]. However, some of the metadata attributes are not frequently available in the news sources and are ultimately discarded in the approach. We thus adopt eight attributes shortlisted as metadata that are considered relevant and available in most news articles. The following are the metadata attributes with the associated definitions:

- **Publisher:** Entity responsible for publishing news sources, e.g., Japan times, The Times of India
- **Subject:** Title of the news article, e.g., U.S. detected its first case of virulent bird flu in commercial poultry in 2017.
- **Description:** Short description of the news article
- **Type:** Type/nature of the news article, e.g., article
- **Source:** URL resource of the news article
- **Language:** Language of the news article, e.g., en_GB, en_US
- **Right:** Authority to publish the news source
- **Date:** Date of publication of news article. However, in some cases, the modification date of news articles is also available. The date of publication is the date at which the news article is published, and the modification date is the last updated date of the news article.

Each metadata attribute is extracted from the online news article. The MS is computed by the following formula [1]:

$$MS = \sum_{n=1}^{8} Presence(attribute_n) \tag{1}$$

$$Presence(attribute_n) = \begin{cases} 1, attribute \notin metadata \\ 2, attribute \in metadata \end{cases}$$

The presence of attributes has a score of 2, while the absence of attributes has a score of 1 [1]. The maximum MS value is 16 if all the attributes are extracted from the news article. Similarly, the minimum MS value is 8 when no metadata attributes are extracted. The metadata of the news article are extracted through the *BeautifulSoup* [32] Python library. It is used for web scrapping by parsing HTML (Hypertext Markup Language) and XML (Extensible Markup Language) content to extract its elements, values and many other attributes.

3.1.2 News Content

Online news content contains information on one or more events that occur in the form of paragraphs, media and references of other linked information available electronically to the public [38]. The content of the news article is ensured by means of currency, timeliness, relevance, accuracy and its impact [26]. To analyze the content of the news source, the data quality attributes available in the content are extracted to quantify the data quality score of the content. Extraction of the quality attributes from the content, the content score (CS) calculation of each attribute and the cumulative score are achieved by automated processes. There are different content attributes considered for the assessment of the content of the news source [1]. However, it is observed that some of them are mostly unavailable in the news sources. The quality attributes shortlisted to assess content include accessibility, relevance, accuracy, clarity, timeliness and reputation. The CS is computed by the following formulas [1]:

$$CS = \sum_{n=1}^{6} Presence(attribute_n) \tag{2}$$

$$Presence(attribute_n) = \begin{cases} 1, Not\ available \\ 2, Partially\ available \\ 3, Available \end{cases}$$

3.1.2.1 Accessibility
The preliminary step of analyzing content is to access online news sources. This ensures that the online news source is available and accessed without any barriers. Moreover, it is also possible that it is available but with restricted access such that it is not possible to access any browser or external tools. In some cases, it is also possible that online news sources are unavailable for future use in digital form.

3.1.2.2 Relevance
Relevance is the most important attribute of the content quality of the online source. In the context of EBS, it is a dependent variable depending upon three further attributes, i.e., affected hosts, an agent that affects the host and the location of the affected host. Furthermore, it is also possible to predict the agent using epidemiological intelligence libraries if it is unavailable. The Spacy [35] natural language processing (NLP) Python library is used to perform named entity recognition (NER) to extract locations, hosts and agents. Some examples of the hosts and agents of avian influenza are chickens, pigs, horses, ducks, gooses, etc. and H5N8, H5N1, highly pathogenic avian influenza, etc.

3.1.2.3 Accuracy
Accuracy is dependent on the information provided by the news sources that are the facts that can be verified and validated. In the context of EBS, it could be that the news content provides information about any health risk, outbreak information or the number of cases. Alternatively, poor relevance can have poor accuracy but not vice versa. Outbreak information is extracted using Spacy [35] by validated outbreak-related keyword tokens in the content. A number of cases are extracted using the pattern-based NLP technique.

3.1.2.4 Clarity
Clarity is the quality of being logical, consistent and completely understandable in terms of content that is similarly reflected in the metadata. Clarity of the article is poor if only the title is available in the metadata, and clarity is adequate

if other metadata attributes are available [1]. Good clarity exists if the subject, description, type, etc. are available in the metadata of the news article.

3.1.2.5 Timeliness

It is important that the content of the news article relates to the current context of the events. Otherwise, the claims may not be considered, or it may be a wrong interpretation. Timeliness is the time of an outbreak saved by detection in EBS relative to the onset of the outbreak [20]. Furthermore, timeliness (days) is calculated by the following equation:

$$Timeliness[days] = T_{alarm} - T_{onset} \qquad (3)$$

where T_{alarm} is the time of the event reported in the event-based system and T_{onset} can be validated from the health information databases.

3.1.2.6 Reputation

The reputation of news sources is extracted using the *MediaRank* [39] algorithm, which is calculated on multiple factors, i.e., popularity, peer reputation, reporting bias and breadth and bottom-line pressure. For example, the general reputation ranking using *MediaRank* [39] of nytimes is '1' and BBC is '5'. Therefore, the general reputation of the news source has an impact on the content quality, as it is computed by considering multiple factors.

3.1.3 The Epidemiological Entity Extraction Approach (E3A)

Event extraction and early warning detection are the key components of EBS [29]. An event is a verified set of processed epidemiological information of an outbreak [3]. It contains attributes such as location, occurrence date associated with epidemiological entities such as disease or unknown syndrome, symptoms, hosts, agents, etc. [3]. More precisely, this information is available in text in the form of spatiotemporal entities (when, where) and epidemiological entities, i.e., disease, host, agent, symptoms, etc. Furthermore, these attributes are extracted from text using NLP techniques.

In the E3A, the title and content of a news article are processed, and then named entities are extracted. It is not sufficient to extract epidemiological (thematic) entities from state-of-the-art name-entity recognition (NER) techniques. These named entities are extracted and classified into four categories: spatial, temporal, thematic and other entities. A pattern-based text mining approach is used for extracting and classifying thematic entities such as hosts (e.g., birds, pigs, horses, etc.) that are affected by a disease and variants of different agents (e.g., H5N1, H5N8, HPAI, etc.). After extracting named entities from the title and content of news articles, a weighted-entity approach is proposed for quantifying their epidemiological context in relation to their corresponding title and content. The resulting spatial, temporal and thematic entities that are recognized as relevant entities in the context of a particular EBS attempt (i.e., specific to proposed work) are termed "RelevantEntities (REs)". The weights are assigned based on two criteria, i.e., 1) title and description of news articles 2) types of entities. Double weights (i.e., 2) are assigned to these entities because of their occurrences in the title of the news articles, as the title is considered the most important element in text mining approaches used for studying the relevancy. However, a weight of 1.5 is assigned to each RE based on their occurrences in the content of the news article. Moreover, the remaining identified named entities are labeled "OtherEntities (OEs)". Last, a weight of 1 is assigned to each OE regardless of their occurrences in the title and content of the news articles. The E3A score (E3S) is calculated to quantify the context of news articles using the following formula:

$$EntityWeight_n = \begin{cases} 2, RE \in Title\ Sentence \\ 1.5, RE \in Content \\ 1, OE \end{cases}$$

$$E3S = \sum_{i=1}^{n} RE\ Weight/TE\ Weight \tag{4}$$

"RelevantEntityWeight" is the sum of the weight of REs (REs extracted from title and content of the news article). However, "TotalEntityWeight" is the sum of the weight of all entities (REs and OEs) occurring in the title and content of the news article. The E3A is applied to 2 groups of news sources to filter the news articles into relevant and irrelevant categories, which is discussed in Sect. 4. The occurrences of REs related to the epidemiological context of news sources that are extracted during the experiments are shown using the word cloud in Fig. 2. The word cloud visualization method is chosen from the existing literature because it provides a simple way to communicate the most frequently used relevant words (i.e., REs in our case from the news articles) using different font sizes indicating their occurrence frequency [25]. The identified REs, as shown in Fig. 2, serve as a starting point for further analysis, as stated in Sect. 4.

Fig. 2. Word cloud of extracted REs

In the next subsections, we detail the concept of each type of entity as well as the techniques adopted to extract them from news.

3.1.3.1 Spatial Entity

A spatial entity is a geographical or spatial location available in the text [22]. Spatial entities are extracted from the text by using the *Spacy* [35] natural language processing (NLP) Python library, which is mainly used for tokenization, named-entity recognition, etc. Examples of spatial entities include Paris, Rome, Berlin, etc.

3.1.3.2 Temporal Entity

Information on date, time and duration available in the text is known as a temporal entity [30]. Temporal entities are important for relating the occurrence of events in news sources. In our proposal, *SUTime* [12] is used for extracting temporal expressions and temporal entities. Some examples of temporal entities include 'last year', 'this Friday' and 'now', which are resolved into '2020', '2021-05-28' and '2021-05-28', respectively.

3.1.3.3 Thematic Entity

Important information related to our context (in particular to health risks) available in the text is known as thematic entities [13]. In our approach, these entities are affected hosts and agents that affect the hosts. Thematic entities in the text are extracted using the *Spacy* [35] Python library with an extended pattern-based approach to extract epidemiological entities. Epidemiological entities are the terms and concepts related to infectious diseases such as hosts, agents, variants and vectors. A pattern-based approach is used to extract named entities (epidemiological entities) in text according to defined patterns. A few examples of thematic entities include birds, H5N1, HPAI, highly pathogenic avian influenza, etc.

3.1.3.4 Other Entity

An entity that never belongs to a spatial entity, temporal entity or thematic entity is called an other entity. A few examples of these entities include quantity: 20, percent: 65%, org: Google, money: 20,000$ and cardinal: three.

4 Evaluation

The purpose of the proposed approach is to filter the relevant news sources by data quality scores. Currently, the proposed work is validated by two groups of news articles, i.e., outbreak-related and irrelevant articles. The ultimate goal of the proposed work is to prioritize outbreak-related news and discard irrelevant news immediately. The details of each group of news items are described in Sect. 4.1.

4.1 Dataset

The dataset of news articles is selected for validation of proposed work having '75' news articles in which the first '25' articles of the dataset contain information about the avian-influenza disease outbreaks, the next '25' articles contain general information (control measures, economic influences, etc.) about avian influenza disease, and the last '25' articles are not health-related news articles. The dataset is small; however, it is more specific to the event outbreak information of avian influenza disease. The preliminary work methodology is validated by a small dataset labeled by experts, whereas subsequent work will be validated with a large dataset labeled by experts. This unstructured information is available in news articles in the form of locations, dates of events with epidemiological entities such as disease or unknown syndrome, symptoms, hosts, and agents. More precisely, this information in news article datasets is used to formulate the spatial-temporal aspects (when, where) and epidemiological aspects, i.e., disease, host, agent, symptoms of the events. Each row in the dataset has a title, text, URL and manually annotated group of news sources. There are two main groups of news articles in the dataset, i.e., irrelevant news (news not related to the health situation) and relevant news (news related to disease outbreaks), which is prioritized by the proposed framework based on quality scores. General information news articles are considered irrelevant in strict evaluation approaches and relevant in flexible approaches. Furthermore, a news article dataset is available at http://shorturl.at/auABP.

4.2   Results

Table 1 shows the top 5 data quality score (DQS) sources of the "relevant" group. *MS* is the metadata score of the news source, *CS* is the content score of the news source, *E3S* is the epidemiological entity extraction score of the news source, and *DQS* is the data quality score computed as the average of the MS, CS and E3S.

Table 1. Top 5 DQS sources in Relevant group

Source	DQS	MS	CS	E3S
Outbreak News Today	0.88	0.94	0.89	0.82
Reuters	0.85	0.94	0.89	0.71
The Japan Times	0.85	0.94	0.89	0.71
nippon.com	0.85	0.94	0.89	0.72
The Northern Daily Leader	0.84	0.94	0.89	0.69

Similarly, Table 2 shows the top 5 data quality score (DQS) sources of the "irrelevant" group. The results clearly differentiate the relevant news and irrelevant news by comparing the DQSs.

Table 2. Top 5 DQS sources in Irrelevant group

Source	DQS	MS	CS	E3S
CNN	0.72	0.88	0.78	0.51
Aljazeera	0.72	0.81	0.67	0.67
Daily Mail UK	0.88	0.66	0.67	0.63
The Guardian	0.70	0.94	0.67	0.50
CNBC	0.69	0.94	0.61	0.52

Table 3. Strict approach

Score Type	Precision	Recall	F-Score
MS	0.44	0.96	0.60
CS	0.53	1	0.69
E3S	0.74	0.56	0.64
DQS	0.62	0.96	0.75

The results are produced using two evaluation approaches: 1) a strict approach (articles with general information on avian influenza are considered irrelevant) and 2) a flexible approach (articles with general information are considered relevant). The performance evaluation of the proposed work for classifying news articles is based on the classification metrics [23]. Classification metrics are calculated from true positives (TPs), i.e., relevant news identified as relevant, false positives (FPs), i.e., irrelevant news identified as relevant, false negatives (FNs), i.e., relevant news identified as irrelevant, and true negatives (TNs), i.e., irrelevant news identified as irrelevant.

The results of the news article dataset, which includes quality attribute values, *MS*, *CS* and *E3S*, are available at http://shorturl.at/foDUV. For every component score, i.e., MS, CS and E3S, a score of **0.72** and higher is considered a significant quality score for filtering the news articles. A score of 0.72 was considered relevant by validation with the manual labels of news articles. The precision, recall and F-score for each DQM using a strict approach are detailed in Table 3. Similarly, precision, recall and F-score for each DQM using a flexible approach are given in Table 4.

Table 4. Flexible approach

Score Type	Precision	Recall	F-Score
MS	0.68	0.80	0.74
CS	0.96	0.90	0.93
E3S	1	0.32	0.48
DQS	0.93	0.76	0.84

The overall performances of different quality measures, i.e., MS, CS, E3S and DQS, with a strict evaluation approach are shown in Fig. 3. Similarly, performances with a flexible approach are shown in Fig. 4.

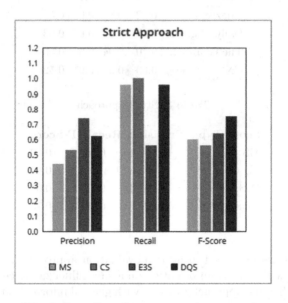

Fig. 3. Overall performance - strict approach

In the strict approach, as shown in Table 3, the DQS computed from the average of MS, CS and E3S produced significant improvements in terms of precision, recall and F-Score compared to individual MS, CS and E3S values. Similarly, the same pattern is observed in the flexible approach, as shown in Table 4, with a notable difference in precision, recall and F-score of the DQSs from the individual scores. However, DQSs in both approaches have a higher value than E3S in terms of recall and F-score, except for the precision measure. Conclusively, due to flexibility and dependency on other components, the false positive rate of DQSs is slightly greater than that of E3Ss.

5   Discussion

The quality of available information in online news sources is a mandatory prerequisite for event-based surveillance systems [14]. Thus, one can benefit from using this approach by marking irrelevant news articles retrieved and performing further analysis on relevant news articles. To filter out relevant news articles based on quality attributes, the approach extends the baseline work of Alomar et al. [1] to take into account all contextual information attributes. This work is currently validated with a smaller dataset with a disease case study of avian influenza for a proof of concept. One can also validate this approach with a large

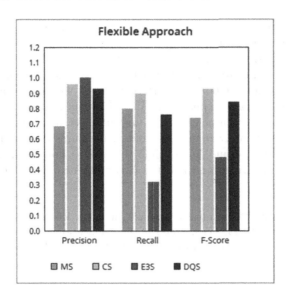

Fig. 4. Overall performance - flexible approach

dataset with avian influenza-related news articles by filtering relevant news articles using the proposed approach.

In the proposed E3A, the weight of the relevant entities is adjusted to determine the context in the news articles. This approach, by weighting the relevant context in news articles, helps filter relevant news in addition to the other components, i.e., metadata and content analysis. Conclusively, the proposed approach produced significant results for the case study of avian influenza. However, it has not been validated with other infectious diseases, but one can try it out with more infectious disease case studies by enhancing the extraction of epidemiological information for those diseases.

6   Conclusion

The proposed research focused on the data quality score computed from the metadata score (MS), content score (CS) with a combination of the epidemiological entity extraction score (E3S) and finally data quality score (DQS), which is the average of the MS, CS and E3S for filtering relevant news articles. The proposed approach is validated using two evaluation protocols, i.e., 1) a strict one and 2) a flexible one. With the strict approach, news is categorized into relevant and irrelevant classes with a precision of 0.62, a recall of 0.96 and an F-score of 0.75. The flexible approach was categorized with a precision of 0.93, a recall of 0.76 and an F-score of 0.84. The MS represents the key attribute aspect enrichment, the CS represents the accuracy, relevance, authority and currency of the content, and the E3S validates the epidemiological context in the news arti-

278   S. M. Alam et al.

cle. The combination of these components resulted in significant improvement in filtering relevant news articles.

Currently, experiments are being conducted on avian-influenza disease news article datasets to filter relevant and irrelevant news. In future work, more data will be integrated in collaboration with experts to extend the avian-influenza dataset and the associated experiments. It could be interesting to investigate and further classify the relevant news articles not only in terms of event outbreaks but also for other specific classes, such as control measures and economic impacts. Further consideration could be possible to analyze non-English, i.e., French, Spanish, etc. news articles and add the capabilities to extract epidemiological information.

Acknowledgments. This study was partially funded by EU grant 874850 MOOD and is catalogued as MOOD023. The contents of this publication are the sole responsibility of the authors and do not necessarily reflect the views of the European Commission.

References

1. Alomar, O., et al.: Development and testing of the media monitoring tool med is YS for the monitoring, early identification and reporting of existing and emerging plant health threats. EFSA Supporting Publications **13**(12), 1118E (2016)
2. Arsevska, E., Roche, M., Falala, S., Lancelot, R., Chavernac, D., Hendrikx, P., Dufour, B.: Monitoring disease outbreak events on the web using text-mining approach and domain expert knowledge. In: Proceedings of the Tenth International Conference on Language Resources and Evaluation (LREC'16). pp. 3407–3411 (2016)
3. Arsevska, E., et al.: Web monitoring of emerging animal infectious diseases integrated in the French animal health epidemic intelligence system. PLoS One **13**(8), e0199960 (2018)
4. Bachmann, P., Eisenegger, M., Ingenhoff, D.: Defining and measuring news media quality: Comparing the content perspective and the audience perspective. The International Journal of Press/Politics, p. 1940161221999666 (2021)
5. Balajee, S.A., Salyer, S.J., Greene-Cramer, B., Sadek, M., Mounts, A.W.: The practice of event-based surveillance: concept and methods. Global Secur. Health Sci. Policy **6**(1), 1–9 (2021)
6. Bastick, Z.: Would you notice if fake news changed your behavior? an experiment on the unconscious effects of disinformation. Comput. Hum. Behav. **116**, 106633 (2021)
7. Batini, C., Scannapieco, M., et al.: Data and information quality. Cham, Switzerland: Springer International Publishing. Google Scholar 43 (2016)
8. Bhuiyan, M.M., Zhang, A.X., Sehat, C.M., Mitra, T.: Investigating differences in crowdsourced news credibility assessment: Raters, tasks, and expert criteria. Proceedings of the ACM on Human-Computer Interaction **4**(CSCW2), 1–26 (2020)
9. Carneiro, H.A., Mylonakis, E.: Google trends: a web-based tool for real-time surveillance of disease outbreaks. Clin. Infect. Dis. **49**(10), 1557–1564 (2009)
10. Cato, K.D., Cohen, B., Larson, E.: Data elements and validation methods used for electronic surveillance of health care-associated infections: a systematic review. Am. J. Infect. Control **43**(6), 600–605 (2015)

11. Chan, L.M., Childress, E., Dean, R., O'neill, E.T., Vizine-Goetz, D.: A faceted approach to subject data in the Dublin core metadata record. J. Internet Cataloging 4(1–2), 35–47 (2001)

12. Chang, A.X., Manning, C.D.: Sutime: a library for recognizing and normalizing time expressions. In: Lrec, vol. 3735, p. 3740 (2012)

13. Cohen, A.M., Hersh, W.R.: A survey of current work in biomedical text mining. Brief. Bioinform. 6(1), 57–71 (2005)

14. Edelstein, M., Lee, L.M., Herten-Crabb, A., Heymann, D.L., Harper, D.R.: Strengthening global public health surveillance through data and benefit sharing. Emerg. Infect. Dis. 24(7), 1324 (2018)

15. Elhadad, M.K., Li, K.F., Gebali, F.: A novel approach for selecting hybrid features from online news textual metadata for fake news detection. In: Barolli, L., Hellinckx, P., Natwichai, J. (eds.) 3PGCIC 2019. LNNS, vol. 96, pp. 914–925. Springer, Cham (2020). https://doi.org/10.1007/978-3-030-33509-0_86

16. Essam, M., Elsayed, T.: Why is that a background article: a qualitative analysis of relevance for news background linking. In: Proceedings of the 29th ACM International Conference on Information & Knowledge Management, pp. 2009–2012 (2020)

17. Ganser, I.: Evaluation of event-based internet biosurveillance for multi-regional detection of seasonal influenza onset. Ph.D. thesis, McGill University (Canada) (2020)

18. Hu, Y., Li, M., Li, Z., Ma, W.: Discovering authoritative news sources and top news stories. In: Ng, H.T., Leong, M.-K., Kan, M.-Y., Ji, D. (eds.) AIRS 2006. LNCS, vol. 4182, pp. 230–243. Springer, Heidelberg (2006). https://doi.org/10.1007/11880592_18

19. Islam, M.R., Liu, S., Wang, X., Xu, G.: Deep learning for misinformation detection on online social networks: a survey and new perspectives. Soc. Netw. Anal. Min. 10(1), 1–20 (2020). https://doi.org/10.1007/s13278-020-00696-x

20. Jafarpour, N., Izadi, M., Precup, D., Buckeridge, D.L.: Quantifying the determinants of outbreak detection performance through simulation and machine learning. J. Biomed. Inform. 53, 180–187 (2015)

21. Kim, M., Chae, K., Lee, S., Jang, H.J., Kim, S.: Automated classification of online sources for infectious disease occurrences using machine-learning-based natural language processing approaches. Int. J. Environ. Res. Public Health 17(24), 9467 (2020)

22. Leidner, J.L., Lieberman, M.D.: Detecting geographical references in the form of place names and associated spatial natural language. Sigspatial Special 3(2), 5–11 (2011)

23. Lever, J., Krzywinski, M., Altman, N.: Classification evaluation (vol 13, pg 603, 2016). Nat. Methods 13(10), 890–890 (2016)

24. Lin, M.Y., Hota, B., Khan, Y.M., Woeltje, K.F., Borlawsky, T.B., Doherty, J.A., Stevenson, K.B., Weinstein, R.A., Trick, W.E., Program, C.P.E., et al.: Quality of traditional surveillance for public reporting of nosocomial bloodstream infection rates. JAMA 304(18), 2035–2041 (2010)

25. Lohmann, S., Heimerl, F., Bopp, F., Burch, M., Ertl, T.: Concentri cloud: word cloud visualization for multiple text documents. In: 2015 19th International Conference on Information Visualisation, pp. 114–120. IEEE (2015)

26. Mandalios, J.: Radar: an approach for helping students evaluate internet sources. J. Inf. Sci. 39(4), 470–478 (2013)

27. Nozato, Y.: Credibility of online newspapers. Convención Anual de la Association for Education in Journalism and Mass Communication. Washington, DC Disponible en (2002): http://citeseerx.ist.psu.edu/viewdoc/summary

28. Organization, W.H., et al.: A guide to establishing event-based surveillance. World Health Organization (2008)

29. Organization, W.H., et al.: Early detection, assessment and response to acute public health events: implementation of early warning and response with a focus on event-based surveillance: interim version. World Health Organization, Technical report (2014)

30. Pustejovsky, J., Castano, J.M., Ingria, R., Sauri, R., Gaizauskas, R.J., Setzer, A., Katz, G., Radev, D.R.: Timeml: robust specification of event and temporal expressions in text. New Directions Question Answering **3**, 28–34 (2003)

31. Rees, E., Ng, V., Gachon, P., Mawudeku, A., McKenney, D., Pedlar, J., Yemshanov, D., Parmely, J., Knox, J.: Early detection and prediction of infectious disease outbreaks. CCDR **45**, 5 (2019)

32. Richardson, L.: Beautiful soup documentation. Dosegljivo (2007). https://www.crummy.com/software/BeautifulSoup/bs4/doc/. [Dostopano: 7. 7. 2018]

33. Rudnik, C., Ehrhart, T., Ferret, O., Teyssou, D., Troncy, R., Tannier, X.: Searching news articles using an event knowledge graph leveraged by wikidata. In: Companion Proceedings of The 2019 World Wide Web Conference, WWW 2019, pp. 1232–1239. Association for Computing Machinery, New York (2019). https://doi.org/10.1145/3308560.3316761, https://doi.org/10.1145/3308560.3316761

34. Valentin, S.: Extraction and combination of epidemiological information from informal sources for animal infectious diseases surveillance. Ph.D. thesis, Université Montpellier (2020)

35. Vasiliev, Y.: Natural Language Processing with Python and SpaCy: A Practical Introduction. No Starch Press (2020)

36. Vaziri, R., Mohsenzadeh, M.: A questionnaire-based data quality methodology. Int. J. Database Manage. Syst. **4**(2), 55 (2012)

37. Wang, R.Y., Strong, D.M.: Beyond accuracy: what data quality means to data consumers. J. Manag. Inf. Syst. **12**(4), 5–33 (1996)

38. Westerman, D., Spence, P.R., Van Der Heide, B.: Social media as information source: recency of updates and credibility of information. J. Comput.-Mediat. Commun. **19**(2), 171–183 (2014)

39. Ye, J., Skiena, S.: Mediarank: computational ranking of online news sources. In: Proceedings of the 25th ACM SIGKDD International Conference on Knowledge Discovery & Data Mining, pp. 2469–2477 (2019)

40. Zhou, C., Xiu, H., Wang, Y., Yu, X.: Characterizing the dissemination of misinformation on social media in health emergencies: an empirical study based on covid-19. Inf. Process. Manage. **58**(4), 102554 (2021)

41. Zhu, X., Gauch, S.: Incorporating quality metrics in centralized/distributed information retrieval on the world wide web. In: Proceedings of the 23rd Annual International ACM SIGIR Conference on Research and Development in Information Retrieval, pp. 288–295 (2000)

AmLDA: A Non-VAE Neural Topic Model

Tomonari Masada[(✉)] [iD]

Rikkyo University, 3 Chome-34-1 Nishiikebukuro,
Toshima City, Tokyo 171-8501, Japan
masada@rikkyo.ac.jp

Abstract. The variational inference (VI) for Bayesian models approximates the true posterior by maximizing a variational lower bound called ELBO. This paper considers the VI for the latent Dirichlet allocation (LDA), a well-studied Bayesian model. The VI for LDA was originally proposed as a variational expectation-maximization (VEM), where we obtain the update equations by setting the derivatives of the ELBO equal to zero. However, its M step requires the analysis of the whole training set, and its E step needs to run the update dozens of times. The stochastic VI (SVI) proposed later has improved the VEM by replacing the M step with a minibatch gradient ascent. Further, a variational autoencoder for LDA called ProdLDA in turn has replaced the E step with a minibatch gradient ascent by using an amortized encoder. Now we can train LDA like a deep neural network. However, ProdLDA marginalizes out the discrete latent variables and thus maximizes an ELBO formulated differently from both the VEM and the SVI for LDA. As a result, ProdLDA suffers from the problem of component collapse. Therefore, we propose a new VI for LDA called AmLDA. As AmLDA maximizes the same ELBO as that which both the VEM and the SVI maximize, it does not suffer from component collapse. Only the parameterization differs because AmLDA uses an amortized network for parameterizing unknown variables. The evaluation was performed over five large datasets. The experimental results show that AmLDA is as effective as the SVI.

Keywords: Topic modeling · Deep learning · Variational autoencoder

1 Introduction

Bayesian probabilistic models are a powerful tool for data analytics. This paper considers *topic modeling*, one among the best adopted Bayesian methods in practical data exploration. Topic modeling is utilized in a wide variety of disciplines including social sciences [12,22] and digital humanities [3,24]. In this paper, we discuss latent Dirichlet allocation (LDA) [2] (see Fig. 1 and Table 1), which is the most fundamental and the best known topic model. LDA remains a source of abundant inspiration to researchers even in deep learning era [15,16,21,25–27].

© The Author(s), under exclusive license to Springer Nature Switzerland AG 2022
J. A. Lossio-Ventura et al. (Eds.): SIMBig 2021, CCIS 1577, pp. 281–295, 2022.
https://doi.org/10.1007/978-3-031-04447-2_19

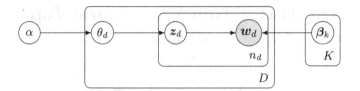

Fig. 1. Graphical representation of LDA [2]. Each plate represents replicates. The number of the replicates is given in the right-hand bottom corner of the plate. See also the caption of Table 1.

The central task of Bayesian modeling is to infer the posterior distribution of latent random variables given observations. This paper focuses on the optimization-based posterior inference called variational inference (VI), which approximates the true posterior by maximizing a lower bound of the log of the marginal likelihood of the observations. This maximization objective is often called ELBO, which stands for the Evidence Lower BOund. The original LDA paper [2] proposes an EM algorithm-based coordinate ascent VI, where the update equations of the unknown parameters are derived by computing the derivatives of the ELBO and setting them equal to zero. The EM algorithm-based VI is also known as variational expectation-maximization (VEM) [17]. The E step of the VEM for LDA updates the local variational parameters governing the document-wise topic probabilities as in Algorithm 1. The M step shown in Algorithm 2 updates the topic-wise word probabilities, which are global parameters, that is, the parameters relevant to every document. However, we can run the M step only after analyzing the whole dataset. This leads to a slow convergence.

The stochastic variational inference (SVI) for LDA [6,7] has made a great progress toward a more efficient and effective VI. The SVI for LDA replaces the M step of the VEM with a gradient-based update, where we only need to analyze randomly sampled subsets, that is, minibatches. The minibatch SVI achieves a faster convergence than the VEM and even improves the effectiveness of topic modeling in terms of predictive probability. However, only the global parameters are updated by a minibatch gradient ascent. The local parameters are still updated by the E step in Algorithm 1, where we need to run the update dozens of times for estimating the topic probabilities for each document. Therefore, the SVI inherits the inefficiency of the E step of the VEM.

The variational autoencoder (VAE) [10] has changed the scenery of the posterior inference for topic modeling [1,4,5,15,23,25]. We often call the VAE-based topic models together as neural topic model. In this paper, we discuss ProdLDA [23], which is a rather straightforward VAE-based version of LDA. ProdLDA differs from LDA by the logistic-normal prior substituting the Dirichlet prior of LDA. The VI for ProdLDA is more efficient than the SVI for LDA, because ProdLDA parameterizes the local variational parameters with an encoder neural network, which amortizes the inference and shares weights and biases across document examples. When estimating the topic probabilities for each document, we only need to perform a single forward pass through the amortized encoder.

Table 1. Generative description of LDA [2]. D is the number of documents. V is the vocabulary size. K is the number of topics. n_d is the length of the dth document. α is the symmetric Dirichlet prior parameter. $\{\boldsymbol{\theta}_1, \ldots, \boldsymbol{\theta}_D\}$ are the parameters of the document-wise topic categorical distributions. $\{\boldsymbol{\beta}_1, \ldots, \boldsymbol{\beta}_K\}$ are the parameters of the topic-wise word categorical distributions. See also Fig. 1.

- For each document $d = 1, \ldots, D$
    - sample mixing proportions $\boldsymbol{\theta}_d \sim \text{Dirichlet}(\alpha)$
    - For each position $i = 1, \ldots, n_d$, sample:
        * topic $z_{d,i} \in \{1, \ldots, K\} \sim \text{Categorical}(\boldsymbol{\theta}_d)$
        * word $w_{d,i} \in \{1, \ldots, V\} \sim \text{Categorical}(\boldsymbol{\beta}_{z_{d,i}})$

However, ProdLDA marginalizes out the discrete latent variables of LDA. Consequently, the VI for ProdLDA maximizes an ELBO differently formulated from that maximized both by the VEM [2,17] and by the SVI [6,7] for LDA. That is, the VI for ProdLDA solves a different maximization problem. This causes a serious side effect called *component collapse*, in which the encoder becomes stuck in a poor local optimum, where all topics are nearly identical. An implementation of ProdLDA[1] tackles the issue by tweaking the optimization. However, we need a more effective remedy than ad hoc deep learning tuning techniques.

This paper proposes a new amortized VI for LDA. Our contribution is two-fold. First, we parameterize both the local and the global parameters of LDA as outputs of their respective neural networks. Consequently, all parameters are updated by a minibatch gradient ascent. This leads to an efficiency comparable to ProdLDA. Second, we marginalize out no discrete latent variables and thus maximizes the same ELBO as that maximized both by the VEM and by the SVI for LDA. In other words, our parameterization is not VAE-based and thus widely differs from that of ProdLDA. Therefore, our proposal does not suffer from the component collapse, which is a serious issue for ProdLDA. This leads to an effectiveness comparable to that of the VEM and the SVI. Table 2 summarizes the comparison. We call our method AmLDA, which stands for Amortized LDA. We suggest that VAE is not the best way to achieve an amortized inference for LDA and possibly also for other topic models.

The rest of the paper is organized as follows. Section 2 introduces LDA and provides a detailed description of the compared methods. Section 3 describes our proposal, AmLDA. Section 4 provides the results of the comparison experiment. Section 5 concludes the paper by suggesting future research directions.

2   Previous Work

In this section, we first introduce latent Dirichlet allocation (LDA) [2] and then gives a detailed introduction of the relevant proposals, that is, the variational expectation-maximization (VEM), the stochastic variational inference (SVI), and the variational autoencoder (VAE) for LDA.

---

[1] https://pyro.ai/examples/prodlda.html .

Algorithm 1. The E step of the VEM for LDA [2]

1: For each document $d = 1, \ldots, D$
2:     Repeat until convergence:
3:         For each position $i = 1, \ldots, n_d$
4:             For each topic $k = 1, \ldots, K$
5:                 $\phi_{d,i,k} = \beta_{k,w_{d,i}} \exp(\psi(\gamma_{d,k}))$ ▷ ψ is the digamma function.
6:             Normalize $\phi_{d,i}$
7:         For each topic $k = 1, \ldots, K$
8:             $\gamma_{d,k} = \alpha + \sum_{i=1}^{n_d} \phi_{d,i,k}$

Algorithm 2. The M step of the VEM for LDA [2]

1: For each topic $k = 1, \ldots, K$
2:     For each word $v = 1, \ldots, V$
3:         $\beta_{k,v} = \sum_{d=1}^{D} \sum_{i=1}^{n_d} \phi_{d,i,k} \delta_v(w_{d,i})$ ▷ $\delta_v(w) = 1$ if $w = v$ and 0 otherwise.
4:     Normalize β_k

2.1 Latent Dirichlet Allocation (LDA)

LDA is a Bayesian probabilistic model for a document set. Assume that we have a set of D documents. We identify each document with its index and refer to the document set by the index set $\{1, \ldots, D\}$. LDA represents every document as a bag of words, that is, as a multiset of words $\boldsymbol{w}_d \equiv \{w_{d,1}, \ldots, w_{d,n_d}\}$, where $w_{d,i}$ is the random variable holding an observed index of the word occurring at the ith position in the document d. n_d is the number of the word occurrences in the document d. We let V denote the vocabulary size and identify each word with its index in the vocabulary set $\{1, \ldots, V\}$. Then, $w_{d,i} = v$ means that we observe a token of the word v at the ith position in the document d.

LDA generates a document set as in Table 1. Figure 1 is the corresponding plate representation. LDA prepares a categorical distribution Categorical($\boldsymbol{\beta}_k$) defined over the words $\{1, \ldots, V\}$ for each topic $k \in \{1, \ldots, K\}$, where we denote the number of topics by K and identify each topic with its index in $\{1, \ldots, K\}$. The parameter $\beta_{k,v}$ is the probability that the word v from $\{1, \ldots, V\}$ is used to express the topic k. Note that $\sum_{v=1}^{V} \beta_{k,v} = 1$ holds for all k. LDA we consider in this paper has no prior distribution for the categorical distributions Categorical($\boldsymbol{\beta}_k$) for $k = 1, \ldots, K$. However, our method can also be applied when a prior, e.g. Dirichlet prior, is attached to these topic-wise word categorical distributions.

As in Table 1, LDA draws topic probabilities $\boldsymbol{\theta}_d \equiv (\theta_{d,1}, \ldots, \theta_{d,K})$ for each document $d = 1, \ldots, D$ from a symmetric Dirichlet prior Dirichlet(α). Note that $\sum_{k=1}^{K} \theta_{d,k} = 1$ holds for every d. LDA then generates word tokens in each document first by drawing a latent topic $z_{d,i}$ from the document-wise topic categorical distribution Categorical($\boldsymbol{\theta}_d$) and then by drawing a word $w_{d,i}$ from the topic-wise word categorical distribution Categorical($\boldsymbol{\beta}_{z_{d,i}}$) for $i = 1, \ldots, n_d$. LDA can be interpreted as a token-level clustering, where $z_{d,i}$ gives the topic to which the word token $w_{d,i}$ is assigned. The set of the latent topic assignments $\boldsymbol{z}_d \equiv \{z_{d,1}, \ldots, z_{d,n_d}\}$ tells which topics are dominant in each document.

Based on the generative process in Table 1, we can obtain the evidence, that is, the marginal likelihood, of the observed word tokens $\boldsymbol{w}_d \equiv \{w_{d,1}, \ldots, w_{d,n_d}\}$ as

$$p(\boldsymbol{w}_d; \alpha, \boldsymbol{\beta}) = \int \Big(\sum_{\boldsymbol{z}_d} p(\boldsymbol{w}_d|\boldsymbol{z}_d; \boldsymbol{\beta})p(\boldsymbol{z}_d|\boldsymbol{\theta}_d) \Big) p(\boldsymbol{\theta}_d; \alpha)d\boldsymbol{\theta}_d \qquad (1)$$

However, the maximization of the evidence in Eq. (1) is intractable. Therefore, the variational inference (VI) [2] instead maximizes the following lower bound of the log of the evidence, called ELBO, for each d:

$$\begin{aligned}
\log p(\boldsymbol{w}_d; \alpha, \boldsymbol{\beta}) \geq \;& \mathbb{E}_{q(\boldsymbol{z}_d)}\big[\log p(\boldsymbol{w}_d|\boldsymbol{z}_d; \boldsymbol{\beta})\big] + \mathbb{E}_{q(\boldsymbol{\theta}_d)q(\boldsymbol{z}_d)}\big[\log p(\boldsymbol{z}_d|\boldsymbol{\theta}_d)\big] \\
& - D_{\mathrm{KL}}(q(\boldsymbol{\theta}_d) \parallel p(\boldsymbol{\theta}_d; \alpha)) - \mathbb{E}_{q(\boldsymbol{z}_d)}\big[\log q(\boldsymbol{z}_d)\big]
\end{aligned} \qquad (2)$$

where $D_{\mathrm{KL}}(q \parallel p)$ stands for the Kullback-Leibler divergence from p to q. In Eq. (2), $q(\boldsymbol{\theta}_d)$ and $q(\boldsymbol{z}_d)$ are the factors of the variational posterior $q(\boldsymbol{\theta}_d, \boldsymbol{z}_d)$ under the mean field approximation $q(\boldsymbol{\theta}_d, \boldsymbol{z}_d) \approx q(\boldsymbol{\theta}_d)q(\boldsymbol{z}_d)$, where $q(\boldsymbol{\theta}_d)$ denotes the variational Dirichlet posterior Dirichlet(γ_d) governing the document-wise topic probabilities $\boldsymbol{\theta}_d$, and $q(\boldsymbol{z}_d)$ denotes the variational posterior representing the token-wise topic assignment probabilities. It can be shown that $q(\boldsymbol{z}_d)$ further factorizes as $q(\boldsymbol{z}_d) = \prod_{j=1}^{n_d} q(z_{d,i})$. Each factor $q(z_{d,i})$ expresses the topic assignment categorical distribution Categorical($\boldsymbol{\phi}_{d,i}$), where the variational parameter $\phi_{d,i,k}$ is an approximated probability that $z_{d,i} = k$ holds.

By maximizing the ELBO in Eq. (2) for all d, the VI for LDA estimates the following parameters: $\boldsymbol{\phi}_{d,i} \equiv (\phi_{d,i,1}, \ldots, \phi_{d,i,K})$, $\boldsymbol{\gamma}_d \equiv (\gamma_{d,1}, \ldots, \gamma_{d,K})$, and $\boldsymbol{\beta}_k \equiv (\beta_{k,1}, \ldots, \beta_{k,V})$. The ELBO in Eq. (2) can be regarded as a function of these parameters. Therefore, we denote it as $\mathcal{L}_d(\boldsymbol{\phi}_d, \boldsymbol{\gamma}_d, \boldsymbol{\beta})$, where $\boldsymbol{\phi}_d \equiv \{\boldsymbol{\phi}_{d,1}, \ldots, \boldsymbol{\phi}_{d,n_d}\}$ and $\boldsymbol{\beta} \equiv \{\boldsymbol{\beta}_1, \ldots, \boldsymbol{\beta}_K\}$. We call $\boldsymbol{\phi}_d$ and $\boldsymbol{\gamma}_d$ local parameter, because they are only relevant to a single document d. In contrast, $\boldsymbol{\beta}$ has a connection with the whole document set and thus is called global parameter.

2.2   VEM, SVI, and VAE for LDA

The original LDA paper [2] provides the variational inference as a variational expectation-maximization (VEM) by computing the derivatives of the ELBO $\mathcal{L}_d(\boldsymbol{\phi}_d, \boldsymbol{\gamma}_d, \boldsymbol{\beta})$ in Eq. (2) for each d with respect to the unknown parameters $\boldsymbol{\phi}_d$, $\boldsymbol{\gamma}_d$, and $\boldsymbol{\beta}$ and setting them equal to zero. The resulting VEM is presented in Algorithms 1 and 2, where the parameters are optimized by a coordinate ascent. The E step in Algorithm 1 updates the local parameters $\boldsymbol{\phi}_d$ and $\boldsymbol{\gamma}_d$ based on the estimation of $\boldsymbol{\beta}$ given by the preceding M step. While $\gamma_{d,k}$ can be updated simply as $\gamma_{d,k} = \alpha + \sum_{i=1}^{n_d} \phi_{d,i,k}$, the update of $\phi_{d,i,k}$ in turn depends on $\gamma_{d,k}$. That is, $\boldsymbol{\phi}_d$ and $\boldsymbol{\gamma}_d$ need to be updated alternately. Therefore, the E step requires dozens of iterations until convergence. Further, the M step in Algorithm 2 updates the global parameters $\boldsymbol{\beta}$ as $\beta_{k,v} = \sum_{d=1}^{D} \sum_{i=1}^{n_d} \phi_{d,i,k}\delta_v(w_{d,i})$ by using $\boldsymbol{\phi}_d$ computed for every document $d \in \{1, \ldots, D\}$. Consequently, the VEM suffers from two inefficiencies. First, the estimation of topic probabilities

Table 2. Comparison of variational inferences for LDA

	VI [2]	SVI [7]	VAE [23]	Ours
No marginalization of discrete variables	✓	✓		✓
Gradient-based update of global parameters		✓	✓	✓
Gradient-based update of local parameters			✓	✓

in each document requires dozens of iterations in the E step. Second, the M step requires performing the E step over the whole document set. These inefficiencies lead to a slow convergence.

To make VI more efficient, we can adopt stochastic optimization, that is, a technique using noisy estimates of a gradient, in maximizing the ELBO. The stochastic variational inference (SVI) for LDA [6,7] addresses the inefficiency of the M step of the VEM by replacing the coordinate ascent with a stochastic gradient ascent. Further, the SVI amortizes the computational cost for updating the global parameters across more data points not by sampling only one document at a time but by sampling hundreds or thousands of documents, that is, by sampling one minibatch at a time. While the SVI proposed by [7] is based on a sophisticated idea of natural gradient, we now have access to many effective gradient-based optimization algorithms, e.g. Adam [9] and AdamW [13]. Therefore, we can achieve an effective inference by tweaking the hyperparameters of the optimization algorithms in a deep learning manner. We denote the VI updating β with a minibatch gradient ascent by SVI. However, the SVI uses the E step in Algorithm 1 with no modification and thus inherits from the VEM the inefficiency of the update of the local parameters ϕ_d and γ_d.

The inefficiency of the E step of the VEM can be addressed by adopting a deep learning based variational inference called variational autoencoder (VAE) [10]. We here discuss ProdLDA [23], a proposal of the VAE for LDA. ProdLDA realizes the estimation of the parameters of the variational posterior $q(\theta_d)$ with an encoder neural network, whose input is a bag-of-words representation of each document $d \in \{1, \ldots, M\}$. In ProdLDA, the Dirichlet prior $p(\theta; \alpha)$ of LDA is replaced by a logistic-normal distribution. The variational posterior $q(\theta_d)$ governing the document-wise topic probabilities θ_d is also replaced by a logistic-normal distribution whose covariance matrix is diagonal. We denote the mean vector and the diagonal elements of the covariance matrix of $q(\theta_d)$ as μ_d and σ_d^2 respectively. The encoder network is trained as a function $\text{Enc}(x_d)$ giving μ_d and the log of σ_d^2 as an output for each document d, that is, $[\mu_d, \log \sigma_d^2] = \text{Enc}(w_d)$, where the bracket means concatenation. Then we can sample document-wise topic probabilities as $\theta_d = \sigma_d \odot \epsilon + \mu_d$, where ϵ is a random noise vector drawn from the multivariate standard normal distribution, and $\odot$ is the element-wise multiplication.

However, it is known that the VAE often suffers from an issue called *component collapse*, where the KL-divergence $D_{\text{KL}}(q(\theta_d) \| p(\theta_d; \alpha))$ from the prior $p(\theta_d)$ to the variational posterior $q(\theta_d)$ is collapsed toward zero. In case of

---

Algorithm 3. The forward pass for computing the local parameters in AmLDA

1: For each document $d = 1, \ldots, D$
2:     For each position $i = 1, \ldots, n_d$
3:         $\phi_{d,i} = \texttt{TokenEncoder}([e_{x_{d,i}}, \bar{e}_d])$ $\triangleright \; \bar{e}_d \equiv \sum_{i=j}^{n_d} e_{x_{d,j}}/n_d$
4:     For each topic $k = 1, \ldots, K$
5:         $\gamma_{d,k} = \alpha + \sum_{i=1}^{n_d} \phi_{d,i,k}$
6:     Detach $\boldsymbol{\beta}$
7:     Repeat N_{local} times:
8:         For each position $i = 1, \ldots, n_d$
9:             For each topic $k = 1, \ldots, K$
10:                 $\phi_{d,i,k} = \beta_{k,w_{d,i}} \exp(\psi(\gamma_{d,k}))$
11:             Normalize $\phi_{d,i}$
12:         For each topic $k = 1, \ldots, K$
13:             $\gamma_{d,k} = \alpha + \sum_{i=1}^{n_d} \phi_{d,i,k}$
14:     Draw S samples $\{\boldsymbol{\theta}_d^{(1)}, \ldots, \boldsymbol{\theta}_d^{(S)}\}$ from Dirichlet($\boldsymbol{\gamma}_d$)

Algorithm 4. The forward pass for computing the global parameters in AmLDA

1: For each word $v = 1, \ldots, V$
2:     $\boldsymbol{r}_v = \texttt{EmbeddingMapper}(\boldsymbol{e}_v)$
3: $\boldsymbol{U} = (\boldsymbol{r}_1, \ldots, \boldsymbol{r}_V)^\mathsf{T}$ $\triangleright \; \boldsymbol{U}$ is a $V \times K$ matrix.
4: For each topic $k = 1, \ldots, K$
5:     $\boldsymbol{\beta}_k = \text{Softmax}(\boldsymbol{u}_k)$ $\triangleright \; \boldsymbol{u}_k$ is the kth column of $\boldsymbol{U}$.

ProdLDA, the component collapse makes all topics nearly identical. As a result, we cannot obtain any meaningful topic extraction. Note that the KL-divergence from the prior to the variational posterior already appears in the ELBO in Eq. (2), which is the maximization objective of both the VEM and the SVI. However, neither the VEM nor the SVI suffer from the component collapse. A possible reason why ProdLDA suffers from the component collapse is that ProdLDA maximizes a differently formulated ELBO. ProdLDA marginalizes out the discrete latent variables $z_{d,i}$ representing token-wise topic assignments. Consequently, ProdLDA replaces the evidence in Eq. (1) with

$$p(\boldsymbol{w}_d; \alpha, \boldsymbol{\beta}) = \int p(\boldsymbol{w}_d | \boldsymbol{\theta}_d; \boldsymbol{\beta}) p(\boldsymbol{\theta}_d; \alpha) d\boldsymbol{\theta}_d \qquad (3)$$

where $p(\boldsymbol{w}_d | \boldsymbol{\theta}_d; \boldsymbol{\beta})$ is the probability mass function of the multinomial distribution defined over vocabulary words $\{1, \ldots, V\}$, whose parameters are obtained as $\sum_{k=1}^{K} \theta_{d,k} \boldsymbol{\beta}_k$. Consequently, the following ELBO, which is different from the ELBO given in Eq. (2), is maximized by ProdLDA:

$$\log p(\boldsymbol{w}_d; \alpha, \boldsymbol{\beta}) \geq \mathbb{E}_{q(\boldsymbol{\theta}_d)} \big[\log p(\boldsymbol{w}_d; \boldsymbol{\theta}_d) \big] - D_{\text{KL}}(q(\boldsymbol{\theta}_d) \, \| \, p(\boldsymbol{\theta}_d; \alpha)) \qquad (4)$$

To the best of our knowledge, it is not known why the maximization of this ELBO suffers from the component collapse. However, we address the issue by maximizing the original ELBO in Eq. (2) in a different but an amortized manner.

In this paper, we propose a new amortized inference for LDA and call it AmLDA. AmLDA maximizes the same ELBO as that which both of the VEM and the SVI for LDA maximize. However, the parameterization differs. AmLDA obtains the unknown parameters as outputs of neural networks, whose input is composed of word embedding vectors. The next section gives the details.

3   Method

AmLDA maximizes the same ELBO as that maximized by the VAE and the SVI for LDA and only differs in the parameterization of the unknown parameters. AmLDA assigns to each word $v \in \{1, \ldots, V\}$ an M-dimensional embedding vector e_v. The word embedding vectors are fed to the neural networks used for computing the following unknown parameters:

- the token-wise topic assignment probabilities $\phi_{d,i} \equiv (\phi_{d,i,1}, \ldots, \phi_{d,i,K})$,
- the document-wise Dirichlet posterior parameters $\gamma_d \equiv (\gamma_{d,1}, \ldots, \gamma_{d,K})$, and
- the topic-wise word probabilities $\beta_k \equiv (\beta_{k,1}, \ldots, \beta_{k,V})$.

The word embeddings are trained jointly with the neural networks. The forward pass for computing these unknown parameters is explained below.

First, the parameters $\phi_{d,i} \equiv (\phi_{d,i,1}, \ldots, \phi_{d,i,K})$ are computed as $\phi_{d,i} = $ TokenEncoder$([e_{x_{d,i}}, \bar{e}_d])$, where $\bar{e}_d$ is the mean of the embeddings of the word tokens occurring in the document d, that is, $\bar{e}_d \equiv \sum_{i=j}^{n_d} e_{x_{d,j}}/n_d$, and $[e_{x_{d,i}}, \bar{e}_d]$ is a concatenation of the two vectors $e_{x_{d,i}}$ and $\bar{e}_d$. A token-wise encoder network TokenEncoder$(\cdot)$ maps the concatenation $[e_{x_{d,i}}, \bar{e}_d]$ to $\phi_{d,i}$.

Second, the posterior parameters $\gamma_d \equiv (\gamma_{d,1}, \ldots, \gamma_{d,K})$ are obtained as $\gamma_{d,k} = \alpha + \sum_{i=1}^{n_d} \phi_{d,i,k}$ for each k. This is the update equation of the E step in Algorithm 1 and can be regarded as a fully connected layer having the fixed weights all equal to 1 and the bias α. However, this simple computation of γ_d has turned out to be suboptimal. We thus additionally perform N_{local} iterations of the pair of the update equations $\phi_{d,i,k} = \beta_{k,w_{d,i}} \exp(\psi(\gamma_{d,k}))$, followed by the normalization of $\phi_{d,i}$, and $\gamma_{d,k} = \alpha + \sum_{i=1}^{n_d} \phi_{d,i,k}$ after making β detached. We have found that $N_{\text{local}} = 2$ works well. We use the resulting γ_d as the parameter of the variational Dirichlet posterior Dirichlet(γ_d) and draw S samples $\{\theta_d^{(1)}, \ldots, \theta_d^{(S)}\}$ from Dirichlet(γ_d). The drawn samples are used for approximating the expectations appearing in the ELBO in Eq. (2).

Finally, the topic-wise word probabilities $\beta_k \equiv (\beta_{k,1}, \ldots, \beta_{k,V})$ are obtained as $\beta_k = $ Softmax(u_k), where u_k is the kth column of a $V \times K$ matrix U. The matrix U is constructed from a set of V row vectors $\{r_1, \ldots, r_V\}$, each of which is in turn computed as $r_v = $ EmbeddingMapper(e_v), where the neural network EmbeddingMapper$(\cdot)$ maps the word embedding e_v to a vector r_v of the same dimension. EmbeddingMapper$(\cdot)$ is intended to give effective topic-wise word probabilities $\{\beta_1, \ldots, \beta_K\}$ based on the word embeddings $\{e_1, \ldots, e_V\}$ and thus is a key ingredient to achieve an effective posterior inference in our method.

The forward pass for the local and the global parameters in AmLDA is summarized in Alogrithms 3 and 4, respectively. Most of the computation can

Table 3. The number of documents and the average document length (in parentheses) of each dataset used in our evaluation experiment

AG_NEWS	DBpedia	YelpReviewFull	YahooAnswers	AmazonReviewFull
120,000	560,000	650,000	1,400,000	3,000,000
(43.17)	(54.48)	(80.86)	(68.05)	(75.28)

be performed efficiently in parallel on GPU. We perform the forward pass in Alogrithms 3 and 4 for constructing a computation graph of the ELBO in Eq. (2) and backpropagate through the forward pass for updating the parameters with a minibatch stochastic gradient ascent, where Adam [9] is used in our experiment.

4 Experiment

4.1 Datasets and Implementation Details

We used five document sets for our comparison experiment. All document sets are from `torchtext.datasets` of PyTorch.[2] We only used the training part. Table 3 shows the number of documents and the average document length of each dataset. We limited the vocabulary size V to 10,000 for every dataset. The tokenization was performed with the `basic_english` tokenizer of `torchtext.data`. Since the datasets were of large size, we randomly selected one percent of the documents as validation set for computing perplexity during the model training.

All compared methods were implemented with PyTorch. We report the evaluation results for the two cases of the number of topics: $K = 50$ and $K = 100$. The word embedding dimension M was set to 200. We set the number S of samples drawn from the variational Dirichlet posterior $\text{Dirichlet}(\gamma_d)$ to 50. The sampling from the Dirichlet posterior was performed by using the reparameterization trick implemented in `torch.distributions.dirichlet` of PyTorch. The token-wise encoder $\text{TokenEncoder}(\cdot)$ mapping the concatenation $[e_{x_{d,i}}, \bar{e}_d]$ to $\phi_{d,i}$ by $\phi_{d,i} = \text{TokenEncoder}([e_{x_{d,i}}, \bar{e}_d])$ was implemented as

$$\phi_{d,i} = \text{Softmax}(\text{Linear}_K(\text{LayerNorm}([e_{x_{d,i}}, \bar{e}_d]))) \tag{5}$$

where $\text{Linear}_K(\cdot)$ and $\text{LayerNorm}(\cdot)$ stand for a fully connected layer of output size K and a layer normalization, respectively. The network $\text{EmbeddingMapper}(\cdot)$ mapping e_v to a vector r_v of the same dimension was implemented as

$$r_v = \text{Linear}_K(\text{LayerNorm}(f_{\text{global}}(\text{Linear}_H(\text{LayerNorm}(e_v))))) \tag{6}$$

where the function $f_{\text{global}}(\cdot)$ is a deep neural network implemented as L layers of $\text{Linear}(\text{LeakyReLU}(x))$. The leaky rectified linear unit $\text{LeakyReLU}(\cdot)$ is simply defined to be $x + \text{ReLU}(x)$ in our implementation. The network $f_{\text{global}}(\cdot)$ worked well when $L = 10$ and $H = 20K$.

---

[2] https://pytorch.org/text/stable/datasets.html.

Table 4. Evaluation results in terms of validation perplexity

Dateset	K	AmLDA	SVI	SVI+	ProdLDA
AG_NEWS	50	475.933	409.784	380.463	**119.380**
	100	381.244	286.391	309.130	**102.908**
DBpedia	50	252.768	204.771	**203.494**	431.744
	100	214.196	**159.573**	160.535	248.482
YelpReviewFull	50	**310.637**	328.413	318.341	836.945
	100	270.478	267.741	**260.798**	428.584
YahooAnswers	50	267.543	273.902	**265.523**	1317.396
	100	221.790	215.594	**211.053**	433.427
AmazonReviewFull	50	309.790	309.061	**304.257**	1648.765
	100	249.104	255.375	**245.986**	733.784

We tuned free parameters based on the perplexity averaged over the validation documents. The perplexity is defined for each document d as

$$\text{Perplexity}(\boldsymbol{w}_d) \equiv \exp\left(- \frac{\sum_{i=1}^{n_d} \log p(w_{d,i}|\boldsymbol{\theta}_d; \boldsymbol{\beta})}{n_d} \right) \tag{7}$$

where the word probability $p(w_{d,i}|\boldsymbol{\theta}_d; \boldsymbol{\beta})$ is computed as $\sum_{k=1}^{K} \theta_{d,k} \beta_{k,w_{d,i}}$. A smaller perplexity means that the variational posterior works better at predicting word occurrences in each document.

The comparison between the VEM and the SVI has already been performed in [6], where the authors call the VEM for LDA "the batch LDA." The performance of the SVI is at least as good as, and often better than, the VEM. Therefore, we compared AmLDA to the SVI for LDA and to ProdLDA. However, we have found that the SVI for LDA can be improved by introducing a neural network parameterizing the topic-wise word probabilites $\boldsymbol{\beta}_k$ as follows. First, we prepare a V-dimensional vector $\boldsymbol{b}_k$ for each topic $k \in \{1,\ldots,K\}$ and additionally a special V-dimensional vector $\boldsymbol{b}_0$. Roughly, the vector $\boldsymbol{b}_0$ is intended to represent the background probability [19]. Second, we define a K-dimensional vector $\boldsymbol{c}_v$ as $\boldsymbol{c}_v \equiv (b_{0,v}+b_{1,v}\ldots, b_{0,v}+b_{K,v})$ for each word $v \in \{1,\ldots,V\}$. Third, we compute a K-dimensional vector $\boldsymbol{t}_v$ by the following forward pass:

$$\boldsymbol{t}_v = f_{\text{SVI}}(\text{LayerNorm}(f_{\text{SVI}}(\text{LayerNorm}(\boldsymbol{c}_v)))) \tag{8}$$

where the function $f_{\text{SVI}}(\cdot)$ is defined as

$$f_{\text{SVI}}(\boldsymbol{x}) \equiv \text{ReLU}(\text{Linear}_K(\text{ReLU}(\text{Linear}_K(\boldsymbol{x})))) \tag{9}$$

Finally, we obtain the topic-wise word probabilities $\boldsymbol{\beta}_k$ for each word v by applying the softmax function as below:

$$\boldsymbol{\beta}_k = \text{Softmax}\big((t_{1,k},\ldots,t_{V,k})\big) \tag{10}$$

We denote this enhanced version of the SVI for LDA by SVI+.

Our implementation of ProdLDA is a clone of that provided at the Web site of Pyro (cf. footnote 1). However, we have found that this implementation is suboptimal. Therefore, we introduced the following modifications. First, the batch normalization was replaced by the layer normalization. Second, the number of the fully connected layers in the encoder were increased from two to five.

4.2 Evaluation Results

Table 4 presents the evaluation of the inference effectiveness in terms of perplexity computed over the validation set. SVI+, that is, the enhanced version of the SVI for LDA, gave the best perplexity for six cases out of ten. We have found that AmLDA works well for large datasets. AmLDA achieved the best perplexity for YelpReviewFull dataset when $K = 50$ and maintained the perplexity comparable to SVI+ in the rest five cases for the three largest datasets, YelpReviewFull, YahooAnswers, and AmazonReviewFull. ProdLDA worked only for the AG_NEWS dataset, which is the smallest one. This may mean that it is relatively easy to tune the hyperparamters of ProdLDA for small datasets. For the rest four datasets, ProdLDA gave a drastically worse perplexity. ProdLDA may require additional elaboration for tackling the curse of component collapse when applied to large datasets. However, such elaboration is beyond our scope [11,14,18,20]. Based on the results in Table 4, we decided to conduct a further comparison between AmLDA and SVI+ in terms of three additional evaluation measures.

Table 5 presents the evaluation of the highest probability words in the topics extracted by AmLDA and SVI+. We quantified the quality of the highest probability words with the following three evaluation measures taken from [1]: normalized pointwise mutual information (τ), external word embeddings topic coherence (α), and inversed rank-biased overlap (ρ). The first two measures estimate topic coherence in different ways. The last one estimates topic diversity. The detailed explanations of these evaluation measures are referred to [1]. We utilized the implementation of these measures available at the corresponding github repository[3]. We computed each measure by using the top 20 highest probability words. First, normalized pointwise mutual information measures how often the highest probability words co-occur in the documents from the reference corpus. As Table 5 shows, AmLDA worked better for the three largest datasets. Second, external word embeddings topic coherence evaluates how similar the word vectors of the highest probability words are. In terms of this, SVI+ was slightly better than AmLDA. Third, inversed rank-biased overlap shows diversity of the extracted topics. AmLDA surpassed SVI+ for nine cases out of ten.

We present the highest probability words of each topic extracted by AmLDA and SVI+ from the datasets AG_NEWS, YahooAnswers, and AmazonReviewFull in Tables 6, 7, and 8, respectively, for randomly chosen five topics when $K = 50$. We have made the word lists by excluding stop words obtained from The Natural

---

[3] https://github.com/MilaNLProc/contextualized-topic-models (cf. [1]).

Table 5. Evaluation in terms of normalized pointwise mutual information (τ), external word embeddings topic coherence (α), and inversed rank-biased overlap (ρ) [1]

Dateset	K	τ		α		ρ	
		AmLDA	SVI+	AmLDA	SVI+	AmLDA	SVI+
AG_NEWS	50	−0.2209	**−0.1569**	0.0813	**0.1099**	**0.9998**	0.9965
	100	−0.2753	**−0.2566**	**0.0822**	0.0782	**0.9999**	0.9990
DBpedia	50	−0.1566	**−0.1076**	0.0868	**0.1362**	**1.0000**	0.9967
	100	−0.1508	**−0.1400**	0.0899	**0.1005**	**0.9997**	0.9985
YelpReviewFull	50	**−0.0722**	−0.1128	0.1156	**0.1278**	**0.9994**	0.9929
	100	**−0.1049**	−0.1202	**0.1092**	0.1091	**0.9992**	0.9884
YahooAnswers	50	**−0.0097**	−0.0832	**0.1693**	0.1248	0.9893	**0.9958**
	100	**−0.1400**	−0.1516	**0.0976**	0.0911	**0.9996**	0.9983
AmazonReviewFull	50	**−0.0951**	−0.1193	0.1020	**0.1097**	**0.9995**	0.9959
	100	**−0.1387**	−0.1477	0.0947	**0.1014**	**0.9997**	0.9936

Table 6. Highest probability words in random topics from AG_NEWS ($K = 50$)

AmLDA	stocks sports pc stock man tokyo called canada match violence los trading indian
	sunday back ibm major mobile intel nuclear workers peoplesoft support israel
	season air six making george advanced zealand dolphins negotiations fannie qualifying
	former investors close capital dead central information reach quarterly better
	open biggest bill nokia disney deals approves postponed correct initially fired
SVI+	microsoft users windows pc digital software office source desktop server competition
	afp announced online phone drug trade america power unit devices launches november
	back cup test victory australia win league champions australian insurance football
	favre dame ties clarett bend gymnastics ore microsoft countries mr robinson
	oracle peoplesoft press french canadian france canada cash blue asian aid hostages

Language Toolkit (NLTK)[4]. The highest probability words selected by SVI+ seem a bit more coherent within each topic. However, it looks like that AmLDA can provide more diverse words as numerically shown by the evaluation results in terms of the inversed rank-biased overlap in Table 5.

---

[4] https://www.nltk.org/.

Table 7. Highest probability words in random topics from `YahooAnswers` ($K = 50$)

AmLDA	within gold infection dna produce iron doctors bond silver birds injury universities
	would looking tell help give please also let time back well look great together
	computer windows file cd pc software programs drive xp program files system
	want need going lot may time job able also trying something new start might
	think yes guys believe girls prefer look american dont agree hot homework personally
SVI+	ibuprofen snacks weaknesses erosion estrogen routers dietary churches ping des
	football match le fifa un stock avoid fish suck il personality les glass unit
	make com number check cards cheap shop dictionary amazon monster people well
	system cd skin boss toes rom paycheck contract gb going plan unlimited juvenile
	money food working project worth jobs plan paid schools market apply stand surgery

Table 8. Highest probability words in random topics from `AmazonReviewFull` ($K = 50$)

AmLDA	role bottles letters grand musicians subtitles wore bulky suction snap drum
	poor happy especially children later batteries woman send common web iron favor
	album make every nothing look sure funny getting although together full worst
	way see film fan fine wish collection trying understand christmas rather difficult
	time first cd buy two game songs sound song play cheap support games metal cord
SVI+	cd album music songs game like one song sound listen fan better voice first
	useful class tape de changed pain musical bottle failed match brother videos
	movie story one like well plot first funny time interesting little character
	disappointed thought daughter expecting excited surprised shipped tea expected
	good product recommend job recomend yarn needless organize supportive exercising

5 Conclusions

This paper proposes a new amortized variational inference for LDA, called AmLDA, where deep neural networks parameterize the unknown distribution parameters, which were directly updated in the VEM and the SVI for LDA. While ProdLDA, a VAE-based LDA, also uses an amortized neural network for document encoding, it suffers from a serious issue of component collapse. AmLDA addresses the issue by maximizing the same ELBO as that which the VEM and the SVI for LDA maximize. The non-VAE parameterization we adopt in AmLDA can also be applied to other topic models. The recipe is as follows: derive the ELBO of your topic model by introducing variational posterior distributions; parameterize relevant unknown distribution parameters, including the parameters of the variational posterior distributions, with neural networks; and tune the hyperparameters of the neural networks and those of the optimizer in a deep learning manner to achieve a better posterior approximation. This recipe of neural parameterization has already been given, for example, by [8] with respect to the grammar induction. It is a promising research direction to improve existing topic models by parameterizing unknown distribution parameters appearing in the ELBO with deep neural networks as we have done in AmLDA and to provide a highly tunable method for exploring topic diversity of a document set.

References

1. Bianchi, F., Terragni, S., Hovy, D.: Pre-training is a hot topic: contextualized document embeddings improve topic coherence. In: Proceedings of the 59th Annual Meeting of the Association for Computational Linguistics and the 11th International Joint Conference on Natural Language Processing - Volume 2, pp. 759–766 (2021)
2. Blei, D.M., Ng, A.Y., Jordan, M.I.: Latent Dirichlet allocation. J. Mach. Learn. Res. **3**, 993–1022 (2003)
3. Brett, M.R.: Topic modeling: a basic introduction. J. Digital Humanities **2**(1), 1–2 (2012)
4. Dieng, A.B., Ruiz, F.J.R., Blei, D.M.: Topic modeling in embedding spaces. Trans. Assoc. Comput. Linguist. **8**, 439–453 (2020)
5. Dieng, A.B., Wang, C., Gao, J., Paisley, J.W.: TopicRNN: a recurrent neural network with long-range semantic dependency. CoRR abs/1611.01702 (2016)
6. Hoffman, M.D., Blei, D.M., Bach, F.: Online learning for Latent Dirichlet allocation. In: Proceedings of the 23rd International Conference on Neural Information Processing Systems - Volume 1, pp. 856–864 (2010)
7. Hoffman, M.D., Blei, D.M., Wang, C., Paisley, J.: Stochastic variational inference. J. Mach. Learn. Res. **14**(5) (2013)
8. Kim, Y., Dyer, C., Rush, A.: Compound probabilistic context-free grammars for grammar induction. In: Proceedings of the 57th Annual Meeting of the Association for Computational Linguistics, pp. 2369–2385 (2019)
9. Kingma, D.P., Ba, J.: Adam: a method for stochastic optimization. CoRR abs/1412.6980 (2014)
10. Kingma, D.P., Welling, M.: Auto-encoding variational bayes. CoRR abs/1312.6114 (2013)

11. Li, B., He, J., Neubig, G., Berg-Kirkpatrick, T., Yang, Y.: A surprisingly effective fix for deep latent variable modeling of text. In: Proceedings of the 2019 Conference on Empirical Methods in Natural Language Processing and the 9th International Joint Conference on Natural Language Processing (EMNLP-IJCNLP), pp. 3603–3614 (2019)

12. Lindstedt, N.C.: Structural topic modeling for social scientists: a brief case study with social movement studies literature, 2005–2017. Soc. Currents **6**(4), 307–318 (2019)

13. Loshchilov, I., Hutter, F.: Decoupled weight decay regularization. In: 7th International Conference on Learning Representations (2019)

14. McCarthy, A.D., Li, X., Gu, J., Dong, N.: Addressing posterior collapse with mutual information for improved variational neural machine translation. In: Proceedings of the 58th Annual Meeting of the Association for Computational Linguistics, pp. 8512–8525 (2020)

15. Miao, Y., Grefenstette, E., Blunsom, P.: Discovering discrete latent topics with neural variational inference. In: Proceedings of the 34th International Conference on Machine Learning, pp. 2410–2419 (2017)

16. Miao, Y., Yu, L., Blunsom, P.: Neural variational inference for text processing. In: Proceedings of the 33rd International Conference on Machine Learning, pp. 1727–1736 (2016)

17. Nallapati, R., Cohen, W., Lafferty, J.: Parallelized variational EM for latent Dirichlet allocation: an experimental evaluation of speed and scalability. In: 7th IEEE International Conference on Data Mining Workshops, pp. 349–354 (2007)

18. Nan, F., Ding, R., Nallapati, R., Xiang, B.: Topic modeling with Wasserstein autoencoders. In: Proceedings of the 57th Annual Meeting of the Association for Computational Linguistics. pp. 6345–6381 (2019)

19. Ponte, J.M., Croft, W.B.: A language modeling approach to information retrieval. In: Proceedings of the 21st Annual International ACM SIGIR Conference on Research and Development in Information Retrieval, pp. 275–281 (1998)

20. Razavi, A., van den Oord, A., Poole, B., Vinyals, O.: Preventing posterior collapse with delta-VAEs. In: 7th International Conference on Learning Representations (2019)

21. Rezaee, M., Ferraro, F.: A discrete variational recurrent topic model without the reparametrization trick. In: Advances in Neural Information Processing Systems, vol. 33, pp. 13831–13843 (2020)

22. Roberts, M.E., Stewart, B.M., Airoldi, E.M.: A model of text for experimentation in the social sciences. J. Am. Stat. Assoc. **111**(515), 988–1003 (2016)

23. Srivastava, A., Sutton, C.: Autoencoding variational inference for topic models. In: 5th International Conference on Learning Representations (2017)

24. Stone, H., Sports, T.: The Push and Pull of Digital Humanities: Topic Modeling the "What is digital humanities?" Genre. DHQ 14(1) (2020)

25. Wang, W., et al.: Topic compositional neural language model. In: Proceedings of the 21st International Conference on Artificial Intelligence and Statistics, pp. 356–365 (2018)

26. Wang, W., Gan, Z., Xu, H., Zhang, R., Wang, G., Shen, D., Chen, C., Carin, L.: Topic-guided variational auto-encoder for text generation. In: Proceedings of the 2019 Conference of the North American Chapter of the Association for Computational Linguistics, pp. 166–177 (2019)

27. Xu, H., Wang, W., Liu, W., Carin, L.: Distilled wasserstein learning for word embedding and topic modeling. In: Proceedings of the 32nd International Conference on Neural Information Processing Systems, pp. 1723–1732 (2018)

Auditing Algorithms: Determining Ethical Parameters of Algorithmic Decision-Making Systems in Healthcare

Asma Aldrees[✉], Cherie Poland, and Syeda Arzoo Irshad

Virginia Tech, Falls Church, USA
{aaldrees,cheriem,syedaarzoo99}@vt.edu

Abstract. The hypothesis we intend to test is the identification of potential sources of bias and/or ethical concerns in healthcare data and to propose methods for reducing or eliminating the bias. To test this hypothesis we have selected an open source dataset focused on the impact of HbA1c Measurement on Hospital Readmission Rates. A detailed analysis will be made of dataset parameters in order to determine whether a given feature or set of features is affecting or biasing the algorithm or results. By testing this hypothesis we hope to identify potential sources of bias and ethical concerns in the data or algorithm and we will identify methods that may beneficially minimize unintended bias in algorithm and/or analysis.

Keywords: AI ethics · Auditing · Responsibility · Accountability · Ethical parameters · Feature engineering · Neural network · Explainability · Healthcare

1 Introduction

As a society, we are being tossed around on a sea of competing ideas, backed by statistics, data, and computer algorithms. The decisions made by algorithms rely on the data used as input and the manner in which the algorithms are programmed by humans. Ultimately all data science, statistics, and AI decisions are human decisions, regardless of the manner or means by which they are wielded. The use and manipulation of algorithms represent opportunities for better understanding of our world. However, algorithms can also encompass, express, and unveil intentional or unconscious bias, bias intrinsically present in the data, and manipulation by competing interests or those with agendas. In this paper we examine various aspects of a fully identified open source healthcare dataset with information about patients with diabetes and asked how we should determine ethical parameters of Artificial Intelligence (AI) algorithms using the healthcare dataset. Transparency and accountability are overarching lessons for AI Ethics, but the relational context in which these lessons arise is just as important.

A. Aldrees, C. Poland and S.A. Irshad—All authors contributed equally to this work.

© The Author(s), under exclusive license to Springer Nature Switzerland AG 2022
J. A. Lossio-Ventura et al. (Eds.): SIMBig 2021, CCIS 1577, pp. 296–309, 2022.
https://doi.org/10.1007/978-3-031-04447-2_20

1.1   Motivation

The motivation for this project is to explore multiple types of bias in datasets and algorithms, assess the ability to discriminate and compare potentially biased data or biasing features involving multiple parameters, hyper-variable data, and multiple data analysis methodologies, within a single large, multi-parameter dataset. The comparison of potential algorithmic modalities, such as model type, feature selection, as well as different types of neural networks and graph networks is due to the authors' interest and non-academic work in detecting and identifying similarities in complex interactions, multi-layer, and multi-step dependencies in the healthcare and complex data domains. A further motivation derived from these interests is to evaluate data triangulation methodologies on a heterogeneous and hyper-variable dataset comprising different attributes in order to improve the accuracy and consistency of categorizations and classifications and to show relatedness in order to improve the trustworthiness of the underlying algorithmic assessments and provide a possible auditing framework for future dataset and algorithmic analysis.

The remainder of this paper is organized as follows: Sect. 2 explains different methods of auditing data. The adopted dataset in this paper is mentioned in Sect. 3 while the analysis and results of the selected auditing methods are provided in Sect. 4. Section 5 discusses the evaluation model for each of the auditing methods. Finally, we summarize and conclude the study of this research paper in Sect. 6.

2   Related Work

Different methods of auditing data are required in order to search for and test for underlying or hidden bias and attributes. Methods encompassing anomaly detection and pattern recognition are required. No single auditing method will likely uncover all potential issues. The breadth and scope of auditing methods creates an algorithmic auditing toolkit that one may use to deeply examine data with various degrees of granularity.

2.1   Post-hoc Interpretability Tools to Audit AI Models

Deep Learning models provide a higher degree of accuracy than the traditional machine learning models when the input consists of large, unstructured data. Similarly, sophisticated ensemble techniques like bagging and boosting are preferred to simpler, more interpretable decision trees as they achieve better performance with structured tabular data. However, there exists a trade-off between accuracy and interpretability. The complex architecture of these models make it hard for the end-user to interpret how the input features have contributed to the model output prediction. Recent works have also revealed the inherent bias in some of these black-box models against minority groups [16,18]. Thus, the pervasive use of these high performing, 'black-box' models in sensitive areas like healthcare and criminal justice raises ethical concerns and a critical need to audit these models for fairness [7,15].

One of the ways to audit these algorithms would be to look into the 'black-box' to understand how the input features are combined to arrive at the model output. In recent times several machine learning interpretability techniques have emerged that can be used to explain the machine learning model results in terms of individual input feature contributions. Current popular interpretability techniques can be categorised into Post-hoc interpretability and Intrinsic Interpretability [17]. Post-hoc methods provide explanations of the model output after the model is trained. Some of the current state-of-art methods include feature attributions (LIME, SHAP), model and data analysis tools (What-if Tool, Fairness Indicators), gradient and concept based testing (TCAV, GRAD-CAM) and datapoint inspection methods (Partial Dependence Plots, Ablation testing). Intrinsic interpretability is achieved by using inherently interpretable machine learning models. In certain scenarios the explanations provided by the post-hoc methods are unreliable. Using inherently interpretable models can overcome this drawback. Models like RETAIN and IMV-LSTM are examples of inherently interpretable RNN based models [5]. RETAIN uses a Reverse Time Attention Mechanism to build a clinically interpretable ML model using the EHR (Electronic Health Record) data. IMV-LSTM uses a mixture attention mechanism in the hidden layers of the RNN to capture the input variable importance in a multi-variate time series set up [9].

Due to proprietary reasons, the inner working of machine learning models may not be publicly available. Post-hoc interpretability techniques can serve as a useful tool to audit such machine learning models. This paper utilises LIME (Local Interpretable Model-Agnostic Explanations) as a technique to audit a black-box machine learning model used in the healthcare domain [22]. SHAP is a successor of LIME and has better interpretability power, but it is considered to be slower than LIME for larger data sets. While LIME creates perturbations around a single data point of interest, SHAP needs to consider all possible permutations to arrive at the result. A more detailed comparison between the two techniques is left to future work.

2.2 AI Fairness Models to Mitigate Bias

Fairness has emerged as an important concern in terms of trust and reliability of the decision-making process based on machine learning models. The implementation of solid AI techniques and tools has intrigued researchers to build capable AI fairness models [16]. The main objective with these tools is to detect, measure, and reduce unwanted bias. Recently, various auditing tools and open-source libraries have been developed to provide a high level of functionality in fairness models. For instance, FairSearch is the fair open-source search API to apply fairness in ranked search results [27]. FairTest tool helps to identify biases between potential outcomes and sensitive attributes [25]. Other handful fairness toolkits incorporate AI to mitigate the bias, such as Themis-ML [2];

the "Fairness-Aware" Machine Learning interface. Also, Fairness Test-Bed; the open-source framework facilitates a direct comparison of algorithms [6].

In this paper, AI Fairness 360 toolkit (AIF360) was adopted to investigate and mitigate the potential bias in the dataset [3]. It is a comprehensive Python open-source package developed at IBM and aims to bring together all sets of fairness metrics, and bias mitigation algorithms [12]. This toolkit focuses on implementing a large variety of debiasing techniques. It recommends the earliest mediation of the dataset because it gives the most flexibility and opportunity to correct occurred bias. Moreover, the AIF360 is the first open-source toolkit that brings together: bias metrics, bias mitigation algorithms, bias metric explanations, and industrial usability. Hence, AIF360 enables stronger collaboration between AI fairness researchers and practitioners, helping for deploying solutions in a variety of industries [3].

2.3   Data Visualization Models to Discern Differences

There are several different types of data visualization models that can be used to discern differences in datasets in order to help identify patterns or anomalies. Knowledge Graphs and Data Triangulation are two methods that provide readily apparent graphical output that end-users find more appealing than examining large charts of floating point numbers. Graphical representations of data are used in a variety of other applications and are readily adapted to algorithmic auditing methodologies.

A knowledge graph comprises a graph data model ontology of attributes and other data that may provide information about relatedness. Knowledge graphs model topical coherence of information based on an assumption that information from the same context tends to belong together. Data are often contextual and knowledge graphs utilize a data interchange standard comprising tuples where each tuple can be considered a small graph [14]. It may also comprise any other associated attributes linked to the data. The primary purpose is classification, clustering, and relatedness that is able to be presented in visual form. The knowledge graph maps heterogeneous types of knowledge. The combined approaches should result in a decrease in disambiguation errors and result in a more discerning clustering of content and inference from the highly heterogeneous data [11]

Machine learning and deep learning models of artificial intelligence can incorporate data triangulation in neural networks in the form of mini-batches of additional data to compare signal to noise ratios, even in noisy datasets. The theory being that the signals will show up consistently across the multiplier iterations of datasets, even if some of the data are incomplete, missing, or excessively noisy. Data triangulation compares qualitative and quantitative data and can be used across all data types and from entirely different sources. Triangulation is a correlation process that attempts to define relational metrics between data while accounting for noise, overlaps, outliers, and density [10]. Neural networks can also be triangulated concurrently with other neural networks in order to refine classification, reduce output error, and provide a better explanation of output results (e.g. explainable AI) [26].

3   Dataset

The "Diabetes 130 US hospitals for years 1999–2008 dataset" is Kaggle's open source collection of over 100,000 clinical database records for patients with clinically diagnosed diabetes. The dataset represents 10 years (1999–2008) of clinical care at 130 US hospitals and integrated delivery networks. It includes over 50 features representing patient and hospital outcomes. The dataset comprises the following attributes available for analysis: patient number, race, gender, age, admission type, time in hospital, medical specialty of admitting physician, number of lab test performed, HbA1c test result, diagnosis, number of medications, diabetic medications, number of outpatient, inpatient, and emergency visits in the year before the hospitalization. Further analysis may be determined based on the similarity of characters in the category [24]. The data are submitted on behalf of the Center for Clinical and Translational Research, Virginia Commonwealth University, a recipient of NIH CTSA grant UL1 TR00058 and a recipient of the CERNER data This data is a de-identified abstract of the Health Facts database (Cerner Corporation, Kansas City, MO) [21].

3.1   Data Preparation

Each model has specific requirements for the type of data it will operate over, and these necessitate different pre-processing techniques. However, in order to provide a consistent comparison across models, each model must receive the same input. We combine these needs by creating types of inputs that multiple models can handle.

4   Models of Analysis

Different models of analysis are used to extract different features from the data. These features, their patterns, and anomalies (if any) are then analyzed to determine whether any bias exists in the underlying data. The expectation of finding bias in any given generic dataset is neutral. While none is overtly expected, history shows that humans have both overt and unconscious bias and that bias may be reflected in unexpected places. We do not expect a single methodology to show bias in the underlying dataset.

4.1   Lime for Model Auditing

Post-hoc interpretability techniques serve as viable model auditing tools as they enable us to understand individual feature contributions to the model output. Local interpretable model-agnostic explanations (LIME) is a popular perturbation based interpretability technique that provides local explanations to black-box models. LIME trains a linear classifier that locally approximates the behaviour of the black-box machine learning model [8].

A perturbed dataset is created by feeding in variations of a single data point to the ML model and noting the corresponding outputs. LIME then trains an interpretable model (for example, a decision tree) on this new dataset of permuted samples, where the samples are weighted by their proximity to the sample of interest. The local interpretable model is used to explain the predictions made by the machine learning model to be audited.

In this experiment, the pre-processed diabetes readmission dataset was subjected to an XGBoost algorithm [4]. The inputs to the model consist of over 30 input features that contain patient information such as number of hospital visits, number and type of medications administered, whether the patient suffered from diabetes, and demographic information like age, sex and race. The XGBoost model was trained to predict if the patient is likely to be readmitted or not. Predicting if a patient will be readmitted to the hospital helps doctors determine the type of treatment to use and also helps the hospital staff in efficient utilisation of scant medical resources like ICU units. The trained XGBoost model is used to generate LIME explanations. The LIME explanation for a single row in the dataset is displayed in Fig. 1.

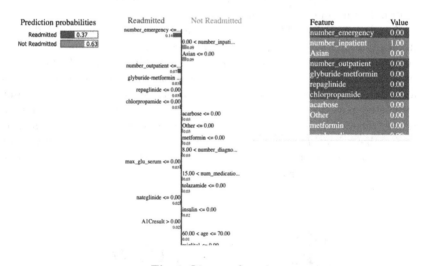

Fig. 1. Lime explanation

These explanations help us understand how much weightage was given to each input feature by the XGBoost model in predicting patient readmission for a specific data instance. In this experiment the different race categories 'Caucasian', 'AfricanAmerican', 'Other', 'Asian' and 'Hispanic' were one-hot-encoded before being subjected to the XGBoost model and subsequent Lime explanations. From the Fig. 1, it can be deduced that the 'Asian' race had more impact on the model output prediction than the other races for the particular data instance being examined. Explanations such as these enable us to audit the algorithms and determine if protected attributes (like age, race, gender) play a significant role in determining the model output behaviour of whether a patient is likely to be readmitted or not. The codebase associated to the LIME model analysis can be found in [13].

4.2 AIF360 Model Analysis

AIF360 toolkit was considered for a comprehensive analysis and mitigation of any potential bias. Therefore, the dataset was transformed into Binary-Label-Dataset required by the AIF360 toolkit. The protected attributes were selected in which the bias was there as gender and race. These attributes partition a population into groups that have a difference in terms of parity received. In this article, we followed the terminologies addressed [3], such as privileged and unprivileged groups. The dataset will be divided into privileged and unprivileged groups based on the protected attribute. A privileged group indicates a values that have been at a systematic advantage, while unprivileged group indicates attribute values that have been at a systematic disadvantage.

Prior to applying fairness metrics to the selected attributes, some statistical analysis was implemented to determine the target attribute (protected attribute). The mean of the readmitted attribute values was computed per gender and race attributes. The analysis results showed that the probability of getting readmission was almost the same between males and females, with readmission percentages of 0.451, 0.469, respectively. This indicated bias absence in gender attribute. However, statistical analysis was implemented over race attribute, which revealed a bias against Asian race which has the least number of readmitted patients comparing with other race values, as shown in Fig. 2. Therefore, race attribute was appointed as the protected attribute. Then, the data types have been encoded into privileged and unprivileged groups. Asian race was denoted as the unprivileged group, while rest all data belonging to race belong to the privileged group.

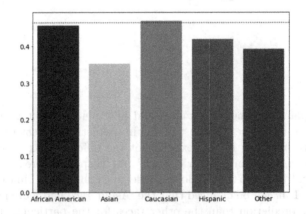

Fig. 2. Proportion of total patients who got readmitted.

Further analysis of bias was implemented by applying AIF360 fairness metrics. The dataset was split into training and testing datasets. Then, the fairness metric (Disparate Impact (DI)) was selected to detect and measure the bias against Asian race. This metric calculates the ratio of the probability of outcomes between the unprivileged (Asian race) and privileged groups (other race attributes). A value of 1 implies both groups have equal benefits, while a value less than 1 implies higher benefit for the privileged group, and a value greater than 1 implies higher benefit for the unprivileged group. We further recast this as $1 - \min (DI, 1/DI)$. For a fairness benchmark, we require that $1 - min(DI, 1/DI) < 0.2$ [20]. Both accuracy and fairness values were computed using a Logistic Regression machine learning model. The DI metric was applied to the training and testing datasets and found to be 0.868 and 0.934, respectively. The DI values were greater than the fairness threshold (0.2), which indicated high bias violations in the model. Figure 3 shows the values of accuracy and fairness metrics on the training dataset.

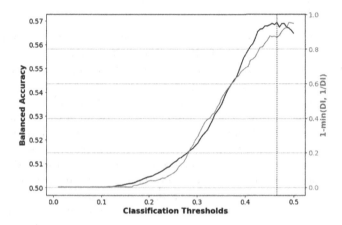

Fig. 3. Accuracy and fairness metrics with bias.

The AIF360 methodology for mitigating the discovered bias was implemented. The dataset was transformed using a pre-processing bias-mitigation algorithm called Reweighing. It assigns different weights to the various entities in the population to ensure fairness. The Reweighted data was then passed through the models for training and testing part and once again the DI fairness metric was measured. The new value of DI metric was found (0.003) in the training dataset, and (0.013) in the testing dataset, as shown in Fig. 4. Both values were smaller than the fairness threshold (0.2), which implied that the bias was mitigated and removed. The codebase associated to the AIF360 toolkit analysis can be found in [1].

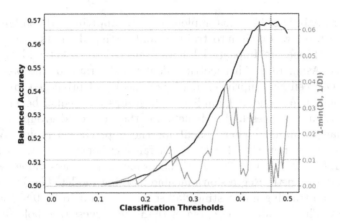

Fig. 4. Accuracy and fairness metrics without bias

4.3   Data Triangulation

Data triangulation was used to compare multiplicative groupings of data. The dataset provided a rich source of information related to medications prescribed to patients who were admitted to hospitals on both an inpatient and outpatient basis. The goal of the original study was to assess collected data to determine reasons for readmission and to determine what changes could be made in order to avoid a subsequent readmission. In the present study, all of the medication were analyzed in at least triple form with age and race as connected comparisons. Additional comparisons were made and cross-compared. Because the data set provides qualitative data for whether prescriptions were prescribed during the medical evaluation encounter or whether they were changed (no, steady, up, down) all modes were assessed together and individually.

The dataset showing all modes of prescription and whether there was any indication of impact on readmission are shown in multi-mode format in Fig. 5 for both insulin (top; 5A) and metformin (bottom; 5B).

A multi-point comparison of different diabetes medications was undertaken by both race and age, considering hospital readmission with and without a change in medication. The data unexpectedly showed that there is an underlying bias in the types of medication given to different races as a factor of age.

Although both age and race appeared to affect hospital readmission (data not shown), the greater anomaly was the apparent bias in the underlying prescription of the medications for diabetes where the differences appear as a differential between a patient's age, given a patient's race. The raw data showed a relatively flat curve with African American patients, but a dramatic frequency difference was seen with Caucasian patients (Fig. 5).

All of the prescribed medications in the dataset were analyzed. The two most commonly prescribed diabetes medications, metformin and insulin, showed the most distinctive bias. Both medications are available in generic form. Both are therefore less expensive and more accessible than the other medications provided in the dataset.

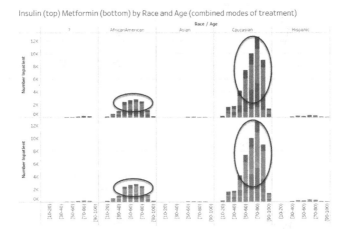

Fig. 5. Differences in number of insulin (top; 5A) and metformin (bottom; 5B) prescriptions for inpatient admissions by age and race with combined modes of treatment.

There were substantially fewer numbers of African Americans than Caucasians participating in the study. However, the difference in power does not account for the curve distinctions which appear with increasing age by race. The curves in Fig. 6 are relatively flat for African Americans in the 40–80 year old age ranges for both insulin and metformin, although prescription of insulin increase slightly in the 60–80 year old range compared to the 40–60 year range.

When the data were normalized over the total number of diabetic medication prescriptions (all diabetic prescriptions in the dataset regardless of race or age), the data showed that medications were similarly prescribed for African Americans and Caucasians overall. However, what was different were the types of medications prescribed and the age at which they were prescribed. The age curves were shifted favoring diabetic prescriptions at a younger age range for African Americans and an older age range for Caucasians. The differences in the curves (shift) has apparently gone unnoticed for years, given that the dataset was published in 2013. It was only extracted in the instant algorithmic audit when a multivariate analysis of the data was utilized in an attempt to more clearly visualize and explain what algorithms may be seeing in underlying datasets.

Expected findings (neutral; no bias) is shown in the normalized 60–70 age group (Fig. 7). However, there is no clear rational basis for the shift of the distinct medication curves based on age and race. The fact that the curves show distinctions which cannot otherwise be accounted for on a disease basis may be indicative of underlying bias in the clinical treatment of diabetic patients. This finding was unexpected. The finding also raises the question of whether and to what degree machine learning algorithms and data science can be used to

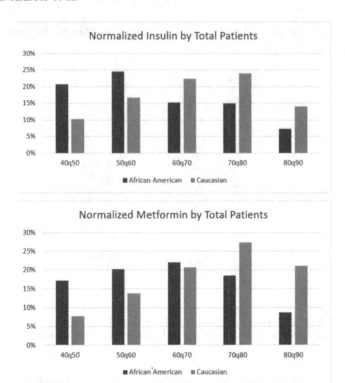

Fig. 6. Normalized metformin and insulin by race and age.

identify treatment disparities so that corrective action may be taken on a policy basis to promote fairness, accountability, and transparency.

5   Model Evaluation

5.1   LIME Model Evaluation

The LIME results showed that 'race' was considered as a significant factor in predicting patient readmission for a particular data instance. These explanations serve as a helpful model auditing tool when the inner workings of the machine learning model are not revealed. The user can just feed in data samples permuted around a sample of interest to the black-box model and store the outputs as a new dataset to train a more interpretable model. Lime however suffers from a drawback of unclear coverage. The explanations provided by LIME are local in nature and the boundary to which these explanations apply is not well defined. 'ANCHORS: High-Precision Model-Agnostic Explanations' is a model-agnostic system proposed by the authors of LIME that generates a set of 'if-then' rules as explanations for model output predictions and overcomes the drawbacks of LIME by providing a clear coverage of the data instances to which the explanations apply [23]. Evaluation of this technique is left to future work.

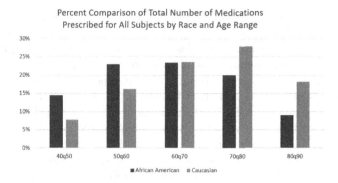

Fig. 7. Percent comparison of total number of medications prescribed for all Subjects by race and age range.

5.2 AIF360 Model Evaluation

This model aims to make the machine learning model fair by mitigating the bias in the adopted dataset. It was evaluated and processed using pandas (Python-Data Analysis Library) and transformed into the form of Binary-Label model required by the AIF360 toolkit [19]. The Disparate Impact fairness metric was applied on the race protected attribute to detect any potential bias. As a result, race attribute showed a bias violation against Asian race. The idea behind using AIF360 toolkit that we were able to detect the bias as well as mitigate the bias, thereby improving the fairness of the model. The Reweighing pre-processing bias mitigation algorithm was applied to reduce the bias. AIF360 is very helpful and easy to use toolkit. It has shown outstanding performance in detecting and mitigating bias and hence improving the fairness of the AI model built.

5.3 Data Triangulation Evaluation

The data were evaluated in comma delimited form in Microsoft Excel and imported into Tableau for visualization. Additional validation and normalization were completed in Microsoft Excel. Data were analyzed in at least triples using well-described Data Triangulation techniques (supra) with a variety of output visualization formats. Outliers and curve differences were immediately visualized and numerical differences were calculated based on standard mean statistical analysis. We did not expect to find distinct medication curves based on age and race in the dataset since it was a public dataset and others have published analytical assessments of the data since 2013.

6 Conclusion and Future Work

This paper introduces various techniques to audit machine learning models. The Data Triangulation methodology identified anomalies in the underlying dataset.

These anomalous curve patterns merits further investigation. What is it about the Caucasian vs African American patients that is generating a different prescription distribution curve? The bias appears in the underlying prescription data itself, based on human clinical prescription of medications, and not in the algorithms used to assess the data. This distinction is important because underlying bias in the data can affect the output of any algorithm applied to it. Determining the rational basis for the anomalous differences in the data will also be important for further work not only in anomaly detection and AI Ethics, but also for clinical treatment protocols. Future work may also include running the data in a CNN and LSTM neural network framework as a generative adversarial network (GAN) model in order to detect anomalous patterns, such as those as previously described by [28].

The Lime results indicated race as a factor in model output predictions. The lime explanation also showed that medicines like repaglinide and metformin contributed significantly in predicting the patient readmission. Interestingly, the data triangulation method discussed above revealed significant bias in the administration of medicines like insulin and metformin to the caucasian and african-american race. The combination of these results lead us to conclude that the type of medicines administered could serve as a proxy for race in determining patient readmission. Moreover, in the AI fairness 360 model, various fairness metrics and bias mitigation algorithms can be applied and compared in future to gain better understanding of the model.

References

1. Aldrees, A.: AI Fairness Model Using IBM AIF360 Toolkit for Patients Readmission. https://github.com/asmaaldrees/AI-Fairness-Model-Using-IBM-AIF360-Toolkit-for-Patients-Readmission. Accessed 20 Nov 2021
2. Bantilan, N.: Themis-ml: A fairness-aware machine learning interface for end-to-end discrimination discovery and mitigation. J. Technol. Hum. Serv. **36**(1), 15–30 (2018). https://doi.org/10.1080/15228835.2017.1416512
3. Bellamy, R.K.E., et al.: AI fairness 360: An extensible toolkit for detecting, understanding, and mitigating unwanted algorithmic bias. CoRR abs/1810.01943 (2018)
4. Chen, T., Guestrin, C.: Xgboost: A scalable tree boosting system. In: Proceedings of the 22nd ACM SIGKDD International Conference on Knowledge Discovery and Data Mining, pp. 785–794. KDD 2016, Association for Computing Machinery, New York, NY, USA (2016). https://doi.org/10.1145/2939672.2939785
5. Choi, E., Bahadori, M.T., Schuetz, A., Stewart, W.F., Sun, J.: RETAIN: interpretable predictive model in healthcare using reverse time attention mechanism. CoRR abs/1608.05745 (2016)
6. Friedler, S.A., Scheidegger, C., Venkatasubramanian, S., Choudhary, S., Hamilton, E.P., Roth, D.: A comparative study of fairness-enhancing interventions in machine learning. In: Proceedings of the Conference on Fairness, Accountability, and Transparency - FAT* 2019 (2019). https://doi.org/10.1145/3287560.3287589
7. Gianfrancesco, M.A., Tamang, S., Yazdany, J., Schmajuk, G.: Potential biases in machine learning algorithms using electronic health record data. JAMA Intern. Med. **178**(11), 1544–1547 (2018). https://doi.org/10.1001/jamainternmed.2018.3763

8. Github: Lime: Explaining the predictions of any machine learning classifier. https://github.com/marcotcr/lime. Accessed 20 Nov 2021

9. Guo, T., Lin, T., Antulov-Fantulin, N.: Exploring interpretable LSTM neural networks over multi-variable data. CoRR abs/1905.12034 (2019)

10. Heath, L.: Triangulation: methodology. In: Smelser, N.J., Baltes, P.B. (eds.) International Encyclopedia of the Social & Behavioral Sciences, pp. 15901–15906. Pergamon, Oxford (2001). https://doi.org/10.1016/B0-08-043076-7/00711-7

11. Huang, H., Heck, L.P., Ji, H.: Leveraging deep neural networks and knowledge graphs for entity disambiguation. CoRR abs/1504.07678 (2015)

12. IBM: Ai fairness: Aif360. https://github.com/ibm/aif360. Accessed 29 July 2021

13. Irshad, S.A.: Auditing-xgboost-model-for-patient-readmission-using-lime. https://github.com/syeda-arzoo/Auditing-XGBoost-model-for-patient-readmission-using-LIME. Accessed 20 Nov 2021

14. Lin, Y., Liu, Z., Sun, M., Liu, Y., Zhu, X.: Learning entity and relation embeddings for knowledge graph completion. In: Proceedings of the 29th AAAI Conference on Artificial Intelligence, pp. 2181–2187. AAAI 2015, AAAI Press (2015)

15. McWilliams, C.J., et al.: Towards a decision support tool for intensive care discharge: machine learning algorithm development using electronic healthcare data from mimic-iii and bristol, uk. BMJ Open **9**(3) (2019). https://doi.org/10.1136/bmjopen-2018-025925

16. Mehrabi, N., Morstatter, F., Saxena, N., Lerman, K., Galstyan, A.: A survey on bias and fairness in machine learning. CoRR abs/1908.09635 (2019)

17. Molnar, C.: A guide for making black box models explainable. In: Interpretable Machine Learning. lulu.com (2019)

18. Obermeyer, Z., Powers, B., Vogeli, C., Mullainathan, S.: Dissecting racial bias in an algorithm used to manage the health of populations. Science **366**(6464), 447–453 (2019). https://doi.org/10.1126/science.aax2342

19. Pandas: pandas/python-data analysis library. https://pandas.pydata.org/. Accessed 29 July 2021

20. Pok, W.: Bias detection and mitigation. https://ambiata.com/blog/2019-12-13-bias-detection-and-mitigation/. Accessed 20 Nov 2021

21. repository, U.M.L.: Diabetes 130-us hospitals for years 1999–2008 data set. https://archive.ics.uci.edu/ml/datasets/Diabetes+130-US+hospitals+for+years+1999-2008. Accessed 29 July 2021

22. Ribeiro, M.T., Singh, S., Guestrin, C.: why should I trust you?: Explaining the predictions of any classifier. CoRR abs/1602.04938 (2016)

23. Ribeiro, M.T., Singh, S., Guestrin, C.: Anchors: high-precision model-agnostic explanations. In: McIlraith, S.A., Weinberger, K.Q. (eds.) Proceedings of the 32nd AAAI Conference on Artificial Intelligence, pp. 1527–1535. AAAI Press (2018)

24. Strack, B., DeShazo, J.P., Gennings, C., Olmo, J.L., Ventura, S., Cios, K.J., Clore, J.N.: Impact of HbA1c measurement on hospital readmission rates: analysis of 70,000 clinical database patient records. BioMed Res. Int. **2014**, 781670 (2014). https://doi.org/10.1155/2014/781670, publisher: Hindawi Publishing Corporation

25. Tramèr, F.V.A., Geambasu, R., Hsu, D., Hubaux, J.M.H., Juels, A., Lin, H.: Fairtest: Discovering unwarranted associations in data-driven applications (2015)

26. Walczak, S.: Methodological triangulation using neural networks for business research. Adv. Artif. Neu. Sys. 2012 (2012). https://doi.org/10.1155/2012/517234

27. Zehlike, M., Sühr, T., Castillo, C., Kitanovski, I.: Fairsearch: A tool for fairness in ranked search results. CoRR abs/1905.13134 (2019)

28. Zenati, H., Foo, C.S., Lecouat, B., Manek, G., Chandrasekhar, V.R.: Efficient GAN-based anomaly detection. CoRR abs/1802.06222 (2018)

Image Processing, Machine Learning, and Semantic Web

Plant Disease Classification and Severity Estimation: A Comparative Study of Multitask Convolutional Neural Networks and First Order Optimizers

Valeria Lucero🅳, Sherald Noboa🅳,
and Manuel Eugenio Morocho-Cayamcela$^{(\boxtimes)}$🅳

School of Mathematical and Computational Sciences,
Deep Learning for Autonomous Driving, Robotics, and Computer Vision Research
Group (DeepARC Research), Hda. San José s/n y Proyecto Yachay,
Yachay Tech University, 100119 Urcuquí, Ecuador
{alejandra.lucero,sherald.noboa,mmorocho}@yachaytech.edu.ec
http://www.yachaytech.edu.ec

Abstract. The detection of plant diseases has been a hot research topic lately, specially since deep learning models and state-of-the-art convolutional neural networks (CNNs) architectures came into play. For this reason, this paper aims to compare several multitask CNN architectures used for: (i) classifying the environmental stress of coffee leaves, and (ii) estimating the severity of diseases that affect coffee plantations. This study is performed in two stages. First, the best performing CNN architecture was obtained from the multitask tests, which was ResNet34. Second, we improved the performance of ResNet34 by training it with six different optimization functions, and three different initial learning rates. This comparison was based on the analysis of different performance metrics such as the classification accuracy, training loss, F1-score, and the required number of epochs to achieve convergence. Our results show that with an initial learning rate of 1×10^{-3}, Adagrad and Adam are the best optimizers for disease classification and severity estimation, respectively. Likewise, stochastic gradient descent shows to be an acceptable optimizer when the momentum hyperparameter is tuned properly.

Keywords: Computer vision · Artificial intelligence · Agriculture technology · Disease classification · Severity estimation · Optimizers · Neural network

1 Introduction

Currently, the demand for agricultural products has increased due to exponential population growth. However, the total land allocated to agricultural systems has decreased. For this reason, farmers cannot afford to lose their crops. One of the largest agricultural productions worldwide is coffee, which is grown

J. A. Lossio-Ventura et al. (Eds.): SIMBig 2021, CCIS 1577, pp. 313–328, 2022.
https://doi.org/10.1007/978-3-031-04447-2_21

in more than 50 countries where Brazil, Colombia, Ecuador, Indonesia, India, and Vietnam stand out significantly [9]. However, the coffee plant tends to be substantially affected by various pests, diseases, and stresses; such as leaf miner, rust, brown leaf spot, and cercospora leaf spots. These conditions cause defoliation and reduced photosynthesis. In other words, they affect the yield and quality of the final product [3]. For this reason a correct and timely detection of these plant diseases is a challenge for farmers. Firstly, because there are several diseases with similar symptoms; and secondly, it is not enough to recognize the type of pest or disease, but it is vital to identify the level of severity. Therefore, detecting plant diseases accurately and timely will allow smart farming systems to recommend precise treatments [17].

On one hand, several machine learning classification models allow farmers to detect crop diseases efficiently. For example, a clustering approach has been used to detect rust disease in coffee leaves. It has also been proposed to detect infection signals of the same condition using graphical pattern matching. For fungal diseases, radon transform and support vector machines have been also proposed [13]. On the other hand, deep learning models have overcome traditional machine learning algorithms in computer vision tasks. Especially, convolutional neural networks (CNN), that allow us to obtain advanced results in computer vision tasks. For example, CNNs have been used to solve leaf disease classification in agriculture. Some of the models and architectures used for coffee leaf disease classification are AlexNet, VGG16, ResNet50, and InceptionV3. However, most of the solutions deal with a single task (i.e., either classification of leaf disease, or the estimation of the severity).

Multi-task learning (MTL) is a concept that recommends sharing the same CNN architecture for more than one task. For example; coffee leaf classification, and severity estimation can be executed at once. Basically, using this approach means that the system is trained once, and both tasks can be inferred. This concept is explained since the initial layer of any CNN model will learn general representations of the input data that involve both tasks, which leads to lower training time [19]. However, when deep learning models are trained there are several optimization algorithms that can be used. For example, there are stochastic gradient descent (SGD), Adam, Adadelta among others that can be selected for a single task or multitask scenario. Normally, the goal of neural network training is to minimize the cost function, (i.e., finding the value that minimizes the difference between the actual and predicted label) [6]. Therefore, choosing the right optimizer become a crucial task for any deep learning approach. For the latter reason, we decided to compare the behavior of six different optimizers in a multitask scenario. To the best of our knowledge, this is the first work focused on studying this topic in detail. Then, the main contribution of this work is to compare different deep learning architectures using a multitask approach with different optimizers.

The remaining of this paper is organized as follows. Section 2 describes the most relevant related works. The proposed methodology and experimental setup are presented in Sect. 3. The experimental results obtained are illustrated and discussed in Sect. 5. Finally, Sect. 6 deals with the concluding remarks and future work.

2   Related Works

Coffee leaf disease classification is a challenging and time consuming handmade task that depends on factors such as leaf size, number of diseases, and the experience of the person in charge. One approach to solve this problem comes with CNN models that learn and process the representation of visual information with multiple levels of abstraction. In the deep learning era, the development of AlexNet established a landmark in 2012. Since then, several state-of-the-art CNN architectures have improved dramatically the results obtained for many computer vision tasks such as image classification, semantic segmentation, object detection, visual object recognition, etc. [17]. Although modern architectures exist, many authors continue to use simple CNN architectures for coffee leaf disease classification. The authors in [13] have presented a CNN with two convolutional layers for coffee leaf rust detection. The main finding of this study are that after applying a thinner segmentation for rust detection, the F1-scores increases from 0.61 up to 0.82. On the other hand, other researchers used a modern approach in comparison with simple models such as InceptionV3 with mini batch gradient descent as the training algorithm [9]. Transfer learning and data augmentation have also been employed by the authors to enhance the generalization of the model and achieved an overall testing accuracy of 97.61%.

In short, some studies have tackled the coffee leaf classification problem obtaining promising results. In this task, the main goal of the CNN model is to decide to which category/disease a certain leaf belongs. In the same way, coffee leaf severity estimation is another task that has fewer studies. The importance of severity estimation is explained due to the help that farmers require in the two aforementioned tasks. The first one is to identify an appropriate treatment according to the amount of damage in the coffee leafs and to predict yield loss for future harvesting. Coffee leaf disease classification is strongly related with healthy crops. Normally, plant disease severity is scored based on a visual inspection by experts. Thus, a deep learning model can also be a solution for this manual estimation problem. For instance, VGGNet, Inception-v3, and ResNet50 were compared using the PlantVillage dataset for estimating the damage in apple leafs. The authors found that VGG16 achieved an accuracy of 90.4% which was superior to the others models [21]. Likewise, *Viena et al.* [20], demonstrated the importance of tuning the hyper-parameters such as mini-batch size, number of epochs, and data augmentation using AlexNet, and Resnet18. The dataset used by the authors was the PlantVillage, but this time they focused on grape leafs. The highest classification accuracy of 90.31% was achieved by AlexNet, with 32 mini-batch size, 50 epochs, and without data augmentation. Besides, the authors did not find a clear correlation between augmented data and improved results.

Typically, in deep learning the final goal is to solve a single problem such as identifying leaf diseases or estimating the stress severity using one or more models. In contrast, MTL has caught the attention of deep learning practitioners since the method consists of a system able to solve more than one task sharing the same architecture [3]. In MTL, the initial layers of the network will learn joint generalized representations of the input data which allow a generalization ability of the model that serve for both tasks [19]. For example, *Manso et al.* developed a system able of classifying and estimating the coffee leaf stress with different numbers of neurons in the hidden layer and different starting learning rates. Their system consists of a single feedforward neural network which obtained a 96.013% of accuracy with the right combination of 40 hidden neurons and a learning rate of 0.1 [12]. Based on the last study, *Esgario et al.* expanded their work adding a detection of more than one stress per leaf and classifying more coffee leaf diseases. Moreover, their approach solution involves a comparison of some state of the art deep learning models. The authors compared AlexNet, VGG16, GoogLeNet, MobileNetV2, and ResNet50 models performance for a single task and multitask approach for identifying leaf diseases and estimating the level of stress. Their findings were that with an accuracy of 86.9% and 95.63%, AlexNet and ResNet50 behave better for multitask disease classification and severity estimation, respectively [3].

In the same way, *Liang et al.* proposed a Plant Disease Diagnosis and Severity Estimation Network called PD^2SE-Net inspired in ResNet as well as ShuffleNet-V2 models. The PlantVillage dataset was used for the experimental part and an overall accuracy of 98% and 91% for disease classification and severity estimation were obtained, respectively. One interesting part of this study is that they tested SGD with momentum (SGDm) and Adam. In this case, SGDm outperforms Adam, which normally is preferred by most researchers thanks to its attributes such as memory requirement and gradient estimation with adaptive learning rates for different parameters [10]. Normally, an important aspect in neural networks training is choosing the right optimizer for a specific task. For instance, *Kandel et al.* proposed a comparative study of six different first order optimizers with different starting learning rates using four different architectures applied for histopathology image classification. The authors found that AdaGrad produced the best performance with a learning rate of $= 10^{-3}$, Adamax whith a learning rate of $= 10^{-4}$ and Adam with a learning rate of $= 10^{-5}$. Likewise, *Suresh et al.* compared three CNN architectures using three optimizers for plant disease classification. The architectures were InceptionV3, ResNet50v2, MobileNetV2; and the optimizers were Adagrad, Adadelta, and Adam. They found that the highest classification accuracy of 99.9% was obtained with Inceptionv3 and Adam [17]. In general, Adam optimizer shows better and faster convergence than other optimization methods such as RMSProp, AdaGrad, and AdaDelta [6,14]. Finally, *Saleem et al.* presented a comparative study of eighteen deep learning models for leaf image classification in general using the PlantVillage dataset. They found that cascaded AlexNet with GoogLeNet improved GoogLeNet; and Xception models outperformed the rest of the models with Adam and Adadelta optimizers combined [15].

3   Methodology

Image classification tasks involve the use of CNNs. In this work the use of five well known CNN architectures and its variants were tested for classifying the biotic stress and estimating the severity of disease in coffee leaves. This approach used the multitask framework models proposed by *Esgario et al.* [3]. This approach consists of two image classification tasks such classifying biotic stress, and estimating the severity in coffee leaves. An overall methodology of this research is presented in Fig. 1. Firstly in stage one, the optimizer chosen for all the models was SGD with momentum due to its fast convergence. Then, 7 architectures were trained using a coffee leaf dataset that is split into training, validation, and testing [3]. Next, all the models were compared in terms of training, validation, and testing metrics such as accuracy, precision, recall, and F1-score. In stage two, the best performing model is selected and tested with six optimizers with different starting and fixed learning rates. Finally, the optimizer that outperform all its contenders is selected for our multitask application.

3.1   Dataset

The dataset used contains 1685 images of healthy and sick arabica coffee leaves that are affected by different biotic stresses (diseases) such as leaf miner, rust, brown leaf spot, and cercospora leaf spot. Besides, each leaf has a label that indicates the percentage of damage (severity estimation) as follows: healthy ($<0.1\%$), very low (0.1%–5%), low (5.1%–10%), high (10.1%–15%) and very high ($>15\%$). The dataset is split into training, validation, and testing. The percentages of the split dataset are 70% for training, 15% for validation, and 15% for testing. This dataset can be considered unbalanced for both tasks: the leaf stress identification and the severity estimation, because the numbers of samples vary for both. The photos were taken from smartphones cameras over an abaxial position (lower) side of the leaves. The resolution of the images are 256×512 pixels in a JPG format. Figure 2 shows a subset of the dataset containing the stress of the leaves, and Fig. 3 shows the level of severity with brown leaf spot stress. The total number of images that the dataset contains are summarized in Table 1. The table can be read as: there are 531 rust affected leaves in the whole dataset, and the are 332 coffee leaves that present a low severity in all the dataset. The original dataset is available at: https://github.com/esgario/lara2018.

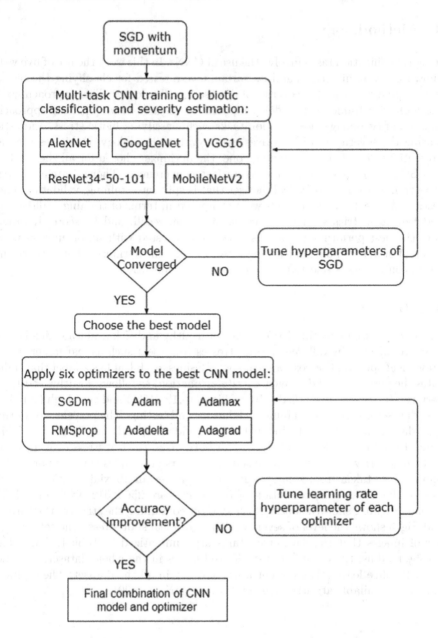

Fig. 1. An overview of the methodology proposed for this work.

3.2 Environment Setup

The CNN architectures were built in Python language due to the availability of very useful libraries and deep learning frameworks as Pytorch. The CuDNN

Fig. 2. Examples of coffee leaves affected by different diseases: (a) healthy leaf, (b) leaf miner, (c) rust, (d) brown leaf spot, and (e) cercospora leaf spot.

Fig. 3. Examples of coffee leaves affected by brown leaf spot with different levels of severity: (a) healthy leaf, (b) very low, (c) low, (d) high, and (e) very high.

library was installed as it increases the speed of training. All the experiments were conducted on a workstation with an Intel(R) Core(TM) i7-8750H CPU @ 2.20 GHz up to 2.21 GHz, 16 GB of RAM and a Graphical Processing Unit (NVIDIA GEFORCE GTX 1060) with the following specifications: 6 GB memory, 1280 CUDA cores, 1708 MHz MHz core clock.

3.3 Deep Learning Architectures

Since the explosion of deep learning in 2012 with the presentation of AlexNet, several CNN architectures have been proposed. Normally, all the architectures are created with the same goal which is to increase the accuracy and simplify the model complexity. Most of the models work for general purposes on a wide range of applications. In our case, the model used has two tasks, which are the disease classification, and severity estimation. These two tasks are closely related since the problems are from the same domain (image classification task). For this study, we have considered well-proved successful CNN models such as AlexNet [7], VGG16 [11], GoogLeNet [18], MobileNetV2 [16], ResNet34, ResNet50, and ResNet101 [4]. Note that AlexNet was the first model that started the deep learning eruption in 2012. Since then, new and updated models have arrived such as

Table 1. Dataset details.

Biotic stress	Samples	Severity	Samples
Healthy	272	Healthy	272
Leaf miner	387	Very low	924
Rust	531	Low	332
Brown leaf spot	348	High	101
Cercospora leaf spot	147	Very high	56
Total	1685	Total	1685

GoogLeNet and VGG16, which inspired their improvements on deeper convolutions and pooling layers. In the same way, ResNet architecture has improved the last models allowing us to train extremely deep neural networks with 150 layers successfully without the vanishing gradient problem. Lastly, MobileNetV2 is a model focused on mobile devices as smartphones which aim to deliver high accuracy while keeping the parameters and mathematical operations as low as possible [1]. In our case, in order to convert these models into multitasks systems, the architectures were modified by adding a new fully connected layer in parallel with the existing one. Thus, the convolutional layers are shared and the classification blocks are individualized. In other words, the model will learn joint features useful for both classification problems.

3.4   Deep Learning Optimizers

The SGD with momentum optimizer was used to train all the architectures during the first step of the proposed methodology. After that, one deep learning model is chosen for an improvement in both tasks based on the the highest accuracy and F1-score in the first step of the analysis. In the next stage, we used six state-of-the-art optimizers to train the previously selected model. The most relevant features of the optimizers are described below:

SGDm: This optimizer improves the traditional SGD because of the momentum added. Basically, the idea behind of this optimizer is to understand the right direction of the gradients, the optimizer should be able to consider the previous position. In short, the momentum needed to continue moving in the right direction is given by the previous update [5].

Adagrad: Previously, all the optimizers before Adagrad used to had a fixed learning rate. Adagrad optimizer was introduced for establishing different learning rates updates for different weights. In other words, this optimizer works with a learning rate adaptation that has the benefit of making especially easy to update. The learning rate changes automatically by dividing the learning rate by the sum of squares of all the previous gradients [6].

RMSProp: The optimizer was proposed to address the problem of the mono-tonically decreasing learning rate that Adagrad presented. This means that the learning rate is so small that Adagrad stops updating the weights. Besides, RMSProp reduces the training time thanks to its learning rate that has an exponential decay [8].

Adadelta: This optimization algorithm intends to do the same job as RMSProp; that is, it will reduce the learning rate monotonously. Adadelta accumulates past gradients over a fixed time window that will guarantee the continuation of the learning process after many epochs [22].

Adam: The adaptive moment estimation method was introduced to combine the benefits of Nesterov momentum [23], AdaGrad, and RMSProp algorithms. Adam calculates discrete learning rates for different parameters similar to Adagrad and Adadelta. Although, the difference and advantage presented by Adam is that it keeps an exponentially decaying average of past gradients. Moreover, Adam is also preferred by researchers because of its reduced memory usage, among other advantages [2].

Adamax: This optimizer is a variation of Adam, which states that uncentered variance tends to infinity. It means, it is based on the infinity norm. It was proposed for working with sparse parameter updates like word embedding [2].

3.5 Training Specifications

For the first stage of this work all the models were trained from scratch using the dataset described in Sect. 3.1. The images of the dataset had to be resized to $224 \times 224 \times 3$ for accomplishing the requirements of the input data of all the models. For all the experiments the dataset was split into proportions of 70-15-15 for the training, validation, and testing, respectively. Likewise, for training and validation part, we used the hyper-parameters described on Table 2. One thing to notice is that the learning rate decreases by a factor of $1/2$ or $1/5$ every 20 epochs. Moreover, the ReLU activation function was used in all the experiments due to its computational efficiency and its reduction of the vanishing gradient problem. After the whole training and validation, the models were tested and the evaluation metrics recorded were the accuracy, precision, recall, and F1-score. After choosing the best model, we move on to the second stage of our methodology, which is testing the model with different optimizers and learning rates. The learning rates are 10^{-3}, 10^{-4}, and 10^{-5}, as it is proposed in [6]. The rest of the optimizers' hyper-parameters are summarized on Table 3.

Table 2. Hyper-parameters of the trained architectures.

Parameter	Value
Optimizer	SGD with momentum
Loss function	Cross-Entropy
Epochs	100
Batch size	32
Learning rate*	0.01
Momentum	0.9
Weight decay	0.0005

* Decreases alternately by a factor of 1/2
or 1/5 every 20 epochs.

Table 3. Hyperparameters of the deep learning optimizers.

Optimizers	Specifications
Adadelta	Learning rate = 0.001, 0.0001, 0.00001, weight decay = 0.0005, rho = 0.9, eps = 1e–8
Adagrad	Learning rate = 0.001, 0.0001, 0.00001, weight decay = 0.0005, eps = 1e–8
Adam	Learning rate = 0.001, 0.0001, 0.00001, weight decay = 0.0005,
Adamax	Learning rate = 0.001, 0.0001, 0.00001, weight decay = 0.0005, eps = 1e–8, betas = (0.9, 0.999)
RMSprop	Learning rate = 0.001, 0.0001, 0.00001, weight decay = 0.0005, alpha = 0.99, eps = 1e–8, momentum = 0.9
SGDm	Learning rate = 0.001, 0.0001, 0.00001, weight decay = 0.0005, momentum = 0.9

4   Results

This section presents the comparative analysis of the CNN architectures to select the best model which leads to the results obtained regarding the improvement in the performance of the best-suited models by using various deep learning optimization algorithms. All the results were evaluated in terms of training, validation, accuracy/loss, and F1-score. The F1-score is considered an important performance metric especially for the case when there is an uneven distribution in the classes just such as our dataset. Therefore, the model that attained the highest F1-score was considered the most suitable architecture for the classification of plant diseases. The three best performing architectures are represented in Fig. 4, and it was empirically observed that they required 75 epochs (an epoch is a complete cycle of training on each image sample in the training dataset) where the accuracy and loss during training and validation converged. The overall performance of the models is also summarized in Table 4. Finally, the results for each learning rate hyper-parameter is presented in Table 5 and Table 6.

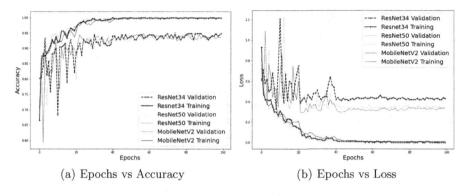

(a) Epochs vs Accuracy   (b) Epochs vs Loss

Fig. 4. Performance plots of the best three CNN architectures.

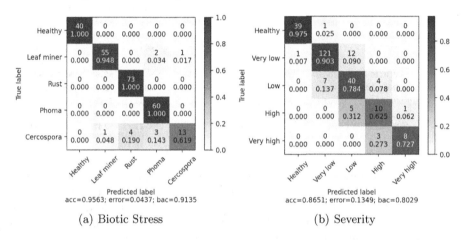

(a) Biotic Stress   (b) Severity

Fig. 5. Confusion matrices for the ResNet34 prediction results

After training each architecture with the same hyper-parameters proposed by [3], we can visualize in Fig. 4 that ResNet34 is the architecture that offers the best results. Figure 5 presents the confusion matrices associated with the prediction results obtained with ResNet34. The biotic stress classification results were consistent for most of the stresses, except cercospora leaf spot, which presented a considerable amount of classification errors. However, severity estimation is a task with increased difficulty compared to biotic stress classification. For this reason, ResNet34 obtained an accuracy of 86.51% presenting difficulty in separating leaves with high and very high severity rates. Although by nature of the confusion matrix, we can observe that most of the errors can be considered of minor importance for this problem as they are located close to the main diagonal.

The results were divided by task (biotic stress, and severity), CNN architecture (AlexNet, GoogLeNet, VGG16, ResNet34, ResNet50, ResNet101, and MobileNetV2), and evaluation metrics (accuracy, precision, recall, and F1-score). The best results are presented in bold in Table 4.

Table 4. Training and validation accuracy/loss, precision, recall, and F1-score along the 100 epochs required to train the deep learning architectures.

Task	Deep learning architectures	Training accuracy	Validation accuracy	Training loss	Validation loss	Accuracy	Precision	Recall	F1-score
Biotic Stress	AlexNet	99.83	92.09	0.01	0.57	90.48	87.08	87.44	87.09
	GoogleNet	99.83	94.47	0.01	0.28	91.27	88.62	87.75	87.95
	VGG16	100.00	94.86	0.00	0.46	87.70	87.50	80.25	81.16
	Resnet34	99.92	94.86	0.00	0.43	**95.63**	**95.64**	**91.35**	**92.82**
	Resnet50	99.83	93.28	0.00	0.35	**95.63**	95.60	90.81	92.35
	Resnet101	99.92	94.07	0.00	0.39	94.05	92.05	90.19	90.95
	MobileNet V2	99.92	93.68	0.01	0.33	93.65	91.90	89.69	90.50
Severity	AlexNet	99.07	84.19	0.01	0.57	86.11	79.39	78.10	78.56
	GoogleNet	100.00	87.35	0.01	0.28	82.54	75.02	80.11	77.19
	VGG16	100.00	90.12	0.00	0.46	85.71	**82.61**	**83.78**	**82.63**
	Resnet34	99.92	85.77	0.00	0.43	**86.51**	81.84	80.29	80.84
	Resnet50	99.92	87.35	0.00	0.35	84.13	78.58	77.43	77.74
	Resnet101	100.00	87.75	0.00	0.39	81.75	76.73	72.44	74.20
	MobileNet V2	99.75	88.93	0.01	0.33	85.71	82.47	79.67	80.54

To continue with stage two, this section aims to improve the performance of deep learning architectures by training the best model obtained from the previous step with different deep learning optimization functions and different initial learning rates. After our tests, ResNet34 was selected as the best performing model for the multitask operation. Table 5, and Table 6 summarize the results obtained. Some important observations are shown below:

- Significant changes were observed in the training/validation accuracy, loss, precision, recall, and F1 score. These changes are not necessarily better.
- The SGD with constant learning rate of 1×10^{-3} and momentum, improve the results of the first stage in the severity estimation with an accuracy of 87.30%.
- In the biotic stress task, the Adagrad optimizer with an initial learning rate of 1×10^{-3} is the best performing optimizer. Moreover, in the severity estimation task, the Adam optimizer with the same initial rate is the best optimizer in general.
- The ResNet34 model trained with the Adagrad optimizer for biotic stress task, achieved the highest validation accuracy and F1-score with 92.89% and 91,35%, respectively.
- The ResNet34 model trained with the Adam optimizer for the severity task, achieved the highest validation accuracy and F1-score with 84.19% and 81.23%, respectively.

Table 5. Performance of deep learning optimizers applied to training and validation using different learning rate values = 1×10^{-3}, 1×10^{-4}, 1×10^{-5} with ResNet 34 in Biotic Stress task

Task	Optimizers	Training Accuracy	Validation Accuracy	Training Loss	Validation loss	Accuracy	Precision	Recall	F1-score
Biotic Stress	Initial learning rate = 1×10^{-3}								
	Adadelta	77.03	77.47	0.87	0.82	76.59	73.60	67.24	64.92
	Adagrad	99.92	92.89	0.01	0.39	**94.84**	**93.87**	**90.04**	**91.35**
	Adam	97.63	93.68	0.16	0.28	94.05	91.48	89.42	90.19
	Adamax	99.49	91.70	0.04	0.42	93.65	92.90	89.65	90.73
	RMSprop	86.53	65.22	0.39	1.58	81.35	79.67	75.73	75.37
	SGD	99.83	91.70	0.01	0.41	93.25	92.74	85.77	86.77
	Initial learning rate = 1×10^{-4}								
	Adadelta	16.69	19.37	1.79	1.80	15.08	6.30	19.30	7.08
	Adagrad	99.07	90.91	0.07	0.32	93.25	91.25	**89.41**	**90.15**
	Adam	99.32	93.68	0.03	0.43	92.86	89.45	87.48	88.28
	Adamax	100.00	92.09	0.01	0.41	**93.65**	**92.03**	88.24	89.56
	RMSprop	97.71	89.33	0.14	0.45	92.06	89.40	89.35	89.30
	SGD	94.66	91.70	0.24	0.29	92.46	90.04	87.36	88.22
	Initial learning rate = 1×10^{-5}								
	Adadelta	17.20	25.30	2.05	2.00	17.46	10.97	21.10	13.03
	Adagrad	84.92	84.98	0.64	0.63	86.11	70.10	75.22	72.45
	Adam	99.75	90.12	0.02	0.48	**93.65**	92.04	**89.00**	**90.10**
	Adamax	97.88	92.49	0.10	0.30	91.67	89.18	86.20	87.17
	RMSprop	99.66	88.93	0.03	0.56	93.25	**93.60**	88.19	89.78
	SGD	72.37	71.15	0.96	0.94	77.38	62.66	66.2	64.07

5   Discussion

All the architectures tested performed decently and some even obtained great results. According to our experiments the model that outperform the others is ResNet34. This can be explained due to its own nature against the others models. For instance, with VGG16, it is well known that after some depth the performance degrades, which is one of the bottlenecks of VGG. On the other hand, with ResNet, the gradients flow directly through the skip connections backwards from later layers to initial filters. In other words, it offers a better performance avoiding the vanishing gradient problem no matter the depth of the model. To continue, the Resnet34 model showed the highest accuracy in Table 4. Nevertheless, the results presented with different optimizers in Table 5 and Table 6 show a decrease in the values of the evaluated metrics. Both the biotic classification, and the severity estimation decreased the accuracy. Except, the SGD optimizer with a learning rate of 0.001 that improves the severity task in terms of accuracy from 86.51% to 87.30%. In addition, it is important to remember that the accuracy of the severity task in this work is low because the dataset is unbalanced. The low accuracy might be caused since the initial learning rate is small compared to the learning rate of the first training (first stage). Recall that the first value taken by the learning rate in the choice of the best model was 0.01. During the first stage, the learning rate of the optimizer was

Table 6. Performance of deep learning optimizers applied to training and validation using different learning rate values = $\times 10^{-3}$, 1×10^{-4}, 1×10^{-5} with ResNet 34 in Severity task

Task	Optimizers	Training accuracy	Validation accuracy	Training loss	Validation loss	Accuracy	Precision	Recall	F1-score
Severity	Initial learning rate = 1×10^{-3}								
	Adadelta	69.92	65.61	0.87	0.82	67.06	36.51	41.47	38.35
	Adagrad	99.75	85.38	0.01	0.39	85.71	79.24	81.70	79.01
	Adam	90.08	84.19	0.16	0.28	85.71	**86.02**	**82.08**	**81.23**
	Adamax	98.22	88.14	0.04	0.42	80.16	71.07	70.54	69.73
	RMSprop	82.80	62.45	0.39	1.58	81.75	82.56	68.94	73.89
	SGD	100.00	85.38	0.01	0.41	**87.30**	85.92	78.90	80.46
	Initial learning rate = 1×10^{-4}								
	Adadelta	19.49	21.34	1.79	1.80	20.63	27.62	24.07	16.63
	Adagrad	98.05	84.58	0.07	0.32	84.13	76.72	72.07	73.80
	Adam	98.47	86.17	0.03	0.43	**84.92**	80.38	**79.51**	**79.77**
	Adamax	99.83	84.58	0.01	0.41	84.13	74.75	74.45	74.47
	RMSprop	90.68	83.40	0.14	0.45	82.14	75.82	74.54	74.87
	SGD	89.15	85.38	0.24	0.29	79.76	69.50	63.58	65.49
	Initial learning rate = 1×10^{-5}								
	Adadelta	3.22	3.95	2.05	2.00	4.37	0.90	20.00	1.72
	ADAgrad	75.25	73.91	0.64	0.63	71.83	41.79	44.23	42.74
	Adam	99.49	83.40	0.02	0.48	82.54	**78.97**	**73.71**	**75.87**
	Adamax	97.20	83.40	0.10	0.30	81.35	74.12	66.25	68.58
	RMSprop	98.81	79.84	0.03	0.56	**82.94**	71.68	72.12	71.84
	SGD	63.14	60.87	0.96	0.94	59.52	38.33	28.84	27.59

not at all fixed because its multiple reduction after 20 epochs. Thus, SGD with momentum with a kind of dynamic learning rate is still suitable for training neural networks. During our experiments SGD with momentum was able to overcome more advanced gradient-based optimizers based on adaptive moment estimation.

6   Conclusion

In this article, a comprehensive comparative analysis has been performed between 7 well known CNN architectures. From the inference of our results, ResNet34 was the best performing model in the first stage of this work. However, in the second stage the results were not as we expected. First, in the stress classification, none of the optimizers were able to overcome the results from the first experiment. Second, after testing all the optimizers with different learning rates, the only result that improved compared with the first stage was again SGDm in the severity estimation task. Therefore, it was shown that SGDm is still a suitable optimizer able to overcome more advanced gradient-based optimizers. Besides, probably one factor that affects the low accuracy in the severity estimation is the unbalanced dataset. Thus, in the future, this work will expand and balance the dataset in order to achieve better results.

References

1. Aloysius, N., Geetha, M.: A review on deep convolutional neural networks. In: 2017 International Conference on Communication and Signal Processing (ICCSP), pp. 0588–0592 (2017). https://doi.org/10.1109/ICCSP.2017.8286426
2. Dogo, E.M., Afolabi, O.J., Nwulu, N.I., Twala, B., Aigbavboa, C.O.: A comparative analysis of gradient descent-based optimization algorithms on convolutional neural networks. In: 2018 International Conference on Computational Techniques, Electronics and Mechanical Systems (CTEMS), pp. 92–99 (2018). https://doi.org/10.1109/CTEMS.2018.8769211
3. Esgario, J.G., Krohling, R.A., Ventura, J.A.: Deep learning for classification and severity estimation of coffee leaf biotic stress. Comput. Electron. Agri. **169**, 105162 (2020). https://doi.org/10.1016/j.compag.2019.105162
4. He, K., Zhang, X., Ren, S., Sun, J.: Deep residual learning for image recognition. In: 2016 IEEE Conference on Computer Vision and Pattern Recognition (CVPR), pp. 770–778 (2016). https://doi.org/10.1109/CVPR.2016.90
5. Jin, R., He, X.: Convergence of momentum-based stochastic gradient descent. In: 2020 IEEE 16th International Conference on Control Automation (ICCA), pp. 779–784 (2020). https://doi.org/10.1109/ICCA51439.2020.9264458
6. Kandel, I., Castelli, M., Popovič, A.: Comparative study of first order optimizers for image classification using convolutional neural networks on histopathology images. J. Imaging **6**(9) (2020). https://doi.org/10.3390/jimaging6090092, https://www.mdpi.com/2313-433X/6/9/92
7. Krizhevsky, A., Sutskever, I., Hinton, G.E.: Imagenet classification with deep convolutional neural networks. Adv. Neural Inf. Process. Syst. **25**, 1097–1105 (2012)
8. Kumar, A., Sarkar, S., Pradhan, C.: Malaria disease detection using CNN technique with SGD, RMSprop and ADAM optimizers. In: Dash, S., Acharya, B.R., Mittal, M., Abraham, A., Kelemen, A. (eds.) Deep Learning Techniques for Biomedical and Health Informatics. SBD, vol. 68, pp. 211–230. Springer, Cham (2020). https://doi.org/10.1007/978-3-030-33966-1_11
9. Kumar, M., Gupta, P., Madhav, P., Sachin: disease detection in coffee plants using convolutional neural network. In: 2020 5th International Conference on Communication and Electronics Systems (ICCES), pp. 755–760 (2020). https://doi.org/10.1109/ICCES48766.2020.9138000
10. Liang, Q., Xiang, S., Hu, Y., Coppola, G., Zhang, D., Sun, W.: Pd2se-net: computer-assisted plant disease diagnosis and severity estimation network. Comput. Electron. Agri. **157**, 518–529 (2019)
11. Liu, S., Deng, W.: Very deep convolutional neural network based image classification using small training sample size. In: 2015 3rd IAPR Asian Conference on Pattern Recognition (ACPR), pp. 730–734 (2015). https://doi.org/10.1109/ACPR.2015.7486599
12. Manso, G.L., Knidel, H., Krohling, R.A., Ventura, J.A.: A smartphone application to detection and classification of coffee leaf miner and coffee leaf rust. arXiv preprint arXiv:1904.00742 (2019)
13. Marcos, A.P., Silva Rodovalho, N.L., Backes, A.R.: Coffee leaf rust detection using convolutional neural network. In: 2019 XV Workshop de Visão Computacional (WVC), pp. 38–42, September 2019. https://doi.org/10.1109/WVC.2019.8876931
14. Okewu, E., Adewole, P., Sennaike, O.: Experimental Comparison of Stochastic Optimizers in Deep Learning, pp. 704–715 (2019). https://doi.org/10.1007/978-3-030-24308-1_55

15. Saleem, M., Potgieter, J., Arif, K.: Plant disease classification: a comparative evaluation of convolutional neural networks and deep learning optimizers. Plants **9**, 1319 (2020). https://doi.org/10.3390/plants9101319

16. Sandler, M., Howard, A., Zhu, M., Zhmoginov, A., Chen, L.C.: Mobilenetv 2: inverted residuals and linear bottlenecks. In: 2018 IEEE/CVF Conference on Computer Vision and Pattern Recognition, pp. 4510–4520 (2018). https://doi.org/10.1109/CVPR.2018.00474

17. Suresh, G., Gnanaprakash, V., Santhiya, R.: Performance analysis of different cnn architecture with different optimisers for plant disease classification. In: 2019 5th International Conference on Advanced Computing Communication Systems (ICACCS), pp. 916–921, March 2019. https://doi.org/10.1109/ICACCS.2019.8728282

18. Szegedy, C., et al.: Going deeper with convolutions. In: Proceedings of the IEEE Conference on Computer Vision and Pattern Recognition, pp. 1–9 (2015)

19. Vandenhende, S., Georgoulis, S., Van Gansbeke, W., Proesmans, M., Dai, D., Van Gool, L.: Multi-task learning for dense prediction tasks: a survey. IEEE Trans. Pattern Anal. Mach. Intell. 1 (2021). https://doi.org/10.1109/TPAMI.2021.3054719

20. Verma, S., Chug, A., Singh, A.: Impact of hyperparameter tuning on deep learning based estimation of disease severity in grape plant. In: International Conference on Soft Computing and Data Mining, pp. 161–171 (2020). https://doi.org/10.1007/978-3-030-36056-6_16

21. Wang, G., Sun, Y., Wang, J.: Automatic image-based plant disease severity estimation using deep learning. Comput. Intell. Neurosci. 2017, 1–8 (2017). https://doi.org/10.1155/2017/2917536

22. Wang, Y., Liu, J., Mišić, J., Mišić, V.B., Lv, S., Chang, X.: Assessing optimizer impact on DNN model sensitivity to adversarial examples. IEEE Access **7**, 152766–152776 (2019). https://doi.org/10.1109/ACCESS.2019.2948658

23. Zhang, Z.: Improved adam optimizer for deep neural networks. In: 2018 IEEE/ACM 26th International Symposium on Quality of Service (IWQoS), pp. 1–2 (2018). https://doi.org/10.1109/IWQoS.2018.8624183

Crack Detection in Oil Paintings Using Morphological Filters and K-SVD Algorithm

Carla Rucoba-Calderón, Efrain Ramos$^{(\boxtimes)}$, and Juan Gutiérrez-Cárdenas

Universidad de Lima, Av. Javier Prado Este 4600, Lima, Peru
{oramos,jmgutier}@ulima.edu.pe

Abstract. Cracks in oil paintings constitute an undesirable but unavoidable effect of time, deteriorating the painting quality. This work proposes a crack detection method that supports the physical restoration process of the artworks, providing a fissure map that allows the artist to visualize the pictorial layer and its flaws. This approach applies three image processing techniques to digitized oil paintings: oriented elongated filters, top-hat morphological filters and a K-SVD algorithm. Then, a post-processing stage based on K-Means is performed on the resulting binary maps to eliminate false positives. Finally, a pixel-by-pixel voting technique is applied to combine the binary maps. Our proposed framework has a better performance detecting craquelure when compared to other methods such as ADA Boost and convolutional neural networks. We obtained a recall of 0.8577, a probability of false alarm of 0.0779, a probability of false negatives of 0.1423, an accuracy of 0.7123, and an F_1 value of 0.7783, which is amongst the best results for the state-of-the-art techniques.

Keywords: Morphological filters · K-SVD · Conservation and restoration of paintings · Digital analysis of paintings · Crack detection

1 Introduction

Oil paintings are continuously deteriorated due to several threats they are exposed to, which can have environmental, biological and anthropological origins [1]. In order to reduce the effect of these alterations, paintings are subjected to a method known as restoration, which is typically carried out by a skilled artist. This manual restoration is based on the analysis of the pictorial layer, an arduous job that relies on the visual capacity of the restorer. The problem with this approach is that irreparable errors are prone to occur during this process, since small damaged areas may not be properly identified by the expert, potentially leading to greater damage and even its total loss [2]. To avoid this purely visual analysis, according to Nikolaidis and Pitas [3], image processing has the potential to be used as an important tool in the restoration process. However, most procedures that use image processing, such as the restoration of the Ghent

© The Author(s), under exclusive license to Springer Nature Switzerland AG 2022
J. A. Lossio-Ventura et al. (Eds.): SIMBig 2021, CCIS 1577, pp. 329–339, 2022.
https://doi.org/10.1007/978-3-031-04447-2_22

Altarpiece [4], are purely digital, and the work of art is still physically subject to damage that will cause its alteration.

To deal with the aforementioned problems, in this work we propose the detection of cracks in the pictorial layer of oil paintings by applying three image processing methods. The first method uses an oriented elongated filter consisting of a set of filters generated by the linear combination of 2D Gaussian kernels. This technique is sensitive to cracks in light and dark areas. The second method uses a top-hat multiscale morphological filter, which consists of the top-hat operation using a square-shaped structure to detect fissures of different sizes. This technique is able to correctly represent the width and branching of the craquelure. The third method uses a K-SVD algorithm, based on a dictionary that is built and adapted to generate signal representations that allow the reconstruction of the images. This technique can correctly detect cracks in dark and smooth areas. All three methods are applied to oil painting images to generate a crack map for each method. Then, k-means is used to reduce the branching and excess width of the detected cracks. Finally, a voting scheme per pixel is applied generating a single fissure map that will support the restorer for their subsequent physical restoration. A very succinct description of a preliminary proof-of-concept developed for our proposal was described in Rucoba [5].

This paper is organized as follows: Sect. 2 presents the state of the art in the usage of digital image processing for the analysis of art and cracks in art images; Sect. 3 presents the proposed methodology for crack detection; Sect. 4 shows the experimental setup; and Sect. 5 shows the discussion of the results of the proposed approach.

2   Digital Analysis of Art

This section describes the state of the art related to the application of digital image processing in the analysis of works of art. We divide the approaches according to their domain of application and the nature of the feature extraction.

2.1   Approaches in the Spatial Domain

In the Digital Processing of the Ghent Altarpiece [14], the authors try to identify fissures and color gaps within the Ghent Altarpiece for its subsequent restoration. Another example is the work by Pei et al. [6], where the detection and restoration of anomalous patterns is applied to ancient Chinese paintings. Pizurica et al. [4], focused on detecting cracks using a Naïve-Bayes binary probabilistic classifier with an input vector composed of attributes obtained from the application of morphological filters. The resulting vectors became categorical predictors that were later counted as binary numbers, being 1 a representation of a crack. On the other hand, Pei et al. [6] applied color enhancement based on saturation modifications, and an adaptive histogram to equalize image lighting. They then concealed the gaps using an algorithm for the detection of damaged pixels and their neighbors, since these would be the candidates to replace the windows. In addition, boundaries had to be defined between the objects in the painting and the background. Some problems with the approach of Pizurica et al. [4] are that very thin fissures are not properly detected, and fine lines (hair and eyelashes) are falsely detected as fissures. The computational cost is also high, requiring 40 min to process and restore 50 images using a 750 MHz CPU PC.

2.2 Approaches in the Frequency Domain

These approaches apply filters in the frequency domain and then take the resulting image back to the spatial domain using an inverse Fourier transform. Cornelis et al. [7] proposed the restoration of the crackle of paintings decomposing the image into animation and texture, where the animation component retains the strong edges of the initial painting, and the texture component consists of the canvas and excess paint in certain areas. This latter component was obtained using a multiscale adaptive threshold in the frequency domain. Likewise, Purkait et al. [8], generate a diffusion scheme that combines an anisotropic diffusion method with a robust high-frequency generation algorithm. This algorithm matches the image on different scales of smaller size and applies a blur operator to each image, to compare the patches with the previously selected images and select the corresponding improved one. The results of Cornelis et al. [7] were positive according to an expert in paintings and restoration, in comparison to an MCA (morphological component analysis) method, since the details were maintained without losing information. However, an increase in processing due to previous transformations required by some images with deformations was noted. Purkait et al. [8] showed an enhancement of the edges and smoothing of the areas with noise, generating loss of information in the final image.

2.3 Feature Extraction Algorithms

These algorithms aim at characterizing the cracks. Giakoumis et al. [9] applied a "Top-Hat" transformation consisting of a lighting component of the image and a non-linear filter that eliminates the edges of the structure. Crack detection was achieved by closing the original image with the filter that obtains the structure and then performing a subtraction with the non-linear filtered image. Although their results detected cracks, there was the need to enhance the illumination of the dark areas of the images. Sizyakin et al. [10] used a methodology composed of three steps. First, a morphological filter was used to separate pixels that are candidates for fissure. Then, a neural convolutional network architecture trained was applied to classify the pixels and distinguish them from false positives. Finally, the positions of the crack pixels were considered using a displacement coefficient. The work of Garg et al. [11], proposed two main stages: the detection of cracks and their classification. For fissure detection, the image started in its negative version, and then a morphological gray-scale top-hat filter was applied. The cracks were then classified to eliminate possible false positives using two classification algorithms: a supervised back propagation algorithm of crack classification, and a fuzzy C-means algorithm of unsupervised crack classification. The results show that the unsupervised classification algorithm was the best among the two tested algorithms, obtaining a better output in most cases.

3   Method for Crack Detection

Our proposed methodology consists of the four stages shown in Fig. 1. In the first stage we pre-process the images by improving the contrast only in the darkest areas of the painting, to support the detection of cracks since areas of low contrast can be challenging. The second stages perform crack detection using three different approaches. The third stage then post processes the crack maps resulting from the three applied crack detection techniques using a semi-automatic grouping method to rule out false positives. The fourth stage combines the three resulting images using a pixel voting scheme.

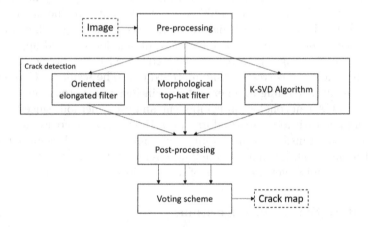

Fig. 1. Scheme of the steps applied for crack detection

3.1   Image Pre-processing

The image is first converted to grayscale I_{org} and a contrast-limited adaptive histogram equalization (CLAHE) is then applied, leading to I_{cl}. Then, the weighted average of the original grayscale image and the image in its enhanced contrast version is obtained. With this approach, only the dark areas will be replaced with the enhanced contrast version, whereas the brighter areas will not be modified, achieving the desired effect. The resulting weighted image I is mathematically given by the following convex combination

$$I = (1 - w)I_{org} + wI_{cl} \tag{1}$$

where $w \in [0, 1]$ is a weighting factor for each pixel. In our approach we obtained this value from the Gaussian blurring of the inverted original image. The application of CLAHE to the image equalizes by controlling the over-amplification of the contrast [12]. Furthermore, it is applied to small portions of the image by limiting the maximum number of pixels in each bin of the local histogram and then redistributing those pixels in the general histogram of the image.

3.2 Crack Detection

This stage is composed of three sub-stages: elongated filters, a top-hat morphological filter, and a K-SVD algorithm. Each of these techniques is independently applied to the input image leading to three different results of crack detection.

a. Oriented Enlongated Filters. These filters are obtained through the linear combination of 2D Gaussian kernels $G(x, y; \sigma)$, where x and y represent the spatial domain, and σ is the constant variance. The application in the spatial domain of this filter leads to

$$\bar{G}'(x, y, w, l) = \frac{1}{2lN + 1} \sum_{k=-lN}^{lN} \left(x + \frac{k}{N} t_1, y + \frac{k}{N} t_2, w \right) \tag{2}$$

where an emphasis on the orthogonal edges was performed based on a vector $n = (n_x, n_y)$ for the directional derivative of G. In (2), the value of w controls the mean width of the filter, $t = (t_x, t_y)$ is an orthogonal unit value for n, and l controls the length of the resulting kernel. After the application of the filter, the images are processed with a hysteresis threshold, which consists of a high and low threshold. The low threshold edges related to high edges are kept, whereas those unrelated to high edges are discarded. The output of this stage is a binary image containing the identified fissures.

b. Morphological Top-Hat Filters. These filters $TH_b(l)$ are applied on b elements with square shape and sizes ranging from 3×3 to $\beta \times \beta$ pixels, where β depends on the width of the cracks. The sizes are based on Cornelis et al. [8]. The results are then thresholded using Otsu's method. Subsequently, the crack maps resulting from the different scales are combined. This process begins with the union of the smaller-scale (3×3) maps to form a base that will receive the larger scales. Due to this effect, only the groups of pixels connected to the base fissure map are kept. Finally, the resulting map is processed by joining the separated pixel spaces and removing small groups of pixels.

c. K-SVD Algorithm. The K-SVD algorithm works as a generalization of the k-means grouping process, and aims to achieve dispersed signal representations through dictionary training rather than relying on predefined dictionaries [13]. This is achieved by iteratively combining the update of the dictionary and the update of the sparse signals. When it works with an atom per signal, it trains a dictionary using the form of gain V_Q (vector quantization), but if there is a unit coefficient for the atom, it performs k-means. The algorithm works on portions of the image $x \in \mathbb{R}^n$ of size $\sqrt{\alpha} \times \sqrt{\alpha}$, and it has a dictionary $D \in \mathbb{R}^{\theta \times k}$, where k is the number of adjusted atoms and L is a restriction stating that each fragment of the image cannot be composed of more than L atoms. Furthermore, the vectors x_l of X are the fragments of the image that the dictionary uses to learn. Each atom in this dictionary D_l is a unit vector in the vector norm l_2. On the other hand, the vector α_l is the scattering coefficient of x_l and $\|\alpha_l\|_0$ is the number of elements other than 0 in that vector. Using this notation, the problem is:

$$\min_{a,D} \|X - D\alpha\|_2^2 \quad s.t. \quad \|\alpha\|_0 \leq L \tag{3}$$

This algorithm is applied in crack detection to enhance the cracking of the image by training the dictionary for each image. To this end, a dictionary D is trained with k portions of the image that have cracks, generating a complete dictionary conditioned to the image. A total of 20 iterations are carried out, and then the dictionary is used to reconstruct the images and keep only the cracks.

3.3 Post-processing

In this stage, a semi-automatic grouping method is applied to each of the images that are obtained in the crack detection phase. This method detects false positives and helps to reduce undesired ramifications. The process begins by connecting the cracks in a list of coordinates, where each crack is divided into segments. Then some characteristics such as length, orientation and spatial density are extracted from these segments. One of the objectives of using these characteristics is to distinguish elements of the painting such as hair, which usually belong to denser regions. These characteristics are then combined into a vector of characteristics, which is used as input to a k-means segmentation. Finally, the clusters identified as not false positives will be kept.

3.4 Voting Scheme

The last stage consists in fusing the previously obtained crack maps from the post-processing stage, in order to keep the advantages of each of the three techniques that were used for crack detection. The approach is a voting scheme that adds the three maps to obtain a single image, where each pixel will receive a value between 0 and 3. This value is the number of techniques that identified the pixel as a crack. If a pixel gets a value of 2 or more, it will be considered to be a crack and will remain in the detected image.

4   Experimental Setup

4.1   Dataset

In this work, digitized oil painting dataset images were used. We generated a dataset that gathers digitized oil paintings from various sources such as Van Eyck's works of art (`http://legacy.closertovaneyck.be`), which are presented as 13 high quality photographs. Oil paintings from the Getty Search Gateway image bank (`https://cutt.ly/WmbszEg`) were also included, providing a total of 63 free access high definition images. Together, both datasets provided 76 high quality images with dimensions ranging from 1600×1600 pixels to 14982×13885 pixels. The images were also divided in a grid of 8 fragments, with dimensions defined by the original size of the images. This resulted in a dataset of 608 images (`https://cutt.ly/wmbsmzE`). Some examples of the fragments of damaged areas of the images to be used are shown in Fig 2.

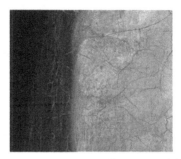

Fig. 2. Cracks examples in the dataset paintings.

4.2 Parameters

We used the values shown in Table 1, which were experimentally tuned using [14] as a starting point. This table presents values used in the pre-processing stage. For instance, the Gaussian filter that was applied to reduce noise of the inverted image had a 45×45 kernel with a standard deviation $\sigma = 15$. A large kernel is applied in order to generate a severe blur of the images, since several anomalies considered as noise can affect the crack detection.

Table 1. Values for the parameters used in the experimentation.

Processing stage	Parameters	Values
Pre-processing	mask size and σ	45×45, 15
Oriented elongated filter	mask size and σ	51×51, 1.4
Oriented elongated filter	thresholds n_1 and n_2	60, 150
Top-hat filter	ratios r_1 and r_2	3 px, 8 px
K-SVD	$\sqrt{\alpha}$	16
K-SVD	dictionary atoms k	128
K-SVD	scarcity constraint L	1

Within the detection techniques, the elongated filter was composed of a Gaussian filter with a 51×51 kernel and a standard deviation $\sigma = 1.4$ in order not to apply a severe blurring. Then, the maximum and minimum thresholds of the Canny edge detector were set to 60 and 150, respectively, reducing the detection of false positives. The radius applied to the filter ranges between $r_1 = 3$ px and $r_2 = 8$ px, which were defined due to the regular width of the cracks. For the K-SVD algorithm, the dictionary training was carried out on the image divided into 16 portions, 128 dictionary atoms and a scarcity constraint with value 1 to make the process more strict. OpenCV was used for image processing and Scikit-learn for the K-SVD technique and the post-processing.

4.3   Crack Detection

The first step of crack detection consisted in enhancing the grayscale image using the CLAHE histogram equalization. A Gaussian filter was then applied on the inverted grayscale image to finally combine resulting images. An example of a pre-processed image is shown in Fig 3. Then, the crack detection process was carried out. Fig 4 shows an example of the results of the three techniques: oriented elongated filter, top-hat filter and K-SVD algorithm, on the same image for a visual comparison of the results. Next, post-processing with K-means was applied. This allowed grouping the crack pixels based on orientation, length and density, allowing the elimination of excess width, branches and false positives as can be seen in Fig 5 and Fig 6. Finally, a voting scheme per pixel was applied: there was a count of how many techniques identified a given pixel as a fissure. If two or more techniques identified it as a fissure, then it was considered as a

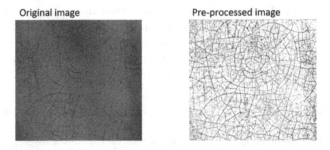

Fig. 3. Comparison of the original and pre-processed images.

Fig. 4. Results of crack detection techniques.

Oriented elongated filter   Top-hat filter   K-SVD algorithm

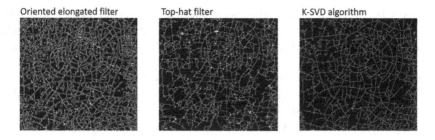

Fig. 5. Results of the post-processed crack maps.

Oriented elongated filter   Top-hat filter   K-SVD algorithm

Fig. 6. Overlapping results of post-processed crack maps.

true fissure. However, if none or only one technique identified it as a fissure, this pixel was not considered to be on the final map. Fig 7 shows the final crack map, where the coincident pixels

Fig. 7. Results of final crack maps.

5   Discussion

To evaluate the results, a ground truth fissure map was manually generated since there are no datasets containing this information. The used images were sections from the Ghent Altarpiece, the same image used with other approaches. We computed the true positives, false positives, false negatives, total fissure pixels (DfPx), total non-fissure pixels (UdPx) and total pixels (AlPx). Using these values we obtained the probability of false alarm (FA), the probability of false negatives (FM), the precision, the recall, and the F_1 metric. Table 2 shows the results obtained with our methodology, which is called *TKF*, in comparison with the results obtained by other works. The methodologies used for this comparison are Boosting Methods (ADA), Support Vector Machines, Connected Neural Networks (NN) [15], convolutional neural networks (CNN) [16], deep characteristics fusion network (DFFN), Bayesian conditional tensor factorization method (BCTF) and convolutional networks with multimodal data (MCNC), the latter developed by [10] and which uses the image in its x-ray and infrared version.

Table 2. Comparison of the obtained metrics

Method	Recall	FA	FM	Accuracy	Metric F_1
ADA	0.8693	0.0920	0.1307	0.5636	0.6839
SVM	0.8530	0.0912	0.1470	0.5612	0.6770
NN	0.8655	0.0877	0.1345	0.5745	0.6906
CNN	0.8481	0.0777	0.1519	0.5989	0.7020
DFFN	0.7488	0.0422	0.2512	0.7081	0.7279
BCTF	0.7896	0.0535	0.2104	0.6686	0.7241
MCNC	0.7673	0.0375	0.2327	0.7365	0.7516
TFK	0.8577	0.0779	0.1423	0.7123	0.7783

It can be seen that MCNC [10] has better precision compared to other techniques. Our methodology has a precision close to that of MCNC, and we obtained the best results in the F_1 metric. Thus, our proposed methodology lies within the limits of other state-of-the-art methods outperforming some of them with respect to some metrics. The values obtained for the false alarm are mainly due to the excess in thickness of some cracks, as well as isolated pixels. The false negatives are being affected by pixels that are in dark areas or areas with color variations, where the techniques failed to properly detect cracks. Similar problems are found in other works that have the same objective. We propose to apply morphological filters, specifically in these areas; however, it would be a fairly manual process and it would depend on the opinion of the person conducting the experimentation, since this part of the restoration is very subjective.

6   Conclusion

We proposed a method for the detection of craquelure in digitized oil paintings using morphological filters and a K-SVD algorithm. Our method started with a pre-processing of the images, enhancing dark areas of the paintings and areas with abrupt color changes. Then, the oriented elongated filter, the top-hat filter and the K-SVD algorithm were separately applied, followed by a post-processing to reduce the number of isolated pixels, the excessive thickness of the cracks, and the unnecessary branching in the crackle. Finally, the voting scheme allowed the final fissure map to keep the pixels identified as fissures by the greatest number of techniques, resulting in a reliable image. The resulting crack maps are expected to support the pre-restoration process of the paintings, reducing the time and effort of experts in detecting crackle for subsequent treatment. Using the detection of cracks as a first step, other tasks oriented to painting maintenance, such as digital restoration or categorization of cracks, can be carried out.

References

1. Instituto Andaluz del Patrimonio Histórico: La biología en la conservación/restauración del patrimonio histórico. IPAH, Sevilla (2019)
2. Conservation, S.F.A.: Cracks on Paintings. Sflac, Florida (2013)
3. Nikolaidis, N., Pitas, I.: Digital image processing in painting restoration and archiving. Int. Conf. Image Process. 1, 586–589 (2001)
4. Pižurica, A., Platiša, L., Ružic, T., Cornelis, B., Dooms, A., Martens, M., et al.: Digital image processing of the Ghent altarpiece. IEEE Sign. Process. Mag. 34(4), 112–122 (2015)
5. Rucoba, C.: Comparación de técnicas de procesamiento de imágenes para la detección de fisuras en pinturas al óleo. Congreso Internacional de Ingeniería de Sistemas; Lima, PE, 27 October 2021
6. Pei, S., Zeng, Y., Chang, C.: Virtual restoration of ancient Chinese paintings using color contrast enhancement and lacuna texture synthesis. IEEE Trans. Image Process. 13(3), 416–429 (2004)
7. Cornelis, B., Haizhao, Y., Goodfriend, A., Ocon, N., Jianfeng, L., Daubechies, I.: Removal of canvas patterns in digital acquisitions of paintings. IEEE Trans. Image Process. 26(1), 1057–7149 (2017)
8. Purkait, P., Chanda, B.: Digital Color Restoration of Old Damaged Mural images. ICVGIP. Mumbai, India (2012)
9. Giakoumis, I., Nikolaidis, N., Pitas, I.: Digital image processing techniques for the detection and removal of cracks in digitized paintings. IEEE Trans. Image Process. 15(1), 1057–7149 (2006)
10. Sizyakin, R., Cornelis, B., Meeus, L., Dubois, H., Martends, M., Voronin, V., et al.: Crack Detection in Paintings Using Convolutional Neural Networks. IEEE Access 8, 74535–74552 (2020)
11. Garg, S., Sahoo, G.: Crack classification and interpolation of old digital paintings. J. Comput. Sci. Appl. 1(5), 85–90 (2013)
12. Zuiderveld, K.: Contrast Limited Adaptive Histogram Equalization, pp. 474–485. Academic Press Professional, Inc. (1994)
13. Elad, M.: Sparse and Redundant Representations: from Theory to Applications in Signal and Image Processing. Springer Science & Business Media (2010)
14. Cornelis, B., Ruzic, T., Gezels, E., Dooms, A., Pizurica, A., Platisa, L., et al.: Crack detection and inpainting for virtual restoration of paintings: the case of the Ghent altarpiece. Sign. Process. (93), 605–619 (2012)
15. Zhang, L., Yang, F., Zhang, Y. D., Zhu, Y. J.: Road crack detection using deep convolutional neural network. 2016 IEEE International Conference on Image Processing (ICIP), pp. 3708–3712 (2016)
16. Fan, R., Bocus, M. J., Zhu, Y., Jiao, J., Wang, L., Ma, F., et al.: Road crack detection using deep convolutional neural network and adaptive thresholding. In: IEEE Intelligent Vehicles Symposium (IV), pp. 474–479 (2019)

CoffeeSE: Interpretable Transfer Learning Method for Estimating the Severity of Coffee Rust

Filomen Incahuanaco-Quispe[1]([✉])(iD), Edward Hinojosa-Cardenas[2](iD),
Denis A. Pilares-Figueroa[2](iD), and Cesar A. Beltrán-Castañón[3](iD)

[1] University of São Paulo, São Paulo, Brazil
fincahuanaco@usp.br
[2] Universidad Nacional de San Agustín de Arequipa, Arequipa, Peru
{ehinojosa,dpilares}@unsa.edu.pe
[3] Pontificia Universidad Católica del Perú - PUCP, Lima, Peru
cbeltran@pucp.edu.pe

Abstract. Coffee is one of the most important agricultural products and consumed beverages in the world. Then, adequate control of the diseases is necessary to guarantee its production. Coffee rust is a relevant coffee disease, which is caused by the fungus *hemileia vastatrix*. Recently, deep learning techniques have been used to identify coffee diseases and the severity of each disease. In this paper, we propose a new interpretable transfer learning method to estimate the severity of coffee rust called *CoffeeSE*. The proposed method consists of four stages: Leaf segmentation, patch sampling, patch-based classification, and quantification/interpretation analysis. On the classification stage, a Brazilian dataset is used to transfer by fine-tuning new weights to a pre-trained classifier. So, this new classifier is tested in Peruvian coffee leaves infected with coffee rust. Our approach shows acceptable quantification results according to an expert agronomist. In addition, an interpretability module of the patch-classifier is proposed to provide a visual and textual explanation of the most relevant pixels used in the classification process.

Keywords: Coffee rust · Transfer learning · Interpretability · Sampling

1 Introduction

Coffee is one of the most popular and consumed beverages worldwide. According to International Coffee Organization (ICO), the global coffee consumption has increased 2.7% per year average over the last five years. As reported by MIT's Observatory of Economic Complexity, in 2019, Coffee were the world's 122nd most traded product, with a total trade of thirty billion dollars.

In Latin America, specifically in Brazil and Peru (countries where the coffee leaves were obtained for this paper), the coffee industry fulfills an important role.

J. A. Lossio-Ventura et al. (Eds.): SIMBig 2021, CCIS 1577, pp. 340–355, 2022.
https://doi.org/10.1007/978-3-031-04447-2_23

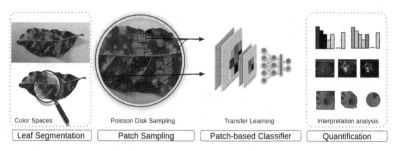

Fig. 1. Flowchart of CoffeeSE proposed method

Brazil is the biggest coffee-producing country in the world, with immense areas of land, needing hundreds of people to manage and operate them to produce huge quantities of coffee according to National Coffee Association; and, Peru is one of the top 20 largest coffee-producing countries in the world according to ICO.

In order to guarantee good quality and productivity of coffee, it is important to recognize coffee diseases in their initial stage [35]. Coffee Rust disease, which is caused by the *Hemileia vastatrix* fungus, is one of the most common and terrible diseases of coffee growing, and, it can cause yield losses of up to 35% and has a polyetic epidemiological impact on subsequent years [37].

The first symptom is small yellowish spores or lesions that appear on the underside of leaves. After that, these spores grow, coalesce and produce distinctive orange colour spores with large irregular shapes. Finally, during the last stage of the disease, the centers of the spores will eventually dry up and turn brown [2].

To set the severity of the Coffee Rust development stage, usually, an empirical method, based on subjective and visual criteria, is applied by farmers or specialists. After that, depending on the severity defined, a amount of fungicide is applied to solve the problem. One of the problems with the empirical method is that some farmers do not have the knowledge or access to specialists to define the severity, and consequently, the control performed tends to be inefficient and may lead to increased risk of crop yield losses [12].

To avoid this problem, different automatic methods, based mainly on artificial intelligence, are proposed to estimate the severity of the Coffee Rust. Those methods can be divided into two groups: 1) Methods based on image processing [19,25]; and, 2) Methods based on deep learning [13,14,26]. Both groups have demonstrated effectiveness in Coffee Rust detection, for that, each step of the proposed method uses a method of one group or another.

In this paper, we propose a new method to estimate the severity of the coffee rust and it is a sequence of four main stages: 1) Leaf segmentation, where is applied the method Grabcut [6] combined with *Luv* color space on uniform partially obscured background.

2) Patch sampling, because each leaf input image has a high dimension and in order to reduce the computational cost, a subset of patches of the image

are selected and used in the next stage [10]. 3) Patch-based classification, each selected patch is classified, as healthy or unhealthy, by applying transfer learning from a pre-trained deep convolutional neural network (Inception-v3 [36]). 4) Severity coffee rust definition, finally, the quantify of healthy and unhealthy patches are calculated in order to define the rust severity scale (based on a previous threshold percentage for each scale).

Additionally, it is important to mention that deep learning architectures (such as deep neural networks, deep belief networks, neural networks, and convolutional neural networks) continue to be thread mostly a black-box function approximator, mapping a given input to classification or prediction output, for that reason, interpretability of deep networks models has gained attention to provide a level of human-understandable justifications for its output [7,41]. We added interpretability criteria in the patch-based classifier stage, where a SmoothGrad method [32] is applied on each selected patch to generate a visual salience and *Lab* color space in combination with k-means clustering method [18] in order to generate a text explanation.

The main contributions of this work are summarized as follows:

- We introduce a sampling method for selecting patches from the coffee leaf and process it preserving the high-resolution image. Traditionally the source image is resized, but that generates a loss of data (i.e. texture information) [10].
- Transfer learning based on Inception-v3 architecture is used to categorize each previous patch selected as healthy or unhealthy.
- Based on SmoothGrad method [32] and *Lab* color space, a multi-modal (visual and textual) explanation is defined for each healthy or unhealthy patch.

The paper is organized as follows. Section 2 describes the background concepts used in the proposed method. Section 3 presents in detail each stage of the proposed method. Section 4 shows the experimental analysis, results obtained and the interpretability stage. Finally, conclusions and future works are given in Sect. 5.

2   Background Concepts

In this section we present concepts related to color spaces, color-based segmentation and transfer learning using Inception-v3, all of them used in the proposed method.

2.1   Color Spaces

The representation of the color in 3D space is led by the trichromatic and opponent color theories [38]. For that, many 3D color spaces have been proposed (i.e. RGB, HSI, CIE XYZ, Lab, and Luv). The RGB color space is easy to understanding and is based on the RGB color model. HSI family color spaces use cylindrical coordinates where the saturation channel (S) is proportional to radial distance, the hue (H) is a function of the angle in the polar coordinate system, and the intensity (I) is the distance along the axis perpendicular to the polar coordinate plane. This HSI is obtained from the RGB by coordinate transformations process [27].

The CIE XYZ color space is based on measurements of the human visual perception and uses positive integers to formulate tristimulus values X,Y, and Z where Y represents the human eye's response to the total power of a light source [3]. The CIELAB or Lab color space is a uniform color space and takes the XYZ tristimulus values of a stimulus and the reference white as input and outputs correlates to lightness, chroma, and hue [24]. The CIELUV or Luv color space is one of the perceptually uniform color spaces where L stands for luminance, whereas U and V represent chromaticity values of color images [28].

The Lab and Luv color spaces are both transformations of the CIE XYZ color space and are used in the leaf segmentation task and interpretability phase in this paper, respectively.

2.2 Color-Based Segmentation

In general, image segmentation methods use the color of each pixel to define regions with homogeneous colors, thus each region pertains to a separate cluster(object) in the image. Those methods depend strongly on the color space applied, there is no single color space that can provide satisfactory results. For this reason, is necessary to choose an adequate color space that provides the expected results. In addition exists segmentation algorithms that use thresholding, clustering methods, histograms, edge detection, and others, those methods are based on properties like gray-level, color, intensity, texture, depth, or motion [29]. But, the most useful property is the color [9], and gray-scale [11,23].

In nowadays some of those methods are combined with color space models because of the relevance of their effective results without involving higher computational cost [21,22,31,39]. For example in [33] is presented a segmentation method based on clustering in colors space in combination with *Graph Cut* method to segment leaf images. Then in [39] and [22] works are presented a comparison of the effect of *Graph Cut* with different colors spaces. Those works evidence our initial intuition about choosing some of those colors spaces. In this paper, we give special attention to Luv color space model and GrabCut method [6]. GraphCut is effective for segmentation of gray-level images, which is based on Min-Cut/Max-Flow [4] algorithm. The main difference of GrabCut with previously works are the interactivity process, the user needs to provide the foreground and background sample. Our goal is automatize this step, offering channel v to GrabCut in replacement of that data. With this approach we solve the initialization problem for the GrabCut method in context of coffee leaves.

2.3 Transfer Learning

In deep learning, Convolutional Neural Network (CNN) is a class of methods that have become dominant in various computer vision tasks and is attracting interest across a variety of domains [40].

The inception style is a generic structure based on blocks, and flexible enough to adapt to many constraints. For example in [36], some techniques to improve CNN architectures are presented, in special architectures based on GoogLeNet (Inception). They offer various design principles for scaling CNN networks in inception architectures. According to the authors, Inception-v3 reduces in $12x$ parameters in respect to AlexNet, and $36x$ VGGNet.

In general, the training process in a CNN is performed in a complex and large dataset considering thousands of epochs. For that, the computational load cost, the memory bandwidth, and capacity have a significant effect on the entire training performance [1]. To reduce that effect, a strategy called Transfer Learning is proposed to use the already pre-trained models to resolve other problems skipping the entire time used in the previous model [42]. We adopt this strategy for our patch-based classifier stage, where an Inception-v3 is adapted by fine-tuning for our domain of coffee rust.

3   Proposed Method

The proposed method called CoffeeSE (Coffee rust Severity Estimator) is composed of four stages: Leaf segmentation, Patch sampling, Patch-based classifier, and finally Quantification and analysis. We show in Fig. 1 the flowchart of the proposed method and each stage is explained in the following subsections.

3.1   Leaf Segmentation

The goal of CoffeeSE is to process the input images of coffee leaves in the original resolution, those images were obtained in semi-controlled conditions (with uniform background). The expected result is to divide the image into two regions, leaf and background. At this stage, the GrabCut method [6] is applied on gray-level coffee leaf image obtained from the channel v of Luv color space decomposition. Figure 2 shows the effect of our approach using GrabCut initialized with channel v. The first column shows the original image of the coffee leaf, the second column shows the channel v of the Luv color space decomposition, and the third column shows the result based on GrabCut and Luv color space.

(a) Coffee RGB image   (b) Channel v of Luv   (c) Masked by Grabcut

Fig. 2. Coffee leaf segmentation scheme

3.2   Patch Sampling

In this stage, a set of patches is getting from the coffee leaf image segmented in the previous stage (Fig. 2c). The binary image or mask of the segmented leaf allows delimiting the sampling method to inner the leaf. Our strategy considers choosing a set of patches from coffee leaf, it is possible to consider a naive strategy, where random positions inner the image, but we can not guaranty a uniform covering.

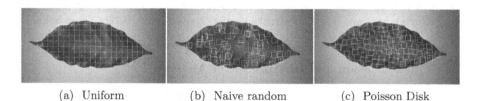

(a) Uniform   (b) Naive random   (c) Poisson Disk

Fig. 3. Patch sampling schemes. Each white box is a candidate patch.

This argument is easily verifiable with Fig. 3b, where we can observe overlays of patches and areas not covered in a naive random approach. Then to solve it, we focus on a particular sampling method called Poisson Disk Sampling [5]. It is an improved method than just a random approach and it is very common in the Computer Graphics area. This method guarantees uniform coverage of the region of interest, in our case the coffee leaf (see Fig. 3c). Both sampling methods choose patches randomly from the image, but just Poisson Disk sampling guaranty less overlap and high coverage of the leaf area as shown in Fig. 3.

3.3   Patch-Based Classification

Deep Learning techniques have shown overcome properties in comparison to Machine Learning techniques to solve many problems related to images. The CNNs are the most outstanding methods for image processing tasks [15]. Transfer learning techniques gain importance because offer the possibility of using pre-trained networks without spending too much computational cost.

In this stage, each previously selected patch needs to be classified as a healthy or infected patch. For this task, we applied the Transfer Learning technique, which includes a fine-tuning task to correct the weight of our classifier. The most effective model for our domain (coffee leaves) was the Inception-v3 [36]. This CNN based in blocks is re-trained with 568 coffee patches in different sizes which were cropped from infected leaves with coffee rust, obtained from image data-set of [12] and Plant Disease Symptoms (PDDB) [16] (Fig. 4).

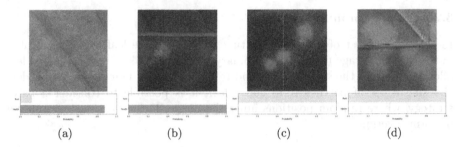

<table>
<tr><td>(a)</td><td>(b)</td><td>(c)</td><td>(d)</td></tr>
</table>

Fig. 4. Patch classification outputs. *a* and *b* probabilities for two random healthy patches(green bar) and *c* and *d* for rust infection (yellow bars). (Color figure online)

3.4 Quantification and Interpretation Analysis

Finally, in the quantification stage is calculated the number of infected patches over total patches to define the coffee rust severity. Recently, Esgario et al. [14] presented a severity estimation method for five levels (Health, Very Low, Low, High, and Very high), based on deep learning. The authors use *Leaf Biotic* term to refer to plant diseases. The main difficulty with this approach is the absence of enough image samples for each level or grade of disease for the training process. It was reflected in the 86.51% of accuracy in the best case for coffee leaves.

Our original strategy of patch counting assumes that is proportional to ground truth based on pixels. The experiments show that the proportions are not constant, because we carry a problem related to scaling and random sampling. Then we decide to model by lineal regression a corrector for our quantification stage (see Fig. 9).

4 Experiments

The flowchart shown in Fig. 5 illustrates the experiment design process. Each part of the experimental flowchart is detailed in the following subsections.

4.1 Coffee Leaves Datasets

We consider a Brazilian dataset [14] from different regions of Espiritu Santo, this dataset provide 1747 leaves of coffee with different biotic stress, but for coffee rust severity grades are: 272 Healthy leaves (grade 0), 229 of grade 1, 77 of grade 2, 23 of grade 3 and 19 of grade 4, the authors used smartphones ASUS Zenfone 2, Xiaomi Redmi 5A, Xiaomi S2, Galaxy S8 and iPhone 6S.

On the other hand, for Peruvian dataset we collected 35 coffee leaf images using Panasonic DMC-F3 camera, with resolution 4000 × 2672 pixels in JPEG format, a process that resolution is so expensive then we re-sample to 2048 × 1024 pixels (same of Brazilian), using nearest neighbor interpolation [8], because this approach conserves texture information (Fig. 6).

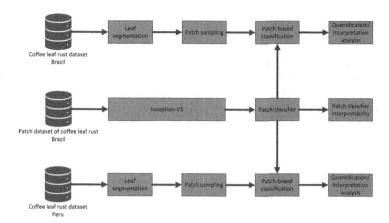

Fig. 5. Experiment design process

(a) From Esgario et al. [14] dataset.

(b) Peruvian coffee leaves

Fig. 6. Coffee leaves, illustrating the semi-controlled datasets used in this study.

We notices that, both datasets have similar semi-controlled conditions, like uniform background and illumination source, the illumination was provided by natural light (changes during the day, producing shadows). That conditions make them compatible for our propose. We use [14] dataset because have enough images for train our patch classifier and then test in our Peruvian dataset with few images, but containing leaves with high level of coffee rust infection.

4.2   Leaf Segmentation

This stage is crucial in our method because impact drastically in patch sampling. In Fig. 7 we show the results of our segmentation process in both datasets, we use a sOrensen index for compare the accuracy of four approach for this task. We confirm our initial intuition about the influence of Luv decomposition of coffee leaf images.

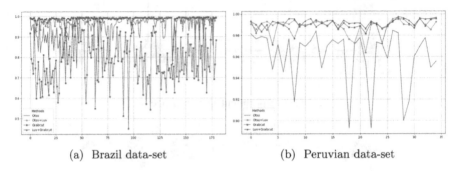

(a) Brazil data-set   (b) Peruvian data-set

Fig. 7. Comparison of four segmentation methods applied in each Brazil and Peruvian leaves, using sOrensen index score.

4.3   Sørensen Similarity Index

The Sørensen index, in statistic is used for comparing the similarity of two samples. It was developed by the botanist Thorvald Sørensen and published in 1948. Sørensen's original formula was intended to be applied to presence/absence data, and is:

$$QS = \frac{2C}{A+B} = \frac{2n(A \cap B)}{n(A) + n(B)}$$

where A and B are the number of species in samples A and B, respectively, and C is the number of species shared by the two samples; QS is the quotient of similarity and it has ranges from $[0-1]$. The Sørensen index is identical to Dice's coefficient which is always in $[0,1]$ range [34].

We have evaluated various predefined architectures such as Inception-v3, MobileNet-v2, ResNet, VGG16, and VGG19. The Inception-v3 network got the better result with 96.99% of accuracy during the fine-tuning process, and we operated with 50, 100, and 500 epochs. The patches were divided into train, validation, and test group. In Fig. 8, we show the graphic of the accuracy and loss evolution of the training process.

During the counting process we notice the big difference between pixel counting (ground truth) and our patch counting approach. We plot that difference in continue curves in Fig. 9. Both curves have similar behavior, but in different scale, it is not constant, then we decide to model that error using a linear regression, producing a corrector for our answer, we plot this new curve based in the corrector in the same Fig. 9 by discontinue lines in green color.

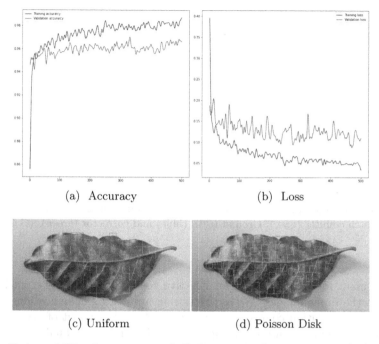

(a) Accuracy   (b) Loss

(c) Uniform   (d) Poisson Disk

Fig. 8. Train and Visual test process (a,b) Fine tuning by 500 epochs. (c,d) Labeled in red boxes the infected patches and in gray healthy patches. (Color figure online)

We can notice in Fig. 8d a patch mislabeled (in red color), it can be explained watching the sensitivity maps presented in Fig. 11, where the main veins of leaves are considered like a mandatory features during the classification process.

4.4 Patch Classifier Interpretability Module

Deep neural networks continue to be thread mostly as a black-box function approximator, mapping a given input to prediction output, for that reason, interpretability of deep networks models has gained attention to provide a level of human-understandable justifications for its output [7]. In this case, we generate a multimodal explanation, that incorporates both visual pointing and textual explanation [17]. In order to understand the deep neural network Inception-v3 during classification process, we focus in one of the most recently interpretability visual pointing methods [20]. On these work is presented a benchmark with nine methods like a Gradients (GRAD), Guided Backprop (GB), Integrated Grdients (IG), Classic Smoothgrad (SG), SmoothGrad^2 (SG-SQ), VarGrad (Var), Random and Sobel Edge Filter. From those methods we choose two of them SmoothGrad and Smoothgrad in convination with integrated gradient. In Fig. 11 is possible to appreciate those two methods [32].

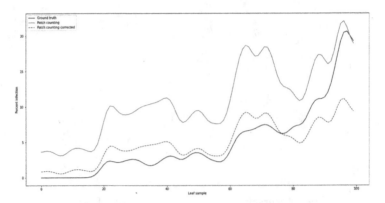

Fig. 9. Patch classification corrector: Adjust patch counting to ground truth based in pixels. Patch counter (gray), Ground truth (blue) and corrector (green). (Color figure online)

The main idea is to choose an effective method for highlight pixels (features) in the input images that are more relevant during classification process. In image classification context, one way to explain the output of deep network is to identify the most important input pixels that impact in final classification. According to Daniel Smilkov [32], it is possible to create a strategy using a gradient map (sensitivity map) called SmoothGrad. There are two aspects in order to make the qualitative comparison [32]. First, the visual Coherence (highlight the object, excluding the background) and second the test discriminativity (image with two objects A and B, for A classification we expect concentration in object A, and vice versa).

Related to visual coherence the Fig. 11 shows in second and third column, we expect highlight the regions with orange, yellow and/or brown spots. We notice in majority cases the veins add a little importance that affect the right classification.

Finally, we use a four-steps method to generate a textual explanation for coffee rust presence based on colour feature for the sensitivity maps obtained previously. The first step consists in obtained a specific region where integrated gradient in combination by smoothgradient defines relevant pixels, the others pixels are set to transparent (white color in the Fig. 12). In the second step, each not transparent RGB pixel is converted to CIE L*a*b* (CIELAB) space color and added them to 1-dimensional array, where each row contains a 3-dimensional array (first dimension is L*, second dimension is a*, and third dimension is b* in the CIELAB space color). The third step consists in used a well-known k-means algorithm [30] to create clusters based on color similarity. In the last step, color centroids (result of the previous step) are compared with ten of the most known colors (black, brown, red, orange, yellow, green, blue, purple, gray and white) based on euclidean distance, finally, the colors with minor distance with each centroid are used for generating the textual explanation (Table 1 and Fig. 10).

Table 1. Final result using our method in Peruvian coffee dataset

Image	Severity %	Grade
01	1.63	1
02	2.36	1
03	6.83	2
04	5.39	1
05	0.60	1
06	11.13	2
07	6.23	2
08	13.27	2
09	14.73	2
10	6.70	2
11	3.15	1
12	2.74	1
13	10.32	2
14	20.49	2
15	13.98	2
16	11.57	2
17	14.33	2
18	11.73	2
19	20.85	2
20	17.68	2
21	22.45	3
22	15.59	2
23	30.29	3
24	15.68	2
25	19.79	2
26	19.63	2
27	19.54	2
28	28.85	3
29	33.67	3
30	30.23	3
31	32.60	3
32	28.46	3
33	30.95	3
34	19.96	2
35	20.26	2

(a) Image **04**, 5.39%

(b) Image **05**, 0.60%

(c) Image **28**, 28.85%

(d) Image **29**, 33.67%

Fig. 10. Visual inspection of Peruvian data-set. Each item shows leaf id and coffee rust percent.

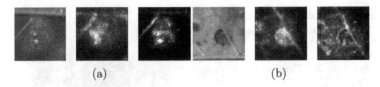

(a)   (b)

Fig. 11. Sensitivity maps: First column coffee leaf region with rust, second column shows smooth gradient map and thrid colum shows integrated gradient in combination by smooth gradient. (Color figure online)

In Fig. 12 each row shows a example of the multimodal explanation method. The first column shows the original region shown in the Fig. 11; the second column shows a specific region where integrated gradient in combination by smooth gradient defines relevant pixels; the third column shows the result of K-Means algorithm with 3 clusters; and, the fourth columns shows the textual colour explanation why that region contains coffee rust.

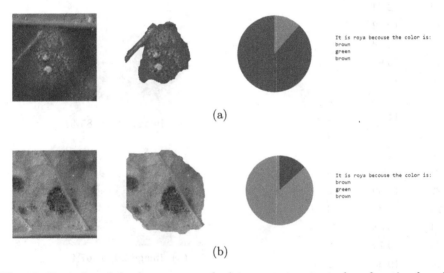

Fig. 12. Examples of the four-steps method to generate a textual explanation based on colour feature.

5   Conclusions and Future Works

To the best of our knowledge, the CoffeeSE proposed method is the first method in the literature that focuses on estimating the severity of coffee rust based on patch classification using an interpretable transfer learning method. Reducing the use of the Deep Learning techniques to specific tasks and maximizing the final user understood.

The proposed method consists of four stages (leaf segmentation, patch sampling, patch-based classification, and quantification) and the experiments are applied to coffee rust datasets of Brazil and Peru. The results, obtained in the Peru dataset, show an accuracy of 95% compared with the severity defined by agronomic inspection and visual quantification methods.

CoffeeSE provides, for experts in coffee rust disease, a visual (Salience maps) and textual explanation in combination with common colors. Increasing the understanding of how our model learns and providing new criteria for experts, to direct and validate the developing model. In contrast, to just provide a percentual number without interpretation.

The sampling method based on the Poisson disk sampling permits us to apply each patch classification in parallel, we will direct our research in that direction. In addition, introduce also micro patchings to reduce the error of the quantification process. Now our approach is limited to 75×75 patch size because inception-v3 supports that minimal size.

Future researches include the extension of the proposed method to estimate the severity of coffee rust on branches and bushes considering the interpretability stage.

References

1. Alzubaidi, L., et al.: Review of deep learning: concepts, CNN architectures, challenges, applications, future directions. J. Big Data **8**(1), 1–74 (2021). https://doi.org/10.1186/s40537-021-00444-8
2. Avelino, J., et al.: The coffee rust crises in Colombia and Central America (2008–2013): impacts, plausible causes and proposed solutions. Food Secur. **7**, 303–321 (2015)
3. Berns, R.: Color and Spatial Vision, pp. 17–35. Wiley, March 2019
4. Boykov, Y., Kolmogorov, V.: An experimental comparison of min-cut/max- flow algorithms for energy minimization in vision. IEEE Trans. Pattern Anal. Mach. Intell. **26**(9), 1124–1137 (2004)
5. Bridson, R.: Fast Poisson disk sampling in arbitrary dimensions. In: ACM SIGGRAPH 2007 Sketches on - SIGGRAPH 2007, pp. 22–32. ACM Press, San Diego (2007)
6. C., R., Kolmogorov, V., Blake, A.: "GrabCut": interactive foreground extraction using iterated graph cuts. ACM Trans. Graph. **23**(3), 309–314 (2004)
7. Chakraborty, S., et al.: Interpretability of deep learning models: a survey of results. In: 2017 IEEE SmartWorld, Ubiquitous Intelligence Computing, Advanced Trusted Computed, Scalable Computing Communications, Cloud Big Data Computing, Internet of People and Smart City Innovation, pp. 1–6 (2017)
8. Danahy, E.E., Agaian, S.S., Panetta, K.A.: Algorithms for the resizing of binary and grayscale images using a logical transform. In: Astola, J.T., Egiazarian, K.O., Dougherty, E.R. (eds.) Image Processing: Algorithms and Systems V, vol. 6497, pp. 305–314. International Society for Optics and Photonics, SPIE (2007)
9. Deng, Y., Manjunath, B.S., Shin, H.: Color image segmentation. In: CVPR 1999, pp. 2446–2451 (1999)
10. Dimitriou, N., Arandjelović, O., Caie, P.D.: Deep learning for whole slide image analysis: an overview. Front. Med. **6**, 264 (2019)

11. Doignon, C., Nageotte, F., de Mathelin, M.: Detection of grey regions in color images : application to the segmentation of a surgical instrument in robotized laparoscopy. In: 2004 IEEE/RSJ International Conference on Intelligent Robots and Systems 2004. (IROS 2004). Proceedings, vol. 4, pp. 3394–3399, September 2004

12. Esgario, J.G.M., Krohling, R.A., Ventura, J.A.: Deep learning for classification and severity estimation of coffee leaf biotic stress (2019)

13. Esgario, J.G., de Castro, P.B., Tassis, L.M., Krohling, R.A.: An app to assist farmers in the identification of diseases and pests of coffee leaves using deep learning. Inf. Process. Agric. (2021)

14. Esgario, J.G., Krohling, R.A., Ventura, J.A.: Deep learning for classification and severity estimation of coffee leaf biotic stress. Comput. Electron. Agric. **169**, 105162 (2020)

15. Fuentes, A., Yoon, S., Kim, S., Park, D.: A robust deep-learning-based detector for real-time tomato plant diseases and pests recognition. Sensors **17**(9), 2022 (2017)

16. Barbedo, J.G.A., et al.: Annotated plant pathology databases for image-based detection and recognition of diseases. IEEE Latin Am. Trans. **16**(6), 1749–1757 (2018)

17. Gilpin, L.H., Bau, D., Yuan, B.Z., Bajwa, A., Specter, M., Kagal, L.: Explaining explanations: an overview of interpretability of machine learning (2019)

18. Hartigan, J.A., Wong, M.A.: A k-means clustering algorithm. JSTOR Appl. Stat. **28**(1), 100–108 (1979)

19. Hitimana, E., Gwun, O.: Automatic estimation of live coffee leaf infection based on image processing techniques. Comput. Sci. Inf. Technol. (CS IT) (2014). https://doi.org/10.5121/csit.2014.4221

20. Hooker, S., Erhan, D., Kindermans, P.J., Kim, B.: A benchmark for interpretability methods in deep neural networks (2019)

21. Jau, U.L., Teh, C.S., Ng, G.W.: A comparison of RGB and HSI color segmentation in real - time video images: a preliminary study on road sign detection. In: 2008 International Symposium on Information Technology, vol. 4, pp. 1–6 (2008)

22. Khattab, D., Ebied, H., Hussein, A., Tolba, M.: Color image segmentation based on different color space models using automatic GrabCut. Sci. World J. **2014**, 126025 (2014)

23. Liu, B., Yin, C., Liu, Z., Zhang, Y.: Automatic segmentation on cell image fusing gray and gradient information. In: 29th Annual International Conference of the IEEE Engineering in Medicine and Biology Society 2007. EMBS 2007, pp. 5624–5627, August 2007

24. Luo, M.R.: CIELAB. In: Luo, R. (ed.) Encyclopedia of Color Science and Technology, pp. 1–7. Springer, Heidelberg (2014). https://doi.org/10.1007/978-3-642-27851-8_11-1

25. Manso, G.L., Knidel, H., Krohling, R.A., Ventura, J.A.: A smartphone application to detection and classification of coffee leaf miner and coffee leaf rust (2019)

26. Marcos, A., Rodovalho, N.L.S., Backes, A.: Coffee leaf rust detection using convolutional neural network. In: 2019 XV Workshop de Visão Computacional (WVC), pp. 38–42 (2019)

27. Plataniotis, K., Venetsanopoulos, A.: Color Image Processing and Applications. Digital Signal Processing. Springer, Heidelberg (2000). https://doi.org/10.1007/978-3-662-04186-4

28. Rahimzadeganasl, A., Sertel, E.: Automatic building detection based on CIE LUV color space using very high resolution pleiades images. In: 2017 25th Signal Processing and Communications Applications Conference (SIU), pp. 1–4 (2017)

29. Rahman, M., Islam, M.: Segmentation of color image using adaptive threshold-ing and masking with watershed algorithm. In: 2013 International Conference on Informatics, Electronics Vision (ICIEV), pp. 1–6, May 2013
30. Sammut, C., Webb, G.I.: Encyclopedia of Machine Learning, 1st edn. Springer, Boston (2011). https://doi.org/10.1007/978-0-387-30164-8
31. Sanchez-Lopez, J.R., Marin-Hernandez, A., Palacios-Hernandez, E.R., Rios-Figueroa, H.V., Marin-Urias, L.F.: A real-time 3D pose based visual servoing implementation for an autonomous mobile robot manipulator. Procedia Technol. **7**(0), 416–423 (2013). 3rd Iberoamerican Conference on Electronics Engineering and Computer Science, CIIECC 2013
32. Smilkov, D., Thorat, N., Kim, B., Viégas, F., Wattenberg, M.: SmoothGrad: remov-ing noise by adding noise. arXiv, June 2017
33. Soares, J.V.B., Jacobs, D.W.: Efficient segmentation of leaves in semi-controlled conditions. Mach. Vis. Appl. **24**(8), 1623–1643 (2013). https://doi.org/10.1007/s00138-013-0530-0
34. Sørenson, T.: A Method of Establishing Groups of Equal Amplitude in Plant Soci-ology Based on Similarity of Species Content and Its Application to Analyses of the Vegetation on Danish Commons. Biologiske skrifter, I kommission hos E. Munks-gaard (1948)
35. Suhartono, D., Aditya, W., Lestari, M., Yasin, M.: Expert system in detecting coffee plant diseases. Int. J. Electr. Energy 156–162 (2013)
36. Szegedy, C., Vanhoucke, V., Ioffe, S., Shlens, J., Wojna, Z.: Rethinking the incep-tion architecture for computer vision. In: 2016 IEEE Conference on Computer Vision and Pattern Recognition (CVPR), pp. 2818–2826 (2016)
37. Talhinhas, P., et al.: The coffee leaf rust pathogen Hemileia vastatrix: one and a half centuries around the tropics. Mol. Plant Pathol. **18**(8), 1039–1051 (2017)
38. Vezina, M., Ziou, D., Kerouh, F.: Color space identification for image display. In: Kamel, M., Campilho, A. (eds.) ICIAR 2015. LNCS, vol. 9164, pp. 465–472. Springer, Cham (2015). https://doi.org/10.1007/978-3-319-20801-5_51
39. Wang, X., Hänsch, R., Ma, L., Hellwich, O.: Comparison of different color spaces for image segmentation using graph-cut. In: 2014 International Conference on Com-puter Vision Theory and Applications (VISAPP), vol. 1, pp. 301–308 (2014)
40. Yamashita, R., Nishio, M., Do, R.K.G., Togashi, K.: Convolutional neural net-works: an overview and application in radiology. Insights Imaging **9**(4), 611–629 (2018). https://doi.org/10.1007/s13244-018-0639-9
41. Yebasse, M., Shimelis, B., Warku, H., Ko, J., Cheoi, K.J.: Coffee disease visualiza-tion and classification. Plants **10**(6), 1257 (2021)
42. Zhuang, F., et al.: A comprehensive survey on transfer learning. CoRR abs/1911.02685 (2019)

Investigating Generative Neural-Network Models for Building Pest Insect Detectors in Sticky Trap Images for the Peruvian Horticulture

Joel Cabrera[✉] and Edwin Villanueva

Pontifical Catholic University of Peru, Lima, Peru
`a20161442@pucp.edu.pe`, `ervillanueva@pucp.edu.pe`

Abstract. Pest insects are a problem in horticulture so their early detection is important for their control. Sticky traps are an inexpensive way to obtain insect samples, but manually identifying them is a time-consuming task. Building computational models to identify insect species in sticky trap images is therefore highly desirable. However, this is a challenging task due to the difficulty in getting sizeable sets of training images. In this paper, we studied the usefulness of three neural network generative models to synthesize pest insect images (DCGAN, WGAN, and VAE) for augmenting the training set and thus facilitate the induction of insect detector models. Experiments with images of seven species of pest insects of the Peruvian horticulture showed that the WGAN and VAE models are able to learn to generate images of such species. It was also found that the synthesized images can help to induce YOLOv5m detectors with significant gains in detection performance compared to not using synthesized data. A demo app that integrates the detector models can be accessed through the URL https://bit.ly/3uXW0Ee

Keywords: Pest insects detection · Data augmentation · Generative adversarial networks · Variational autoencoders · Deep learning

1 Introduction

One of the main problems in horticulture is the presence of pest insects, which can affect the productivity and quality of crops. In Peru, this problem represents a great challenge due to the artisanal nature of the activity and the lack of affordable technological tools to deal with local pests. The usual way that horticulturists deal with the problem is through the scheduled and indiscriminate application of pesticides, which generates a negative impact on the environment and people [2].

One way to improve the current approach of dealing with insect pests is by getting timely information on insect species and their distribution in crops.

Supported by Pontifical Catholic University of Peru.

J. A. Lossio-Ventura et al. (Eds.): SIMBig 2021, CCIS 1577, pp. 356–369, 2022.
https://doi.org/10.1007/978-3-031-04447-2_24

This can help implement on-necessity pesticide application strategies, which can reduce production costs and environmental impacts. A simple way to sample insect populations in crops is through the deployment of sticky traps [2]. These are pieces of colored sticky paper that attract and immobilize insects when land on them. Despite the cheapness of sticky traps to get insect samples, the process of identifying the specie of the captured insects is a time-consuming task that requires specialized personnel. In this sense, computer vision methods are highly desirable to automate this process [3, 18].

In recent years, some deep learning based models have been proposed to identify insect species in sticky trap images with interesting results [4, 6, 10, 13, 16, 18, 19]. However, inducing this type of models requires considerable amounts of training images of the target species so that the model can learn the particular patterns of the species. Obtaining a sizeable set of images of pest insects is generally one of the most difficult part in the model construction process. For the case of Peru, at the best of our knowledge there is not a public collection of images of the most relevant insect species for the Peruvian horticulture.

In this paper we investigated the application of synthetic data generation techniques, such as generative neural models, in order to build a sizeable and realistic set of training images that serve to induce effective models for the identification and classification of insect species in sticky traps for Peruvian horticulture. The investigated models are three recent neural network architectures: Conditional Deep Convolutional Generative Adversarial Network (DCGAN) [5, 12], Confitional Wasserstein GAN (WGAN) [1] and Conditional Variational Autoencoder (VAE) [8]. These techniques are evaluated in their usefulness to induce effective insect classifiers and compared against the classical data augmentation technique based on image perturbations (rotations, mirroring, modifications of brightness, contrast, etc.).

The rest of the paper is organized as follow. Section 2 describe the data collection and pre-processing, the generative models and the detection model considered in the study. Section 3 presents the results and evaluation of the generative and detection models. Finally, in Sect. 4 we conclude the work with a summary and future works.

2 Materials and Methods

2.1 Data Collection and Pre-processing

For training the generative models we collected an initial set of images of the following insect species relevant in the Peruvian horticulture: *Prodiplosis longifila*, *Liriomyza huidobrensis*, *Brevicoryne brassicae*, *Trips tabaci*, *Bemisia tabaci*, *Macrolophus pygmaeus*, *Nesidiocoris tenuis*. For the last three species we use images of the "Yellow Sticky Trap Dataset". For the other species we scraped web pages with information of pest insects. All the images were pre-processed (cut, filled and scaled) to obtain patches of 64×64 pixels containing each one a single insect. The number of collected images for each specie is showed in Table 1.

Table 1. Total of pest insects images per species and source.

Species	Total of images	Source
Prodiplosis longifila	35	Web
Liriomyza huidobrensis	112	Web
Brevicoryne brassicae	58	Web
Trips tabaci	53	Web
Bemisia tabaci	5807	Yellow Sticky Trap Dataset
Macrolophus pygmaeus	1619	Yellow Sticky Trap Dataset
Nesidiocoris tenuis	688	Yellow Sticky Trap Dataset
Total	**8372**	

The collected dataset was further increased using a series of image transformation procedures, commonly used as image data augmentation techniques. We applied: random horizontal and vertical flip, random rotation and color jitter. Figure 1 shows the result of applying these transformation procedures several times to a single base image.

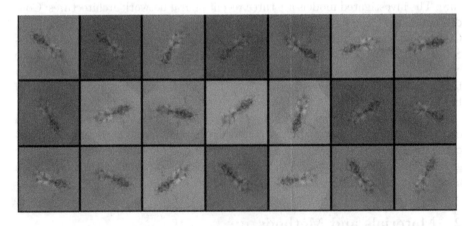

Fig. 1. Images resulting of applying traditional image data augmentation procedures to a single insect image (upper-left image).

2.2 Generative Models

We implement generative models that learn to synthesize pest insect images to be used as data augmentation procedures for subsequent classifier induction. The models implemented are conditioned in the species to be generated. All generative models are adjusted with the data generated as described in the previous section. Next we describe the implemented generative models.

Conditional Deep Convolutional Generative Adversarial Network (DCGAN). This model, initially proposed in [5,12], is composed by two modules: a generator and a discriminator, which are trained in an adversarial game. The goal of the generator is to synthesize images that are similar to the original ones and the discriminator tries to discriminate the original images from the synthetic ones. The output of the discriminator is used as feedback to the generator to improve the quality of the images and fool the discriminator so this can not discriminate if an image is real or fake. Both modules are trained jointly in order to facilitate the task to the generator at the beginning of the training. If the discriminator is pre-trained to discriminate the images, the generator would not have the opportunity to learn to produce good quality images. Figure 2 shows the high level architecture of the DCGAN with its integrating modules.

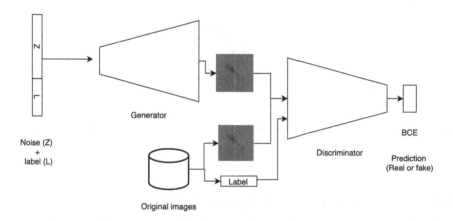

Fig. 2. High level architecture of the generative DCGAN model used to synthesize images of pest insects.

The generator is composed of five transposed convolutional layers. Each layer, except the last one, is followed by a batch normalization layer and ReLu as activation function. In the last it is used the tanh activation function. The input of this module is a vector of length 64 of random noise concatenated with a one-hot label vector of the image class (insect specie) to be generated.

The discriminator is composed of four convolutional layers, each one followed by a batch normalization layer and LeakyRelu as activation function. In this case the inputs of the module are the original images or the fake ones concatenated with the one-hot label vector as channels.

Conditional Wasserstein GAN (WGAN). This model, originally proposed in [1], replaces the second module of the traditional GAN, (the *discriminator*) with a module named *critic*. Instead of classifying the images into real or fake labels, the critic outputs a numerical score that indicates how realistic an image is. This score brings more information to the generator to improve the image generation. In order to ensure that the output score is valid, the critic needs to be 1-Lipschitz continuous (1-L). In other words, the norm of the gradient should be at most 1. A penalty factor is added to the loss function to enforce 1-L continuity, this factor is calculated with the interpolation between real and generated images. Figure 3 shows the high level architecture of the WGAN model.

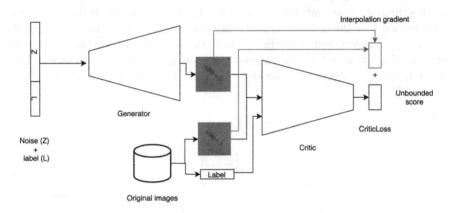

Fig. 3. High level architecture of the WGAN [1] model used to synthesize images of pest insects.

Conditional Variational Autoencoder (VAE). This model, initially proposed in [8], is composed of an encoder and a decoder. The encoder has as input the original image concatenated with the one-hot label vector of the image class. It encodes the image to a set of normal distributions. Then, a vector is sampled from these distributions and concatenated again with the one-hot label vector in order to be passed to the decoder. The decoder reconstructs the image from this vector. The decoder is used to generate images from a random noise vector concatenated with the one-hot label vector of the target class. Figure 4 shows the high level architecture of the VAE model.

2.3 Generation of Sticky Trap Images

The trained generative models were used to synthesize sticky trap images to train and validate insect species detectors. We construct yellow sticky trap images by placing model-generated insect images randomly in an area of dimensions compatible with what is found in real settings. Original images obtained in the pre-processing step (Sect. 2.1) are also considered to be placed in the resulting images using a mixing ratio. In the experimental phase we test different mixing ratios. To simulate realistic conditions we also consider the addition of different objects in the sticky traps images, like sticks, rocks and random noise. All the

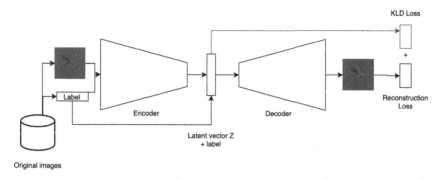

Fig. 4. High level architecture of the model VAE [8] model used to synthesize images of pest insects.

information about the class of the images added, the location of the pest insects in the image as bounding boxes and the proportion of generated and real images is stored in separated files. These files were required to train the detection model.

2.4 Detection with YOLOv5

In order to detect the pest insects in the yellow sticky traps images we use the pretrained model YOLOv5m [7] and fine tuned it in the custom datasets. In this version of the model, Cross Stage Partial Network (CSPNet) [14] is used as the model back- bone and Path Aggregation Network (PANet) [9] as the neck for feature aggregation (see Fig. 5). The head is retrained to make the prediction of the desired classes and bounding boxes of the species of insects.

3   Results and Discussion

In this section we describe the experiments performed and results obtained. First, we evaluate the three types of generative models described above in their ability to reproduce the diversity of the insect images of each target specie in the original dataset. Next, we present results about the usefulness of the synthesized datasets to induce good models for detection and classification of pest insects in sticky trap images.

All models were implemented in Python language using the Pytorch deep learning library. Experiments were carried on a Lambda Deep Learning Work-station (lambdalabs.com) with two GeForce RTX 2080 Ti GPU cards installed in a system running Ubuntu 18.04.5 LTS operating system.

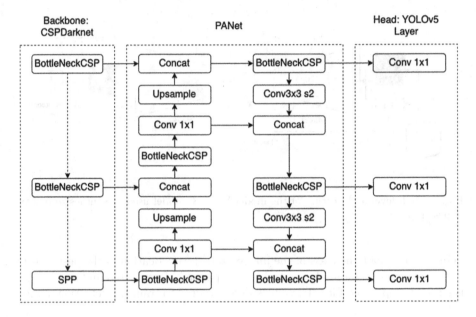

Fig. 5. YOLOv5 Architecture [7] (SPP: Spatial Pyramid Partial Network, CSP: Cross Stage Partial Network, Conv: Convolutional layer)

3.1 Performance Evaluation of Pest Insect Image Synthesis

Each trained generative model was qualitatively and quantitatively evaluated on its ability to generate realistic insect images and their variabilities of the target species.

For the qualitative evaluation, we generated 500 images of each insect specie with each generative model. Then, we applied the t-SNE technique [11] to find a low-dimension representation of the images. This procedure was also performed in the original image set obtained in Sect. 2.1. Figure 6 shows a scatter plot of the 2D representation of the original images reduced with t-SNE. Figures 7, 8 and 9 show equivalent representations for the images generated with each generative model. We can visually appreciate that the models WGAN and VAE seems to have learned closely the distribution of the original image set. All separated clusters and overlapped clusters in the original set are also reproduced in the synthetic sets generated with that models. The DCGAN model seems to have had difficulty learning the variety of the images in most species since it tends to produce very similar images for each specie (very narrow clusters in the t-SNE representation in Fig. 7), problem known as mode collapse.

To have a more objective analysis of the capabilities of the models in learning the varieties of each species, we calculated the Universal Divergence (UD) [15]. The UD metric assess the divergence between two distributions: the distribution of the t-SNE embedding of the original images of a given insect species against the distribution of the t-SNE embedding of the model-generated images of the

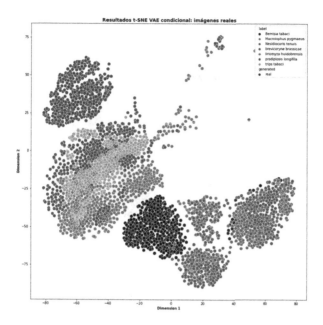

Fig. 6. Two-dimensional t-SNE representation of 3500 original pest insects images. Colors identify the insect species.

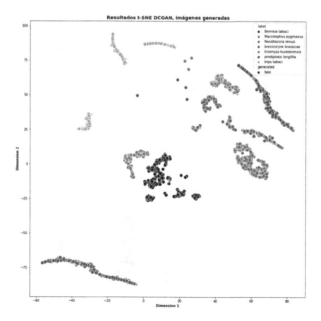

Fig. 7. Two-dimensional t-SNE representation of 3500 pest insects images generated by the DCGAN model. Colors identify the insect species.

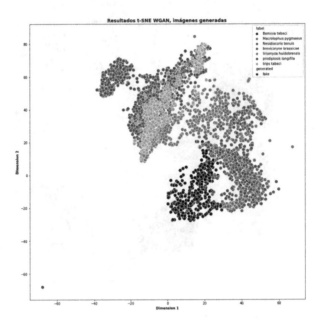

Fig. 8. Two-dimensional t-SNE representation of 3500 pest insects images generated by the WGAN model. Colors identify the insect species.

Fig. 9. Two-dimensional t-SNE representation of 3500 pest insects images generated by the VAE model. Colors identify the insect species.

same insect species. Lower UD values mean that the distributions are closer. Table 2 shows the resulting UD metrics for each insect species and generative model. These results suggest that VAE and WGAN have similar capabilities to capture the distribution of the original images, being the VAE model slightly better, as evidenced in the average UD. We also verify that DCGAN model present the most divergent distributions compared to the original images, which was also observed in the qualitative evaluation (Fig. 7).

Table 2. Divergence between real images and genereted images per model and species.

	DCGAN	WGAN	VAE
Bemisia tabaci	7.207	7.431	7.058
Macrolophus pygmaeus	6.953	7.227	7.264
Nesidiocoris tenuis	7.247	6.604	6.878
Brevicoryne brassicae	6.759	6.022	6.070
Liriomyza huidobrensis	5.721	5.880	5.742
Prodiplosis longifila	7.707	6.278	5.997
Trips tabaci	7.475	6.507	6.494
Average	7.010	6.564	**6.500**

3.2 Evaluation of Pest Insect Detection and Classification

To further assess the utility of the synthetic data, we induced YOLOv5m models with such data and evaluated their performance in identifying and classifying insect species in test sticky trap images.

Following the procedure described in Sect. 2.3 we generated six sets of sticky trap images, each set containing 300 yellow sticky trap images, each image with around 100 insects of the seven target species. Figure 10 shows an example of a generated sticky trap. The difference between the sets is the proportion of the synthetic pest insects added to the sticky trap. We tested the following proportions: 0% (only real images), 20%, 40%, 60%, 80% and 100% (only synthetic insect images). Figure 11 shows an example of the output of a YOLOv5m model (bounding boxes and species labels) in some sticky trap image.

To evaluate the detection performance of the YOLOv5m models we use the area under the curve precision-recall (AUC) in testing data. We evaluate this metric per species. Table 3 shows the AUC metrics of the models trained with the 6 different proportions of synthetic data and for each species. We can observe that in five of the seven species the AUC metric improves when we use a fraction of synthetic data in the training set. In some cases the increase in performance has been more than 14% (Liriomyza huidobrensis). In the species Prodiplosis longifila and Trips tabaci no performance improvement was observed with any proportion of synthetic data. For the case of Prodiplosis longifila, this species is quite different from the rest, as observed in the t-SNE plot (Fig. 6), so its

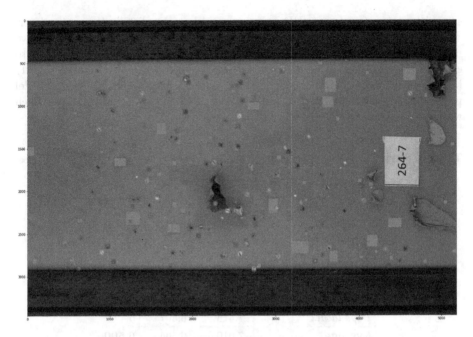

Fig. 10. Example of sticky trap image generated with 20% of synthetic pest insects images and other elements found in real settings.

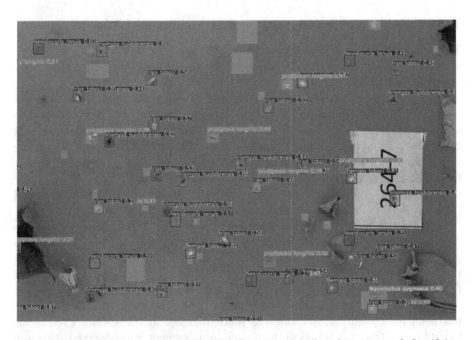

Fig. 11. Example of an output of the YOLOv5m model after detecting and classifying the insects in a sticky trap image.

Table 3. AUC metrics of different YOLOv5m models (columns) trained with different proportions of synthetic data and differentiated by insect species (rows). Last column indicates the percentage difference in AUC of the best model using synthetic data in relation to the model trained without synthetic data

Species	# Imgs.	Use of generated imgs.						Max. Diff.
		0%	20%	40%	60%	80%	100%	
Bemisia tabaci	5807	0,91	0,91	0,92	0,87	**0,93**	0,90	**2,10%**
Macrolophus pygmaeus	1619	0,70	0,68	0,72	0,72	0,75	**0,81**	**10,60%**
Nesidiocoris tenuis	688	0,61	0,52	**0,65**	0,36	0,44	0,49	**4,00%**
Brevicoryne brassicae	58	0,47	**0,51**	0,37	0,26	0,40	0,47	**4,50%**
Liriomyza huidobrensis	112	0,81	0,81	0,87	0,86	0,89	**0,95**	**14,60%**
Prodiplosis longifila	35	**0,77**	0,75	0,61	0,44	0,44	0,51	**0,00%**
Trips tabaci	53	**0,52**	0,49	0,45	0,44	0,42	0,42	**0,00%**

identification is not problematic and the generation of synthetic data is not very helpful. For the species trips tabaci, this has high overlapping with Brevicoryne brassicae. Probably the base images of these species with which the generative models were constructed have not had enough diversity to capture discriminating features and it would be necessary to have more real data to learn more details about these species.

A demo web app was deployed integrating the detector models and a simple user interface. The user can submit its sticky trap images and obtain the resulting detection bounding boxes as in Fig. 11. This tool can be accessed through the url https://bit.ly/3uXW0Ee.

4   Conclusion

Automating the identification of insect pests in sticky trap images is highly desirable. However, this is a challenging task due to the difficulty in obtaining sizeble sets of training images. In this article we studied the usefulness of three generative models in synthesizing pest insect images (DCGAN, WGAN and VAE) in order to increase the training set and thus facilitate the induction of identification and detection models. In a series of experiments with images of seven insect species of interest for the Peruvian horticulture we demonstrated that the WGAN and VAE models are able to capture the variability of the images of such species. Additionally, it was found the synthetic data generated by such models can help to induce YOLOv5m detectors with significant gains in identification performance compared to not using synthesized data.

The present work can be extended with the use of novel generative models. One example of this is the model SAGAN [17] that use self–attention layers in order to learn better spatial and structural information from the images. This can be important to induce the model to learn features like the shape of the insects that can be more relevant differences between the species than texture or color, which are well learned with generative models based on convolutional layers

(DCGAN, WGAN and VAE). Also the final detection model can be improved to protect it from adversarial attacks with images not related to pest insects and avoid wrong detections and classifications.

Acknowledgement. The authors gratefully acknowledge Artificial Intelligence Group of Pontifical Catholic University of Peru (IA–PUCP) for the support with the computational infrastructure for the experimental part of the present study.

References

1. Arjovsky, M., Chintala, S., Bottou, L.: Wasserstein generative adversarial networks. In: Precup, D., Teh, Y.W. (eds.) Proceedings of the 34th International Conference on Machine Learning. Proceedings of Machine Learning Research, vol. 70, pp. 214–223. PMLR (2017)
2. Cañedo, V., Alfaro-Tapia, A., Kroschel, J.: Manejo Integrado de plagas de insectos en hortalizas Principios y referencias técnicas para la Sierra Central de Perú (2011)
3. Cho, J., Choi, J., Qiao, M., Kim, H., Uhm, K., Chon, T.S.: Automatic identification of whiteflies, aphids and thrips in greenhouse based on image analysis. Int. J. Math. Comput. Simul. **1**, 46–53 (2007)
4. Espinoza, K., Valera, D.L., Torres, J.A., López, A., Molina-Aiz, F.D.: Combination of image processing and artificial neural networks as a novel approach for the identification of Bemisia tabaci and Frankliniella occidentalis on sticky traps in greenhouse agriculture. Comput. Electron. Agric. **127**, 495–505 (2016)
5. Goodfellow, I.J., et al.: Generative adversarial networks (2014)
6. Huang, J., Zeng, M., Li, W., Meng, X.: Application of data augmentation and migration learning in identification of diseases and pests in tea trees. In: 2019 Boston, Massachusetts July 7- July 10, 2019. American Society of Agricultural and Biological Engineers (2019)
7. Jocher, G., et al.: ultralytics/yolov5: v5.0 - YOLOv5-P6 1280 models, AWS, Supervise.ly and YouTube integrations (2021)
8. Kingma, D.P., Welling, M.: Auto-encoding variational bayes (2014)
9. Liu, S., Qi, L., Qin, H., Shi, J., Jia, J.: Path aggregation network for instance segmentation. In: Proceedings of the IEEE Conference on Computer Vision and Pattern Recognition (2018)
10. Lu, C.Y., Arcega Rustia, D.J., Lin, T.T.: Generative adversarial network based image augmentation for insect pest classification enhancement. IFAC-PapersOnLine **52**(30), 1–5 (2019)
11. van der Maaten, L., Hinton, G.: Viualizing data using t-SNE. J. Mach, Learn. Res. **9**, 2579–2605 (2008)
12. Radford, A., Metz, L., Chintala, S.: Unsupervised representation learning with deep convolutional generative adversarial networks (2016)
13. Rustia, D.J., Chao, J.J., Chung, J.Y., Lin, T.T.: An online unsupervised deep learning approach for an automated pest insect monitoring system. In: 2019 ASABE Annual International Meeting (2019)
14. Wang, C.Y., Liao, H.Y.M., Yeh, I.H., Wu, Y.H., Chen, P.Y., Hsieh, J.W.: CSPNet: a new backbone that can enhance learning capability of CNN (2019)
15. Wang, Q., Kulkarni, S.R., Verdu, S.: Divergence estimation for multidimensional densities via k-nearest-neighbor distances. IEEE Trans. Inf. Theory **55**(5), 2392–2405 (2009)

16. Xia, C., Chon, T.S., Ren, Z., Lee, J.M.: Automatic identification and counting of small size pests in greenhouse conditions with low computational cost. Ecol. Inform. **29**, 139–146 (2015)
17. Zhang, H., Goodfellow, I., Metaxas, D., Odena, A.: Self-attention generative adversarial networks (2019)
18. Zhong, Y., Gao, J., Lei, Q., Zhou, Y.: A vision-based counting and recognition system for flying insects in intelligent agriculture. Sensors **18**, 1489 (2018)
19. Zhou, H., Miao, H., Li, J., Jian, F., Jayas, D.S.: A low-resolution image restoration classifier network to identify stored-grain insects from images of sticky boards. Comput. Electron. Agric. **162**, 593–601 (2019)

Making Licensing of Content and Data Explicit with Semantics and Blockchain

David Gatta[1], Kilian Hinteregger[1], and Anna Fensel[1,2](✉) ![ORCID]

[1] Department of Computer Science, University of Innsbruck, Technikerstr. 21a, 6020 Innsbruck, Austria
{David.Gatta,kilian.hinteregger}@student.uibk.ac.at
[2] Wageningen Data Competence Center and Consumption and Healthy Lifestyles Chair Group, Wageningen University and Research, 6708 PB Wageningen, The Netherlands
anna.fensel@wur.nl

Abstract. Creation and reuse of content and data are on the rise. Tracing of who, when and how has created and modified content and data in an explicit manner becomes paramount for transparent, explainable, efficient and fair digital ecosystems. We specifically address a challenge that there is currently no uniform method to link data and content with licenses explicitly, immutably and in a traceable way (with authentication). Thus we have created a blockchain-based method which makes it possible to attach semantic licenses with data and content. Ethereum and the Data Licenses and Clearance Center - "DALICC", a software framework for automated clearance of rights, are used as a bases for our prototype implementation for the license annotation (see: https://github.com/kilian hnt/dalicc-license-annotator). Particular care is taken to ensure that the solution remains generic. Its practical feasibility, such as compliance with requirements, particularly, authentication, affordable deployment and usage costs, is positively evaluated.

Keywords: Data · Content · Licenses · Semantics · Immutability · Blockchain · Etherium

1 Introduction

Creation of derivative data works is often accompanied by legal uncertainty about usage rights and high costs in the clearance of licensing issues. As one of the solutions to lower the costs of rights clearance and stimulating the data economy, the Data Licenses Clearance Center - DALICC project [1] has developed a software framework that supports automated clearance of rights issues in the creation of derivative data works. The solution is based on semantic technology, to ensure explicitness in license representation and decision making processes.

This paper addresses a further challenge, namely, that currently there is no uniform method to link data and content with licenses in an explicit and traceable manner. Currently license information is often only available as a human-readable text, but in our digitized world, it would be advantageous if computers could also read and interpret the rights granted in order to clear license issues quickly, as enabled by DALICC. However, DALICC, solutions on which it is built (such as ODRL, that can be also used to make license information explicit [2]) and other potentially relevant solutions (such as PROV-O [3] and SOLID [4], for assisting people to define how their data are managed) are not providing a possibility to link assign semantic licenses to owners in an immutable and traceable manner. The latter, however, is possible to make on blockchain, in a practical manner for tracing the ownership and right information of primary and derivative works. Therefore, this work aims to find such appropriate method to attach semantic licenses to data and content. To achieve this, an approach with a blockchain was chosen to design the entire system in a decentralized and therefore trustworthy manner. Inherent traceability of a blockchain is especially important for the use cases such as content and data creation and reuse. Specifically, the Ethereum platform was chosen for the implementation, because it is one of the most popular platforms for decentralized applications in the world [5].

The paper is structured as follows. The problem statement, our approach with functional and non-functional requirements are discussed in the next section. Further, the implementation section explains the chosen technologies and provides details about backend and frontend of the implementation. Finally, the evaluation and the conclusion sections conclude the paper.

2 Problem Statement

DALICC helps to determine which content and data can be shared with whom to what extent under which conditions. There is yet currently no standardized way to license digital content to allow both - machines and humans - to read and interpret the rights granted. In this section, we discuss the requirements of an application that can address this problem, continuing with the description of the technologies we chose to realize a prototype of the application and finally our implementation and evaluation.

2.1 Functional Requirements

The following functional requirements are placed on the application to meet the given problem by us. An unauthenticated user is a user who does not have any credentials. Hence, an unauthenticated user must not be signed in to make some actions. In contrast, an authenticated user is a user who has confirmed his/her identity so that each of his/her actions can be assigned to him/her. A licensor is an authenticated user who has already licensed data or content and is only referred to as the licensor in the context of these data or content. The requirements, that relate to the basic functions of the solution, are as follows (see also Fig. 1):

- An authenticated user must be able to license a file.
- The licensor of a specific file must be able to change the license of the file.
- An authenticated user must be able to license the content of a URI.
- The licensor of a specific URI must be able to change the license of the URI.
- An unauthenticated user must be able to get the license information associated with a specific file.

- An unauthenticated user must be able to get the license information associated with a specific URI.

2.2 Non-functional Requirements

In addition to the above mentioned functional requirements, the application must meet additional non-functional requirements. These are provided to ensure that the application has a certain level of security and trustfulness:

- There must be no authority that can act independently and can falsify license information, i.e. the representation of the licensor and the representation of the license.
- The license information must be publicly stored somewhere, so that anyone can see it.
- The license information must be secured so that no one can change it, except the licensor itself.
- To save storage, only a unique reference of the licensed data should be stored and not the entire data.
- The licenses should be represented by a reference to a license in the DALICC License Library [6].
- The whole licensing process should cost acceptably for the users (e.g. less than 1€) to ensure a realistic and practical solution for different industries (e.g. creative industries).

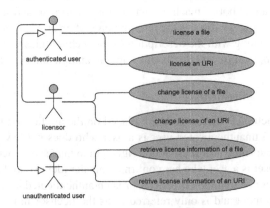

Fig. 1. Functional requirements visualized using a use-case diagram.

3   Implementation

The source code of the implemented application, as it is detailed further, is published openly on GitHub [7].

3.1 Technology Choices

According to Antonopoulos and Wood [8], a DApp is an application that is mostly or entirely decentralized. Additionally, a DApp has no downtime and is continuously available as long as the decentralized platform, which the application is using to provide the service, is operating. Thus DApp is well suited for the backend of the application. The application is mostly implemented using HTML, CSS and JavaScript.

Ethereum is a platform for building decentralized applications [9, 10]. It combines the blockchain technology, introduced by Nakamoto [11] and a Turing-complete programming language, to make it possible to execute computer programs called smart contracts. These properties of the Ethereum network make it a solid base to meet the application requirements.

The SHA-3 family consists of four cryptographic hash functions and was released by the National Institute of Standards and Technology (NIST) in 2015 after nine years of research [12, 13]. This hash algorithm is well suited for this application and its application Vue.js, CryptoJS, web3.js, Bignumber.js and Axios are used from javascript libraries.

3.2 Backend and Frontend

Backend Logic. The backend logic of the application is built on top of the Ethereum Platform. It is split up in three smart contracts, and is visualized in Fig. 2.

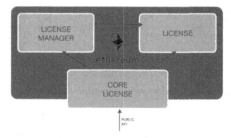

Fig. 2. Simplified visualisation of the smart contracts and their relations.

The components are interacting as follows when performing their core functions:

- *Creation of the Core-License contract.* Once the Core-License Contract is created, it also creates the License-Manager contract. The constructor of the License-Manager contract is called and as the parameter, the address of the Core-License contract is passed. This address later serves to check whether the call comes from the Core-License contract or not.
- *Licensing some data or content.* To license some data first the SHA3-256 hash of these data must be calculated. Then the function licenseData (uint hashValue, string memory licenseUri) of the Core-License contract must be called, which takes the hash value of the data as the first parameter and the URI of a license as the second parameter.

- *Changing the license of some data or content.* Changing the license of certain data can be done in the same way as described in the previous step. It should be noted that only the licensor itself can change the license.

Frontend. The frontend of the application was realized as mentioned above as a web application using Vue.js. The connections between the technologies are as follows web3.js is used to communicate with the Ethereum backend. The backend is set up before the application is published and the address of the Core License contract gets inserted into the slot provided in the code of the frontend. Bignumber.js is used to work with the hash values created by CryptoJS and to submit them to the backend using web3.js. The license titles and URI's get retrieved using an AJAX request from the DALICC License Library. In Fig. 3 we can see a simplified overview of the interactions between the frontend and the backend when a user licenses a file.

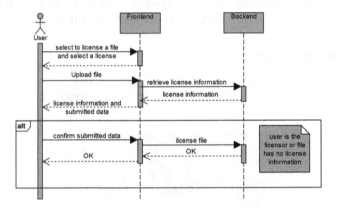

Fig. 3. Simplified sequence diagram for licensing a file.

The workflow for using the solution is as follows. To license a file or retrieve its license information, the user is guided through various steps. First, the user is prompted to choose if he/she wants to license content (step 1, 2 and 3), named as "license your work", or to retrieve license information about content (step 1 and 2), named as "retrieve license information", as shown in Fig. 4. This selection is made by clicking on the respective button. Subsequently, he/she has to follow these steps:

1. The user gets asked to choose whether he/she want license an URI or a file. If the user wants to license a URI or a file, then he/she can select a license from the DALICC License Library using an autocomplete combobox. The licenses are loaded from the DALICC License Library with an AJAX request. If the DALICC License Library is not reachable, the user gets displayed a warning and a predefined collection of licenses from the DALICC License Library. If the user only wants to retrieve the license information, the licenses do not get retrieved from the DALICC license library and the user cannot select a license.

2. In this step, the user must enter a URI in a text box or select a file using a file input field. Subsequently, he/she confirms his/her request by pressing a button. Then the SHA3-256 hash value of the URI or the file content is calculated which is used to retrieve the license information from the backend. To require no authentication and thus, a DApp able browser, the web3 provider Infura [14] is used. Now the license information is displayed to the user if it exists. If the user is the licensor or if the content is not already licensed then the user can continue with step 3. Otherwise, the user cannot continue with the process. To check if the user is the licensor the address given in the injected web3 API is compared with the licensors address retrieved from the backend.

3. Start licensing: in the last step the user can check his/her submitted data and then he/she can confirm and start the process by pressing the "start licensing" button. The SHA3-256 hash value is calculated and passed by the contract to the web3 Javascript interface. Depending on the user's DApp Browser, he/she receives a notification about the incoming transaction which he/she has to confirm. If he/she confirms the transaction, in our application the returned hash is displayed.

Fig. 4. Frontend positioning and entry page (licensing and license retrieval).

4 Evaluation

Building the application as a decentralized application on top of the Ethereum platform helped to meet the TRADE principles from the FAIR TRADE Framework [15]. Here, the property "Autonomous" of the FAIR TRADE Principle is not fully fulfilled, because the data in the blockchain is immutable and cannot be deleted. The blockchain is distributed and published all over the world and thus the data saved there can be accessed globally by anyone [8]. Since the only information that gets saved in the Ethereum network is the Ethereum address of a licensor, the hash value of the licensed data and the URI of a license, it does not get in conflict with the requirements. The licensor still has the choice of whether to remain anonymous behind the Ethereum address or indicate that he/she is the licensor.

Moreover, there are five cases, where the cost differs:

1) Deploying of the smart contract system, which has to be done only once.
2) License data or content when the smart contract for the license was not already created.
3) License data or content when the smart contract for the license was already created.
4) Modifying the license of some data or content when the smart contract for the new license was not already created.
5) Modifying the license of some data or content when the smart contract for the new license was already created.

These five cases were tested using the Rinkeby test network [16], an Ethereum test network that simulates the conditions of the main Ethereum network, so that developers can test their smart contracts for free, approaching the real life deployment settings. We have received the following results:

1. The smart contract system was deployed three times and each time the Gas (refers to the fee, or pricing value, required for the execution of code on the Ethereum platform) used was 1521249.
2. This case was tested five times with the results shown in Table 1.

Table 1. Gas costs for licensing where the license contract does not exist.

License URI	Hash value	Gas used
https://www.dalicc.net/license-library/CreativeCommonsAttribution20Austria	1	609177
https://www.dalicc.net/license-library/GnuFreeDocumentationLicense	2	609081
https://www.dalicc.net/license-library/BSD-4	3	587853
https://www.dalicc.net/license-library/GNU_GPL_v3	4	587913
https://www.dalicc.net/license-library/MIT	5	587829

3. Also this case was tested five times with the results shown in Table 2.

Table 2. Gas costs for licensing where the license contract exists.

License URI	Hash value	Gas used
https://www.dalicc.net/license-library/CreativeCommonsAttribution20Austria	10	78788
https://www.dalicc.net/license-library/GnuFreeDocumentationLicense	11	78692
https://www.dalicc.net/license-library/BSD-4	12	77782
https://www.dalicc.net/license-library/GNU_GPL_v3	13	77842
https://www.dalicc.net/license-library/MIT	14	77758

4. This case was tested five times with the results shown in Table 3.

Table 3. Gas costs for modifying the license of some data where the new license contract does not exist.

License URI	Hash value	Gas used
https://www.dalicc.net/license-library/Cc010Universal	10	570487
https://www.dalicc.net/license-library/OdcOpenDatabaseLicense	11	570583
https://www.dalicc.net/license-library/TheZlibLibpngLicense	12	570559
https://www.dalicc.net/license-library/Wtfpl	13	570379
https://www.dalicc.net/license-library/EclipsePublicLicense20	14	570583

5. This case was tested five times with the results shown in Table 4.

Table 4. Gas costs for modifying the license of some data where the new license contract already exists.

License URI	Hash value	Gas used
https://www.dalicc.net/license-library/MIT	10	60284
https://www.dalicc.net/license-library/CreativeCommonsAttribution20Austria	11	61314
https://www.dalicc.net/license-library/GNU_GPL_v3	12	60368
https://www.dalicc.net/license-library/BSD-4	13	60308
https://www.dalicc.net/license-library/GnuFreeDocumentationLicense	14	61218

Assuming a Gas price of 3 Gwei and assuming that 1 Ether has a value of 111 Euro, we get the prices shown in Table 5. Those results show us that we can expect that the cost will be acceptable for businesses (under 1€) and therefore, the non-functional requirements are met.

Table 5. Prices for interaction with the smart contract system.

Action	Price
Deploying contract	0.50657€
Licensing data with not existing license contract	around 0.20€
Licensing data with existing license contract	around 0.03€
Modifying License of data with not existing license contract	around 0.20€
Modifying License of data with existing license contract	around 0.02€

Finally, we must check if the implemented application also meets the functional requirements. Confirming these, we have ensured that the licensing attachment processes through the app are executable, in a user-friendly manner. As described in the implementation of the frontend, the user has the option of specifying a URI or selecting a file, then retrieving the license information of the data, licensing the data or changing the license of the data, if he/she is allowed to. Since Infura is used as a web3 provider to retrieve the license information, the user does not need a DApp-enabled browser and hence, does not need to authenticate for retrieving license information. Now also the functional requirements have been met, so all the requirements that have been placed on the application are met.

5 Conclusion

A solution to explicitly attach licenses to data and content has been created and published as an open source, basing on the DALICC License Library. For this purpose, an approach using the Ethereum platform was designed and implemented to keep the system trusted, autonomous, distributed and decentralized. Thus, a licensing system has been created which preserves the integrity of the license information and also provides a high availability of that information. We also paid attention to usability during the implementation and tried to keep the learning curve flat. To do this, the user is guided through the licensing process step by step and unnecessary steps have been automated. We have also evaluated the costs for the user, identifying them as being acceptable for typical possible usage purposes. One limitation here is that we evaluated the simplest scenarios (one-step processes of license management): in more elaborated real life settings it would be necessary to study aggregated costs of multiple transactions (modifications of licensing, multiple files, etc.) typical of data publication scenarios. Further investigations may address the integration of the solution into practical settings, e.g. defining the authorities set up managing such traceable explicit licensing, as well as associated workflows and responsibilities. This may vary from domain to domain, and handled differently in different cases: some may be more centralized (e.g. insurance data, with few parties) and some more distributed (e.g. smart cities, with multiple parties).

Acknowledgements. This work is supported by the smashHit European Union project funded under Horizon 2020 (grant number: 871477) and by the Austrian Federal Ministry of Transport, Innovation and Technology (BMVIT) DALICC project (grant number: 855396).

References

1. Pellegrini, T., Mireles, V., Steyskal, S., Panasiuk, O., Fensel, A., Kirrane, S.: Automated rights clearance using semantic web technologies: the DALICC framework. In: Hoppe, T., Humm, B., Reibold, A. (eds.) Semantic Applications, pp. 203–218. Springer, Heidelberg (2018). https://doi.org/10.1007/978-3-662-55433-3_14. DALICC project: www.dalicc.net
2. Steyskal, S., Polleres, A.: Defining expressive access policies for linked data using the ODRL ontology 2.0. In: Proceedings of the 10th International Conference on Semantic Systems, pp. 20–23 (2014)
3. Lebo, T., et al.: PROV-O: the PROV ontology. W3C Recommendation (2013)
4. Buyle, R., et al.: Streamlining governmental processes by putting citizens in control of their personal data. In: Chugunov, A., Khodachek, I., Misnikov, Y., Trutnev, D. (eds.) EGOSE 2019. CCIS, vol. 1135, pp. 346–359. Springer, Cham (2020). https://doi.org/10.1007/978-3-030-39296-3_26

5. ADApp Statistics. https://www.stateofthedapps.com/stats
6. Panasiuk, O., Steyskal, S., Havur, G., Fensel, A., Kirrane, S.: Modeling and reasoning over data licenses. In: Gangemi, A., et al. (eds.) ESWC 2018. LNCS, vol. 11155, pp. 218–222. Springer, Cham (2018). https://doi.org/10.1007/978-3-319-98192-5_41
7. DALICC License Annotator. https://github.com/kilianhnt/dalicc-license-annotator
8. Antonopoulos, A.M., Wood, G.: Mastering Ethereum: Building Smart Contracts and DAPPs. O'Reilly Media, Newton (2018)
9. Wood, G.: Ethereum: a secure decentralised generalised transaction ledger. Ethereum Project Yellow Paper **151**(2014), 1–32 (2014)
10. Buterin, V.: A next-generation smart contract and decentralized application platform. White paper 3.37 (2014). https://github.com/ethereum/wiki/wiki/White-Paper
11. Nakamoto, S.: Bitcoin: a peer-to-peer electronic cash system (2008)
12. Dworkin, M.J.: Sha-3 standard: permutation-based hash and extendable-output functions. Technical report (2015)
13. NIST: NIST releases Sha-3 cryptographic hash standard (2015). https://www.nist.gov/news-events/news/2015/08/nist-releases-sha-3-cryptographic-hash-standard
14. Infura. https://infura.io
15. Domingue, J., Third, A., Ramachandran, M.: The fair trade framework for assessing decentralised data solutions. In: Companion Proceedings of the 2019 World Wide Web Conference, pp. 866–882. ACM (2019)
16. Rinkeby Test Network. https://www.rinkeby.io

Deep Neural Networks Based Solar Flare Prediction Using Compressed Full-disk Line-of-sight Magnetograms

Chetraj Pandey$^{(\boxtimes)}$, Rafal A. Angryk, and Berkay Aydin

Georgia State University, Atlanta, GA 30302, USA
{cpandey1,rangryk,baydin2}@gsu.edu

Abstract. The efforts in solar flare prediction have been engendered by the advancements in machine learning and deep learning methods. We present a new approach to flare prediction using full-disk compressed magnetogram images with Convolutional Neural Networks. We selected three prediction modes, among which two are binary for predicting the occurrence of $\geq$M1.0 and $\geq$C4.0 class flares and one is a multi-class mode for predicting the occurrence of <C4.0, [$\geq$C4.0, <M1.0] and $\geq$M1.0 within the next 24 h. We perform our experiments in all three modes using three well-known pretrained CNN models—AlexNet, VGG16 and ResNet34. For this, we collect compressed 8-bit images derived from full-disk line-of-sight magnetograms provided by the Helioseismic and Magnetic Imager (HMI) instrument onboard Solar Dynamics Observatory (SDO). We trained our models using data-augmented oversampling to address the existing class-imbalance issue by following a time-segmented cross-validation strategy to effectively understand the accuracy performance of our models and used true skill statistics (TSS) and Heidke skill score (HSS) as metrics to compare and evaluate. The major results of this study are (1) we successfully implemented an efficient and effective full-disk flare predictor for operational forecasting using compressed images of solar magnetograms; (2) Our candidate model for multi-class flare prediction achieves an average TSS of 0.36 and average HSS of 0.31. Similarly, for binary prediction in (i) $\geq$C4.0 mode: we achieve an average TSS score of 0.47 and HSS score of 0.46, (ii) $\geq$M1.0 mode: we achieve an average TSS score of 0.55 and HSS score of 0.43.

Keywords: Solar flares · Deep neural networks · Solar magnetograms

1 Introduction

Solar flares are the large eruptions of electromagnetic radiation originating from the inner solar atmosphere and extending out to the outermost atmosphere of the Sun, which can last minutes to hours, and they often transpire as a sudden flash of increased brightness on the Sun observed near its surface [1]. Although there exists observational precursors, the actual physical cause of this phenomenon is

© The Author(s), under exclusive license to Springer Nature Switzerland AG 2022
J. A. Lossio-Ventura et al. (Eds.): SIMBig 2021, CCIS 1577, pp. 380–396, 2022.
https://doi.org/10.1007/978-3-031-04447-2_26

still unsolved, which hinders the validation process of statistical or data-driven flare forecasts. Recent studies [2,3] shows promising results when solar flare prediction is posed as a computer vision/image classification task and deep architectures are employed.

Solar flares are categorized into five major classes according to their peak X-ray flux level : X $(> 10^{-4} \text{Wm}^{-2})$, M $(> 10^{-5} \text{Wm}^{-2})$, C $(> 10^{-6} \text{Wm}^{-2})$, B $(> 10^{-7} \text{Wm}^{-2})$, and A $(> 10^{-8} \text{Wm}^{-2})$ [4]. These flare classes are measured in logarithmic scales (i.e., M3.2 is 10 times stronger than C3.2 flare). Although, the explosive heat of a solar flare cannot reach all the way to the Earth, the electromagnetic radiation and energetic particles certainly can induce the intense variation in near-Earth magnetic field, causing potential disruptions to many stakeholders such as the electricity supply chain, airlines industry, astronauts in space and communication systems including satellites and radio. The X-class and M-class flares are rare events and hence the scarcity of data give rise to the class-imbalance issue which further complicates the learning process for deep learning models, where the large amount of data is considered to be crucial for achieving meaningful generalization.

Most of the current flare prediction models are active region-based, that is, predictions are issued for a certain region on the Sun. Active regions are the temporary areas on the Sun characterized by especially strong and complex magnetic fields. These regions frequently produce various types of solar activity and are well-suited for predicting the occurrence of flares. For an operational system—system which is ready to use with the near real-time data for making real-time predictions—individual predictions from active regions are aggregated to provide a final prediction result. However, due to the strong projection effects near the limbs of the Sun, such predictions are limited to the active regions in

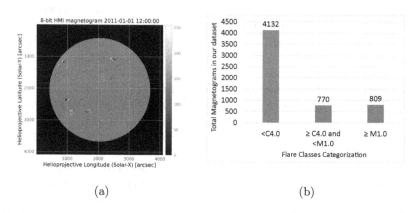

(a)   (b)

Fig. 1. (a) A pictorial representation of the compressed 8-bit image derived from the line-of-sight magnetogram as observed by SDO/HMI on 2011–01–01 12:00:00 UT. (b) The total number magnetograms for each target class label we use in this study; i.e., <C4.0 class, ≥C4.0 to <M1.0 and ≥M1.0 class flares.

central locations, which is not ideal for operational systems. Full-disk predictions are therefore more appropriate to complement the active region-based counterparts and provide a crucial, often overlooked, element to these near real-time operational systems.

Convolutional Neural Networks (CNN) [5] based deep learning architectures have been very popular for over a decade now for computer vision problems where data are labeled images. In this experiment, we use 8-bit compressed magnetogram images where the pixel value ranges from 0 to 255 derived from full-disk line-of sight solar magnetograms which contains 4096 × 4096 raster map of the one dimensional magnetic field strength values on the sun typically ranging from $\sim \pm 4500$G. Using compressed images instead of high depth solar magnetograms do not show any reliable magnetic field information however, they represent the shape parameters of active-regions which includes the projected shape of sunspot at an angle. Considering the limited scope of active region-based flare prediction counterparts, where the prediction is limited to central location (up to $\pm 70°$) of a full-disk magnetogram due to severe projection effect on the limbs of the Sun, with compressed full-disk magnetograms we incorporate the entire information including the active-regions present on the limbs. Although the 8-bit compressed magnetograms may induce information loss to some extent; however, considering the depth and complexity of deep learning models, it may be a more suitable choice to use images as it elevates the model's computational efficiency while training and predicting the flaring events in real-time.

In this paper, we address the task of training robust full-disk flare prediction models and explore different prediction modes (i.e., predicting the occurrence of $\geq$C4.0 and $\geq$M1.0 class flares in binary mode, and <C4.0, $\geq$C4.0 to <M1.0 and $\geq$M1.0 in multi-class mode with a prediction window of 24 h) and assess the impact of such formulation of the prediction problem with three different CNN architectures. As mentioned earlier, we use compressed images of full-disk line-of-sight magnetograms obtained from Helioseismic and Magnetic Imager (HMI) onboard Solar Dynamics Observatory (SDO). These images do not require further preprocessing and are available in near real-time (often <30 min). An example compressed solar magnetogram image is demonstrated in Fig. 1.(a). These compressed images contain 4096 × 4096 pixels which we resize to 512×512 pixels for our experiments. We use a transfer learning based approach with three landmark CNN models, AlexNet [6], VGG16 [7] and ResNet34 [8]. We customize these models as per our requirement of two classes in binary mode and three classes in multi-class mode with single-channel input image and analyze the performance of each model.

In the long run, we intend to employ these models to create more reliable and robust flare prediction ensembles in an operational setting. Robust prediction of solar flares is a central problem in space weather forecasting and has many practical implications. Many of the severe solar storms are associated with a strong-flare and deep learning-based prediction models have the potential to help understand intrinsic magnetic field configurations that lead to a flare. We also note that the models trained in our work are not active region-based and they only use data derived from line-of-sight magnetograms.

The remainder of this paper is organized as follows. In Sect. 2, we present the related work on solar flare predictions using machine and deep learning models. In Sect. 3, the data collection and preparation strategies are presented. In Sect. 4, we present the overview of the model architectures we use for solar flare prediction. In Sect. 5, we present our detailed experimental evaluation, and, lastly, in Sect. 6, we present our final remarks on this work including its limitations and discuss future work.

2 Related Work

The convolutional neural network (CNN) [5] is a class of deep neural network architecture with sparse neuron connections inspired by biological processes [9] to imitate the animal visual cortex. Recently, there have been several attempts to predict solar flares using deep learning models. Nishizuka et al. presented a Deep learning model based on a multi-layer perceptron for solar flare forecasts for $\geq$C1.0 and $\geq$M1.0 class [10]. In this study, they used 79 manually selected features (well-known physical precursors) extracted from multi-modal solar observations, which are vector magnetograms, 131 Å AIA images, and 1600 Å UV continuum images. Their models require a preliminary feature extraction process to prepare the data to feed the deep learning model.

Similarly, Huang et al. [11] presented a CNN-based flare forecasting model with two convolutional layers with 64 11×11 kernels where they used solar active regions patches extracted from line-of-sight solar magnetograms within ±30° of the central meridian. In this work, their models are trained to predict $\geq$C1.0-, $\geq$M1.0-, and $\geq$X1.0-class flares from active regions in central locations. While they show significantly high accuracy (>0.66 true skill statistic) for $\geq$M1.0 class, the models are limited only to certain areas of the observable disk, overlooking the significant portion that has information on other active-regions, and thus have limited operational prediction ability. In [2], Park et al. applied a CNN-based hybrid model which combines GoogleLeNet [12] and DenseNet [13]. Their model is trained to predict the occurrence of a $\geq$C1.0 class within the next 24 h. They use data from both HMI magnetograms, as well as magnetograms from Michelson Doppler Imager (MDI) onboard Solar and Heliospheric Observatory (SOHO), the predecessor of HMI/SDO. This allowed them to use a substantially higher number of images for training (entire MDI dataset, one image per day, for training and HMI dataset for testing); however, it should be noted that these two instruments are currently not cross-calibrated for use in forecasting and may lead to spurious or deficient patterns being discovered.

Li et al., in [3], also use a CNN-based model to issue binary class predictions for both $\geq$C1.0 class and $\geq$M1.0 class flares within 24 h using Space-Weather Helioseismic and Magnetic Imager Active Region Patches (SHARP) data [14] extracted from solar magnetograms located within ±45° of the central meridian excluding the magnetograms samples that has multiple sunspot groupings (or NOAA-defined active regions). This again limits the scope of the prediction to easier-to-predict active regions. They use undersampling and data augmentation to remedy the class-imbalance issue and create a non-chronological dataset by randomizing the process of data splitting for a 10-fold cross validation. While such data splitting leads to higher experimental accuracy scores, it often fails to deliver similar real-time performance as discussed in [15].

In this work, we build a set of models using compressed full-disk line-of-sight magnetograms with pretrained deep learning models to predict the occurrence of flaring events (for $\geq$C4.0 and $\geq$M1.0 class in binary modes and <C4.0, $\geq$C4.0 to <M1.0, and $\geq$M1.0 class in multi-class mode) with a prediction window of 24 h. We will use bi-daily full-disk images sampled at 00:00 UT and 12:00 UT, and labeled based on the existence of a flaring event within the next 24 h. For this, we create a dataset by using a non-chronological splitting of data into four time segmented partitions for both binary and multi-class flare predictions. We use 8-bit compressed images of full-disk line-of-sight solar magnetograms with a modified version of the pretrained AlexNet, VGG16 and ResNet34 models for all of our experiments. To remedy the existing class-imbalance issue in the dataset we use data-augmented oversampling.

3   Data Preparation

We use an image dataset derived from full-disk line-of-sight HMI solar magnetograms. HMI provides various magnetic field products at high spatial and temporal resolution. We select two images derived from magnetograms at 00:00 UT and 12:00 UT each day from December 2010 to December 2018. These images are not the original full-depth magnetic field rasters but rather are compressed JP2 images created from magnetograms (i.e., pixel values ranging from 0–255). We retrieve our images from a public data API, Helioviewer [16], which provides 4096 × 4096 compressed images of magnetograms closest to the requested timestamp. While preparing our final dataset, we skip the timestamp if the observation time of the available image and requested image timestamp is more than six hours.

We use a prediction window (i.e., forecast horizon) of 24 h. The bi-daily observations of magnetograms are labeled based on the maximum of peak X-ray flux within the next 24 h, converted to GOES flare classes; e.g., if the maximum intensity flare for the next 24 h (starting from the image's observation time) is an M1.2 flare, then we tentatively label the image as 'M'.

We collect a total of 5,711 solar magnetograms where there are 81 X-class flares, 728 M-class flares, 2,324 C-class flares, and 2,578 are <C1.0[1]. To perform the task of multi-class flare prediction we choose a threshold of C4.0 where flare <C4.0 are considered to be flare-quiet instances and $\geq$C4.0 class are further subdivided into two flaring classes. The main motivation to choose this threshold is that in most cases, the flares above C4.0 are observed to be associated

---

[1] While there may be A-, B- and lower C-class flares in our $< C4.0$ category, they are often referred to as *flare-quiet* (or *no-flare*) category, because these flares are weak and may not be detected properly during solar maxima due to high background X-ray flux.

with Coronal Mass Ejection (CME) events with notably higher speed that can make impact on the near-Earth space. Furthermore, using C4.0 as the threshold ensures approximately equal number of instances i.e. 770 and 809 images for two flaring classes ($\geq$C4.0 to <M1.0 and $\geq$M1.0) and we refer to them as mild-flares and strong-flares respectively in the scope of this paper as shown in Fig. 1.(b).

When preparing the dataset for $\geq$C4.0 class in binary prediction mode, if the maximum X-ray intensity of flare is weaker than C4.0 (<C4.0), the observations are labeled as "no-flare" and greater than or equal to ($\geq$C4.0) are labeled as "flare". In doing so, we collect 4,132 "no-flare" instances and 1579 "flare" instances. Similarly for $\geq$M1.0 class flares prediction in binary prediction mode, we do not include mild-flares ($\geq$C4.0 to <M1.0) to train our models. The objective for excluding those instances is to make the decision boundary for $\geq$M1.0 class wider so that the model could generalize better. For this, we collect 4,132 "no-Flare" instances and 809 "flare" instances for $\geq$M1.0 class binary prediction mode.

As we will describe later in the experimental evaluation, we create our cross-validation (CV) dataset partitions based on the tri-monthly partitioning of total images. The average class-imbalance ratio in our entire dataset for binary prediction in $\geq$C4.0 class mode is $\sim$1:2.6 (flare:no-flare). On the other hand, due to scarcity of X- and M- class flares, for $\geq$M1.0 class flares, after excluding the mild-flares from no-flare instances, the data distribution is highly imbalanced, $\sim$1:5 (flare:no-flare). Similarly for multi-class prediction, the two of the flaring classes (mild and strong) are nearly balanced, but no-flare class is still the majority class. The imbalance ratio is $\sim$1:1:5 (strong-flare:mild-flare:no-flare).

4 Model Architecture

A general architecture of a CNN model in a classification problem consists of convolutional layers with *ReLU* activation function followed by a pooling layer and finally one or more fully connected layers with a *softmax* function to give the prediction probabilities of each class [17]. In CNNs, each convolutional layer has a set of kernels (filters), which are trained to extract complex features from the input data. After the convolutional layer, we use ReLU activation which adds non-linearity to the model. To summarize the outputs from a convolutional layer by reducing the size of the output map, a pooling layer is used. Pooling layers maximize or average the spatial size of output from the convolutional layer and reduce the number of computations. A fully connected layer is the traditional neural network where nodes in one layer are densely connected with nodes in another fully connected layer. To overcome the problem of overfitting in such deep networks, usually a dropout layer [18] is added, which ensures the random sparse connectivity between the nodes in two fully connected layers [19].

In this study, we implement three of the well-known CNN-architectures: AlexNet, VGG16 and ResNet34 models to make binary and multi-class flare predictions. In the first place, we use AlexNet model [6] because of it's simplicity in the architecture which consists of 5 convolutional layers, 3 maxpool layers,

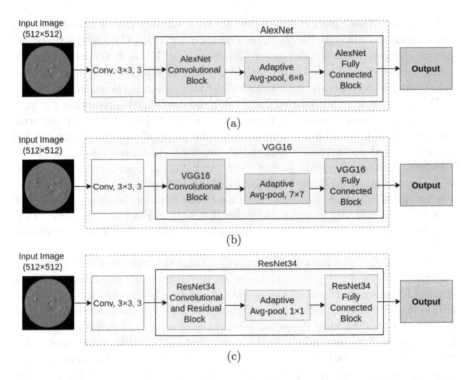

Fig. 2. An overview of three deep learning architectures we use (a) AlexNet-, (b) VGG16-, (c) ResNet34-based models for both the binary and multi-class flare prediction. Models produce a set of probabilities determined based on the prediction mode.

1 adaptive average pool layer, and three fully connected layers. Secondly, we consider a deeper architecture, VGG16 [7], to study whether the performance improves with more layers as it complements the AlexNet model by adding more convolutional layers to the network and using same-sized smaller convolutional kernels of 3 × 3 for all convolutional layers whereas AlexNet uses variably-sized kernels of 11 × 11, 5 × 5 and 3 × 3. VGG16 consists of 13 convolutional layers, 5 maxpool layers, 1 adaptive average pool layer, and 3 fully connected layers. Finally, we use another landmark CNN model, ResNet34 [8]. It further complements the VGG16 architecture by allowing the network to train deeper layers with less number of parameters. However, it is different from AlexNet and VGG16 in the sense that it takes residuals from each layer and uses them in the subsequent connected layers. ResNet34 has 34 convolutional layers where the first layer has a kernel of 7 × 7 and the rest have 3 × 3 kernels with one max pool layer, one adaptive average pool layer and one fully connected layer. The main motivation for selecting these architectures is to understand how the performance changes with different architectures with increasing number of layers and we use the simplest architectures giving consideration to the size of our dataset which is relatively small for deep learning models.

We use all these three models with the transfer learning based approach and exploit the pretrained model weights to improve model training performance in two modes: binary and multi-class where the final layer outputs two and three softmax probabilities respectively. The above architectures trained on binary modes outputs two softmax probabilities for two classes which are then interpreted as no-flare and flare. Similarly, for multi-class modes, the models output three softmax probabilities interpreted as no-flare, mild-flare and strong-flare.

These models are pretrained on the ImageNet dataset [20] which requires a 3-channel image as input to the network. Since the data we use are compressed images of solar magnetograms (which are greyscale), we add a convolutional layer at the beginning of the network which accepts 1-channel input with a 3×3 kernel using size-1 stride, padding and dilation, and outputs a 3-channel image as shown in Fig. 2. This added CNN layer is initialized using Kaiming Initialization in "fan-out" mode [21] for all three models in both binary and multi-class modes. Furthermore, to efficiently exploit the pretrained weights regardless of the architecture of these models, which expects input of different dimensions with 3-channels, we use an adaptive average pooling layer in each models after complete feature extraction using convolutional layer and just before the fully-connected layer to match the dimension on our image input size of 512×512.

5 Experimental Evaluation

To train a deep learning model with higher predictive accuracy scores, it is essential to configure the hyperparameters, select an optimization algorithm, and a proper loss function. In addition, it is equally important to prepare the dataset that allows the models to generalize better while training and is sufficiently representative to validate the models. In this section, we elaborate our dataset settings, model implementation, and hyperparameter configurations we have used in this work that directly influence the performance of our models. Furthermore, we present the results of our experiments and the skill scores that characterize the predictive performance of our models in a near-operational setting.

5.1 Experimental Settings

Dataset: In this work, we used compressed images of full-disk line-of-sight magnetograms in bi-daily fashion sampled at 00:00 UT and 12:00 UT for each day. These images are labeled based on maximum GOES peak X-ray flux from 00:00 UT to 24:00 and 12:00 UT to next day 12:00 UT. We ready our cross-validation by dividing our entire data into four time-segmented partitions for both $\geq$C4.0 and $\geq$M1.0 class predictions in binary prediction modes and <C4.0, $\geq$C4.0 to <M1.0, and $\geq$M1.0 in multi-class modes. Each of these partitions has three months of data from all years included in the entire dataset. The data in Partition-1 contains images from the months of January to March, Partition-2 from April to June, Partition-3 from July to September, and Partition-4 from October to December.

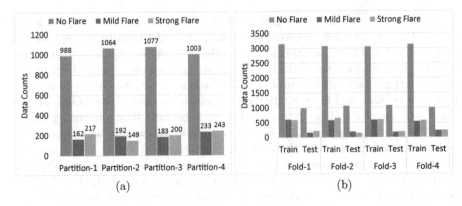

Fig. 3. (a)Time-segmented distribution of data in tri-monthly separated partitions indicating the number of instances for each classes (no-flare, mild-flare and strong-flare) (b) Distribution of 4-fold CV dataset into training and test set created from time-segmented partitions.

Here, this partitioning of the dataset is created by dividing the data time-line from Dec 2010 to Dec 2018 into four partitions on the basis of months rather than chronological partitioning, to incorporate approximately equal distribution of flaring instances in every fold for training and testing the model. As mentioned earlier, we perform two variations of binary predictions: (i) for $\geq$C4.0-class flares, we denote mild-flare and strong-flare as flaring instances and (ii) for $\geq$M1.0 class flares, we exclude the mild-flares, i.e. $\geq$C4.0 to $<$M1.0 from the dataset with a motive to increase the separability in two classes of flares and no-flares. In doing so, all of the four partitions for both the binary prediction modes includes approximately equal number of flare instances. For multi-class prediction mode, we include our entire dataset and the respective partitions contain almost equal number of instances for mild-flare and strong-flare across each partitions as shown in Fig. 3.(a).

We then create the 4-fold CV dataset from the aforementioned partitions where we use three partitions for training the model and the remaining one for testing (validating) the model, ensuring that both the training and test set has data from each year (i.e., Dec 2010 to Dec 2018). First fold (Fold-1) of our 4-fold CV dataset contains data from January to March as the test set and the rest 9 months as training set. Similarly, the second fold (Fold-2) contains the data from April to June as the test set and the rest 9 months of the data as the training set. We use data from July to September and October to December as the test set in the third fold (Fold-3) and fourth fold (Fold-4) with the remaining 9 months of data as the training set respectively. Note that, each fold in 4-fold CV dataset for three different prediction modes: (i) $\geq$C4.0-class binary prediction mode considers mild-flare and strong-flare as flare class (ii) $\geq$M1.0 binary prediction mode do not include the mild-flare into the dataset and denote strong-flares as flare class and (iii) multi-class mode includes the entire dataset as shown in Fig. 3.(b).

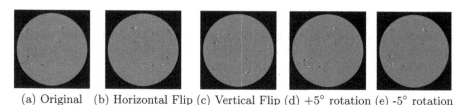

(a) Original   (b) Horizontal Flip (c) Vertical Flip (d) +5° rotation (e) -5° rotation

Fig. 4. (a) An example compressed magnetogram observed by HMI on 2011–01–01 12:00:00 UT (b) Augmented data sample after applying horizontal flipping. (c) Augmented data sample after applying vertical flipping. (d) Augmented data sample after applying +5° rotation. (e) Augmented data sample after applying −5° rotation.

Implementation: In our experiments, we trained the AlexNet, VGG16 and ResNet34 models with Stochastic Gradient Descent (SGD) as an optimizer and Negative Log-Likelihood (NLL) as our loss function for both binary and multi-class predictions. This implementation of loss function is the generalized version of cross-entropy loss and is not limited to the binary classification problem, hence we use logarithmic-softmax as an activation to the output layer to make it compatible with NLL loss. The NLL loss we use to train our CNN model is:

$$L = -\frac{1}{N} \sum_{i=0}^{N} \sum_{j=0}^{J} y_j \cdot log(\hat{y}_j) + (1 - y_j) \cdot log(1 - \hat{y}_j) \tag{1}$$

where y_j represents the actual j^{th} class label, $\hat{y}$ represents the predicted class label for the jth class and N is the batch-size. For binary predictions, $j = 2$ and for our multi-class prediction mode, $j = 3$. To track the performance improvement of our model, we validate our model with test data in every epoch. An important setting of these experiments is the use of dynamic learning rate which is initialized at 0.01 and reduced by a factor of 10%, if the validation loss do not improve for four consecutive epochs. We use the mini-batch strategy to obtain a faster convergence where the weights are updated after each batch and all of our models are trained up to 80 epochs until weights stability.

We perform four experiments using the 4-fold non-chronological CV dataset and with each architecture in both binary and multi-class prediction modes. Although all of our data partitions have approximately equal numbers of flaring instances, there still exists a prevailing class-imbalance issue. To address the class-imbalance issue, we use data-augmented oversampling; i.e., we oversample the training data after data augmentation only for flaring instances in both binary and multi-class prediction modes so that every batch includes balanced flare and no-flare instances. We use three data-augmentation techniques: vertical flipping, horizontal flipping, and +5° to −5° rotations only on flaring instances included in the training set. Note that the rotations are limited to 5°C as to not impact the preferred locations of active regions (which are limited to activity belts [22]). The Fig. 4 shows the augmented samples of compressed images of magnetograms. These augmented images are then concatenated to the original training set and then we oversample the flaring instances to create balanced batches for training. Considering the limited amount of data, using oversampling and data augmentation has an advantage that makes the use of entire acquired data, when compared to undersampling [23].

To quantify the performance of our models, we create a classical contingency matrix for both of our binary operating modes, which includes information on True Positives (TP), True Negatives (TN), False Positives (FP) and False Negatives (FN). Note that, in the context of our flare prediction task, flare class in either of the modes is considered as the positive outcome while no-flare is the negative. Using these four outcomes we use two widely used performance metrics in space weather forecasting, True Skill Statistics (TSS, shown in Eq. 2) and Heidke Skill Score (HSS, shown in Eq. 3) to evaluate our models.

$$TSS = \frac{TP}{TP + FN} - \frac{FP}{FP + TN} \tag{2}$$

$$HSS = 2 \times \frac{TP \times TN - FN \times FP}{((P \times (FN + TN) + (TP + FP) \times N))} \tag{3}$$

Here, $N = TN + FP$ and $P = TP + FN$. Furthermore, for multi-class prediction modes we employ multi-category TSS and HSS as shown in Eq. 4 and 5 respectively [24].

$$TSS = \frac{\frac{1}{N} \sum_{i=1}^{K} n(F_i, O_i) - \frac{1}{N^2} \sum_{i=1}^{K} N(F_i) N(O_i)}{1 - \frac{1}{N^2} \sum_{i=1}^{K} (N(O_i))^2} \tag{4}$$

$$HSS = \frac{\frac{1}{N} \sum_{i=1}^{K} n(F_i, O_i) - \frac{1}{N^2} \sum_{i=1}^{K} N(F_i) N(O_i)}{1 - \frac{1}{N^2} \sum_{i=1}^{K} N(F_i) N(O_i)} \tag{5}$$

where $n(F_i, O_j)$ denotes the number of predictions in category i that had actual observations (ground truth) in category j, $N(F_i)$ denotes the total number of predictions in category i, $N(O_j)$ denotes the total number of observations in category j, and N is the total number of instances in testing set.

TSS values range from -1 to 1, where 1 indicates all correct predictions, -1 represents all incorrect predictions, and 0 represents no-skill, often transpiring as the random or one-sided (all positive/all negative) predictions. It is defined as the difference between True Positive Rate (TPR) and False Positive Rate (FPR). One important characteristic of TSS is that it does not account for class-imbalance ratio in the dataset and hence treats false positives (FP) and false negatives (FN) equally.

Similarly, HSS measures the forecast skill of the models over an imbalance-aware random prediction and it ranges from $-\infty$ to 1, where 1 represents the perfect skill and 0 represents no-skill gain over a random prediction. It is common practice to use HSS for the solar flare prediction models (similar to weather predictions where forecast skill has more value than accuracy or single-class precision), due to the high class-imbalance ratio present in the datasets.

5.2 Evaluation

Our flare prediction model is trained as a CNN-based binary classifier where we predict flares in two binary modes with $\geq$C4.0 and $\geq$M1.0 as thresholds and a multi-class classifier where we predict flares <C4.0 as no-flares (NF), $\geq$C4.0 to <M1.0 as mild-flares (MF), and $\geq$M1.0 as strong-flares (SF). The output of our model is binary (flare/no-flare) predictions and multi-class (no-flare/mild-flare/strong-flare) within the next 24 h. We compare the predictions of our models with maximum GOES peak X-ray flux at 00:00 UT and 12:00 UT with a prediction window of 24 h. We use TSS and HSS metrics to measure the predictive performance of our models.

We summarize the skill scores of all our models in Table 1. The table contains the average skill scores for all three models in binary and multi-class prediction modes with standard deviations across 4-folds computed with confidence level of 95%. These are the stable final epoch cross-validated results obtained by training the models for 80 epochs and validating in every epoch, however, since the ResNet34 model doesn't get fully stable until then, so we compute the average of last five epochs in all prediction modes.

We employ 4-fold cross-validation using the tri-monthly partitioned dataset for evaluating our models as discussed in Sect. 5.1. The TSS and HSS scores obtained from our CV experiments for all three models in binary modes (i) $\geq$C4.0 class and (ii) $\geq$M1.0 class are shown in Fig. 5 and Fig. 6, respectively. After training all of our models, we get our best results using the AlexNet model for both binary as well multi-class modes. For binary predictions in $\geq$C4.0 class modes, all three architectures have relatively low fluctuations with the highest TSS and HSS scores obtained using the AlexNet model. When higher C-class flares filtered from the dataset, we observe an overall increase in both TSS and HSS scores with an exception at Fold-3 results. However, in doing so, the scores have a greater fluctuations across the folds for all the models. While the skill score fluctuations are common in flare prediction studies, Partition-2 includes the most difficult instances to predict, which essentially perturb the overall trend.The best results of our models are comparable to the state of the art deep learning-based flare predictors in the combined performance and and hence provides the evidence that applying a deep learning-based approaches has a high potential for full-disk flare predictions.

Table 1. Average TSS and HSS skill scores with standard deviation measured at 95% confidence level for all of our models

Models	Binary ($\geq$C4.0)		Binary ($\geq$M1.0)		Multi-class	
	TSS	HSS	TSS	HSS	TSS	HSS
AlexNet	**0.47 ± .06**	**0.46 ± .03**	**0.55 ± .09**	**0.43 ± .11**	**0.36 ± .04**	**0.31 ± .02**
VGG16	0.43 ± .05	0.42 ± .04	0.47 ± .08	0.43 ± .05	0.30 ± .04	0.29 ± .04
ResNet34	0.42 ± .06	0.41 ± .05	0.46 ± .08	**0.46 ± .07**	0.26 ± .05	0.28 ± .05

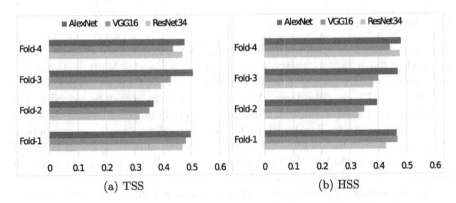

Fig. 5. (a) Binary ($\geq$C4.0) prediction performance of our models measured in TSS for each fold in 4-fold CV. (b) Binary ($\geq$C4.0) prediction performance of our models measured in HSS for each fold in 4-fold CV.

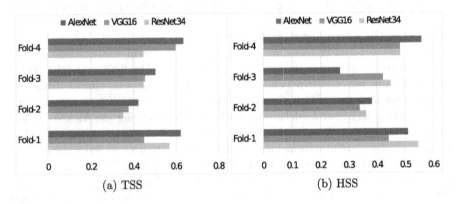

Fig. 6. (a) Binary ($\geq$M1.0) prediction performance of our models measured in TSS for each fold in 4-fold CV. (b) Binary ($\geq$C4.0) prediction performance of our models measured in HSS for each fold in 4-fold CV.

In addition to binary modes, we also evaluated the performance of our trained models in multi-class mode, using multi-class versions of TSS and HSS. Similar to the earlier experiments, AlexNet-based models provided relatively better scores compared to Resnet34 and VGG16 which is presented in Fig. 7 showing the detailed results for each folds. The averaged scores in the last column of Table 1 show that both the skill scores have a relatively low fluctuation ($\sim \pm 0.02$) and our model creates stable predictions for flare prediction. The better predictive performance of AlexNet over other two reasonably advanced models in all of our experiments can be attributed to it's simplicity in the architecture (in terms of number of layers) and the total number of instances in our dataset which is relatively small for deep learning based models.

We also present a set of aggregated contingency tables to better explain the performance of multi-class predictors in Fig. 8. Note that the individual cell

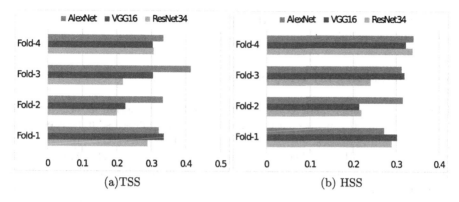

Fig. 7. (a) Multi-class prediction performance of our models measured in TSS for each fold in 4-fold CV. (b) Multi-class prediction performance of our models measured in HSS for each fold in 4-fold CV

	Predicted		
	NF	MF	SF
NF	3660	276	196
MF	472	150	148
SF	385	176	248

(a) ResNet34

	Predicted		
	NF	MF	SF
NF	3428	461	243
MF	390	202	178
SF	285	231	293

(b) VGG16

	Predicted		
	NF	MF	SF
NF	3148	801	183
MF	276	367	127
SF	176	385	248

(c) AlexNet

Fig. 8. 4-fold aggregated confusion matrices for multi-class predictions where NF, MF, SF indicates no-flare, mild-flare, and strong-flare respectively for three models (a) ResNet34 (b) VGG16 (c) AlexNet

values are found by summing the values from four contingency matrices obtained in each fold. As expected, multi-class classification is a more difficult prediction problem and the results often show greater shifts between neighboring class label pairs (NF-MF and MF-SF). The aggregated confusion matrix show that, for all three models, mild-flare class has a higher number of false-negatives, which is anticipated, since it lies as the border class between the other two and there is a resemblance of phenomena and therefore a strong likelihood of misclassifying a C5.0-class flare as no-flare ($> C4.0$), or C9.0 flare as strong-flare ($> M1.0$). This is more visible in the aggregated confusion matrix for AlexNet, which is our best model for multi-class predictions, suggests that, the higher number of false-negatives are in the neighboring classes (e.g., NF predicted as MF). Finally, our results show that the predictive performance of AlexNet-based models are satisfactory and can be used under operational settings, first, because it gives more robust results, and second due to its simpler architecture allowing a computationally efficient platform for near real-time predictions even in the case of large ensembles.

6   Conclusion and Discussion

In this work, we implement CNN-based binary flare prediction models for both $\geq$C4.0 and $\geq$M1.0 class prediction modes and one multi-class flare prediction model with three classes: (i) <C4.0 as no-flare class , (ii) $\geq$C4.0 to <M1.0 as mild-flare class, and (iii) $\geq$M1.0 as strong-flare class using transfer learning with AlexNet, VGG16 and ResNet34 models. We built efficient flare prediction models having predictive performance comparable to state-of-the-art models using full-disk line-of-sight magnetograms which overcome the prediction ability of active region-based models where the prediction is limited to central locations (within $\pm$70o). Furthermore, we select a specific threshold of C4.0 for flare prediction since most of the eruptive flares (flares with associated CMEs) are observed to have peak X-ray flux above C4.0 and has an ability to make an impact on near-Earth space in most cases.

For our experiments to make binary predictions in $\geq$M1.0 class mode, we exclude the data instances indicating the mild-flares to widen the decision boundary for flare and no-flare instances. In order to mitigate the prevailing issue of class-imbalance across our dataset, we use data-augmented oversampling. Based on our experimental results, we observe that AlexNet based model outperforms other two models in both the binary and multi-class prediction modes. This result can be attributed to AlexNet's simple architecture and the total number of images in our dataset which may not be sufficient for depeer models like VGG16 and ResNet34. The results of all cross-validated experiments suggests that the AlexNet model can be used in an operational setting to perform near-real time flare predictions. To reproduce this work, the source code and detailed experimental results can be accessed from our open source repository [25].

It is also important to mention that our models use point-in-time observations of magnetogram images and do not identify the active regions contributing to the corresponding flaring event. Furthermore, the Eastern limb flares (whose active regions only become visible after predictions are issued) limit the prediction capabilities of our models due to unavailable active region information. Subsequently, we intend to use other deeper variants of CNN-based architectures along with integration of different dimensions of solar data products such as vector magnetograms, intensitygrams, dopplergrams, and extreme ultraviolet images. One important aspect of this work is the utilization of a more practical threshold of C4.0 in flare forecasting which is discussed in literature but not considered in practical implementation, therefore, we will continue our experiments by optimizing these thresholds for different architectures and modes to further improve the flare prediction models. To improve the performance of our current models we also aim to build hybrid models by combining active region-based counterparts to obtain more robust ensemble flare prediction models.

Acknowledgements. This project is supported in part under two NSF awards #2104004 and #1931555 jointly by the Office of Advanced Cyberinfrastructure within the Directorate for Computer and Information Science and Engineering, the Division of Astronomical Sciences within the Directorate for Mathematical and Physical Sciences, and the Solar Terrestrial Physics Program and the Division of Integrative and Collaborative Education and Research within the Directorate for Geosciences.

References

1. Shea, M., Smart, D., McCracken, K., Dreschhoff, G., Spence, H.: Solar proton events for 450 years: the carrington event in perspective. Adv. Space Res. **38**(2), 232–238 (2006)
2. Park, E., Moon, Y.J., Shin, S., Yi, K., Lim, D., Lee, H., Shin, G.: Application of the deep convolutional neural network to the forecast of solar flare occurrence using full-disk solar magnetograms. Astrophys. J. **869**(2), 91 (2018)
3. Li, X., Zheng, Y., Wang, X., Wang, L.: Predicting solar flares using a novel deep convolutional neural network. Astrophys. J. **891**(1), 10 (2020)
4. Fletcher, L., et al.: An observational overview of solar flares. Space Sci. Rev. **159**(1–4), 19–106 (2011)
5. Lecun, Y., Bottou, L., Bengio, Y., Haffner, P.: Gradient-based learning applied to document recognition. Proc. IEEE **86**(11), 2278–2324 (1998)
6. Krizhevsky, A.: One weird trick for parallelizing convolutional neural networks (2014)
7. Simonyan, K., Zisserman, A.: Very deep convolutional networks for large-scale image recognition (2014)
8. He, K., Zhang, X., Ren, S., Sun, J.: Deep residual learning for image recognition (2015)
9. Matsugu, M., Mori, K., Mitari, Y., Kaneda, Y.: Subject independent facial expression recognition with robust face detection using a convolutional neural network. Neural Netw. **16**(5–6), 555–559 (2003)
10. Nishizuka, N., Sugiura, K., Kubo, Y., Den, M., Ishii, M.: Deep flare net (DeFN) model for solar flare prediction. Astrophys. J. **858**(2), 113 (2018)
11. Huang, X., Wang, H., Xu, L., Liu, J., Li, R., Dai, X.: Deep learning based solar flare forecasting model. i. results for line-of-sight magnetograms. Astrophys. J. **856**(1), 7 (2018)
12. Szegedy, C., et al.: Going deeper with convolutions. In: 2015 IEEE Conference on Computer Vision and Pattern Recognition (CVPR). IEEE, June 2015
13. Huang, G., Liu, Z., Maaten, L.V.D., Weinberger, K.Q.: Densely connected convolutional networks. In: 2017 IEEE Conference on Computer Vision and Pattern Recognition (CVPR). IEEE, July 2017
14. Bobra, M.G., et al.: The helioseismic and magnetic imager (HMI) vector magnetic field pipeline: SHARPs – space-weather HMI active region patches. Solar Phys. **289**(9), 3549–3578 (2014)
15. Ahmadzadeh, A., Aydin, B., Georgoulis, M.K., Kempton, D.J., Mahajan, S.S., Angryk, R.A.: How to train your flare prediction model: revisiting robust sampling of rare events. Astrophys. J. Supplement Ser. **254**(2), 23 (2021)
16. Muller, D., et al.: JHelioviewer: visualizing large sets of solar images using JPEG 2000. Comput. Sci. Eng. **11**(5), 38–47 (2009)

17. Alzubaidi, L., et al.: Review of deep learning: concepts, CNN architectures, challenges, applications, future directions. J. Big Data **8**(1), 1–74 (2021). https://doi.org/10.1186/s40537-021-00444-8

18. Srivastava, N., Hinton, G., Krizhevsky, A., Sutskever, I., Salakhutdinov, R.: Dropout: a simple way to prevent neural networks from overfitting. J. Mach. Learn. Res. **15**(56), 1929–1958 (2014), http://jmlr.org/papers/v15/srivastava14a.html

19. Albawi, S., Mohammed, T.A., Al-Zawi, S.: Understanding of a convolutional neural network. In: 2017 International Conference on Engineering and Technology (ICET). IEEE, August 2017

20. Deng, J., Dong, W., Socher, R., Li, L.J., Li, K., Fei-Fei, L.: ImageNet: a large-scale hierarchical image database. In: 2009 IEEE Conference on Computer Vision and Pattern Recognition. IEEE, June 2009

21. He, K., Zhang, X., Ren, S., Sun, J.: Delving deep into rectifiers: surpassing human-level performance on imagenet classification (2015)

22. Pulkkinen, P.J., Brooke, J., Pelt, J., Tuominen, I.: Long-term variation of sunspot latitudes. Astronomy Astrophys. **341**, L43–L46 (1999)

23. Ahmadzadeh, A., Hostetter, M., Aydin, B., Georgoulis, M.K., Kempton, D.J., Mahajan, S.S., Angryk, R.: Challenges with extreme class-imbalance and temporal coherence: a study on solar flare data. In: 2019 IEEE International Conference on Big Data (Big Data). IEEE, December 2019

24. WWRP/WGNE Joint Working Group on Forecast Verification Research: Forecast verification issues, methods and FAQ, January 2015. https://www.cawcr.gov.au/projects/verification/

25. DMLab: Source Code. https://bitbucket.org/gsudmlab/fulldisk_simbig/src/master

Prediction of Soil Saturated Electrical Conductivity by Statistical Learning

Carlos Mestanza[1]([⊠]) [iD], Miguel Chicchon[2][iD], Pedro Gutiérrez[1][iD],
Lorenzo Hurtado[1][iD], and Cesar Beltrán[2][iD]

[1] Universidad Nacional Agraria La Molina, Lima, Peru
cmestanza@lamolina.edu.pe
[2] Pontificia Universidad Católica del Perú, Lima, Peru

Abstract. The diagnosis of saline soils requires the analysis of electrical conductivity in saturated soil paste extract. Its analysis is expensive, tedious, and highly time-consuming, therefore, commercial laboratories analyze the aqueous extract in a 1:1 ratio and then transform the value into saturation extract using equations. The research aimed to calibrate a statistical learning method to predict the electrical conductivity adapted to Peruvian conditions. For this, we apply different models from highly interpretable to black-box, such as multiple linear model, generalized additive models, Bayesian additive regression tree, extreme gradient boosting trees, and neural networks. In general, the models with beast predictive power were neural network and extreme gradient boosting trees, and the beast interpretable was Bayesian additive regression trees. The generalized additive models present the best balance between prediction power and interpretability with low application on extremely salty soils.

Keywords: Soil analysis · Pedometry · Machine-learning

1 Introduction

Salts in the soil limit the exchange of water and nutrients with plant roots. Consequently, they retard the growth and development of many plants [27] though three effects: water deficit, nutritional imbalance, and specific ion toxicity [26]. Soil salinity is one of the largest global challenges in the arid and semi-arid regions that severely affects agricultural production [11]. The Peruvian coast has an average of 5.7 hectares per agricultural unit [15], concentrating the largest amount of land for agro-industrial production purposes. The arid conditions of this region make the soils vulnerable to salinization processes. [13] highlights that despite the success of agro-exports in the coastal region, the excessive use of water and the climate cause serious drainage and salinization problems.

The management of saline soils begins with the diagnosis of the degree of salinization. The most common indicator of the degree of salinization is electrical conductivity in saturated soil paste extract (EC_{SE}) measured in deciSiemens per meter ($dS.m^{-1}$) and determines the concentration of all soluble

J. A. Lossio-Ventura et al. (Eds.): SIMBig 2021, CCIS 1577, pp. 397–412, 2022.
https://doi.org/10.1007/978-3-031-04447-2_27

salts in soil [10]. Nevertheless, saturated paste analysis is tedious, highly time-consuming, and requires skills and expertise to reach saturation point. Commercial laboratories choose to analyze electrical conductivity (EC) in other extracts instead of saturated soil paste. In Peru, the use of the extract in 1:1 soil over water mass ratio is regulated by the supreme decree number 013–2010-AG. To interpret the value, it is necessary to transform this measure to its equivalent in soil paste extract. [20] proposes a multiplicative factor of 2.2 to do the transformation, but he attributes the creation of the factor to simple experience or expert judgment. In Peru, a multiplicative factor of 2 (LASPAF Factor) is used, which is regulated for national use. The origin of the factor is unknown and it is possibly an adaptation of [20] original text (1984). Although strong linear relationships between EC_{SE} and EC have been reported, the coefficients entering these relationships are not constant, but vary according to the area of interest [18]. This suggests the need to calibrate a transformation method adapted to the local conditions of the Peruvian soils. The variability of soils in different regions of Peru can be characterized with other properties such as particle size content, organic carbon, and cation exchange capacity.

The transformation from one value to another is a regression problem and can be worked with different statistical and computational methods. In soil science, the branch that optimizes the use of numerical methods to understand and solve problems is called pedometry. [29] notes that the methods range from linear regression, generalized linear model (GLM) and generalized additive models (GAM) to regression trees, random forests, neural networks, genetic programming and fuzzy systems. Those mentioned include machine learning and statistical methods, but [5] high-lights the difference between the two, while statistical methods focus on inference, which is achieved through the creation and fitting of a project-specific problem-ability model, machine learning concentrates on prediction by using general-purpose learning algorithms to find patterns in often rich and unwieldy data. A mixed approach is statistical learning, [16] explain that it is a sub-field in statistics, focused on supervised and unsupervised modelling and prediction. A balance is sought between low prediction error and high power of interpretation. The purpose of the research was to calibrate a statistical learning method to obtain the electrical conductivity in saturated soil paste extract. As objectives it was raised (i) identify the method with the lowest prediction error and (ii) interpret the relationship between the predictors and the electrical conductivity.

2   Related Work

Most of the records in transformation methods are using linear equations. [31] and [14] were the pioneers in proposing equations to transform the value, both coincide by a factor close to 3 applicable for different textural classes of soil. Similarly, and for all soil textures [18,28,37] and [24] they propose factors close to 2 but include the intercept parameter. Table 1 summarizes the proposal of different authors to transform the extract in 1:1 to soil paste extract. They all agree to use a single predictor, but some propose different equations based on the textural classes of soils. Some aspects to highlight is the low number of samples used for the model, the high coefficient of determination, and the range of electrical conductivity that does not exceed 40 $dS.m^{-1}$.

Table 1. Transformation equations proposed by different researchers. The number of samples (n) used, coefficient of determination (R^2) and range of electrical conductivity in soil paste extract (EC_{se}) reported by the author are presented. The R square (R_c^2) and Root Mean Square Error ($RMSE_c$) were calculated with the testing set. NA: data not available.

Equation	n	R^2	EC_{se}	R_c^2	$RMSE_c$
$EC_{se} = 3*(EC)$ [31]	30	NA	NA	0.57	4.9052
$EC_{se} = -0.77 + 3.01*(EC)$ [14]	127	0.96	0.10–22.4	0.63	4.5897
$EC_{se} = 2.20*(EC)$ [20]	NA	NA	NA	0.93	1.9354
$EC_{se} = 1.46 + 1.79*(EC)$ [37]	170	0.85	0.165–108	0.93	1.9849
$EC_{se} = -0.57 + 1.93*(EC)$ [28]	NA	0.96	NA	0.95	1.7111
$EC_{se} = -0.44 + 2.15*(EC)$ [32]	18	0.99	0.22–17.68	0.94	1.8086
$EC_{se} = 0.14 + 2.26*(EC)$ [24]	1408	0.89	0–20	0.92	2.1300
$EC_{se} = -0.117 + 1.83*(EC)$ [18]	198	0.97	0.47–37.5	0.94	1.8698

Different countries and localities use different extracts and transformation methods to obtain soil paste extract. [8] in China proposed different equations based on the saturation percentage that depends on the clay content in the soil using extracts in 1:5. Their results show that the slopes of the equations tend to vary based on the con-tent of saturation percentage, the link with the textural class, or the particle size becomes evident. [1] also worked in 1:5 extract for Egyptian soils, but with controlled experiments where they used artificial soils to which they modified the salinity conditions, as a result obtained the required equation. Everything indicates that each country seeks an adequate calibration for its local conditions since the methods and soils are variable.

The current trend is to map the electrical conductivity in the territories. [2] used the Victoria - Australia database (5158 samples) to relate electrical conductivity to particle size distribution, textural class, soil order, pH, rainfall, and elevation. His initiative is preliminary to understand the variation of the EC with respect to factors that vary in space. [23] combined spectral information from sentinel 1 and 2 satellites with electrical conductivity to produce maps of China. These approaches cannot be applicable to data from Peru since there is no georeferenced information to relate to spatial information or factors that vary in space.

3   Methodology

3.1   Dataset Description, Pre-processing and Exploratory Analysis

A total of 6068 samples were collected from the sample inventory of the soil laboratory of National Agrarian University La Molina. Twenty-two of the 25 regions (political limits) of Peru were collected, except Apurimac, Madre de Dios and Ucayali regions. The analysis of samples was carried out based on the provisions of supreme decree number 013–2010-AG: electrical conductivity of extract in 1:1, pH in suspension soil - water 1:1, total equivalent carbonates by acid digestion, soil organic carbon by Walkley and Black method, Cation Exchange Capacity with ammonium acetate at pH 7.0, exchangeable cations by atomic absorption spectrophotometry, particle size fractions by Bouyoucus hydrometer method, effective Cation Exchange Capacity by sum of cations, Exchangeable Sodium Percentage by calculus, and Base Saturation by calculus. Table 2 summarizes the description of the variables used.

Table 2. Dataset description.

Variable	Symbology	Units
Electrical conductivity in extract 1:1	EC	$dS.m^{-1}$
Sand fraction	SAND	$10g.kg^{-1}$
Silt fraction	SILT	$10g.kg^{-1}$
Clay fraction	CLAY	$10g.kg^{-1}$
pH	pH	No units
Total Equivalent Carbonates	TEC	$10g.kg^{-1}$
Soil Organic Carbon	OC	$10g.kg^{-1}$
Cation Exchange Capacity	CEC	$cmolc.kg^{-1}$
Exchangeable Calcium	eCa	$cmolc.kg^{-1}$
Exchangeable Magnesium	eMg	$cmolc.kg^{-1}$
Exchangeable Potassium	eK	$cmolc.kg^{-1}$
Exchangeable Sodium	eNa	$cmolc.kg^{-1}$
Exchangeable Acidity	eAlH	$cmolc.kg^{-1}$
Exchangeable Sodium Percentage	ESP	No units
Base Saturation	BS	No units
Electrical conductivity in saturated soil paste extract	EC_{se}	$dS.m^{-1}$

Missing values and anomalies were detected prior to the analysis. Mice library [4] in R language [30] was used to identity instances with missing values. Instances with missing values in the response variable were removed and the predictors were imputed using predictive mean matching. Samples with anomalous values were eliminated using as criteria: pH values greater than 11 and less than

3, soil organic carbon greater than 10 $10\,g.kg^{-1}$ (detection limit of the Walkley and Black method), and samples with electrical conductivity in saturated soil paste extract greater than 50 $dS.m^{-1}$. Anomaly detection analysis (outliers) was performed using a multivariate method based on random forest implemented in the outForest library [25] and based on [7]. Each variable is regressed onto all other variables and the root mean square error ($RMSE_j$) for the j variable is calculated. The difference of the observation (y_i) and prediction ($pred_i$) is calculated and the ratio between these two values is considered to measure the magnitude of the outlier (s_{ij}). A threshold of 3 was established to determine if an observation is an outlier.

$$s_{ij} = \frac{y_i - pred_i}{RMSE_j}, s_{ij} > 3 \tag{1}$$

The statistical summary was generated to report the values in which the models can be applicable. [12] proposed group soils based on the sensitivity of crops to salt content (EC_{se}), not salty soils (>0.75), Slightly salty (0.75–2), Moderately salty (2–4), Strongly salty (4–8), Very strongly salty (8–15) and Extremely salty ($\geq$15). The frequency analysis was performed on the classes described.

3.2   Modelling

The dataset was divided into a training set (60%), validation (20%) and testing (20%) using caret library [19]. The training set was used to calibrate the models, the validation to determinate the most appropriate hyperparameters, and test to error metrics. Interpretable models and black box models were used to follow the objectives. The multiple linear regression (MLR) and generalized additive models (GAM) were the ones with the highest interpretability. [16] describes them as supervised methods where the MLR assumes an approximately linear relationship between the predictors and the response, while GAMs allows the incorporation of nonlinear functions to the predictors. Tree models are useful when there are non-linear relationships and interactions between predictors. The Bayesian additive regression trees (BART) is a Bayesian nonparametric approach that allows to identify and explain the most important components to explain the variation of response variable [9], for this research we place it as an intermediate model between interpretable and black-box. Extreme gradient boosting trees (XGBoost) and neural network (NN) are completely black-box models whose advantage is a high predictive power and allow us to evaluate the capabilities of the other models.

Predictors for MLR and GAM were selected based on expert criteria, degree of interpretability, and significance of the coefficients. Once the model was proposed, the influencing values were determined based on the difference in fit, Cook distance, covariance ratio, hat values and were eliminated. The BART model was worked with the bartMachine library [17]. Initially the default values were used to then execute the out of sample RMSE method and determine the optimal number of trees. The hyperparameters were selected based on the lowest RMSE obtained with the validation set. The parameter k regulates the variance of the mean (σ_μ) and was tested from 0.5 to 20 with jumps every 0.5 units. Hyperparameters ν and q establish the probability distribution of the residual variance (σ) and were tested as 2, 3, 4, 5 and 0.85, 0.90, 0.95, respectively. We use BART to select the most important predictors, for that, the variable inclusion proportion was calculated [3] as the proportion of times each predictor is chosen as a splitting rule divided by the total number of splitting rules appearing in the model. [9] recommend 20 trees to use in the procedure and we fix the number of repetitions and permutations in 100. The XGBoost and NN models must determine the most suitable hyperparameters. The validation set was used to calculate the metrics and thereby select them. The XGBoost hyperparameters were tested for tree maximum depth (2–12), minimum child weight, proportion of subsamples, column sample by tree, gamma, lambda, alpha, eta and tree number, and were 2–12, 1–8, 0–1, 0–1, 0–0.5, 0.001–100, 0.001–100, 0–1, and 1–1000 respectively. The parameters for NN were layer1 and layer2 (4, 8, 16, 32, 64, 128, 256), drop-out1 and dropout2 (0.0, 0.1, 0.2, 0.3, 0.4, 0.5), L2 regularized (0.00001, 0.0001, 0.001), learning rate (0.0001, 0.001, 0.01) and batch size (32,64,128). The procedures for xgboost and neural networks were run with the packages xgboost and Keras in R language [4].

3.3   Goodness of Fit Measures

To evaluate the quality of the model, different parameters must be calculated that show the prediction capacity and the fitting of the new data to the model. The root mean square error (RMSE) tells how concentrated the data are around the line of the best fit, the coefficient of determination (R^2) measures the amount of the variance explained [34], mean absolute error (MAE) is a direct measure of the error, and concordance correlation coefficient (ρ_c) what is a correlation between the two reading that fall on the 45° line through the origin [22]. [6] comments that the Lin concordance coefficient is adequate when you want to evaluate the agreement between the same variable evaluated with two different apparatus or methods. To evaluate the predictive power with the increase in salinity, the RMSE was calculated for the test set divided into the ranges proposed by [12].

4   Results and Discussion

4.1   Data Preprocess and Exploratory Analysis

The original dataset contained 6068 instances, 112 contained missing data. Twenty-nine were eliminated because they did not contain the response variable and 83 were imputed. Forty-three samples outside the allowed limits were eliminated (pH, EC_{se}, OC) and anomalous values were eliminated. OutForest detected 827 instances with outliers in the predictors and 385 in response.

Instances with outliers in the response variable were eliminated and the 300 (5% of 6000) with the highest weight in the predictors were selected to transform them into missing values and then imputed with predictive mean matching. Finally, the dataset was reducing to 5611 instances and 17 variables. Table 3 reports the statistical summary of the dataset; the data have great variability of soil characteristics. [32] worked soils with sand contents between 22 and 88 $10\,g.kg^{-1}$, compared to them we have sandier and clayey soils. The regular range of EC_{se} for creating equations fluctuates between 0.1 to 18 $dS.m^{-1}$ ([24] and [22]), only [37] expanded to extreme saline soils. The most frequent soils are nonsaline (1105), slightly (1376), moderately and strongly salty (2034), and the less frequent are very strongly (600) and extremely salty (496). This feature suggest that the distribution of the variable tends to a log-normal or gamma distribution.

Table 3. Statistical summary of dataset variables.

Variable	Mean	Standard deviation	Minimum	Maximum
EC_{se}	5.31	7.29	0.03	45.40
EC	2.65	3.66	0.02	24.40
SAND	72.23	22.02	8	100
SILT	19.59	15.47	0	76
CLAY	8.18	8.58	0	49
pH	7.61	0.82	3.49	9.80
TEC	2.02	4.27	0	42.50
OC	0.47	0.69	0.01	7.29
CEC	8.71	6.14	1.12	40.64
eCa	5.67	4.58	0	30.84
eMg	1.44	1.18	0.08	8.87
eK	0.57	0.55	0.02	3.99
eNa	0.51	0.64	0.02	4.55
eAlH	0.05	0.32	0	4
ECEC	8.24	5.58	1.12	38.04
ESP	0.07	0.07	0	0.61
BS	0.97	0.13	0.04	1.00

4.2 Multiple Linear Regression

When proposing a model with all predictors, the variable with the greatest strength was EC. All investigations related above ([14, 18, 20, 24, 28, 31, 32, 37]) use it as the only predictor. We incorporate one of the particle sizes (SAND, SILT, CLAY) as a predictor, due to its influence on water retention in the soil.

It was not possible to incorporate the three particles due to the high correlation between then and the one that presented the best linear association was SAND. TEC was the second variable, the existence of carbonates is closely related to arid soils [27] and their dissolution directly affects salinity. Finally, all the selected predictors were significant ($p - value < 0.05$). The analysis of influencing values detected 372 instances that were extracted to fit the model. The assumption of normality of residuals and homogeneity of variances were not fulfilled due to the nature of the variable. However, the low probability values in Table 4 suggest that it is possible to trust the inference about the model, except for eMg. The MLR had a good fit to the data ($R^2 = 0.95$, $\rho_c = 0.97$), but a slightly low mean predictive power ($RMSE = 1.7059$).

Table 4. Parameters estimated by linear regression model.

Coefficient	Estimate ± SE	t-value (p-value)
Intercept	-0.1851 ± 0.0594	-3.118 (0.0018)
EC	1.9137 ± 0.0070	272.392 (<0.0001)
SAND	0.0055 ± 0.0007	7.414 (<0.0001)
TEC	-0.0503 ± 0.0073	-6.912 (<0.0001)

Unlike factor used in Peru, the result shows that a factor of 1.91 is more appropriate to transform EC to EC_{se}. The t statistic was used to compare the value of the EC coefficient with the value of 2 under the null hypothesis that the value is equal to 2. As a result, the null hypothesis was rejected ($p < 0.0001$) and we can affirm that the factor used in Peru is different from ours. Table 7 shows that the predictive power is adequate up to very strongly saline soils and above this predictive power is being lost. The absolute of t value is an indicator of the importance of the variables, the most important is EC and the others are secondary due to the large difference in the numerical value of t. The relationship between SAND, eMg and ESP is direct, the increase of any of them slightly increases the EC_{se}. Generally, saline soils are associated with arid conditions. [33] explains that arid and semi-arid conditions generate little development in soils and [21] adds that they are naturally sandy. [35] show that areas where evapotranspiration is greater than precipitation tend to accumulate salts due to lack of washing.

4.3   Generalized Additive Models

Based on the results of the MLR we used the gamma location-scale family to absorb the heterogeneity of variances by modelling the scale parameter separately. In addition, 71 influential observations ($|residuals| > 2.5$) were eliminated from the model. Figure 1 shows that the assumptions of the model are fulfilled, the distribution selected was the appropriate one. The fit of the model was similar to that of the MLR ($R^2 = 0.95$, $\rho_c = 0.97$), but the prediction error was slightly better ($RMSE = 1.6850$). As in the MLR, Table 7 shows that predictive power is lost as there are higher salinity soils. The GAM models allow the incorporation of nonlinear relationships, in this way, different predictors were selected compared to the MLR (Table 5). In particle size, SAND was replaced by CLAY as its influence is more related to salinity, and eNa and CEC replaced TEC because they affect the amount of water required for the saturation extract. In the case of MLR, these predictors were not selected because their relationship with EC_{se} are nonlinear. The extreme association between EC_{se} and EC requires that the coefficients of the interaction be included, all of which are significant. Data variability (scale) was controlled using EC as a predictor. The effective degree of freedom (edf) value show how many parameters were required to adjust the predictor to response. The interaction terms were modelled quadratically ($edf = 2$) and cubic ($edf = 3$) form. All predictors required complex shapes ($power > 3$) to fit the response.

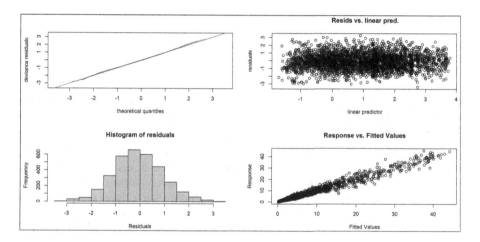

Fig. 1. Diagnostic-plot for GAM model. The upper left figure shows the fit to the selected distribution, upper right the homogeneity of variances, lower left the distribution of the residuals and the lower right the fit to the proposed model.

4.4 Bayesian Additive Regression Trees

The adequate number of trees based on the model was 100 and the hyperparameters k, ν and q were set to 2.5, 5, and 0.90. The results of the Markov Chain - Monte Carlo (MCMC) interactions show that the convergence stats in 1000, we established a burn in at 2000 interactions and took 3000 interactions after that. The BART model had a good fit ($R^2 = 0.94$) and a lower predictive power ($RMSE = 1.8573$) than MLR and GAM. Although the results were not as expected, the model is useful for selecting predictors. [3] explain that the

Table 5. Parameters estimated by generalized additive models.

Intercept	Estimate ± SE	Z-value (p-value)
Parametric coefficients		
Mean	0.9384 ± 0.0042	222.2 (<0.0001)
Scale	3.7867 ± 0.0271	139.6 (<0.0001)
Variable	edf	χ^2 (p-value)
Spline smooth coefficients		
EC	48	132192 (<0.0001)
CEC	7	152 (<0.0001)
eNa	6	142 (<0.0001)
CLAY	5	302 (<0.0001)
Interaction terms		
EC and CEC	2	15.92 (0.0076)
EC and CLAY	3	75.55 (<0.0001)
eNa and EC	3	38.6 (<0.0001)
Scale coefficients		
EC	24	838.29 (<0.0001)

BART model allows to select predictors in a nonparametric way, unlike other alternatives this allows to detect complex relationships with the response variable. The Fig. 2 shows the results of predictor selection with BART. Following the result, the only predictor that should be considered in the models is the EC, the others have similar importance with the exception of eAlH and BS. These results should be taken with caution since the excessive relationship between EC and EC_{se} may obscure the strength of the association with the other predictors. The BART model allows evaluating how the predictors affect the response (partial dependence). Figure 3 shows the partial dependence of the EC, CEC, OC and SAND on the response variable (EC_{se}). EC shows a linear association, as assumed in other investigations. The pH trend to increase in acid to basic soils, but there is a drastic change to the pH of 7.8. [36] mentions that from a pH of 8.5 soils tend to be sodic, this method can be used to adjust the critical value to local conditions in Peru, but requires more detail in the interaction with other factors not considered in this experiment. The relationship with OC is inverse, increasing the organic carbon content promotes ion stabilization, reducing saline conditions. The relationship with the sand is very irregular, it can be associated with powers greater than three.

4.5 Extreme Gradient Boosting Trees

Extreme Gradient Boosting (XGBoost) is a scalable end-to-end tree boosting system proposed by [38]. The general idea is to build new models on top of each other such that the new models rectify the mistakes made by the existing

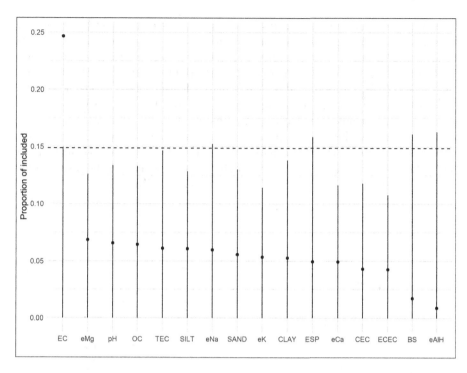

Fig. 2. Variable selection by global max and global SE method in BART. The points represent the variable inclusion proportion for the data. Dashed horizontal line is the 0.95 quantile distribution of the maximum values of the proportions obtained through permutations for all variables, considered in the global max method to include a variable. And the horizontal lines are the limit that the value of the proportion must exceed the variable in the global SE method to be included.

models. XGBoost introduced a distributed weighted quantile sketch algorithm for approximate tree learning and sparsity-aware algorithm for sparse data. A grid search on hyperparameters with 10-fold cross-validation was carried out to find the best model based on R^2 metrics. The final hyper parameters used were tree maximum depth (4), minimum child weight (6), proportion of subsample (0.75), column sample by tree (0.95), gamma (0.1), lambda (1.0), alpha (0.001), eta (0.15) and tree number (118). The model generated with the optimized parameters of Table 6 obtained the prediction metrics of $R^2 = 0.95$, $MAE = 0.81\,dS.m^{-1}$ and $RMSE = 1.63\,dS.m^{-1}$. The importance of the variable in the XGBoost model shows that the EC is the most important and the importance of the other predictors is depreciable.

4.6   Neural Network

A neural network takes an input vector of 17 variables and constructs a nonlinear function to predict the response. The minimum unit is a non-linear function known as a neuron or node, which when grouped with others that have the same level form a layer. A hyperparameter search based on the number of hidden layers was performed, obtaining better results with a hidden 2-layer neural network architecture. The final hyper parameters used were Layer1 (256), Dropout1 (0.3), Layer2 (4), Dropout2 (0.0), L2 (0.0001), learning rate (0.004) and batch size (64). The output of each node corresponds to a RELU activation function except for the output layer with sigmoid function. To avoid overfitting, the L2 regularization and the dropout technique were used in each layer. The optimizer used was RMSPROP with a reduction of 0.1 in the learning rate when the MAE metric has stopped improving in the last 20 epochs. The final model was obtained using the best prediction and fit of the tested models (Table 6).

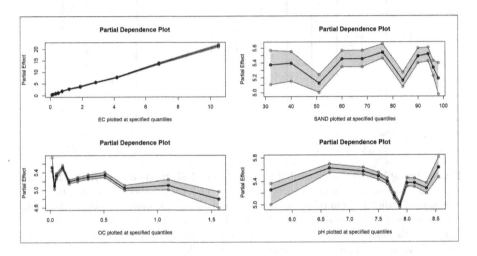

Fig. 3. Partial Dependence Plot of predictors from 2.5% to 97.5% quantile. Black line represents the average prediction of EC_{se} and blue lines are the credible intervals.

4.7 Models Comparison

Overall metrics show that the NN and XGBoost were the ones with the best predictive power and fit to the data (Table 6). The models proposed in the literature (Table 1) are lower in predictive power (RMSE) but similar in fit (R^2) to those proposed in this research, with exception of the LASPAF model, which has good predictive power ($RMSE = 1.68$ and $MAE = 0.90$) and fit to the data ($R^2 = 0.95$ and $\rho_c = 0.97$) despite being a simpler model. An advantage of simpler models (LASPAF and MLR) is that they can be used by the user manually, they can be used without problems by people who are not data scientist. The difficulty of the NN and XGBoost lies in the computational cost, implementing them in a system for direct use by customers is a challenge outside the scope of this research.

Table 6. Metrics comparison between existing models and proposed models.

Model	RMSE	R^2	MAE	ρ_c
LASPAF	1.6820	0.95	0.9034	0.97
MLR	1.7059	0.95	0.8888	0.97
GAM	1.6850	0.95	0.8210	0.97
BART	1.8896	0.94	0.9298	0.97
XGBoost	**1.6334**	0.95	0.8140	**0.98**
NN	**1.6253**	0.95	0.8335	**0.98**

There is a big difference between the global values of RMSE and by classes of saline soils. Table 7 shows that up to moderate salinity levels ($EC_{se} < 8\,dS.m^{-1}$) the GAM model is better at estimating EC_{se} than the NN and XGBoost models. At levels of very strongly ($8 - 15\,dS.m^{-1}$) and extremely ($> 15\,dS.m^{-1}$) salty its predictive power decreases compared to the NN and XGBoost, however the differences are small. The data show that the LASPAF method is good for situations where there are no salinity ($< 0.75\,dS.m^{-1}$) or extremely salinity which are rare situations in conditions of saline soils.

Table 7. Root Mean Square Error of models by saline soil classes.

Model	$EC_{se}(dS.m^{-1})$					
	0.75	$0.75 - 2$	$2 - 4$	$4 - 8$	$8 - 15$	>15
LASPAF	**0.1878**	0.3454	0.9715	1.5479	2.4664	4.0523
MLR	0.2768	0.3177	0.9209	**1.4511**	**2.3711**	4.2640
GAM	**0.1805**	**0.3006**	**0.7469**	1.3458	2.3088	4.3698
BART	**0.2458**	0.4539	0.8298	1.6736	2.5751	4.7851
XGBoost	0.2528	**0.3001**	**0.7691**	1.4544	**2.1887**	**4.1487**
NN	0.2735	**0.3083**	**0.7938**	1.3531	2.2148	4.1516

The disadvantage of the black-box models (XGBoost and NN) was that they only indicate the most important variables for the model. In comparison, the interpretable models (MLR, GAM and BART) show the shape of the relationship between the predictor and the response, being able to use this information to understand and up-date the theoretical framework behind it for the local situation in Peru. The influence of secondary predictors on predictive power is reflected in the interactions detected by the black-box methods.

5   Conclusions

Neural Networks followed by Extreme Gradient Boosting Trees were the methods with the lowest overall prediction error, however, the difference with computationally simpler methods is too small. Generalized Additive Models has potential use for soils with regular salinity conditions but loses predictive power in extremely saline soils. Multiple Linear Regression and Bayesian Additive Regression Trees are not recommended methods for prediction, but they are useful tools to understand the theoretical framework of electrical conductivity in saturated soil paste extract. All methods reaffirm, that is, electrical conductivity in extract 1:1 is the most important predictor. The influence of the other predictors is low, but it contributes to the improvement of the predictive power, especially in the methods that detect interactions between them.

References

1. Aboukila, E.F., Norton, J.B.: Estimation of saturated soil paste salinity from soil-water extracts. Soil Sci. **182**(3), 107–113 (2017). https://doi.org/10.1097/ss. 0000000000000197
2. Benke, K.K., Norng, S., Robinson, N.J., Chia, K., Rees, D.B., Hopley, J.: Development of pedotransfer functions by machine learning for prediction of soil electrical conductivity and organic carbon content. Geoderma **366** (2020). https://doi.org/ 10.1016/j.geoderma.2020.114210
3. Bleich, J., Kapelner, A., George, E.I., Jensen, S.T.: Variable selection for BART: an application to gene regulation. Ann. Appl. Stat. **8**(3) (2014). https://doi.org/ 10.1214/14-aoas755
4. Buuren, S.v., Groothuis-Oudshoorn, K.: mice: Multivariate imputation by chained equations in R. J. Stat. Softw. **45**(3) (2011). https://doi.org/10.18637/jss.v045.i03
5. Bzdok, D., Altman, N., Krzywinski, M.: Statistics versus machine learning. Nat. Meth. **15**(4), 233–234 (2018). https://doi.org/10.1038/nmeth.4642
6. Camacho-Sandoval, J.: Coeficiente de concordancia para variables continuas. Acta Médica Costarricense **50**, 211–212 (2008)
7. Chandola, V., Banerjee, A., Kumar, V.: Anomaly detection. ACM Comput. Surv. **41**(3), 1–58 (2009). https://doi.org/10.1145/1541880.1541882
8. Chi, C.M., Wang, Z.C.: Characterizing salt-affected soils of songnen plain using saturated paste and 1:5 soil-to-water extraction methods. Arid Land Res. Manage. **24**(1), 1–11 (2010). https://doi.org/10.1080/15324980903439362
9. Chipman, H.A., George, E.I., McCulloch, R.E.: BART: Bayesian additive regression trees. Ann. Appl. Stat. **4**(1) (2010). https://doi.org/10.1214/09-aoas285
10. Daliakopoulos, I.N., Tsanis, I.K., Koutroulis, A., Kourgialas, N.N., Varouchakis, A.E., Karatzas, G.P., Ritsema, C.J.: The threat of soil salinity: a European scale review. Sci Total Environ. **573**, 727–739 (2016). https://doi.org/10.1016/ j.scitotenv.2016.08.177
11. El hasini, S., Halima, O.I., El. Azzouzi, M., Douaik, A., Azim, K., Zouahri, A.: Organic and inorganic remediation of soils affected by salinity in the sebkha of sed el mesjoune - marrakech (morocco). Soil Tillage Res. **193**, 153–160 (2019). https:// doi.org/10.1016/j.still.2019.06.003
12. FAO: Guidelines for soil de-scription. FAO, Rome (2006)
13. Gamboa, N.R., Marchese, A.B., Tavares Corrêa, C.H.: Salinization in Peruvian North Coast Soils: Case Study in San Pedro de Lloc, book section Chapter 7, pp. 141–159 (2021). https://doi.org/10.1007/978-3-030-52592-7

14. Hogg, T.J., Henry, J.L.: Comparison of 1:1 and 1:2 suspensions and extracts with the saturation extract in estimating salinity in saskatchewan soils. Canadian J. Soil Sci. **64**(4), 699–704 (1984). https://doi.org/10.4141/cjss84-069
15. INEI: 4to censo nacional agropecuario (17/08/2021 2012). http://censos.inei.gob.pe/cenagro/tabulados/
16. James, G., Witten, D., Hastie, T., Tibshirani, R.: An Introduction to Statistical Learning. Springer Texts in Statistics. Springer (2021). https://doi.org/10.1007/978-1-4614-7138-7
17. Kapelner, A., Bleich, J.: bartMachine: machine learning with Bayesian additive regression trees. J. Stat. Softw. **70**(4) (2016). https://doi.org/10.18637/jss.v070.i04
18. Kargas, G., Chatzigiakoumis, I., Kollias, A., Spiliotis, D., Massas, I., Kerkides, P.: Soil salinity assessment using saturated paste and mass soil: water 1:1 and 1:5 ratios extracts. Water **10**(11) (2018). https://doi.org/10.3390/w10111589
19. Kuhn, M.: Building predictive models in rusing the caret package. J. Stat. Softw. **28**(5) (2008). https://doi.org/10.18637/jss.v028.i05
20. Landon, J.R.: Booker Tropical Soil Manual (2014). https://doi.org/10.4324/9781315846842
21. Legros, J.: Major Soil Groups of the World: Ecology, Genesis, Properties and Classification. CRC Press, Boca Raton (2012)
22. Lin, L.I.K.: A concordance correlation coefficient to evaluate reproducibility. Biometrics **45**(1) (1989). https://doi.org/10.2307/2532051
23. Ma, G., Ding, J., Han, L., Zhang, Z., Ran, S.: Digital mapping of soil salinization based on sentinel-1 and sentinel-2 data combined with machine learning algorithms. Regional Sustain. **2**(2), 177–188 (2021). https://doi.org/10.1016/j.regsus.2021.06.001
24. Matthees, H.L., et al.: Predicting soil electrical conductivity of the saturation extract from a 1:1 soil to water ratio. Commun. Soil Sci. Plant Anal. **48**(18), 2148–2154 (2017). https://doi.org/10.1080/00103624.2017.1407780
25. Mayer, M.: outForest: multivariate outlier detection and replacement (2021). https://CRAN.R-project.org/package=outForest
26. Miura, K.: Nitrogen and Phosphorus Nutrition Under Salinity Stress, book section Chapter 16, pp. 425–441 (2013). https://doi.org/10.1007/978-1-4614-4747-4
27. Omuto, C., Vargas, R., El Mobara, A., Mohamed, N., Viatkin, K., Yigini, Y.: Maping of salt-affected soils: technical manual. FAO, Rome (2020)
28. Ozkan, H., Ekinci, H., Yigini, Y., Yuksel, O.: Comparison of four soil salinity extraction methods. In: 18th International Soil Meeting on Soil Sustaining Life on Earth, Managing Soil and Technology, pp. 22–26 (2006)
29. McBratney, A.B., Minasny, B., Stockmann, U. (eds.): Pedometrics. PSS, Springer, Cham (2018). https://doi.org/10.1007/978-3-319-63439-5
30. RcoreTeam: R: A language and environment for statistical computing (2021). https://www.R-project.org/
31. Richards, L.: Diagnosis and improvement of saline and alkaline soils. United States Department of Agriculture, Washington (1954)
32. Sonmez, S., Buyuktas, D., Okturen, F., Citak, S.: Assessment of different soil to water ratios (1:1, 1:2.5, 1:5) in soil salinity studies. Geoderma **144**(1–2), 361–369 (2008). https://doi.org/10.1016/j.geoderma.2007.12.005
33. Sposito, G.: The Chemistry of Soils. Oxford University Press, Oxford, 2 edn. (2008)
34. Wadoux, A.M.J.C., Malone, B., Minasny, B., Fajardo, M., McBratney, A.B.: Estimating soil properties and classes from spectra, book section Chapter 9, pp. 165–214. Progress in Soil Science (2021). https://doi.org/10.1007/978-3-030-64896-1

35. Weil, R., Brady, N.: The Nature and Properties of Soils. Pearson, London, 15 edn. (2017)
36. Zaman, M., Shahid, S.A., Heng, L.: Guideline for Salinity Assessment, Mitigation and Adaptation Using Nuclear and Related Techniques (2018). https://doi.org/10.1007/978-3-319-96190-3
37. Zhang, H., Schroder, J.L., Pittman, J.J., Wang, J.J., Payton, M.E.: Soil salinity using saturated paste and 1:1 soil to water extracts. Soil Sci. Soc. Am. J. **69**(4), 1146–1151 (2005). https://doi.org/10.2136/sssaj2004.0267
38. Chen, T., Guestrin, C.: XGBoost: a scalable tree boosting system. In: 22nd ACM SIGKDD International Conference on Knowledge Discovery and Data Mining, pp. 785–794 (2016)

Author Index

Printed in the United States
by Baker & Taylor Publisher Services